GLOBAL ISSUES
beyond
Sovereignty

FIFTH EDITION

MARYANN CUSIMANO LOVE
The Catholic University of America

ROWMAN & LITTLEFIELD
Lanham • Boulder • New York • London

Executive Editor: Traci Crowell
Assistant Editor: Deni Remsberg
Executive Marketing Manager: Amy Whitaker
Interior Designer: Rosanne Schloss

Credits and acknowledgments for material borrowed from other sources, and reproduced with permission, appear on the appropriate page within the text.

Published by Rowman & Littlefield
An imprint of The Rowman & Littlefield Publishing Group, Inc.
4501 Forbes Boulevard, Suite 200, Lanham, Maryland 20706
www.rowman.com

6 Tinworth Street, London SE11 5AL, United Kingdom

British Library Cataloguing in Publication Information Available

Library of Congress Cataloging-in-Publication Data Available
ISBN 978-1-5381-1733-0 (cloth : alk. paper)
ISBN 978-1-5381-1734-7 (pbk. : alk. paper)
ISBN 978-1-5381-1735-4 (electronic)

♾™ The paper used in this publication meets the minimum requirements of American National Standard for Information Sciences—Permanence of Paper for Printed Library Materials, ANSI/NISO Z39.48-1992.

This book is dedicated to my husband Rich and my children Maria, Ricky, and Ava, who support me every step of the way.

And thank you to the Dominican Sisters of Iraq, CRS Iraq, and JRS Iraq, who inspire us to imagine and create a more peaceful world.

Brief Contents

■ ■ ■

Contents

■ ■ ■

Figures and Tables

■ ■ ■

FIGURES

TABLES

About the Author

■ ■ ■

DR. MARYANN CUSIMANO LOVE holds a PhD degree from Johns Hopkins University and is associate professor of International Relations in the Department of Politics of the Catholic University of America in Washington, DC. She serves on the board of the Arms Control Association, the Advisory Board of the Catholic Peace Building Network, the Board of Jesuit Refugee Services, and the US Catholic Bishops' International Justice and Peace Committee, where she advises bishops on international affairs and US foreign policy and engages in diplomacy at the United Nations and with the US government. She has also served on the Department of State's Core Group on Religion and Foreign Policy, charged with making recommendations to the secretary of state and the Federal Advisory Commission on how the US government can better engage with civil society and religious actors in foreign policy. She is an international affairs editor at *America* magazine. She served as a Fellow at the US Commission on International Religious Freedom, a Pew Fellow of International Affairs, and a Fellow at the US Naval Academy Stockdale Center for Ethical Leadership. Dr. Maryann Cusimano Love has also authored the *New York Times*–bestselling children's books *You Are My I Love You, You Are My Miracle, You Are My Wish, You Are My Wonders, Holiducks, Alphaducks,* and *Sleep, Baby, Sleep.*

Preface

■ ■ ■

WE ARE IN A RACE between cooperation and catastrophe, across a host of global issues. Environmental problems, refugee flows, drug and human trafficking, cyberattacks—all these issues cross borders faster than sovereign states are able or willing to respond.

Global problems move at internet speed; governments do not move so quickly. This creates gaps in what citizens expect the state to do, and what countries have the capacities to do. Effective responses to global issues require better cooperation among more actors. There are more people on the planet than ever before in human history, over 7.6 billion people, and that total is expected to increase to 9–11 billion people by the year 2050. There are more sovereign states than ever before, 193 countries. With more states and more people than ever before, we need more and better means to cooperate and coordinate to address global issues.

This book investigates global issues that move beyond sovereignty in both the nature of problems and solutions. *How can we bridge the gaps between the sovereign states we have, and the coordinating capacities we need, to address the global issues we face?* Global challenges are fast, fungible, fluid, and decentralized, and borders are more permeable. How can global issues be tackled in a system that is based on sovereignty? How does globalization facilitate both global problems and attempts to manage them? How do the debates over globalization and sovereignty frame our understanding of these issues? This book examines the rising importance of nonstate actors and prestate actors and global issues, and the challenges to changing institutions. What policy responses are available and advisable? As states struggle to manage global issues and adapt to the rapid changes of globalization, what is the future of sovereignty? No world government exists or is likely. Yet unilateralist state policies cannot dictate outcomes to most global issues either. Globalization exacerbates and creates governance gaps. What policies are available and advisable to bridge the gaps between the state-based system we have, and the coordinating capacities we need? These are challenges for globalization and sovereignty going forward.

Global issues are facilitated by globalization's fast open technologies, open markets, and open societies. Even the most powerful countries cannot solve or stop these issues alone. The power of the private sector is growing (both legal and illegal, for-profit and nonprofit), while state power is flat or in some places declining. This does not mean sovereignty is going away. Sovereign states face capacity gaps, jurisdiction gaps, participation gaps, legitimacy gaps, and ethics gaps in their efforts to address global issues. Sovereign states team up with a variety of actors to address global issues, contracting out functions to the private sector, sharing functions with other sovereign states, coordinating functions through IGOs, and relying on prestate actors also.

Global Issues: Beyond Sovereignty provides a thesis and a common narrative throughout the "issue" chapters. The range of responses to manage global issues are compared and discussed throughout. While private sector actors have means to impact transnational issues, they do not have a public mandate to do so. Countries increasingly must learn how to play well with others; this is easier said than done. Attempts to manage global issues flow through three channels: public sector responses, private sector responses, and mixed public–private partnerships. All three channels are explored throughout the book, uniting the issue chapters in a common discussion of challenges and responses. The conclusion presents lessons learned for theory and practice from managing global issues. To facilitate interactive methods, discussion questions are provided in each chapter. To reach different types of learners, each chapter contains photos and figures. Key terms are highlighted throughout the text, with definitions of the key terms provided at the end of each chapter.

News headlines and policy makers are consumed with pressing global issues. But none of these important global issues are captured by the traditional view of International Relations (IR) as the activities of states. People are dying, but states cannot save them. The strongest states in the system cannot solve these problems alone; their institutions are not wired for it, and they are scrambling to come up with effective responses. Nearly a third of the people on the planet live in the weakest states in the system. These fragile states cannot provide roads and drinking water, basic law, order, and governance. Their citizens are the most vulnerable, yet these states are the least able to respond to the challenges of globalization. The worst of these states are what I call kleptocracies; their kleptomaniacal leaders treat the government as ATM machines, to be used for personal enrichment. Half the people on the planet live without basic freedoms (in both "strong" and "weak" states); their governments deny them the abilities to participate in, know of, or hold their governments accountable for the activities undertaken in their name. The worst of these states are predatory, deliberately killing the very citizens they are supposed to protect. Sovereignty—the ideas that governance aligns with territory, and that those outside the geographic boundaries have no authority to meddle in internal affairs— is not neutral or theoretical or helpful for many of the people on the planet. For example, nearly 6 million people have died in the Congo, as many Jews have died in the Holocaust, in a conflict driven by weak sovereignty, the quest to control natural resources to sell to the lucrative global market that powers our cell phones, and problems spilling over central Africa's leaky borders.

Too many IR books and ideas about how the world works have not yet caught up with real-world practices. The pressing problems we face move across borders, yet ironically our policy responses, and our textbooks, are too often state-focused. Many IR books are heavy on discussions of what states are doing to address global issues, with less developed discussions of how private sector actors, nonstate actors, and prestate actors address global issues. This statist bias leads to a demographic bias. Since most heads of state are older men, texts that focus primarily on state actions place less attention on the activities of most of the people on the planet, the youth and women who make up the majority of the world's population. Too often women and youth are discussed in International Relations as victims, rather than address- ing their agency and contributions. In contrast, this book examines the contributions of youth, women, and nonstate actors.

Other global issues books are often an eclectic mash up of topics, headlines du jour, with an "and now this!" organizational scheme. The presentation to students is disjointed, not clear. The approach is often a "scare 'em and leave 'em" presentation of a global horror show of problems, without clear arguments about the connections among the issues, integrated discussions of solutions, or balance in terms of reporting progress made in addressing global issues. *Global Issues Beyond Sovereignty* presents students with both the good news and the challenges of global issues, and the ways actors are adapting responses.

Many International Relations treatises emphasize continuity rather than change. In contrast, this book puts change front and center, with all its warts. Change is rarely linear and predictable; a major theme of this book is the unintended consequences of globalization, particularly policies intended to open societies, markets, and technologies. Many International Relations books present a binary approach to global issues and nonstate actors, presenting them as either "good" or "bad." There tends to be a binary approach also to sovereignty, which is presented either as waning (with the EU and rise of IGOs offered as evidence), or sovereignty is presumed to be as strong as ever (as evidenced by Brexit). Instead of an either/or frame, this book takes a both/and approach. Globalization presents both benefits and unintended challenges. Sovereignty both remains and adapts. Concrete examples and illustrative cases are discussed throughout.

I am grateful for the support and patience of my family and children Maria, Ricky, and Ava Rose during the long hours I was at work on this book. I am also thankful for the lively discussions with my students, and colleagues: to Dr. Richard Love, my colleague at the Peacekeeping and Stability Operations Institute at the US Army War College, and my husband, for his thoughtful comments as "first reader"; to the people I interviewed in Iraq, Korea, Northern Ireland, Nigeria, Nicaragua, Ghana, Japan, the Amazon, Italy, the United Kingdom, the United Nations, Washington, DC, and elsewhere; to Senator Sam Nunn, Lord Desmond Browne and colleagues at the Nuclear Threat Initiative; to Secretary of State George Shultz, Secretary of Defense Bill Perry, Ambassador Jim Goodby and colleagues at the Hoover Institution at Stanford University; to my colleagues at the Catholic Peacebuilding Network, including Daniel Philpott, John Paul Lederach, Jerry Powers, David Cortright, Scott Appleby, George Lopez, William Headley S.C.Sp., Msgr. Hector Fabio from Colombia, Myla Leguro from the Philippines, Marie Dennis, Peter John Pearson from South Africa, Ferdinand Muhigirwe S.J., from Eastern Congo, and all my colleagues at Notre Dame's Kroc Institute of Peace; to Drew Christiansen, S.J., Katherine Marshall, and colleagues at Georgetown University's Berkley Center; to Major General William Burns, Ambassador Bill Burns, Ambassador Mary Ann Glendon, and the bishops and staff at the US Conference of Catholic Bishops; colleagues at *America* magazine; to Bill Barbieri, Patricia Andrasik, Bob Destro, Fred Ahearn, Steve Schneck, and colleagues at the Institute for Policy Research of Catholic University; to Nobel Laureates Mairead Corrigan Maguire, Jody Williams, Beatrice Finn, Muhammed Yunus, and Mohamed El Baradei; to H.E. Archbishop

Bernardito Auza, Archbishop Tomasi, Pierce Cordan, and colleagues at the Holy See Mission to the United Nations; to Cardinal Peter Turkson and Flaminia Giovanelli and colleagues at the Vatican Dicastery for Integral Human Development; and to colleagues at Catholic Relief Services, Jesuit Refugee Services, Talitha Kum, the US Commission on International Religious Freedom, US Institute of Peace, Global Priorities, and the Arms Control Association. I am thankful to Traci Crowell and the team at Rowman and Littlefield. All errors of course are entirely my own.

We must cooperate or die. Humans have faced this challenge before. What's different today is the scale and speed at which we need to cooperate. With the greatest number of people and countries ever on planet earth, we need the greatest cooperation and coordination to navigate globalization's fast moving challenges.

Yusra Mardini of the Refugee Olympics Team, Summer Olympics 2016, Rio de Janeiro, Brazil.

1

Global Problems, Coordinated Solutions, Networked Sovereignty

■ ■ ■

How leaky are the borders of man-made states!

How many clouds float over them scot-free, how much desert sand sifts from country to country, how many mountain pebbles roll onto foreign turf in provocative leaps! . . . Only what's human can be truly alien. The rest is mixed forest, undermining moles, and wind.

—Wisława Szymborska, Nobel Poet[1]

Put down the national flags. Look up from the numbers and look to the future.

—Bono

We are in a race between cooperation and catastrophe.

—Senator Sam Nunn

I want everyone to think refugees are normal people who had their homelands and lost them.

—Yusra Mardini, Olympic athlete and Syrian refugee[2]

Around the world, responsible nations must defend against threats to sovereignty not just from global governance, but also from other, new forms of coercion and domination.

—President Donald Trump[3]

GLOBAL ISSUES MOVE BEYOND BORDERS, from cyberthreats to refugees. This book investigates global issues that move beyond sovereignty in both the nature of problems and solutions. Disease and pollution cross borders without passports. *How can we bridge the gaps between the sovereign states we have, and the coordinating capacities we need, to address the global issues we face?* Borders are more permeable, and threats are fast, fungible, fluid, and decentralized. How can global issues be tackled in a system that is based on sovereignty? How does globalization facilitate both global problems and attempts to manage them? How do the debates over globalization and sovereignty frame our understanding of these issues? This book examines the rising importance of nonstate actors and global issues, and the challenges to changing institutions. What policy responses are available and advisable? As states struggle to manage global issues and adapt to the rapid changes of globalization, what is the future of sovereignty?

Many global issues represent the downside of globalization. **Globalization** is the fast, interdependent spread of open economy, open technology, and open society infrastructures. Globalization is not new, but aided by modern information technology, the current period of globalization is quicker, thicker, deeper, and cheaper than previous periods of globalization. **Sovereignty** in international relations is the theory that each geographic territory has one autonomous, recognized governing authority. **Sovereign states** in practice have four characteristics: land, population, a government in control of the land and population, and international recognition. In practice, international recognition is key; the borders, population, and government of sovereign states may all be contested, but only the other sovereign states determine who is "in the club" of sovereign states.

OLYMPIAN AND REFUGEE

Consider the story of Yusra Mardini. She was forced to leave school and flee her home in war-torn Syria as a refugee. Nearly, a half million people have been killed in the Syrian civil war. Half the Syrian population have fled the war; six million people dispersed within Syria, and another six million, like Yusra, escaped outside of Syria. Sixteen-year-old Yusra and her sister fled the bombs of Damascas, and found passage in a boat that promised to take them to safety. Unscrupulous human traffickers put too many people onto an unseaworthy vessel. Yusra and her sister became heroes when they saved the lives of the 20 refugees on their small, overcrowd boat. When the motor died and their boat floundered in the Aegean Sea, Yusra jumped into the water and swam for three and a half hours. She pulled the sinking boat to safety until they were intercepted by a rescue boat, all the while smiling so as to reassure the younger refugee children. Yusra was a competitive swimmer before the war. After her escape from Syria, she returned to swimming, earned a spot on the Olympic swim team, and swam in the Olympic Games under the Refugee Olympic team flag.

Olympic athletes usually parade behind flags of their countries. Olympic athletes work hard to master their sports. They are blessed with good genetics from their families, financial support from corporate sponsorship as well as from their families and communities, and good coaching and practice time from their schools and athletic leagues. Yet when an Olympic athlete wins a competition and rises to the medal stand, the only affiliation that matters is the country from which the athlete hails. The anthem played and flag flown during the medal ceremony are of the winning athlete's country, not their family crest, sports' league colors, not the brand or ditty of their sponsoring corporation, or religious hymn of the community praying for them. All that matters is the athlete's country.

This Olympic picture is the unquestioned, default model most of us carry in our heads concerning international relations. According to this view, we live in a world of countries, of sovereign states, and the 7.6 billion people of the world are divided up by those geographic borders, sorted into 193 countries. We march through life ruled by our country's flag; the sovereign state calls the tunes. The lucky happen to be born in powerful or prosperous states. For those who won the birth lottery, they have a better chance of developing their talents, of being the best they can be, and of reaching their full human development. The powerful and prosperous states send hundreds of athletes to the Olympic games. People who are born into less powerful and poor states have fewer chances of "climbing the medal stand," rising to the top of the world, of reaching their full potential. For those born into the most desperate conditions in the poorest states, they may not even be able to reach the full height of their genetic code, stunted in their growth by malnutrition, poverty, and disease. From the pageantry of states at the Olympics, to the similar display of sovereign flags at the United Nations, this is the simple, old story of global politics most of us are told. It is not really true.

NONSTATE ACTORS AND PRESTATE ACTORS

If we look closer, there is another story hiding in plain sight, a story of the global issues that move beyond sovereignty. There are now more refugees fleeing war and persecution than at any time since World War II. These people, like Yusra Mardini, who were either failed by their states or in some cases hunted by their states, competed at the Olympics as the Refugee Olympic team. There are **four types of nonstate actors**—both for profit, nonprofit, legal, and illegal nonstate actors. Yusra's Olympic story illustrates the rising power of all four types of nonstate actors.

The entire pomp and pageantry of the Olympic games are not organized by states at all, and not by the governments of countries, but by nongovernmental organizations (NGOs), legal, nonprofit, civil society organizations. The International Olympic Committee organizes the games, the International Sports Federations set the rules of the games, and the National Olympic Committees determine which athletes will compete. These nonprofit NGOs rely on the support of for-profit multinational corporations, MNCs, to pay for the games. Legal, for-profit MNCs provide 95 percent of the funding for the Olympics, via sales of broadcast rights, sponsorships, and licensing fees. These legal, nonstate actors work hard to manage the threats posed by illegal, nonstate actors, from illicit for-profit international criminal organizations and drug sellers, to illegal nonprofit terrorist organizations. The athletes are tested repeatedly for illegal drugs, sold by global criminal networks. The International Olympic Committee works to secure the athletes and guests against attacks, not by the armies of states, but attacks by terrorist and criminal networks, by violence caused by nonstate actors. Human trafficking rings do a brisk business in sexual services at every major athletic event, from the Superbowl to the World Cup to the Olympics. Sporting events tend to draw men with money away from home and looking for pleasure, and human trafficking networks move their supplies of young

Figure 1.1 Types of Nonstate Actors

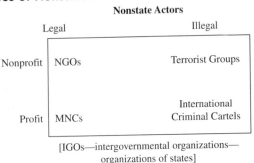

[IGOs—intergovernmental organizations— organizations of states]

Source: Dr. Maryann Cusimano Love

bodies to places where there will be market demand. Religious groups mobilize to counter the human trafficking rings, alongside NGOs who work to prevent and raise awareness about human trafficking at these sporting events. Doctors and health-care companies work to develop and distribute vaccines and medicines, to stop the spread of global diseases that accompany the millions of people moving across borders. Elite athletes with enough money may "shop" for citizenship, to have the opportunity to compete in the games on a team for which it is easier to "make the cut." Refugees and stateless athletes, like Yusra Mardini, compete in the Olympics as a part of the Refugee Olympic team.

The flags of countries may fly as the Olympic medals are given out, but that picture is misleading; the whole enterprise is organized, operated, and financed by nonstate actors. Yusra's story illustrates all four types of nonstate actors: she fled terrorists, was transported by international criminal traffickers, was rescued and assisted by humanitarian NGOs, and swam in the Olympics with the help of the international NGO the Olympic Federation, as well as for-profit MNC sponsors like Coca Cola. Some nations (cultural groups who share a common history, language, ethnicity, and/or religion) who are not recognized as sovereign states also compete at the Olympics. Nonstate actors are active even at the Olympics, alongside all the symbols, anthems, and flying flags of sovereign states.

From trade to trafficking, global issues move beyond borders. Sovereign states, even the most powerful countries, cannot solve or stop these issues alone. This does not mean sovereignty is going away; it simply means that effective responses to global issues require adaptive coordination among more actors. There are more people on the planet than ever before in human history, over 7.6 billion people, and that total is expected to increase to 9–10 billion people by the year 2050. There are more sovereign states than ever before, 193 countries. Most of these sovereign states are very new; almost three-quarters of states originated after World War II. Twenty states are even newer, appearing after the end of the Cold War in 1991. Although the sovereign state system dates back to the 1648 Treaty of Westphalia, only a handful of today's sovereign states existed in 1648 and signed the Treaties of Westphalia (i.e., France, Spain, Sweden, the Netherlands). Most of today's sovereign states originated in the decolonization movement of the late twentieth century. With more people and more states in more contact than ever before, more adaptation and coordination among a variety of actors with varying capacity is needed. No world government exists or is likely. Yet unilateralist state policies cannot dictate outcomes to most global issues either. Globalization exacerbates and creates governance gaps. What policies are available and advisable to bridge the gaps between the state-based system we have, and the coordinating capacities we need? These are challenges for globalization and sovereignty going forward.

States are not the only important actors in global politics. **Prestate** actors exist today that predate the sovereign state by thousands of years. For example, **religious actors** are **prestate actors**; they existed millennia before the creation of the modern sovereign state system, and many of these religious institutions performed functions that later have also been performed by states (providing law, schools, health care, and social services, keeping records of births and deaths, etc.). Other prestate actors include **nations**, cultural groups such as the Iriqois and the Kurds. Some multinational corporations (MNCs) existed before the advent of sovereign states. Some international criminal cartels existed before the sovereign states in which they operate. For example, the Camorra mafia group existed before the foundation of the Italian state. Most nonstate actors, such as MNCs and NGOs, are newer; there has been an explosive growth of these organizations in the last hundred years and particularly in the most recent decades since the creation of the Internet.

Sovereign states are actors in international politics, but so are nonstate actors and prestate actors. These different characters play simultaneously on the global stage, and each bring different capacities to global issues. The Olympics particularly showcase the activities of legal, nonstate actors working across borders, but some global issues are more dangerous. The attacks of September 11, 2001, also demonstrated global issues that move beyond sovereignty. Nonstate actors used nonmilitary means to attack primarily nongovernmental targets. Nineteen terrorists, primarily from Saudi Arabia but who represented no state, inflicted massive casualties and approximately 3,000 deaths against citizens from the most powerful state in the international system as well as from 80 other countries. They used commercial airlines, the tools of global transportation and commerce, to attack, and chose as their primary targets the twin towers of the World Trade Center, symbols of global capitalism. Members of the Al Qaeda terrorist network operate across sovereign borders through cells in an estimated sixty-five countries. Seventeen of the September 11, 2001, suicide bombers were Saudis, with two Egyptians. They had been living in the United States, trained in Afghanistan, and organized and financed in Germany, England, and Spain with information and money sent to them from companies, nongovernmental organizations (NGOs), and individuals around the world. The Al Qaeda financial network drew from the diamond trade in Sierra Leone and the heroin trade in Afghanistan, effectively linking the terrorist network with global crime and drug trafficking networks. The hijackers exploited the very global transportation, communication, and economic systems they protested—and which they believed carry undue and unwanted US and Western influence around the world. Their high-visibility attacks were planned to maximize global media exposure. The terrorists used globalization to fight globalization. They turned globalization against itself, using globalization's open society, open economy, and open technology infrastructure to wage their protest against modern patterns of power, and to call for a return to "the good old days" of the sixth century.

None of these important global actions is captured by the traditional view of International Relations as the activities of states.

Many global issues represent the downside of globalization. **Globalization** is the fast, interdependent spread of open economy, open technology, and open society infrastructures. Globalization is not new, but the speed, reach, intensity, cost, and impacts of the current period of globalization are. Earlier periods of globalization moved trade, missionaries, and colonizers far more slowly, with the speed of frigates. Now people and products cross borders in hours. Ideas and capital move around the globe at the touch of a keystroke. Global (or trans-sovereign) problems move across borders, and cannot be solved by any one country alone. Nonstate actors are important players both in creating and managing global issues—from legal groups such as NGOs, and multinational corporations (MNCs) to illicit groups such as international crime cartels and terrorist organizations. The rise of global challenges is made possible by the very changes that have been facilitated and celebrated by many policy makers: the rise of democracies and liberal, capitalist economies, and advances in technology, transportation, and communication. The rise of global problems is full of irony. It is physically difficult to limit the flow of particular peoples and goods at a time when technological, market, and societal forces make such movement easier than ever before.

Although globalization did not create problems that go beyond borders, it has facilitated and intensified them. For example, although terrorism existed long before, the modern period of globalization certainly facilitates the work of terrorist groups such as ISIS and Al Qaeda. Open economies, societies, and technologies give terrorists the opportunity to take its complaints to a global stage, to act at a distance cheaply, to perpetrate greater casualties using global technologies, and to elicit greater fear by playing in front of cameras and satellites that broadcast its members' actions instantly and globally. Globalization gives breakdowns in state authority and capacity and global problems greater reach, speed, intensity, and impact.

Sovereignty is the form of political organization that has dominated the international system since the Treaty of Westphalia in 1648. Sovereign states have exclusive and final jurisdiction over territory, as well as the resources and populations that lie within such territory. A system based on sovereignty is one that acknowledges only one political authority over a particular territory and looks to that authority as the final arbiter to solve problems that occur within its borders. Sovereign states have four characteristics, three of which are negotiable: territory, population, a government with control over the territory and population, and international recognition. In practice, only international recognition is nonnegotiable. If a political entity has territory, population, and a government but lacks international recognition, such as the Palestinian Authority, then it is not considered a sovereign state. Once a state is internationally recognized, such as Somalia, it does not matter if it lacks a government with the ability to control the territory and population, if territory is contested, or if population varies widely (because of large refugee flows, for example). Many states are fragile states. They have international recognition as a state, so may enter into treaties and international law, but the government may lack the capacity to provide law and order over all its territory and citizens.

The term "nation" is not synonymous with the term sovereign state. The distinction is not just academic. Each year, tens of thousands of people die trying to make their nations into states. A **nation** is a group with a common cultural, linguistic, ethnic, racial, or religious identity—such as the Sioux nation of the US plains or the Kurds in Iraq, Turkey, Iran, Armenia, and Syria. There are 8,000 nations. A **sovereign state** or country, however, is an internationally recognized unit of political authority over a given territory, such as the United States of America or Iraq. There are 193 sovereign states. National boundaries—where various ethnic or linguistic groups are located—are elastic and often do not coincide with sovereign state boundaries. For example, the Basques live on either side of the border between Spain and France, and the Kurds live in the region straddling Iraq and Turkey.

Despite the widespread use of the term, there is no such thing as a **nation-state**; 8,000 does not equal 193. Every sovereign state has many nations living in it. The very culturally homogenous Japan has a half million Americans living in Tokyo alone, Norway has over

700,000 citizens who immigrated from foreign countries, 89 percent of the people living and working in the United Arab Emirates are not UAE citizens. Chinese diaspora live around the world in great numbers, and move with Chinese trade, even into the "hermit kingdom" of North Korea.[4] History is blood spattered with horrific attempts to create nation-states, from Hitler's white supremacist plan to create a Nazi Germany for the white Aryan race only, to the Rwandan genocide attempt to rid Rwanda of Tutsis, and to the Balkan wars of ethnic cleansing. None of these attempts to create a one-to-one correspondence between a single nation and the borders of a sovereign state have worked, and they are even less likely today in an era of globalization. Open economies and open technologies intermingle people across national lines, and the rise of open societies means there are fewer dictatorships able and willing to segregate and outlaw marriages and other interracial or multicultural unions, as used to be common in the age of colonialism, apartheid in South Africa, and segregation in the United States. White supremacist, nationalist, and racist regimes are on the rise today and try to limit the mixing of national groups. Some outlaw changing religions. Fragile states exemplify places where nationalist agendas threaten to tear apart sovereign states, from Spain to Iraq; the United States is not immune.[5] This book does not use the terms "nations" and "states" as synonyms, because they are not; people die every day over the distinction.

GLOBAL PROBLEMS AND THE GLOBALIZATION DEBATES

Globalization creates a world of paradox. Global transportation, communication, and economic interdependence make possible the vision of a closer human family. Millions of people cross an international border every day, and a million new people get access to the Internet every day. Dangerous diseases, however, use the same global infrastructure that tourists do. Although capital flows of trillions of dollars cross borders each day, most poor people and poor countries see little of it. Building the global infrastructure of open economies, technologies, and societies creates great benefits, but globalization also carries significant costs that are often not equitably dispersed, especially to the world's poor.

Some[6] argue that globalization is a means to bring peoples and cultures together; rout tyrannical governments; easily and cheaply spread information, ideas, capital, and commerce; and transfer more power than ever before to civil society and networked individuals. For advocates, curtailing globalization would be immoral. Global poverty is a problem—and globalization is the key to solving it. The world's most impoverished countries are those that are least globalized.

Critics, however, see globalization as trampling sovereignty,[7] or as bringing "undesirable" races or people "from shithole countries" across borders. Nationalists today often repackage past racism and rebrand their focus as "cultural," as when Nazi propaganda was updated and used in the Brexit campaign.[8] Others decry globalization as neoimperialism wearing a Nike swoosh symbol, extending the web of global capitalism's exploitation of women, minorities, the poor, and developing regions. It fouls ecosystems, displaces local cultures and traditions, mandates worship at the altar of rampant consumer capitalism, and deepens the **digital divide**, the gap between those who have access to computers, the Internet, and modern information technology (and other asymmetries) between the global haves and have nots. The private sector has gotten richer, while governments have become poorer, leading to fewer resources for governments to mitigate or respond to the challenges of globalization.[9]

Opposition to globalization comes from many different camps, right and left. Many critics share a common view that globalization puts profits before people. Globalization benefits a few at the top at the expense of the rest.[10] Environmental, human rights, and labor advocates charge that globalization brings a race to the bottom in human rights and environmental standards as businesses extend their reach to benefit the corporate bottom line. Local laws and control may be sacrificed to international regimes that are controlled by a few powerful states or corporations. These regimes are not democratic, representative, or transparent. Critics see globalization as a new form of imperialism—whether corporate, cultural, or Western—that is immoral and unjust. Liberal consumer advocates such as Ralph Nader, conservative protectionists such as Brexit voters in the UK, radicals such as Al Qaeda, and anticorporate activists such as anti-McDonald's farmer Jose Bove in France have little in common other than their opposition to globalization. For these opponents, the biggest question is how to stop globalization and the harms that come from it. Ironically, most use the tools of globalization (the Internet, social media, global technology, and modern telecommunications) to protest globalization.

Opponents and advocates see globalization differently in part because the costs and benefits of globalization are asymmetrically distributed rather than shared equally. Capitalism is criticized for disparities between rich and poor in terms of income, political power, participation, and opportunities. In parallel, the worldwide spread and intensification of capitalism that globalization represents is criticized for exacerbating capitalism's excesses and exporting the resulting problems to the entire world, as in the 2008 global economic recession. For example, global income inequality is increasing in the latest phase of globalization, both within and across countries. In the past, economic and productivity growth would benefit all; "a rising tide would float all boats." Since 1980, economic growth has primarily benefited the top 1 percent, who have seen immense increases in income, while the earnings of the middle and lower classes have been flat or declining for the past forty years.[11] The wealth of the world's sixty richest individuals surpasses the combined wealth of half of the world's population. Global hunger is on the rise in many parts of the world due in part to climate change hurting small subsistence farmers. The world is backsliding in recent years in the battle against hunger and malnutrition, erasing a decade's progress in decreasing hunger.[12] While the percentage of people living in extreme poverty has decreased, half of the people on the planet live on less than $5.50 a day, and 70 percent live on less than $10 a day. Many poverty statistics are government reported and often understate the problem. Half of the people living in extreme poverty are children. Children are more than twice as likely to live in extreme poverty than adults. In sub-Saharan Africa and South Asia the number of people living in extreme poverty has increased. One-third of sub-Saharan African countries experienced declining incomes for the bottom 40 percent of their populations.[13] Some countries are poorer than they used to be. Many of those are countries with oil-dependent economies, such as Venezuela and Nigeria, and/or that have experienced conflict, such as Iraq and Syria. Extreme poverty is particularly destructive in Africa, the world's youngest countries where malnutrition stunts children's cognitive and physical development, limiting lives, and lifetime earning potential. Forty-three percent of Africans live in poverty, and many of the "middle-class" live dangerously close to the poverty line.[14] Critics say globalization widens the gap between rich and poor. Advocates say the lack of globalization causes such poverty.

Does globalization increase income inequality, making the rich richer and the poor poorer? Debates rage over this question, and there is some evidence on each side. On the one hand, China and India have moved their economies toward more industrial and high-tech sectors, and so have been able to benefit from foreign direct investment (FDI), and incomes have improved. Plenty of poverty remains in these countries, especially among women and people in rural areas, and the rate of economic growth has slowed. But because of the large populations in China and India, growth in income, life expectancy, and education there allows advocates for globalization to claim that globalization is decreasing global poverty (even though China still retains a great deal of government control over the economy, so China does not follow the Western consensus for globalization). Even in China and India, poverty reduction has been overstated due to problems with economic measurements, and lack of accurate and transparent figures from the Chinese communist government. Poverty is much worse in sub-Saharan Africa and economies in transition (such as those in Eastern Europe). The world's poorest countries have experienced declining income rather than economic growth, gains in life expectancy, and education made immediately after decolonization flatlined or reversed in many countries (e.g., life expectancy in Chad is fifty years). African countries find their agricultural products shut out of global markets due to protectionist agriculture policies. Their cheaper labor is excluded from developed country markets due to restrictive immigration policies. These countries do not benefit from FDI, which goes to more developed economies rather than to the poorest economies. Income inequality has increased within countries as well as among countries.

Wealth is only one indicator of global asymmetries. Countries and communities with oil economies have seen declining health, longevity, and environmental damage. Decisions about globalization are made in corporate boardrooms and state capitals generally in economically developed states. Toxic waste from developed countries, however, is shipped to the world's poorest communities as some corporations exploit regions where environmental legislation or enforcement is weak. Most foreign direct investment and corporate shareholder profits go to developed states. Globalization's costs and benefits are unequally distributed, with poor people and poor countries too often not participating in the full benefits that globalization may bring. Maximizing the benefits of globalization while minimizing or managing the challenges is difficult because the institution we generally task with managing global problems—the sovereign state—cannot do the job alone, particularly as governments have become poorer. The private sector has gotten richer, while governments have become poorer over the past four decades, leading to fewer resources for governments to mitigate the challenges of globalization.

Another part of the debate is over the pace of globalization or "hyperglobalization," the rapid changes in the scope, speed, and spread of globalization in the information age. This calls into question the role of checks and balances on markets, from governments, civil society, social safety nets and unions. Globalization has been ascendant since the end of World War II, but the pace and nature of globalization changed after the 1980s and 1990s, when changes in technology and politics ushered in a period of "hyperglobalization." Former US president Ronald Reagan and former British prime minister Margaret Thatcher pursued faster and larger free trade agreements and faster growth rates, while cutting government and social safety nets, cutting worker retraining for new jobs, and cutting labor unions' abilities to counter the growing power of corporate elites. The development and privatization of information technologies was met with policies that widely distributed these technologies, particularly former US senator and vice president Al Gore's legislation to make the Internet free and available to the public, which drastically lowered information costs, making hyperglobalization possible. China and India modernized and opened their economies to international trade at this time, but did so with heavy government involvement. This "hyperglobalization" period concentrated the benefits of globalization in very few hands and reduced job and income security, thus undermining democratic and public support for globalization. When world crises disrupted hyperglobalization, public support for it reduced. Capitalism should not be run like a casino; investments should be based on sound reason, data, and evidence. **Casino Capitalism** is the economic system's drive for short-term, quick profits over slower, lower-risk growth. This pressure for fast, risky, high returns, creates banks and financial companies who gamble with investor's money, creating and spreading high risk over the larger financial system. When unregulated Casino Capitalism collapsed into a global economic recession in 2007, the pace of globalization slowed, and people increasingly petitioned governments and other actors to intervene to reign in excesses. By this view, the period of hyperglobalization lasted from 1980 to 2007. After the worldwide recession of 2007–2008, and the increase in refugees from the Libyan and Syrian civil wars, support for globalization has been more mixed since, with increased calls for protectionist tariff and trade measures and fortified borders.

Most of the clashes between globalization's proponents and skeptics are peaceful, carried out in op-ed pages, in consumer boycotts, and on the floors of parliaments. But as globalization disrupts work and living patterns, and as global economic busts show the volatility of integrated global financial markets, frustrations are also rising. Nationalist politicians blame social and economic problems on anything foreign—immigrants, refugees, foreign made products, international trade deals, international organizations. Growing income inequality between the 1 percent and everyone else also undermines the legitimacy and support for policies that have facilitated globalization since the end of World War II. Robots and automation take jobs, particularly of store and factory workers, causing economic and social dislocations, and weaker labor unions and weaker government social safety nets are not able to soften the blow for those globalization has left behind.

This book takes a third way in these debates: Globalization is neither inherently good nor evil—but both. Terrorists and tourists alike use the same global infrastructure. Global issues are the unintended side effects of globalization. As globalization either advances or maintains its place in modern life, so will both opposition to globalization and its unintended adverse effects. To better harness and spread the benefits of globalization, we must take these adverse effects and the ethics of globalization seriously and work to better contain globalization's challenges. As the sides become more polarized, this third way is often overlooked. Proponents do not adequately recognize globalization's failures, while opponents do not fully recognize its benefits. Some proponents argue that the way to address global inequities and poverty is more globalization more quickly, more "hyperglobalization" and full speed ahead. Some opponents argue for a return to an imagined "good old days" before globalization. Some opponents argue that globalization should not be fixed but abandoned, and attempts to lessen globalization's downsides are misplaced, akin to asking cannibals to eat more politely with forks. Creating a kinder, gentler "globalization with a human face" allows unjust systems to persist longer rather than tearing them down. Ironically, opponents to globalization use the tools of globalization (global media, social media, and the Internet, for example) to organize, mobilize, and publicize their opposition to globalization. And proponents of globalization use the arguments of opponents who are concerned with serious poverty and environmental problems to justify more globalization, arguing that only greater globalization will increase living standards and eventually leave more disposable income to address environmental problems. Too often, both sides talk past each other.

The same is true in the sovereignty debates. Some argue sovereignty is dead, while others argue it is insurgent and unchanging. I argue instead for a third approach: Sovereignty remains, but is changing in important ways, and must adapt to allow greater coordination among the largest number of people, states, and nonstate actors in human history, in order to face the complex and intertwined global issues we created.

Understanding pressing global issues means understanding that globalization creates both benefits and challenges that states cannot control or solve alone. Because the problems go beyond sovereignty, so must the solutions. But going beyond sovereignty to manage global problems does not mean the creation of a world government that dictates outcomes. Variety, subsidiarity, and solidarity are keys to resilience and ethical legitimacy. A variety of creative adaptations and new coordination mechanisms are being and must be created. These adaptations also carry unintended consequences for the state. The growth of the private sector, often with the aid of deliberate policy choices by states, now often dwarfs the capacity of the public sector, even in strong states. In their attempts to manage pressing global problems, states contract out and form networks and alliances with the private sector (NGOs and MNCs) and with other states and multilateral organizations (IGOs). States enter into these partnerships voluntarily, expecting help in managing global problems. Yet in doing so, states may intentionally (through tax cuts and government downsizing) and unintentionally (through unintended consequences) lose some autonomy, authority, and legitimacy as they embrace the rising capacity of other actors.

Which policy path will we choose going forward: hyperglobalization or nationalism/unilateralism/protectionism? Or a patchwork quilt variety of networks and reforms to globalization, that address inequities, build democratic support and legitimacy, yet do not "throw out the baby with the bathwater?" Do we put our foot on the gas, on the brake, or do we retune and reinvent and take a new path? Globalization is decentralized and widely implemented in social, technological, economic, and political structures around the world. We can't uninvent it or delete it from human thought and practice. What we make of it or do about it going forward is up to us, however. We are blessed, or cursed, to live in interesting times.

THE DIFFICULTIES IN ADDRESSING GLOBAL ISSUES

Global issues are difficult to solve for many reasons. First, states and the private sector have to figure out how to control or contain them without closing off economies, societies, or technologies. Second, because their very nature precludes unilateral solutions, global issues are harder to tackle because they require coordination among a greater number of actors. Third, they are complex because they entail both state and nonstate actors, which creates coordination problems. Effective action requires complex coordination among states, NGOs, IGOs, MNCs, and other nonstate actors. These groups have different interests, capabilities, and constituencies. As more groups attempt to coordinate action, more opportunities are created for policy to go awry. As a British minister for the environment explained,

> We face new dilemmas—of problems that cross boundaries, of issues that no single government can control, and of shared risk. Nowhere is this collectivity more true than with the environment. Pollution, global warming, ozone depletion, and loss of species do not respect borders. . . . Globalization—in the form of increasing trade, the communications revolution, and increasing cultural exchanges—means that . . . governments have less influence over activities and economic sectors that were formerly under their control. . . . Some people refer to the effect this has on governments as "loss of agency." But the need for intervention in the public interest has not diminished—it is just that the locus has changed. Activities that were formerly national are now international, but the institutional capacity to deal with them has yet to evolve . . . we must manage the changing responsibilities of governments, business and civil society, forming new partnerships, learning from each other, finding new ways of harnessing the expertise and legitimate concerns and aspirations of each.[15]

Fourth, global issues are challenging because they often take place in the economic and social spheres, where the arm of liberal capitalist states has the shortest reach. Fifth, addressing global issues is difficult because these problems blur the borders between domestic and foreign policy. As domestic constituencies become mobilized over global issues, policy makers find their tasks complicated because they must address and coordinate the interests of additional groups. Domestic labor, environmental, and industry groups mobilize for international discussions of pollution or climate change, for example. Politics does not stop at the water's edge. Efforts to manage global issues may stumble over contentious and unsettled domestic policy debates. For example, Brazilian government policies toward global climate change involve discussions of the rights of indigenous peoples and the private industries that cut, burn, and extract minerals in the Amazon rain forests.

Global issues signal a fundamental change, integrating domestic and foreign policy:

> Foreign policy as we have known it is dead . . . because it is no longer foreign.. . .The distinctions between domestic and foreign are gone. Look at the issues: The . . . fight against drugs and crime has major international components. Our stolen cars end up in El Salvador or Guatemala or Poland.

Our drugs come from Peru or Pakistan or Burma or elsewhere and transit almost anywhere. Crime cartels spread tentacles from Nigeria or Russia or Colombia. Today, it is inconceivable to consider a coordinated attack on crime without working a part of the strategy in the international arena. . . . International terrorism has reached our shores. . . .We cannot deal with the threats to our environment, to assaults on biodiversity with domestic policy. Ozone layer depletion and global warming cannot be addressed by domestic environmental regulations alone. Over and over again, we find issues that are domestic in consequence, but international in scope. These are the consuming issues of the twenty-first century.[16]

Global issues also can be difficult for states to address because of institutional gaps between the sovereign states we have and the policy responses we need. Capacity gaps, jurisdiction gaps, participation gaps, legitimacy gaps, and ethical gaps all plague efforts to address global issues (these are discussed more fully in the concluding chapter). Existing institutions were not created to handle these problems, and they may be slow to change, resist taking on new functions that may divert resources from their traditional missions, and have difficulties coordinating with other institutions. Finally, contracting out or cooperating with the private sector and multilateral organizations to combat or contain global problems may unintentionally further undermine sovereignty.

YESTERDAY: WHERE SOVEREIGNTY CAME FROM

Most sovereign states are new. The international system has not always been organized around sovereignty. Empires have been common historically, including China, Japan, and the Ottoman Empire. Prior to the Treaty of Westphalia in 1648, there were overlapping jurisdictions of political authority with no clear hierarchy or pecking order among them.[17] In this European feudal system, claims to authority were diffuse, decentralized, and based on personal ties rather than territory. Medieval European subjects faced simultaneous and competing claims for allegiance to the pope, the king or the emperor, the bishop, and local feudal princes, dukes, counts, lords, and so on.[18] Taxes and military service could be required of a person from several different authorities within the same territory. A person's bonds to an authority figure were based on personal ties and agreements, and "political authority was treated as a private possession."[19] This made secession problematic because contractual obligations might not survive a person's death.

Rather than land, authority claims often were based on the divine—on spiritual connections or on the legitimacy of lineage to the Church (and in the days before the Reformation, that meant the Roman Catholic Church). Secular and spiritual authority were intertwined. Kings were anointed with holy insignia (e.g., British monarchs have the title "Defender of the Faith"), emperors were crowned as "servants of the apostles," and popes and bishops needed the support of nonclerical leaders to gain and retain power. Both the Church and the Holy Roman Empire sought to fill the vacuum left by the fall of the Roman Empire and made universal claims of authority.

People, not territory, were the primary objects of rule, and "rule was per definition spiritual" rather than spatial.[20] In the struggle between the papacy and the Holy Roman Empire for control, both institutions were weakened in ways that helped new forms of political organization to emerge.

There were many reasons why the feudal system declined and the sovereign state emerged. The rise of long-distance trade in the late Middle Ages created both a new merchant class of elites and the need for a new political system that could better accommodate the mercantilist economic system. The Church was against the exchange and loan of money and the taking of oaths, but currency and contracts were crucial to long-distance trade. Trade also required more precise and consistent measurements of time, weights, jurisdiction, and private property. As Hendrik Spruyt notes,

> [t]he result of this economic dynamism was that a social group, the town dwellers, came into existence with new sources of revenue and power, which did not fit the old feudal order. This new social group had various incentives to search for political allies who were willing to change the existing order. The new trading and commercial classes of the towns could not settle into the straitjacket of the feudal order, and the towns became a chief agent in its final disruption. . . . Business activity could not be organized according to the . . . system of personal bonds. . . . Contracts could not depend on the initiating actors. Sometimes these contracts might have to carry through beyond the death of the original contractors.[21]

The rise of a new economic system with its own needs, however, was not enough to bring about the rise of the sovereign state. The currency of other ideas aided the development of the concept of sovereignty. Martin Luther and the Protestant Reformation, Henry VIII and his Anglican separatists, the rise of scientific knowledge and explorations of the non-European world, along with the new merchant elites, challenged the authority and legitimacy of the Church in Rome. Roman ideas of property rights—which stressed exclusive control over territory—also were on the rise.[22] Ideas of individual autonomy and freedom from outside interference, later captured by Immanuel Kant, were important in the development of sovereignty. According to Daniel Philpott, these religious ideas that gave rise to today's modern conceptions of human rights played a vital part.[23] Nicholas Onuf cites three conceptual crucial antecedents to the genesis of sovereignty: *majestas*, or the idea that institutions inspire respect; *potestas imperiandi*, or the ability to coerce and enforce rules; and the Protestant idea of stewardship, or rule on behalf of the citizens of the body politic, not the personal rule of the Middle Ages.[24]

Besides conceptual changes, sovereignty also emerged because of changes in practical political balances. Sovereign states were more effective and efficient at waging war and conducting trade than were competing political organizations.[25] Elites who benefited from the new form of organization sought to delegitimize actors who were not organized as sovereign states by excluding them from the international system.

Other forms of political organization competed with the sovereign state to succeed the feudal system: the city-state, the urban league, and the empire. Hendrik Spruyt believes that the sovereign state eventually won out for three main reasons. First, states were better able to extract resources and rationalize their economies than were other forms of political organization. Second, states were more efficient and effective than were medieval forms of organization, especially at being able to "speak with one voice" and make the external commitments necessary to the new trading system. And third, social choice and institutional mimicry meant that sovereign states selected out and delegitimized other actors who were not sovereign states.[26]

Out of these changes in ideas, economics, and political balances came the eventual acceptance of the sovereign state. Authority was now based on exclusive jurisdiction over territory. Identity became based on geography: You were where you lived—a citizen of French territory, not primarily a member of the Holy Roman Empire or the community of Christians or the Celtic or Norman clans.

In theory, the sovereign state had a monopoly on the legitimate use of force within a territory. Sovereignty was reciprocal. One state recognized the others' exclusive jurisdictions over their territories and the populations and resources that resided on their lands; in return, they recognized that state's exclusive jurisdiction over its territory and everything on its land.[27] From the beginning, sovereignty was based on a social compact. Sovereignty never meant that all states had equal power or resources—some had vast lands, populations, and resources, while the capabilities of other states were meager. But sovereignty meant that only other sovereigns had legal standing in international agreements. States were the main unit of the international system.

From its origins in Europe, the idea and practice of sovereignty spread around the globe as Europeans conquered and carved up the planet into colonial territories. Sovereignty (with its territorial limits) came into conflict with the unlimited, universal Chinese, Japanese, and Ottoman empires, but eventually sovereignty came to dominate worldwide, whether by force or accession. When European colonies became independent after World War II and later when the Soviet bloc disintegrated between 1989 and 1991, the political units that emerged sought sovereign statehood, not recognition of other forms of political organization.

Sovereignty is an equalizing concept. Internally, governments organize themselves in whatever fashion they choose: monarchy, dictatorship, republican constitutional parliamentary system, autocracy, theocracy, etc. Externally, however, all a state needs is international recognition as a sovereign state.

TODAY: SOVEREIGNTY CHALLENGED

While the modern international system is built on the foundation of sovereignty, today, it is under siege, in practice and in theory. There have always been weak states, and distinctions between the theory and the practice of sovereignty, yet both de jure and de facto sovereignty are now under assault more than ever. The sovereign state will continue to be the main unit in the international system for some time, but the operation and legitimacy of sovereignty are being undermined by both external and internal dynamics.

The mid-twentieth century was the "high water" mark for sovereignty and strong states. "Big government" was "in" around the world, in communist states, fascist states, military dictatorships, and even in capitalist democracies (where state power had grown in order to fight the Great Depression and two world wars). The idea of sovereignty was also strong. As European colonial empires broke up after World War II, the newly independent communities chose to organize as sovereign states, rather than as tribes, nations, empires, or other organizing units.

Negative sovereignty is a sovereign state's legal right to nonintervention from other states, even in cases when a state abuses its own citizens. Historically, negative sovereignty was widely accepted and commonplace. Rather than protecting their own citizens, many sovereign states brutally killed tens of millions of their own people, from Nazi Germany's Holocaust to Stalin's purges in Russia to Mao's Cultural Revolutions in China to Pol Pot's killing fields in Uganda. After the end of the Cold War, and a series of humanitarian crises in the 1990s (the famine in Somalia in 1993, the Rwandan genocide in 1994, the ethnic cleansing and wars in the Balkans) international norms began to change, away from sovereignty as right (of nonintervention) to sovereignty as responsibility, **R2P**, or the Responsibility to Protect. States have the primary responsibility to protect their own citizens. When states are unable or unwilling to protect their own citizens, or worse, when states kill their own citizens, these moral and political failures impact others. The Universal Declaration of Human Rights (UNDHR) asserts human rights and dignity should not be undermined by the sovereign state in which people are born or reside. States committed themselves to prevent and protect people against genocide, war crimes, and crimes against humanity in the Genocide Convention and other international laws. R2P furthers these commitments.[28]

This R2P principle was established in UN Security Council 1674, adopted April 28, 2006, accepting "the responsibility to protect populations from genocide, war crimes, ethnic cleansing, and crimes against humanity." Primary responsibility lies with the state itself for protection of its own citizens. But in cases where states are unable or unwilling to protect their own people, others also have responsibilities to act to protect civilians. R2P calls for diplomatic and humanitarian assistance. The UN General Assembly also affirmed the R2P (in (A/RES/60/1). States are not obligated to intervene militarily to prevent genocide, but R2P does keep the door open for states to request the Security Council to authorize force for civilian protection missions. As Patrick Stewart notes,

Sovereignty cannot be a blank check. It implies fundamental responsibilities, not simply privileges. It is not enough to say all governments can act as they wish, with no regard for other nations or their own citizens. And when governments ignore these standards and violate rules, they cannot expect others to turn a blind eye. They should expect consequences. This was a conception of sovereignty on which both George W. Bush and Barack Obama, for all their differences, agreed. Sovereignty is fundamental, but it also contingent. When countries sponsor terrorism or pursue weapons of mass destruction in violation of international rules, or when they make war on their citizens, they risk forfeiting their expectation of sovereign inviolability. . .sovereignty cannot simply mean independence. It must be framed as responsibility.[29]

Sovereignty is under siege in practice. Sovereignty is challenged externally by the globalizing dynamics of open markets, open societies, and open technologies, which make the borders of even strong states permeable by outside forces. Sovereignty is also under siege internally from the rise of internal conflicts and subnational movements, as well as from the reinforcing crises of economic development (resource scarcity, environmental degradation, population growth) that undermine the international and internal legitimacy on which sovereignty stands. Both of these dynamics have led to a growing number of fragile and collapsing states. But even the strongest states in the system cannot effectively manage global issues alone.

Nearly one-third of the people on the planet, about two billion people, live in fragile or failing states. Africa and the Middle East are home to the world's most fragile states.[30] Not coincidentally, countries in Africa and the Middle East remain embroiled in civil wars, in places such as Syria, Iraq, the Democratic Republic of Congo, Sudan, and Afghanistan.[31] The effects of these civil wars do not remain internal. Refugees flee these conflicts in droves. Terror and insurgent groups active in one civil war cross borders and destabilize other states. The challenges of fragile states are felt beyond their borders.

A state is in a process of collapse when its institutions and leaders lose control of political and economic space. When state authorities can no longer provide security, law and order, an economic infrastructure, or other services for citizens, then government retracts and the countryside is left on its own. Political space broadens as outside actors usurp (as in Syria and Lebanon) and intervene (as IGOs and NGOs enter to provide relief services necessitated by state breakdown). Economic space contracts as the informal economy takes over beyond state control, and as localities resort to barter, as occurred in Somalia.[32] In the power vacuum left by state collapse, global problems thrive. For example, as Al Qaeda fighters were pushed out of Afghanistan, they moved to Sudan, Somalia, and Yemen—other areas where state control is weak.

When states implode, more than the residents are affected. In an interdependent world, the event can hurt distant international actors. Refugee flows, disease, terrorism, crime, drug smuggling, ethnic conflict, and civil war all thrive as the state recedes and often spread beyond borders. NGOs, IGOs, and criminal organizations are all drawn to collapsed states, whether to help restore law and order or to exploit its absence.

Some scholars believe that the international system used to be based primarily on **"positive sovereignty,"** the actual, empirical ability of a state to control its political and economic space, to provide public safety and public services for the people living within a country's territory. It is a state's ability to "provide political goods for its citizens . . . the sociological, economic, technological, psychological, and similar where-withal to declare, implement, and enforce public policy both domesti-cally and internationally."[33] Weak states existed, but not for long, as it was considered perfectly legitimate for an outside power to conquer and absorb a weak state. The "old sovereignty game" recognized but did not protect weak sovereignties. They were vulnerable links in the interna-tional system's food chain. Their digestion by more powerful states was internationally sanctioned behavior.

This changed with the rise of Woodrow Wilson's idea of self-deter-mination, with the discrediting of the concept of "salt-water colonial-ism"[34] and the end of colonial empires, and with the rise of democracy. The "new sovereignty game" is increasingly based on "negative sover-eignty," the formal-legal entitlement to freedom from outside interfer-ence and the de jure norm of nonintervention.[35] Thus, the current norms and practices of the international system create conditions that allow weak, ineffectual quasi-states to exist.

Sovereignty is also under siege from internal pressures and conflicts that weaken state institutions. Many states in the developing world are undergoing related crises of rising populations needing education and jobs, poverty, disease, environmental degradation, and internal conflict. Corruption flourishes as survival is endangered, a "get mine" mentality permeates public life, and people don't expect to live long enough to face consequences for their actions. High external debt diverts government budgets from critical public health, education, and social welfare invest-ments to making interest payments that further profit Western banks. Where political institutions are seen as weak and ineffective to meet public needs, cynicism, hostility, and armed conflicts multiply. Most African countries now struggle to respond to this "perfect storm" of poverty, environmental pressures, and political instability. The oppor-tunity for conflict among societal groups increases as resources shrink.

Reinforcing economic and political crises are not restricted to Africa. GNP in the former Soviet states fell by as much as 30 percent after the Cold War, while major armed conflicts in the region qua-drupled in the 1990s.[36] Pressure on (and disillusionment with) fragile state institutions grows as the state fails to break (or contributes to) the scarcity cycle and as the chasm grows between the lesser-developed and the developed states. States that are confronted with reinforcing crises can "harden," resorting to increased repression in an attempt to establish control.[37] Repressive tactics are costly, however. Civil institutions of the state atrophy (and economic and social performance often suffer) as power and resources concentrate in the military and police. State legitimacy and authority is further undermined, and opposition grows with the increase in repressive tactics.

The result is not just a crisis of a particular regime but of the sovereign state itself. Any regime that wins power will face extremely denigrated (to nonexistent) state institutions and societal bases of state power. Thus, the related crises of poverty and internal conflict undermine the foundations of sovereign power. Many areas of Afghanistan respond entirely to tribal and local authorities, not the sovereign state. After decades of warfare, arms are readily available, leaving the state with nothing close to a monopoly on the use of force.s NGOs, IGOs, and states aid Afghanistan, many worry not only about the capacity of any new government but also whether the area is governable.

Sovereignty also is undermined by external trends that have been heralded since the end of the Cold War: the opening of societies, economies, and technologies. Strong states are not immune to the problems of globalization, as shown by global air pollution problems, and terrorist attacks. Developing states are also caught in a bind. Leaders are attracted to the prospect of wealth promised by democracy, capitalism, and technology (which can strengthen the state), yet they fear the loss of control and the decentralization of power that these processes entail (which can weaken the state). Capitalism, democracy, and technology can devolve power away from central state institutions and undermine the state's ability to control its borders.[38] Many developing states desire international capital and jobs, but the process of liberalizing economic and political systems can be quite destabilizing. Citizen demands on government cannot wait until new institutions are built and put into place, so developing states are in the challenging position of trying to modernize and democratize their institutions as these same institutions try to solve critical problems. Democratization is difficult; as Jack Snyder and Edward Mansfield note, it is like changing the steering wheel while driving the car.[39]

The end of the Cold War increased the pressure on many weak states. More states compete for less overseas development assistance. The standard of living dropped precipitously in many states that had received Cold War assistance, such as North Korea (where famine has been a problem in recent years). The underlying ineffectiveness of state political and economic institutions becomes clear without the mask of Cold War aid and alliances. The authority and legitimacy of the state suffer because the state cannot meet citizen expectations, and living standards decline.

The world is increasingly segregated into two zones—peace and turmoil—with a widening gap between the advanced capitalist democracies and the underdeveloped nondemocratic states, as Max Singer and Aaron Wildavsky argue. They argued the stabilizing solution to this dilemma was the advancement of democratization, economic liberalization, and development so that more states would move from the "zone of turmoil" to the "zone of peace."[40]

It is not that simple. Democratization and economic liberalization can undermine already fragile state institutions. During the transition period, attempts to establish open societies and markets can further move a weak state into the zone of turmoil. Even in largely peaceful and prosperous market democracies, cyber attackers and drug markets thrive. US life expectancy has declined precipitously due to the opioid drug crisis, in the most steep decline since the influenza outbreak of World War I. The speed of technological change disrupts economies, causing turmoil even in developed democracies. Singer and Wildavsky argued that the zone of peace (even with its problems of drugs and crime) is preferable to the zone of turmoil (with its starvation and war), but surely their argument needs qualification—at least to check the expectations of fledgling democracies. Singer and Wildavsky's zone of peace is not the Promised Land. Democratization and economic liberalization carry their own costs in terms of global issues. Even strong, wealthy states with healthy internal institutions cannot unilaterally defeat global problems.

Open Economies

Open economies are on the rise, facilitated by global technologies and open societies. Historically, developed countries have long promoted international trade and global capitalist economic systems, sometimes even through force, while also trying to protect some domestic markets from international competition. US tensions with China and Japan in the nineteenth and twentieth centuries concerned the opening of Asian markets to US goods.

European imperialism in Asia, Africa, and the Americas also served commercial interests. From the trade in spices, slaves, and rum to the extraction of precious metals, foreign commerce drove earlier periods of globalization. US imperialism in Latin America and the Pacific was also conducted in the name of promoting trade and opening commerce. The American empire—in the form of US protectorates in Puerto Rico, Guam, Samoa, Virgin Islands, and Hawaii, among others—was acquired largely to assist US commercial interests in their efforts to expand foreign trade. The United States forcibly created the country of Panama (by seizing territory from Colombia) in order to build the Panama Canal to facilitate trade. Military intervention in Guatemala in 1954 was done largely to protect the interests of the United Fruit Company. As one US trade official argued, "For most of America's history, foreign policy has reflected an obsession with open markets for American business. . . . Business expansion abroad was often seen as an extension of the American frontier, part of the nation's manifest destiny."[41]

Given these ties between colonialism and free market economics, it is no wonder that many citizens in developing countries are suspicious of globalization and the spread of international trade and capitalist systems. Many question just how "free" trade is among unequal trading partners and how "open" developed economies are to the goods (especially agricultural products) of lesser-developed countries. Developed countries retain **protectionist measures**, policies that shield local companies from competition from foreign companies through a variety of means including tariffs, subsidies, and quotas. Protectionist obstacles are high in agriculture, the products in which developing countries enjoy comparative advantage. Some see free trade and monetary policies as neoimperialism, with multinational corporations and international economic organizations such as the IMF and World Trade Organization (WTO) now infringing on the sovereignty of developing states in place of the colonial armies of a previous era. Trade ministers in developed countries counter that open markets, for all their imperfections, perform better than do state-controlled markets.

The Cold War was caused in part by this clash between state and market economies, with the United States opposed to the Soviets closing Eastern European markets to Western goods and trade. During the Cold War, many in the West believed that the superior economic performance of capitalist, free-market systems would eventually bring state-controlled, communist economic systems to their knees. US diplomat George Kennan presciently predicted that the demise of the Soviet sphere would come about not through the external military confrontation of a globalized and militarized US containment policy, which the United States could not afford, but through the West's building of strong, internal open societies and open markets. Eventually, the Soviet bloc would be "unable to stand the comparison."

If economic recovery could be brought about and public confidence restored in Western Europe—if Western Europe, in other words, could be made the home of a vigorous, prosperous and forward-looking civilization—the communist regime in Eastern Europe . . . would never be able to stand the comparison, and the spectacle of a happier and more successful life just across the fence . . . would be bound in the end to have a disintegrating and eroding effect on the communist world.[42]

His prediction was confirmed when the Cold War ended largely nonviolently. The Marshall Plan and forty-five years of a concerted policy of building open economic and political institutions in Western Europe succeeded in rebuilding a continent destroyed by war. Such rebuilding never took place in much of Eastern Europe. Eventually, even the top leaders of the Soviet Union were forced to admit that their economic system was in need of reform when Gorbachev came to power in the USSR in the 1980s.

The last Soviet leader, Mikhail Gorbachev, made **perestroika** reforms, efforts to improve the productivity and efficiency of the USSR's state-controlled economy and polity. He wanted to cut down on vodka abuse on the job, decrease bureaucratic red tape, and increase worker and industry accountability. Quickly, these internal attempts to reform and strengthen the communist system unleashed massive dissatisfaction with the existing system, underlined by the Chernobyl nuclear disaster. Gorbachev's reforms tapped into consumer and social unrest over shortages and poor economic performance (e.g., exploding television sets in Moscow were a common cause of hospital emergency room visits). The legitimacy of the communist model was undermined, accelerating the pace of Gorbachev's initially modest reforms into the eventual overthrow of the entire system. Gorbachev soon learned what the Chinese are now grappling with: that it is difficult to uncork just a little economic freedom.

With the demise of communist regimes in Eastern Europe and the former Soviet Union, and with the demise of state-controlled economies and authoritarian regimes in Latin America, many in the West assumed that "the West won" the Cold War's economic battle. As Paul Krugman put it, "Governments that had spent half a century pursuing statist, protectionist policies suddenly got free market religion. It was . . . the dawn of a new golden age for global capitalism." In addition, there was a sea change in the intellectual Zeitgeist: the almost universal acceptance, by governments and markets alike, of a new view about what it takes to develop. This view has come to be widely known as the "**Washington Consensus**." . . . It is the belief that . . . free markets and sound money [are] the key to economic development. Liberalize trade, privatize state enterprises, balance the budget, peg the exchange rate, and one will have laid the foundations for an economic takeoff.[43]

The "Washington Consensus" has broken down. Many in the developing world have long criticized the "Washington Consensus" as adverse to the poor. They question the desirability of interconnected economies built on a "one-size-fits-all" Western model. They also point out that Washington rarely followed its own advice, as the United States runs large budget deficits, and the United States and Europeans have protectionist agriculture measures. Today, however, the United States has done an "about-face," with the Trump administration's support of tariffs, trade wars, and historically large debt.

The global economic recession of 2007 undermined the Washington Consensus. The crisis began in the United Kingdom and United States, with bad housing loans mixed in with good loans, in complex, little-regulated and little-understood investment bundles called "derivatives." Bankers and investors believed this made sense because risk was widely divided among financial institutions across the globe, and in any case, they had purchased insurance from highly rated global insurance companies like AIG, which would insulate them from losses if the investments went bad. They thought widely dividing the risk lessened it. Instead, it put contaminated or "toxic" assets on the books of so many financial institutions, that all were vulnerable when the housing bubble burst. Rising foreclosures and investors pulled their money out of the market. Financial institutions fell like a line of dominoes; banks and insurance companies did not have the capital on hand to cover all the losses. Stock markets crashed and credit markets froze, hurting all, not only the people who had profited in the "subprime mortgage" fiasco. The cascading financial crises revealed many underlying structural problems. Markets operate best when they operate under law and transparency, but regulations and transparency were weak or nonexistent in this case. Global capitalism is prone to market booms and busts, and cascading crises, but many leaders believed markets would regulate themselves, and market problems would come from developing countries in a "it can't happen here" mentality. More than twenty years earlier, Susan Strange predicted this type of "Casino Capitalism" where extreme market volatility destroys lives due to innovations in financial markets; the sheer size of markets; commercial banks turning into investment banks; the rise of Asian economies; and the shift to corporate self-regulation.[44]

She warned that these economic changes were happening faster than our abilities to understand the political consequences. Many countries are now less inclined to accept economic advice from the United States and Britain, since the economic crisis began in those countries' markets.

Of course, "free-market religion" was never established universally, even before the Great Recession. Peruvian economist and policy maker Hernando de Soto points out that world's poor lack formal and protected property rights, and thus are shut out of the formal economy, in capitalist states from Latin America to the Middle East.[45] While many states "talk the talk" of capitalism, developed countries also retain popular, protectionist, agriculture subsidies and restrictions on certain foreign products. China is a state-run not a free market economy, albeit more open to global trade than in previous decades. Around the world, corruption is a huge obstacle to economic development. Women do not have property rights in many countries. As countries privatize state-owned industries, the process is vulnerable to distortion by corruption, as occurred in Russia. There are still states, such as North Korea, with closed economies. Others, such as China, Vietnam, and Cuba, try to attract foreign capital and investment and encourage some privatization of the economy, while the central government still owns and plays a key role in many industries.

Yet the spread of capitalism, some contend, helps to spread peace and democracy as well. People with economic rights may demand political rights. There is some evidence of this today in Iran and in China, where a growing middle class increasingly demands an end to political corruption, and where there are now contested local elections. Thomas Friedman argues that capitalism and economic interdependence bring peace. The economic price of war is too heavy for countries whose economies are deeply intertwined, who both supply Dell computers for example. "**The Dell Theory**" stipulates: No two countries that are both part of a major global supply chain, like Dell's, will ever fight a war against each other as long as they are both part of the same global supply chain."[46]

US and Western dominance of international economic regimes draws criticism from many people around the world. The European Union (EU), WTO, IMF, and World Bank were all created by the United States and its developed allies. Developing countries often have little say in the rules and regimes that govern the global economy. This power imbalance impacts access to essential medicines, for example. For many years, the WTO's rules favored Western pharmaceutical companies that were interested in protecting their patents and profits over developing countries that needed affordable generic medicines to save lives and fight pressing public health crises, such as HIV/AIDS. In the first modification of WTO rules, a process for access to essential medicines for poor countries was created.[47] China initiated the Asian Infrastructure Investment Bank, along with forty-five other countries, as an alternative to the international institutions dominated by the United States and Western countries.

However, even though open economies often perform better than their state-run counterparts, they also carry many costs, including cascading economic crises.[48] Resentment over a widening gulf between rich and poor states and developed countries' dominance of the global economy leads to protests of globalization. The transition to capitalist economic structures also can destabilize states. Some dispute that markets and democracy go hand in hand. Amy Chua argues that "Exporting free market democracy breeds ethnic hatred and global instability." When market liberalization helps "foreign minorities" earn disproportionate wealth, the local majority suffers economically, and this lights the match to violence. Wealthy ethnic minorities, from Chinese in Southeast Asia to Croatians in the former Yugoslavia, become violently hated, at the same time as emerging democracy "empowers the impoverished majority, unleashing ethnic demagoguery, confiscation, and sometimes genocidal revenge."[49]

Instability provides openings for organized crime to step into the vacuum, as has occurred in Russia. The old communist order was pulled down, but new laws and institutions that support free market economies are weak, and much turmoil can arise in the interim.

Decreased regulation and increased transborder trade decreases the opportunities for shipments to be searched or monitored. Electronic monitoring and other mechanisms can replace physical searches, but these digital search mechanisms are invented and often implemented by the private sector. Thus, states lose, or share with private actors, significant control over their borders, one of the hallmarks of sovereignty.

"Dirty money" follows many of the same paths as "clean money." The same emerging global financial infrastructure useful to legal businesses also increases the opportunity and ease of conducting and covering illicit economic activities, such as the smuggling of narcotics and nuclear materials. Profits from illicit activities can be hidden in legal investments, sprinkled into front companies, bank accounts, and small investments across a range of industries and states. With cryptocurrencies and electronic markets, the money trail can move quickly and be erased as investments can be changed and moved with a keystroke.

Attempts to freeze and seize the monies of criminal groups and terrorist organizations show how difficult it can be to track and stop illicit cash in interdependent economies.

Open economies also decentralize power as more and more actors have autonomous economic power and the central government loses its ability to control economic activities in a global marketplace, including governments' abilities to tax, issue money, and even perform security functions. Nonstate actors can issue money now, as digital currencies, particularly decentralized, anonymous cryptocurrencies like Bitcoin, move monetary policy outside the state. Microsoft founder Bill Gates's annual income is more than the annual GNP of many states. On the illegal side, the income of prominent drug lords often overwhelms and distorts the legal economy in a state because it is difficult to control or regulate.

States increasingly contract out military and security functions to private sector companies. Privatization has expanded exponentially, and now private companies operate killer drones, interrogate and torture terrorists, spy for the government, train armies, provide security in war zones with private armies for Ambassadors, Embassies and military installations, and are part of state military operations. As states turn to private sector companies to do state military and intelligence services, states lose some capacity and experience to do this work. For example, 70 percent of the US intelligence budget now goes to private sector companies. As described by one intelligence officer, "We can't spy if we can't buy."[50]

As a former contractor notes, "Private military contractors perform tasks once thought to be inherently governmental, such as raising foreign armies, conducting intelligence analysis and trigger-pulling. . . . The United States has developed a dependency on the private sector to wage war, a strategic vulnerability. Today, America can no longer go to war without the private sector."[51]

This long-term trend is accelerating. Some in the Trump administration propose amplifying this trend by turning the US war in Afghanistan over to private sector mercenary armies, private military contractors hired to conduct combat operations. They argue that there should be a private Viceroy for Afghanistan, and the model should be the old British East India Company that carried out colonization for the British Empire.[52] Push back against this trend usually only occurs when an abuse by military contractors comes to light in the media, as occurred when Blackwater company killed seventeen Iraqi civilians in 2007. Increased government oversight usually fades with the headlines.[53]

Today, push back to open economies' free trade agreements and integrated markets is growing, as seen in the United Kingdom's Brexit vote, and President Trump's tariff wars. Anxieties over income inequalities, job insecurities, and flat or declining middle-class incomes drives protests like the "Yellow Vest" protests in France, and the earlier "Occupy Wall Street" movement protests. In the United States, nearly all the jobs created in the last decade have been temporary, part time, or contract "gig" economy jobs, such as Uber drivers.[54] China's model of a state-directed economy appeals to many. As robots and IT displace more workers, pressure will continue for reforms to address economic imbalances. How can we enjoy the benefits of open economies while managing and minimizing its downsides? While economic change continues, and while states try to "call balls and strikes," the game has changed. The economic "players" are in the private sector and the world is their playing field; they get to call the shots.

Open Societies

Today, there are more open, democratic societies than in previous periods of history, as shown in this graphic. As recently as 1993, most countries in the world were autocracies. Today, one country, China, accounts for most of the people living in autocracy. Four out of five of the world's most populous countries are democracies. Democratization is not even, but occurs in fits and starts and with reversals. Democratic advancement has stalled for the past decade and some backsliding is occurring, even in established democracies.[55]

Francis Fukuyama argued that the end of the Cold War also signaled the end of history, by which he argued that "a remarkable consensus concerning the legitimacy of liberal democracy as a system of government has emerged throughout the world, as it conquered rival ideologies like hereditary monarchy, fascism, and most recently communism."[56] Although liberal democracy has not triumphed and may never prevail in all areas of the globe, Fukuyama contends that the twentieth century was marked by great battles of competing ideologies, and that at the Cold War's end no alternative *universal* ideology of consequence existed to challenge ideas of liberal democracy. According to Fukuyama, liberal democracy "gives fullest scope" to satisfying "all three parts of the soul [desire, reason, and spirit] simultaneously."[57] However, Fukuyama's thesis is challenged today by the rise of authoritarianism in some democracies (such as the Philippines and Eastern Europe), the

Figure 1.2   Rise of Open Societies

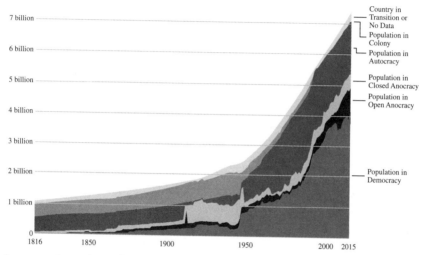

Increased number of people living in democracies

Source: World Population by Political Regime they live in (OWID 2016) OurWorldinData.org/a-history-of-global-living-conditions-in-5-charts/

rise of China, as well as by the ideas of some Islamic extremist groups that are intent on challenging Western government forms and promoting fundamentalist Islamic rule. Democratization is not a straight line; it ebbs and flows.

Democratization rose in the historical **"fourth wave" of democratization,** which included the dramatic democratization of the former Soviet states in the 1990s. This fourth wave was "more global in its reach . . . affecting far more countries and more thorough than its predecessors."[58] Democracy is not new and has been around in one form or another since the ancient Greeks. What is new, however, is the number of states from a variety of regions that are turning to representative government forms with free multiparty elections and the protection of individual and minority rights including free speech and free press, freedom of association, freedom of movement, and freedom of religion. For the first time in history, about half of the world's governments are either democracies or in transition to democracy.

In the first wave of democratization in the 1800s, universal suffrage was extended in states that were committed to democratic principles so that more than white male property owners could vote. This movement toward democracy ended as monarchies and authoritarian rulers sought to reestablish control in many states after the "springtime of freedom" in Europe in 1848–1849. Although the first wave expanded democracy within societies and sought to spread democracy in Western Europe and North America, these same states were involved simultaneously in carving up the non-Western world into colonial empires in profoundly nondemocratic ways.

The second wave of democratization occurred during and after World War I as many states believed that autocracies were more to blame for starting the war than were democratic states. However, many of the democracies established after World War I were weak, such as Germany's Weimar Republic, and many of these states reverted to authoritarianism as fascism swept the globe.

The third wave of democratization occurred with World War II as colonial powers were no longer able or willing to hold onto their overseas empires, and a tidal wave of decolonization swept the globe. The number of independent states tripled from 1945 to 1979, and many of these former colonies turned to democratic government forms. Once again, however, this wave of democratization was followed by reversals. After historic initial democratic elections, many leaders would not hand over power to others, barring further elections. This pattern was pernicious in Africa, where some of the world's oldest leaders reign over the world's youngest populations. Ironically, the Cold War also caused some democratic backsliding, as the United States and the West supported noncommunist but nondemocratic regimes. "By some counts, one-third of the globe's democracies had fallen under authoritarian rule by the late 1970s,"[59] as personal rule, military rule, or single-party autocracy replaced democratic political participation and institutions in developing states. Even though there were reverses, with each wave the number of democracies overall increased, as states such as India joined and stayed in the community of democracies.

The fourth wave of democratization differs from previous eras in two important respects. First, it was not the result of a single external event such as World War I or World War II. Although the end of the Soviet empire led many Eastern European states into the democratic experiment, other states such as Portugal, Spain, and South Africa turned to democracy for reasons other than (and prior to) the end of the Cold War.

Second, the most recent wave of democratization differs from its predecessors in scope and intensity. More states on more continents are becoming more democratic than ever before. This wave is not restricted to Europe or to former colonial empires, and this wave is more intensive, entailing a restructuring of political and economic institutions.

While the fate of these newly emerging democracies is by no means secure, the fourth wave of democratization has advantages that previous movements could not claim. The simultaneous trends of open markets and open technologies support and facilitate political openings. Previous reformers did not have instant Internet posts or satellite television immediately reporting advances or backsliding to an international audience. Previous reformers also did not have to liberalize political institutions as a prerequisite to receiving international capital investments, whether from international lending institutions such as the World Bank or IMF or from private investors who believe the rule of law as practiced in democratic societies secures a better business environment. The growth of civil society internationally may also help solidify the current wave of democratization.

Democracy has beat the odds. Four decades ago, policy makers and scholars thought such extensive advancement of democratization was unlikely, a utopian dream. The opening of societies may lend itself to more open economic systems, as people with some say in their political futures tend to desire openness in their economic futures as well.

Democracy spread for several reasons (of course, there are significant disagreements over how best to promote democracy in practice).[60] Global media and cheap and ready access to information technology can help democratization. Democracies are more likely to have free market and free trade capitalist economies (encouraged by international financial institutions) and to have more prosperity and better records of economic development. Democratic protections of property rights and individual liberties provide a rule of law that fosters a more stable investment and business climate and better protects the larger number of citizens now traveling abroad and taking advantage of more advanced transportation and communication links. Perhaps most important, developed democracies tend not to go to war with one another, a phenomenon known as **democratic peace theory**.[61] Democracies are not more peaceful overall. They tend to go to war with nondemocracies, and the transition period of democratization can be fraught with conflict. But democracies don't go to war with other democracies; on this the empirical record is strong.

Democratization is not easy, carries costs, and is vulnerable to reversals. Transitions to democracy can be destabilizing in the short run, as "[d]emocratization typically creates a syndrome of weak central authority, unstable domestic coalitions, and high-energy mass politics."[62] Democratic elections and liberal protections—of human rights, rule of law, and separation of powers—may not coincide.[63] If privatization and liberalization of the economy are occurring simultaneously with democratization efforts (as is often the case), then corrupt, powerful corporate or criminal organizations may gain assets and influence before the civic institutions of public control and accountability are established (as occurred in Russia, and other post-Soviet states such as Ukraine, Tajikistan, Uzbekistan, Kazakhstan, etc.). Any one of these transitions would be highly complex and destabilizing for a society. The simultaneous and often sudden overlapping of these transitions only increases the level of difficulty for polities and increases the pressures for fragmentation that can undermine states.

The historic "fourth wave" of democratization has crested today. The expansion of democratization has stalled for the last decade. While there has been some backsliding since the high point of the fourth wave a decade ago, declines so far have been modest.

Future directions are unknown. China's growing economy may attract more countries toward its authoritarian model. States such as China and Vietnam, partly open their economic systems to achieve prosperity and development without allowing significant political freedoms. Many states, particularly in Africa and the Middle East, retain authoritarian political systems. Greater economic relations with China may legitimize, reward, and "normalize" their nondemocratic regimes. The Trump administration has removed democratization as a US foreign policy objective from the US National Security Strategy, reversing decades of US foreign policy. President Trump regularly praises dictators while criticizing democratic allies. US foreign policy no longer incentivizes and encourages democratization as a means to closer trade and policy relations with the United States.

Open Technologies

The exponential growth and dizzying speed of new information, communication, and transportation technologies present special challenges for sovereign states, which struggle to keep up with the technology changes and uses of private actors. Asymmetries in speed, information, and technological adaptation change not only the threats states must respond to, but also the tools states have, and the way they do their jobs. The new technologies change the power and social dynamics under which governments operate. Sovereign states have the authority and legitimacy to act, but the private sector often has more capacity and agility. States are expected to protect citizens and critical infrastructure, but 85 percent of critical infrastructure are privately owned and operated. States have been tinkering, working to find more effective ways to work with the private sector in managing technology change and threats. In practice, this is hard to do. State actions to create and exploit new technologies for military purposes, such as the creation of drones, the Internet, and cyberwarfare, are then used by nonstate actors against states. These technologies democratize and privatize war.

Developed countries tend to be enamored with technological advances, and it is easy to understand why. Technology made possible the settlement of the American continent and still undergirds the US military's preeminent position in the world today. Cellular phones connect areas that are otherwise difficult to reach, making services such as mobile medicine and mobile banking available to remote areas.

Over 4.2 billion of the world's 7.6 billion people have Internet access. Ninety-five percent of North Americans use the Internet, and 85 percent of Europeans, while only 36 percent of Africans have access.[64] US scientists, industry, and government invented the computer and developed the Internet. The first modern computer, developed in 1946 to calculate firing trajectories for artillery shells, "could execute the then-astonishing number of 5,000 arithmetic operations per second . . . weighed 30 tons, filled an enormous room at the University of Pennsylvania, consumed 150,000 watts of power, and used 18,000 vacuum tubes."[65] The slang term "bugs in the system" literally referred to insects in these huge machines that interfered with operations. Computing power has increased one trillion fold from 1956 to the present. The computers that sent astronauts to the moon had the processing power of a pair of Nintendo consuls.[66]

Many theorists argue that technology drives globalization and that the digital divide between rich and poor countries has made the rich richer and the poor poorer, undermining sovereign states. Technology also makes economic transactions less tied to geography, and easier for digital commerce and economic transactions to avoid government taxes, thus weakening sovereign authority and resources. Technology has unintentionally undermined sovereign authority, decentralized power, and opened markets and societies.[67] To some extent, this presents a "chicken-or-egg" question. Although technology may in some sense "drive" the process of globalization, technological advances do not occur in an economic or political vacuum. Sustained political and investment decisions drive technological advances. Scientists did not suddenly develop powerful supercomputers, tiny microchips, and fiber optic telecommunications links by accident. These advancements came about through sustained investment, supported by political and social policies that harnessed resources in pursuit of technological progress and innovation as tools to advance economic and political goals. The first mainframe computer and the Internet were developed by the US Department of Defense working in close connection with universities. Then-Senator Al Gore wrote the legislation that created the public access to the internet, making the military-created technological advancement freely available for public and commercial use.

However, like their counterparts, open technologies also undermine sovereignty and make global challenges possible. Technology moves legal and illegal information, people, and goods more quickly and efficiently than ever before across borders without the consent or even knowledge of sovereign authorities. Drug cartels and terrorists use drones. The US military's technological dominance is also its Achilles heel. The invention and decentralized spread of information technologies brings many tools for advancing open markets and open societies. These technologies can also be used to undermine democracies and markets. The speed of technological change challenges the abilities of our democracies and markets to appropriately adapt. State-centric responses of improving laws, enforcement, and international state-to-state cooperation on these issues are not enough. The private sector is larger and more technologically proficient than the government. Private sector self-policing is occurring, and states experiment with various attempts at public–private networks in technology areas. Increasingly, states contract out foreign policy technology needs to the private sector, creating new vulnerabilities and challenges.

TOMORROW: DEBATES ABOUT THE FUTURE OF SOVEREIGNTY

There are three main views about the future of sovereignty. According to the first view, we are witnessing the end of the state. The second view argues that sovereignty is unchanged; states are still the primary actors in international politics, and other actors (NGOs, IGOs, MNCs) exist and operate only as much as allowed by states. The third view holds that the sovereign state continues to be an important actor on the world scene, especially in the military security realm, but that sovereignty is changing, especially as the state increasingly shares or loses power to markets and nonstate actors. I further argue that the decline in war and violence has the unintended consequence of deflating sovereignty in its "strong suit," the application of organized military force over territory. Sovereign states have capacity for centralized violence that is less needed. In other issue areas where action is needed, for example, environmental protection or cybersecurity, violence is less relevant. Sovereignty is associated with law and order, autonomy, and independence, in an era when other actors increasingly provide law and order, and globalization curtails autonomy and independence.

The first view contends that sovereign states are a "nostalgic fiction" in the global economy. States "are little more than bit actors." Decisions over investments, production, and exchange rates "are made elsewhere by individuals and institutions over which they have little practical control." Although tempting, attempts to raise tariffs and assert national economic controls will ultimately fail because supply chains are decentralized and global, making "national origin" labels difficult if not meaningless. Is a Toyota made in Mississippi a Japanese car? Private sector resources dwarf those of states. Thus, states are losing their capacity to respond to economic bumps in the road, and so regions are becoming more important. "There are now tens of millions of teenagers around the world who, having been raised in a multimedia-rich environment, have a lot more in common with each other than they do with members of older generations in their own cultures." Although it may still be politically popular to talk about states as the important actors, "it is a bald-faced economic lie."[68]

The second, opposing view argues that nothing fundamental has changed. Weak states have always existed, and sovereignty has always been what Stephen Krasner terms "organized hypocrisy," challenged in theory and practice.[69] Examples of problematic sovereignty only show how embedded the concept of sovereignty is.[70] It continues to be our default assumption. Changes in the environment do not readily or easily translate into institutional changes. Sovereign states persist over time, even when their functions are not in sync with a changed international environment because of vertical and horizontal linkages:

> Vertical depth refers to the extent to which the institutional structure defines the individual actors. Breadth refers to the number of links that a particular activity has with other activities, to the number of changes that would have to be made if a particular form of activity were altered. . . .With regard to both breadth and depth, sovereign states have become increasingly formidable institutions. They influence the self-image of those individuals within their territory through the concept of citizenship, as well as by exercising control, to one degree or another, over powerful instruments of socialization. With regard to breadth, states are the most densely linked institutions in the

contemporary world. Change the nature of states and virtually everything else in human society would also have to be changed. Hence, even though environmental incentives have dramatically changed since the establishment of the state system in the seventeenth century, there is little reason to believe that it will be easy to replace sovereign states with some alternative structure for organizing human political life.[71]

Despite interdependence, weak states, and compromised or problematic sovereignty, the sovereign state is not retreating. The costs of changing to an alternative system would be prohibitive, and people cannot conceive of a plausible alternative to sovereignty.

Others in this school of thought argue that no such fundamental change away from sovereignty is imminent because existing states have little incentive to alter the system. States are the gatekeepers to the international system, so it is difficult for actors other than states to be accorded equal participation in that system. States still protect their sovereignty, as the United Kingdom's Brexit from the EU illustrate. The growth of the European Union provides only a **"pooled sovereignty,"** the sharing of decision-making power among states in a cooperative system. The EU is a regional, shared, alternative model to traditional sovereignty, but there are few other serious challengers to sovereign arrangements. ISIS wanted to destroy the Western sovereignty model and replace it with a religious caliphate uniting all Muslims, but their quest has faltered to re-create a pre-Westphalian organization. Hendrik Spruyt argues that, for sovereignty to be replaced, there must be competition among alternative models of organization—as there was at sovereignty's initiation after competition with the urban league and city-state. If anything, sovereignty is becoming more entrenched because nationalist, ethnic, and religious challenges to sovereignty reinforce the state as a prize worth fighting for. Although sovereignty is not the optimal institutional arrangement, new institutional challengers have not yet arisen. Sovereignty took centuries to emerge, Spruyt argues. It is too early to declare its demise, and many countries (although not all) tried to reinvigorate state institutions and state spending to respond to the global economic crisis.

Another "nothing much has changed" perspective argues there is no such thing as globalization, only Americanization. This view contends that we are witnessing the advance of one incredibly powerful state—the United States—rather than the retreat of the state.[72] This view paraphrases Mark Twain's famous observation by noting that the territorial state is being "buried too soon." Challenges to the existing sovereign state do not mean its death but that "pride of place [will go] to whatever authorities are able to organize and maintain superior armed force. This implies that their requiem for the Westphalian state is premature. So far, no promising alternative to the territorial organization of armed force has emerged.[73]

To this assertion, I argue "Yes, but so what?" Sovereignty is a hammer in a networked world less responsive to hammers, a more connected world that responds better to more diverse social pressures and economic tools. Sovereignty's signature skill set remains the application of centralized coercive force over territory. In a world in which violence is declining, the state's superior organization for war matters less. Conflict remains part of the human condition, but conflicts are less violent,[74] and nonviolent tools are twice more effective than violence.[75] Even where violent conflict remains, state violence is less able to offer a way out for countries caught in the conflict trap, in recurring cycles of violence and poverty.[76] Yes, states still have armies, navies, and air forces to project centralized military power over territory. But private actors also have these coercive forces. And this "go to move" is less effective against the decentralized violence of our age. The sovereign state's centralized, territorial violence can destroy things and control land. This is less effective against decentralized networks common today, which are less connected to a specific piece of land (terrorists, drug, and criminal cartels), and have few things. Sovereigns retain military powers that are less useful against today's threats, and are less able to prevail against nonstate threats in an interdependent world. Today's threats are adaptive, fast, fungible, networked, and cost little to assemble (though they may cause high cost impacts). The state's coercive powers are very costly to assemble, but they are more fixed, less fungible, slower to deploy, less networked, and less able to deliver a decisive knock-out blow. Thus they are less effective against today's threats from prestate and nonstate actors. Even the strongest states increasingly "contract out" even military, law enforcement, and intelligence functions to private companies. The state persists, but its capacity has not grown as fast relative to the private sector's capacity.

States can compel order through force or threat of violence. But there are many and increasing ways to establish order without force or threat of violence. Order can be orchestrated by attraction. States excel in compellence, at a time in which social groups are changing norms away from hierarchical violent force. The law and order functions of states are primarily confined to limited pieces of land, at a time when more globally connected markets, societies, and technologies need rules that go beyond borders. States have no monopoly on law and order, on creating rules or norms. States have no monopoly on attractive powers, on economic, social, moral, and communication powers. Relative to the private sector, the state is more constrained in its capacity to act effectively in the economic and social spheres that increasingly affect citizens' everyday lives. There is a mismatch between the types of power states have, and the types of power needed to address pressing global issues. Due to these capacity and jurisdiction gaps, states are less able to "go it alone." Sovereign states contract out, network, and partner with others to enhance capacity, jurisdiction, and achieve objectives, for normative reasons (e.g., a responsibility to protect citizens, a duty to serve the public, constitutional norms, the "golden rule," professional standards), as well as for practical reasons (to gain resources, respect, legitimacy, re-election). Actors pressure states to address global issues, and so states improvise, or risk losing support and resources from domestic and international sources. As state aim to be effective and enhance capacity, states become less autonomous, less independent, and less in control.

Today, I argue we have increasingly **networked sovereignty**. Sovereignty is increasingly connected in networks—sideways to other states and nonstate actors, upwards to pooled sovereignty organizations, and downward to local actors. There is no "one size fits all" network model. Choice of the linked networks varies by issue area and political forces.

This messy mix is not fixed and hierarchical, but relational and changing. Which actors or network will prevail on any global issue area are context and network dependent. The "nothing much has changed" with sovereignty argument is based on a faulty premise and faulty metrics. It imagines a linear, competitive, winner-take-all, hierarchical change process whereby a singular organization dethrones sovereignty. Lacking evidence of a new, single organizational unit to supercede or overthrow sovereignty, they erroneously conclude sovereignty remains fundamentally unchanged. Their argument does not imagine a mixed and multiple, collaborative and competitive, change process. The sovereign state persists, but people and states also rely on other networks, reviving old and building new state and nonstate networks. Old pre-state networks use new tools, and use their relationships to tackle new issues. New multilateral state networks, private NGO networks, for profit networks, and public–private networks are also built. The sovereign state is not dethroned, it is rewired with new connections. There is experimentation, tinkering, and learning. Some of the networks work better than others; others are "duds." All are resourced and evaluated through highly politicized processes. Through networks the state may expand its capacity and jurisdiction, but this may come at the expense of autonomy, legitimacy, and independence.

Too often the views on sovereignty are unhelpfully considered as zero-sum, either/or, and thus talk past one another. This book tracks changes or adaptations in the sovereign state without signing its death certificate.

A mixture of actors "govern the globe."[77] The sovereign state is part of the mix, but does not always play the starring role. The diffusion of power to other actors is contested and contextual, not automatic, linear, and is not consistently or globally "good" or "evil" in general. Authority flows from many streams. Actors may attract authority based on technical expertise, competence, moral principles, institutional credibility, or by delegation, according to Martha Finnemore et al. The governance activities of nonstate actors, simultaneous with the activities of sovereign states, do not represent linear "progress" or "decline, and must be managed by what Anne-Marie Slaughter calls "webcraft" and network analysis, rather than "statecraft."[78]

This third view sees the state changing as its functions change.[79] Today, either other actors increasingly fill functions previously done by states, or no one fills them. For example, Susan Strange discusses ten important functions or authorities claimed by states that are on the decline. First, the state is responsible for defending national territory against foreign invasion, but in developed countries, the threat of foreign invasion is declining or minimal, thereby eroding this source of state authority. Second, the state is responsible for maintaining the value of its currency, but inflation in one country can spread to others, revealing that this responsibility is now a more collective one. Third, the state used to choose the appropriate form of economic development, but open economies now allow market pressures from the IMF, World Bank, and private investors to limit state choice and force convergence on a narrow range of development models. Fourth, the state used to be responsible for correcting the booms and busts of market economies through state spending to infuse money into public works or other state enterprises. President Franklin Delano Roosevelt fought the Great Depression in the 1930s in the United States by initiating large public works projects, building national parks, the Tennessee Valley Authority dams, and highways and bridges to put people back to work and get the economy moving again. But this option is more difficult for governments now, given the market pressures to keep government spending at a minimum. Fifth, states used to provide a social safety net for those who were least able to survive in a market economy by providing assistance to the very old and young, sick, disabled, and unemployed. Today, market pressures are leading states to cut back on their social welfare benefits and protective regulations. Sixth, states used to have the ability to set appropriate tax rates to pay for government public works or social benefits spending. Today, all states are pressured by international market forces to keep tax rates to a minimum, thereby limiting their autonomy and authority to raise funds. Seventh, states used to have great autonomy in control over foreign trade, especially imports. Today, government intervention can only affect the margins because most of the decisions that concern trade flows are the "aggregate result of multiple corporate decisions."[80] Strong international market forces pressure governments to reduce obstacles to cross-border trade.

Eighth, governments used to take responsibility for building the economic infrastructure of the state "from ports and roads to posts and telegraphs. . . . Even where governments, as in the United States, looked to private enterprise to find the necessary capital, they never hesitated in revising the laws on landed property so that landowners could not easily obstruct the infrastructural investment."[81] Today, public utilities are being privatized, and the key infrastructure needed in modern economies are communications technologies, most of which do not depend on government's control over territory. Infrastructure development decisions are being made in corporate boardrooms, not state offices. Eastern European states are being integrated into the modern telecommunications grid not by governments primarily, but by private corporations that recognize the profit margins that are available to the corporation that gets there first. States may have built the infrastructure of highways, but firms and private actors are building and extending the information superhighways.

Ninth, states used to be able to create or allow public or private monopolies to dominate the local market, but today international market pressures impose greater costs on state governments that try to maintain monopolies. Finally, states used to entertain one "special kind of monopoly—that of the legitimate use of violence against the citizen or any group of citizens."[82] Now, the globalization of the arms trade and easy access to technology make the means of violence more readily available to nonstate actors. Strong and weak states alike are losing their monopolies on force, as evidenced by the chemical attack on the Japanese subway and the destruction of the World Trade Center in the United States.

We are witnessing the incredibly shrinking state. States continue to exist, but their powers are not as extensive as they used to be, and other actors take or share power with states over key functions or sectors. The result is "a ramshackle assembly of conflicting sources of authority" in which individuals' loyalties and identities will not necessarily lie with the sovereign state but are spread among professions, civic groups, ethnic ties, firms, etc., just as state power is becoming diffused.[83] As more power shifts away from states and toward markets, accountability and democracy may decrease because corporate leaders are not subject to democratic accountability and market forces cannot be voted upon.

Other theorists agree that we are in a period of transition or turbulence[84] in which the sovereign state is increasingly under challenge but not obsolete because alternatives to sovereignty have not established themselves. James Rosenau argues that not just markets but also increasingly skilled individuals are driving the changes. He believes access to computers and cell phones connected by the Internet, modern transportation, etc., have led to a "skill revolution." People who are plugged in have become better able to assess, compare, and contrast large amounts of data; are more sophisticated in critiquing the information provided to them by states and in seeking alternative information; and are better able to articulate and mobilize around goals. "It is unimaginable that people have not learned and become more complex in order to adapt to an increasingly complicated world."[85] In an evolutionary way, people are adapting to changes in their environment. "People have become increasingly competent in assessing where they fit in international affairs and how their behavior can be aggregated into significant outcomes."[86] Thus, the globalization of democratization is no accident, because the telecommunications revolution that is fueling the skills revolution is global. A people plugged in is a people empowered to bring about change, to end apartheid in South Africa, to tear down the Berlin Wall and the communist empire, and to challenge the dictatorship in Tiananmen Square. Democratization is not linear or automatic, as we have seen in the lack of new democracies since 2011. Rosenau believes the skills revolution makes governments more responsive to citizens' needs and more democratic, whereas Strange and others believe that increased market and corporate power reduces democracy and accountability.

Because of the digital divide, the rate of change is not uniform. But even though "the information-rich are getting richer at a quicker rate than the information-poor, the trend line is conceived to slope in the same upward direction for both groups."[87] Citizens in lesser-developed countries (where poverty and repressive regimes may limit access to technology) are also becoming more skillful, as seen in the Arab spring uprisings, organized on Facebook. As people become more skillful, they also become less deferential. Traditionally, state legitimacy and compliance derived from constitutional and legal sources. Under these circumstances, individuals were habituated to compliance with the directives issued by higher authorities. They did what they were told to do because . . . that is what one did. As a consequence, authority structures remained in place for decades, even centuries, as people unquestioningly yielded to the dictates of governments.[88]

Today, because of the skills revolution, a pervasive "authority crisis" exists as people are increasingly inclined to question authority and have the means to do so. Legitimacy now derives not from tradition but from performance. States are no longer the only key actors, and they must manage and compete with a variety of organizations. Sovereignty continues to limp along—not because of its strength, but more by default because none of these new organizations has displaced sovereignty.

This authority crisis leads actors into a struggle to reconstitute political authority. This struggle to give coherence to multiple, overlapping, and unclear structures is called "Complex sovereignty."[89]

Another approach contends that sovereignty is losing its identification with territory. Richard Rosecrance argues, "In economies where capital, labor, and information are mobile and have risen to predominance, no land fetish remains. Developed countries would rather plumb the world market than acquire territory. The virtual state—a state that has downsized its territorially based production capability—is the logical consequence of this emancipation from the land."[90] By shedding outmoded functions to nonstate actors and by downsizing territory, states are adapting their logic to market forces. When the Treaty of Westphalia was signed, the economic system was mercantilist and land-based. Wealth and power depended on the control of land, access to raw materials, and control of the means of production. In a world of slow-moving ships and horseback messengers, capital and labor were fixed in place, not mobile. Increasing power meant increasing land, and thus the European colonial empires were born. It is no accident that under this economic system, the political organization that developed—sovereignty—directly correlated authority to territory. But now the economy has changed, and states are changing to reflect the new reality. The new economic system is based on information, technology, and services—none of which depends on the control of land. In a world of open borders and economic flows—and people who have access to computers, phones, the Internet, e-cash, and other advanced technologies—the means of production, capital, and labor are mobile. States have access to raw materials through trade, not conquest. Thus, for states with modern, information-based economies such as Japan, territory is not the source of their power, so conflict over territory becomes passé. For states with less-developed economies that are still land-based (and primarily dependent on natural resource extraction or agricultural exports), territory will not become passé and may still be a source of conflict. A population explosion may make land important again. But these trends are not sustainable in the long term because land does not produce a better return than knowledge, so states with lots of land (such as Russia) may not be especially powerful in the new economy. Knowledge allows more extraction and more efficient and effective utilization of resources. States recognize the success of "virtual" states such as Japan and will try to emulate them and thus develop modern economies that are less shackled to land.

The virtual state no longer commands resources as states did in the mercantilist yesteryear. It negotiates, deriving its power from direct foreign investment, an educated workforce, and market savvy, not from military superiority or control over territory. This brings a crisis for democratic politics as states lose some of their autonomy over electing and enforcing policy to unelected, nonstate actors. Citizens can, however, vote with their feet if they are unimpressed by their state's performance.[91]

Do global problems challenge not only the interests of states (as the traditional realist International Relations theory stipulates) but also the very architecture of states? How can global issues be managed in a system of sovereign states? Do the responses to global issues (greater reliance on private sector MNCs or NGOs, for example) change or undermine sovereignty? Are alternatives to sovereignty evolving as people struggle to respond to global problems? Or is the state becoming more entrenched as people rely on old responses to combat new threats?

THE NEW SECURITY DILEMMA

"War made the state and the state made war," has been a key theme in social science. Security has been the dominant realm of sovereign states, but this is changing. In previous eras, threats came from strong states. The "old security dilemma" was how one country could contain another strong state without provoking self-defeating counteractions. This spiral of insecurity was noted in arms races, the outbreak of World

War I, and the Cold War. Military actions intended for defense could backfire, trigger escalation ladders, and further decrease one's own security. Thus, attempts to increase a state's security instead made it more insecure, setting off a self-defeating spiral of counteractions by others.

Today's spiral of insecurity entails unintended consequences not just from states but also nonstate actors. States invested in information technology to establish battlefield dominance, but found these same technologies made them vulnerable to cyberattacks. States built military drones and the internet to advance their security, but now find these being used against them by private actors. Western states supported the advance of open societies, open markets, and open technologies, but now find these same channels also create vulnerabilities.

The old security dilemma was how states could protect against strong states without making themselves more vulnerable. The **new security dilemma** is how actors protect against global issues, leveraging networks of state and nonstate actors, without taking actions that make these issues more severe. Globalization plus weak states and global issues add to the new security dilemma. Globalization gives breakdowns in state authority and capacity and global issues greater reach, speed, intensity, and impact. Borders are more permeable, and threats are decentralized, fast, fungible, and fluid. How should we respond to the problems of weak states and nonstate threats without making these problems worse? Responding with old tools, such as military force, may not be effective. For example, terrorism is worse in war zones. The Bush administration did not intend to make terrorism worse by invading Iraq, but it did. Invading Iraq in response to the 9/11 terrorist attacks on the United States had the unintended consequence of creating Al Qaeda in Iraq and subsequently, the breakaway group from Al Qaeda in Iraq, ISIS. There was no Al Qaeda in Iraq prior to the US invasion (understandable, as Al Qaeda is a Sunni violent extremist organization and Iraq is a Shi'a country). After the US invasion of Iraq, Al Qaeda in Iraq was created to take advantage of the popular opinion opposed to US military occupation of Iraq. The United States removed Iraq's dictator, Saddam Hussein, from power. This removed Hussein's armed and dangerous Republican Guard forces from power. They became the leadership of ISIS, which broke away from the newly formed Al Qaeda in Iraq terrorist group. Using military force may make terrorist organizations stronger because they can appeal to messianic visions and attract heightened international attention.

Failure to respond to nonmilitary threats, like environmental degradation, allows these problems to grow until they present threats of instability and violence that cannot easily be met by force. For example, the US military notes climate change is a security threat. High-intensity storms erode military bases and equipment, and climate change migrants exacerbate conflicts. But military forces can do little to manage climate change.

The new security dilemma requires leveraging a variety of state and nonstate networks to address global issues, creating more powerful nonmilitary tools (including more effective involvement of the private sector), and the retooling of military forces to meet nonstate threats. State military force is not sufficient to combat global problems, which often stem from economic or other causes. Threats are decentralized, as are the resources needed for the fight, which are not primarily military. We must go beyond the military tools of sovereignty to address global issues that go beyond sovereignty. When the strongest military in the strongest state (the United States) needs the private sector to help manage security problems (traditionally, the state's strong suit), then sovereignty is changing.

Globalization has downsides. New security dilemmas challenge people and states. This does not mean that sovereignty is dead. Human history has and will witness many different social organizing frameworks. The sovereign state is in no danger of disappearing. But we cannot expect that the sovereign state will emerge unchanged from this period of rapid change. For globalization to be both sustainable and just, its costs must be clearly understood and addressed. Sovereignty and globalization carry many benefits, but there is nothing sacrosanct about either. The following chapters further unpack the question. *How can we bridge the gaps between the sovereign states we have, and the coordinating capaciti 's we need, to address the global issues we face?*

KEY TERMS

DISCUSSION QUESTIONS

1. Who is Yusra Mardini? What's her story?
2. What are "the Olympics picture" default model assumptions concerning international relations? What's the reality?
3. How does Yusra's story illustrate all four types of nonstate actors?
4. Despite widespread use of the term, there is no such thing as a "nation-state." Why is that? What's the difference between nations and sovereign states? Why does the difference matter?
5. "History is blood spattered with the attempts to create nation-states." What are some examples?
6. What is old about globalization? What is new about globalization?
7. Which of the criticisms of globalization resonate with your experiences, or those of your family or community? Which of these criticisms do not seem persuasive to you?
8. Have you seen or experienced examples of the digital divide? What kind of "spillover effects" can the lack of access to information technology have for a community?
9. Democratic peace theory does not mean that democracies are more peaceful than other forms of government. Can you think of any examples of democracies going to war with nondemocratic states?
10. Which of the concepts of the future of sovereignty (nothing much has changed, pooled sovereignty, or networked sovereignty) is most persuasive to you, and why?

NGO leaders fight poverty.

2

Nongovernmental Organizations

Politics in Transnational Networks

■ ■ ■

Poverty is sexist. There is nowhere on earth where women have the same opportunity as men. Nowhere. But the gender gap is wider for women living in poverty. For **130 million girls** without an education. For **one billion women** without access to a bank account. For **39,000 girls** who became child brides today. For women everywhere paid less than a man for the same work. Around the world, there are 130 million girls who are not in school. That's so many girls that, if they made up their own country, it would be bigger in population than Germany or Japan. Denying girls what an education offers—a fair shot, a path out of poverty—means that women can work the land but can't own it; they can earn the money but can't bank it. Funding girls' education isn't charity but investment, and the returns are transformational. When you invest in girls and women, they rise and they lift their families, their communities, their economies and countries along with them. They rise and they lead. It's not alms, it's investment. It's not charity, it's justice.

—Bono, lead singer of U2[1]

WHY IS BONO AT CONCERTS, on television, on the Internet, in the halls of Parliaments and Congress, at the United Nations, with his NGO The One Campaign, reminding us of our moral responsibilities to help the poor, particularly women and girls? Why are actors wearing "Poverty Is Sexist" shirts to televised awards shows? Why have Oprah Winfrey, Melinda Gates, Sheryl Sandberg, joined this campaign for girls education and equality? Why do NGOs leverage celebrity activism to raise awareness to global issues? Because it works.

Charities and churches have long worked to help the world's poor. Yet the size and sophistication of the "**third sector**" is growing, of NGOs, nonprofit and nongovernmental organizations. The creative ways they organize is new. The method of using **transnational advocacy networks (TANs)**, NGOs working together across borders to address global problems, is new, and is yielding impressive gains. NGO networks are particularly effective in raising issues which states have not effectively addressed, from landmines to extreme poverty. Networks of NGOs, working with like-minded states, persuaded the countries of the world to adopt the **Millennium Development Goals (MDGs)** to cut extreme poverty by half. The MDGs created specific goals and benchmarks for reducing poverty, from increasing girls' education to decreasing maternal mortality rates. NGOs worked with governments to implement the goals, and kept the pressure on to reach these commitments. The MDGs were largely successful, and were replaced with more specific **Sustainable Development Goals (SDGs)**, a set of seventeen goals with associated benchmarks, to decrease poverty, and increase prosperity, environmental quality, peace and justice by the year 2030.[2] Bill Gates called these goals "The best idea for focusing the world on fighting global poverty that I have ever seen." Progress was uneven. The world met the goal five years early of raising half of the people out of extreme poverty. Yet the goal of decreasing women's deaths in childbirth by two-thirds was not met. Gains in girls' education were met in some places with increased violence against girls who go to school, by groups like the Taliban and Boko Haram who want to block girls' education. This is why NGOs, and their high-profile spokespersons, continue to focus attention on raising girls and women out of poverty traps. Girls and women are more likely to be malnourished, to lack access to education, and to be deprived of property rights. Girls and women who can't go to school, can't own property or have a bank account, lack nutrition, and health services are trapped in poverty, no matter how hard they work. NGOs are working to take down these structures that keep women and girls trapped in poverty. Empowering girls and women supercharges anti-poverty efforts. Educated women can educate their own children, raise the nutrition and healthcare of the entire family, and women spend most of their income on their children and families, at much higher rates than men, who are more likely to divert income on alcohol, gambling, and other purposes that do not reduce poverty. Investing in girls and women brings a higher return on investment for development.

Leveraging celebrity activism is a way to reach people who might otherwise not consider or engage with global issues. Poor girls, refugees, polluted waters are not usually covered by global media. These global issues are not thought to sell advertisements, the way that sports news will. But celebrities are constantly in the global media spotlight, so when high-profile people address global issues, cameras follow them. Bono fights global poverty. Angelina Jolie advocates on behalf of refugees. George Clooney works to stop wars in Sudan. Leonardo diCaprior works for environmental protection; Matt Damon works for access to clean water. Leveraging the media platforms and access to policymakers that these high-profile people can offer, NGOs can mobilize action on global issues. Bono and others worked the halls of Congress, Parliaments, the UN, and EU, winning over conservatives by quoting scripture and discussing religious obligations to help the poor. The SDGs continue the efforts of the MDGs to address global issues in sustainable ways.

In a similar story of NGOs affecting foreign policy, NGO activist Jody Williams had had enough. NGOs had warned governments about the dangers of landmines for years, but governments were not taking sufficient action. Long after wars were over, antipersonnel landmines remained in more than ninety countries, killing and maiming an estimated 26,000 people each year—or creating one new landmine victim every twenty minutes.[3] Landmines violate the **laws of war,** the national and international military rules that govern behavior of combatants during conflict (such as the Geneva Conventions and the US military code of justice), because they cannot distinguish between combatants and civilians. Many victims of landmines are children, who, out of curiosity, pick up these shiny but dangerous objects. Many governments found landmines to be cheap weapons of war. They did not want to stop using them, and they did not want to pay for difficult and often deadly mine-removal programs.

Jody Williams used the personal computer in her kitchen to organize the many NGOs that had a stake in this fight. Using what was then a newish technology of email, she inexpensively, quickly, and efficiently brought diverse groups on board and founded the **International Campaign to Ban Landmines (ICBL),** a global network of actors in over 100 countries working to ban landmines and help landmine survivors. With the help of the Canadian government, the ICBL brought pressure to bear on governments to quickly ban, remove, stop producing and stockpiling antipersonnel landmines, and to increase landmine education and reduce the pain and suffering of landmine victims. The ICBL enlisted celebrity spokespeople such as Princess Diana in a direct media campaign that bypassed obstructionist governments and made emotional appeals directly to the public. Internally, governments were pressured by their own populations. Externally, they were pressed by the coalition of NGOs and states such as Canada, which led the movement to ban landmines. In record time, the ICBL succeeded in getting states to adopt an international treaty banning antipersonnel landmines in December 1997. In one of the world's most widely accepted treaties, one hundred sixty-four states are parties to the **Ottawa Convention,** officially titled the Convention on the Prohibition of the Use, Stockpiling, Production and Transfer of Anti-Personnel Mines and on Their Destruction, despite opposition from the United States. In each year since the **Mine Ban Treaty** entered into force, landmine use, production, and stockpiling has decreased, while landmine decommissioning, education, and services to landmine victims has increased. The ICBL continues to be active, using a network of NGOs in 100 countries to monitor compliance with the treaty, and pressuring states that have not joined the treaty to do so. **Jody Williams,** leader of the ICBL, won the Nobel Peace Prize for her efforts.[4] In every decade since, another disarmament treaty has successfully followed the landmines model.

The **Cluster Munitions Coalition,** a similar global network of NGOs active in over 100 countries, working in tandem with like-minded states and with the landmines campaign, succeeded in getting a cluster munitions ban in 2008. Cluster munitions' unexploded ordinance work like antipersonnel landmines. Similar to the landmines ban, **the Convention on Cluster Munitions** treaty bans the use, production, transfer, and stockpiling of cluster munitions, and requires removal of the weapons and assistance to victims of cluster munitions. A majority of countries, including a majority of NATO countries, are parties to the treaty. The United States is not, but has not used cluster munitions since 2003 and had a policy from 2008 to 2018 of removing cluster munitions from US arsenals and war plans. The Trump administration has reversed course.[5] Today, the landmines campaign and cluster munitions coalition have merged, working together on monitoring and compliance of the treaties.

The **International Campaign Against Nuclear Weapons** (ICAN) followed the landmines model, with the support of Jody Williams and many of the landmines and cluster munition campaign leaders. These networks employed a pincer movement of internal pressure from civil society with external pressure from governments,[6] joining networked civil society activismy NGOs in 101 countries with the leadership of like-minded countries. One hundred and twenty-two countries voted in favor of The **Treaty on the Prohibition of Nuclear Weapons** in 2017.

Like the landmine and cluster munitions ban, the treaty bans using, developing, testing, producing, manufacturing, acquiring, possessing, transferring, basing, stockpiling, using or threatening to use nuclear weapons or other nuclear explosive devices. A majority of countries had already banned nuclear weapons; the Nuclear Ban Treaty unites and extends the separate nuclear weapons free zone treaties into one international treaty. The United States and other nuclear powers exploded over 2,045 nuclear weapons from 1945 to the present. The United States exploded over 1,100 of those nuclear weapons, after the atomic bombings of Hiroshima and Nagasaki. During the Cold War, the United States exploded nuclear bombs on ourselves repeatedly (on Nevada, New Mexico, Colorado, Mississippi, California, Hawaii, etc.), as well as on many Pacific islands (the Marshall Islands, the Bikini Islands, etc.), to test the destructiveness of nuclear bombs. Nuclear bombs have been dropped all over the world. Other countries bombed Australia, Algeria, Ukraine, Kazakstan, Russia, China, India, Pakistan, French Polynesia, Kiribati, South Africa, and North Korea. The nuclear ban treaty calls on signatories to provide assistance to victims and help with environmental remediation efforts of the people and places hurt by those thousands of nuclear weapons exploded. The treaty closes a legal loophole. All other weapons of mass destruction were banned previously because they violate the laws of war (chemical weapons, biological weapons); now nuclear weapons are also prohibited. None of the nine nuclear weapons states have signed the treaty. But the ban is a way to increase both internal and external pressure on the nuclear states to honor the commitments they have made to more deeply reduce their nuclear arsenals,[7] in the Nuclear Nonproliferation and other treaties. **Beatrice Finn** and ICAN won the Nobel Peace prize for the work of NGOs in banning nuclear weapons.

Nuclear bomb survivor Setsuko Thurlow spoke at the Nobel prize ceremony.

I speak as a member of the family of hibakusha—those of us who, by some miraculous chance, survived the atomic bombings of Hiroshima and Nagasaki. For more than seven decades, we have worked for the total abolition of nuclear weapons. We have stood in solidarity with those harmed by the production and testing of these horrific weapons around the world. People from places with long-forgotten names, like Moruroa, Ekker, Semipalatinsk, Maralinga, Bikini. People whose lands and seas were irradiated, whose bodies were experimented upon, whose cultures were forever disrupted. We were not content to be victims. We refused to wait for an immediate fiery end or the slow poisoning of our world. We refused to sit idly in terror as the so-called great powers took us past nuclear dusk and brought us recklessly close to nuclear midnight. We rose up. We shared our stories of survival. We said: humanity and nuclear weapons cannot coexist.[8]

In each of these cases, strategic networks of NGOs were able to lift and move action on global issues despite the opposition or indifference of the world's most powerful states.

These examples illustrate four main themes that I will explore in this chapter. First, not only are the power and number of NGOs increasing but also they are more frequently joining forces in transnational advocacy networks, or mobilizations of principled actors who are committed to social change.[9] Second, NGOs are active in more sectors, taking on increased functions that were once the sole preserve of states, such as arms control, and serving as the legal monitors of arms control treaty compliance. Third, NGOs use tactics that are aimed directly at the public, multinational corporations (MNCs), and intergovernmental organizations (IGOs). They are not focused only on governments—and this is one of their greatest strengths, particularly when they create ways around gridlocked politics of states. NGOs come with weaknesses, however, including democracy deficits, North–South divisions, and coordination complexity. Fourth and finally, these changing ideas and practices of transnational politics affect sovereignty.

NGOs: PEOPLE POWER

NGOs predate the current period of modern globalization, yet their numbers, sizes, budgets, ranges of activities, power, transnational networks, and levels of international recognition have drastically increased in recent years—to the point where scholars note that "we are in the midst of a global 'associational revolution.'" According to Lester Salamon and the Johns Hopkins University Center for Civil Society Studies, if the nonprofit sector were a country, it would have the fifth largest economy in the world.[10]

Nongovernmental organizations are not new. Parts of civil society are ancient, such as religious societies and universities. Morroco's University of Al Karaouine is the world's oldest still operating university, dating from 859. The European Universities of Bologna, Salamanca, Oxford, and Cambridge followed two centuries later in the eleventh and twelfth centuries. Trade unions and the international antislavery movement date to the 1700s, also predating most of today's sovereign states.

Yet the number, power, resources, and reach of nongovernmental organizations have exploded in the late twentieth and early twenty-first centuries, facilitated by globalization's open societies, open economies, and open technologies. The fall of repressive communist, fascist, monarchical, and dictatorial regimes, and the spread of democracies, created space for civil society to grow, with greater legal protections for freedoms of association and of speech. Open technologies increased the opportunities and decreased the costs of organizing and operating NGOs, while the development of free market, open economies have allowed private philanthropic groups to arise and thrive.

NGOs are an odd category, defined negatively by what they are not rather than by positive definitions of what they are. NGOs are not governments, but they may receive resources from or offer resources to governments, or they may only involve themselves in certain areas or issues with the permission of governments. NGOs are a broad and eclectic group, however, and some never accept government aid. Other NGOs, such as Catholic Relief Services, derive significant portions of their budgets and resources from governments as states contract out developmental assistance to NGOs. Private sector charity and remittances account for the bulk of development assistance; government assistance accounts for a shrinking portion of assistance. For example, the Gates Foundation, run by richest man in the world, Microsoft founder and Windows inventor Bill Gates, commands more resources than more than half of the world's countries.

NGOs range from small, grassroots groups run on shoestring budgets to huge international organizations with deep pockets, from single-issue outfits to umbrella organizations. NGOs are private-sector organizations but are often assumed to be public interest groups, which leads to contention. Who elects NGOs and who do they speak for? Many in the United States refer to NGOs as PVOs, or private volunteer organizations. But the term volunteer can be misleading, because international NGOs often have permanent, full-time, paid professional staffs. NGOs are nonprofit groups. Although community development banks or Habitat for Humanity often turn a profit, the resources generated are reinvested in the community. Profit is not the organization's primary goal, but a means to achieving the NGO's goals such as stabilizing communities by developing homes and businesses in poor areas where banks will not lend money.

Counts of NGOs vary, although scholars agree that their numbers are increasing. They are often referred to as part of civil society or as the third sector (government and for-profit businesses being the other two sectors).

The Union of International Associations tracks NGOs and IGOs and listed 21,224 traditional international NGOs, such as universal membership organizations and internationally oriented national organizations. Another 33,153 special NGOs (such as religious orders) brings a total of 54,377 international NGOs.[11]

LAWYERS, GUNS, AND MONEY

Despite their rising numbers, NGOs raise some puzzles. NGOs have no armies; states have the guns. NGOs *command* no money, but rely on voluntary charitable contributions. NGOs collect no taxes and can compel no one to follow them or to contribute to their treasuries. So if others have the guns and money, what is the source of NGO power? NGOs trade in the currency of ideas, norms, especially ideas of good and evil, right and wrong, and NGOs often try to use these norms to change the rules and laws. The ideas compel, even when the organizations cannot. NGOs attract support more than they can enforce compliance. The landmine and cluster munitions examples illustrate this. States had the weapons and bigger budgets, but NGOs were successful in convincing people of the merits of their norms and ideas, which they then successfully advocated be turned into law. While only states can sign the laws, NGOs work to help write them, market them, convince people to adopt them, and follow up afterwards to monitor compliance with the new law, and encourage greater societal transformation to the norms and laws.

Many NGOs are transnational **moral entrepreneurs,** agents who act as reformers or crusaders to change rules out of an ethical concern to curtail a great evil.[12] Their very names are often cast as moral imperatives, groups of NGOs that work together across borders to promote common values or issues. The previously discussed International Campaign to Ban Landmines, the Cluster Munitions Coalition, and the International Campaign Against Nuclear Weapons are examples of transnational advocacy networks of NGOs working together across borders.

Governments have legal authority, but advocacy NGOs rely on moral authority. Generally, where states have military power and MNCs have economic power, the strength of NGOs lies in their idea power. They seek to occupy the only high ground available to them, the moral high ground. If an NGO can succeed in redefining a problem as a moral issue, then it will have a greater chance of prevailing, because states and MNCs may not be able to speak credibly as bastions or brokers of morality. Religious organizations in particular often have well-developed ethics and rich institutions, resources that are useful to transnational advocacy networks and greatly needed today given the ethical and institutional gaps of globalization (discussed in the conclusion). For example, consider the importance of church networks and leaders in abolishing slavery, as well as the importance of Archbishop Desmond Tutu in the South African Anti-Apartheid movement. Morally, religious organizations have legitimacy speaking on moral issues and a treasure chest of well-developed ideas available for use by transnational advocacy networks. Tactically, religious organizations can pool their power with other religious and civil society groups and use their direct pulpit access to citizens (who may be business or government decision-makers) as well as their ability to attract media.[13] Although secular NGOs may not command institutional networks (such as schools and hospitals) that are as extensive as those of religious organizations, they also develop and trade in moral ideas, such as when environmental transnational advocacy networks construct and promote environmental ethics.

NGOs often practice what I term **resurrection politics**,[14] taking an issue previously deemed "dead on arrival" and raising it up onto the political agenda. They often do this by "putting a human face" on global issues, reframing the issue in terms of its human impacts and moral imperatives, rather than a far-distant or technical concern. For example, the head of the World Bank and the US Treasury Secretary told NGOs campaigning for debt relief of poor countries, the Jubilee debt relief movement, that the issue was dead. There was no political movement for the issue. Governments were not going to forgive the debt of poor countries, even though countries had paid back their debts but were still paying interest, and much of the money had profited wealthy countries and banks, and corrupt leaders, rather than poor people. Voters in rich countries did not care about the issue, something economists and technical experts debated but most citizens had little knowledge of. The NGOs instead raised the issue onto the political agenda, effectively reframing the issue as a moral and religious imperative. Rather than a technical issue restricted to debates of international economists, NGOs opened access and relevance of the issue to a wider audience, pointing out that all the Abrahamic religions require debt forgiveness for the poor. The NGOs flipped the issue, from dormant to active. NGOs have practiced Resurrection Politics in numerous campaigns, from the ban on landmines to cluster munitions to the prohibition of nuclear weapons. All of these issues were previously deemed impossible nonstarters. NGOs breathed new life into these issues, broke through the frozen politics of the status quo, and prevailed. As Jody Williams, Nobel Laureate of the landmines campaign, told me, "Don't believe governments and industry when they tell you it can't be done. They said the same thing about the landmine campaign."

NGOs have information power, and **information politics** is an important tool of NGOs. Especially when networked transnationally, NGOs may have access to grassroots information about how particular policies affect vulnerable people, information that governments, MNCs, or IGOs overlook or do not have. Margaret Keck and Kathryn Sikkink note that NGOs often strategically use information politics, credibly gathering information and moving it to where it may have the most impact. For example, the ICANN transnational advocacy network gathered information about the victims of nuclear weapons tests, and the humanitarian impact of nuclear weapons. The TAN brought indigenous people and nuclear weapon survivors and doctors to speak at the United Nations, as well as at international meetings leading up to the Nuclear Weapons Ban negotiations. While this information was known to the local communities and activists, they moved that information where it would have the greater chance of political impact.

Symbolic politics is a tool of NGOs, using potent symbols, pictures, colors, flags, or religious images, to connect or make sense of an issue far away with something closer to heart or more understandable. Symbols can work on a more intuitive or emotional level than facts and figures, and can cut through the noise or the apathy regarding an issue. For example, religious NGOs working on climate change invoke the symbol of St. Francis of Assisi, an eleventh-century saint known for his love of nature, the poor, and peace. Old images of St. Francis can help people understand what's at stake in newer global environmental issues using images that invoke ancient religious beliefs, obligations and practices of caring for nature.

Transparency politics is another important tool of NGOs, efforts to create greater openness and public access, in order to allow greater scrutiny, honesty, and detection of corruption and poor practices. Globalization brings many asymmetries, in costs, benefits, and access to information. For example, corporate polluters know what toxins they are creating and dumping. The people downwind or downstream do not know what toxins they are breathing or drinking. Transparency is opening public access to information that some governments and corporations want to keep closed to public oversight. People with greater and cheaper access to information technologies can work to force greater transparency. Transparency and sunshine politics are important tools for NGOs. By expanding the information base of a public's or elite's discussion of previously closed matters, NGOs often practice **"Dracula" politics**, a type of transparency politics that works to expose particularly bad deeds to public light. The fictional character Dracula could not survive in the light of day. NGOs apply the same process to global issues. Will a particular policy or practice be able to survive in the daylight? For example, slavery today is everywhere illegal. Slavery can only exist if the public is "kept in the dark" about cases of modern-day slavery. Simply exposing slave networks can go a long way toward eliminating them. Transparency alone can do much to shrink corruption, and lessen both government and corporate abuses. Opening the decision-making process to greater transparency helps to reframe issues as moral issues, again moving the issue to where NGOs have some home court advantage.

For example, **Transparency International** is an NGO that rates countries according to how corrupt they are, and publishes an annual, public report about global corruption. No country wants to be on Transparency International's annual list of most corrupt places. Simply by creating a transparent, publicly available, global rating system, TI has done much to expose and correct for the corrupt stealing of public funds and resources . NGO action to counter human trafficking are also examples of transparency politics. Slavery is illegal everywhere. Simply exposing human trafficking can bring about greater attention and resources to combating it. When transparency is opened, and bad behavior or policies are exposed, and the bad actors and actions exposed are specifically identified and held up for public scrutiny, it is called **"name and shame"** politics. For example, Volkswagon broke laws, polluted, cheated, and covered up their violations by installing computer programs in 11 million vehicles that tampering with the emissions controls, turning the cleaning devices on only to pass auto emissions tests, and otherwise emitting toxins while driving. Volkswagon was aware it was violating laws and polluting; Volkswagon customers and governments around the world did not have this information. Transparency, and simply naming and shaming Volkswagon, worked to change the bad behavior. Another example of name and shame is the naming of New England Patriots owner, Robert Kraft, as soliciting sex from women trapped in human trafficking. The "Me Too" movement of publicly identifying men accused of sexual crimes, uses name and shame politics.

Accountability politics is an important tool of NGOs, holding organizations, governments, and corporations responsible to comply with their previously stated commitments. NGOs contrast an organization's words with their deeds, and challenge them to live up to their legal and moral obligations, and to their mission statements, corporate advertising image, and values. NGOs can hold organizations accountable either to **hard law** (legal obligations) or to **soft law**, community or group norms and standards. NGO campaigns against child labor and poor working conditions in factories are efforts to hold companies accountable to the positive public image and brands they have created.

NGOs use **forum shopping**, to move and press the issues they are concerned about in a more favorable arena. For example, NGOs take concerns about sweatshop labor conditions to consumers in developed countries rather than to the governments that allow exploitive sweatshops such as Vietnam. Vietnam is a communist country that bars freedom of speech, freedom of press, freedom of association, and where it can be dangerous to criticize government policies, including labor and trade policies that allow the exploitation of workers. Because local politics is blocked in Vietnam, NGOs take their concerns to the consumers who buy products made with slave or sweatshop labor. NGOs' network power gives them the abilities to identify more favorable forums and the capacities to move the issue across sovereign state borders. For example, with the help of human rights NGOs, the families of four US churchwomen who had been abducted, raped, and murdered while serving the poor in El Salvador in 1980 sued the Generals responsible in court in the United States. Feeling that justice was blocked in the political system of El Salvador, NGOs helped to move the issue to the United States, where there are stronger legal protections on human rights and greater access to the international media, and where many of the perpetrators of these crimes had moved in their retirement. Those responsible for the torture and deaths of the churchwomen, and the assassin of Roman Catholic Archbishop Oscar Romero (who was murdered with a single bullet through the heart while saying mass at a hospital chapel), had trials reopened in different venues. What can possibly be accomplished by this? The women and the Archbishop are dead and the civil war has ended. But NGOs trade in ideas. Those involved with these cases want "to deter other would-be torturers and assassins from committing such acts," and to send "a message to military commanders around the world that they can be held responsible for their failure to act, as well as for their direct actions, and that the United States is not a safe haven for such people."[15] The trials help shed light on the poor human rights practices of governments, as well as open a new forum for hearing other cases blocked by local governments.

One type of forum shopping is what Margaret Keck and Kathryn Sikkink describe as a **"boomerang politics,"** in which issues can move around blocked local politics.

Governments are the primary "guarantors" of rights, but also their primary violators. When a government violates or refuses to recognize rights, individuals and domestic groups often have no recourse within domestic political or judicial arenas. They may seek international connections finally to express their concerns and even to protect their lives. When channels between the state and its domestic actors are blocked, the boomerang pattern of influence characteristic of transnational networks may occur: domestic NGOs bypass their state and directly search out international allies to try to bring pressure on their states from outside.[16]

While true, I note that NGOs forum shop or go global for other reasons as well, even when local politics are not blocked. Even when an NGO enjoys a good relationship with the local government, as Jody Williams and the ICBL enjoyed with the Canadian government, the goal may require activating a global advocacy network. Or NGOs may perceive a better target internationally, even when local politics are not blocked. For example, religious and environmental NGOs successfully pushed for conflict minerals transparency laws, in which companies that use minerals from warzones must disclose this information, so customers, shareholders, and investors can make informed choices. The government of the Democratic Republic of Congo works to stop armed actors and insurgents from conflict and illegal mining. But by targeting the EU and United States, the markets and home of many of the companies that use conflict minerals, advocates believed it would place greater pressure on companies to clean up their supply chains, and ensure that illegal actors were not profiting from war. Since the US conflict minerals transparency act passed, more companies have cleaned up their supply chains, and violence has declined in the extractives areas of the DRC. Transparency and forum shopping work well together.

Leverage politics is when NGOs use the power, platform, or resources of celebrities and stronger network members on behalf of weaker network members to move a global issue forward. When Bono campaigns to eradicate global poverty especially for poor girls and women, the One Campaign is leveraging his power as a celebrity to bring attention to poor women who otherwise would not attract media or public policy attention. Leverage politics does not require celebrities. NGO networks that include members from poorer countries as well as richer countries can use the resources of the rich on behalf of the poor, even when those with greater resources are not celebrities. The NGO Doctors without Borders leverages the skills of physicians to help the needy regardless of sovereign borders.

NGOs have **network power**. The increased speed and adaptability of their organizational mode provides benefits. They are typically organized as flatter, more flexible organizations than governments, IGOs, or MNCs. This may give NGOs greater speed and adaptability to respond to pressing global issues or to get their views to the media faster than some government bureaucracies.

Some NGOs can use their reputational power as a "force multiplier" to enhance their values, ideas, and information power. Reputational power may derive from important, well-known, or respected figures who are members of the group, or it may come from the NGO's own track record of strong advocacy. For example, The Elders are a group of respected senior public figures who use their reputations to draw attention to key global issues, often issues of war and peace. The NGO was founded by the late South African president Nelson Mandela and includes many Nobel Laureates, such as South African human rights defender Archbishop Desmond Tutu, former Irish president Mary Robinson, and former US president Jimmy Carter. Like an MNC, an NGO may build a "brand name" around the quality and reliability of the organization's information products. Some NGOs emphasize building such reputational power through quality reports, analysis, and information products—for example, Transparency International's work on corruption worldwide, and the International Campaign to Ban Landmines' annual Landmines Monitor report on global compliance with removing landmines and helping victims.

NGOs use media and communications power as a force multiplier for their values, ideas, and information power. Although NGOs vary in their skills with social media and access to global media, they do have certain media advantages. Social and global media simplify issues to attract wider audiences and compete against ever-shorter sound bites to sell their products. If NGOs often emphasize how policies or practices affect vulnerable individuals or groups, or how global issues present clear moral choices, then they may be able to attract media attention. NGOs can use media as a megaphone for their message if they understand the care and feeding of the media and can deliver compelling stories and good pictures with clear good guys and bad guys framing in arenas where government, IGO, or corporate responses may be slow or lack credibility. Because MNCs may have huge marketing investments in their brand names and do not want these brands sullied or their reputations trashed, even the threat of negative media coverage can bring greater attention to an NGO's ideas. This "name and shame" power is uneven, however. Products, commodities, and companies that are unbranded do not have a "name" to protect, so are less moved by "shame and name" campaigns. Communications and media power are important to groups that trade in ideas. NGOs, like others who can persuade but cannot compel, must be good salespeople as well as good preachers to effectively mobilize their ideas.

NGOs also have female power. Women are underrepresented in the governments of states and in leadership positions in MNCs and IGOs. But women are better represented as both leaders and members of NGOs. Women make up the majority of people on the planet, but many governments, MNCs, and IGOs throw away or underutilize the talents of more than half their populations. This can be a moral and strategic advantage for NGOs. They can provide a means for women to participate in and affect international structures that may otherwise exclude them. If women perceive NGOs as more likely to represent their interests, then this may add to popular support and reputational advantages for NGOs. Like human society in general, NGOs are certainly not free from gender conflicts. Relative to other institutions, however, NGOs are more likely to be run by and for women, taking up issues—such as women's rights, human trafficking, and female genital mutilation—that other institutions ignore.

NGOs also have the power of individuals. They do not accept the traditional view that states are the fundamental unit in international politics and that individuals can have little effect. Believing individuals can make a difference, they create ways for them to do so. Without getting bogged down in the question of which came first, the idea or the activist, activists are central to NGOs.[17] Individuals may start NGOs, splinter NGOs, and use NGOs as vehicles for both personal and community expression and activism. Even when NGOs network internationally in large campaigns, testimonials of how global problems affect real people are an enormous strength for NGOs, helping to put a face on global politics.

NGOs can more strategically use the power of personal stories if a wider society empathizes with them, either as innocent civilians, or because people can envision themselves in their shoes. A "poster child factor" also helps NGOs gain sympathy and concrete identification with their cause from either elites or masses.

Another source of power for NGOs can be consumer power. If an NGO can credibly argue a connection between a corporate policy and some objectionable wider practice, then it can marshal the market power of customers, consumers, or shareholders through boycotts or pressure on advertisers and shareholders, among other forms of market pressures. This can put an economic price on objectionable practices that may make corporations or states notice and respond to NGO concerns. Consumer and shareholder campaigns directly pressured McDonalds and Starbucks not to use polystyrene (Styrofoam) packaging. Today, these groups continue campaigning to reduce plastics, such as plastic drinking straws. Tuna companies label their products as "dolphin safe" as a result of consumer pressures to change their fishing practices to protect against killing dolphins while fishing for tuna.

Outlining these potential sources of power for NGOs does not mean that all organizations have all of these resources at all times. Some NGOs have denser networks that allow them to pool or access greater resources than others with fewer or sparser networks. Some issues are easier to put a face on than others. Environmentalists who are concerned with global climate change have emphasized on the effects on polar bears rather than people. This framing makes it difficult to translate the concerns of climate change into more concrete attention to those, particularly the poor, whose lives are most adversely affected. If ideas are a crucial source of power for NGOs, then clearly some ideas are better than others, and some play better to particular audiences than do others. Some NGOs can craft an easily recognizable and universally sympathetic message better than others. NGOs that promulgate values and ideas with greater resonance will have advantages over NGOs with narrower and less appealing idea bases. For example, it may be easier to mobilize against child labor than to save the dwarf wedge mussel. As in all things political, context matters in assessing NGO power. It is easier to sell the idea that child labor is wrong in rich countries than in poor countries.

Different NGOs have different resources, expertise, networks, issues, and contexts. However, NGOs use their variegated supplies of people power in several common ways. NGOs raise consciousness regarding issues with elites, masses, or both. NGOs often practice resurrection politics, taking issues previously thought dead on arrival (such as landmines and debt relief), and raising them up onto the public and political agenda. NGOs also practice ideas, information, transparency, accountability, and symbolic politics, expanding the idea base surrounding issues by introducing new or discrediting accepted information, or introducing alternative norms by which to evaluate information. NGOs frame or reframe issues. NGOs change language, beliefs, and symbols surrounding issues (which may later translate into behavioral changes). NGOs move issues to a forum more amenable to a favorable response. NGOs practice leverage politics by enlisting celebrities to bring attention and leverage to their cause.[18]

NGOs change government, IGO, or MNC policy, or individual behavior. They adapt or create institutional structures or advocacy networks to further particular issues. NGOs practice Dracula politics, transparency politics, and sunshine politics, shining a light on problems and shaming and naming perpetrators. Like Dracula, many abusive international practices can only persist in the dark, and die off when exposed to the light of day. NGOs monitor compliance with norms or regimes once created, making actors live up to the promises they make.

Yet NGOs come with their downsides as well. Coordinating action among a wide variety of eclectic organizations with different agendas, cultures, and operating procedures is difficult. The abilities of NGOs to work well with states, IGOs, and MNCs in combating transsovereign problems is often inhibited by poor communication and coordination among the various groups, who may not like, trust, or understand each other. IGOs, MNCs, and government foreign policy organizations too often deal with NGOs in an ad hoc, nonsystematic manner. Increased numbers of NGOs in complex combinations make coordination, communication, transparency, and accountability difficult, as is determining that groups should be included in government and IGO decision processes. NGOs may compete against one another for the supremacy of their ideas, funding, and recognition. As private-sector organizations, whom do NGOs speak for or answer to beyond their own governing boards or contributors? NGOs have asymmetrical resources and influence, and even within NGO advocacy networks, conflicts arise between Northern and Southern NGOs. Who guides the network? Southern NGOs are critical of donor-driven development, where the rich people drive the action based on what they are interested in. However, media power and reputational power can also be tools to check and balance rising NGO power. For example, public pressure against the Red Cross decision to use funds donated to the victims of September 11 for other purposes indicates these tools can yield results. Many NGOs adopt voluntary codes of conduct and publish their budgets to encourage transparency and accountability. The same questions that plague corporate codes of conduct, however, may be raised regarding NGOs: How seriously are these codes implemented, and what are the sanctions if voluntary codes are not implemented? Because NGO power frequently derives from moral and reputational capital, NGOs may have greater incentives to address democracy deficits than other organizations.

NGOs AND GLOBALIZATION: OPEN SOCIETIES

Open societies, open technologies, and open economies make it easier to establish, organize, and run NGOs. We are witnessing an explosion of NGOs worldwide precisely when liberalizing trends are spreading. The spread of democracy lowers the barriers to forming NGOs. Some of the hallmarks of democracy are freedom of expression and freedom of association.

Certainly, the democratization process encourages the creation and spread of NGOs as part of the effort to build civil society. Nondemocratic governments may make NGOs illegal, fearing they may form a base of opposition to the government. Organizing people in states with closed political systems—North Korea, for example—can be a dangerous proposition to the activist, who risks imprisonment, torture, and death.

The fears of authoritarian governments are justified because NGOs have worked to bring about the fall of nondemocratic regimes. Lester Salamon notes that "Under Pope John Paul II, Catholic churches in Warsaw, Gdansk, Krakow, and elsewhere in Eastern Europe provided a crucial neutral meeting ground and source of moral support for those agitating for change in the latter 1980s. The Lutheran Church played a comparable role in East Germany."[19]

NGOs also have been instrumental in pressing for open societies and advocating for human rights and democratization. During and after World War II, NGOs kept the issue of human rights on the international agenda when state representatives meeting to construct the postwar international organization (which became the UN) tried to exclude or water down such concerns. States were skeptical about including human rights in the UN Charter. They feared a loss of sovereignty over internal treatment of their citizens if the topic were broached in the UN Charter. But NGOs such as the American Jewish Committee, the American Bar Association, the National Association for the Advancement of Colored People, and the League of Women Voters reminded states that the failure to protect individual and minority rights after World War I had contributed to the conflict and genocide of World War II. Sustained lobbying by NGOs ensured that respect for human rights became one of the four purposes of the United Nations set forth in its Charter, and that the Charter called for the creation of a UN Commission on Human Rights. NGOs provided expert advice and research and helped to draft language and lobby for the adoption of the **1948 Universal Declaration of Human Rights**, the international agreement that forms the foundation of international human rights law, and other subsequent human rights treaties.[20]

NGOs often are created as the locus of resistance to nondemocratic regimes. One dramatic example was the emergence of NGOs in opposition to the military dictatorships in Argentina and Chile in the 1970s and 1980s. Citizens who criticized or were seen as threats to these regimes, as well as many who happened to be in the wrong place at the wrong time, became the desaparecidos, or the "disappeared." They were kidnapped, imprisoned, tortured, and killed. In a final insult, the children of many of the disappeared were sold to childless military couples. "One torturer estimated that about sixty babies passed through [his clandestine detention center], and that all but two—whose heads were smashed against the wall in efforts to get their mothers to talk— were sold."[21]

Children were tortured in front of their parents, and parents in front of their children. Some prisoners were kept in rooms no longer or wider than a single bed. And the torture continued for days, weeks, months, even years, until the victim was released or, more often, killed. The sadistic brutality did not always even end with the death of the victim. "One woman was sent the hands of her daughter in a shoe box." The body of another woman "was dumped in her parents' yard, naked but showing no outward signs of torture. Later the director of the funeral home called to inform her parents that the girl's vagina had been sewn up. Inside he had found a rat."[22]

In a heroic response to such brutality, a small group of middle-aged mothers of disappeared children organized in 1977. Calling themselves the "Mothers of the Plaza de Mayo," at first they numbered only fourteen. Frustrated in their attempts to locate their children, they began a silent vigil every Thursday afternoon in the main square of Buenos Aires in front of the president's residence and seat of government. Although the women were subject to harassment and attack (some of them even disappeared themselves), they continued their efforts to draw attention to the atrocities of the military government. They were followed by the "Grandmothers of the Plaza de Mayo," who attempted to trace and recover the trafficked children and babies. Quickly, the numbers of these groups swelled across Latin America, and they soon became the NGO known as Federación Latinoamericana de Asociaciones de Familiares de Detenidos-Desaparecidos (FEDEFAM, Federation of Families of Political Prisoners and Disappeared Persons). Working with a wide transnational network of NGOs, they fought the military dictatorships and their brutality, always at great personal risk to themselves. When the dictatorships eventually fell, these groups helped to build democracies, strengthen the legal protections for human rights, and reunite political prisoners with their families.[23]

NGOs promote open societies in many ways. They expose the abuses of regimes by tracking facts and disseminating information, as well as by mobilizing public opinion to try to end the abuses and improve conditions. They communicate with decision-makers locally and globally, dispensing information and advocating for legal changes. They are direct service providers, offering education, advocacy, and legal aid services. They teach citizens what their rights are and "how to act upon them."[24]

NGOs AND GLOBAL TECHNOLOGIES

Open technologies also greatly assist the formation and maintenance of NGOs, as seen in the landmines case. Any group with Internet access can mobilize people and circulate information globally. Cheap and easily available information technologies allow citizens to more easily gather and disseminate information and ideas, identify members, solicit funds, network with others, and coordinate activities. Decentralization of phone and communication companies has made it more difficult for governments to control access to or censor use of the Internet. Many governments still work to censor the Internet, although as former president Clinton put it, the attempt may be as futile as "nailing Jello to a wall."[25]

NGOs also rely on satellites and drones to independently gather information, particularly in difficult to access areas. They use social media as well as news media to directly communicate with the public, publicize their causes, raise money, and pressure governments. For example, humanitarian NGOs use "ambulance drones" to send medicines to remote areas. Human rights NGOs use commercial satellites to monitor human rights abuses, refugee flows, and famine. Actor George Clooney gave his income from Nescafe coffee commercials to buy satellite time for NGOs to monitor genocide and human rights abuses in Sudan and South Sudan. Environmental NGOs use satellites and drones to directly collect information on environmental quality, independent of government sources. For example, NGOs use drones and satellites to detect pollution and destruction of the Amazon rainforest.[26] NGOs use these technologies to create pincer movement pressure, inside and outside the area where the global issue is most severe. They use the satellite and drone information to conduct their own projects, and to pressure governments, intergovernmental organizations, and citizens to directly address global issues. Media attention of their reports and activities also raises public attention and funding to NGOs. Cell phone and mobile payment apps allow citizens to immediately contribute to NGOs in the midst of natural disasters and humanitarian crises.

NGOs also actively work to expand the reach of open technologies. Typically, international NGOs work with local counterparts, thereby spreading technology. For example, when the NGO Inclusive Security, first known as Women Waging Peace began, one of the first projects it funded was equipping women's peace organizations with laptop computers and providing training in the use of the Internet and social media strategies. In similar ways, environmental NGOs press for the adoption of cleaner, greener technologies, such as water- and air-filtration systems that make it possible for factories to emit fewer toxic pollutants into the environment. Public health NGOs disseminate health technologies such as mobile medical apps and filtration systems for drinking water as part of their disease eradication programs. Development NGOs disseminate technologies for agriculture, irrigation, water systems, and electrification. However, there is a digital gap. NGOs in developed countries have better technologies and are better able to integrate new technologies in their work than NGOs in poorer communities and countries.

NGOs AND OPEN ECONOMIES

The rise in NGOs is also facilitated by open economies. The information economy brings advantages for NGOs that trade in ideas and information. Economic liberalization also allows money to flow freely across borders, allowing NGOs to solicit and contribute money across sovereign jurisdictions. In addition, capitalism encourages the growth of the private sector, of which NGOs are a part. Free market economies tend to emphasize grassroots, private-sector responses to societal problems rather than top-down, state-sponsored solutions. NGOs thus fit with the entrepreneurial and pluralistic norms of capitalist societies.

The rise of new businesses and technologies also leads to the creation of new NGOs. Some of the richest beneficiaries of open economies often donate some of their wealth into creating new NGOs. Microsoft Founder (and world's richest man) Bill Gates created the Bill and Melinda Gates Foundation, one of the world's most well-endowed

NGOs, primarily dedicated to fighting global disease. Gates and Warren Buffett (often the world's second richest man), created the Giving Pledge, inviting billionaires to commit to giving away the majority of their wealth to NGOs and philanthropy. About 140 billionaires have committed to donating the majority of their wealth. Michael Bloomberg, billionaire financier and former Republican mayor of New York City, signed the Giving Pledge, and has made the largest university donation in history to Johns Hopkins University. He supports global health NGOs and NGOs that help cities become more sustainable, through his Bloomberg Foundation.

Google founders Sergey Brin and Larry Page each created their own charities. Amazon founder Jeff Bezos, and Facebook Founder Mark Zuckerberg, also created family foundations through which they support NGOs.

Billionaires who experienced hardship before becoming wealthy often start NGOs. Freed from communism in Hungary in the old Soviet Union allied state of Hungary, businessman George Soros has created NGOs such as the Soros Foundation and the Open Society Foundation, and donated his money to advancing human rights and democracy through existing NGOs such as Amnesty International.

Privatization of the economy is even encouraging the growth of NGOs in China.

The Chinese government and Communist party refer to it as "small government, big society." They want to shrink government, and they want to grow society, that is, they want to shift functions from the government sphere to the private sphere. . . .The vehicle for doing this, in part, is to create a private nonprofit sector that can shoulder some of the social tasks that have traditionally, in recent Chinese history, been state functions.[27]

There are limits to the independence of Chinese NGOs. China is a state-run economy that closely controls civil society. Yet, the small government, big society approach shows the spread of ideas concerning the value of the private sector, even in repressive countries.

NGOs vary in their receptiveness to open markets, however. While some trade and professional associations lobby to expand free-market arrangements such as the WTO, social advocacy NGOs in the labor, development, environment, and human rights arenas are often skeptical of economic globalization—as seen in the regular protests against the IMF, World Bank, and WTO.

NGOs AND STATES

NGOs work with donor states to aid people in weak or failing states, as relief and development organizations such as Catholic Relief Services are doing in ministering to the needs of Afghan, Syrian, and Somali refugees. Donor governments increasingly prefer to funnel aid through NGOs rather than give it directly to recipient foreign governments that may be neither efficient nor accountable in their use of the funds. In states undergoing transitions, new institutions may be weak and lack proven track records.

Governments believe that aid funneled through NGOs is more politically acceptable than direct government-to-government assistance. They believe that NGOs can better reach the grassroots level and are more efficient because they involve less bureaucratic red tape and over-head. They also believe that working with NGOs helps to develop the private sector.

Many see contracting out to NGOs as a win-win situation. The government "has found an efficient, less costly means of carrying out its legislative mandate, while the [NGO]s have discovered a relatively dependable source of money, available in large sums."[28]

There are downsides, however. NGOs risk losing the perception of their autonomy and independence from governments if they rely too heavily on state sources for funding, which can compromise an NGO's reputational power. One NGO executive director described the question of accepting funding from the USAID as the dilemma of not wanting "to look like the tool or the fool of the United States government."[29]

NGOs are also concerned about the potential for conflict of interest between their goals and the goals of government donors. NGOs are concerned about becoming dependent on states for resources and potentially neglecting their traditional bases of support. They do not want to change their focus to fit more closely with government priorities in order to attract state funding. The "strings" that may come attached to accepting government funds (such as the "Buy American" requirement that goes along with US aid dollars) may detract from their program principles (such as whenever possible, to buy locally to help the local economy). And NGOs fear that the reporting and accounting procedures required of government contractors may make them more bureaucratic, entangle them in red tape, and drive up costs (which donors wanted to avoid by funneling aid through NGOs in the first place).

When recipient governments are cut out of the aid loop because of corruption or weakness, animosity may develop between state institutions and NGOs. For example, in Haiti, short-term concerns for quick and accountable projects may come at the cost of developing long-term state capacity in crucial sectors such as education and public health.[30]

As citizens turn to NGOs as service providers, the state may be further undermined, which can perpetuate a feedback loop. NGOs may become involved to attend to problems that states are not addressing. In so doing, NGOs may further undermine the capacity and legitimacy of states, which can exacerbate transsovereign problems rather than fight them.

As an increasing number of states collapse, this is becoming a larger issue. Many NGOs do not wait for a state invitation before entering a country to provide services. This is especially true in countries such as Somalia, where there has not been an effective state since 1991. If NGOs fulfill the functions of states where there are no functioning sovereignties, then how are sovereign states rebuilt? Some NGOs are not concerned with the question. Individuals in need, not states, are their priorities. They regard sovereignty not only as a right to nonintervention (negative or de jure sovereignty) but also as a responsibility to provide some benefit to citizens (positive or de facto sovereignty). If states are unable or unwilling to fulfill their responsibilities toward individuals in need, then NGOs must step in.

The NGO known as Doctors Without Borders (Médicins Sans Frontières) developed specifically out of the creed that physicians would provide medical assistance where needed, regardless of whether government actors existed or welcomed them. Save the Children developed out of the efforts of a British woman, Eglantyne Jebb, to provide aid to the children victimized by World War I, regardless of whether they were the citizens of a winning or losing state in the conflict. Similarly, Amnesty International began in 1961 with the efforts of a London lawyer, Peter Benenson, to win the release of some Portuguese political prisoners. His campaign soon developed into a worldwide watchdog and advocacy organization for human rights. Amnesty International is fundamentally concerned with protecting the human rights of individuals and groups. It is less concerned with the effect its activities may have on state capacities. Faith-based NGOs likewise are concerned with higher principles. The major world religions existed before the advent of the modern sovereign state, and they likely will be around long after its demise. Although not necessarily antagonistic to states, faith-based NGOs feel they answer to a higher power than the state.

Understandably, then, NGO–state relations are often adversarial because NGOs are often created to curb the abuses of states or to attend to issues that states ignore. In Central America in the 1970s and 1980s, NGOs were targeted by the state, particularly four types of NGOs—human rights, training, humanitarian, and organizations that represented those citizens uprooted by the violence and civil wars:

> Physical attacks on NGOs started in the 1970s. . . . Governments have tried to destroy human rights NGOs since their creation. They have endured because of personal courage, the mix of financial, technical, and political support received from international NGOs, and survival strategies crafted to suit local conditions. For example, the Catholic Justice and Peace Commission and El Salvador's Tutela Legal operated under the umbrella of church protection. . . . Most survived because of strong international links and small, low budget, decentralized administrative operations; some . . . perished. NGOs documenting and researching issues related to uprooted populations were also intimidated because of their infringement into policy areas considered the armed forces' preserve.[31]

Today, environmental defenders are often targeted for violence and murder, particularly in environmentally endangered areas, such as the Amazon.

One sign of the adversarial relationship between states and NGOs is the establishment of "front" NGOs by governments "to infiltrate and gather information on the NGO community. These 'government NGOs' are of particular concern in the field of human rights."[32]

NGOs AND STATE FUNCTIONS

Not only do some NGOs commandeer more resources than do many states but also the activities of these organizations increasingly impinge on functions that previously were jealously guarded by states. NGOs carry out health, education, welfare, and development functions, especially in weak states. NGOs had greater capacity than impacted states in responding to the earthquake in Haiti or the Ebola crisis in West Africa. Even in strong states, NGOs are increasingly active in issues such as economic and environmental policy making, and even arms control.

Although only states make laws and sign treaties, NGOs increasingly help to write laws and treaties, lobby for their acceptance, and monitor compliance with them. NGOs were critical to the creation of the treaties banning landmines, cluster munitions, and nuclear weapons, and it is NGOs that monitor the compliance with these treaties. NGOs may have more technical competence and capacity than states, and some states enlist NGOs to represent them in international meetings, for example, on international environmental issues.

NGOs play an increasingly prominent role in international environmental institutions, participating in many activities—negotiation, monitoring, and implementation—traditionally reserved to states. . . . For better or worse, NGOs are now a regular part of the cooperative process. Within limits, they address delegations as a state would. They participate actively in the corridor diplomacy that is so central to negotiations, receive documents, present proposals, and are consulted by and lobby delegations. These changes are all relatively new. . .[33]

Because environmental problems are indifferent to state borders, and the information and technical expertise needed to make environmental policy often exceeds the capacity of states, NGOs provide valuable services on environmental issues. They can track environmental problems and effects on resources across borders, presenting the wider perspective needed to write treaties and create and monitor regimes. For example, in negotiations on climate change, "NGOs set the original goal of negotiating an agreement to control greenhouse gases long before governments were ready to do so, proposed most of its structure and content, and lobbied and mobilized public pressure to force through a pact that virtually no one else thought possible when the talks began."[34] NGOs also provide policy research and development, serve on government delegations, participate in small working-group meetings at international negotiations, monitor state commitments, report on negotiations, lobby participants, and facilitate negotiations. NGOs even have legal standing in most of the major environmental treaties negotiated in the last decade.

NGOs also develop and implement "soft law," or the voluntary codes that often serve as stepping stones to the eventual passage of "hard law." Finally, NGOs may change attitudes and behavior directly, changing the ideas held by individuals and institutions. In this way, NGOs may work to manage pressing global problems with or without the cooperation or capacity of states.

NGOs WORKING BEYOND SOVEREIGNTY

NGOs go beyond sovereignty not only in their organization, membership, and activities across borders but also in their ideas and the targets of their activities. If the public sector is shrinking or not growing as fast as the private sector, then the nonprofit part of the private sector may be needed as a counterweight to the for-profit private sector. Citizens who believe globalization is out of balance, or tilted in favor of corporations, look to NGOs to serve as a check or counterbalance. Networks of international environmental NGOs, for example, directly pressure MNCs and the public to change environmental behavior. They do not restrict themselves to lobbying governments and IGOs for strengthened legislation or treaties. By taking their arguments directly to corporations, consumers, and public opinion worldwide, NGOs operate beyond sovereignty. McDonald's stopped using styrofoam cups and burger packaging largely in response to NGO-fueled direct-public and consumer-pressure campaigns.[35] NGOs often prefer direct action campaigns to legislative campaigns because state actions to pass and enforce laws on particular environmental problems can be slow and are only effective within a country's territory with enforcement measures. Direct corporate and consumer campaigns, on the other hand, can achieve results across borders without government legislation or enforcement. Convincing individuals not to purchase products made from rainforest wood can be more effective in preserving rain forests than pursuing government legislation.

Religious organizations also work beyond sovereignty, often targeting their activities directly toward individuals and communities. Religious organizations reach globally with rich, interconnected institutions in health care, education, relief and development, and refugee and resettlement services. These institutional infrastructures are so extensive, well developed, and multifaceted that some consider it misleading to consider a religious organization "just another NGO" because NGOs may be more singular in focus and rarely run global networks of schools and hospitals, for example. Too often, when religious organizations are considered at all in international relations, they are presented as parties to ethnic and nationalist conflict and opposed to globalization, change, and modernity (or what some have termed "Jihad versus McWorld"). Samuel Huntington, among others, predicts an inevitable clash of civilizations with religious groups at war—that is, of the West versus the rest.[36] There are alternative views, however. Corporations and states are neither the only engines of globalization nor its only beneficiaries. Religious organizations have long been globalizing forces,[37] spreading ideas, institutions, flows of people, and capital across international borders. Today, religious organizations (like other civil society groups) continue to play active roles in globalization as both global actors and mediating institutions, responding to the challenges of globalization and offering alternative ethical visions of it (beyond market or consumer dynamics).

NGO ideas go beyond sovereignty. Corporations see the world as a market. In this material world, people are all customers, shareholders, or investors. States see globalization as a world to be governed. People are either governed or ungovernable, citizens or those beyond government and posing problems (e.g., illegal immigrants, refugees, terrorists, and criminals). Social advocacy NGOs, however, present alternative ethical visions, seeing a world in which we are all people with fundamental human dignity. Rather than mere opposition to globalization as the clash of civilizations "Jihad versus McWorld" formulations suggest, NGOs present more varied and constructive reactions, to create a globalization that puts people first. Their formation of transnational networks that work to acknowledge and bridge North–South conflicts may represent one of the best ways for globalization to proceed "with a human face," thereby unleashing greater human potential than can mere materialism—and for more of the planet than currently participates in the benefits of globalization.

As NGOs (sometimes in partnership with IGOs or MNCs) fill functions instead of states and challenge the ideas of states, what effect does this have on sovereignty? Keck and Sikkink note, "If sovereignty is a shared set of understandings and expectations about state authority that is reinforced by practices, then changes in these practices and understandings should in turn transform sovereignty."[38]

The state is not going away. Rather, it is increasingly networking and contracting out. As states downsize and decentralize in response to the pressures of globalization, and as states innovate in response to global problems, nonstate actors such as NGOs perform functions previously assumed by states and promote ideas that have unintended consequences for sovereignty.

KEY TERMS

1948 Universal Declaration of Human Rights, 71
accountability politics, 64
Beatrice Finn, 57
boomerang politics, 65
Cluster Munitions Coalition, 56
"Dracula" politics, 63

forum shopping, 64
hard law, 64
information politics, 62
International Campaign Against Nuclear Weapons (ICAN), 56
International Campaign to Ban Landmines (ICBL), 55

DISCUSSION QUESTIONS

1. Scholars note that we are in the midst of a global associational revolution. What do they mean by that? What evidence of this do you see in your experiences and your community?
2. NGOs have no armies, compel no taxes, and cannot command followers. So why are they increasingly effective?
3. Who is Jody Williams? What's her story? Why did she win the Nobel Prize? How did she inspire other TAN movements?
4. Before reading this chapter, did you know that most countries in the world have banned nuclear weapons? Why did nuclear bomb survivor Setsuko Thurlow speak at the 2017 Nobel Prize ceremony? Why have most countries in the world banned nuclear weapons?
5. The MDGs and SDGs were voluntary goals. So why have they worked so well?
6. Open societies, open technologies, and open markets create conditions that facilitate the creation of NGOs and the types of politics they use, such as information politics, leverage politics, transparency politics, accountability politics, name and shame politics, etc. Which of these types of politics have you experienced? Describe.
8. How do NGOs move beyond sovereignty? What evidence of this trend have you seen in your own experiences and communities?

Dr. Maryann Cusimano Love

Student Nike protest.

3

Multinational Corporations

Power and Responsibility in Global Business Networks

Georgetown University is committed to protecting the rights of workers producing university-licensed apparel.

—Rachel Pugh, Georgetown University spokesperson

We're trying to tell Nike in the clearest terms through this protest that Georgetown University stands up for our values.

—Lily Ryan, Georgetown University student

Hear the prayers we make today for all women and men who are deprived of the fruit of their labors and find tears rather than joy in their work. We pray especially for the Nike workers in Vietnam who suffer exploitation at the hands of their employers. They are denied the dignity you, God, have bestowed upon them.

—Father Drew Christiansen, S.J., Georgetown University

We support the students and student athletes in their efforts to advocate for Hoya apparel we can wear with pride.

—Georgetown University Student Association

Nike has been deeply committed to workers and improving conditions in contract factories for more than twenty years, and that commitment remains as strong today as ever. Our investment in transparency and commitment to protect worker's rights is unwavering.

—Sabrina Oei, Nike Spokesperson

GEORGETOWN UNIVERSITY STUDENTS AND OTHER college students protested at university campuses and Nike Town stores around the world and across the country. Nike is the world's largest sports apparel company and holds lucrative contracts to produce college sportswear and use college sports teams to advertise its products. Through groups like **United Students against Sweatshops (USAS)**, students urged their universities to ensure that Nike kept promises to uphold good human rights, labor, and environmental practices and allow independent verification of factory conditions, or else to cut ties with Nike. Independent, credible reports listed numerous serious violations at Nike factories, including the factories that produced Georgetown University, Cornell University, and University of Washington logo clothing. The independent reports found illegal practices such as workers not getting paid, workers exposed to toxic chemicals, workers forced to work overtime and doors locked to prevent their leaving, and the firing of pregnant workers. Yet Nike refused to allow the independent monitoring group into its factory. After pressure and negotiations, the entire University of California system, the University of Washington, Boston University, Northeast University, and many others ended their Nike contracts and instead contracted with others, such as Under Armour, who agreed to fair treatment of workers and independent monitoring of factories.[1]

Georgetown Women's athletes covered over the Nike logos on their team equipment, in protest of the poor pay and poor treatment of workers at Nike factories. As activist Jim Keady told the Georgetown athletes, "Nike has a problem. So does Georgetown . . . . Student athletes have power. It's the student athletes that drive the multi-billion industry that is college sports. No cooperation, no money. They have power to change the situation. And I'm hoping they will use that power in this case."[2]

Globalization makes a business such as Nike possible. The founders of Nike began by selling Tiger athletic shoes, a Japanese brand, in the US market in 1964. Phil Knight (later Nike's cofounder and CEO) soon realized that rather peddle another company's brand, he could use the global supply chain to produce shoes inexpensively in Asia and sell them in developed economies for a handsome profit. Over time, Nike has shifted production from Japan and South Korea to Vietnam, Indonesia, and Cambodia in search of lower costs. While the exact labor costs are not disclosed but are protected as competitive business information by Nike and other companies, the trend lines are clear. Nike and other companies not only claim they pay minimum wage but also admit in their internal corporate reporting that between one-third and one-half of their factories do not meet wage and safety standards. Eighty percent of workers are girls and women with little power, who earn about 42 cents an hour, and work long hours (forced and unpaid overtime, six days a week working ten or more hours a day) in difficult conditions. While conditions and pay in some factories have improved since complaints were first raised by Students against Sweatshops regarding exploitation by Nike and other garment and sportswear companies. But Nike itself identifies low wages, excessive overtime, and prohibitions on unions and organizing as problems in its factories, in Nike's Corporate Social Responsibility reports. Public records do not show what factory workers earn to make a pair of Nikes, but they do show that Nike pays the Asian factories approximately $25–28 for a pair of shoes (which includes the cost of materials, factory overhead and factory profit, in addition to worker wages), adds transportation and marketing costs plus a profit, and sells the pair to a retailer for $50. The retailer then adds its costs and profits and sells the product to consumers for $100 and up.[3]

But why buy Nike shoes rather than another brand? The sportswear market is competitive and crowded. More than sportswear, Nike sells ideas. In Greek mythology, Nike is the winged goddess of victory, which gave rise to the company's signature winged "swoosh" symbol and the practice of making its products into wearable advertisements. Through aggressive global marketing and promotions, Nike sells an image, a lifestyle, and a creed more than a product. Close your eyes and you would be hard-pressed to tell the difference between Nike shoes and other brands. Nike is selling the dream of being a world-class athlete, the desire to belong to the club of premier athletes, and the inspiration to become the best you can be. You may never be able to play basketball like superstars LeBron James or Michael Jordan, but you can wear the same brand of shoes. As one Nike official puts it, "We don't know the first thing about manufacturing. We are marketers and designers."[4] Nike pioneered the process of creating a market through product design, promotion, and innovative global advertising, and of associating the Nike brand swoosh with world-class athletes, male and female, of every race, from the inner cities to the more privileged classes. Nike went from $2 million in sales in 1972[5] to more than $34.5 billion in revenues in 2018[6]—or more than the GDP of oil-rich Bahrain and 114 other states.[7] And Nike is willing to pay for the marquee endorsement, spending over $8 billion for celebrity athlete endorsements between 2002 and 2016, and famously paying a $1 billion endorsement contract with basketball star LeBron James.[8]

The same global media that made Nike a household name and a billion-dollar company, however, also made it vulnerable to charges of labor and environmental abuses. NGOs and activists concerned with labor, environment, and human rights brought public attention to the sweatshop practices of Nike factories abroad and the disconnect with Nike advertising themes of empowerment, diversity, and women's equality. Reports of sexual harassment of women workers in Nike production facilities in Asia and of seven-year-old children stitching soccer balls in Pakistan gained media and consumer attention. A young woman in China making Nike shoes would have had to work nine hours a day, six days a week, for fifteen centuries to earn the yearly salary of Nike CEO Phil Knight.[9]

At first, Nike's response to the critics was denial. The factories are subcontractors to Nike, the company argued; therefore, the employees who made Nike products were not company employees, and Nike was "powerless" to change subcontractors' behavior. When abuses at Nike's Indonesian factories came to light in the early 1990s, the Nike general manager in Indonesia responded, "It's not within our scope to investigate. I don't know that I need to know."[10] The workers were lucky to have jobs at all, Nike representatives maintained, and it was not the company's fault if governments in developing countries had poor labor or environmental laws or enforcement. More than 80 percent of the workers are young women. The company says these workers are good at sewing. Critics say they are more docile and easily intimidated than older workers or men. "I don't think the girls in our factories are treated badly. It's better than no job at all, than harvesting coconut meat in the tropical sun," said a company official.[11] But as the controversy grew, so did negative media coverage (undermining Nike's $280 million annual advertising budget at the time).[12] Reports continued of women being beaten by supervisors and forced to work sixty-five hours a week for $10 in pay without bathroom or meal breaks. Nike began to admit there were "isolated problems" that it was determined to correct, yet an internal audit done by the company and leaked to The *New York Times* revealed that workers in one factory were exposed to 177 times the legal limit of carcinogens, with 77 percent of the workers suffering from respiratory problems. Rather than being unaware, the company knew of the problem.[13]

In 1998, consumer boycotts and shareholder unrest grew while company profits fell. CEO Phil Knight announced a new course for the company. Nike would (1) increase the minimum age of its workers to sixteen in apparel factories and eighteen in shoe factories; (2) follow US Occupational Safety and Health Administration standards for air quality at factories abroad, especially seeking substitutes for the adhesives that were causing respiratory problems in workers; and (3) allow local NGOs and independent auditors to monitor and release information about the company's subcontracting factories. Nike joined corporate responsibility groups such as the Apparel Industry Partnership, the Fair Labor Association, the Global Alliance for Workers and Communities, and the **United Nations Global Compact**, which is a voluntary UN initiative in which businesses promise to adopt sustainable and socially responsible practices in their businesses, and to report on how well they are keeping their promises. Nike also increased community development loans for small business and education projects in the areas of its overseas production facilities.[14]

Nike believes it is now a leader in **corporate social responsibility (CSR)**, in which businesses self-regulate (or work together with other businesses and NGOs) to improve their environmental and human rights impacts. Some observers credit Nike with raising standards and awareness of the issues across the apparel industry. Critics charge the pronouncements are more public relations efforts than real accomplishments and that Nike's corporate codes of conduct are voluntary and unenforceable. Nike still does not pay workers adequate wages or allow consistent monitoring by international NGOs that might be more critical to participate in monitoring. College students organized into groups such as the Workers Rights Consortium, the Clean Clothes Campaign, and United Students against Sweatshops to pressure suppliers of college sportswear not to use sweatshop labor. Nike has withdrawn advertising sponsorships of athletic programs at many colleges and universities such as Brown University, the University of Michigan, and even for a time Phil Knight's alma mater, the University of Oregon, due to student protests of Nike and activism in these groups. While collegiate licensing is only a small part of Nike's overall business, image is everything for a company like Nike, especially image among young athletes, the company's key market. As CEO Phil Knight acknowledged, "The brand is sacred. I messed that up."[15]

The Nike example illustrates pressing debates that will be discussed in this chapter about the rising power and global reach of **multinational corporations (MNCs)**. Do MNCs raise labor and environmental standards internationally or are they leading a global race to the bottom? Are states effectively able to regulate MNCs, or do MNCs have increasing power over states? Are MNCs exercising their power responsibly, and how do they interact with other actors (NGOs, IGOs, and states) in setting standards for responsible corporate behavior? Are corporate codes of conduct a way to go beyond sovereignty to manage pressing global problems and to make private actors better stewards of the public good? Are they nontariff trade barriers or protectionist measures that hurt development in the Global South? Or are they merely a way for corporations to deflect state regulation and public criticism? What are the effects on sovereignty?

THE GLOBAL REACH OF MNCs

Multinational corporations are enterprises that control and manage commercial ventures and operations outside their countries of origin.[16] Fueled by open economies and distributed technology, enhanced financial mechanisms and the ease of transborder trade, their power and influence is growing dramatically. Of the world's hundred top economies, sixty-nine are corporations and thirty-one are countries.[17]

MNCs are not new. Foreign investment, banking, resource extraction, trade, and production were part of imperial expansion and colonial trade by the Romans, Venetians, Genoese, English (British East India Company), and Dutch (Hudson Bay Company). What is new is the global reach and influence of modern multinational firms. In 1969, there were 7,000 MNCs.[18] By 2008, there were 79,000 multinational parent corporations with 790,000 foreign affiliates worldwide.[19] Today, the world's largest companies generated $30 trillion in revenues, $1.9 in profits, and employ 67.7 million people.[20] The sheer scope of these entities represents a rise in private, nonstate power across the globe.

MNCs are a diverse and eclectic group. MNCs are organized internationally to achieve several corporate objectives: open new markets and gain access to new consumers, acquire natural resources at lower costs, and produce efficiencies through the reduction of production and labor costs or by taking advantage of lower environmental regulations and taxes. Some allow "host" subsidiaries greater autonomy; others insist on a high degree of "parent" company control. They range from corporations such as Royal Dutch Shell Oil and British Petroleum, which extract raw materials and natural resources; to manufacturers such as Apple, Samsung, Siemens, Coca Cola, Walt Disney Corporation, and Volkswagon, which produce consumer goods; to companies such as Lloyd's of London, Barclays, and Credit Suisse, which offer banking, investment, insurance, and consulting services. Many MNCs are hybrids of these functions—such as IBM, which sells computer and business products and provides consulting services.

MNCs are not simply companies that engage in foreign trade or market their products abroad. MNCs engage in **foreign direct** investment (FDI) and carry out production in foreign countries. They engage in FDI because local firms have a "home court advantage." They are more knowledgeable about local business practices and consumer tastes, and it is generally less costly for local firms to do business in their home markets. Foreign firms that seek entry into a locality have an incentive to "hook up" with local firms. FDI is when an individual or a company in one country buys control or a significant degree of influence on the management of a business in another country. FDI may take many forms: buyouts of a foreign subsidiary, joint ventures, licensing agreements, or strategic alliances. The top recipients of FDI are the United States, the United Kingdom, and China, while all of Africa combined receives only 3 percent of global FDI.[21]

MNCs AND THE GLOBALIZATION DEBATES

The global reach of MNCs can be a positive force for profits as well as development. MNCs can assist in transferring capital and know-how to the developing world and often bring in capital goods and technology. They may create jobs and assist in developing training and education programs. MNCs also provide avenues for access to other international markets and exposure to the region that may result in additional investment. MNCs often have the incentive to develop a host state's infrastructure to maximize commerce. For example, **Muhammed Yunus** won the Nobel Prize for offering microcredit to the poor through Grameen Bank in Bangladesh. Others followed his lead. Standard Chartered Nakornthon Bank works with poor villages in rural Thailand, offering training and small, low-interest loans for microdevelopment. As a result, "[i]ncome levels skyrocketed. . . . People returned to work in the village. The payoff rate for loans was 100 percent, and our bank now has a loyal base of customers. The project has been so successful that development agencies and the government have kept asking how it was done."[22]

But there is also a downside. MNCs can overwhelm a locality and drive traditional firms out of business. MNCs normally insist on maintaining control over technology, management, and intellectual property, which means that technology and expertise are not transferred to the host state. CEOs, boards of directors, and shareholders may all be located in developed countries so that MNC decision-making and profits flow disproportionately back to developed economies. MNCs often become advocates at the local level for changing local systems in favor of gaining preferential treatment. These take the form of tax breaks, favorable laws, dispute resolution mechanisms, and ownership and property rights. In seeking lower-cost alternatives globally, MNCs exploit resources, labor, and the environment, leading critics to charge that MNCs lead a race to the bottom in worker, regulatory, safety, and environmental standards.

For example, one IGO, the UN International Labor Organization assesses that there are 218 million child laborers worldwide, with seven in ten working in agriculture. Child labor, or workers aged between five and fourteen years of age, may make up as much as 63 percent of Mali's labor force and could number nearly 200 million in India.[23] Some of these children work for MNCs or their subcontractors, such as in high-profile cases (e.g., Nike and others using children to sew soccer balls) and as forced child slave labor in Africa picking the cocoa beans for major chocolate companies like Nestle. Yet MNCs counter these arguments by noting that working conditions are generally no worse and are often better than those of the local employers, and prominent MNCs are likely to comply with standards that are higher than those maintained locally.[24] They also argue that age and wage standards cannot be universal but must be considered in the context of local economies.

MNCs AND OPEN ECONOMIES

It is no surprise that many MNCs are in the forefront of lobbying to increase free market economic systems and reduce barriers to FDI and trade.[25] Whether through regional trading blocks such as NAFTA, CAFTA, or the EU, or multilateral free trade agreements such as GATT and the WTO, MNCs in general seek to decrease tariff and **nontariff barriers** to trade and investment, as well as decrease state control of state subsidies to key industries. Nontariff barriers are measures other than taxes that restrict imports or exports, such as quotas, "buy local"/ rule of origin mandates, arcane licensing procedures, or domestic subsidies of local companies to protect them from foreign competition. In practice, this varies by MNC and country. Companies that receive subsidies favor continuing them (such as the oil and coal industries which receive "corporate welfare"), and industries that are hurt by foreign competition pressure governments for protection such as tariffs, particularly in agriculture. MNCs lobby states and multinational organizations to open up economies to market forces. In the democratizing states of the former communist bloc, Latin America, and South Africa, MNCs are pressing for protections of private property and the free movement of goods and capital in their liberalizing economies. Once established, MNCs or their local affiliates often try to get the local host states to protect their advantages by enacting exclusionary laws and giving the established MNCs monopoly advantages. Host countries can be subject to intense pressure to acquiesce to MNC investment already in place and to appease international pressure to open their economies and markets. Each year, developed states spend over $250 billion in **agricultural subsidies,** payments to local farmers and agricultural producers, to prevent goods from developing countries from reaching their markets.[26] One outcome of these subsidies is to distort the global market and protect or insulate a firm or sector that would lose its competitive advantage and fail were the protections or subsidies not in place. This is why developing countries question how "free" the free market and free trade really are—free for whom?

Many MNCs have pushed hard for harmonizing international law, although some prefer to exploit differences in legal codes in local venues that profit foreign companies. For example, the Union Carbide Chemical Corporation was responsible for the worst industrial accident in history. Its plant in Bhopal, India released 41 tons of poisonous gas, killing 15,000 people and inflicting permanent disabilities on 150,000 more.[27]

> As people ran with their families, they saw their children falling beside them, and often had to choose which ones they would carry on their shoulders and save. This image comes up again and again in the dreams of the survivors: in the stampede, the sight of a hundred people walking over the body of their child. Iftekhar Begum went out on the morning after the gas to help bury the Muslim dead. There were so many that she could not see the ground—she had to stand on the corpses to wash them.[28]

After the accident, Union Carbide worked to see that a more lenient judge in India would hear the case so that the company could avoid having to face a stricter US judicial system that might have imposed hefty fines. After years of legal battles, the MNC agreed to pay survivors generally $2,857 for each death (a few received as much as $4,286). Ninety-five percent of the victims who were compensated received only $500. These are the gross figures; subtract the legal fees, administration costs, and sometimes bribes survivors had to pay to stake their claim, and most survivors actually netted much less. These settlements are low even by Indian standards. The standard compensation offered by Indian Railways is $5,714 for accidental death and $3,429 for disability, which is disbursed quickly and with minimal additional fees.[29] Unfortunately, this case is not an anomaly. Victims of MNC negligence or abuse rarely win remedy, due to the overwhelming power advantages of MNCs.[30]

While some companies prefer to take their chances with local legal codes, most MNCs have a powerful interest in harmonizing global laws to decrease transaction costs. It is costly for them to do business internationally when each country has separate standards and rules for, among other things, trade, investment, intellectual property rights, legal accountability, and contract rights. MNCs push for greater harmonization to decrease their costs and risks and create a better business climate, and they stress that developing states benefit as well from such measures. They argue that international trade, global supply chains, and FDI helps developing economies and that developing states are better served by a system of established rules with transparent and regular procedures for making rules than by trying to negotiate ad hoc agreements with more powerful actors on a deal-by-deal basis. In general, developing countries have agreed and voluntarily signed up for these international agreements out of a desperate desire to attract MNCs and FDI that may bring jobs and alleviate poverty in their countries. Often, developing states fear that not to acquiesce will mean that FDI and jobs will go elsewhere and that they will be left behind. Not surprisingly, there is unequal bargaining power among the parties. Developing states riddled with poverty cannot compete with the deep pockets of MNCs that lobby state governments and the international bodies that create the rules of the road for international trade. Developing countries often lack the resources to send delegations to the international meetings that decide the rules, thus denying them a seat at the table as the rules are debated and made.

The spread of capitalist economic systems and MNCs has also brought global pressures for deregulation, on the assumptions that markets are self-correcting and that government-imposed regulations often introduce market distortions, inefficiencies, and competitive disadvantages for regulated firms. Markets are not automatic and self-correcting, though. Market distortions, failures, and a "no rules" approach can encourage fraud and abuse, which undermine international markets, as happened in the 2007 global economic recession caused by the previously unregulated financial derivatives "dark markets." The meltdown of global markets brought greater attention and efforts for international regulation of these markets. Prior warnings were disregarded, that the unregulated derivatives market was ripe for fraud and abuse, and could cause a global financial meltdown. Today, many of those reforms are being undermined or repealed.

MNCs AND OPEN TECHNOLOGIES

Cheap, easily available global information and transportation technologies make the growth of MNCs possible. New technology also creates new industries and presents the hope of "leapfrog" development for some developing countries. For example, Bangalore, India, is now a thriving center of the computer services industry. India is aided by an educated workforce that speaks English and a time zone differential that allows Indian computer programmers to service the information systems of companies in many developed countries while the companies' main workforces sleep. Although this model is not replicable in all developing countries, many developing countries aspire to the Bangalore model as they seek to profit from the global economy and technologies. It is not only large corporations that benefit from global technologies, but also medium, small, and even microbusinesses that can go global thanks to the Internet and shipping companies such as FedEx and United Parcel Service. Australian sheepskin slippers, Turkish towels, and Mexican crafts can be marketed and sold to consumers globally without large overhead investments and access to global resources and shipping can facilitate just-in-time manufacturing.

MNCs may disperse technologies in the countries where they operate as a part of their business presence, but some MNCs restrict technology transfers out of concern for retaining proprietary and competitive advantages. MNC and state interests regarding technology transfers are not always correlated either. The US government wanted limits on the sale of powerful computer encryption technologies so that law enforcement officers would have the keys to crack the codes of illicit actors using encrypted communications. Businesses did not want a lucrative new market in encryption programs regulated—and business won. States often want to restrict the sale of sensitive technologies that can have military applications, whereas MNCs may favor trade in dual use technologies. The German, British, and US governments fought the Persian Gulf War in 1990 and 1991 against an Iraqi army that German, British, and US firms had supplied with weapons and the ingredients to make chemical weapons.

MNCs AND OPEN SOCIETIES

The relationship between MNCs and open societies, human rights, and democracy is hotly contested. In states such as China, Indonesia, and Nigeria, MNCs have pursued a capitalist economic agenda without pushing hard for democratic political reforms or human rights protections. In corporatist societies (such as Chile and Argentina in the 1970s), authoritarian regimes ally with and co-opt business elites, protecting business interests while repressing democratic rights and principles. Order is central for the stable, efficient, and profitable conduct of commerce. Political upheavals, even those associated with democratization, create costs and uncertainties for the investment, production, and trade of MNCs.

Do MNCs favor repressive regimes as a way of ensuring a stable, orderly, and favorable business environment? It depends. In some cases, MNCs have hurt human rights and democracy. In Nigeria, Shell Oil was accused of helping to arm and finance a repressive military government, as long as the government helped to keep Shell's oil flowing. According to Mr. Austin Onuoha of the Nigerian Center for Social and Corporate Responsibility, the oil companies claim to invest millions in "community development," but the money they spend to hire security forces is counted as part of their Corporate Social Responsibility (CSR) projects. Royalty and licensing agreements between the government and oil companies on how oil money will be split are not made public, and Nigerians see little benefit from the oil industry. The World Bank estimates that Nigeria has received over $350 billion from the oil industry since 1960, but corrupt business-government practices mean that the money has not benefited the Nigerian people, 70 percent of whom live on less than $1 a day.[31] Exxon–Mobil, Chevron-Texaco, and Petronas, with the aid of World Bank loans, have been building and operating an oil pipeline since July 2003 in Chad and Cameroon, extremely poor countries with two of the most corrupt governments in the world according to ratings of government corruption by Transparency International.[32] These governments are not democratic, and human rights and environmental abuses have been reported in the project. The government of Chad has illegally diverted World Bank loans for military purchases. According to Fr. Antoine Berilengar, SJ, a representative on the Petroleum Revenue Oversight and Control Committee in Chad, the oil companies do not hire local workers to build the pipeline, but instead bring in foreign workers, who do not pay local taxes and are less concerned about environmental and human rights abuses in Chad.[33]

Others disagree, noting that MNCs want human rights protections for their own workers, and rule of law to protect their property rights and investments.[34] MNCs may not favor repressive regimes for several reasons. Arbitrary exercise of police powers and military brutality affect MNC executives, workers, and citizens alike. Repressive regimes may rule by force rather than law, but respect for law (and particularly for property rights) is crucial for successful business transactions. Without the rule of law, business transactions become risky, uncertain and potentially more costly. Empirically, the record is mixed. Some industries, particularly the oil, mining, and extractive industries, invest and set up businesses where the natural resources are, even if the government regimes are repressive. Other industries have more mobility and choice in where they establish operations, and can encourage countries to improve their transparency, accountability, democracy, and human rights records.

The effects of MNCs on human rights can cut both ways. Sometimes just the presence of a multinational corporation can place the international media spotlight on local worker conditions, creating a "race to the top."[35] Concerned with protecting their image, companies will pressure local governments to improve workers' conditions or take the initiative to do so themselves. A multinational's instinct to protect its reputation, and thereby its bottom line, can have the beneficial side effect of exporting a concern for human rights. This may be MNC specific, however. Not all companies have a brand to protect; image-conscious branded products have a greater concern for reputation than do unbranded or extractive industries. Thus, even though MNCs in general tend to promote open economies and open technologies, their record of promoting open societies (including respect for human rights) is contested and mixed.

RISE OF PRIVATE POWER: DO CORPORATIONS RULE THE WORLD?

We are witnessing the rise of private power. Even in developed states, private standard-setting bodies, contract law, and private arbitration mechanisms now fulfill regulatory functions once performed by states.[36] In emerging information technology sectors, this trend of private governance is particularly pronounced. For example, Internet commerce is often untaxed and self-regulated by companies, not by governments. A private body assigns Internet domain names and adjudicates disputes.

The critique that corporations rule the world[37] runs even stronger given the unequal bargaining power of developing states against MNCs. In developing states, grinding poverty leads states to court corporate investments because the private sector has more money than the public sector, and state-to-state aid and investment is drying up. Developing states often do not have the capacity to check corporate power, as law and order and institutions may be fragile at best in countries without resources to adequately pay, staff, equip, and train government officials. As corporations enter developing states, they often do so free of taxes (in export processing or free trade zones). The largest companies are also able to avoid taxes even in developed states. For example, the majority of corporations avoid taxes through off shore tax havens, loopholes, and clever, complex processes which manipulate accounting to show "losses," and which move profits to shell company "affiliates" and locales such as Panama, as documented in the **Panama Papers** investigative journalism projects.[38] Some companies receive government "bail outs" despite bad business behavior. On the assumption that some MNCs were "too big to fail," the Emergency Economic Stabilization Act of 2008 was passed to secure the US financial system, and authorized the US Treasury to spend up to $700 billion in order to acquire risky mortgage-backed securities and make capital available to banks in order to stimulate lending. Export processing and free trade zones are often free of other government regulations (environmental and worker safety law enforcement).

MNCs encourage the multilateral organizations to pressure developing states to privatize their remaining state-controlled industries, such as telephone systems. Although it is done in the name of rationalizing economies and making them more efficient, privatization may also bankrupt governments because poor countries do not have the tax bases to finance basic government services—education, public health systems, clean water, roads, public safety, customs, courts, and law and order. When telephone revenues, for example, are the primary government income and the business is privatized, after the initial windfall in money from the sale of state-owned industries, states may lack financing for basic government activities.

Many states have no tradition of payment of personal income taxes, and governments are too weak to be able to get citizens to pay taxes (this is a problem in Russia, Italy, and many Caribbean states). Because so many goods and incomes go untaxed, states charge exorbitant tax rates on those few goods or people that they are most able to tax—for example, automobile imports, or imports of washers and dryers. This creates greater incentives to smuggle, commit fraud, and evade taxes because taxes on the few pay for the services provided to the many. Inability to finance basic good governance makes all government ripe for corruption because government workers are not paid a living wage and need to supplement their income with "overtime" (the euphemism for bribery in the Caribbean). Thus, governments in developing states often do not have the capacity to challenge or contain the power of corporations, and the actions of corporations (to lower their tax rates, privatize industries, and pay government bribes) may actually contribute to the weakness of state structures and governance.

Developing states sign agreements that allow corporations to operate in their territories; such arrangements are examples of bargaining among unequal parties. A developing state is signing a contract with a gun to its head—the gun being grinding poverty, unemployment, and death—and it is trying to lure corporations with its low wages and lack of unionization. A state has less ability to wrest many guarantees of good behavior, local management power, and so on, from a corporation when poverty is a state's comparative advantage. The corporation has many poor states from which to choose, and it is often not building plants and capital investments from scratch but is contracting out to local subsidiary agents. The corporation can easily find another poor country that will accept its business. Literally, beggars can't be choosers.

Even strong states cannot contain corporate power alone because MNCs operate across international borders, and jurisdiction often stops at the border. Attempts to harmonize legal codes to help law enforcement work multilaterally across borders or to rein in corporate power are weak and often without teeth. They often are exports of Western contract law and procedures that are advantageous to corporations. They show how corporations can get laws that work for them rather than how states can effectively counterbalance the weight of corporations.

The rise of private contract law epitomizes the rise of private power in the global age. A relatively few MNCs exercise power to create law in their own interest and for their own benefit. Developed states not only condone this practice but also support the trend because they hope to rationalize commercial disputes and benefit from increased tax revenue from their MNCs. The result is that local governments, especially in the developing world, experience a loss of control and influence over trade practices within their borders.

MNCs worldwide are seeking ways to fashion enforceable rights. One way they do this is by expanding private contract rights in order to avoid foreign laws. This is generally not a difficult challenge. The three most common ways of doing so are through **choice of law, stabilization, and arbitration clauses**. These clauses ensure the protection of property rights, right of entry into new markets, and the availability of natural resources. The effect of these clauses is not only to avoid the law of a host state but also to develop a legal system outside traditional sovereign courts. It sets up external and private law to resolve disputes, based on the concept of the sanctity of the contract and party autonomy. Courts allow these contractual decisions, often with little or no respect for the public policy concerns of host states. Courts will often refuse to hear a controversy where clauses using alternative dispute resolution (ADR) or arbitration exist in a contract. For example, when Mexico denied Metalclad, a New Jersey company that wanted to build a hazardous waste disposal site in Mexico, permission to build a facility because of concerns about the site's environmental impact, the NAFTA court initially ordered Mexico to pay $16.7 million to Metalclad in breach of contract compensation for earnings Metalclad could have received if it had been allowed to proceed. This amount was later reduced on appeal. The case remains an example of the tension between private contract rights and sovereign concerns such as environmental safety.

Choice of law clauses are perhaps the most common among the three and allow a party to avoid local law and remove issues from local courts by predetermining where controversies will be resolved and under whose law the controversy will proceed. Arbitration clauses determine who has the authority to decide controversies and usually include a reference to the specific rules that will guide arbitration. Arbitration courts have established procedures and remedies that can be adopted or amended by the terms of a contract, and the arbiters have powers similar to those of sovereign courts.[39] A stabilization clause freezes the law at the time the contract is entered into and prevents law made after a contract enters into force from having any effect on a controversy's ultimate disposition.

These clauses allow a contract to avoid the laws of sovereign states and propel controversies to a "supranational" legal arbitration body or to a court outside a local jurisdiction. Thus, they insulate foreign corporations from uncertain and unfamiliar locales, which facilitates predictability and reduces market uncertainty, yet this worldwide body of private law runs counter to the sovereign concept of regulating affairs within one's state borders. These contract provisions are increasingly offensive to local legal and political institutions and affront the concept of equal dignity of sovereigns. The contract terms effectively let the parties opt out of local jurisdictions. Private contract also gives MNCs a procedural advantage since many parties in the developing world lack the expertise needed to enter into agreements with a full appreciation of the costs and consequences. Firms located outside such traditional centers of commerce such as New York, London, and Geneva may also lack the resources to fully protect their rights under contract. The travel costs alone may make pursuing a dispute prohibitively expensive.

While MNCs work to enlarge the private sector and earn profits, they also can facilitate the illicit economy. Money laundering, for example, is facilitated by the international banking, and financial services industries, crypto currencies, and even online gaming. An estimated $2.8 trillion are laundered through banks every year.[40] Money laundering involves complex financial and product transactions that mask and perpetuate the underlying criminal activity that generates the illegal gains. Money laundering finances the most egregious crimes in the global age from terrorism and drug trafficking to human trafficking, illegal arms transactions, and nuclear smuggling. It propagates corruption and corrupt regimes by providing an avenue for using illegal proceeds. Money laundering also provides a way to avoid taxes.

The underlying purpose of money laundering is to conceal the true source of the funds for free use in the open market. The mechanisms for laundering money are complex and diverse and often involve multiple transactions among several (and sometimes unsuspecting) parties, fraudulent alterations of prices for goods, and outright bribes and kickbacks. Money laundering is illegal, but some MNCs prefer the benefit of the infusion of capital. The most common form of money laundering is transfer pricing, where prices are falsified on import and export transactions in order to generate artificial values. The difference between the fair market value and the artificial value is pocketed. Real estate transactions and securities trades, often between related parties and improperly priced and paid for in order to shift money across borders, offer creative avenues for generating illegal capital flight. Money laundering activities must first hide the source of the illegally received proceeds and then provide a legitimate explanation for the proceeds. Through complex, layered transactions, money laundering blends criminal proceeds into the licit economy.

Most laundered money winds up in the United States and Europe through Western banks. As the beneficiaries of such an enormous inflow of capital, the banking and financial establishment traditionally favors informal money laundering controls and reporting requirements. Government efforts to curtail money laundering have failed in the past because of the lack of "buy-in" from the private banking and business sector. The attacks of September 11 changed how many political and commercial leaders view money laundering, and they increased state and IGO pressure to regulate these industries. However, state anti–money laundering policies rely on industry self-reporting of suspicious financial activities. Even in strong, developed states, governments do not have the capacity to curtail money laundering without cooperation from the private sector, which demonstrates the extent of private power.

PRIVATE POWER AND PUBLIC RESPONSIBILITY

Does the rise in private power mean MNCs can act with impunity and with no responsibilities to the common good? No. States still regulate corporations, although, as the previous section demonstrated, MNCs may have the ability to forum shop—to have a dispute heard in a forum more amenable to their interests—and may have deeper pockets and better lawyers to evade states' regulatory capacities. However, other bodies are stepping in to fill these governance gaps. IGOs increasingly regulate global commerce, and MNCs are increasingly self-regulating, in part because of greater attention to corporate social responsibility (CSR).

There has been an explosion of CSR mechanisms for MNC voluntary self-regulation, especially in the past decade. They fall into several categories. First are **internal codes of conduct** and statements of company core values. Most MNCs have such in-house codes of conduct. The first generation of these CSR statements were frequently broad, general guidelines. Second-generation CSR statements are more concrete and specific, such as the commitment of Levi Strauss and other companies to reduce carbon emissions by 25 percent and increase use of renewable energy by 20 percent. Optimists say these codes of conduct are important barometers of changing corporate culture. They are attempts to educate and socialize large workforces into common values, such as the belief that good corporate citizenship is as important as bottom-line profit margins. Even broad guidelines can be helpful as a first step to more specific standards and concrete benchmarks. They are also useful because they provide a public commitment by companies to particular values. If company behavior falls short later, then the codes of conduct statements give reformers a basis to discuss criticisms. Skeptics argue that the codes are little more than window dressing designed to diffuse criticism and deter regulation, that they are frequently so vague and general that they cannot be implemented or measured, and that they are unenforceable because they are voluntary.

The second genre of CSR measures are **sector-wide agreements** among companies within an industry to adopt certain standards or shared best practices. Sector-wide agreements can vary from narrow technical codes on specific industrial processes to broader statements of larger CSR commitments such as the Apparel Industry Partnership to improve working conditions in the garment industry. Some sectors may develop regimes or private professional bodies to monitor and report on implementation and compliance with the standards. Many rely on the companies themselves to choose methods of monitoring and transparency to show implementation and compliance with adopted codes.

The third approach is to develop general CSR codes that are not specific to particular organizations or industries. The **UN Global Compact** challenges businesses to comply with ten principles drawn from UN treaties concerning human rights, labor, the environment, and anti-corruption. Since its creation in 2000, the Compact has grown to include about 10,000 companies and 3,000 nonbusiness signatories in over 160 countries in a voluntary "leadership platform for the development, implementation and disclosure of responsible corporate practices." Over two-thirds of members report that the compact helps them develop and implement more robust CSR policies and share lessons learned.

The compact's ten principles are quite broad. Other CSR codes are more focused, such as the Ceres (Coalition for Environmentally Responsible Economies) principles on environmental responsibility. Ceres created the Global Reporting Initiative, an independent, international standards organization that helps more than two-thirds of the world's largest MNCs apply their CSR standard reporting framework. Ceres also coordinates the Investor Network on Climate Risk to understand the economic costs and social risks from climate change.

The Caux Round Table Principle for Business was created in Caux, Switzerland, to provide ethical guidance for business leaders to engage in moral capitalism. All of these overarching corporate goals rely on companies to decide their own monitoring and transparency measures. The International Standards Organization (ISO) has its own set of standards, as does the Council on Economic Priorities (Social Accountability standards). These standards create soft law, with more specific operational guidelines and measurable benchmarks to monitor progress and implementation of CSR goals. As industries "buy into" labeling and accreditation, they agree to undergo regular inspections and audits by accredited auditors.

There are vigorous debates over whether CSR is effective, and regarding which codes, standards, and reporting techniques work better to raise corporate behavior and improve labor, human rights, and environmental practices. Some critics argue that internal audits are more rigorous because only people familiar with the processes and layouts of particular factories will know where to look for problems or abuses. Others argue that internal audits lack credibility because companies have few incentives to blow the whistle on themselves. This leads to arguments in favor of external auditing procedures, but again this raises questions of competence and independence. Although using professional auditors trained in particular standards sounds like an attractive way to ensure more reliability and comparability of results over time and across companies, critics argue that auditors hired and paid by industry have few incentives to issue negative reports and "bite the hand that feeds them." NGOs argue they can offer independent assessments and should be a part of the process, but this again raises the questions of which NGOs should be involved and how qualified they are to make assessments. Some corporations do not see NGOs as unbiased and believe NGOs will never acknowledge improvements in corporate practices or issue favorable assessments. Some corporations such as Nike choose to involve local NGOs as a form of outreach to the local community where facilities are located. International NGOs question whether local NGOs are more easily manipulated to issue favorable reports because they may fear losing local jobs or may not have the resources or access to complete information to make fully informed and more critical judgments. Finally, reporting varies widely. Some reports are little more than press releases, while others are substantive and concrete assessments. The Global Reporting Initiative works to increase the comparability, credibility, and consistency of CSR reporting to help make "apples-to-apples" comparisons, and to highlight best practices.

The UN also works to increase CSR through the Guiding Principles on Business and Human Rights. These establish the responsibilities of countries to create and enforce laws that protect against human rights violations by MNCs, including commitments for businesses run or subsidized by the state. On the other hand, the United Nations has also increased outreach to businesses in public–private partnerships, particularly to reach the Sustainable Development goals. Pubic private partnerships vary widely on topic and breadth, from public health campaigns to development projects to help provide market access for indigenous microbusinesses.[41]

This explosion of CSR codes and implementation techniques shows a rising acknowledgment of the power of private governance and the power of corporations to implement social and economic change. It testifies to increased attention among corporations to the "triple bottom line," a rising awareness that the environmental and social as well as economic concerns can affect business.

But why is there such growth in CSR standards and attention? Margaret Keck and Kathryn Sikkink argue that blocked politics cause activists to take their grievances to other forums,[42] including pressuring MNCs to focus on issues ignored by states. Because groups cannot lobby for environmental or human rights change in China or Vietnam, NGOs and moral entrepreneurs search for a forum where democratic politics, independent media, voters, and consumers can exert some pressure for change rather than be excluded. MNCs based in developed democracies are open to civil society pressures, whereas authoritarian states may be less susceptible to these pressures. Blocked politics explains some of the increased attention to CSR, but not all of it.

Corporations often argue that they are not the correct targets for labor, environment, and human rights demands, and that governments should be pressured to change. Yet even in democratic countries, MNCs are targeted for CSR campaigns rather than governments, even though politics are not blocked and procedures exist for citizen advocacy. Moving away from state activism and toward CSR campaigns focused on MNCs is a way for NGOs to focus their resources and to get more bang for the buck. NGO resources are constrained, so dividing them among 193 countries may mean there will be too few resources for any one NGO to be effective, reach critical mass, and overcome threshold effects of inertia and the status quo. NGOs find that if they successfully lobby MNCs to raise standards, the effects will be felt broadly across borders, rather than in one country only.

There are other reasons for the increased number and attention to CSR codes as well. Virginia Haufler studied private standard setting across a variety of sectors and industries and concluded that risk assessments, concern for reputation, and corporate learning were critical factors in adoption and implementation of CSR standards.[43] Previous crises certainly can alert decision-makers to the risks of ignoring CSR. For example, the Ceres environmental principles were created in response to the Exxon Valdez oil spill.

Only publicly traded companies are vulnerable to **shareholder activism**. **Unbranded products**, generic products that companies do not advertise or invest in to develop a particular name, image, or following, are less vulnerable to consumer boycotts and negative publicity. But ideas matter in pressuring corporations to address global issues. Even unbranded food products are vulnerable to claims about health and safety. And not all brands are equally vulnerable to CSR pressures. It matters what values and ideas the brand proclaims. Nike is vulnerable not just because it is an identifiable brand but also because it advertises values of diversity, emancipating young people, and women's equality. This makes it more vulnerable to brand devaluation by charges that women are being abused and children forced to work in diverse countries. Similarly, Mattel Toys has been a leader in the Business

Alliance for Secure Commerce because, as its chief security officer put it, "The last thing we can afford is Barbie on drugs." A shipment of Barbie toys compromised by drug traffickers would be extremely harmful to the toy's wholesome role model identity in a way that would be less damaging to a shipment of toilet bowl cleaner. It is not just the brand, but the ideas behind the brand that give traction to CSR efforts.

Several factors are important in determining whether an MNC will adopt CSR standards. The internal leadership of the company is important. Anita Roddick, founder of The Body Shop, was a force for CSR within her global franchise and throughout the wider business community.

Company culture, the competitive environment, and consumer demand are important. Chiquita Brands International, the banana importer and exporter, addresses issues of child labor and environmental impacts of its supply chain, and has adopted some of the industry's most enlightened age and wage policies. But if grocery stores and consumers do not factor CSR into buying decisions, then CSR policies may not be sustainable, either because leadership will backslide if companies believe CSR policies are a drag to their costs that competitors avoid and consumers do not reward, or because the company goes under.

Shareholder activism also can spur attention to CSR as investors pressure companies to improve their practices on social or environmental issues, or as investments are withdrawn from companies with poor practices or ratings. For example, the Interfaith Center on Corporate Responsibility, a coalition of over 300 religious investors from the Catholic, Jewish, and Protestant communities with a combined investment total of over $400 billion, promotes socially responsible investing. Shareholder and investor activism does not produce quick results, but the effect is like water on stone, a slow reshaping that can produce great effects over time. Media attention to corporate shortcomings spurs MNC attention. Companies engage not only in immediate damage control within a targeted company but also in longer-range policy change across companies as MNC leaders learn lessons from the crises of others. NGOs threaten to use the sticks of negative media publicity, protests, consumer boycotts, and shareholder activism, but they can also offer the carrots of positive attention to favorable examples of CSR. Too often, however, NGOs rely more on the sticks than the carrots. Finally, IGOs and states can offer incentives for positive CSR behavior and threaten regulation or adversarial treatment to companies with negative CSR records. A combination of these factors leads companies to decide whether and which CSR policies may enhance their reputation, change their market share, or reduce their risks of adverse consumer, media, IGO, government, or shareholder reactions.

Through the CSR movement, MNCs are finding that open societies, open technologies, and open economies cut both ways. These infrastructures facilitate the operations and profits of MNCs. Yet global technologies that broadcast MNC advertising also serve as an instant and global megaphone for news of corporate abuses. Open societies allow critics to organize and apply political pressure to MNCs, and open economies allows consumer and shareholder market pressures to be brought to bear on MNCs.

MNCs, STATE FUNCTIONS, AND SOVEREIGNTY

Beyond social, environmental, and economic regulatory and arbitration functions, MNCs perform security functions once reserved for states. MNCs today operate killer drones, interrogate and torture terrorists, spy for governments, train foreign militaries, provide security in war zones with private armies, and are part of military operations. MNCs removed the nuclear, chemical, and biological weapons of states of the former Soviet Union, and conduct homeland security and de-mining operations. Functions traditionally reserved for the state are increasingly contracted out to private companies. For example, in 1978, when the negotiation process for the chemical weapons convention (CWC) began, few government officials had more than superficial knowledge of the chemical industry. US arms control negotiators requested assistance in the negotiation process from the chemical industry. Recognizing the importance and effect of the chemical weapons ban for their industry, the chemical manufacturers assisted the US government. An industry group, the Chemical Manufacturers Association (CMA), helped develop procedures for onsite inspections and participated in special sessions of the Conference on Disarmament. What resulted was an unprecedented industry–government partnership in forging an effective treaty. For industry, opposition to the treaty not only would have resulted in negative publicity but also would have risked the creation of a treaty that was technically unsound and detrimental to industry interests.

The private sector has a critical role to play in protecting critical infrastructure from illicit activities, from terrorism to cybercrime. Between 85 and 90 percent of critical infrastructure in the United States is privately owned. Critical infrastructures are systems whose incapacity or destruction would have a debilitating effect on a state's defense or economic security. They include telecommunications, electrical power systems, gas and oil industries, banking and finance, transportation, water supply systems, government services, and emergency services. The attacks on September 11, 2001, highlighted security concerns over physical and electronic threats to critical infrastructures. Such threats are global, blur public–private distinctions, and render states, commercial interests, and individuals mutually vulnerable and interdependent.

There are limits to what governments can effectively do to provide adequate security in the absence of private cooperation. Private infrastructure owners are in the best position to understand the technology and vulnerabilities and must recognize their stake in infrastructure protection. Many challenges to effective public–private cooperation exist. Trust needs to be established between stakeholders. Public–private lines of communication and response activities need to be clarified. Technical training and expertise needs to be furthered in both sectors. Government and industry leaders must recognize the need for cooperation. Process buy-in is essential to success.

Governments of the strongest states are ceding security functions to private companies. For example, more private company contractors than government troops served in the war in Iraq. The US and Russian governments used private security companies to disassemble former Soviet nuclear weapons through the Cooperative Threat Reduction program, as well as to conduct de-mining operations in support of troop deployments. In Afghanistan, 75 percent of US forces are contractors. Eric Prince, former head of Blackwater, a private military company, wants private contractors, not government troops, to fight the war in Afghanistan and run the country in a company-run protectorate. While the Trump administration considers such a move, the Afghan government pushed back, stating "Under no circumstances will Afghanistan allow the counterterrorism fight to become a private, for-profit business."[44]

Private organizations are increasingly seen not just as contributors to global problems but as crucial players in designing and implementing effective global solutions. We are witnessing a creative period as new private organizations arise and increased partnerships are formed with business to manage pressing global problems. As MNCs become the target of citizen demands for social, environmental, and economic goods, ideas of authority change. As governments cede or contract functions to the private sector (even security functions), state power, capacity, legitimacy, and authority change relative to other actors—and thus sovereignty is changing.

KEY TERMS

agricultural subsidies, 91
arbitration clauses, 97
choice of law, 97
corporate social responsibility
  (CSR), 87
foreign direct investment (FDI), 88
internal codes of conduct, 100
Muhammed Yunus, 89
multinational corporations
  (MNCs), 87

nontariff barriers, 90
Panama Papers, 96
sector-wide agreements, 100
shareholder activism, 103
stabilization clause, 98
unbranded products, 103
UN Global Compact, 101
United Students against
  Sweatshops (USAS), 84

DISCUSSION QUESTIONS

1. Why have college students and student athletes held protests of Nike? What does the Nike brand stand for? Why is Nike particularly vulnerable when criticisms of labor and human rights violations are raised?

2. Why have companies used children to sew soccer balls or harvest cacao for making chocolate? What are the pros and cons of those types of practices for MNCs? Why is child labor a problem for a community's long-term economic development?

3. Multinational Corporations use global supply chains and distribution channels. This makes them able to pursue a "race to the bottom," to pursue cheap labor in countries with little legal enforcement of international standards. Yet MNCs may also raise standards by adhering to higher labor and environmental standards than local businesses. What evidence do you see of MNCs bringing a "race to the bottom," or a lifting of standards?

4. Which types of countries have been able to profit from the globalization of new information technologies toward their own development? Which types of countries are not good candidates for "leapfrog development" through technology?

5. How do MNCs aid democratization and open societies, and in what circumstances are MNCs an obstacle to open societies?

6. Do "corporations rule the world?" Why or why not? In what specific ways are MNCs more powerful than states, or able to evade the laws of states?

7. Who was Muhammed Yunus and why did he win the Nobel Prize?

8. What can be done to combat the tax evasion and corruption exposed by the Panama Papers?

9. Why do companies adopt voluntary corporate social responsibility codes of conduct? Are these effective? For example, why does the Mattel toy company want to maintain certain standards for its products?

UN Photo/Leonel Grothe

UN peacekeeping operations in the Central African Republic.

4

Intergovernmental Organizations

Coalitions of Countries

■ ■ ■

The United Nations was set up not to get us to heaven, but to save us from hell.

—Winston Churchill

Our own land and our own flag cannot be replaced by another. But you can join with other nations, under a joint flag, to accomplish something good for the world that you cannot accomplish alone.

—Eleanor Roosevelt[1]

Never before in history has so much hope for so many people been gathered together in a single organization, the United Nations. I hold, to assure you that the Government of the United States will remain steadfast in its support of this body.

—President Dwight D. Eisenhower[2]

The United Nations MDGs helped to lift more than one billion people out of extreme poverty, to make inroads against hunger, to enable more girls to attend school than ever before and to protect our planet. Yet for all the remarkable gains, I am keenly aware that inequalities persist and that progress has been uneven.

—Ban Ki-moon, UN Secretary General

The United States ought not to forget that the emerging European Union is one of its greatest achievements: it would never have happened without the U.S. Marshall Plan.

—Helmut Schmidt, former German Chancellor[3]

There is no such thing as the United Nations. If the U.N. secretary building in New York lost 10 stories, it wouldn't make a bit of difference.

—John Bolton, US National Security Advisor[4]

DID YOU EVER WONDER WHY it is possible for you to board an airplane in one country and land in another country? How are you able to walk into your local store and buy goods from many foreign countries? How is it possible that you can study abroad, receive mail and telephone calls from people in other countries? Intergovernmental organizations (IGOs) and international law work every day to make globalization possible and to make it real. IGOs are the unnoticed, unsung, but critical infrastructure, working away in the background, making exchanges among sovereign states and the flows of people, commerce, and ideas across foreign borders possible, effective, and orderly. IGOs are like bridges and highways; we use them every day to move around and conduct our business, but we rarely notice or think about them until they break down.

IGOs present a paradox. They are increasingly criticized in national political debates, from the UK's Brexit vote to the US Congress' votes to reduce UN funding. IGOs are criticized for being weak and ineffective, yet oddly, they are simultaneously criticized for being too strong, for running roughshod over national sovereignty. IGOs are created by sovereign states; sovereign states are their members, yet IGOs are sometimes criticized for not being sufficiently docile to or representative of the interests of some sovereign states. US politicians decry that the WTO has been unable to do what no sovereign state, the United States or others, has likewise been unable to do: force China to respect intellectual property rights, international patent and copyright rules. US policy makers are not happy about criticisms of US and Israeli foreign policy made by other countries in the UN General Assembly, and Russia and China deplore the UN's criticisms of their human rights abuses. Saudi Arabia does not appreciate being called out for their support of terrorist groups. Developing counties criticize IGOs for being too responsive to the agendas of rich countries at the expense of the world's poor. Nongovernmental organizations lament how long it takes to get international agreement and action through IGOs on issues from climate change to reducing global arms flows. Yet despite these contradictory criticisms of IGOs as being both too weak and too strong simultaneously, when troubles arise, whether from global disease or climate change or financial crisis, the first question policy makers and citizens ask is "What are the UN/and other IGOs doing to respond to this global issue?" Protestors gather and demonstrate at IGO meetings, such as UN and G-20 meetings. Like all human institutions, IGOs have many flaws. Yet if IGOs truly were ineffective and unimportant, no one would bother to show up, picket and protest.

IGOs come in many varieties. They are groups formed voluntarily by states to coordinate actions and facilitate cooperation in a variety of issue areas. **Formal IGOs** are established by treaties, charters, or conventions, have permanent headquarters, secretariats, have member states, and a structure. **Informal IGOs**, such as the **G-7** or **G-20** groups, are groups of countries that meet regularly to address common issues, but do not have permanent headquarters, staff, or membership dues. Some are universal membership organizations, like the **United Nations** and the Universal Postal Union. Other IGOs are regional, such as the **Organization of American States (OAS)**, the **African Union (AU)**, or the **Organization for Security and Cooperation in Europe (OSCE)**. Some are supranational, such as the **European Union (EU)**, which binds its twenty-eight members into a common market, money, and laws. Others issue nonbinding recommendations, such as the **Food and Agriculture Organization's (FAO)** early warning recommendations for famine assistance to countries experiencing food shortages. Some IGOs like the United Nations are open forums that can be used to address multiple issue areas. Other IGOs only deal with specific issue areas, such as **NATO, the North Atlantic Treaty Organization**, a military defensive alliance among twenty-nine countries, or the **International Atomic Energy Organization (IAEA)**, which works to advance safe, secure and peaceful nuclear technologies, or the WTO, which coordinates common trade rules for its 160 members.

IGOs and global issues go hand in hand. The oldest IGOs are older than most of today's sovereign states. IGOs were created in the 1800s to manage problems that went across borders, from war to slavery/human trafficking to environment and health problems, which not even the strongest sovereign states could handle alone. Practically, as cross border commerce, transportation, and communication increased, so did the need to regulate and manage these flows. Principles also moved across borders, as global norms spread, such as the antislavery movement. This chapter will describe the expansion of IGOs, discuss some of the key IGOs working to manage globalization's open economies, open technologies, and open societies, and conclude with the opportunities and challenges of IGOs managing global issues.

The vast majority of today's IGOs were created after World War II, with the goal of preventing another horrific world war among the major powers. The United States led the effort to create the United Nations, which became an "umbrella" intergovernmental organization. Many specialized IGOs that predated the UN became associated with the UN as part of the UN system.

As the number of countries and the world population increased, so did the need for coordinating mechanisms. As described by IGO scholar Madeleine Herren,[5]

> International organizations further substantiated processes of nation-building . . . . A history of international organizations is a history of globalization . . . international organizations developed parallel to the spread of modern nation states. . . . An increasingly connected world asked for transnational contacts in almost every field.

IGOs have largely succeeded in advancing many of the goals countries charged them with, yet IGOs simultaneously have problems. The world is more peaceful and more prosperous than it was seven decades ago when modern IGOs were created, by any measure and any study. People were horrifically poor throughout most of human history. Today, we have a global population of 7.6 billion people, more people than ever before in human history, yet there are fewer people living in extreme poverty, fewer people dying of starvation, more people going to school, more middle-class and rich people, living longer, healthier lifespans. While global population has been increasing, the numbers of the world's poorest people have been decreasing, both in relative and absolute numbers. There are many reasons for this. The expansion of democracies and free market economies have done much to lift people out of poverty, and new technologies help fight disease and help people access information. Yet IGOs have also worked continuously on expanding peace and prosperity, and their coordinating functions have helped build the rules of the road for the global market, fighting disease, and committing to common benchmarks for eradicating poverty (first the Millennium Development Goals, now the Sustainable Development Goals). In previous centuries, countries that wanted to expand their economies went to war to invade and conquer territory. For example, the Japanese have few domestic sources of energy, so in the twentieth century, they invaded neighbors to access energy. Today, countries do not need to conquer territory in order to access what they need; they can trade in a global market built by rules largely created and monitored in IGOs. In previous centuries, plagues spread across trade routes and countries unchecked, decimating populations. Today, IGOs like the **World Health Organization** monitor and intervene to combat global diseases. When Ebola hit West Africa in 2015, it was quickly contained and curtailed with the intervention of IGOs, to help support local governments who lacked the capacity to stop the epidemic. IGOs have many weaknesses, and may favor rich countries and people over poor. Yet despite their limited resources, bureaucratic inefficiencies, and uneven political support, IGOs have helped advance a world of greater peace and prosperity.

Despite what you read in the headlines, we are not in a world at war, but we are experiencing more peace and prosperity than ever before, no matter how you measure it. There are fewer major wars than ever before, even though we have more people living on our planet than ever in human history (7.6 billion people), in more countries than ever before (193), with over 8,000 nations (groups of people united by a common language, religion, ethnicity, culture, and/or historical tradition). Combined, these countries command over 20 million soldiers.

Figure 4.1 World Population Living in Extreme Poverty, 1820–2015

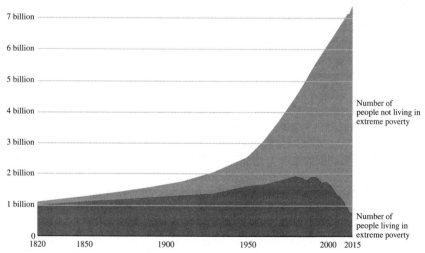

Source: OWID based on World Bank (2019) and Bourguignon and Morrisson (2002)

Yet there are fewer wars than ever before, currently twelve **major armed conflicts** (wars or major armed conflicts are defined as conflicts in which more than 1,000 people die in battle-related deaths in a year). There are no international wars, the scourge of the twentieth century that IGOs were created to combat. All major armed conflicts are civil wars. So while the numbers of people and countries has been increasing, the number of wars has been decreasing at the same time. The number of major armed conflicts, the casualties of war, the types of war, and the geography of war are all shrinking. This is not magic or happy accident. It is the product of hard work, including the coordinating activities of IGOs.

THE EXPANSION OF IGOs

The number of IGOs has rapidly expanded over the past two centuries, in parallel with the growth of the number of sovereign states and the growth of NGOs and civil society. At the start of the 1900s there were a handful of IGOs. Today, there are nearly 5,000 IGOs.

The more states there are, and the more complex and integrated economies and technologies are, the greater the need is for coordinating mechanisms by which people can manage global issues that cross borders. A series of River Commissions were created in the 1800s to manage commerce, pollution, and transportation on critical European waterways, the busy critical infrastructure of the era (before automobiles and airplanes). The Rhine Commission was established in 1815, followed by similar commissions for the Elbe (1821), the Douro (1835), the Po (1849), and the Danube (1856). These were followed by some of the oldest IGOs that continue to function today. The International Committee of the Red Cross (1863) was founded by international convention as an IGO (although many people perceive it to be an NGO). Other early IGOs are the International Union of Telecommunications (1865, originally called the Telegraphic Union), the Universal Postal Union (1874), and international bodies to prevent the spread of diseases, later organized into the International Office of Public Health (1907), the precursor to today's World Health Organization. A series of multilateral conferences on peace, security, and development began after the Napoleonic Wars two centuries ago. These conferences met from time to time, and later were institutionalized with regular meetings and staff, in first the League of Nations and later the United Nations. Unlike the early single issue and limited membership or regional organizations, the United Nations became an umbrella organization under which separate technical bodies could come together, and it became a universal membership organization in which nearly all sovereign states participated.

Values and norms of human rights and peaceful cooperation were intermingled with the pragmatic reasons for creating IGOs. Normatively, more leaders in civil society and states wanted to create forums for people to peacefully work together, as industrialization and mass conscription armies made war more deadly than ever before. International organizations were created simultaneously in both government and civil society realms. Government and civil society interacted, learned from and influenced each other. The international movement to ban slavery, the International Olympic Movement, the creation and adoption of the Geneva Conventions to limit war crimes and abuses in war, the creation of international scientific and academic bodies, the creation and spread of international religious and missionary organizations, industry organizations to support international railways, and the founding of international organizations all occurred simultaneously and these actors influenced each other. Nonstate actors attended government and intergovernmental conferences, and intergovernmental organizations adopted organizational forms (secretariats, unions) innovated by nonstate actors.

THE UNITED NATIONS

The United Nations was planned while World War II was still being fought. President Franklin Roosevelt coined the name in 1942. Allied leaders of the United States, Britain, Russia, and China met in the Dumbarton Oaks Conference in Washington, DC, in 1944, to negotiate the general principles for an international organization. The first attempt at an international organization, the League of Nations, was proposed by President Woodrow Wilson and created in 1920. It was ineffective in preventing World War II for many reasons, including the fact that although the United States proposed the IGO, it never joined the organization. In creating the United Nations, the United States and other countries worked to build a stronger IGO, informed by lessons learned from the earlier attempt. Invitations were sent around the world, and in April of 1945, representatives of fifty-one countries gathered in the United States, in San Francisco, and created the United Nations. Today, the UN has 193 member states, as well as delegations of observers from NGOs and other groups, who may participate in some UN discussions but do not have a vote.

The UN Charter notes the four main purposes of the organization: "to maintain international peace and security, to develop friendly relations among nations, to cooperate in solving international problems and in promoting respect for human rights, and to be a centre for harmonizing the actions of nations."[6] The UN has helped advance all four of these purposes. War and human rights violations have decreased since the UN' founding, in part due to actions coordinated at the UN. There is less war than ever before, and studies show that UN peacekeeping operations have helped to advance peace. Countries that receive **UNPKOs** have a better track record of achieving sustainable peace than countries in conflict which do not receive UNPKOs. The UN serves as a forum for advancing peaceful international relations and has become a center for discussion and activities to coordinate international actions, including the advancement of human rights.

There are six main bodies for carrying out these UN purposes: the General Assembly, the Security Council, the Secretariat, the Economic and Social Council, the International Court of Justice, and the Trusteeship Council, which was created to help countries in their decolonization transition to independent states, and now is largely inactive. All countries are members of the General Assembly, which discusses global issues and issues resolutions; each country has one vote. The General Assembly votes whether or not to admit states as members, thus providing or withholding international recognition, a crucial characteristic for would-be sovereign states. The assembly also elects members of other UN bodies—judges for the International Court of Justice, rotating members of the UN Security Council, etc. The United Nations is not a world government, and the General Assembly is not a world legislature. But over time the UN has served as an important forum where states negotiate international treaties, such as the 1968 Treaty on the Nonproliferation of Nuclear Weapons (NPT) and the UN Framework Convention on Climate Change, discussed in later chapters.

The **UN Security Council (UNSC)** is responsible for addressing issues of international peace and security, including voting to send in UN peacekeeping forces to a conflict. The UNSC has fifteen countries as members: five countries are permanent members with a veto—the United States, Russia, China, the UK, and France. The remaining ten member countries serve two-year terms and are elected by the General Assembly to serve on the UNSC. Sixty countries have never served on the UNSC, but may be invited to participate in meetings (without a vote) if the issues under consideration concern them. Others regularly consult with the UNSC, including NGOs, leaders of the International Committee of the Red Cross (technically not an NGO but an IGO because it was created by international law), and other states that contribute troops to UN peacekeeping operations. Polarized politics during the Cold War made consensus and action by the UNSC difficult.

In the first 40 years, the UNSC authorized only seventeen peace-keeping operations (PKOs). With the fall of the Soviet Union and the end of Cold War gridlock, the UNSC became quite active, authorizing fifty-six operations over the past 30 years, four times as many PKOs as in the earlier era. Peacekeeping operations (PKOs) have also become more ambitious. Earlier PKOs were often more modest observer forces, witnessing a truce or ceasefire, or traditional missions, patrolling a buffer area between combatants. Some of the first UNPKOs of the post–Cold War period failed, in Rwanda and Somalia, giving a poor public percep-tion to UNPKOs. PKOs since have learned and improved from these initial failures. Next-generation PKOs are more robust, larger, more expensive, and more engaged in multidimensional activities, including building peace, reforming security forces, carrying out disarmament and demobilization of combatants, and enforcing civilian security. These more robust PKOs have worked. Joshua Goldstein in his book "Winning the War on War" demonstrates that the recent rise in PKOs is directly responsible for the decrease in major armed conflicts during the past three decades. Conflicts where UN peacekeeping operations were sent had more peaceful outcomes than conflicts without UNPKOs.[7]

As scholars from the renowned Peace Research Institute of Oslo note, "The increase in the deployment of UN 'blue helmets' is a key driver of the gradual decline in the number and severity of armed con-flicts worldwide since the mid1990s . . . ." Peacekeeping reduces the level of violence in conflict. Peacekeeping also decreases the duration of conflict. Peacekeeping increases the longevity of peace. [UNPKOs] con-tain the lethality of wars as well as preventing them from re-erupting or spreading. . . . There has been a gradual shift over the last two decades from more restrictive to more robust PKO mandates. Our study shows that it is mainly these more ambitious PKOs that are "winning the war on war."[8]

The secretary-general of the United Nations supervises the Depart-ment of PKOs, which is part of the Secretariat of the UN. While only the UNSC can authorize sending UNPKOs, the secretary-general may present issues to the UNSC for their consideration. The United Nations does not have a standing army. When the UNSC votes to send in PKOs, the secretary-general must ask member states to contribute troops. While the United States contributes money toward PKOs, the countries that contribute the largest numbers of troops to PKOs are from Africa and South Asia: Ethiopia, Bangladesh, India, Pakistan, Rwanda, Nepal, Egypt, Senegal, Indonesia, Tanzania, and Ghana. More recently, China volunteers troops to PKOs.

The secretary-general is both the chief administrator and a global diplomat who works to persuade and mobilize people to address global issues. The UN Secretariat is made up of international civil servants who serve the United Nations in UN Offices in New York, Geneva, Vienna, Nairobi, and 140 countries.

The **Economic and Social Council (ECOSOC)** is where most of the activities of the United Nations take place. NGOs can apply for consultative status at the United Nations through ECOSOC; 7,000 NGO representatives participate in UN activities at the UN headquarters building in New York City, NY. Others participate at UN facilities in Geneva, Switzerland and other UN offices. Nearly 3,000 NGOs have consultative status with the UN ECOSOC. ECOSOC is the United Nations' main forum for addressing economic and social issues, and is tasked with coordinating the activities of the many specialized agencies, some of which existed before the United Nations, such as the International Labor Organization and the World Meteorological Organization.

Many specialized, functional agencies are associated with the UN, called the UN Family or the UN System. These are geographically dispersed, from the **World Health Organization (WHO)** in Geneva to the Food and Agriculture Organization in Rome. Some UN agencies were created and co-report to the General Assembly, such as the United Nations Children's Fund (UNICEF), the United Nations Development Fund for Women (UNIFEM), the UN High Commission on Refugees (UNHCR), the World Food Program (WFP), and the United Nations Environment Programme (UNEP).

The last of the UN major organs is the **International Court of Justice (ICJ)**. Based in the Hague, the Netherlands, the ICJ is available to hear international law disputes of UN member states if states ask the ICJ for its interpretation. The ICJ is not an international supreme court. It has no jurisdiction over individuals, is not a criminal court, cannot pursue cases or investigations independently, and serves only when member states ask it to hear a specific case between countries and both disputants agree to abide by ICJ findings. The court can hear two types of cases: contentious cases of international legal disputes between UN member states who submit the case to the ICJ, and requests for advisory opinions on legal issues submitted by UN specialized agencies and organs. Fifteen judges are elected by the UN General Assembly and UNSC to serve on the ICJ for 9-year terms. By tradition, these judge positions are distributed geographically, with three judges from Africa (one from Francophone Africa, one from Anglophone Africa, one from Arab Africa), three from Asia, two from Latin America and the Caribbean, two from Eastern Europe, and five from Western states. These totals include one judge from each permanent member of the UNSC. By law, no country can send more than one judge concurrently. The ICJ meets at the Peace Palace, facilities owned and operated by an NGO, the Carnegie Foundation.

There are many critics of the United Nations. Developing countries critique the United Nations for being a tool of the richer, more powerful countries against the poorer, less powerful countries, a new, more "politically acceptable" form of colonialism. For example, the UNSC's five permanent members reflect the victorious powers at the end of World War II rather than the most powerful countries today. Three European countries are permanent members of the UNSC, while not a single African country is a permanent member, leading to charges of neocolonialism, particularly when the UNSC votes to send troops to Africa. While many agree with this critique, that the permanent members of the UNSC are not representative of today's realities, there is no consensus and no political will to change the composition of the UNSC. The UNSC is already "deadlocked" when the five permanent members cannot agree on a course of action, in places such as Syria. Simply increasing the number of permanent members of the UNSC would make it more difficult to get the needed unanimous agreement, so expansion of the permanent members of the UNSC would actually weaken its ability to act. There is also no consensus for "swapping out" old members for new. Former colonial powers, such as France, are not volunteering to exit the permanent members of the UNSC, and rising powers such as India, Japan, Germany, and Brazil do not agree on which country ought to be offered a coveted permanent spot on the UNSC. So while all agree it is a flawed structure, there is no agreement on what would be a better structure or how to get the required votes to change the structure.

Developed countries criticize the UN for wasting resources, for bureaucratic inefficiencies and at times even corruption. Since richer countries pay a larger share of the UN operating budget than poorer countries, this is a perennial source of criticism. The UN has undertaken reforms to downsize, economize, and to increase transparency, efficiency, and accountability, particularly around the millennium and seventieth anniversary of the UN. But critics say more reforms are needed.

Nondemocratic countries criticize the UN for meddling in internal, sovereign affairs. By this view, whether Saudi women drive or children work in factories is a matter for national governments to legislate internally. According to this view, international bodies of "outsiders" should not try to impose "one-size-fits-all" policies on countries, which may be at odds with local cultures or practices.

Democratic countries criticize the UN for not doing enough to promote human rights. The UN is not a league of democracies, but is open to all countries regardless of regime type. Because nondemocracies and countries with poor human rights records are UN members, and because no country has a perfect human rights record, this allows countries that violate human rights to serve on UN human rights bodies. The UN's original body, the High Commission on Human Rights, was disbanded for this reason, and a successor body created, the UN Human Rights Council. UN members elect 47 countries to serve 3-year terms on the UNHRC, with seats allocated by regional groups: thirteen seats for African countries; thirteen for Asian countries; six for Eastern Europe; eight for Latin American/ Caribbean countries; and seven for Western European and others. Countries are supposed to take into account the human rights record of states when UN members vote for which countries should serve on the Council. In practice, a few members of the forty-seven countries serving on the Human Rights Council have poor human rights records, such as Saudi Arabia and Cuba. Some argue that this de-legitimizes the Council and undermines human rights. This is why the Trump administration has withdrawn the United States from the Human Rights Council. Others argue that the only way to "raise the bar" for human rights is to engage violators, rather than simply "preaching to the choir."

OPEN ECONOMIES AND IGOs

International organizations have been most successful in creating the rules of the road to better integrate and coordinate the international economy. During World War II, leaders of the allied powers met in Bretton Woods, New Hampshire, and decided to create several international economic organizations to help rebuild and better integrate the world economy. The lack of common rules over money, exchange rates, trade, and tariffs exacerbated international tensions leading to two world wars as well as the global economic depression. Leaders wanted to improve economic rules and relations to create more stability, prosperity, and peace. They created several international economic institutions (the World Bank, the International Monetary Fund, GATT) that continue to operate today and have created many new economic treaties and organizations (the World Trade Organization) to implement these agreements.

The **World Bank** (first only the International Bank for Reconstruction and Development, now including other organizations) was originally created in 1944 to help European countries rebuild after World War II. These origins gave it a focus on providing loans to governments for large infrastructure projects—dams, road, bridges, electrical grids, and irrigation systems. In 1947, the bank made four loans totaling $447 million dollars. With de-colonization, the World Bank group's focus shifted to helping newly independent countries access loans. Today, the World Bank's mission has shifted to eradicating extreme poverty and increasing prosperity for the world's poorest by helping both government and the private sector have access to finance. The International Bank for Reconstruction and Development can make loans to middle-income and poor countries with good credit ratings. The International Development Association can make loans to the poorest countries. The International Finance Corporation can make loans to private sector groups in developing countries, while the International Center Investment Dispute Resolution offers mediation and arbitration services for investors, and the Multilateral Investment Guarantee Agency offers political risk insurance to investors and lenders, and in order to encourage others to invest in developing countries. One hundred eighty-nine countries are now members of the World Bank, with offices in 130 locations. In 2015, over $60 billion in loans were made to 302 development projects.

The World Bank is a bank, not a charity, and it is criticized for this tension between its banking and poverty eradication goals. It offers loans and services to governments and investors, and as such is criticized for servicing the needs of bankers and investors more than the concerns of poor people. The bank is criticized for "donor driven development" and imposing the "Washington Consensus," being more responsive to the concerns of rich countries (which provide the bulk of the Bank's budget) than poor countries or people. Although the Bank employs people from many countries who work on projects around the world, the Bank is headquartered in Washington, DC, thus leading to concern that the Bank is more responsive to US interests than the needs of the world's poor. This is a long-standing criticism; in the 1950s, many of the Bank's most powerful proponents (such as the Rockefeller family), supported the Bank as a counter to communism and state-controlled economies, and a means to help private sector investors and companies gain access to and build markets in developing countries. That focus remains, and some parts of the bank earn profits by loaning money, for example, to build malls or luxury apartments or help mining companies; those profits are then used for the World Bank programs that serve poor people. World Bank loans come with strings attached, which advance privatization but may harm other goals such as access to education, equity, or environmental protection. For example, in the 1980s and 1990s, the bank required countries to enact "structural adjustment policies," which included selling public assets (e.g., public utilities such as electrical or telecommunications services) to private companies. Many oligarchs and businessmen profited from these sales, which further concentrated wealth (and often exacerbated corruption), while poor citizens experienced cuts in public services, and were stuck with paying the bill for these loans to governments. The public assumed the debts for these projects while often private companies and individuals reaped the profits. Rather than lift the poor out of poverty, many poor countries were left owing huge debts to banks. The banks (both international development banks and private banks) make money on the interest paid on the debts, whether or not the projects ever worked out. This creates a moral hazard; the banks make money off the poor, whether or not the poor ever benefit even indirectly from the proposed projects. Sometimes the projects harm the poor directly. Large infrastructure projects often displaced poor people whose land was grabbed to build the dams, etc. World Bank financed projects, such as gold mining, oil and other extractive industries, harm the environment and the subsistence farmers and fishermen who live off the land polluted by extractive industries. For example, the poison cyanide is used in gold extraction; when this leaks or leaches from the mines into local lands and water supplies, people and farm animals die. The World Bank argues that these mining, oil, and extractives industries provide a path out of poverty for poor countries, and bring in tax revenues that governments can later spend on building schools or roads or providing health services. Poor people who live in these communities argue that extractive industries make them worse off, not better off. Their water is poisoned, their land is taken, the mining jobs go to foreign workers, the profits go to foreign businesses and corrupt officials in remote capital cities, the roads built are for mining trucks not local use. Governments use brutal police or military tactics to protect the businesses. This harms local communities (particularly indigenous communities and women) and increases conflicts, rather than helping them.

The World Bank Group has made many reforms in response to these criticisms. Adoption of the Millennium Development Goals (MDGs) and Sustainable Development goals (SDGs) has increased attention to eradicating extreme poverty. The bank has also increased transparency and accountability of bank programs. Critics argue these reforms are "window dressing," and do not address the underlying structural disconnect, that many World Bank programs help the rich at the expense of the poor. Whatever one's assessment of the Bank's development projects, these programs are small compared to the size of the global economy and private foreign direct investment. These critiques are criticisms of the larger global economy, foreign direct investment, and specific industries (extractives) in general, as well as particular World Bank programs and procedures. Regardless of how well the bank reforms particular projects, the larger criticisms of globalization will remain.

The World Bank's largest contributions may come not from its lending programs but from its information and analysis services. The World Bank gathers data and generates reports tracking global economic performance, prosperity, development, and poverty. This information is a public good, available to all. While multinational corporations can hire analysts to create proprietary reports just for them on global economic trends, World Bank reports provide a public library of important information on the global economy available to help governments, businesses, schools and universities, and citizens to understand and plan. For example, one World Bank research project of Paul Collier and colleagues on the **"Conflict Trap"** asked why some countries were able to recover from pernicious cycles of violence and poverty, while other countries remained stuck in cycles of war that impoverished the country. The researchers found that countries with the following particular characteristics were more likely to remain stuck in negative cycles of violence: if the country has a previous history of armed conflict within the last 5 years; a youth bulge; a flat or declining economy; and a natural resource–dependent economy. Countries which diversified their economies beyond natural resource–based economies diversified the paths out of poverty, and created economic opportunities that were not as easily seized by armed actors as natural resources can be. Diversified economies could provide jobs for young men, thus making them less vulnerable to recruitment for violence by armed actors. The Conflict Trap research is important not only because it helps people understand and help prevent some of the economic roots of war but also because this World Bank research raises direct criticism of previous World Bank approaches to development (those which financed natural resource extraction projects in countries with a youth bulge that had experienced prior conflicts). The information functions of IGOs can be very important.

The **IMF International Monetary Fund** was also created during World War II at the Bretton Woods conference in order to rebuild and stabilize the global economy after the shocks of the global economic depression and wars. The IMF focuses on stabilizing exchange rates, monetary and fiscal policy. As a nearly universal IGO, with 189 member states (only North Korea, Cuba, Andorra, Lichtenstein, and Monaco are not IMF members), the IMF works to prevent financial crises and contagion, to stop financial problems in one country from spilling over and dragging down the wider international financial, currency and economic system. According to the IMF, its "primary purpose is to ensure the stability of the international monetary system—the system of exchange rates and international payments that enables countries (and their citizens) to transact with each other."[9]

Over time, the IMF's mission has widened beyond exchange rates and monetary policy to include the stability of the global economic system. After the 2007–2009 global recession, the IMF's mandate "was updated in 2012 to include all macroeconomic and financial sector issues that bear on global stability."[10] The IMF now works "to foster global monetary cooperation, secure financial stability, facilitate international trade, promote high employment and sustainable economic growth, and reduce poverty around the world,"[11] although monetary policy is still a main focus. Headquartered in Washington, DC, the IMF (like the World Bank group) also imposes conditionality on its loans. Those "Washington Consensus" requirements have forced countries to focus on producing goods for international export (rather than domestic consumption) so that countries will have access to international "hard currencies" with which to repay their loans (the IMF does not want or allow countries simply to print more local currency in order to repay their foreign loans with worthless local money). These conditions originally referred to economic policies recommended for Latin American countries in the 1980s and 1990s.[12] Critics contend they became a "one-size-fits-all" standard package of economic policies for all developing countries which included cutting government spending (even on schools and public health), raising interest rates, devaluing the currency, to control inflation and attract international investment and trade. What was good for international investors was often not good for local citizens, particularly the poor. Many countries followed the IMF conditions and did not experience greater prosperity or stability. The same previous criticisms raised against the World Bank, and the global economy more generally, are also leveled at the IMF.

Other IGOs focus on harmonizing rules to promote international trade. Business needs law, regulations, and consistent rules to exist and prosper. A lack of rules or inconsistent procedures creates inefficiencies, problems, risks, and losses for business. The General Agreement on Tariffs and Trade (GATT) treaty from 1947 fundamentally changed economic policymaking, by creating common and transparent processes for how countries can regulate imports and exports of most goods. This helps businesses operate and trade across borders. As the number of countries increased and the amount of global trade increased, more economic rules of the road were needed. **The World Trade Organization (WTO)** was created to be the common institution to administer a growing number of economic agreements, including GATT, the General Agreement on Trade in Services (GATS), the agreement on Trade Related aspects of International Property Rights (TRIPS), agreements on agricultural trade and reducing subsidies in agriculture, and provision of dispute resolution processes for trade-related disputes.

REGIONAL IGOs

Some of the most powerful open-economy IGOs are regional. The precursors to today's European Union (EU) began after World War II. European countries needed to rebuild their economies after the war, and wanted to better integrate their economies into a common market to grow their prosperity and to prevent another European war. The United States encouraged European economic integration. US Marshall Plan Aid for European reconstruction after World War II was conditional upon the European countries creating and joining the Organization for European Economic Cooperation, and coordinating and integrating their economies (countries which refused did not receive Marshall Plan aid). This helped pave the way for the creation of the European Coal and Steel Community and the European Common Market, which later developed into the EU's common European market with a common currency, the Euro. The EU began with six original members turning the industries of war (coal and steel) into economic cooperation and integration for peace. The EU has grown to include more than twenty-eight countries, in an umbrella organization of many associated European institutions that foster open movements of goods, services, money, ideas, and people.[13] The most open labor markets in the world are among EU members, whose citizens can freely move and work across borders.

Despite the advancement of free markets and the creation of many IGOs to support trade, there still are not global free markets in agriculture or labor. While more money and products than ever before can move freely across borders in international commerce, people cannot. Capitalists can sell their stuff, but workers cannot sell their labor freely in the global market or move across borders to follow jobs. Also trade in agriculture, a labor-intensive industry, is still highly restricted and subsidized. There are many reasons for this, including domestic politics, national health and environmental standards in food, and national security concerns as countries want to retain domestic food production. Because food is a necessity, some countries argue that it should not be treated like trade in "widgets," and outsourced. Not many countries are willing to follow the Saudi example, giving up most domestic food production to rely primarily on the international market to feed the country.

Restrictions in labor and agriculture markets show the limits of open economies, and the limits of IGOs. Developing countries criticize the hypocrisy of these restrictions, noting that developed countries pursue free trade in markets for which they have comparative advantage (e.g., finished goods, high technology products, financial and information products), yet restrict markets in which developing countries have comparative advantages (in labor and agriculture). While progress has been made in reducing agricultural subsidies and trade barriers, many still remain.

The **Asian Infrastructure Investment Bank (AIIB)** is a new multilateral development bank created to foster infrastructure development in Asia. This is the first major IGO created by China, against the opposition of the United States, who wanted countries to continue to use the existing multilateral institutions initiated by the United States. The AIIB is less concerned about lending money to dictatorships or regimes with poor human rights records. The AIIB was launched along with China's **"Belt and Road Initiative,"** an effort to boost China's trade by building a global network of ports, highways, railways, and pipelines to enhance China's dominance of regional trade routes.

The number and power of IGOs pursuing open economies has greatly increased in recent decades, but these trends are reversible, not automatic. Countries can leave IGOs, as the UK demonstrated with its contentious, narrow vote to "Brexit" from the EU. And countries can flout or try to change IGOs, as the Trump administration did by instituting protectionist US tariffs undermining the WTO.

OPEN TECHNOLOGIES AND IGOs

Some of the oldest IGOs were created to deal with the newest technologies. The International Telegraphic Union, later renamed the International Telecommunications Union (ITU), was formed in response to the then "emerging" technology of the telegraph. Today, the ITU addresses issues of satellite and cellular technologies never imagined in 1865. Anyone who uses a cell phone interacts with the ITU. According to the ITU

> We allocate global radio spectrum and satellite orbits, develop the technical standards that ensure networks and technologies seamlessly interconnect, and strive to improve access to information and communication technologies (ICTs) to underserved communities worldwide. ITU is committed to connecting all the world's people—wherever they live and whatever their means. Through our work, we protect and support everyone's fundamental right to communicate. **Today, ICTs underpin everything we do.** They help manage and control emergency services, water supplies, power networks and food distribution chains. They support health care, education, government services, financial markets, transportation systems, e-commerce platforms, and environmental management. And they allow people to communicate with colleagues, friends, and family anytime, and almost anywhere. With the help of our global membership, ITU brings the benefits of modern communication technologies to people everywhere in an efficient, safe, easy, and affordable manner.[14]

The technology IGOs have some of the most innovative and adapting organizations. Public–private partnerships were the norm in the technology IGOs long before this mode spread to other IGOs and government actors. For example, the ITU is a hybrid organization. It is a universal membership organization with all 193 sovereign states as members. But the ITU also includes leading academic institutions, ICT regulators, and a global "Who's Who" of over 700 leading technology companies.

The **Internet Corporation for Assigned Names and Numbers (iCANN)** is an NGO, not an IGO that manages the Internet address book. Quite deliberately, iCANN is not an IGO, as the United States and Internet users fear an IGO would allow repressive governments to try to censor and distort the Internet. But iCANN has some IGO-like characteristics, including a Governmental Advisory Committee with representatives from 170 sovereign states to provide input on Internet governance. In the beginning of the Internet, one person (Jon Postal) in California, a computer science researcher at the University of California Los Angeles and the University of Southern California in California, assigned IP addresses and Internet domain names. The Internet was created by academics working with the US government. As Al Gore passed legislation to grow the Internet and create public access to the Internet for citizens and the private sector, the US Commerce Department oversaw the work of iCANN. But since October 2016, iCann was released from US government oversight, and is governed by a hybrid multistakeholder model that envisions consensus among key Internet users—businesses, NGOs, governments, academics, and citizens. The US government agreed to this model rather than yield to pressure to turn iCANN over to an IGO such as the ITU (International Telecommunications Union), fearing governments would use a traditional IGO structure to harm the Internet.

The **International Standards Organization (ISO)** is likewise a hybrid organization. Also set up as a voluntary NGO, not an IGO, the members are standards organizations, one representing each country. Some of these member standards organizations are governmental, and some are not, but companies and individuals cannot be ISO members. The ISO promotes international industrial, commercial, and proprietary standards. The standard-setting process is undertaken by ISO members, but the standards themselves are voluntary. The ISO is an independent body, but it was one of the first organizations recognized with consultative status by the UN Economic and Social Council, and the ISO was created at the request of and with the cooperation of the UN.

Many of these open technology organizations were created before there was a United nations, and were later moved within the UN family of specialized agencies and updated to handle modern technology issues, such as the UIC, the French acronym for the International Union of Railways (Union Internationale des Chemins de fer), created in 1922, and headquartered in Geneva.

Many of the technology IGOs are not headquartered in New York, NY, where the UN headquarters is located, or in Washington, DC, where many world financial organizations are located. The International Civil Aviation Organization is headquartered in Canada, where it works with countries and industry groups to develop consensus on practices and policies "in support of a safe, efficient, secure, economically sustainable and environmentally responsible civil aviation sector." These common standards and practices include everything from the use of biometric passports to safety audits. Civil aviation is the safest modes of transport, with millions of international flights and fewer than 300 deaths per year.

Modern aviation is one of the most complex systems of interaction between human beings and machines ever created. This clockwork precision in procedures and systems is made possible by the existence of universally accepted standards known as Standards and Recommended Practices, or SARPs. SARPs cover all technical and operational aspects of international civil aviation, such as safety, personnel licensing, operation of aircraft, aerodromes, air traffic services, accident investigation and the environment. Without SARPs, our aviation system would be at best chaotic and at worst unsafe.[15]

IGOs, like the **International Atomic Energy Agency**, continue to be created to standardize the rules and harmonize the use of new technologies. US president Dwight Eisenhower proposed the creation of the International Atomic Energy Agency, to promote the peaceful uses of nuclear technology for nuclear medicine, energy, and research, for the benefit of all people, while restricting the spread of nuclear weapons.[16] Like other key US military generals in World War II, Republican Dwight Eisenhower had been skeptical of the US use of atomic bombs against Japan. Leading US military officers in World War II including General Eisenhower, General MacArthur, General Curtis LeMay, General Hap Arnold, Admiral Leahy, Admiral Halsey, Admiral Nimitz all agreed that Japan was beaten and suing for peace in the spring of 1945, and the atomic bombings were unnecessary to end World War II, a finding that was confirmed by the US Strategic Bombing Survey report in 1946.[17] Eisenhower was the only US president to criticize the US atomic bombings of Hiroshima and Nagasaki.[18] Initially, Eisenhower proposed that the United States give its remaining atomic weapons to the UN for destruction. Later as president, Eisenhower's "Atoms for Peace" proposal was made in 1953 and implemented in the creation of the IAEA in 1957.

Today, the IAEA's 169 member states work on issues from advancing seafood safety, food security, nuclear medicine and cancer control, and nuclear energy. The IAEA helps set up and enforce the world's five nuclear weapons-free zones in Latin America and the Caribbean, the South Pacific, Southeast Asia, Africa and Central Asia. The United States, Russia, and other smaller nuclear weapons states are not allowed to move or keep nuclear weapons in these nuclear weapons free zones. The IAEA also monitors the **1968 Nuclear Nonproliferation Treaty (NPT)**, in which nonnuclear weapons states committed to use nuclear technology for peaceful purposes only and not develop nuclear weapons, while nuclear weapons states committed to disarm and greatly reduce their nuclear arsenals. Only five countries are not signatories to the NPT: Israel, India, Pakistan, North Korea, and South Sudan.

The IAEA conducts international inspections and verification work in 181 countries to ensure that nuclear materials and technologies are safe and not diverted for military uses.

OPEN SOCIETIES AND IGOs

Some of the strongest regional, and weakest universal, IGOs are those promoting and defending open societies, human rights, and democracy. This is understandable because democracy was the minority government form until recently. Today, many countries remain with poor human rights records and which are not democracies, such as China, who thus have little incentive to create strong IGOs to protect and promote opposing government forms. Also existing democracies may "backslide," as occurs today where "populist/nationalist" leaders have been elected in many countries who undermine democratic institutions such as free press and opposition parties, and who violate human rights. Throughout most of human history, people were at the mercy of their local ruler for how well or how poorly they were treated. There were few international organizations or laws to "raise the bar," to inspire, encourage, or pressure governments to respect human life and dignity.

This has only begun to change very recently. World War II was a wake-up call, a shock to the conscience for many. For centuries, Europeans and Westerners had long fancied themselves "civilized" and "more advanced" than other cultures and countries, which they regarded as having more brutal and barbaric practices. The British Magna Carta, the US Declaration of Independence/Constitution/and Bill of Rights created open society norms and institutions which began to protect human life and dignity and check governmental power for some people (mostly white, male, property owners) in some countries (mostly in the global North). The Europeans and Westerners treated colonized and indigenous peoples brutally, as well as women and minorities in their own countries, but they believed that in general they maintained a higher standard than the rest of the world.

The atrocities of World War II called these assumptions into question. Europeans killed Europeans by the millions, in greater numbers and more atrocious ways than previously imagined possible. White supremacist, fascist dictators tortured and slaughtered millions whom they believed to be racially and culturally inferior. While the dead were still being counted and buried, a "Never Again" movement emerged that stronger international protections for human life and dignity were required to protect people when their own sovereign states could not or would not. Eleanor Roosevelt led the charge, and in 1948, the countries of the world agreed to a common set of principles, the Universal Declaration of Human Rights (UDHR), which for the first time established common, universal, international standards for human rights and responsibilities. Getting any global agreement at all was nearly miraculous, let alone the sweeping agreement on civil, political, economic, and social rights and responsibilities contained in UDHR. At the time, the wounds of world war were still fresh, colonial and independence movements were in conflict globally, the Cold War opposing blocks were solidifying with Soviet occupation of Eastern Europe and revolution in China, and military occupation of defeated World War II countries was ongoing.

Despite all these conflicts, the UDHR embraced universal principles, declaring that "All human beings are born free and equal in dignity and rights," and "Everyone is entitled to all the rights and freedoms set forth in this Declaration, without distinction of any kind, such as race, color, sex, language, religion, political or other opinion, national or social origin, property, birth or other status. Furthermore, no distinction shall be made on the basis of the political, jurisdictional or international status of the country or territory to which a person belongs."[19] The UDHR contains thirty articles including political rights (free speech, freedom of association, and freedom to participate in government), economic rights (to a job, food, health care, housing, education, labor unions, property and intellectual property rights, etc.), as well as social rights (freedom of religion and conscience, consensual marriage, rights to nationality and to participate in the cultural life of the community).

Saying the words didn't magically or immediately make them come true. It would take many decades of hard work for more people to be able to stand up to their governments, demand and enforce the rights set forth in this document. Implementation is ongoing and uneven globally. Despite its uneven application, the UDHR declaration gave people some purchase to stand on to advance their claims, some legitimacy and credibility to their efforts, and a north start to guide them and connect them with others around the world. To be able to reach for and build open societies based on human rights and democracy, we first had to be able to name our goals. In the more than 70 years since these principles were declared, specific laws, institutions, and practices have been built to implement these principles. Freedom of movement is still quite restricted. As discussed in the chapter on refugees, despite the 1951 Convention on refugees, people fleeing for their lives are still prevented freedom to move to safety. In many peaceful countries, though, freedom of movement is expanding through the increase of "neighbor admission" coordinated, preclearance policies. Nearly one-third of countries have agreements with their neighbors to enforce common external border policing and customs policies, in return for open movement among citizens of these neighboring countries. The largest region allowing open movement for citizens of member states is the **Schengen Zone** in Europe among twenty-six countries and over 400 million people. Other similar zones are the **CARICOM** zone of twelve Caribbean countries, the East African Community of six countries, the Gulf Cooperation Council of five Persian gulf states, the Nordic Passport Union of five countries of northern Europe, the Andean Community of four Latin American countries, and the CA4 agreement among four Central American countries. Another ten countries have free bilateral movement agreements with their neighboring country, such as Ireland and the United Kingdom have Belarus and Russia, India and Nepal, and Australia and New Zealand.[20] These agreements allow states to exercise coordinated border control with a two-tier system at exit and entry points. Citizens of the European Shengen zone and similar agreements are put in the equivalent of the "Easy Pass" lane. These citizens have been screened in advance using common rules; their identity cards and security risks have been precleared, represent less threat, so they move more easily across borders among member countries applying common screening rules. For outsiders, more rigorous processing takes place at the border.

The strongest IGOs promoting open societies are regional organizations created by and comprised of European democracies, part of the European Union organizations. Greater European cooperation, coordination, and unification had long been a goal for many. The end of World War II provided the opportunity to create intergovernmental institutions to promote open societies in Europe. After the horrific human rights abuses before and during World War II, including the Holocaust, followed by Soviet communist expansion, Europeans created institutions to promote democracy and protect human rights in Europe. Wanting to go farther than the UN's Universal Declaration of Human Rights, the Europeans created binding law and an international court and parliament to enforce it. The European Convention on Human Rights and the European Human Rights Court were established even before many of the economic integration IGOs that later coalesced into the EU. Over time, this led to the creation of a common, elected, European parliament, and the expansion of the EU to twenty-eight countries. EU membership is only open to democracies. To become a member of the EU, countries must have stable political institutions "guaranteeing democracy, the rule of law, human rights and respect for and protection of minorities."[21]

Other regional IGOs were also created with open society goals as part of their missions, but none are yet as strong as the European IGOs. Unlike the European IGOs, all of the other regional IGOs contain both democracies and nondemocracies as members, so have mixed records and are less strong in their capacities to enforce human rights and democracy. As the quantity and quality of democracies increase around the world, the strength of these IGOs may also increase, as is gradually occurring with the Organization of American States (OAS) and the OAS' Inter-American Commission on Human Rights, and the Inter-American Human Rights Court. These IGOs are used not only to draw attention to abuses in fragile democracies or states with poor human rights records, but also to "raise the bar" in countries with longer democratic traditions. For example, globally women and children often suffer domestic violence and have difficulty getting protection from the police and court systems, even in democracies. Three young girls were killed by their father when the state of Colorado refused to enforce a domestic violence restraining order against him in 1999. The police failed to act when the man kidnapped the girls, and ignored repeated pleas from the mother to enforce the court order. When the man drove up to the police station and opened fire on the police, they shot him. The bodies of the dead girls were found in his pickup truck. The US Supreme Court ruled against the woman and (dead) girls, saying they had no constitutional right to police enforcement of the restraining order. The case eventually moved to the **Inter-American Human Rights Commission**, the first time that a US survivor of domestic violence received a judgment in an international body.[22]

The third regional human rights system was established in Africa in the 1980s, after most countries had achieved independence from colonialism. The African Commission on Human and People's Rights and the African Court on Human and People's Rights enforce the African human rights charter, as part of the African Union (AU) system. The Asia-Pacific region is the only region that has not been able to establish a regional human rights system analogous to the European, Inter-American, and African bodies. Some in the region fear that due to the presence of many human rights violating countries in Asia, should any regional treaty or IGO emerge it would be "watered—down" and not a strong advocate for universal human rights. The Southeast Asian subregion has created a human rights IGO under **ASEAN, the**

Association of Southeast Asian Nations, but lacking a regional human rights charter this body can only reference general international rights. However, understandable for the region, it has worked on issues of women and migrant workers' rights.

The UDHR landmark international commitment to human rights has no single, mandatory enforcement mechanism. It is implemented by national governments, and some states ignore components with which they disagree. As discussed previously in the UN section, because UN member states include nondemocracies and states with poor human rights records, the UN Human Rights Commission and UN bodies have been uneven in their work to advance open societies. However, the UN High Commissioner for Human Rights was established to create a strong watchdog and advocate to investigate and advance human rights concerns. The Office of the High Commissioner for Human Rights supports the Commissioner. The UNHCHR has been effective in raising human rights crises and concerns that may not be getting sufficient attention in other bodies, such as the systematic rape of women in war zones.

Other IGOs also have taken up some of the implementation work. In addition to the UDHR, many other international laws were enacted after Hitler's white supremacist genocide against Jews and others, to try to prevent such atrocities. After World War II, the allies had to decide what to do with Nazi war criminals. The British and Russians wanted simply to assassinate the Nazi leaders, to punish them and to end their ability to continue to attract followers. The United States disagreed, wanting to establish the principles of the rule of law, that no one is above the law, and that law applies even during wartime. The United States also wanted to preserve and present the world with the evidence of Nazi atrocities, to prevent Holocaust deniers and white supremacist apologists from denying the crimes ever occurred, or were "that bad." The Nuremburg trials after World War II were hastily assembled to make key Nazi officials stand trial for war crimes and crimes against humanity. The **1948 Convention on the Prevention and Punishment of the Crime of Genocide** expanded international humanitarian law, applying whether the offenses took place in war or peacetime, and expanding concepts of human rights to apply not only to individuals but also to communities. Genocide is defined as acts committed to "destroy, in whole or in part, a national, ethnical, racial or religious group." This includes killing, causing serious bodily, or mental harm to members of the group, inflicting conditions of life (such as forced migration or starvation) calculated to destroy the group, preventing births and/or forcibly transferring children away from the group. The law includes both government officials and private citizens who plan, conspire, incite others, order others, are complicit, and attempt to commit genocide, in whole or in part, whether or not perpetrators are effective in their efforts or act on behalf of the state.[23]

More separate international tribunals were created in the 1990s to prosecute cases of genocide, war crimes, and crimes against humanity, such as the International Criminal Tribunal for the Former Yugoslavia, and the International Criminal Tribunal for Rwanda. This costly pattern of creating new ad hoc courts each time major atrocities occurred (including hiring prosecutors and judges, establishing means of gathering evidence, establishing offices, finding resources and funding) was not efficient. Led by a lead American prosecutor from the Nuremberg trials, a permanent court responsible for such offenses was created, the **International Criminal Court (ICC)**. The name is a misnomer: it does not hear cases of international crime. The court only hears cases of genocide, war crimes, and crimes against humanity, and then only as a "court of last resort," when countries ask the ICC to hear a case, either because they are unable or it would be difficult for them to address it, or when the UN Security Council refers a case to the court. The governments of countries experiencing civil war have "their hands full" fighting the war. Simultaneously gathering evidence for prosecution, or tracking suspected war criminals who may have fled internationally, is a difficult and expensive task. Many national courts may be operating at full capacity prosecuting other more usual crimes (theft, murder), and do not have resources or experience in prosecuting this specific type of international crime. The cases may also be politically controversial, so many countries prefer to have an external, independent judicial handle these expensive cases. Thus, by definition the ICC only gets some of the world's worst cases, which no one else wants and that are hardest to try.

The court has been controversial. It took time to create the court from the treaty ratification in 2002 until its first prosecution in 2010. Building a permanent headquarters in took time and money. The first prosecutor focused more on indictments than prosecutions. But the chief criticism of the ICC has been that it has focused on Africa. While true, the ICC only has jurisdiction over its members, and Africa is the Court's largest group of members. Previous wars in other regions were heard by the predecessors to the ICC (the International Criminal Tribunal for the former Yugoslavia, Nurembuerg, and Tokyo trials), but the ICC was not in existence at the time of those crimes. Since the ICC was created, most wars occurred in Africa, so African countries themselves asked the ICC to hear most cases. Countries in other regions at war are not ICC members (Iraq, Syria, North Korea, Israel, Palestine, Sri Lanka) so the court has no jurisdiction in those cases. While the UNSC could refer cases from outside the ICC's jurisdiction, non-ICC members (China, the United Sates) are UNSC permanent members, and they block movements for the ICC to expand and hear cases from other countries. The ICC independent prosecutor has preliminary investigations underway in other regions, including Afghanistan, Iraq, Colombia, Venezuela, and the Philippines, but many of those countries are undertaking their own investigations and prosecutions and thus have not asked the ICC to step in. All the ICC's initial prosecutions were in Africa. The ICC independent prosecutor is African, and she points out this means that all the victims served and reparations paid are to African victims. This charge of "neo-colonialism" has increased particularly since the ICC indicted current African leaders, the President of Sudan and the Vice President of Congo. Some say this shows the ICC is working in its mandate to stop impunity and show that no one is above the law. The ICC may be "working" on the cases it does not hear; its existence may help pressure countries to hear such cases in their national courts of first resort, to preclude such cases from being taken up by the ICC, the court of last resort. Thus measuring the ICC's success by convictions may be a poor metric, if the purpose of the ICC is to create incentives to put itself out of business, to encourage national courts to hear such cases and to prevent such atrocities from occurring in the first place by chipping away at the culture of impunity.

CONCLUSIONS: OPPORTUNITIES AND CHALLENGES FOR IGOs MANAGING GLOBAL ISSUES

The challenge of first-generation, nineteenth- to twentieth-century IGOs was to herald in the birth of a huge number of new sovereign states, to "equip" them with common rules of the road for interaction, to facilitate trade and economic interactions, and to prevent or moderate war among states. Great progress has been made on all these fronts. At the same time that there are more people and more countries in the world than ever before, there is also greater peace and prosperity. The share of people living in extreme poverty is decreasing. Today, major war is greatly decreased, and war is civil war, not war among states. IGOs have helped facilitate these trends of prosperity and peace. IGOs have harmonized the rules of trade. And UNPKOs, while limited and strained for resources, have shown positive results; countries where

UN PKOs have gone have a better track record of sustaining peace than countries without UNPKOs.

The challenges going forward are in some ways the growing pains and challenges of success. How can a larger number of more powerful IGOs secure the gains made thus far, while adapting to address new challenges, larger populations, new countries, and countries of rising power? While the number of IGOs and their missions and functions have increased, ironically the political support for IGOs among the countries originally founders of IGOs has decreased. From Brexit to US Congressional budget cuts to IGOs, the founding countries are taking stock of their traditional policies supporting IGOs. Taking stock can be useful for any organization, a moment of adaptation to new times bringing opportunities for reform. Or IGOs may be undermined by a move toward less coordinated, more nationalistic and antagonistic foreign policies, from tariff and trade wars to go-it-alone military interventions.

As IGOs have become larger, more universal organizations, the original members may feel estranged from the norms or priorities of newer members. As new members gain access to IGOs, they seek to use them to benefit their own populations, just as the original founders (the United States, the United Kingdom, and other European countries) did at the time of the founding of these organizations. It is not surprising that IGOs are under scrutiny. Particularly given the different perspectives and goals of very divergent states, all who consider themselves the "masters" of the IGOs, it would be surprising if the work of these IGOs did not draw very different criticisms from all corners. But as providers of international public goods, the challenge is not to "throw the baby out with the bath water." How can IGOs be improved, not undermined, in their provision of public goods and services, from safe commercial air traffic to the smooth movement of goods across borders?

IGOs are perhaps at their "awkward adolescent" stage. After just undergoing a huge growth spurt and testing their new powers, they have experienced some setbacks, including some pushback from the countries that created them. IGOs will have to devise ways to adapt with the times, while also growing public legitimacy and support among younger generations, as the older generations, who created many IGOs, die. Will IGOs survive this passing of the mantle? To do so, IGOs must increase both their efficiency and legitimacy simultaneously.

A planet growing in population and numbers of countries needs coordinating mechanisms. IGOs face flaws and challenges, but they also provide useful and important coordinating networks, described by those who work at the UN as "The United Nations belongs to the world, and works for the world." While this describes the consensual basis that allows the UN and many other IGOs the ability to operate, it is also simultaneously what some nationalists find objectionable.

KEY TERMS

1948 Convention on the Prevention and Punishment of the Crime of Genocide, 134

African Union (AU), 111

ASEAN, 133

Asian Infrastructure Investment Bank (AIIB), 126

Belt and Road Initiative, 126

Economic and Social Council (ECOSOC), 118

European Union (EU), 111

formal IGOs, 111

Food and Agriculture Organization's (FAO), 111

IAEA (International Atomic Energy Organization), 111

ICC (International Criminal Court), 135

IMF International Monetary Fund, 124

informal IGOs, 111

Inter-American Human Rights Commission, 133

International Court of Justice (ICJ), 118

Internet Corporation for Assigned Names and Numbers (iCANN), 127

major armed conflicts, 114

NATO (North Atlantic Treaty Organization), 111

Organization for Security and Cooperation in Europe (OSCE), 111

Organization of American States (OAS), 111

Schengen Zone, 132

UN, 111

UN Security Council (UNSC), 116

UNPKOs, 116

WHO, 118

World Bank, 121

WTO, 125

DISCUSSION QUESTIONS

1. Describe the paradoxes presented by IGOs.
2. Why do IGOs and global issues go hand in hand?
3. Despite what you read in the headlines, we are not in a world at war, but we are experiencing more peace and prosperity than ever before, no matter how you measure it. What evidence supports this claim?

4. Consider your family or community's history from thousands of years ago until today. How have these global trends of greater peace and prosperity impacted your community or family?

5. Why has the number of IGOs rapidly expanded over the past two centuries, in parallel with the growth of the number of sovereign states and the growth of NGOs and civil society?

6. What values and norms helped bring about the creation of IGOs? What pragmatic reasons were there for creating IGOs?

7. Why have the number of UNPKOs increased since the end of the Cold War? Why does this matter?

8. Describe some of the criticisms of the UN. Despite these problems, what contributions has the UN made?

9. What reforms has the World Bank made in response to critics?

10. Why is it that although more money and products than ever before can move freely across borders in international commerce, people cannot. Why is that?

11. What is China's Belt and Road Initiative? How does this differ from other countries' policies to halt or lessen international trade and migration?

12. "The United Nations belongs to the world, and works for the world." Describe why this statement simultaneously describes the positions of both those who laud and those who loathe the United Nations.

Dr. Maryann Cusimano Love

Talitha Kum anti-human trafficking network.

5

Religious Actors and Global Issues

God and Global Governance

■ ■ ■

Everyone has the right to freedom of thought, conscience, and religion, and this right includes freedom to change his religion or belief and freedom to manifest his religion or belief in teaching, practice, worship and observance.

—Article 18, Universal Declaration of Human Rights

From the 18th century onwards a succession of European sages predicted that modernization would produce the end of religion....Today it is secularization theory that is dead rather than religion. Religion continues to flourish... The answer to *Time* magazine's question back in 1966—Is God Dead?—is thus an emphatic "no." God has not only survived the acids of modernity. He has learned how to use the tools of modernity to spread His message.

—John Micklethwait and Adrian Wooldridge[1]

Religious Leaders act as bridges between the grassroots and the organizational levels. If you access this bridge, you will be able to access the heart of the people you want to reach.

—Sheikh Mohamed Gemea, Al Azhar University, Egypt

RELIGIOUS ACTORS ARE NOT NONSTATE actors; they are *prestate* **actors.** Thousands of years before the concept of sovereign countries was ever invented, religious organizations created institutions and performed (and still perform) functions that are today associated with sovereign states. Religious organizations had laws, courts, schools, universities, hospitals, media, humanitarian aid departments, diplomatic emissaries, etc., and registered births, marriages, and deaths, millennia before sovereign states ever created such institutions or engaged in these activities. Religious organizations predate the Treaty of Westphalia of 1648 and the modern sovereign state system by millennia. Only a very small number of today's 193 sovereign states have been around since 1648. Most sovereign states are very new, only created after the end of European colonialism after World War II or after the end of the Soviet Empire in 1989. The sovereign state is a newcomer around the world today, often with limited response capabilities to global issues, while religious transnational networks are well established, including in areas where the capacity and legitimacy of the sovereign state are limited. Religious actors **bring 3 "Is"** to global issues: institutions, ideas, and imagination. Institutions provide the "goody bag" of health, food, education, development, and emergency services, provided by networks of religious institutions, hospitals, schools, charities, etc. Ideas are the religious norms and reasons for actions on global issues. For example, **Laudato Si** a Catholic environmental encyclical that communicates ideas about the religious responsibilities to care for God's creation. This high level of religious teaching, an official letter from Pope Francis, includes the ideas that form the common ground of many religious traditions regarding care for creation. It decries that environmental problems disproportionately kill and harm the world's poorest people. The final "I," imagination is key to envision positive futures on global issues.

For example, indigenous religious leaders and Catholic leaders from the Amazon established a transnational advocacy network, **REPAM,** to protect the indigenous peoples of the Amazon from personal, community, and environmental destruction. Indigenous leaders have given testimony at the Inter-American Human Rights Commission, the United Nations, the EU parliament, and others, about the illegal logging, illegal mining, and illegal fishing that are destroying the Amazon. Using their religious institutions, they take their ideas where it will have the most political impact, to imagine and work toward a better future.

Religious actors are the oldest, largest, continually functioning transnational actors on the planet. Of the over seven billion people on the planet, 85 percent of the world's people describe themselves as being religious, believing in God/a supreme being. Nearly one-third of the world's population are Christians, and nearly 24 percent follow Islam. Catholicism is the world's largest single religious sect with over 1.1 billion Christian followers. About 85 percent of Muslims follow some version of Sunni Islam.

All the world's major religions precede the sovereign state by millennia. Hinduism is over 4,000 years old. Judaism is over 3,500 years old. Buddhism is 2,500 years old. Christianity is over 2,000 years old. Islam is 1,400 years old.

These religious groups differ in their global spread or reach. Many religions never "left the cradle" of their birth. Ninety-nine percent of Hindus and Buddhists are in Asia, where these religions were born. Most of the religiously unaffiliated are in China, an atheist communist

Figure 5.1 Major World Religions

% of world population

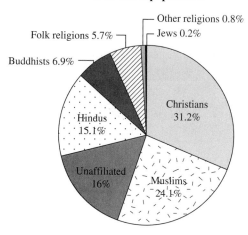

Number of people in 2015, in billions

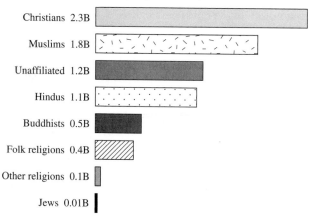

Christians are the largest religious group

Source: Pew Research Center demographic projections

Figure 5.2 Geographic Distribution of Religious Groups

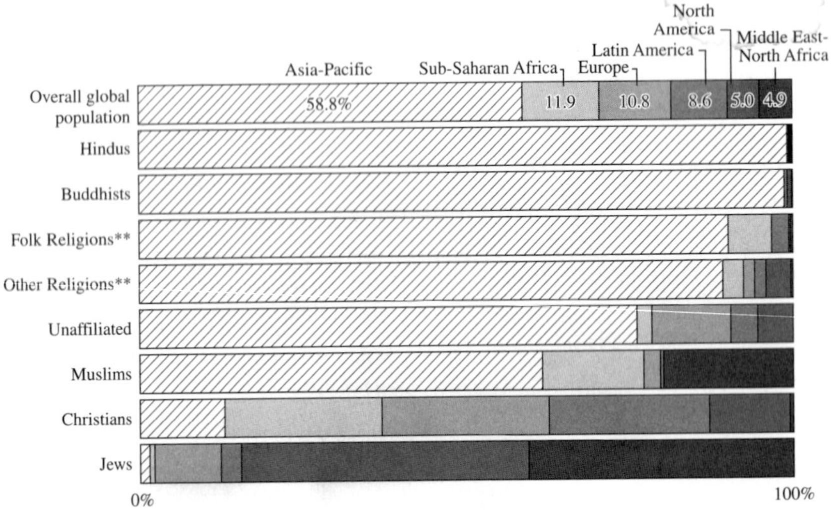

Percentage of each group's total population that lives in particular regions

Source: Pew Research Center's Forum on Religion & Public Life. Global Religious Landscape, December 2012

state that discourages and/or persecutes religion. Islam originated in the Middle East, part of Asia, and most Muslims live in Asia and the Middle East. The world's fourteen million Jews live primarily in two countries, Israel and the United States.

The exceptions are Christian groups. Christianity has spread globally beyond its region of origin (the Middle East) to all geographic areas. Christian communities are under siege in Christianity's "cradle," but are thriving elsewhere. A century ago two-thirds of Christians lived in the global North, in Europe and North America. Today, that number is reversed; two-thirds of Christians live in the global south. All global religions may choose to address global issues, helping the poor or protecting the environment, for example. However, these religious demographics mean that transnational networks of Christian groups will be more available to address global issues.

Religious networks thus have ample capacities to influence global politics *directly* by reaching citizens and communities directly, through their own activities, laws, and institutions. They run vast networks of institutions—hospitals, schools, universities, relief and development organizations, and even businesses, in addition to houses of worship. They provide social services and emergency assistance, often to people outside their faith community, and thus build better relationships across faith communities. They control land and property. People willingly give money to their religious organizations, without being forced to by tax law, and these resources can also be used to fund programs. People receive news and information from religious media, including information about religious groups often overlooked or underreported on state-controlled or commercial media. Religious frames of reference intricately permeate people's lives, and TANs spread these ideas. Religious actors educate people, provide health care, provide emergency and charitable assistance, and make laws. Religious networks develop, project and distribute norms and ideas through numerous means—universities, schools, media. They also advocate for the governments of countries and IGOs to change government policies regarding various global issues, but governmental advocacy is only one of the ways in which they operate.

RESURGENT RELIGION AND CHALLENGED STATES

Religion is resurgent around the world at precisely the time when states are challenged. During the mid-twentieth century, states were strong and religion was repressed by a variety of regime types. Communist regimes around the world imposed atheism and state attacks on religious actors and organizations. Mosques, churches, synagogues, monasteries, and religious schools and properties were destroyed by communist states. Religious leaders and organizations were persecuted, often killed and imprisoned. Fascist and military dictatorships likewise repressed religious actors that conflicted with the state. Secularism rose in European states, bringing *Time* magazine to publish a famous edition with the cover "God is Dead." This proved incorrect. With the end of the Soviet Empire, the fall of military and other dictatorships, and the advance of democratization, religion rebounded. Religious beliefs and actors went underground during periods of repression, but had not been "wiped out." Religious actors helped to end repressive regimes, and rebounded at the end of the twentieth century.

Strong global religious networks meet weakened and stressed state institutions, with a variety of results.

States are under siege externally from a host of global problems that easily cross borders, facilitated by globalization's open economies, societies, and technologies. Global problems—such as disease, terrorism, drugs and crime, environmental degradation, refugee flows, cyber threats, and the proliferation of WMD—plague strong and weak states alike. The problems do not stop at state borders, but state capacities and authority to address these problems usually do stop at the borders. States are charged with responding to these problems, but they lack effective capacities and institutions to do so. No one state can solve or manage any of these problems alone, yet states lack effective means of coordinating or compelling action across borders. Failures to adequately address global problems undermine the authority and legitimacy of states (and associated IGOs), as citizens become dissatisfied with the institutions' continued inability to adequately meet pressing challenges. Even the strongest states in the system find their sovereign institutions are inadequate to meet global challenges.

The weaker states in the system have an even more tenuous grasp on these problems. In addition to external challenges, these states also face grave internal challenges, as reinforcing crises of poverty and security further undermine capacity, authority, and legitimacy of state institutions, creating failed and failing states with ungoverned and ungovernable territories. One-third of the world's population live in failed or failing states, without basic governance capacities to meet citizen demands. People still face problems, but state institutions are less able to meet and manage these problems alone.

At precisely the moment when state institutions struggle to meet pressing global problems, religious institutions and networks are resurgent worldwide. Global religious networks have both physical resources (personnel, money, technical competence, institutional structures from hospitals to schools) and moral resources (ethical and legal codes, popular support, moral legitimacy) to address many global problems. In regions of continued, prolonged conflict (such as Colombia) and areas of postconflict reconstruction (Burundi, Rwanda, Afghanistan, Iraq), when old regimes have been discredited but new institutions have not yet been built, religious institutions and leaders often step into the vacuum to help bridge these institutional gaps.

In strong and weak states alike, states "contract out" a host of social service functions to religious organizations. From emergency relief and development programs that serve the poor to a host of health and education functions, states partner with religious organizations in providing needed social services for a variety of reasons. Religious organizations, with their long-standing grassroots networks, including low-paid clerics and volunteers, may simply be able to deliver social services more cheaply and effectively than state institutions. These efficiency gains are often the motivating force when strong states (including developed democracies) partner with religious organizations to provide services. In weak, failed, or failing states, religious organizations may have capacities, reach, and legitimacy that states lack. Strong religious networks and institutions (hospitals, schools, universities, relief, and development organizations) may be in place in places where state institutions are weak or nonexistent. For example, faith-based organizations have been key in global efforts to reduce HIV/AIDS, malaria, TB, and ebola, particularly in Africa. Religious health networks have effectively delivered health services in areas without state public health institutions. Whether partnerships develop by choice or by necessity, usually such public–private partnerships are consensual and serve the interests of both state and religious organizations. Religious organizations may have mandates to serve the poor and feed the hungry, and government service contracts or partnerships may allow them to serve more needy people. Governments may have authorities and responsibilities to aid people, but may lack the institutional capacities, so turning to religious and other private sector actors is a way to quickly "rent" and use networks and capabilities that would take states much longer to try to build.

Muslim clerics are working with IGOs, NGOs, and the government to reduce maternal and infant mortality rates by increasing health education, immunization, and use of health services. For example, UNICEF is engaged with hundreds of religious leaders in Northern Nigeria to increase polio vaccination and community use of other health services. Muslim cleric Sheik Abubakar Gumi described the need for religious leader engagement on public health issues.

> Up until a few years ago, people in Muslim-majority communities stayed away from health centres, rejected polio vaccines and other routine immunizations even if they were brought to their doorstep due to misconceptions, suspicions, and socio-cultural norms. But this changed with the engagement of religious leaders, who have succeeded in mobilizing people against behaviours that have put the lives of women and children at risk.[2]

Interfaith anti-malaria projects fight malaria and also help increase social cohesion among different identity groups. For example, in Nigeria, mosques and churches serve as important distribution points for mosquito nets and information in the fight against malaria in Nigeria. One quarter of all African malaria cases come from Nigeria. Malaria routinely stunts worker productivity in adults, but it is deadly to children. Working with international NGOs and IGOs, Archbishop Onaiyekan and the Sultan of Sokoto formed the Nigeria Interfaith

Action Association. They trained health-care workers and distributed 60 million insecticide-treated bed nets to 30 million families via their respective religious networks. Religious leaders are a trusted source of information regarding how mosquito nets must be consistently used to be effective. Mosques and churches are critical distribution points, reaching areas where no public health clinics exist. States often turn to religious organizations for services in the economic and social realms, where liberal, capitalist states have the least reach.

Religious organizations are increasingly active even in the law and order, security and peacebuilding realms. For example, religious actors fight drug cartels and organized crime. Dozens of Mexican priests have been killed in recent years for standing up to drug cartels.[3] Religious leaders were key in combating organized crime in Italy. As Mexico faces increasing violence from global drug cartels, Mexican churches collaborate with their religious colleagues in Italy and Colombia to share their expertise and lessons learned in combating organized crime. It is dangerous work, but in the absence of effective state institutions, religious institutions often step in to fill the gap. Religious organizations may be able to bring their moral authority and legitimacy to bear on problems in ways states cannot, especially where state institutions are seen as corrupt and part of the problem, as in Mexico and Colombia.

There are challenges when states contract out to religious organizations, as discussed in Chapter Three. Does reliance on religious networks serve the short-term goal of providing needed services, while ignoring or delaying the long-term goal of developing adequate state institutional capacity to provide essential services? Religious organizations must avoid "capture" or "neutering" of their creeds and practices at the hands of the state. Countries that do not establish a state religion must avoid establishing religious monopolies and ensure that religious organizations do not favor their own congregants or use state monies to proselytize.

Religious organizations and states operate differently regarding sovereignty. Religious organizations have a moral mandate to help "God's children," and do not stand on the sidelines and wait until state institutions are ready and able to provide services. Westphalia created a nonintervention norm for other states that does not apply to religious actors, who answer to a higher authority than state sovereignty. Some NGOs, like "Doctors Without Borders," also act wherever people are in need, whether or not it has the prior permission of the sovereign state. But a key difference with the NGO comparison is that religious organizations are both domestic and external actors; global religious organizations have believers and branches in countries around the world, and are not only external actors. Thus, religious organizations often put people before states. Many religious organizations would concur with the position stated in Vatican II, The Church in the Modern World, "The social order and its development must constantly yield to the good of the person, since the order of things must be subordinate to the order of persons and not the other way around, as the Lord suggested when he said that the Sabbath was made for man and not man for the Sabbath."[4] Religious organizations often begin with the protection of human life and dignity over deference to sovereignty.[5] The UN and the US government have moved toward this position in adopting the Principle to Protect, "the idea that sovereign states have a responsibility to protect their own citizens from avoidable catastrophe, but that when they are unwilling or unable to do so, that responsibility must be borne by the broader community of *states*." But putting that principle into practice has been limited by state interests and concerns of state sovereignty.[6]

In a minority of cases, religious groups and actors seek to take over either all or part of the governing functions of states; they seek to integrate their religion in the governing institutions of states. Religious groups and institutions in some areas of the world, scandelized and discouraged by the corruption and incompetence of state structures, have sought to overturn and fill the functions of states themselves as theocracies, in places such as Iran and Afghanistan under the Taliban. In other areas, short of fully establishing theocracies, states "contract out" the law to religious codes such as sharia law governing Muslim communities in some states of northern Nigeria. When resurgent religions with exclusionary and integrationist political theologies meet the vacuums created by weak and failing states, peace and democratization are endangered, as well as the lives and religious freedom of nonmembers to the resurgent exclusionary faith. This occurs in a dangerous minority of cases, but this potential is why religious actors in politics are often seen as "enemies of the state."

RELIGION AND GLOBALIZATION

Religion and globalization have always gone hand in hand. The quest to understand and encounter the transcendent runs deep in humans, because we are social animals, the impulse to share religious ideas and practices with others also runs deep. Religions have track records of spreading globally, from the spread of Confucianism and Zoroastroism in earlier millennia, to the work of Paul and the disciples to spread

Christianity from a small swath of Galilee to large tracts of the globe in just a few years, to the rapid spread of Islam and evangelical Protestantism today. That process continues, but with a few modern wrinkles. As discussed in chapter 1, globalization is not new; traders and missionaries left their marks in previous periods of globalization. But globalization today is quicker, thicker, deeper, and cheaper than previous periods of globalization. Ideas move at the speed of a keystroke, as fast as the mobile or Internet or satellite connection, and so cheaply as to create much greater global volume. This creates a tipping point for today's global interactions; the difference between modern globalization and its predecessors is not just one of quantity, but of kind, quality, intensity, and scope. More people in more strata of societies are affected by more aspects of global networks more quickly than in previous periods, when people, ideas, and goods spread with the speed of frigates.

This fast modern phase of globalization, spreading interdependent open society, open economy, and open technology networks, creates unintended challenges for states for which states are not well equipped to handle. The very principles of sovereignty are being challenged in theory and in practice. One-third of the world's population live in weak failed and failing states, where sovereign states lack the capacity to provide citizens with basic necessities: security, law and order, food and clean drinking water, access to health, education, and opportunities for jobs. An overlapping set of half the world's people live in states with repressive governments that do not protect citizens but abuse the basic human rights of their own people. The worst of these are predatory states engaged in genocides or democides, killing their own citizens they are charged with protecting. Even strong states, even rich, developed, democratic states struggle in responding to a host of global problems from nuclear threats to the spread of diseases to environmental threats.

Chapter 2 described the ways in which transnational civil society networks come together to address many of these global issues, and gave examples of religious organizations effectively joining forces with secular NGOs from debt relief to the landmine campaign. Faith-based groups now have historic opportunities to practically and importantly influence international and local politics. This is due to the intersection of several related trends: the modern period of globalization, the falling costs and rising opportunities presented by communications technologies, the rising power of NGOs, including faith-based organizations, and the rising power of transnational advocacy networks. The results are important opportunities for what I refer to in chapter 2 as *resurrection politics,* a politics of life and hope, in which faith-based groups in coalition with secular NGOs take issues thought previously dead on arrival, raise them up onto the political agenda, reframe issues with values and powerful images, and thereby change the political space to include those previously marginalized, by drawing on the language and symbols of faith.

While religious organizations can and do work with NGOs, they are in many ways not "just another NGO." Global religious networks *can* function as transnational advocacy networks, yet the category does not quite fit. Global religious networks have much greater institutional and ideological depth than most transnational advocacy networks. They work across wider time and issue horizons. They have longer histories of continuously working as networks across a wide range of issue areas; they are not assembled ad hoc primarily for single-issue advocacy. They are not only advocacy networks, but have great functional capacity across a wide range of functional areas. For example, the Catholic church is the largest single sect religion in the world (Islam has slightly more followers, but these are divided among Sunni and Shi'a sects). The Catholic Church operates over 200,000 schools, serving more than 52 million students. The Church also runs more than 5,000 hospitals; 16,000 clinics, 14,000 homes for the aged and disabled, 8,000 orphanages, 11,000 nurseries, and 25,000 other social service agencies.[7] Catholic relief and development organizations serve needy populations in every country. This kind of institutional breadth and depth is not quantitatively or qualitatively comparable with NGO structures.

Conventional wisdom is that globalization sets the forces of modernity against the forces of tradition, in ways that undermine religious groups.[8] I take issue with that view.[9] Religion is resurgent around the world, and many faith-based groups are facilitated and empowered by globalization.[10] Religious organizations work beyond sovereignty, often targeting their activities directly toward individuals and communities. Corporations, NGOs, and states are neither the only engines of globalization nor its only beneficiaries. Religious organizations have long been globalizing forces, spreading ideas, institutions, flows of people, and capital across international borders. Today, religious organizations, in partnership with other civil society groups, are opening up new political space, responding to the challenges of globalization and offering alternative ethical visions of it.

RELIGION AND OPEN ECONOMIES

God and money have been on mixed terms over the millennia. On the one hand, religions sometimes seem discouraging about money. All of the world's major religions emphasize that humans should not enslave themselves to money and possessions. All the Abrahamic faiths (Judaism, Christianity, Islam, and all their offshoots) share teachings that humanity should pursue God, not pursue "idols" and "false gods," such as the pursuit of economic gain at the expense of spiritual development. It is lawful to own property if economic gain is pursued and used ethically. Money should serve the purposes of God and community and not be gained or used in ways that exploit persons or for personal aggrandizement at the expense of pressing communal needs. The same teachings hold in non-Western religions, that the pursuit of money and possessions can corrupt human beings and communities, leading people away from enlightenment, enslaved by their possessions and by performing nonmeaningful work only for the purpose of earning money.

For these reasons, all the major religions prescribe charity and generosity toward the poor, and limitations on debt (which is why religious organizations joined NGOs in the **Jubilee** transnational advocacy network pressing for debt relief, using biblical language calling for Jubilee debt relief for the poor). The stance toward lending money has been a particularly provocative point. Early Christianity and Islam placed prohibitions on moneylending for interest, while Judaism placed restraints on the amount of interest that could be charged and to whom. The Torah also urges debt forgiveness every seven years. Charging interest raises concerns about abuse of the poor, as well as concerns about greed and excessive wealth creation without work. Catholic restrictions on moneylending were one of the economic factors that led to the creation of the sovereign state. The rise of long-distance trade and merchant classes required economic activities that previously had not been sanctioned by the Church. Over time both Christianity and Islam allowed for moneylenders to earn some profits, but profits were restricted in scale to the work and risks investors added to the enterprise (leading to a separate Islamic banking system so that Muslim communities could be certain financial services followed Islamic values, much as many Jews turn to "koscher" products to be certain that food is prepared consistent with Jewish dietary restrictions). Moneylending often contributed to anti-semitism and violent pogroms over the centuries, as non-Jewish communities turned to Jewish moneylenders as a means to circumvent the moneylending restrictions placed by their own religious faiths, but then faulted "greedy Jewish money lenders" for providing needed financial services.

On the other hand, today, it may sometimes seem difficult to discern the impact of ancient religious restrictions on the use of money. Religious organizations and leaders have often amassed great wealth, in land, church buildings including universities and hospitals, artwork, as well as cash donations. The fall of communism in the USSR and the old Soviet empire has created resurgent opportunities not just for capitalism in previously communist countries, but also for capitalist religions, for religious organizations to fund raise and offer church members economic as well as spiritual counseling. Religious organizations and leaders apply the principles of open markets and modern capitalism to their churches, and reap great benefits. Religious books (such as the best-selling *Left Behind* novel series, and Rick Warren's *A Purpose Driven Life*), music, movies, even health clubs and theme parks are big businesses. More than one thousand megachurches exist internationally, each drawing congregations of over two thousand worshipers per week, using organizational methods that consciously mimic corporate culture. **Megachurch** leaders describe themselves as **"pastorpreneurs,"**[11] using the same niche marketing and economies of scale principles as other successful businesses. As megachurch pastor and televangelist T.D. Jakes describes it, "Jesus is the product. When the product is excellent, it doesn't require a big sales pitch."[12]

The advancement of open economic systems worldwide greatly aids the spread of religious ideas and organizations globally. As John Micklethwait and Adrian Wooldridge argue,

"The God Business" is huge. Global market competition now applies to religions, each vying for followers by providing "total service excellence. These pastorpreneurs don't just preach on Sundays. They don't just provide services for the great rituals of birth, death, and marriage. They keep their buildings open seven days a week, from dawn to dusk, and provide a mind-boggling array of services," from banks, pharmacies, schools, to tax and real estate services and skateboarding parks.[13]

Religious organizations offer franchises more flexible than McDonald's, with boutique branches to serve specific demographics, such as biker churches or sports-enthusiast churches. New religious franchises are making big inroads against the traditional religions, such as mainstream Protestant and Catholic faiths, but are also attracting followers who were previously nonreligious or "unchurched." This is not just a US phenomenon. South Korea is home to the world's largest megachurch, with over 800,000 members.

The spread of capitalist economic forms has advanced the development, number, and capacity of all private sector organizations, including religious organizations, even in "Godless" communist China. The opening of the Chinese economy has coincided with the rise in religion in China. Despite the state's official stance against religion, Christians now outnumber members of the communist party in China. Most follow a very individualistic-style of Christianity in small congregations of "**house churches**," which are groups who meet to worship in people's homes to avoid the persecution that might ensue from meeting publicly in official churches. "Nobody reports us as long as we don't sing," explains one congregant.[14] Because the state still officially persecutes many believers and restricts religious practice, the numbers in China may actually be much higher. Some estimate that China could be the world's biggest Muslim country, as well at the biggest Christian country, by 2025.[15]

Religion's resurgence is also aided by global capitalism in another way. As capitalism spreads its market values globally, many look to religions as a counterweight to the market's excesses, as a source of values that the market does not supply. Pope Francis calls for a **globalization of solidarity**, an international, systematic concern for the poor and marginalized, for a global economy that serves people, rather than the globalization of indifference to the poor and vulnerable that too often is promoted. For example, indigenous and Catholic religious leaders are working together in transnational advocacy networks, to protect the Amazon from exploitation.[16]

In China, many look for a source of values that they do not see in corrupt market and government institutions. A Chinese government economist, Zhao Xiao, argues that market values are not enough; they can encourage efficiency, but not honesty or selflessness, for example. For these the market needs God. "Only through faith can the market economy have a soul."[17]

This view is shared by many in less-developed countries, who look to religion as a source of social justice. Economic and political systems favor elites, while some religious organizations speak courageously on behalf of the poor. Religion thrives among the poor, with religious organizations often serving the poor in basic ways (provision of food, health services, education) that state and other institutions do not provide. Pippa Norris and Ronald Inglehart argue religion is most important in the least-developed majority of the world, but they echo the Marxist/secularist arguments that as scarcity decreases so does religion. This ignores evidence from emerging economies such as China, India, and the former Soviet Union, where religious institutions and practices are increasing while prosperity also increases.[18] The problem in recognizing religious resurgence in developed economies may stem from measurement errors and differing religious expression. It may be that religion is practiced differently from poor countries to rich countries.[19] The poor may be more communal as they reach out to extended family and neighbors in the quest for survival, and they may likewise be more communal in religious expression, joining and attending religious organizations and services. Demography shows they may have little choice, as the poor are often highly concentrated and crowded. Religious practices in rich countries may be more individualistic and personal, less defined by congregating face-to-face in brick-and-morter places. For many, religion may be a matter of "Believing without Belonging," according to sociologist Grace Davie.[20] This is evident in the volume of people who watch religious programs and read religious books, but may not regularly attend religious services. The poor may not be able to afford religion by technology or through buying religious products, so the old-fashioned (and free) bricks-and-mortar route may be the more available and therefore more prevalent means of religious expression. The rich have more options, and so may express their religious behavior more like their consumer behavior. This is true in the United States and many Latin American countries, where people frequently change religions just as they change other consumer brands. In some places, people may practice "vicarious religion"; they may not regularly attend services, but neither do they change brands. They engage virtually, but expect their traditional religious brand to be there for them when they need it (i.e., for a family wedding or funeral), like a public utility. Lived religion is a moving target. These behaviors may be different from historic measures of religion (weekly attendance in pews/mosques/synagogues), but it may not signify a loss of religion.

Still, the triumph of the market has led some to concern that the search for money overwhelms the search for the divine, and that the importance of material possessions in a global consumer culture crowds out spiritual concerns. Yet after the global economic meltdown of 2007, many religious organizations reported huge increases in attendance and requests for social services. This can be interpreted in two ways. As Norris and Inglehart note, people can turn to religion when they have few other options to deal with problems of resource scarcity. But also, even prosperous people still see in religion a source of social justice that may be lacking in market and government structures. Concern for social justice and for changing unjust social structures can be attractive to poor and prosperous alike. All the major world religions have always had a focus on care for the poor, leading to a focus among religious groups on both short-term charity and emergency assistance and long-term economic development. A large percentage of foreign aid funding is channeled through religious NGOs. Religious actors and organizations' concern with the poor and social justice fueled the Jubilee debt relief and eradicate poverty campaigns, discussed in chapter 4. Because of this historic association, religious organizations who align too closely with market forces without sufficient care for the poor may lose legitimacy, as their behavior is perceived as inauthentic.

Consistent with religious traditions of care for the poor, religious organizations and leaders often raise concerns about whether global financial institutions such as the International Monetary Fund, World Trade Organization, and World Bank, and specific free trade agreements adequately address the needs of the world's poor.[21] Religious leaders often pressurize the leaders of MNCs to protect the poor and the environment in the areas in which they do business. For example, religious leaders are concerned that the poor often bear the costs of oil or natural mineral extraction, but do not share in the economic benefits that derive from exploiting these natural resources. Therefore, African Jesuit priests from the Congo to Cameroon are engaged in transparency and shame and name projects, gathering information on the profit-sharing agreements between MNC oil and mining companies and governments, to follow the money trail, learn why the poor did not benefit, and pressure changes so that the poor will benefit more from such arrangements in the future.[22] Catholic Relief Services Extractive Industries programs likewise urge MNCs to "publish what they pay," and to fully respect human rights and the environment.[23] Religious organizations engage in shareholder activism to encourage MNCs to adopt more socially responsible business practices with better impacts on the poor and the environment.[24] Thus, many religious organizations attempt to use the tools of the global economy, in order to create a global economy that better serves the needs of the world's poor and vulnerable people.

RELIGION AND OPEN TECHNOLOGIES

Conventional wisdom holds that religion and science and technology are opposed. This view is mistaken. Some religious organizations oppose some scientific theories and technological practices, exemplified by the debates over cloning, stem cell research, abortion, and evolution. Religious groups continue to monitor and challenge the ethical bases of technologies, from nuclear weapons to health care. But religious organizations are also significant beneficiaries of global transportation and communication technologies. Technologies from papyrus scrolls to Phoenician ships have always been the back-story of religious advancement and dissemination. Twenty-first-century global technologies help religious groups organize, proselytize, mobilize, and conduct their core ministries in ways that are revolutionizing religion.

At the time of Westphalia, the dawn of new technologies created problems for organized religious hierarchies. Specifically, the Gutenberg printing press undermined the authority of clerics' views of scriptures, the Bible, and religious texts, and literally allowed laymen and women for the first time to hold and read their own copies of holy books, and reach their own conclusions. This technological opening created religious and organizational openings, as new Protestant and reform religious groups were formed based on individual, not communal, ideas of faith and authority.

Social media, the Internet and other cheap, decentralized, and readily available information technologies are creating similar changes today. The "Gutenberg Bible" of the twenty-first century is no single text in a single medium; instead, there are thousands of religious texts and videos from all the world religious traditions available through a myriad of mediums, low, and high-tech, new and old-tech applications—Facebook, Twitter, cell phones, websites, radio, and TV. Today's connective information technologies from computers to televisions to wireless devices bring religious materials from the Koran and the teachings of the Dalai Lama as well as the Bible to exponentially more people than ever read a Gutenberg Bible. People now have more religious resources than ever before available to them at the touch of a keystroke or the push of a button on their TV. This allows people to reach their own conclusions on religious matters with less intercession from traditional religious hierarchies and clerics.

Technology also allows individuals to partake in religious ceremonies and practices from the comforts of their homes, without ever having to set foot in a mosque, synagogue, or church. People who have never been persecuted have house churches. This further privatization of religion creates challenges and opportunities for religious organizations. For old brand religions that do not adapt to new technologies, attendance is diminishing at their traditional religious services. Why travel to an inconvenient brick-and-mortar location for a service whose music and sermon may not be as compelling as what is readily available online, on the television, or on DVD? Why go, on Sunday morning or Saturday night or any inconvenient time when one can participate in religious ritual at any hour any day? For new religious organizations and religious organizations that adopt a variety of new technologies, this creates opportunities for new outreach and new services (including the vast array of one-stop-shopping services from counseling to theme parks to food courts and childcare available at many megachurch complexes). Many religious organizations have been very successful by creating new "value added" attractions not available through remote venues. Believing without belonging has reached a new expression; believing with virtual belonging, to listening, viewing, or online communities.

Humans are social animals and religious organizations offer supportive social communities; therefore, there will always be a market for "old time" religion, offered up face-to-face and hand-to-hand. Big life event religious rituals—births, deaths, marriages—will always be in-person events. However, even "old time religion" services are taking cues from corporate and entertainment culture, with more friendly Walmart-type "greeters" rather than stoic ushers helping congregants to seats, and more professional high-quality audio and video performances replacing lower-quality music and visuals.

Religious organizations are scrambling to keep up with the speed of technological revolutions, a race made difficult by the age discrepancies between many older clerics and younger congregants with different technological skills and expectations. Religious organizations that do not use the new technologies (that retain paper religious bulletins rather than create sophisticated websites and online presences) often find they may have difficulties attracting younger followers, who look for information about religious services and activities online, using the same technologies for the sacred as they use in the secular areas of their lives. Religious organizations without virtual presences do not exist to many younger believers.

Religious organizations that skillfully adapt and use the new technologies find efficient force multipliers for their ministries and messages. These networks and communications are not totally free but are mediated, by service and content providers and users, who combined, define the search terms and content. But mediation is decentralized and diffuse, especially compared with more hierarchical controls of previous media and religious authorities. Iranians challenging election results by chanting "God is good," all use Facebook, Twitter, blogs, cell phone photos and uploads to disseminate real-time information about their religious groups' activities to a global audience, despite government actions to try to restrict their communications. Ironically, even conservative, Orthodox, and fundamentalist religious groups use the new technologies to preach and reach more people. Small sects in remote locations are no longer prisoners of their geography, but they can preach views and reach followers cheaply at a distance to a potentially global audience.

As discussed in the terrorism chapter, religiously identified terrorist groups like Al Qaeda also skillfully use new technologies to promote their views, plan operations, raise funds, train, and communicate among members.

Because religious groups often attract followers across class and generational lines, many must remain literate in both old and new technologies, using print media, radio, television, and other older media to communicate with followers, in addition to streaming video, Facebook, and podcasts. Used well, these new technologies can be a vital way to connect more of the human family in new ways, and sensitize followers to global religious issues, for example, to problems of global poverty, in ways that might otherwise be more difficult. The resurgence of religion has been facilitated by cheap, widely available, global communication technologies. This helps people find God in Cyberspace, and helps religious organizations efficiently communicate, organize, do their work, and raise funds.

The cheaper cost and wider availability of global transportation technologies also dramatically changes the lived experiences of the world's religions. Many more Muslims now make pilgrimages to Mecca, Buddhists travel to **Lumbini** (a world heritage site and pilgrimage site in Nepal, by tradition the birthplace of Buddha), and Catholics travel to the Vatican than ever before. According to the fifth principle of Islam, **Hajj**, Muslims are required once in a lifetime to go on a Pilgrimage to Mecca in Saudi Arabia, if the individual has the means to do so. So many Muslims now have the means to do so (thanks to the cheaper cost and wider availability of global transportation technologies), that Saudi authorities now must use 6,000 cameras to monitor and manage the crowded pilgrims, to avoid congestion and stampedes, as millions converge on the same holy sites at the same time.

Similarly, anyone can now be a missionary, at least for short-term mission projects. Millions do short-term mission or charity work, given the opportunities afforded by "Twinning" relationships of religious communities in developed and developing countries and global "mission trips" and the service-learning voluntourism industry. Religious tourism and mission-centered "voluntourism" are thriving industries, complete with their own trade shows and trade associations. Over a million Americans volunteer overseas each year, many through religious organizations and programs.[25]

Religious groups are not only concerned about the ethical repercussions of technology but also with the ethical distribution of technology. Religious groups work to mitigate the "digital divide," by offering access and training in technologies at religious schools and centers. For example, Jesuit Refugee Services, Catholic Relief Services, Church World Services, and other faith-based NGOs offer livelihood and development programs for the poor in rural areas via access to the technologies of religious organizations. Sudanese refugees sell their handicrafts online via web access and training provided by religious organizations. Resurgent religions are filling functions not filled by challenged sovereign states.

Global technologies also help religious organizations in another way, as people turn to religion as a counterforce to environmental destruction. For example, religious organizations are increasingly active to combat global climate change. They are concerned that overconsumption and toxic technologies are polluting "God's green earth," and that we have religious responsibilities to address environmental problems, which disproportionately harm the world's poor. Abrahamic religions believe that God created the world and entered into a covenant with humanity to be careful stewards of God's creation. The Coalition on the Environment and Jewish Life notes that "For Jews, the environmental crisis is a religious challenge. As heirs to a tradition of stewardship that goes back to Genesis and that teaches us to be partners in the ongoing work of creation, we cannot accept the escalating destruction of our environment and its effect on human health and livelihood. Where we are despoiling our air, land, and water, it is our sacred duty as Jews to acknowledge our God-given responsibility and take action to alleviate environmental degradation and the pain and suffering that it causes. We must reaffirm and bequeath the tradition we have inherited that calls upon us to safeguard humanity's home."[26]

The poor suffer most from environmental damage, so global environmental concerns dovetail with religious concerns with caring for the poor.

RELIGION AND OPEN SOCIETIES

Religious actors have frequently been a key player in democratization in recent decades. Religious actors have mobilized and legitimized democracy movements. Examples include the **People's Power** movement, which removed the Marcos dictatorship in the Philippines; the **Velvet Revolutions** in Poland and East Germany that peacefully removed communist regimes; the **Anti-Apartheid movement** in South Africa that led to the peaceful transition of power away from racial segregation; and the **US civil rights movement**, which used peaceful protest to end Jim Crow laws of racial segregation and exclusion. Research by Stephan and Chenoweth on the success of nonviolent resistance movements may help explain why and how religious actors aid democracy movements. To the extent that religious groups join in nonviolent resistance movements, help mobilize large-scale participation, and remove their support from repressive regimes, they expand civic participation in peaceful prodemocracy movements.

International Relations theory traditionally has had little to say to cases like this. Religion was viewed as either unimportant in world politics, or as undemocratic; both views are false. With modern globalization, the opening of societies has greatly aided the advancement of religion. Religion is resurgent in formerly communist states, showing "godless communism" to have had a much more tenuous grasp on the populations than many previously imagined. But religious organizations have also helped to bring about democratization, in places such as the Philippines and Poland.

Historically, analysis of religion and democratization quickly turned to discussions of *which* religion helped democratization, and which ones did not. Conventional wisdom was that Protestant religions aided democratization, while hierarchical Catholicism and human rights hindered Islam did not. "As an egalitarian religion profoundly opposed to hierarchy, Protestant Christianity would seem to enjoy a powerful affinity with democracy."[27] The facts did not always substantiate this thesis. From Cromwell to colonialism to Apartheid to Jim Crow, in many cases Protestant religions did not advance democracy. Today, the world's largest democracy, India, is a predominantly Hindu and Muslim country. The world's largest Muslim country, Indonesia, is also the world's third largest democracy. A more nuanced research focus is needed, which explores which elements of religions under what conditions help or hurt democratization.

The answers parallel the results on religion, war, and peace. Religious groups advance democratization if they hold political theologies that embrace human rights and democracy, and if they work toward autonomy or **differentiation of political and religious institutions**. Religious groups that hold exclusionary political theologies and that prefer integration with state institutions do not advance democracy. For example, in bygone centuries, the Catholic Church preferred integration with state power, and often supported nondemocratic regimes that supported the Catholic religion, in places like Spain, Portugal, Brazil, and Chile. The Catholic Church's political theology became more inclusive after the **Second Vatican Council (1962–1965)**, a historic ecumenical gathering that created religious laws more clearly supportive of institutional separation with state structures, and unambiguously supportive of human rights, religious freedom, democracy and development. After Vatican II, the Catholic Church became a powerful aid to democratization in many places around the world. Seventy-five percent of the thirty countries that democratized after the Second Vatican Council were predominantly Catholic countries.

The question many raise today is whether Islam can make a similar transition. As Indonesia, India, and Turkey illustrate, Islam is compatible with democracy. The issue is in the details: which specific version of Islam espousing which ideas and political institutions, in which contexts. The record of democracy in Arab Islamic states is poor, untouched by the waves of democratization that have upended authoritarian regimes in all other parts of the globe. Yet nearly half of the world's Muslims live in democratic or partly free states, suggesting alternative futures should more variants of Islam emerge in Arab countries that espouse institutional separation and "Islamic concepts that favor democracy such as *shurah* (consultation), *ijma* (consensus), and *ijtihad* (independent interpretive judgment)."[28]

Put another way, how can religious and state institutions each develop what Alfred Stepan calls the **"twin tolerations,"** or mutually agreed-upon boundaries that respect the institutions of both state and religious organizations. "Democracy is a system of conflict regulation that allows open competition over the values and goals that citizens want to advance,"[29] including religious values and religiously motivated goals. The challenge is not banishing religion from politics, but negotiating the boundaries within which the competition can take place, in ways that respect the institutions of both state and religious organizations. There is no exact one-size-fits-all answer, but stable democracies have to address the questions of "the minimal degree of toleration democracy needs from religion and the minimal degree of toleration that religion needs from the state for the polity to be democratic. Religious institutions should not have constitutionally privileged prerogatives which allow them authoritatively to mandate public policy to democratically elected officials. The minimal degree of toleration of religion needs from democracy... is not only the complete right to worship, but the freedom of religious individuals and groups to publicly advance their values in civil society, and to sponsor organizations and movements in political society, as long as their public advancement of these beliefs does not impinge negatively on the liberties of other citizens, or violate democracy and the law, by violence."[30] Nonviolence and religious freedom go hand in hand and help form the basis of stable democracies.

Even where nonviolent religions are free to flourish, however, religion alone does not bring democracy. Other conditions matter. Catholicism was the majority religion in Poland with a long tradition of autonomy from the state. This gave church structures greater impact in their battles with the communist regime. Minority religions may not have the same impact or legitimacy. As Nigerian Archbishop Onaiyekan describes the Catholic church's role in advancing democracy and anti-corruption in Nigeria, "In my country, people at times accuse us of not doing enough to influence the political fortunes of our nation. They point to the example and the record of Church action in a country like Philippines or Poland. I always remind them that Nigeria is neither the Philippines nor Poland. The Archbishop of Abuja does not have the same political clout as the Archbishop of Manila or of Warsaw. In the countries where the church is a dominant force, by mere fact of her relative numerical strength, the responsibility to be proactive and indeed to be very much in the frontline of peace building activities is clear and evident. In other countries, where the church is just one out of many religious groups, it will be up to the local church to assess and work out how far it can effectively move. In my country Nigeria, Catholics form no more than about 25 percent of the population. We know that we can only offer our own suggestions to the solutions of the problems of the nation. We have no way to force our position on anyone, not even our Catholic members in public office. I must say however, that because of the coherence and objective merits of what we have to say, our message generally receives very good reception, well beyond the confines of the Catholic faith. Experience has shown that the church can always bear witness to justice and peace even in situations where it may be of very weak numerical strength."[31]

Even minority religious groups can play important roles, with the help of modern technologies and global networks. They can be "eyes and ears," windows into authoritarian regimes, providing information about internal conditions in countries (including human rights abuses and breaches of peace) when states cannot or will not do so, for example, in Sudan or Sri Lanka. This information can be invaluable, and over time can aid democratization and protection of human rights.

Again, religious freedom turns out to be a kind of "canary in the coal mine" for other human rights and freedoms necessary for democracy to function; perhaps this is why religious freedom was the first item on the US Bill of Rights. "Throughout most of history the demand for religious freedom has come from religious minorities, dissenters... this is not good enough. Let us make religious freedom the demand of majorities who understand that their own fates hang in the balance as well, if not today, then tomorrow. If we do not protect the religious freedom of even the smallest and weakest religious minorities, we are setting a precedent that will come back to haunt us. For if religious freedom—freedom of conscience—is not protected, the political freedoms of the right to vote, as well as freedom of speech, assembly, and press are certainly not safe."[32]

GETTING RELIGION RIGHT

The trends of resurgent religions in a world of challenged states means the opportunities are increasing for religious groups, of all persuasions, to influence politics. The impact of religion in world politics is neither always good or evil, everywhere a cause of war or peace, democracy or authoritarian rule. We have to make more distinctions than that. To "get religion right" in world politics, states and citizens will need to think and act in more serious and nuanced ways, and build the institutional capacities to engage with religious actors and factors.

Religion can be a source of peace and democratization when religious groups seek separation from state structures and espouse inclusive political ideas including the protection of human rights. When states control or restrict religion, violence is more likely. Religious identity markers are often coopted and manipulated in conflicts that are primarily about control over resources or political power, not souls and doctrine, but once these religious elements are unleashed in nationalist and ethnic conflicts, the conflicts can be more difficult to solve. Religious peacebuilding is an important and underappreciated tool by states that lack institutional capacity in peacebuilding.

Globalization does not staunch religion, but may increase the quest for tradition and meaning in a material, uncertain, and fast-changing world. And globalization offers new tools to religious organizations who adapt and harness the technology, markets, and social networking possibilities of globalization to the traditional focus of faiths. Religious maps are changing, as demographics change, some traditional religions adapt or do not, while new groups compete. Religious practices and expressions change, as technologies and economies change, and many become those who believe but do not belong. But the part of human nature that seeks to understand the relation of humans to each other, to the cosmos, and to the Divine seems in no danger of extinction. Religions have always gone beyond sovereignty, but that process is now on steroids, aided by the technologies and ideas prominent in our age. And as religious organizations respond to the failures of states and to globalization's gaps, loyalties may be created or intensified that do not coincide with the boundaries of states, and are causing complications for states that seek to control or stamp out religious impulses and organizations. To borrow from Mark Twain, news of the death of religion has been overstated. Modernization and globalization have redrawn the map of religion in society, but they have not erased religion from society. Actually, the opposite has occurred. How to engage with resurgent religious actors and factors in a world of challenged states, how to extend the map of religious freedom, peace and democracy to more areas of the world—these are the challenges of our time. We will continue to pay a high price if we fail to "get religion right," to engage with religious actors and factors in world politics.

GETTING RELIGION WRONG IN WORLD POLITICS

The reasons go back over two millennium. In his *History of the Peloponnesian Wars*, the Athenian general and historian, Thucydides, warned against the corrosive impact of religion in world affairs. Thucydides was impatient with the traditional Greek practice of attributing success in battle to having the favor of the gods. He argued that religious ideas and ethical norms had no place in world affairs, where material military power reigned supreme. Long before the creation of the modern sovereign state system, he articulated many components of what would later be incorporated into the "Realist" worldview.

This view of world affairs gained traction after the Crusades, the Inquisition, programs, and the religious wars of the Middle Ages. The Roman Empire spread Christianity globally, and the collapse of the Roman Empire led to centuries of overlapping and contested political organization and authority. In the medieval world, rule was spiritual not spatial, religion was communal not individual, and religious and secular authority were intertwined and overlapping. But such ultimate power led to corruption, undermining the legitimacy of both church and government, and fueling opposition. The Reformation created new ideas about religion and authority, including individual autonomy and freedom from outside interference. A century of wars in Europe were fought over these new religious ideas and authorities, and these wars such as the 30 years war in turn undermined the old system. Changes in technology undermined the old system. The invention of the printing press meant that individuals could own, read, and interpret scriptures on their own. They could also disseminate scientific information, free of the communal interpretations of Church authorities and their monk and religious scribes. During the Enlightenment, religion was often at odds with science, as Catholic and Protestant churches opposed scientific and academic inquiry that seemed to challenge literal readings of the Bible, such as Copernicus', Kepler's, and Galileo's views that the earth revolved around the sun. Changes in the economy added fuel to the fire; the Roman Catholic Church was against loaning money and swearing oaths, even though contracts and currency were required by the new economic system of long-distance trade. The modern sovereign state was born in the 1648 Treaty of Westphalia, in which the boundaries of rule were no longer determined by religion but by geography. The principle of noninterference in the domestic affairs of sovereign states originally referred to respecting the religious preferences of other states.

Many believed Westphalia signaled the final separation of the sacred from the sovereign in world affairs. It did not. The bloody history of colonization around the globe showed that Westphalian noninterference applied primarily to Western countries organized as sovereignties. Non-Western peoples and other forms of political and religious systems were ripe for forced religious conversion and military and political conquer. Westphalia did not guarantee religious freedom, as is sometimes mistakenly inferred. States were, and are, still able to try to control and mandate religious practices within their borders, and also still try to promote these ideas and systems abroad.

The French and American Revolutions struck blows for religious freedom, furthering the separation of church and state. For example, the **First Amendment of the US Constitution** states that "Congress shall make no law respecting an establishment of religion, or prohibiting the free exercise thereof; or abridging the freedom of speech, or of the press; or the right of the people peaceably to assemble, and to petition the Government for a redress of grievances." While only binding upon the United States, other countries were inspired to include similar language in their own laws and constitutions. Thomas Jefferson felt so strongly about this accomplishment that his authorship of Virginia's Statute of Religious Freedom (which he wrote first, and was predecessor to the First Amendment) was one of the only three accomplishments he dictated be listed on his tombstone (the others were his authorship of the Declaration of Independence and his founding of the University of Virginia, *not* his service as the third president of the United States). It was not until 1948, however, that respect for religious liberty was recognized internationally, in Article 18 of the Universal Declaration of Human Rights. Religious freedom is still abused and restricted, serving as a powerful component of religious conflict today. Marxism and Communism believed religion to be an unscrupulous scam on the poor and working classes, and worked hard to stamp out religion from the people and large territories they controlled in the twentieth century. By their economic materialist view, religion was the destructive "opiate of the masses" that would quell demands of the poor and working classes for justice and revolution and con them out of better conditions, by convincing them that it didn't matter if the rich oppressed them, since material possessions didn't matter anyway, and their rewards would come in heaven.

Ironically, throughout the twentieth century (through wars against German imperialism, Nazism and fascism, and Marxism and communism), both the so-called Idealist and Realist approaches to international politics believed that religion ought to be kept out of politics. Idealists believed in the importance of ideas such as democracy, but believed states should only promote secular ideas; religion belonged in the private, personal sphere, not in the arena of public or world affairs. While many Cold War Realists denounced the rise of "Godless" Communism, they were also "Godless" in their approaches to world politics. They believed that religious ideas and actors were unimportant in world politics. Only the material military and economic power of states mattered; therefore, religious ideas and identities ought to be a private matter, not the concern of secular states. The Realist view formidably dominated both the theory and practice of world politics in the past century. One study of International Relations scholarship showed that 92 percent of hypotheses and 94 percent of variables used by scholars were Realist.[33] Competing theoretical approaches, such as idealism, complex interdependence theory, Marxism/dependency theory, post-modernism, all likewise discount the role and study of religion in international politics. Methodology plays its part, as quantitative approaches dominate the IR academy, while studies of religion often use more historical and qualitative methods.

Not only IR scholars were wrong about religion. Sociologists also practiced and promoted the "secular theory," that modernization meant the demise of religion.[34] Since religion was based on primitive, primal, and superstitious views, as societies modernized and science and technology advanced, religion would recede. "Voltaire predicted that Christianity would wither as man became more enlightened. Marx argued that religion was a tool of ruling class exploitation that would disappear with the birth of a classless society. Nietzsche proclaimed that "God is dead. God will remain dead. And we have killed him."

By the 1960s, it looked as if the prophets of secularization were being proved right. Christianity was withering in the former heartland of Christendom—Europe. Developing countries from India to Iran were in the hands of avowedly secular governments. And two of the world's biggest countries—Russia and China—were run by Communist Parties that were dedicated to proving that Marx was right. But the great secular 'isms'-socialism, capitalism, and Pan-Arabism—all lost their luster. In fact secularization theory always underestimated the power of religion."[35] These views were not restricted to Universities, but statesmen, soldiers, and government bureaucrats widely held these views as well. *The Economist* magazine published an obituary for God. No wonder that one survey of major world politics journals from the last 20 years of the twentieth century found a mere six articles on religion.[36] Why study religion if it is dying and unimportant in world politics?

All these views minimizing the importance of religion in world affairs, from Thucydides to communists, idealists, and realists are based on several misconceptions. First, they confuse prescription with empirical description, an "ought" (religion ought to be kept out of world politics) with an "is" (religion is unimportant in world politics). Second, the belief that religion ought to be kept out of world politics was based on a false assumption that religion could only play a destructive role in world affairs. By definition (because little careful empirical or analytical work was done to investigate these claims), religions caused wars, poverty, and oppression. The ways in which religion aided peace, democracy, human rights, and development were not given much attention. Third, they confuse the demise in the power of the Roman Catholic and Protestant churches over affairs of state since Westphalia, and the demise in attendance at mainstream religious houses of worship primarily in Europe, with the demise of religion writ large. They also confused belonging with believing. People who don't attend church, synagogue, mosque, or other religious communities and services still believe in God and religious principles. The growth in religion in populations outside of Europe (including the United States), and the growth in new religions and non-Western religions were erroneously deemed as anomalies, temporary exceptions that would eventually succumb to the European trends. Fourth, they believed that advances in technology and economics undermined religion, creating a more material and individual-focused consumer world, more opposed to the divine. They failed to understand the ways in which religions could flourish using the new economies and technologies. Finally, the prevalence of materialist views (power politics or economics matter, not ideas) and Realist views (states are the primary actors in world politics) meant that religious actors and dynamics had two strikes against them. Since religious actors are nonstate actors who thrive on and promote ideas, they were consistently ignored, underestimated, and misunderstood by most of the leading scholars and practitioners of world politics over the past several centuries. Soviet leader Joseph Stalin dismissively asked, "How many divisions does the Pope have?"[37] His point was that leaders without armies are powerless. Ironically, many leaders and scholars who vehemently opposed Stalin nevertheless agreed with his assessment of the unimportance of religious actors. In further irony, just a few decades after Stalin's dismissive comment, the Soviet Union hired assassins to try to murder Pope John Paul II, because the first Polish Pope inspired and supported the anti-communist Solidarity movement in Poland. The Pope was wounded but lived, helping to bring about the demise of communist rule in Poland followed by the death of the Soviet Union itself. The Pope never commanded any divisions in Poland against the Soviet military superpower, but religious ideas and organizations, in combination with other factors, helped to end the Soviet empire and the Cold War. This history is very much on the minds of Chinese leaders as they repress religious groups in China today.[38]

The world has been ill-served by this dismissal of the role of religion in world politics. The secular government of the Shah of Iran was replaced by a fundamentalist Shi'a Islamist theocracy in 1979. Thirty years later, the world is still perplexed in navigating relations with the Iranian regime. From Iran's Middle Eastern neighbors to its former European colonial conquerors to its former ally the United States, few have clear insights into the religious dynamics and institutions that underlie the Iranian regime. Progress would be improved on critical issues from nuclear power and weapons to terrorism and drug trafficking with better understanding and engagement of religious factors and actors.

The end of the Cold War, the Balkan Wars of the 1990s, and the rise of violent strains of Islamic fundamentalism and terrorist groups like Al Qaeda gives new appreciation to the role of religion in world politics.[39] But as one fallacy loses ground (that religious actors and dynamics are unimportant), another fallacy remains, that religious actors and dynamics can play no constructive role[40] in world politics. The one-sided theory extols only the destructive qualities of religion, even though in practice, people, governments, and IGOs rely extensively on religious actors in response to the problems of failed and failing states. Religious actors provide a host of critical functions, from providing humanitarian relief during wars and natural disasters, economic development, education, health care (from maternal and child health to immunization, HIV/AIDS care and prevention, to malaria prevention), providing on-the-ground information about human rights abuses, protecting refugees and displaced persons, to building peace and reconciliation in conflict-prone areas, and safeguarding the environment. Religious actors in coalition with civil society groups form effective transnational networks. Religious groups operate in and across state borders, and they are less inhibited by the Westphalian nonintervention principle that can often cripple the responses of states and IGOs to pressing human needs.

Unfortunately, our ideas about how the world works have not yet caught up with these practices. According to a leading study, "miscalculating religion's role has led to failure to anticipate conflict or has actually been counterproductive to policy goals. It has kept officials from properly engaging influential leaders, interfered with the provision of effective development assistance, and at times harmed American national security." From diplomacy to development to defense, "policymakers and practitioners have largely been wary of directly addressing religion." Concerns over separation of church and state, prevalence of the Realist worldview, lack of education and training in religion, failure to recruit individuals for government service with education and expertise in religion, and failure to create career tracks for soldiers, intelligence analysts, or statesmen specializing in religion and international affairs (as there are career tracks for economic expertise, for example) are some of the many reasons for the failure to effectively engage with religious factors and actors.[41]

These critiques of the US government apply equally well to many governments and IGOs around the world, who struggle in determining how secular states and organizations can account for and interact with religious actors and factors.

RELIGION, WAR, AND PEACE

Does religion incite violence or bring peace? It depends. This context-driven ambiguity is the "Ambivalence of the sacred," as Scott Appleby notes.[42] Where religious freedom is respected, there is peace. Where religions are repressed, there is greater conflict.

The world is becoming more religious, at the same time as the world is becoming more peaceful. With the end of communist regimes that outlawed religion in Russia and Eastern Europe, and with more accommodating policies (compared to the cultural revolution time period) toward religion in China, 85 percent of the world's people today self-identify as religious. As discussed earlier, peace is breaking out around the world, with major wars declining and marked declines in battle deaths (war is a conflict with over 1,000 battle deaths in a year).[43] Do religious actors help build peace or foster war?

Wars are rarely fought directly over religious dogmas, as in the Crusades. Religions are often a source of peace, nonviolence, and reconciliation, as in the Velvet Revolutions ending communism and Soviet control, and the experiences of religious peacemakers worldwide. Atheistic communist regimes alone caused over 100 million deaths in the twentieth century. The secular wars and violence of the twentieth century, the most violent century in human history, caused much greater loss of human life than religious wars by many orders of magnitude, contrary to the view of religions as a source of war.[44] This does not excuse religiously based violence, but merely puts the issue in context as a corrective to popular misperception.

All the world's major religions place premiums on peace and limitations on war and violence. Yet political leaders often manipulate and pervert religious identities and language for their own gain, to justify war and try to motivate followers to risk their lives for causes that are not particularly religious in nature. What is often referred to as "religious war" is instead a false, deliberate, and cynical perversion of religion to gain a veneer of legitimacy to mask the self-interest or national interest reasons for pursuing conflict, according to a United Nations University study.[45]

There is some truth to this claim. Many of what are often referred to as religious wars either are not or have only partial or tangential relation to religious disagreements. For example, most journalists and pundits described the cause of conflict in the Balkans as a combination of "ancient ethnic and religious hatreds."[46] But the leaders who plunged the region into conflict, such as war criminal Slobodan Milosevic, were communist political leaders with no religious ties or credentials before the breakup of the Soviet Union. After the end of the communist system, these leaders sought to reinvent themselves as nationalists who also invoked religious identities, to justify themselves to anti-communist voters and save their political careers. Poor economics and leaders who stoked conflict were pivotal in bringing violence to Yugoslavia. As the economic situation deteriorated in Yugoslavia, politicians sought to protect their own groups. Leaders exploited identity differences to blame scapegoats, explain away economic woes, and distance themselves from their communist pasts, often magnifying their messages of hate via the media. Thus while groups from different religions (among other differences) fought in the Balkans, the conflict drivers were more secular than sacred.[47]

While one can question the religious motivations and qualifications of nationalist leaders such as Milosevic, the problem with this analysis is that it diminishes the deep power of religion once unleashed into conflict, even if unleashed for cynical and self-interested purposes. In the Balkans, "between them the Croat and Serb nationalists demolished an estimated 1,400 mosques. They destroyed birth records, work records, gravesites, and other traces of the Bosnian Muslim people...Mass expulsions (of Catholics and Muslims by Serbs) and a campaign of terror including murder, forced labor, beatings, and other abuses nearly erased the Croat, Muslim, and Roma (gypsy) populations from the region." Yes, the religious elements of violence were manipulated by nationalist leaders, and they were not "inevitable." Nevertheless, "the sad truth is that the war in the former Yugoslavia featured a prominent religious element."[48]

It is true that all the major world religions arrive at similar conclusions regarding the primacy of peace and limitations on war and killing, particularly the protection of civilian noncombatants. These religious norms held by all the Abrahamic religions—Christianity, Islam, Judaism, as well as non-Abrahamic traditions—Buddhism, Hinduism, etc., informed the development of international and national laws limiting conflict and defining war crimes. The Geneva Conventions, the Laws of Armed Conflict, and the United States and other countries' military codes of justice, portions of the UN charter, as well as the charters of many regional security organizations such as NATO, all owe a debt to religious traditions concerning the primacy of peace and limitations on conflict.[49] Vast common ground exists among world religions on issues of peace, war, and human development. These shared values are underappreciated and underutilized in the quest for peace and development.

Violence of many religiously motivated extremists is decried and not sanctioned by the world's mainstream religions. Christian leaders condemn the violence of the Lord's Resistance Army in Uganda, and Muslim leaders condemn Al Qaeda's violence.[50] The perpetrators of religious violence are generally minority groups acting without the blessing of the majority of their co-religionists, because these groups pervert religious teachings by overturning the religious injunctions against violence.

However, there are problems with this logic. The very religious pluralism that is upheld and applauded by modern and Western governments has a downside: who speaks for Christianity, Hinduism,

Buddhism, Judaism, Islam? The ever-growing diversity and the "splinter sect" phenomenon facilitated by modern technologies and communications means every person has the ability to interpret religious texts and traditions in their own ways, and the ability to more easily gain like-minded followers using the tools of globalization. Decrying "This is not *true* Christianity," or "this is not *true* Islam" does not get us very far. It may be helpful to deny mainstream legitimacy to violent cults, and to try to clarify and contain the spread of violence from the wider audience of adherents to a religious tradition. But it does nothing to stop the activities of violent religious groups.

Further, it glosses over the problematic passages that offend other faith groups and are often used as religious justifications for violence. Rabbi David Meyer, Imam Sohaib Bencheikh, and Jesuit priest Rev. Yves Simoens S.J. enumerate a number of these "Painful verses" within each of their own faith traditions. Too often interfaith dialogue stresses the commonalities among religious groups but avoids the tough issues that are sources of division. In Christianity, some translations of the gospel of John emphasize that "the Jews killed Jesus," justification that has been used in anti-Jewish programs (even though Jesus and his apostles were also Jews). One of Islam's "painful verses," is the Prophet Mohammed's saying "Kill he who changes his religion," used by some to threaten ex-Muslims with death. The Jewish Torah tells the Israelites to wipe out the rival Amalekite tribe in Palestine, which some use to justify killing their modern descendants. For believers who do not hold literal interpretations of sacred texts, but who engage in contextual and historic interpretation, these passages do not justify violence.[51] Fundamentalists from all religious traditions hold to more literal interpretations, but the vast majority of fundamentalists also do not espouse violence, and instead interpret these passages with greater priority to the much more frequent passages urging love of neighbor, peace, and unity.[52] But religiously motivated groups who espouse violence often use these problematic passages to overcome religion's traditional prescriptions against violence, and to fuel the fires of conflict. Ignoring these passages or downplaying them as "not representative of *real* religion" does not do much to douse the fire.

Violence is usually overdetermined. Wars and other forms of violence have many causes—routinely economic and political, at times abetted and intensified by religious factors. Discerning religious violence involves separating rhetoric from reality. For example, the conflict between Israel and the Palestinians is commonly referred to as a Holy War. However, the conflict centers over land, borders, water rights, freedom of movement, property rights, citizenship rights, demographics, and government control and sovereignty. The vast majority of Israeli Jews are secular, not practicing Jews. Not all Palestinians are Muslims; Christian Palestinians are also quite adversely affected by Israeli policy. Certainly control over religious sites and movement of religious leaders are contentious issues. But by no means is the conflict exclusively or even primarily religious.

Conflicts in Northern Nigeria between Christians and Muslims have troubled this populous African oil state. At first glance, the violence would seem to be clearly religious. Boko Haram burns churches and conflicts ensue over imposition of Muslim Sharia law. However, the Sultan of Sokoto, His Eminence Alhaji Muhammad Sa'adu Abubakar III, and Nigerian Archbishop John Onaiyekan of Abuja, serve as co-chairs of the Nigeria Inter-Religious Council. Together, these two religious leaders represent about 95 percent of Nigerians, and they do not believe the conflict is primarily over religion. Nigeria is caught in the **conflict trap**, a pattern of recurring violence that occurs in countries with a youth bulge, flat or declining economy, a natural resource–dependent economy, and a history of previous violence. Conflicts over land, water, frustration with corrupt and incompetent government, and frustration with persistent poverty despite the riches of an oil economy, fuel dissatisfaction, in addition to tribal conflicts. In the Yoruba lands of southwest Nigeria, Christians and Muslims have a history of peaceful intermarriage, shared extended families, and harmonious living. Yet religion can be used to intensify conflicts, if religious leaders are not vigilant to stop this. The sultan notes that many "religious intensification" factors in Nigeria come from abroad, such as Pentecostals who create huge gatherings of hundreds of thousands of Nigerians while predicting that apocryphal end times call for extreme actions, and extremist Wahhabi Muslims from the Middle East and Taliban elements from Chad and Niger who also polarize. Nonreligious factors may form the roots of conflict, but religious factors can serve as tinder to spread and intensify conflict. They work together to deescalate conflict, and to disrupt calls to violence.[53]

The problem isn't religion per say, which is neither always peaceful or always violent. The problem is determining the specifics: under what conditions will what sorts of religions in what sorts of contexts aid peace or war? The answer turns significantly on *religious freedom* and the autonomy between church and state, or the lack thereof. Conventional wisdom views religious freedom at the margins of foreign policy, a subset of human rights concerns to be trumped by more pressing strategic or security concerns. However, research shows that religious freedom is actually a security concern. Where states seek to repress religion, violence often ensues—violence by the state against religious minorities, violence by majority groups who take their cues from state policy, and violence by religious minorities trying to protect their communities and beliefs.[54] Political scientist Daniel Philpott shows two important variables in whether religions will aid war or peace: differentiation and political theology, meaning institutions and ideas. Differentiation is the degree to which state and religious institutions are autonomous, separate and draw on their own sources of authority. When such differentiation is consensual (both state and religious organizations desire and seek differentiation), peace is likely. Neither party uses violence to subjugate the other, and minority religious groups are likewise secure from repression so they also do not seek violent redress. When state and religious organizations are integrated not differentiated (when state and religious authority overlap or are merged), trouble begins. If integration is not consensual (if the status was forced by either party), conflict remains either openly or repressed as parties would prefer greater autonomy. Even if the integration of state and religious institutions is consensual, if the political theology of the religion is exclusionary, conflict also ensues, as other religious groups seek protection from repression. Religion aids peace and democracy when institutions are differentiated and ideas embrace human rights and tolerance.

In practice, there are three types of violence in which religion is a component: religion as a component of nationalist identity politics; violent fundamentalist groups (some of whom use the technique of terrorism, sometimes due to apocalyptic views); and "just war."[55]

The most common form of religious violence is when religion is one component of the Molotov cocktail of violent nationalism. Recall that a nation is not a state. A nation is a group bound together by ethnic, racial, linguistic, cultural, historic, or religious identity. There are over 8,000 national groups around the world, and only 193 internationally recognized sovereign states. Most war is civil war, violence inside states rather than between states, and most civil wars involve conflicts over whether particular national groups should secede from or take over leadership of the state. National groups may be excluded from economic and political opportunities; their language or cultural traditions or human rights may be repressed by majority or ruling groups; or they may have previously ruled and be seeking a return to power. Religion is often invoked as one of the components of national identity, as in the Balkans. Religious differences may pale next to economic or political conflict triggers, and religious differences may not matter when economic times are good and politics are stable. But because religious differences are easier to name and target than perhaps other more entrenched but less transparent economic and political factors, religious identity can be used to spread, intensify, legitimize, and sacralize nationalist identity violence. It can be invoked (and often manipulated) by leaders of nationalist violence, although it is rarely the stand-alone or tentpole factor driving all nationalist violence. Nationalist identity violence spiked with the end of the Soviet empire. While recently this type of violence is receding, it is too early to tell whether the downward trend will continue.

The second form of religious violence perhaps most dominant in media headlines and in the minds of political elites today is violence by extremist religious groups. Violent extremists are themselves minorities within their larger religious traditions and those who promote violence are minorities within the minorities. Nevertheless, very small groups can have large impacts, particularly when they use the techniques of made-for-media terrorism and suicide bombings as force multipliers, to gain publicity and generate fear far in excess of the actual damages done by the attacks, as explained in chapter 8. The term "fundamentalism" is hotly contested. Many within the religious traditions from which fundamentalist groups hail decry the term, saying these groups do not represent the basic "fundamentals" of the faith at all but instead distort the faith. But the term can be useful across a wide variety of faith traditions to denote a "pattern of religious militance by which self-styled true believers attempt to arrest the erosion of religious identity, fortify the borders of the religious community, and create viable alternatives to secular structures and processes."[56] They feel endangered by secular and religious outsiders (who can be foreigners, those of another or no religion, as well as insufficiently zealous members of their own religion), in danger of losing members and their traditions dying off. They believe the world is divided unambiguously into good and evil, pure and impure, orthodox and infidel, often seen through "an apocalyptic framework: the world is in spiritual crisis, perhaps near its end, when God will bring terrible judgment on the children of darkness." They "tend to be exceptionalists," believing "themselves to living in a special dispensation—an unusual, extraordinary time of crisis, danger, or apocalyptic doom: the advent of the Messiah, the Second Coming of Christ, or the return of the Hidden Imam; and so on."[57] The urgency of this "special time requires true believers to make exceptions, to depart from the general rule of the tradition." Fundamentalists are minorities within their own religious traditions. A multiyear, multivolume study on fundamentalism by scholars such as Scott Appleby, Gabriel Almond, and Martin Marty, found only ten fundamentalist movements.[58] The vast majority of adherents to fundamentalist religious views are not violent. They feel their group and values are under siege, they want to safeguard and advance their group and values, but they do not espouse violence. However, for the minority of fundamentalists who do preach violence, this is how they do it: they select passages and elements from their religious traditions that seems to justify violence against evildoers (e.g., by cherry-picking elements from various religious traditions' versions of just war tradition); they ignore the religious traditions' injunctions against violence arguing that "extreme times call for extreme measures"; they chastise religious leaders and authorities who call for peace as "heretics"; and they convince particularly young, marginal, vulnerable, aggrieved people who have little or incomplete education or formation in their faith traditions, that violence is a sacred duty and that the glories of martyrdom await. In Appleby's terms, when there is weak religion, when people are not well educated in their own religious traditions (due to persecution or illiteracy, for example), they are vulnerable to such manipulations of their religious traditions. In Philpott's terms, these groups hold exclusionary political theologies that espouse violence, and they seek to integrate their religion with the institutions of the state so as to repress other religions and non-believers.

In the decades since the September 11 attacks in the United States, this type of religiously motivated violence is often high on the minds of policy makers because of the greater lethality of terrorist attacks in warzones (discussed in the terrorism chapter). While terrorist attacks are rare overall, their number and lethality per incident have been rising in war zones, resulting in greater attention to these types of violence. Greater political and religious reconciliation in Iraq, Syria, and Afghanistan would lessen all violence there, including religiously motivated violence and terrorist attacks.

The final, most rare, form of religiously motivated violence is when violence is sanctioned as a self-defensive "just war" necessary to oppose grave evil.[59] Just War Tradition (JWT) is a centuries-old guide to thinking about when it is morally justifiable to go to war (*jus ad bellum*) and how to fight war in an ethical manner (*jus in bello*). The morality of war is "always judged twice," considering both just reasons for going to war and means to fight war.[60] Before entering combat there must be a just cause such as self-defense, discerned by a right authority intent on peace and protecting the common good, using force only as a last resort, when success is possible and the harms of war will not be disproportionate to the reasons for going to war. Upon conducting hostilities, the means used must protect noncombatants and be proportionate and discriminate, not total. These JWT criteria offer a means for soldiers, statesmen, and citizens alike to consider whether and how to ethically use force. JWT stakes out the middle ground between committed non-violence (pacifism) on the one side, and political realism (realpolitik) on the other. In contrast to both, JWT holds that even under the extreme conditions of warfare, we are all moral beings capable of moral behavior and required to live up to our capacity for ethical treatment of other human beings. While JWT was honed by Western Christians (often Europeans), many of the key elements of just war thought predated Christianity, and are shared by a wide variety of cultures. JWT owes a debt to Africa,[61] to pre-Christian Greek and Roman law and customs, and to Judaic traditions that parallel JWT. The Islamic tradition of jihad (or justifiable holy war) also contains many parallels with JWT,[62] including just cause (self-defense and protection of the global Muslim community from threatened extinction), right authority, and protections on noncombatants and limitations on the conduct of war.[63] Parallels to JWT are found across cultures and religious traditions, from ancient Indian, Chinese, Hindu, Persian, Japanese Samurai, Aztec traditions, to the Shaolin kung fu monks, and the Plains Indians.[64]

Religiously sanctioned just wars are extremely rare. Most wars are not just, but are civil wars in which moral breaches occur on all sides, both prior to and during the conflict.[65] In the most violent twentieth century, only World War II somewhat met the criteria of a just war of self-defense, made necessary because of the failure of a decade's worth of other attempts to combat and contain Nazi evil. However, elements of JWT are routinely hijacked by the previously described violent fundamentalist groups. Different groups in different places distort JWT in common patterns: they claim an "emergency" context, in which the threatened extinction of their group and their values justifies the resort to violence in a common obligation to resist great evil. They ignore the components of the tradition that require that war be a last resort, invoked by right authority. And they not only disregard the prohibitions on deliberately targeting and killing noncombatants and other restrictions (proportionality, etc.), they do so intentionally, to attract greater attention to their causes precisely because they are flagrantly violating entrenched norms and laws shared universally.

There are three typical religious approaches to peace: nonviolence (sometimes called pacifism); just peace attempts to prevent violence, end violence, and rebuild societies after violence in just and sustainable ways so that violence will not return; as well as just war, which attempts to stop and limit violence.

JWT reminds us that peace is always the ultimate objective, and that is almost never justified. JWT also works to lessen and contain conflicts already begun. Regardless of whether the prior *jus ad bellum* conditions were met (and usually they are not), JWT still works to try to contain the conflict by limiting the means of warfare. But JWT tells us nothing about how to avoid war and build peace.

The second religious approach to peace is frequently called pacifism, but practitioners of this approach believe the term "nonviolent resistance" to be more accurate. Nonviolence is much more effective than violence. Nonviolence is more than twice as likely to succeed compared to violence, and nonviolence is much more likely to result in democratization and to prevent future outbreaks of violence, according to statistical comparisons of violence and nonviolence by Chenoweth and Stephan, and others.[66]

There is nothing "passive" about choosing nonviolence, and action is required to oppose great evil. This approach was practiced most memorably by Hindus led by Mahatma Gandhi to overturn British colonial rule in India in the 1940s, and by Christians led by Rev. Martin Luther King to oppose discriminatory rule in the United States during the Civil Rights movement of the 1950s and 1960s. Nonviolent resistance was also effective during the collapse of the Soviet empire, and of the South African apartheid state. People may espouse nonviolent resistance for secular reasons and often nonviolent groups partner with others, for example, with peacebuilders engaged in preventing or ending violent conflicts.

The final religious approach is just peace, and religious peacebuilding.[67] I contend that religious groups pursue Just Peace, based on several principles and associated practices. **Participation** expands the peace process to include women, youth, and victims of the conflict. **Restoration** is people building, rebuilding the whole human person and communities, economically, psychologically, and socially, not simply rebuilding roads and bridges destroyed by war, but rebuilding the human infrastructure. **Right relationship** is building respectful social connections among groups polarized and harmed by conflict. **Reconciliation** is healing the wounds of war, using truth telling, acknowledgment, and other means of restorative justice. **Sustainability** is putting in place just social structures so that peace will last.

Religious peacebuilders engage in a wide variety of holistic, relationship building practices during the entire conflict cycle, from conflict prevention to mediation and conflict resolution to postconflict reconstruction. States have severe capacity gaps in peacebuilding—states know how to fight wars, but they have little institutional capacity to prevent violence and to carry out postconflict reconstruction. The peace states seek is constrained by state sovereignty, national interest, and short time horizons, and emphasizes construction of material and state infrastructure. States have little-to-no capacity in reconciliation among conflicting groups, posttrauma healing and rebuilding of human relationships and communities. Religious organizations bring considerable capacity and legitimacy to these tasks, particularly reconciliation, healing, and relationship building. Because most conflicts are internal, state institutions are often inadequate to the tasks of peacebuilding. They may be seen as illegitimate (as one of the parties to the conflict) and incapable (weak, failed and failing states are often the sites of violent conflicts).

Resurgent religions can be extremely helpful to states challenged by peacebuilding. Failures to engage with religious groups in conflict prevention, conflict mediation, and postconflict reconstruction cost lives and lengthen wars. In conflicts with religious components, as in Iraq today, religious groups can be invaluable guides to the contours of the conflict (which states often do not understand), and partners in helping to defuse the religious components. But even in conflicts that are not religiously based, such as the Congo, religious peacebuilding can be invaluable as states lack the capacity and moral authority to build peace while religious organizations may have both. In many parts of the globe, like the Congo, religious institutions are the only actors left with much capacity and legitimacy, in the vacuum created by failed and failing states.

CONCLUSIONS

Religious actors are prestate actors. Ancient transnational networks are using new means to combat modern global issues, from climate change to human trafficking.

KEY TERMS

3 "I's," 142
Anti-Apartheid movement, 160
conflict trap, 174

differentiation of political
and religious institutions,
161

DISCUSSION QUESTIONS

1. Why are religious actors referred to as prestate actors? Why does this distinction matter?
2. Why did *Time* magazine publish a famous edition with the cover "God is Dead?" Why was this view common in the mid-twentieth century? Why did the headline prove incorrect?
3. Today, how are ancient transnational networks using new means to combat modern global issues? Give examples. What evidence do you see of religious actors addressing global issues, in your experiences and communities?
4. Describe some of the common ways of "getting religion wrong" in International Relations. What evidence of these do you see in news headlines or public discussion?
5. Describe the Conflict Trap. How do these factors describe many of the wars today?
6. Is the Israeli Palestinian conflict a religious war? Why or why not?
7. Why was the bloodiest century in human history not caused by religious conflict?
8. What evidence is there of religious actors aiding peace and democratization?
9. What conditions lead to religious engagement in conflict?
10. What happens when religion is resurgent, while many sovereign states are challenged, as is the case today? What evidence do you see of religious actors "filling the gaps" where states lack capacity?

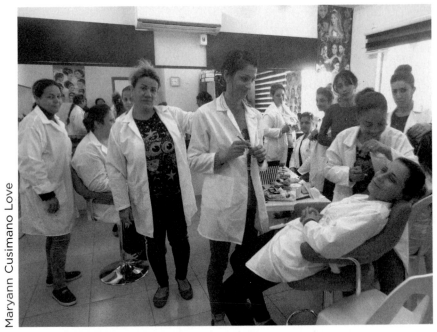

Maryann Cusimano Love

Jesuit refugee services job training program in Iraq.

6

Refugees, IDPs, and Migrants
People beyond Borders

■ ■ ■

The real tragedy is that these deaths are preventable. We need to ensure safe passage for all refugees and migrants, but also address the reasons people are migrating in the first place.

—Bill O'Keefe, Catholic Relief Services.[1]

There is no shame in being a refugee if we remember who we are. We are still the doctors, engineers, lawyers, teachers, students we were back at home. It was war and persecution that drove us from our homes in search of peace. That is refugee. That is who I am. Join me. Stand with us.

—Yusra Mardini,[2] Olympic swimmer and UN Good Will Ambassador for the UN High Commission of Refugees

My grandfather was one of the most famous poets in all of Somalia. Whenever I didn't feel well, he would recite his poems to me as we watched the sun set. His poems were like medicine. One morning, I woke up to a scary sound like angry bees coming from the street outside my window. There was gunfire everywhere. Was this what war sounded like? We couldn't play outside anymore. Everyone was frightened. My grandfather wrote me a short poem, and we read it aloud together: "When I get older, I will be stronger. They'll call me freedom, just like a waving flag."

—K'Naan,[3] musician, Refugee

We in the USA should embrace refugees, not fear them. The words on the Statue of Liberty shouldn't be an empty promise.

—Madeleine Albright,[4] refugee, and former Secretary of State

Turning away refugees is incompatible with America's values and our image of who we are.

—Henry Kissinger,[5] refugee, and former Secretary of State

RUMI TELLS ME of the night they fled ISIS. "I was a student at the University of Mosul, but Daesh (ISIS) took the University, took Mosul. A half million of us, we left before they took Mosul. My family we went with others from Mosul to the Christian villages in Nineveh. We were safer there. The Kurdish peshmerga fighters were protecting the minority villages. But then our cell phones started ringing. The peshmerga were leaving us, going back to Kurdistan. Daesh was coming and the Iraqi forces had run away. They wouldn't protect us. So we left with nothing but the clothes on our backs, squished three families into my uncle's car, my little cousins were crying, eighteen people in a car made for six. We saw many dead bodies, many bad things along the way. The drive to Erbil usually takes less than an hour. It took us eighteen hours. The roads were impossible, the largest traffic jam I've ever seen, clogged with cars, trucks, everyone was fleeing. In the end, we abandoned the car and went by foot. This was very hard on my father, who is old. It was over 100 degrees in the sun, and many people were collapsing with heart attacks, from stress, fear, the heat. We made it into Erbil and headed for St. Joseph's Church. We knew we'd be safe there. But the grounds were already full, so we headed nearby to Mar Elian Church, and camped there. People were sleeping in the church, on the pews, on the church grounds. For the first few nights we slept on the grass. Later, we got some tents, but these were not very good. We were wet whenever it rained. We hoped the fighting would stop, and we could go home quickly, but that didn't happen. We are stuck here. It is not safe to go back. But we cannot go forward.[6]

Rumi is not alone. Today, there are over 65 million people forced to flee homes, the largest number of refugees since the end of the Second World War. As I toured refugee camps in Iraq I heard many such stories. For young people like Rumi, fleeing may effectively end your education, limiting your present and future paths for jobs, earnings, health, and happiness. The average time of displacement is seventeen years for people forced from their homes. This is particularly problematic for youth. Missing out on schooling impairs their lifetime job and earning potential. It can be hard or impossible for displaced children and youth to resume their schooling. War and flight pulls them out of school, and lack of access to schools, including language, financial, and cultural barriers, can preclude them from resuming their studies along their flight path.

Many people, like Rumi, endure multiple displacements, as refugees may flee several times searching for safety. Minority communities are often decimated; before the US wars in Iraq, there were over a million Christians in Iraq, but today there are fewer than 200,000. These ancient communities are some of the last people on the planet who still speak Aramaic, the language of Jesus. Over one million Iraqis fled Iraq's sectarian violence into neighboring Syria, settling mostly in the capital Damascus, only to find themselves in the cross hairs of war again when Syria later plunged into violence.

Avin's family fled Syria when the Syrian civil war broke out. Avin was studying to be an engineer, but that path is closed to her now. There is no room in the local schools for displaced students, they do not speak the language, and they do not have money for private schools, or papers. She cannot get academic transcripts or other official documents transferred out of a war zone. Relief groups like Jesuit Refugee Services provide transitional education programs focused on language and computer skills and providing some simple employment skills like baking and haircutting which may help displaced families transition to new employment. Avin takes part in language, computer, and job training classes in the Jesuit Refugee Services community center in Erbil, Iraq. Finding even temporary work like cutting hair will be difficult due to the high unemployment rate in Iraq; she will not be an engineer, closing economic and development opportunities not only for her but also for her family and future children.[7]

Nearly a half million people have died in the Syrian civil war, between thousands of armed groups and the brutal dictatorship of President Assad, who indiscriminately bombs his own people with barrel bombs and even chemical weapons. Over half the country has fled the violence. Over six and a half million people fled within Syria, and another 5.6 million fled outside Syria. Most, like Avin, fled to a neighboring country. Turkey, Lebanon, and Jordan host most of the world's Syrian and Iraqi refugees; Pakistan and Iran host most of the world's refugees from neighboring Afghanistan. Avin follows her friends and neighbors who have fled using social media apps like Viber and WhatsApp. Some continued on to Turkey. From there some purchased transport in overcrowded, flimsy boats to travel across the Mediterranean Sea to Europe. Thousands have died at sea. Children's trauma healing drawings in the refugee centers tell their stories. "When I grow up I want to be a lifeguard, so I can save my friends who cannot swim."

"When I grow up I want to be a police man, so I can protect people." "When I grow up I want to be a builder, so I can rebuild my home and my church." "When I grow up I want to go home, to see my house and my dog and my fig tree."[8]

While the Middle Eastern wars in Syria, Afghanistan, and Iraq push people from their homes, in Africa conflict, famine, droughts, and food insecurity, also push record numbers of people to leave home. Josefa nearly died in the Mediterranean Sea, the world's deadliest border, while attempting to cross from Africa to Italy. She treaded water and clung to the board of a smashed fishing boat, while other children and women around her drowned. She was saved by the Spanish NGO Proactiva Open Arms, after Libyan and Italian government authorities passed her by.[9] In search of food, she was forced from her home in Cameroon. Cameroon suffers from food shortages due to climate change, and competition for food from Nigerian refugees who fled Boko Haram, and refugees fleeing civil war in the Central African Republic.[10] Josefina traveled north to Libya to board a boat to cross the Mediterranean Sea. Previously, dictators in North Africa, such as Muammar Gaddafi in Libya, prevented migration flows through their countries. The fall of dictators and the ongoing civil wars and unrest in North Africa has created vacuums of authority which are exploited by corrupt leaders, unscrupulous human smuggling and trafficking gangs. People flee famine, drought, and violence in Africa, making their way north to Libyan traffickers, who torture, beat and kidnap them, often holding them hostage until family members can pay ransom for their release. At the high point of the exodus in 2015, a million displaced persons came to Europe; over 300,000 sailed on the Mediterranean Sea from Libya. EU countries have since blocked these migration routes by giving money to Libya and Turkey to stop the migrants, and by increasing Libyan interceptions in the Mediterranean. They have offered money to African countries willing to repatriate migrants. They have also harassed humanitarians, who obey international law requiring sea rescue, with fines and court charges aimed at stopping the rescues. For example, Sarah Mardini, sister of Olympian Yusra Mardini, was arrested in Greece for her work with a charity rescue boat, an example of "the criminalization of solidarity."[11] Over 34,000 migrants have died in the Mediterranean since 2000. In 2016, over 5,300 migrants died while trying to flee for their lives. The actual death toll is likely much higher, as many deaths are unreported, and criminal gangs who traffick persons do not report deaths. Yet despite the headlines about migration to Europe and the U.S., fewer than 1 percent of refugees permanently

Figure 6.1 Major Source Countries of Refugees

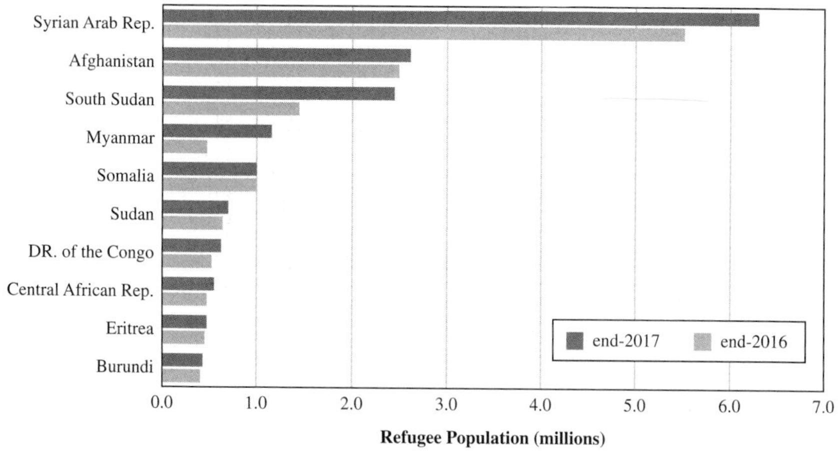

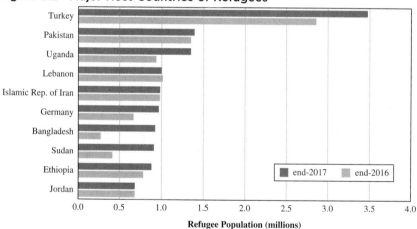

Source: United Nations High Commissioner for Refugees

Figure 6.2 Major Host Countries of Refugees

Source: United Nations High Commissioner for Refugees

resettle in foreign countries. Of 68.5 million forcibly displaced persons, fewer than 102,800 resettle abroad. Germany and Sweden lead as third-party resettlement countries.[12]

Of all the preceding examples, only Avan from Syria is a refugee. Those like Rumi in Iraq who fled violence and persecution by moving to another region of their home country are not refugees but internally displaced persons, never crossing an international border. The millions, like Josefina, fleeing for their lives from drought, famine, starvation, and natural disasters, are classified as migrants, not refugees; they cross an international border but are not fleeing because of a well-founded fear of persecution.

The **1951 UN Convention on Refugees** is the cornerstone of national and international laws on treatment of refugees. The key principle is **nonrefoulement**; a refugee must not be returned to a country where they face serious threats to their life or freedom. The law defines a **refugee** as any person who "owing to well-founded fear of being persecuted for reasons of race, religion, nationality, membership of a particular social group, or political opinion, is outside the country of his nationality, and is unable to return to it." Those escaping natural or economic disasters, and those displaced within their countries, are not refugees. Consider the musical "The Sound of Music." The Von Trapp family, on the run from the Nazis, certainly were fleeing a well-founded fear of political persecution. But while they were hiding in the convent or climbing the Alps, they were not yet refugees but internally displaced persons. Only when they crossed an international border did they satisfy the international legal definition of refugee, and qualify for asylum status in the country they entered.

WHY DOES IT MATTER HOW REFUGEES ARE DEFINED?

For people on the move, the legal definition of refugee seems full of arbitrary distinctions that only lawyers understand or love. People move to save their lives from a variety of threats to their survival: war, famine, violence, persecution, natural disasters, failed economies. But only some death threats count in international law as a "well-founded fear of persecution," and only some of those who are fleeing qualify for the ancient legal principle of **asylum,** affording international protections as refugees. The people traveling together for safety in caravans, presenting themselves to border agents at US ports of entry are not illegal immigrants. They are following the law, presenting themselves to government officers to make a formal asylum claim. Unlike migrants who are primarily single adults who seek to evade border agents in order to blend into the receiving country's economy, these asylum seekers are primarily families with children and unaccompanied children. They enter the country through legal ports of entry and present themselves to petition government authorities for asylum. They primarily come from the "Northern Triangle" countries of Honduras, Guatemala, and El Salvador, where during the Cold War the United States sent guns and money to support "anti-communist" combatants in these civil wars. When the Cold War ended, the guns and violence remained, leading many families and children today to flee the violence of government and criminal gangs.

The refugee definition matters because 145 countries are parties to the UN Convention and thus by international law are *not* supposed to turn away refugees but are expected to offer them asylum. The Convention commits the signatories not to return someone to a country where she/he would be in danger, in addition to offering protection to refugees by granting them the same rights as other foreigners living in their society. It also stipulates that states should not impose penalties on refugees when they have entered the country illegally or return a refugee to a country "where his life or freedom would be threatened on account of his race, religion, nationality, membership of a political social group or political opinion."[13] This does not mean that receiving countries are obligated to offer refugees citizenship. The law states only that host countries are not allowed to forcibly return refugees to their countries of origin, since to do so would be a death sentence, serving as an accomplice to murder, akin to sending Jewish refugees back to the Nazis during the Holocaust. International law is enforced by national governments; however, many countries today are violating the law regarding asylum and non-refoulement.

Based on the definition of a refugee as a person with a "well-founded fear of persecution" for reasons of race, religion, nationality, political opinion, or membership in a particular social group, the refugee definition is commonly understood to include three essential elements: (1) there must be a form of harm rising to the level of persecution, inflicted by a government or by individuals or a group that the government cannot or will not control; (2) the person's fear of such harm must be well founded—the US Supreme Court has ruled that a fear can be well-founded if there is a one-in-ten likelihood of its occurring; (3) the harm, or persecution, must be inflicted upon the person for reasons related to the person's race, religion, nationality, political opinion, or membership in a particular social group.[14]

Historically, the international definition of "refugee" has been interpreted primarily in the context of male asylum seekers, to the prejudice of women refugees. Male political dissident Andrei Sakharov of the former Soviet Union, who was persecuted for denouncing communist totalitarianism, was the classic image of a refugee. In these Cold War cases, an adjudicator had little difficulty recognizing that the harm suffered amounted to persecution, forming the basis for refugee protection.

But women and children make up 80 percent of refugee and internally displaced populations, and the claims of women asylum seekers often differ from those of men. "First, women often suffer harms which are either unique to their gender, such as female genital mutilation or forcible abortion, or which are more commonly inflicted upon women than men, such as rape or domestic violence. Second, women's claims differ from those of men in that they may suffer harms solely or exclusively because they are women, such as the policies of the Taliban in Afghanistan. And third, women often suffer harm at the hands of private individuals such as family members who threaten them with 'honor killings' or abusive spouses who batter them, rather than government actors."[15] Most judges and border agents are men, so rarely do women have their cases adjudicated by women. For example, women in Eastern Congo are routinely raped and mutilated as a weapon of war; over 5.4 million people died in the wars in the Democratic Republic of Congo from the late 1990s until today, and thousands more continue to be killed in violence since, in conflict facilitated and fueled over natural resources such as the coltan used in cell phones. UN Special Rapporteur on violence against women, Ms. Yakin Erturk noted "the scale and brutality of the atrocities amount to war crimes and crimes against humanity."[16] Girls as young as five and grandmothers as old as eighty are not immune to gang rapes, rapes with tree limbs, guns, machetes. Mothers are raped while their husbands and children are tied to trees and forced to watch. In a stunning betrayal, the victims are shunned, blamed for their own attacks which humiliate the family, or because they are infected by the attacks with HIV/AIDs and other diseases, or because many are impregnated with the children of these criminals and enemies.[17]

Do women fleeing rape or female genital mutilation[18] qualify as refugees? They are fleeing a well-founded fear of persecution due to membership in a social group (their gender), and they cross international borders and cannot return. But the UN Convention does not mention gender specifically, and various courts have ruled differently. Most immigration judges are men, so women asylum seekers rarely have their cases considered by women, who might have better understanding of their plight. International law cases are generally heard by domestic systems and courts, so each country (and sometimes different courts within the same country) can apply or interpret the law differently, and there is no "International Supreme Court" to appeal to for final decision or arbitration among conflicting decisions by lower courts. Some judges, concerned that allowing refugee status to women fleeing female genital mutilation would open up new refugee claims, have argued that female genital mutilation is an accepted "cultural practice" and does not rise to the threat status protected by the UN Convention. Some have argued that if women did not fight effectively against their rapists, then women were to blame for being raped. Others have ruled that the practice threatens the life and health of women due only to their membership in a social group (their gender), and therefore constitutes a well-founded fear of persecution as covered by the UN Convention.

What about women fleeing domestic violence? Should they be accorded refugee status? Rodi Alverado was sixteen when she married Francisco Osorio in Guatemala. Her husband brutally beat her and vowed to kill her. "Osorio raped and sodomized Rodi, broke windows and mirrors with her head, dislocated her jaw, and tried to abort her child by kicking her violently in the spine. Besides using his hands and his feet against her, he also resorted to weapons—pistol-whipping her and terrorizing her with his machete." Rodi's repeated attempts to obtain protection failed. The police and the courts refused to intervene because it was a "domestic matter" and because her husband was a former army soldier. Rosa fled to the United States, where her case was unresolved for over a decade. While she was eventually granted asylum, women still struggle to have gender-based violence considered in decisions on refugee status. While gender-based claims can no longer be summarily dismissed, they are still rarely accepted, and must be considered on a case-by-case basis.[19]

Unfortunately, Ms. Alverado's case is not an exception. "Honor killings" are the practice of murdering a woman in order to reclaim the family's "honor." A woman who is accused of socially unacceptable behaviors may be killed or brutally mutilated in order to wipe out the "blemish" on a family's good name. Offenses include walking without a male relative escort, being a victim of rape, kissing or engaging in sexual behavior out of wedlock, flirting, failing to serve a meal on time, seeking divorce, or seeking to choose one's own marriage partner rather than accede to an arranged marriage. In one case, "a husband murdered his wife based on a dream that she had betrayed him. In Turkey, a young woman's throat was slit in the town square because a love ballad had been dedicated to her over the radio. . . a 16-year-old mentally retarded girl who was raped in the Northwest Frontier province of Pakistan was turned over to her tribe's judicial council. Even though the crime was reported to the police and the perpetrator was arrested, the Pathan tribesmen decided that she had brought shame to her tribe and she was killed in front of a tribal gathering."[20]

In some countries, the practice is legal; in others, the law looks the other way as vigilante practice takes over. Estimates are that 5,000 women are killed in honor killings each year, but as the crime is generally unreported and unprosecuted, firm statistics are scarce.[21] In India alone, for example, the UN cites that 5,000 women are murdered each year because their bridal dowries are deemed insufficient. Honor killings have been reported to the United Nations (UN) in Afghanistan, Bangladesh, Great Britain, Brazil, Ecuador, Egypt, India, Iraq, Iran, Israel, Italy, Jordan, Pakistan, Morocco, Sweden, Turkey, Uganda, and the United States.

Slaves and victims of human trafficking are also people on the move who are accorded little protection. There are 26 million slaves in the world today, more than ever before in human history. Slavery is nowhere legal, but the practice persists around the world, according to the UN. Seventeenth-century slaves were considered valuable property to be defended, but twenty-first-century slaves are primarily women and children; they cost little and are easy to replace and thus are considered disposable.[22] Eighty percent of people trafficked are women and girls, and more than 50 percent are minors.[23]

Human traffickers use a variety of methods. Children are kidnapped to work as child soldiers, as laborers in industries that value their small size and nimble fingers, for example, the Indian carpet industry, and as camel jockeys in the Gulf States. Women and girls in poor countries answer employment ads for legal jobs in developed countries as domestic workers, waitresses, and so on. When they report to the employer, they hand over their passports and ID so the employer can supposedly photocopy and verify the information, and use the documents to arrange border crossings. The girls soon learn they have been enslaved into the sex trade. They have no documents, are moved illegally across borders and sold in slave markets, are brutally beaten, and are told that if they work hard they can pay back their "debt" to the brothel owners for room and board to earn their freedom. Many do not know their whereabouts, do not speak the language to be able to ask for help, do not know their rights, are incarcerated in the brothels, and report that the police are often customers, not would-be rescuers. Those that do risk beatings or death and are able to escape may find themselves imprisoned for prostitution and illegal immigration (even though they were forced into both). If deported back to their home countries, they are often ostracized by their families and communities for bringing dishonor to the family (and/or for being infected with HIV/AIDS, a common fate of those in the sex industry), and are then vulnerable to fall back into the hands of traffickers. Whereas the victims of trafficking are too often prosecuted rather than protected, traffickers often bribe local law enforcement and avoid prosecution. The United States works to pressure foreign governments to do more to prosecute human trafficking and protect victims through the **Trafficking in Persons Victims Protection Act,** a law that seeks to prevent human trafficking, protect victims, and prosecute traffickers. But too often victims are not able to access help even when there are laws on the books to supposedly protect them.[24]

While human rights groups argue that women fleeing honor killings, domestic violence, genital mutilation, or human trafficking meet the standard of "a well-founded fear of persecution," many governments have disagreed. An Afghan woman fleeing the abusive practices of the Taliban government, a Jordanian woman fleeing the practice of honor killing, and a Somali woman fleeing genital mutilation were all denied political asylum and refugee status and were ordered returned to their persecutors.[25] The legal definition of refugee matters quite intimately to people on the move.

GLOBALIZATION HELPS PEOPLE MOVE

Today, there are more than 68.5 million refugees and forcibly displaced people around the world; 25.4 million are refugees and 40 million are **IDPs.** Eighty percent of refugees are women and children. Many are victims of protracted conflicts and have not been able to return home for several years or even decades. The average time of displacement for a refugee is 17 years. Three countries are responsible for sending almost 50 percent of the world's refugees: Syria, Afghanistan, and South Sudan.[26]

People are pushed into leaving home by war, violence, persecution, disease, environmental degradation, famine, economic crises, and natural disasters. People are pulled into leaving home by more attractive circumstances elsewhere (peace, jobs, and educational opportunities), compared to less promising conditions at home. Countries court rich or educated workers from abroad. But countries resist foreign population flows of refugees and economic migrants, perceiving more vulnerable populations as a liability, a strain on public services and budgets, and a source of societal instability and violence, even though the data shows the opposite. Trying to prevent population flows, many countries keep refugees warehoused in camps, separated from society, unable to farm or work, or return to normal social patterns. Food to the camps may be rationed or cut back to encourage refugees to return home (whether or not conditions are safe for them at home). Families are often separated in camps, crime and rape too often occur, and the armies or militants who chased refugees from their homes may enter the camps and continue their violence.

Refugee flows mostly originate in the developing world. Sadly, the top sending countries reads like a Who's Who of conflict and instability. Most refugees come from just five countries: Syria, Afghanistan, South Sudan, Somalia, and Myanmar account for 68 percent of the world's refugees. Syria, Afghanistan, and South Sudan combined account for almost half of all refugees. Those seeking refuge are usually headed for neighboring countries. Developing countries receive 85 percent of the world's refugees. The world's poorest region, sub-Saharan Africa, hosts nearly a third of the world's refugees. The largest receiving countries in the world are Turkey, Pakistan, Lebanon, Iran, Jordan, Ethiopia, Kenya, Uganda, Germany, and Chad.[27]

In addition to these continual refugee flows there are an estimated 244 million migrants around the world. Contrary to popular myths, **migrants** account for only 3 percent of the world's population, and move from middle-income countries to more developed economies. Sixty percent of migrants move to Asia and Europe. The top sending countries are India, Mexico, Russia, China, Bangladesh, Syria, Pakistan, and Ukraine, and they move to more developed countries such as Saudi Arabia, the United States, Germany, the United Kingdom, and the Russian Federation, facilitated by open societies, open technologies, and open economies. Younger workers go to graying countries and communities where population is aging and declining and workers are needed. Ironically, the oldest countries and municipalities suffering population decline, that need younger migrants the most, have the most anti-immigrant views. Seventy-five percent of migrants are workers between the ages of 20 and 64, and they have counteracted population decline in Europe. Foreign workers are the backbone of Persian Gulf states and far outnumber citizens. In the United Arab Emirates, Qatar, Kuwait, and Saudi Arabia, more than 85 percent of the population are migrants. Sixty-four countries have higher per capita immigration rates than the United States (14 percent), such as Australia, where 28 percent of the population is foreign born, Canada, where 22 percent were born outside Canada,[28] Singapore (62 percent), Jordan (40 percent), Lebanon (33 percent), Switzerland (28 percent), Sweden (19 percent), and Ireland (16 percent). Low birth rates and aging populations in many developed countries (particularly in Europe) create labor shortages, particularly for manual labor as well as labor shortages in the information technology and health-care sectors. Companies encourage migration so they may recruit needed workers. The fastest growing population of migrants is in the Middle East, where workers move to be part of oil-rich economies. Since 2007 migration reversed between the United States and Mexico, as Mexico's economy has grown; over 1 million people who were born in Mexico and working in the United States returned to their homeland. Migrants send a portion of their income back to their families in their countries of origin. Globally, **remittances** totaled over $600 billion in 2015, a large portion of many developing countries' economies.[29]

Developed states have resorted to ever-new technologies and strategies intended to deter, divert, and preempt migrant flows along their borders. Aiming to detect illegal "human freight," British border authorities in Calais send trucks through X-ray scanners and use thermal imaging and carbon monoxide tests to identify people's heat and breathing inside freight containers.[30] In the world's most dangerous migration route, thousands risk their lives every year by crossing the Mediterranean Sea in unsafe boats; over 34,000 people have died while trying to cross the Mediterranean into Europe since 2000.[31]

Sovereign borders do not keep out people flows. Most enter legally at airports and ports. Migrants and asylum seekers often benefit from the same information, technology, and dwindling transportation costs that made globalization possible in the first place. They can resort to services provided by illegal smuggling networks that specialize in human trafficking via air and road transportation, or global container trade.[32] And they are drawn to take dirty and manual labor jobs that the local population does not want to do. For example, citizens of the United Arab Emirates and those in many other Persian Gulf states receive government subsidies from the country's oil income. They are not interested in working construction jobs in the searing desert heat; those jobs are done by foreign workers.

Sovereign institutions struggle to respond to the needs of migratory populations. Plagued by application backlogs, the often-inefficient systems have created a general "impression of governmental incompetence and incapacity."[33] Applications can take years to process—one asylum-seeker in Britain was detained for eight years[34]—but asylum seekers and migrants do not have a voice or a vote in the democratic politics of their host countries.[35]

Economic migrants, however, are becoming increasingly powerful in the political systems of the countries they left. Monies sent home from emigrants are "one of the most visible manifestations of today's migration,"[36] and have become a huge income source in many developing countries. Remittances total more than 613 billion dollars. India is the world's largest recipient of remittances, receiving more than $69 billion dollars per year, followed by China (64 billion), the Philippines (33 billion), and Mexico (31 billion).[37] Behind foreign direct investment, remittances are the second largest component of external financing in the Latin America, and provide an important lifeline to countries such as El Salvador, Guatemala, and Honduras.[38]

"**Remittance management**" serves as an example of a public–private partnership beyond sovereignty, involving the governments and the private sector in both home and host countries. As remittances exceed official development assistance, Western governments like to think of the monies sent to local communities as development aid that can alleviate poverty in developing countries.[39] Because these flows could be even higher if the transfer was handled more efficiently, governments work to cut transfer costs and foster competition between banks. Banks are eager to increase their share in a market that has been dominated by transfer agencies like Western Union and informal operators. The World Bank supports efforts to transmit remittances digitally via mobile phones and Pay Pal, making transfers faster and cheaper.[40] Public and private actors are interested in improving existing channeling structures, and Western governments also work to stop black market money transactions beyond sovereignty. Expatriate migrants form hometown associations through which remittances are pooled and used for local community projects in their respective home countries, provinces, and villages. Home town associations serve as transnational advocacy networks, shining a light on local issues and impacting community development policies.[41] Programs have been largely successful, and according to the World Bank, monies "appear to be a more stable source of external financing and to be more evenly distributed among and within countries" than other foreign investment sources.[42]

Migrants are also powerful voting constituencies in elections in their home countries. Elections now go beyond sovereignty, as Mexican Presidential candidates campaign in California, Texas, and Florida to earn the votes of Mexicans who have emigrated to the United States, but can cast absentee votes in elections in Mexico.[43] From the Philippines to Iraq and South Africa, overseas citizens vote in state and federal elections in their home countries of origin.[44]

NGOs SERVING PEOPLE ON THE MOVE

NGO numbers and capabilities to serve as advocates and provide services for the displaced have increased as a result of the expanded communications and networking capacities allowed by globalization. On the pro side, NGOs provide much-needed services to vulnerable populations who are truly beyond sovereignty, often not served well by either the governments of sending countries or host countries. NGOs can be powerful advocates and watchdogs for the rights of people on the move, providing a voice for those who otherwise would have no voice in international politics, and bringing attention and pressure on abusive and corrupt governments and policies. On the con side, NGOs operate at the intersection between the global and the local, and are challenged to walk on that fault line when international practices or concerns do not match local ones. Do international NGOs impose one-size-fits-all packages of services, or do the people served have an ability to articulate and participate in meeting their own needs, both short- and long-term? Are the practices of NGOs transparent and accountable? When governments are corrupt or abusive, do NGOs have the ability to challenge this, or must they "go along to get along," looking the other way or participating in corrupt practices in order to be able to do their jobs and serve people on the move?

NGOs provide services for people on the move at all stages of their movements: NGOs provide emergency relief and everyday food, clothing, shelter, medical, legal, and educational services to refugee settlements and IDP camps, assist in postconflict resettlement and reconstruction efforts once they can return home, as well as guide them through the complex asylum process in receiving countries. Suffering from budget cuts, the UNHCR (the Office of the **United Nations High Commissioner for Refugees,** traditionally the lead agency for refugee relief) increasingly relies on NGOs for the work on the ground. At the same time, donor governments have shown a tendency to directly contact and work through NGOs, which are frequently viewed as a more flexible and cheaper alternative to working through governments.[45] Unlike the UNHCR, NGOs also do not need the permission of sovereign governments to assist IDPs in relief efforts that go beyond sovereignty.[46]

Field NGOs, both indigenous and international, play a crucial role in the "on-site" assistance of refugees and IDPs. Their very presence can be essential for the safety of displaced people, as they serve as a deterrent against violent attacks inside and outside the confinements of their camps.[47] Basic onsite services generally include the distribution of food rations and provision of health care to meet everyday needs. NGOs may provide trauma and psychological counseling, human rights education, and legal assistance.

Other NGO activities are geared toward the future and designed to increase the self-reliance and dignity of displaced persons. As discussed earlier, Jesuit Refugee Services offers education, sewing, computers, baking, salon, small business, and handicraft opportunities to help refugees and internally displaced persons return to work and become self-sufficient. Refugee assistance may include micro development loans and access to financial services. NGO work on the ground often involves long-term development projects as well, from clean water to infrastructure to environmental protection, reforestation, and soil conservation projects, as NGOs work to ensure that local communities also benefit from services, so as not to sow enmity between refugees, IDPs, and receiving communities.

While many of these initiatives can revive local economies and reduce strains between local and refugee populations, NGO supply structures can also have detrimental effects. NGO services may undermine state structures that are already too weak to perform these functions and provide for their own people. In the case of large, long-term refugee camps in Tanzania, the local benefits of NGO services were so dramatic that the UN called the full repatriation of the refugees to their home countries "the worst-case scenario for the [nearby villages] in terms of access to services utilized in the camps for local populations who have no other facilities to turn to."[48] Governments are not oblivious to the possible effects of these parallel NGO structures. Governments may be wary and monitor NGOs because "their population usually feels more related to (foreign) NGOs, who are, after all, their main service providers, than to their government. This erodes the government's base of support."[49] Nondemocratic governments, like Sudan, are suspicious of NGO projects involving civic or human rights education, wary that it might lead people to question the ruling elite.

NGO relationships with local governments are usually complicated. NGOs walk a fine line: cooperation with local governments may be necessary to help provide refugees with security and access local economic systems. However, NGOs serve as watchdogs and advocates for refugees, and must be accountable to their donors, so NGOs are often critical of government actions, which may put their personnel and programs in danger, as when the government of Sudan expelled many foreign NGOs assisting refugees from Darfur.[50] NGOs may avoid confrontations with the government for fear that governments might take revenge and close them down. In these situations, NGOs working in transnational networks have advantages because it is easier for them to join forces and discuss their experiences with international human rights agencies, who may publicize and decry government abuses without revealing local NGO sources.[51]

The sheer number of different NGOs, both local and international, creates competition between NGOs and poses challenges for the coordination of relief efforts and long-term development. NGOs need to coordinate their activities among themselves and with fellow international actors. In times of emergency, local organizations may be "pushed aside" and "cannibalized" by larger and better-equipped international NGOs, which might also seek to recruit their personnel. Sometimes collaboration between NGOs is further complicated by the fact that some NGOs have become hybrid organizations with diffuse agendas, and might also be accountable to their donors (DONGOs) or the local government (GONGOs). As local NGOs are attuned to their community's needs and problems, their "embeddedness" can also affect their "objectivity." There is a risk that NGOs might become entangled in power politics as humanitarian operations can be used to justify foreign interventions and facilitate convenient supply lines for troops and warring factions.

Conversely, critics argue that NGOs (as the operational arm of the international donor community) too often acquiesce to local practices and fail to use the "power of the purse" to ensure basic rights of those refugees whose status has remained in limbo, sometimes for whole generations. NGOs campaign against "refugee warehousing," which refers to refugees who have been living in refugee camps for five or more years and are deprived of the right to work or move freely. Host governments often isolate refugees, who remain cut off from local markets and dependent on international aid, in an attempt to reduce the attractiveness of their country as a permanent resettlement site.

NGOs face a number of "balancing act" challenges: short- vs. long-term activities; relief and development vs. justice and peacebuilding activities; activities that address symptoms or underlying causes. For example, Catholic Relief Services had been active in relief, development, refugee, and IDP work in Rwanda for more than three decades when the Rwandan genocide broke out in April 1994, killing 800,000 and displacing over a million more. CRS had known of the underlying fault lines in Rwandan society but had not attempted to resolve them, instead working around them to deliver relief and development services. As Fr. Bill Headley of CRS described it,

> Peace had not been part of the mission of CRS. It had not been part of what we did. We had competencies in agriculture, health, education

and a number of other social service disciplines. . . And so, CRS did its development work and did it well. What we were not prepared to do was make peace. When the genocide occurred, CRS' projects were wiped out in days; many of the people we had served became the "well-fed dead." After and partly because of the genocide, CRS took a hard look at itself. This introspection called us to realize that we could no longer just address the symptoms of conflict-stimulated crisis: burned out houses, food shortages and refugee movements. We also had to attack the systems and structures that underlie oppression and poverty. . . Today, peacebuilding is an agency-wide priority for CRS.[52]

CRS's story is not unique among NGOs. All organizations must balance concerns over mission-creep with questions of long-term effect and sustainability. Is success providing emergency food assistance reliably for years to refugees who are in limbo, restricted to camps, not allowed to move forward or move back? Or is success helping refugees to make new lives abroad and resolving conflicts so they may repatriate back home, creating sustainable livelihoods so they will not need future emergency food aid? Organizations that serve refugees must adapt with the needs of changing populations and situations.

NEVER AGAIN: THE HISTORY OF THE UNHCR

The Office of the United Nations High Commissioner for Refugees was created with the experience of World War II and the Holocaust in mind, but has had to adapt since its inception. On May 13, 1939, the **S.S.** *St. Louis* passenger ship set sail from Hamburg, Germany. Nine hundred of its 937 passengers were German Jews fleeing Hitler's Nazi regime to join relatives or start new lives in the Americas. But when the ship arrived in Havana, the Cuban government refused entry to the passengers. The captain then sailed the ship to Florida, but the US government also refused to admit the refugees; the Coast Guard even fired a warning shot to turn the ship away from the US coastline. The ship's passengers, dubbed "the Voyage of the Damned," then appealed to other countries to save them from the certain death awaiting should they be returned to Nazi Germany. Belgium, Holland, France, and England eventually admitted the refugees, but the first three countries were overrun by the Nazis within months. The *St. Louis* passengers died in the Holocaust along with other European Jews who were unable to escape. Only the few passengers admitted into England survived.[53]

After the Nazi regime's ouster and the end of World War II, memory of the Holocaust galvanized international human rights groups. The establishment of the Universal Declaration of Human Rights, the International Convention to Prevent Genocide, and the United Nations High Commissioner for Refugees were all informed by the Holocaust and the motto "Never again." The 1951 UN Convention on Refugees' definition of a refugee as any person who "owing to well-founded fear of being persecuted for reasons of race, religion, nationality, membership in a particular social group, or political opinion, is outside the country of his nationality, and is unable to return to it," becomes more understandable in the context of the Holocaust. Had this treaty been in force before World War II, the thinking went, countries would not have been allowed to turn away Jews fleeing Nazi persecution. People fleeing persecution, refugees, ought to be allowed protected status and not be forcibly returned to their home countries and the peril that awaits them there.

The Cold War left its mark on the Refugee Convention. As the world became split into the Communist East and the Democratic West, the refugee definition was used to embarrass the Soviet Union and Eastern bloc countries. Defectors leaving the Soviet bloc by definition were welcomed into the West as refugees. They did not have to prove that they particularly or personally had a well-founded fear of persecution, as did those coming from Africa or other regions. Soviet defectors were welcomed as refugees simply because they hailed from a communist state, and the existence of these defectors was used in the propaganda war between East and West to show the deficiencies of the communist system (how good could the communist dream really be if people were fleeing it?). This policy was abruptly changed when the Berlin Wall fell in 1989 and the USSR dissolved in 1991. The reversal shocked many defecting from Russia shortly after the political changeover, who were surprised to find they no longer had special treatment, and had to show a well-founded threat of persecution to themselves particularly, as did any other asylum applicant.

The UNHCR began in this climate after World War II. With a three-year mandate, it was believed to be a temporary agency that would close its doors after having resettled those people displaced by World War II. Unfortunately, wars and persecution continued. The UNHCR mandate was extended every five years to serve the growing number of people that were displaced in the wars of colonial independence in Asia and Africa during the 1950s, 1960s, and 1970s.[54] As an international agency of the United Nations, the UNHCR dealt with refugees displaced across borders, tending to refugees' needs in the relatively sheltered environment of their new host countries. Toward the end of the Cold War, the increase in civil wars in which civilians were a common target of violence brought new challenges to the UN relief agency. Originally, with a mandate to serve only refugees, the UN extended the organization's mission to also serve IDPs (the internally displaced) in 1992 in response to the war in Bosnia Herzegovina, and appointed Francis Deng as the Representative on Internally Displaced Persons.[55] The decision heralded the beginning of a new era in which the UNHCR's mandate of assisting and protecting refugees was expanded to include IDPs, thus going beyond sovereignty.

As the former state of Yugoslavia broke apart in civil wars in the Balkans, the problems associated with only helping refugees became apparent. Slobodan Milosevic, president of the former Republic of Yugoslavia and head of its armed forces, was the first head of state to be placed on trial for crimes against humanity and violations of the Geneva Conventions and the laws of war; he died in prison before the trial's end.[56] Milosevic's charges were due to his acts of ethnic cleansing, attempting to force ethnic Bosnians, Croatians, and Albanians out of lands he wanted to claim for Serbia. In this case, if the UNHCR only tended to people's needs after they left their homes and crossed an international border, was the UNHCR in some way aiding and abetting ethnic cleansing? Some argued that the UNHCR should attend to the needs of internally displaced persons before they crossed international borders and became refugees. It was not enough to help refugees after the fact; UNHCR should be working to prevent the dire circumstances that caused people to flee. More narrow political interests were also in play. Western European countries were interested in preventing refugee flows. If people could be encouraged to stay in their home countries, it would relieve the strain on host countries caused by refugee flows.[57] In Bosnia, the UNHCR was thus tasked with creating safe areas of "humanitarian space" for civilians, so they would not have to leave. Once the fighting broke out, however, the UNHCR faced an impossible mission. As the conflict moved, previously "safe areas" became areas of war. UNHCR often had to negotiate with the warring parties in order to get aid shipments through to the civilian population, and the UNHCR could not protect civilians from hostile factions determined to implement ethnic cleansing. The UN introduced peacekeeping troops, UNPROFOR, to try to stabilize the situation. But the introduction of UN peacekeeping troops undermined UNHCR's role as a neutral provider of humanitarian aid, and the peacekeepers' limited mandate made them ineffective and unable to provide the support UNHCR needed. A mission to save people from refugee miseries thus "took on the characteristics of preventing flight rather than changing conditions."[58]

The case of the former Yugoslavia illustrates the ongoing difficulties the UN and relief agencies face in trying to deliver humanitarian assistance in the midst of conflict. It also shows that while people and relief agencies move beyond sovereign borders, state actors can undermine attempts to help IDPs and refugees. States pushing people out may not want outsiders "meddling" in their affairs, and states receiving refugees may not want them and may try, despite the refugee convention, to make it difficult for refugees to enter their countries and unattractive for them to stay.

Migration Trends

Not one of the September 11, 2001, attackers entered the United States as a refugee claiming asylum. As discussed in the chapter on terrorism, most terrorist attacks are perpetrated in warzones, by local, not foreign-born citizens. Similarly the crime rate among migrants is lower than the crime rate among the domestic population. Nevertheless, after September 11 attacks, and after the war in Syria, refugee and asylum and immigration programs came under increased scrutiny, and anti-immigration platforms thrived in the politics of Western countries. Today, President Trump has greatly reduced refugee admissions. In the past, the United States allowed refugees hurt by US foreign wars to enter the United States. Following the Vietnam War, the United States welcomed 800,000 refugees displaced by those wars. Following the Cold War, the United States allowed 130,000 refugees admission. As the number of refugees worldwide is at an all-time high, President Trump has slashed refugee admissions to an all-time low, allowing only 22,491 claims, the lowest number of refugees admitted in over four decades.[59] He seeks to deport thousands of Vietnamese refugees who have lived in the United States for over two decades, since they arrived as children. Statistics cannot do justice to the suffering these families experience.[60]

PROSPECTS FOR THE FUTURE

People are hardwired to survive. Thus, people have always moved to flee violence, persecution, disease, famine, disaster, and to find a better place in the world for themselves and their families. The modern period of globalization makes it easier than ever before for people to move across sovereign borders. The challenges presented by people on the move will not go away.

The push factors of war, violence, persecution, disease, environmental degradation, famine, economic crises, and "natural" disasters show no signs of abating. In fact quite the opposite has been true. With more people than ever before on the planet, people are building large and permanent nonsustainable settlements, in coastal and vulnerable areas, while weather cycles are ever more deadly and costly. As global climate change increases, sea levels rise and weather patterns change, forcing people to move. The United Nations estimates 200 million **environmental refugees** will exist by 2050, dwarfing the numbers of "political" refugees by orders of magnitude. We are already seeing these "environmental refugees." Residents of Pacific Islands have had to move as rising seawaters have submerged their lands. As one evacuating islander put it, "All those big countries like America and Russia and in Europe are making all the pollution, but we are the ones who are suffering for it." New Zealand, one of the few countries to acknowledge and plan for environmental refugees, has agreed to accept 11,000 Tuvaluan island residents who will be forced to leave their home.[61]

Additionally, the flow of 24/7 information gives pull factors a loud megaphone with global reach. There has always been inequality in the world. But people today are more likely to know that there are places in the world where people don't suffer from war, violence, persecution, disease, environmental degradation, famine, economic crises, and disaster, and to know how to get there. Demographic trends ensure that pull factors will be with us for some time. Developed countries are graying, while developing countries have majorities of young people of working age. Developed countries need to import labor to sustain their economies, lifestyles, and aging populations.

Addressing push factors alleviates the root causes that force people unwillingly out of their homes. To protect people in their home communities from forced displacement, governments and the private sector must work together to foster peace, build sustainable economies and stable environments, and protect human rights.

Stopping and prosecuting practices such as human trafficking, female genital mutilation, honor killings, and other violence against women, will help protect women and allow them and their children to remain in their homes. Some progress has been made, as the United States and the UN have enacted anti trafficking laws and conventions that pressure action by other states.[62] Much work remains to be done, however, as millions are still victims of these practices, in developed and developing countries alike.

These issues are linked. For example, people may be forced from their homes due to food shortages, but famines are political rather than natural disasters. Even when crops fail or drought prevails, food is generally available in other parts of the country or region, but food is not distributed to vulnerable populations for political reasons. Food may be used as a weapon by conflicting sides, as in the Somali famine of 1992.[63] Starvation may be used to punish rebels, to achieve ethnic cleansing, to make a population docile or to flush out insurgents, as in Sudan, or the Irish potato famine of 1846–1850. And refugee camps may be deprived of food in order to push refugees out of host countries. Alleviating the underlying conflicts and environmental degradation that cause food shortages prevents not only starvation, malnutrition, and the related diseases that prey on compromised immune systems, but it also prevents refugee flows.

Lessening push factors also decreases pull factors, which are often a matter of relative gains. Leaving home is never easy and extracts a host of social, political, economic, emotional, familial, and spiritual costs. These costs loom larger and life abroad looks less attractive when life at home holds more promise.

But minimizing push and pull factors will not eradicate them. People will vote with their feet as long as global inequalities persist in human security; political and religious rights and freedoms; education, job, and economic opportunities; and safe environments. Personal security will always trump deference to sovereignty. As long as people continue to move, and governments respond insufficiently to the needs of people on the move, NGOs and IGOs will continue to step into the gap, serving in critical capacities and at times challenging states. Larger networks of people, money, and services exist and work in these gaps of sovereignty.

Previous forms of political organization took a more flexible approach toward migratory populations. As sovereignty tied territory to jurisdiction, people were no longer defined as "children of God" or other more mobile identities, but primarily as citizens of a particular geographic space. Civic rights and governmental responsibilities depended on where you lived. Counterintuitively, today attempts to harden and militarize borders against population flows have the unintended consequence of increasing the number of permanent illegal aliens resident in developed countries. When borders are more permeable, people prefer to move back and forth with circumstances or with the employment market, retaining their homes abroad. But as immigration becomes more restrictive, the cost and danger of border crossings make trips back and forth too difficult and risky. Families become split, and efforts to keep out illegal aliens work perversely to wall them in. Attempts to manage population flows must begin with the recognition that developed economies critically depend on imported labor and will continue to do so as their populations age. A globalization that protects and defends capital flows but not people flows is highly problematic, leads to pernicious injustices, and fuels security problems. From the Democratic Republic of Congo to Europe, improperly handled population flows can lay the groundwork for conflicts to come.

The growth of international humanitarian law, such as the International Conventions on Refugees and Human Rights, and the practices of NGOs and IGOs are expanding the notions of human rights and governmental responsibilities regardless of a person's residence or country of origin. As states increasingly contract out aid and social service functions to NGOs, they aid the growth of nonstate actors, which work to promote ideas of portable human rights regardless of geographic borders. People have fundamental human rights regardless of the countries they find themselves in. States and MNCs have an interest in expanding human rights beyond sovereign borders, if only to protect their own industries and populations from conflict and instability. We need to move from reactive responses to flows of people after the fact, to more proactive responses to the underlying causes that force people to move.

KEY TERMS

1951 UN Convention on
   Refugees, 188
asylum, 188
environmental refugees, 204
honor killings, 191
IDP, 193
migrants, 194
nonrefoulement, 188
refugee, 188

remittances, 195
remittance management, 196
S.S. *St. Louis*, 200
Trafficking in Persons Victims
   Protection Act, 193
United Nations High
   Commissioner for
   Refugees, 197

DISCUSSION QUESTIONS

1. Consider the stories of Rumi from Iraq, Avin from Syria, and Josefa from Cameroon. Only one of these young people meets the definition of refugee. Why?

2. Most refugees and displaced people are children. What is the immediate impact on their education? What long-term impact will this have on their entire lives?

3. What is asylum? Why is it an ancient legal principle?

4. What is the difference between asylum seekers and migrants? Why are people traveling in caravans and presenting themselves to border officials at legal ports of entry into the United States?

5. What is the legal definition of refugee? Who is included in that definition? Who is left out? What sorts of "fleeing for your life" do not count for legal protections? Why does this definition matter to people on the move?

6. Eighty-five percent of refugees and displaced persons are hosted in poor, developing, often neighboring countries. Why do those with the least resources host the most refugees and displaced persons? Why do most refugees and displaced persons not seek resettlement in rich countries, but instead stay closer to home?

7. Most refugees and displaced persons are women and children. Why do more men stay behind and more women and children flee?

8. What are honor killings? Why can many men literally "get away with murder," if they kill a woman?

9. Slavery is illegal. So why are there so many modern-day slaves? What methods are used by human traffickers?

10. Most migrants are workers from middle-income countries. Why do many developed countries depend on foreign workers? Do you see or have any experiences of this trend in your communities?

11. Why are 85 percent of the people in Saudi Arabia migrants, not citizens?

12. How do migrants have economic power?

13. What was the story of the SS St. Louis? Why was it called the "voyage of the damned?" What does the motto "Never Again" mean regarding refugees?

14. Environmental refugees are increasing, dwarfing the numbers of "traditional" refugees. What evidence do you see of this trend of people moving due to storms and "natural disasters"?

15. Describe the "balancing act" NGOs face in helping forcibly displaced people.

16. Famines are political rather than natural disasters. What does this mean? Can you think of any examples?

Dr. George Awuni, CRS partner at the sub-Saharan Agriculture Research Institute, Ghana.

7

Environment and Health

Caring for Our Common Home

■ ■ ■

We must care for Earth, our common home.

—Pope Francis, Laudato Si

Pollution causes 16 percent of all deaths globally, three times more deaths than AIDS, tuberculosis, and malaria combined; and fifteen times more than all wars and other forms of violence. It kills more people than smoking, hunger and natural disasters. In some countries, it accounts for one in four deaths. Pollution disproportionately kills the poor and vulnerable . . . Children face the highest risks because small exposures to chemicals in utero and early childhood can result in lifelong disease and disability, premature death, as well as reduced learning and earning potential.

—The Lancet Medical Journal, Commission on Pollution and Public Health[1]

IT WAS SUPPOSED TO BE the rainy season. I didn't once use my umbrella or raincoat in the weeks I spent in Ghana. For poor, subsistence farmers who live on what they can grow or gather by hand, such changes in the weather patterns are a death sentence, literally. Farmers rely on getting three harvests per season of simple staples (sweet potatoes, corn, grains) that they can then store and use to feed their families all year, particularly to feed their growing children. Meeting the nutritional needs of children from the womb through puberty is critical; the nutritional needs of growing infants and children are more critical than the needs of adults, who merely need to maintain the brains and bodies they have already built. Children die or experience lifetime health and cognitive impairment if they are deprived of necessary nutrition when young. The world's countries with the youngest populations, in Africa and the Middle East, are majority children and youth. They are also the world's poorest countries, and those experiencing the worst impacts of environmental pollution and climate change.

They were supposed to be harvesting the first crop and planting the second when I arrived, but the rains had not come, so there was no first harvest, and no second planting. The best they could hope for was the rains to come and salvage the end of the season, but all their hard work would not yield enough food for their people. Children with distended bellies and slim, stick legs played nearby, sure signs of childhood malnutrition, starvation from lack of food. The world's youngest countries, like Ghana, are trying to adapt quickly to environmental changes against an unmerciful deadline with death. The majority of Ghana's population are children; getting enough food and nutrients in the early years are key for a child to reach full physical and cognitive potential. Hunger kills, and the children who survive childhood hunger are stunted in their development, doomed to a life of earning less and achieving less than children who receive enough food. Forty percent of children in northern Ghana suffer from malnutrition. These trends are particularly troubling because Ghana is nowhere near the poorest country in Africa. Ghana is a middle-income African country with more stable governance, higher education levels, and without war.

George Awuni and his team of university professors and agronomists at the sub-Saharan Agriculture Research Institute are working hard to help African farmers adapt to climate change. He and his colleagues are working to develop new seed strains and new farming methods to help Ghana's farmers yield better harvests despite changing climate. Nongovernmental organizations such as Catholic Relief Services partner with government aid providers such as USAID, and major corporations like Monsanto also sponsor the work. Pope Francis' environmental encyclical, **Laudato Si: Care for Our Common Home,** inspires the work of NGOs such as CRS to work at the intersections between environmental harm and its impact on the poor.

But even if Dr. Awuni and his team succeed in developing promising new seeds and techniques on the test farm, getting these out to Ghana's farmers is difficult. The "roads" are nonexistent and impassable much of the time. Farmers must walk hours to see demonstrations of new seeds and methods. Farmers have no money to buy new seeds. They rely on collecting and saving some seeds from last season's crop in order to plant next season's crop. When a crop fails they lose not only their food, but their seed for next year's planting.

Most subsistence farmers are women, who lack any access to formal banking systems, loans, or credit. Poor farmers often do not have **formal land title** or property rights for the land they farm. When European countries seized land as they colonized much of the world, this made a mess of traditional, indigenous land rights. Indigenous peoples with **communal land rights** and oral contracts were not recognized by European colonizers with their system of individual property rights and written contracts. Decolonization couldn't "put Humpty Dumpty back together again." Add in poor governance and corruption in many places, and you have a lack of land rights for the poor, conflicts over land rights, and poorly protected land rights in many parts of the developing world. Lack of property rights limits the poor's options and capacity to adapt. The poor people who live on and farm the land often do not have, or cannot prove with a written document, their rights to the land they farm. For many, they must stay on their land with continued occupation to demonstrate ownership. If their land is destroyed by drought or flood and stops producing, they do not have the ability to adapt, to sell the farm, move, and acquire land rights to farm in another place.

Women in developing countries often rely on producing "a little extra" beyond what their family needs to subsist, and they sell these products at the market. Market women the world over rely on small sums to send their children to school and purchase medicine and health care for the family. Facing crop failures from climate change, the poor in Ghana turned to cutting down trees to sell as charcoal. But the short-term strategy of selling charcoal to survive has a long-term cost, setting in motion a negative feedback cycle. Trees are needed to avoid erosion, to enrich the soil, and to maintain soil quality. Cutting down trees as a short-term survival strategy undermines long-term survival by degrading and eroding the soil, leading to poorer future harvests.

People in developed countries often struggle to understand these realities. Farmers in rich countries can turn on their irrigation systems when the rains don't come. If the crops fail they receive payment from their crop insurance company so that the farmers don't lose money. They grow crops primarily for sale and export not personal consumption; they do not starve if they experience a poor season. Farmers in rich countries are older; they don't worry about killing children and child malnutrition for the next generation if a crop fails. If the climate changes, farmers in rich countries adapt what they grow, using new seeds and growing methods to be more draught tolerant. They have access to loans, banks, and credit to cover the costs of any changes in seeds or fertilizers or pests or changes in farming processes or technologies. They have written papers and title to prove they own the land they farm, so they can use the title to their land and farms as collateral to get credit and bank loans. They can sell the farm, pick up and move and buy land elsewhere if need be. None of these conditions apply to farmers in poor countries.

Climate change not only causes less food in the mouths of poor children, it also deprives them of schooling and water. Women depend on growing enough to feed their families, and to have a little extra to prepare and sell at the market. This market income is used to pay for their children's school fees and family medical expenses. Without extra produce to sell at the market, women lack money to send their children to school and to afford doctors, vaccines, and medicines. Free public education is often unavailable and inadequate in many poor countries, as is access to water and basic health care. Lack of access to clean water means children, particularly girls, are charged with walking long distances to haul water for their families. Climate change causes draughts, floods, and changes in the access to drinking water, sending children and girls walking farther in search of potable water for their families. Girls and children carrying water are not in school; they are also more vulnerable to harm and trafficking the farther they walk searching for water. Children, particularly girls, without schooling are condemned to a lifetime of poverty.

Subsistence farmers and ranchers cannot pick up and farm or raise livestock in "greener pastures" when changes in weather patterns, new diseases, and pests wipe out their crops and animals. Lack of food and an inability to make a living in rural areas sends millions of young people to the cities in search of jobs, food, and opportunities outside of farming. This can lead to conflict and political upheaval, when governments cannot provide enough food and jobs for growing populations. According to the US military, climate change is a tipping point or "force multiplier," facilitating and exacerbating the fault lines of conflicts around the world. For example, the "Arab Spring" political upheavals began as conflicts over food, rising food prices, and government corruption in dealing with the issues. The Syrian Civil War began in part when a record drought uprooted millions of young Syrians who moved to the capital city. The government's failure to adequately respond to the people's needs led to protests for the removal of dictator Bashar al-Assad. The Syrian regime responded with brutal violence, which destabilized the world and continues as the world's worst war today.

For farmers in developed countries, climate change is a nuisance. For subsistence farmers in poor countries, climate change is a death sentence.

COST SHIFTING

This example illustrates why environmental problems can be so difficult to solve or manage. Cost shifting is common in environmental problems. The people who pollute the environment often do not see or experience the harms of their actions. They derive profits from environmental exploitation, and push the costs of those activities to others, particularly to the poor, those with the least resources to protect themselves from or adapt to environmental harms. Inequalities in the distribution of costs, benefits, information, and power mean that often those who pollute the environment may not even see the harm they cause, while those who experience environmental harm may not be able to seek redress. Environmental costs are shifted from old to young, from rich to poor, from white to brown, from men to women, from the well-connected and well-organized to the less-well-connected and less-organized.

An example of cost shifting is what's known as the **resource curse**. In many regions around the world where oil or other natural resources are extracted, the communities where the mining, drilling, or extraction takes place become poorer with worse environmental conditions, particularly compared to communities not dependent on natural resource extraction, rather than experiencing greater prosperity or benefits of economic development. Research on the resource curse shows that countries which are highly dependent on natural resource extraction have lower economic development and less democratic, more corrupt and less effective governance than countries with more diverse economies.[2] In resource curse regions cost shifting is going on. Companies and corrupt officials enrich themselves from the resource extraction, while shifting the costs to the local community, who must bear the environmental and health costs and consequences and poor governance, which worsens poverty.

Because of these disparities in power, it is not surprising that environmental damage is worsening, because those who do the damage face few consequences, and those who feel the consequences have little power. As discussed in the chapter on international crime, **environmental crimes** (illegal logging, fishing, mining, oil extractions, hazardous waste dumping, etc.) are the third largest category of global crime, behind drug trafficking and counterfeit goods and medicines. Illegal logging is widespread in countries in the Amazon region, Central Africa, and Southeast Asia. In these places 50–90 percent of logging operations are illegal.[3] Environmental crimes are profitable, and they are also easy to get away with.

Environmental problems have increased in parallel with rising global consumption rates and rising population. The world's population has more than tripled since 1950 when we had 2.5 billion people on planet earth. Today we have 7.6 billion people, and are expected to continue to grow to 10 or 11 billion people by 2050. These growing populations are not existing at subsistence consumption levels as indigenous peoples have lived for millennia. Instead, growing consumption rates accompany growing population; a *growing expectation of western levels of consumption* along with growing population are denuding the planet at alarming rates. If we were content with the standard of living of indigenous peoples, or of India, where there are more vegetarians, more public transport, and less consumption of fossil fuels, we could accommodate the rising population. But if people aspire to live at US or Australian levels of consumption, we will need over five planet earths! Even at Chinese or Brazilian consumption levels, we would need two planet earths. Despite the best efforts of space explorers like Elon Musk, we only have one planet Earth.

Growing population with growing consumption has depleted the Earth's resources, causing unintended, cascading impacts such as deforestation, decreased soil quality and soil erosion, decreased water quality and increased water pollution, increased air pollution including carbon pollution and climate change.

LAND: DEFORESTATION AND SOIL LOSS

More people on the planet has meant more logging, as people cut down trees to clear more land to grow more food, and also as logging increases the sale of trees to build homes, infrastructure, furniture, and for fuel. But trees are the planet's lungs, cleaning the air of pollutants; trees capture carbon and turn it into oxygen. Trees preserve soil quality and prevent soil erosion. Trees also prevent flooding and preserve water quality, by keeping debris out of water ways.

Higher population coupled with higher consumption rates has cleared the planet of old growth forests. Forests the size of the country of Panama are lost each year. Forests provide canopy that moderate temperature and hold moisture. Forests provide organic matter to the soil, and roots to hold and enrich the soil. Trees are the living bones that structure the ecosystem; other plants, animals, and necessary microscopic soil organisms all live in a codependent relationship. When the trees are removed, the entire ecosystem is destroyed.

The Amazon rain forests are rapidly disappearing, threatening the indigenous peoples who call the rainforest home. Without political power, native voices are often not heeded in environmental discussions, but their voices are critical in environmental protection.

Figure 7.1 World Population over the Last 12,000 Years and UN Projection until 2100

Source: Our World in Data

It is essential to show special care for indigenous communities and their cultural traditions. They are not merely one minority among others, but should be the principal dialogue partners, especially when large projects affecting their land are proposed. For them, land is not a commodity but rather a gift from God and from their ancestors who rest there, a sacred space with which they need to interact if they are to maintain their identity and values. When they remain on their land, they themselves care for it best. Nevertheless, in various parts of the world, pressure is being put on them to abandon their homelands to make room for agricultural or mining projects which are undertaken without regard for the degradation of nature and culture.[4]

Without forests, a negative feedback cycle is set in motion. Without the trees, land quickly dries out, organic matter is lost, needed soil organisms die, and the land becomes barren. The United Nations Food and Agriculture Organization reports soil loss of over 30 million hectares a year, due to erosion and decreasing soil quality, at precisely the time when the growing population requires more arable land capable of sustaining agriculture and food production. As the land becomes less fertile, people cut down more trees, in order to make money from the sale of the trees, and in order to clear more land for farming, continuing the negative feedback cycle.

Figure 7.2　World Population and Cumulative Deforestation, 1800–2010

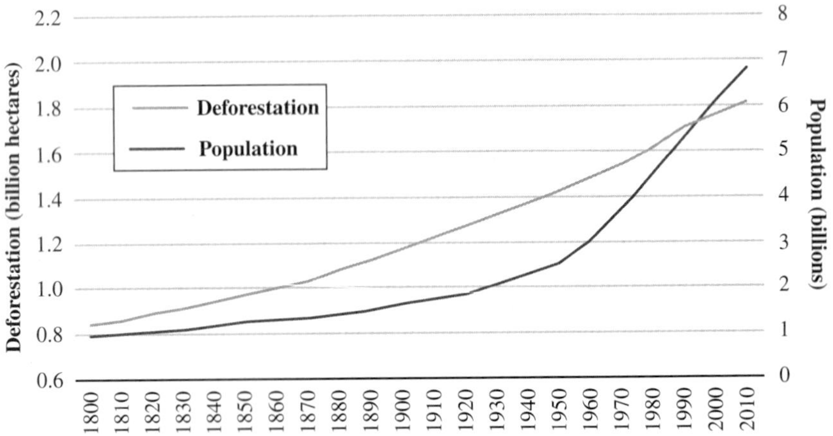

Source: Williams, 2002; FAO, 2010b; UN, 1999

BIODIVERSITY AND EXTINCTION

Cutting forests destroys habitats and leads to species loss and loss of biodiversity. Eighty percent of land animals and plants live in forests; many die when their homes are destroyed. Today species are dying off at the highest rate ever recorded in history, by some estimates 1,000 times higher extinction rates than normal levels. From 1970 to the present, we have killed off over 60 percent of the mammals, fish, birds, and reptiles on the planet. According to Mike Barrett of the World Wildlife Federation,

> We are sleepwalking towards the edge of a cliff. If there was a 60 percent decline in the human population, that would be equivalent to emptying North America, South America, Africa, Europe, China and Oceania. That is the scale of what we have done. This is far more than just being about losing the wonders of nature, desperately sad though that is. This is actually now jeopardizing the future of people. Nature is not a "nice to have"—it is our life-support system.[5]

The extinction of species endangers humans as well. For example, monoculture is now common in agriculture, making crops vulnerable to pests or diseases that can wipe out single cultivars. Seventy-five percent of the global food supply comes from five animal species and a mere dozen crops.[6] Protecting and expanding biodiversity in the food supply makes agriculture more resilient in the face of threats, at precisely the time when food production needs to increase by 70 percent to provide food for the earth's growing population.

The **Convention on Biodiversity** commits countries to consider biodiversity protection a common concern of humankind, and to take measures to conserve all levels of biodiversity—of genetic material, of species, and of entire ecosystems. The Convention entered into force on December 29, 1993, and calls for conservation, sustainable use, and fair sharing of the benefits derived from the use of genetic materials.

All countries, and the European Union, are parties to the convention, except for the United States. But countries have not implemented their commitments, and the loss of biodiversity continues unchecked.

The treaty calls for fair sharing of benefits of biodiversity in response to the problem of **biopiracy,** in which seeds and plants and indigenous knowledge from poor countries are patented by individuals and companies in rich countries. Then the companies charge local farmers and producers for growing and selling the seeds and crops they have grown for generations. They are threatened with lawsuits and cannot continue practices of creating seed banks or certain traditional medicines without paying fees to MNCs who now own the intellectual property, patents, and copyrights for these. Although multinational pharmaceutical companies use the populations of developing countries for human testing of potential medicines in the research and development phases, these poor people and countries often do not share in the benefits of these medicines once they are approved because the poor cannot afford the cure. The Biodiversity Treaty's benefit sharing norm was created to ensure that the poor share in any products made from their local biomaterial and indigenous knowledge. But in practice, companies and scientists from rich countries have better lawyers and knowledge of Western patent law. In one infamous case, a Colorado man, Larry Proctor, bought some yellow beans at a Mexican farmer's market, and then successfully filed and received a patent for a bean (he dubbed it "Enola") that had long been grown in Mexico. A coalition of NGOs, academics, and agricultural groups such as the Consultative Group on International Agricultural Research (CGIAR) and the Center for International Tropical Agriculture (CIAT), fought for and eventually succeeded in the repeal of this bean patent. Through examining the CIAT gene banks, collections of seeds and genetic materials maintained by the Center for International Tropical Agriculture, they were able to show identical beans to what the patent holder claimed to be his "invention." But the fight took over ten years and lots of resources, and during that time the man shut down the normal trade and the use of the yellow Mayocoba bean.

To conserve biodiversity, protect the food supply, and protect against biopiracy, the UN Food and Agriculture Organization (FAO) in partnership with agricultural research centers around the world, have set up over 1,700 **seed banks and gene banks**. These are the "back up" systems for our food supply, to help reconstitute a crop or area devastated by drought or disaster. The success of the "**green revolution**" in agriculture in the 1960s was the creation of more productive and resilient crops which fed millions of people and saved the growing people from starvation. The downside of the green revolution is the overreliance on a few strains of crops and seeds, and the loss of the biodiversity of the food supply. Genebanks and seedbanks work to preserve biodiversity, but these conservation and research centers are often threatened by poor support from governments and sponsors. The gene bank in Aleppo, Syria, was overrun by the Syrian Civil War. The gene bank in Venezuela suffers from the country's blackouts due to the poor economy, which stop the flow of electricity to the seed bank and endanger the collections. Researchers are constructing an online database, the aptly named Genesys, to share information about the gene banks' collections, but the database is not complete. The Consultative Group on International Agricultural Research (CGIAR) is a public–private partnership of governments, IGOs, regional groups, and private foundations, who work together to protect this biodiversity by fostering "sustainable agricultural growth through high-quality science aimed at benefiting the poor through stronger food security, better human nutrition and health, higher incomes and improved management of natural resources."[7]

Paşca Palmer, executive secretary of the UN Convention on Biological Diversity, is pushing for countries to deepen their attention and commitment to protecting biodiversity with more specific targets, like the Paris Climate Accords for climate change. Unlike more easily seen environmental problems, she worries that "biodiversity is a silent killer. By the time you feel what is happening, it's too late. I hope we aren't the first species to document our own extinction."[8]

WATER

Water is life; polluted water kills. About 2 million people die each year from polluted water, and 1 billion people are sickened by unsafe water. Although 71 percent of the earth's surface is water, less than 0.3 percent of the world's water is fresh, accessible, surface, water. Trees play a critical role in holding top soil, preventing silt and run-off from despoiling water supplies. With fewer trees preserving fresh water for drinking and human use, water quality has been decreasing around the world.

Water pollution comes from many sources: industrial pollution from factories; agricultural runoff from farms; oil pollution from oil spills; dumped sewage and untreated waste water; storm water runoff; and trash swept into water, particularly plastics. According to the United Nations, 80 percent of wastewater goes untreated, dumping human and animal waste and toxins directly into freshwater ecosystems used for drinking water.[9] Sewage and waste water dumping cause a variety of diseases, including cholera, dysentery, Hepatitis A, typhoid, and giardia. According to the World Health Organization, 30 percent of the global population lacks access to safe drinking water at home. More than 2.3 billion people lack access to toilets and latrines. Without access to clean water and soap for hand washing, diseases reign. Access to water and sanitation is worse in poor, rural areas, and worse in war zones.[10]

Water pollution is also a problem in the United States. According to the Environmental Protection Agency (EPA), 44 percent of assessed stream miles, 64 percent of lakes, and 30 percent of bay and estuarine areas are not clean enough for fishing and swimming. The EPA also states that the United States' most common contaminants are bacteria, mercury, phosphorus, and nitrogen. These come from the most common sources of contaminates, that include agricultural runoff, air deposition, water diversions, and channelization of streams.

So much plastic is dumped into the world's waterways, or is washed away into waterways during increasing high-intensity storms, that the Pacific garbage patch is visible from space. Animals eat the plastic, mistaking it for food, and we eat the plastic, as it makes its way into our water and food supply. Our drinking water, 100 percent of sea turtles, 60 percent of sea birds, and all fish tested have plastics in them.[11] Plastic breaks down into micro plastics, about this size of a letter on this page, and a size easily ingestible by fish, animals, and us, with poor health consequences.

Water pollution from both agricultural runoff and runoff of fertilizer from lawns creates large algae blooms, which removes oxygen from the water, suffocating plants and marine life. This causes huge fish kills, at a time when rising population levels increase demands for fish. As fish populations are diminished by poorer water quality, overfishing also undermines the health of many ecosystems. Overfishing has drastically reduced the variability and viability of marine life. According to research by the London Zoological Society, marine populations have decreased by 50 percent since 1970, in parallel with a 50 percent increase in demand for fish. Ninety percent of the world's fisheries are either overfished or fully exploited. Yet the world needs more fish to support more people.[12]

Water also absorbs pollution and chemicals in the air. Higher carbon emissions and higher carbon pollution in the air also means more carbon in the oceans. The oceans have absorbed over one-third of all carbon emitted since the 1700s. More carbon in the oceans creates more acidic water, which endangers marine life, particularly coral reefs and shellfish. Ocean acidification is sometimes called "osteoporosis of the sea," because it eats away at the calcium and minerals used by coral reefs and shellfish to build their shells and structures. Acidification also intensifies algae blooms, which removes oxygen from the water, creating dead zones that suffocate and kill marine life. Shellfish such as oysters, crabs, clams, lobsters, and shrimp, are particularly vulnerable to acidifying waters, along with the communities that rely on eating and fishing these harvests.[13] Coral reefs are disappearing at an alarming rate. For example, living coral at the Great Barrier Reef has diminished by more than half in the past 30 years. These reefs are the homes supporting whole ecosystems of marine life. As marine life loses its habitat it also dies off.

Water scarcity affects 40 percent of people, particularly the world's poorest people. This number is expected to increase, as underground reservoirs are increasingly tapped and threatened, and as rising population and consumption numbers drain water supplies, while climate change causes more extreme droughts and contamination of fresh water from sea flooding. Water is life, so even politicians otherwise averse to environmental protection recognize and are rallying around protection of water quality.

WASTE, CHEMICAL, AND HAZARDOUS WASTE DUMPING

The United States leads the world in garbage. We are producing more waste than any other country, and more than at any time in human history. Although the US population accounts for only 5 percent of the world's population, the United States creates 30 percent of the world's garbage, waste that fouls ecosystems both at home and abroad. Much of this waste is easily preventable. For example, between 30 and 40 percent of the US food supply is wasted.[14] The produced waste can top 50 percent, as American consumers don't eat our fruits and vegetables, especially if they have a bump or blemish. Rather than donating food to food pantries or composting food waste (only one-in-ten Americans has access to composting), it ends up in landfills. The single largest component of landfills is food waste. This adds to air pollution, because of the anaerobic decay process in landfills which produces large amounts of methane, a greenhouse gas (compost produces little methane).

The amounts of waste are truly staggering. The United States throws away enough iron and steel to continuously supply all the automakers in the country. A University of Utah study found that

> in the U.S. industry moves, mines, extracts, shovels, burns, wastes, pumps and disposes of 4 million pounds of material in order to provide one average middle-class American family's needs for one year. Americans waste or cause to be wasted nearly 1 million pounds of materials per person every year. This figure includes 3.5 billion pounds of carpet landfilled, 3.3 trillion pounds of CO2 gas emitted into the atmosphere, 19 billion pounds of polystyrene peanuts, 28 billion pounds of food discarded, 360 billion pounds of organic and inorganic chemicals used for manufacturing, 710 billion pounds of hazardous waste and 3.7 trillion pounds of construction debris. If wastewater is factored in, the total annual flow of waste in the American Industrial system is 250 trillion pounds. Less than 2 percent of the total waste stream in the United States is recycled.[15]

E-waste is the fastest growing type of waste, and the United States also leads the world in e-waste. E-waste includes all sorts of electronics—old refrigerators, computers, cell phones, television sets, vacuum cleaners, electronic toys, hair dryers, and other consumer electronic devices. Each American throws away an average 176 pounds of e-waste per year. The global average is far less waste, about 13 pounds per person per year.[16]

Unfortunately, much of the waste is not as benign as spoiled milk. Energy production creates lots of hazardous waste. Mining and metals production use deadly chemicals like cyanide and lead. Modern industries use a host of toxic chemicals in production. The companies profit from the products, then often pass on the pollution costs to others, by releasing the toxins into the air, water, and land. Chernobyl, Ukraine, La Oroya in Peru, Love Canal in the U.S., Koko, Nigeria, and Bhopal, India—people around the world have been killed and sickened by toxins.

As countries learned of the harmful public health and environmental costs from chemicals and hazardous waste, regulation and enforcement of hazardous waste procedures increased in developed countries.

Countries in the global south also increased their environmental regulations, but their governments have less capacity to enforce their laws. This led to the perverse **toxic trade**, in which hazardous waste from rich countries is shipped to poor countries for disposal, to avoid "cradle to grave" accounting and safe disposal costs.

Often there is no "trade," but simply illegal dumping of radioactive waste, chemical waste, industrial waste, medical hazardous waste, dredging, sludge, e-waste, and trash. Sometimes the illegal cargo is simply dumped at a dock or beach or into the water at night, under cover of darkness, as was the case when Ivory Coast was dumped on illegally in 2006, and 100,000 people were sickened and 17 died. Sometimes a local landowner is paid a small fee for leaving the waste on his property, without full disclosure about the nature of the material being "stored" on their property, as happened in Koko, Nigeria. Sometimes local officials are bribed to "look the other way." When residents wake up coughing and sickened by unknown toxins dumped on them by unknown culprits, finding out who dumped what on whom, and helping victims when doctors do not know what toxins victims were exposed to, is very difficult. Finding the culprits, holding anyone responsible for their illegal actions, let alone cleaning up the environment despoiled by the dumping, is nearly impossible. Those who created the waste know what's in it, and those who dumped the waste also know, but they aren't talking.

The Basel Convention on the Control of Transboundary Movements of Hazardous Wastes and their Disposal is an international environmental agreement regulating the toxic trade. Developing countries want a ban on the toxic trade, but instead the convention requires informed prior consent of the receiving country before toxins are shipped and accurate labeling of shipments. Article 4 also calls for countries to reduce hazardous waste. The Convention does not ban the toxic waste flow, but it seeks to make the toxic trade more transparent and consensual. An amendment to the Convention that would ban toxic waste trade has been signed by eighty-six countries, but has not entered into force. Nearly all countries, including Canada and the European Union, are parties to the Convention, which took effect in 1992. The United States is not a party to the convention.

Other international agreements have been more successful in limiting or banning specific toxic substances. **The Rotterdam Convention (1998)** requires accurate labeling, prior informed consent, and sharing information about bans of certain toxic chemicals and pesticides such as asbestos and DDT. Information sharing and informed consent are the goals of this treaty, so that companies from countries which banned certain chemicals from domestic use and production, could not sell those products abroad without notification. Nearly all countries, including Canada and the European Union, are parties to the Convention, which took effect in 1998. The United States is not a party to the convention.

The Stockholm Convention on Persistent Organic Pollutants (2001) bans the most toxic chemicals, which do not break down but last a long time, persist in the environment and bio-accumulate through the food web, and pose a risk of causing adverse effects to human health and the environment.

Countries agreed to ban nine of the "Dirty Dozen" most harmful chemicals initially, and to strictly reduce the use of the pesticide DDT to only malaria control. More harmful chemicals have been added to the ban list since, and the convention's working group and scientific review and research process allows members to continue to identify and protect against the most harmful chemicals. Nearly all countries, including Canada and the European Union, are parties to the Convention, which took effect in 2004. The United States and Israel are not parties to the convention.

The newest of these types of international environmental agreements is the **Minamata convention** (2017) limiting and safeguarding mercury use, a highly toxic chemical used extensively in industrial processes and products, from thermometers to lights. The Convention is named after the Japanese town of Minamata, where the Chisso corporation dumped mercury waste from fertilizer production directly into the Bay, causing poisoning, death, disease, and birth defects in the entire population of humans, fish, and animals who eat fish, such as cats. Japanese eat a diet based on fish, but the fish in the Minamata Bay were full of mercury, due to the 27,000 tons of mercury that Chisso dumped in the bay, beginning in 1956. Despite complaints from fishermen and the local community, and University reports showing mercury poisoning caused "**Minamata disease,**" the company denied that its mercury dumping into public waters was harmful, and continued to dump massive quantities of mercury for over a decade. Mercury poisoning harms the brain and sensory system, causing loss of sight, hearing, touch, tremors, brain damage, and birth defects. The Convention calls on countries to prevent mercury poisoning by limiting the use of mercury and safeguarding mercury storage and waste disposal. Mercury does not dissolve or dissipate, so mercury dumped a long time ago can still harm people today. Mercury pollution moves with air and water and fish, and is not constrained to its place of original contamination, so global cooperation is needed to protect human and fisheries health. The United States is a party to the convention, along with Canada and the EU and a fast growing majority of countries.[17]

AIR POLLUTION, CLIMATE CHANGE

We need clean air to breathe. Clean air is composed of oxygen, nitrogen, water vapor, and inert gases. Not surprisingly, with more industrial processes spewing substances into the air, and fewer trees and more people burning trees and fossil fuels, we have seen the destructive increase of air pollution, including carbon pollution. Air pollution is increasing the world over, killing more people than diseases like HIV/AIDS, malaria, etc. Common air pollutants include lead, particulate matter, nitrogen oxides, sulfur dioxides, ozone, carbon monoxide, and carbon dioxide. These pollutants interact with the environment to produce further harmful chemical reactions, such as acid rain and depletion of the earth's protective upper ozone layer.

Increased air pollution leads to increased health problems, such as asthma, allergies, and lung disease. Asthma and allergy rates are increasing, in parallel with rising rates of air pollution. Asthma is the inflammation, swelling, constricting, and spasms of the airways; it can be deadly. Rates of asthma have been steadily rising for 30 years, along with the deaths from asthma. Research shows that exposure to air pollution early in life increases the development of asthma and allergies; air pollution also exacerbates asthma and allergies, making them worse.[18]

Particulate matter, a mixture of solid particles and liquid droplets that can include smoke, soot, dirt, and dust, is dangerous for our lungs, whether the particles are coarse (larger) or fine (smaller). Deforestation adds to the release of particulates, as soils no longer contained by tree roots dry out and blow away as dust. Construction, industrial-scale farming, clear-cutting, mining, especially mountain top removal coal mining, and fracking all release particulates into the air, as does burning things—whether it is waste, wood, fossil fuel, or burning in industrial production processes.

Perhaps one of the most successful cases of international environmental cooperation are the efforts to protect the ozone layer. Air pollution of **chlorofluorocarbons** (CFCs), a chemical widely used in refrigerators and air conditioners, had created a "hole" in the atmosphere's protective layer of ozone, which shields humans from the most harmful UVB rays of the sun. With ozone protection compromised, skin cancer rates, cataracts, sunburn, and other cancer rates increased. The world came together to create the United Nation's first universally adopted conventions, the **Vienna Convention for the Protection of the Ozone Layer,** which was an agreement over how to work together to protect the ozone layer, and the **Montreal Protocol,** which banned the production of CFCs. Through these interventions, ozone coverage is increasing and is expected to heal by 2070, if present trajectories continue.

Just as acid waters kills coral reefs and dissolves the shells of oysters, clams, and shellfish, acid rain kills trees, plants, harms fish, and damages stone and buildings. Statues on the national mall in Washington, DC, had their faces and details "melted away" by acid rain. Coal-fired power plants release sulfur dioxide and fertilizer runoff from farms and automobile emissions release nitrous oxide into the atmosphere. This acidifies rain and acid rain falls, often on downwind areas hundreds of miles away from the source pollution, on communities that did not cause the problem.

To mitigate air pollution, including acid rain, the Europeans created the Geneva Convention on Long-range Transboundary Air Pollution in the 1970s. It entered into force in 1983. Over fifty primarily European states are parties to the Convention. The United States and Canada are also parties to the convention.

Acid rain is one way in which air pollution causes further, unintended impacts when air pollutants interact in larger chemical and biosphere reactions. Another way air pollution causes further harm is global climate change. Certain air pollutants, such as nitrous oxide, methane, and especially carbon dioxide, capture heat and act like a blanket, holding warmth in the atmosphere closer to the earth's surface rather than letting the heat dissipate.

Trees are huge **carbon sinks,** capturing carbon so it is harmless. With fewer trees, more carbon is released into the atmosphere, exacerbating global climate change. Carbon levels are at their highest levels ever, and so are global temperatures, and extreme weather events.

Electric power generation, transportation, and industry contribute the bulk of carbon dioxide and greenhouse gases. The earth's average surface temperature has risen more than 1.6 degrees in the last century; most of the temperature rise has occurred very rapidly in the past 35 years, in parallel with rising carbon emissions. This excess heat then causes a host of cascading, unintended reactions.

A 1.6 degree temperature may not sound like much, but it is the difference between ice and water. Glaciers are melting in every part of the world, and the snow caps are melting from the world's mountain tops. The earth's great ice sheets are rapidly melting in Greenland, the Arctic,

Figure 7.3   Atmospheric CO2 Concentration (ppm)

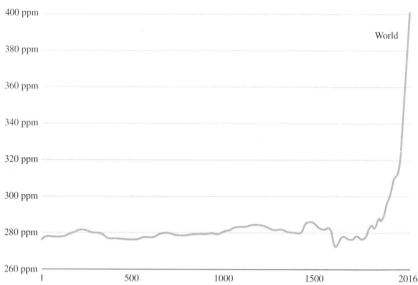

Global average long-term atmospheric concentration of carbon dioxide (CO2), measured in parts per million (ppm)

Source: Our World in Data; Scripps CO2 Program

and the Antartic. The remaining ice is much thinner, and more vulnerable to continued rapid melt. Ice reflects and deflects the sun's rays and heat. When the ice melts, the earth loses this natural "heat shield" and even more warming occurs.

The melted ice has raised sea levels by 8 inches over the past century, but the rate of sea level rise has doubled in the past two decades. A 1 foot or 3 foot rise in sea level may not seem like a dramatic change, but most of the world's population live along the coasts, and two-thirds of the world's largest cities, with populations over 5 million, are in low lying coastal areas not much above sea level, along with the farmland that supports them. The world's largest financial centers are in vulnerable coastal cities (New York, Hong Kong, Singapore, Shanghai, San Francisco, etc.). Rising waters cause coastal erosion, and storm floods and tidal waters enter into river systems and bays and farmlands, contaminating fresh water supplies, killing food crops, destroying housing and businesses, and displacing people.

These changes disrupt weather patterns, bringing more severe storms, flooding, droughts, and fires. Insurance companies testify that the severity of storms and extreme weather events is increasing; each year of late breaks records for the catastrophic losses insurance companies pay to cover the costs of extreme weather. People are made homeless and forced to migrate by these increasing storms, as when 200,000 US citizens of Puerto Rico have moved to the mainland following hurricane Maria, which destroyed the island. The UN expects 150 million climate change migrants by 2050.

As discussed earlier with the example of Ghana, climate change undermines agriculture, changing the flowering times and performance of plants. And the countries most impacted by climate change are poor countries, particularly in sub-Saharan Africa, who have the fewest resources to adapt to climate change. All of Africa produces only 3 percent of the world's carbon emissions, yet they suffer disproportionately the costs imposed on them by rich country emitters.

Black carbon is sooty, particulate matter from burning fossil fuels in gas or diesel engines, coal-fired power plants, and also from burning wood and other biomass. The particulate matter from black carbon inserts itself into the tissue of the lungs.

The **United Nations Framework Convention on Climate Change** was created to marshal the countries of the world to tackle the problems of climate change. It entered into force in 1994. The Convention committed states to reduce greenhouse gas emissions in order to prevent the worst impacts of climate change. The convention did not create binding emissions limits, but created means by which states could negotiate such limits. For example, the Convention created the **Intergovernmental Panel on Climate Change**, a process by which thousands of preeminent scientists around the world provide the best and cutting-edge research on the state of climate change, in order that the countries of the world share information, and base policy on high-quality scientific consensus. The parties to the treaty meet in annual conference of the party (COP) gatherings, to negotiate more specific and more binding commitments to reduce carbon emissions. **The Paris Climate Agreement** was reached at the COP 2015 meeting, and committed countries to developing their own national plans to reduce emissions, in order to limit the global temperature rise to under 1.5 degrees C. The United States signed the Paris Agreement, but President Trump has subsequently withdrawn the United States from the agreement. Many US states, including California and New York, are continuing work to reach the Paris Accord commitments, with or without the US national government. Because the United States emits so much carbon, without the United States on board, the world has little chance of meeting the Paris Agreement targets.

HEALTH AND DISEASE

The world has made great strides toward better health in recent decades. Once-common diseases such as smallpox, polio, and guinea worm have been eradicated. Effective vaccines, for example, against measles, mumps, and rubella, are today more widely available, widening the circle of protection from those once-common and deadly diseases. Lifespans have doubled around the world over the last century, with significant gains from 1990 to 2015, the timeframe of the Millennium Development Goals.

The countries of the world committed to the Millennium Development goals (MDGs) in 2000, and through this common focused effort, were able to improve some key aspects of human health by 2015, the "report card time" for the MDGs. The MDGs were a series of global goals that countries agreed to work together toward. States, IGOs, NGOs, and the private sector all undertook efforts, sometimes working together, sometimes independently, to make progress toward the MDGs. The MDGs support each other in a positive feedback loop; gains in one area help bring gains in others. For example, great gains were made in educating girls. Since girls and women are often responsible for food preparation and home health care in households around the world, gains in female education and literacy also helped raise families into better health, and helped attain the health-related MDGs, including the MDG pledges to reduce child mortality, improve maternal health, and combat HIV/AIDs, malaria, and other diseases.

These efforts were very successful. The child mortality rate was cut in half from 1990 to 2015. More children are surviving childhood, thanks in part to increased childhood vaccination against killer diseases. Measles vaccinations increased, for example, and the cases of measles subsequently decreased by 67 percent.[19]

Maternal health also improved, with a 45 percent decline in maternal death during childbirth. The rates of women receiving prenatal care increases, as did women giving birth with assistance from trained health-care personnel.

Progress was made against killer diseases. Over 7 million lives were saved from HIV/AIDs. The rate of people taking antiretroviral therapy (ART) medicine to control their HIV/AIDs infection increased 1700 percent, a dramatic life-saving increase from a mere 800,000 people receiving ART treatment in 2003 to 13.6 million people taking ART medicines in 2013. At the same time new HIV infections declined by 40 percent.

Malaria was reduced, and over 6 million lives were saved. The malaria infection rate was reduced by 39 percent, and this helped reduce the number of people dying from malaria by 58 percent. Simple interventions helped save lives from malaria. For example, approximately a billion anti-malaria mosquito nets were distributed to countries suffering most from malaria in sub-Saharan Africa.

Over 37 million lives were saved from tuberculosis, due to gains in preventing, diagnosing, and treating tuberculosis. The tuberculosis death rate fell 45 percent, and the rate of people suffering from TB fell 41 percent.

Malnutrition was reduced by almost half. In 1990, 23 percent of people in developing countries suffered from malnutrition, but by 2015, only 12.9 percent of people in developing countries suffer from malnutrition. The number of people living in extreme poverty has likewise been cut in half. In 1990 half the planet lived in extreme poverty of less than $1.25 a day. By 2015, 14 percent of people lived in the world's worst poverty.

Yet of all the MDGs, the least progress was made against the environmental health goals, MDG 7, Ensure Environmental Sustainability. Gains were made in access to safe drinking water and access to toilets or latrines. The proportion of people who practice open defecation because they lack access to sanitation facilities has been cut in half. But the improvement rates were not as high in this area compared to the other MDGs.[20]

To expand progress, the eight MDGs have now been replaced by a larger set of more specific targets, the seventeen Sustainable Development Goals (SDGs). All United Nations Member States adopted the 2030 Agenda for Sustainable Development in 2015. Goal 3, Healthy Living for All, contains all the previous MDG health goals combined, but it also adds attention to global public health structures. For example, good health for all requires some access to doctors and nurses, yet "45 per cent of all countries and 90 per cent of least developed countries (LDCs) have less than one physician per 1,000 people, and over 60 per cent have fewer than three nurses or midwives per 1,000 people."[21]

These SDGs give more attention (six specific SDGs) to environmental goals than the MDGs did (with only one MDG on the environment). The concern is that environmental damage may reverse the progress made toward prosperity and well-being over the past decades. To protect the gains made, and advance them, greater attention is given to environmental protection in the SDGs. Goal 6 is to expand access to clean water and sanitation. Goal 7 is to ensure access to energy for all that is affordable, reliable, modern, and sustainable. Goal 9 is to build sustainable and resilient infrastructure, and Goal 11 is to build sustainable and resilient cities. Goal 12 is a commitment to creating sustainable consumption patterns. Goal 13 is to take urgent action to stop climate change and its impacts. Goal 14, Life Below Water, commits to conserve the oceans, waterways, and marine life. Goal 15, Life on Land, commits to protection of the earth's ecosystems, including forests and protecting biodiversity. As with the MDGs, the goals are devised to work together, so that progress against poverty and hunger (SDGs 1 and 2) will also improve health (SDG 3) and environment (SDGs 6, 9, 11, 12, 13, 14).

Environmental harms disproportionately sicken and kill poor and powerless people for a number of reasons. Poor people are more likely to be subsistence farmers, fishermen, or ranchers, thus their lives and livelihoods are more directly tied to natural resources. When these resources are poisoned, they are poisoned. When the resources are scarce, they suffer. Poor people also often live in environmentally vulnerable areas, and they have the fewest resources to protect themselves against environmental harms. Thus although they consume the least and cause the least environmental damage, they suffer most from environmental degradation. According to the Lancet Commission Report on Pollution and Public Health,

> Nearly 92 percent of pollution-related deaths occur in low- and middle-income countries. Within countries, pollution's toll is greatest in poor and marginalized communities. Children face the highest and, disability, premature death, as well as reduced learning and earning potential.[22]

In a warmer, wetter world, some infectious diseases are spreading. Insects such as mosquitoes thrive in the conditions of climate change, therefore mosquito-born illnesses such as West Nile virus, dengue, and Zika are on the rise. The same is true of tick-carried diseases, such as Lyme disease. Flesh-eating bacteria thrive in the warmer water temperatures created by climate change.

Hotter weather increases heat-related illnesses such as heatstroke. More frequent extreme weather events such as floods, storms, storm surge, droughts, and wildfires, take their tolls on human health.

> These events can exacerbate underlying medical conditions, increase stress, and lead to adverse mental health effects.[4] Further, extreme weather and climate events can disrupt critical public health, healthcare, and related systems in ways that can adversely affect health long after the event.[3]

Globalization and Environmental Issues
Globalization's fast, interdependent systems of open markets, open societies, and open technologies facilitate environmental damage. Can globalization also help solve environmental problems?

OPEN MARKETS AND THE ENVIRONMENT

The spread of Western-style consumer capitalism has taken a toll on the environment. But are there any ways in which open market forces can help environmental protection?

Some argue that economic growth is the answer to environmental problems, that environmental degradation will be self-correcting. As countries develop and become more prosperous, they will have the resources to engage in environmental clean-up. This is called an **environmental Kuznet's curve,** based off the inverted (upside-down) U-shaped graph economists call a Kuznet's curve. According to this theory, economies go through a "dirty development" phase of economic development; so initially as countries develop their economy, the levels of pollution increase. But that reaches a limit (at the top of the inverted U curve), after which increased economic prosperity tends to correlate with increased environmental protection. The idea draws from an implied "levels of need" whereby only after basic economic needs are met do people worry about environmental protection. These optimistic economists point to the history of economic development in the United States and Europe as evidence. Pollution was high during industrialization. Smokestacks belched toxins and soot into the air, Europe lost its forests, and rivers in the United States caught fire due to oil spills and industrial contamination. But as economies grew and prospered, eventually resources were diverted to environmental clean-up. The Cuyahoga River in Cleveland, Ohio, no longer catches fire, even if water quality is still not safe for fishing and swimming.

It would be nice if environmental problems were self-correcting by some economic hidden hand. But there are a few problems with this theory.

First, many environmental problems cannot be "fixed" later on. People killed by environmental degradation cannot be brought back from the dead. Babies born with birth defects due to environmental toxins cannot be given new limbs. Children poisoned by lead cannot be given back their brains and IQ levels prior to lead poisoning, which cannot be cured or reversed. Species, once extinct, cannot be resuscitated. Old growth forests, once cut down, cannot be replaced by massive,

1,000-year-old, living trees. Melted glaciers cannot be refrozen. Rising sea levels cannot be returned to prior, lower sea levels. Many toxins, once dumped into the ecosystem, have very, very long lives. For example, the town of **Chernobyl**, poisoned by nuclear radiation due to a nuclear power plant accident in 1986, will not be inhabitable for 30,000 years.

Secondly, the theory takes data from the 1700s to 1980s time period from the United States and Northern Europe, and assumes that model will be generalizable to the whole planet. But the scale of those environmental problems and the size of the populations are not comparable to today. The environmental problems of less than 1 billion people in one region who share culture may be much more easily remediated than those of a world of nearly 8 billion people, all over the planet, from 8,000 different national groups. At this larger scale of the problem we encounter tipping points and points of no return and nonlinear change, that were not as severely experienced with the smaller case.

Third, the process of environmental clean-up in the United States. and Europe was not automatic, but required the effective democratic political mobilization of masses of citizens, demanding changes in laws and policies. Thus there were critically important other conditions, beyond just economic prosperity levels, which were required to bring about environmental clean-up in the United States and Europe, such as democracy, free speech, freedom of association, independent media, and effective civil society organizations. Only when these organizations mobilized and pressured elected officials to take action, did the laws and the policies begin to change. In many of the countries experiencing environmental degradation today, such as China, there are none of those intervening structures and processes. Citizens cannot effectively raise their voices on environmental issues to the authoritarian government. Fear of being voted out of office will not incentivize leaders to take environmental action. China's state-run industries, and the ties between industry and government, may preclude consumer-pressure campaigns from having an impact on corporate behavior. The "economic growth correlates to environmental remediation" cases the optimistic economists point to were democracies. China and other countries experiencing environmental damage today are not democracies. Economic correlation is not the same as environmental causation.

Fourth, the world has seen tremendous economic growth over the past century, and particularly since the end of World War II and since the start of the information age. Yet despite these vast economic improvements, environmental damage continues to worsen, including in the world's most advanced economies. The United States is the world's richest country, yet is facing many declining environmental conditions, calling into question the theory of the environmental Kuznet's curve.

There are other open market means to improve the environment. Customers can pressure companies to improve their environmental practices. Companies in free market competition will want to protect their brands from association with environmental harms. Toy companies do not want to endanger their health of their child customers or endanger their brand name with lead paint. Mrs. Paul's fish does not want a costly product recall due to contaminated fish. Companies like McDonald's changed packaging to respond to consumer demand for more environmental sustainability. McDonald's also announced a plan for reducing its carbon footprint by 30 percent by 2030. However, as we saw in the chapter on MNCs and the student campaigns to pressure Nike, consumer advocacy pressures and corporate brand protection strategies only have a chance against companies which have branded products. Unbranded products, such as those sold at the Dollar Store, have no brand name, reputation, advertising, or brand investment to protect.

Another open market mechanism for environmental protection is shareholder activism. The Interfaith Center for Corporate Responsibility is an NGO which advises other NGOs and investors in how to use their financial leverage to pressure companies to address social justice issues such as climate change. They pressure companies to move away from fossil fuels, and encourage companies to develop strategies for greener investments and processes.

Many private investors, particularly colleges and universities, are divesting from carbon companies and the fossil fuel economy and instead investing in green technologies. Fossil fuel divestment is the removal of investments in companies which support fossil fuels from an investment portfolio of stocks, bonds, and investment funds, for example, not investing in oil companies. Pension funds and investment funds make this option increasingly easy by offering customers options that include a portfolio of investments that exclude carbon companies. Universities have investment power as they face decisions of where to invest their employees' pension funds and their university endowment investment portfolios. Individuals and groups can exercise their economic rights and market pressures to invest in green companies and divest from fossil fuels, but only on publicly owned and traded companies. Private companies are not vulnerable to shareholder activism, as their stock is not publicly owned and traded.

Because the United States is the world's leader in waste, many companies can be persuaded to reduce their pollution and reduce their carbon foot print in order to reduce waste, reduce toxic liability, and increase profits and improve their bottom line. This is the path that Ray Anderson took to make his company, Interface, produce carbon neutral carpet, in a very petroleum- and carbon-intensive industry, carpet. Many insurance companies and banks are likewise increasing their investments in green technologies, as they are concerned that climate change is harming their business model. Insurance companies have to absorb higher costs and payouts due to higher property damages from climate change's more high-intensity storms. Climate change is bad for business.

Similarly, many towns, provinces, and municipalities are investing more in green infrastructure, green energy, and green technology because it makes economic sense to do so. Many towns and states, like Burlington, Vermont, and the town of Georgetown, Texas, are becoming powered entirely by renewable energy. As Georgetown's republican mayor Dale Ross explains, his motivations are market-driven not ideological. "Cheaper electricity is better. Cleaner energy is better."[23]

Other market-based approaches to environmental issues can be more complex. **Cap and trade** is a system that creates incentives for companies to engage in deeper environmental protection by putting a price on pollution and allowing companies to profit from environmental protection. This system worked well in an agreement between the United States and Canada to reduce acid rain. In order for cap and trade systems to work, the cap or limit on toxic emissions has to be set accurately to protect human health, and there has to be strong enough government capacity to enforce the cap and monitor the trade. Companies that reduce emissions more than necessary can then sell their excess "credits" to companies that are having a harder or more expensive time meeting their obligations. Factories won't all have the same emissions levels, but the aggregate can be a cleaner environment for a lower cost than a "one-size-fits-all" regulatory framework. The acid rain cap and trade system worked better than its most ardent promoters had dreamed, bringing emissions down faster and at lower cost than all estimates, drastically reducing acid rain. However, although carbon cap and trade systems show promise, they have had a rocky start. The first systems such as the EU's Emissions Trading System, the Regional Greenhouse Gas Initiative (among US northeastern states, with Canadian provinces), and California's cap and trade system have all underperformed. This has not stopped other countries from creating their own carbon cap and trade systems. Countries from Australia to China to Mexico are interested in cap and trade systems. Perhaps they can learn lessons from and outperform the initial models.

The complexity of the systems and the transparency and effectiveness of government monitoring are challenges. Others criticize cap and trade systems more fundamentally as "environmental indulgences," paying a fee to sin, to pollute. Critics ask why pollution is OK with a permit, and whether the caps are low enough to protect public health and the environment.

Another, simpler market-based approach is to charge a carbon tax. While taxes are unpopular, they do penalize bad behavior such as pollution, and begin to remove the "externality" of polluters shifting the costs of their pollution to others. With carbon taxes, those emitting carbon will have to pay for their emissions. Tax revenues can then be used for environmental protection and remediation, and for investments in green technologies and green infrastructure, such as enhanced public transportation. Gas taxes are an "old school" form of carbon taxes, and Europeans have long had higher gas taxes than the United States, which subsidizes car travel. But gas taxes are often criticized as being regressive, meaning they are harder for poor people to pay. Some European capitals have combined gas taxes with "no drive" zones, banning from city centers tour buses and vehicles other than those of residents and low carbon delivery and mail trucks. By opening city streets to more bicycles and pedestrians, and increasing the costs to drivers more consistent with the costs fossil fuel emissions impose on others, these governments are attempting to create price structures that will alter environmental practices.

OPEN SOCIETIES AND ENVIRONMENTAL ACTION

Globalization has witnessed an increase in democracies around the world. There are now more democracies and democratizing countries than ever before in history. This should be good news for environmental protection, as democracies tend to have better records of environmental protection than nondemocratic states. For example, Western Europe had a much better record of environmental protection than Eastern Europe during the Cold War. After the Cold War ended and Eastern European countries democratized, they began to clean up their pollution and adopted much cleaner environmental standards.

Communities are capable of cooperating to manage common resources and avoid **"the tragedy of the commons,"** in which a common resource is destroyed. Nobel Prize **winner Elinor Ostrom** studied communities which successfully cooperated to manage environmental common resources. She showed that eight principles work to avoid the destruction of a common resource. Democracies are more likely to have conditions which allow groups to develop these institutions for commons management than nondemocracies.

> 1. Define clear group boundaries.2. Match rules governing use of common goods to local needs and conditions.3. Ensure that those affected by the rules can participate in modifying the rules.4. Make sure the rule-making rights of community members are respected by outside authorities.5. Develop a system, carried out by community members, for monitoring members' behavior.6. Use graduated sanctions for rule violators.7. Provide accessible, low-cost means for dispute resolution.8. Build responsibility for governing the common resource in nested tiers from the lowest level up to the entire interconnected system.[24]

Democracies provide multiple levels at which citizens and policy makers can address environmental issues, which Ostrom discusses as being a necessary condition for resolving environmental commons problems. These multiple levels are both a blessing and a curse. It means there are multiple fora, from the local level on up, at which interested citizens can press for environmental action. It also means there are multiple venues in which polluters can try to block environmental action.

Through elections and constitutions, democracies create checks and balances in which voters have regular opportunities to replace low-performing politicians with officials who may better address pressing issues of the time, such as environmental issues. Citizens have freedom of speech, freedom of association, freedom of religion, and free and independent media by which to share information about environmental problems and to propose environmental solutions.

Multiparty democracies with Green Parties tend to have better representation of environmental issues. The need to create political coalitions can raise environmental concerns even among non–Green-party members.

But just because democracies give citizens channels by which they *can* mobilize on environmental issues, does not mean that they always will. Many issues compete for citizens' attention, people are busy, and can detach from politics. Particularly when environmental issues take a long time to address, public attention can wane.

This is described by Anthony Downes as the **issue attention cycle**. When an environmental issue reaches an "alarm" stage and receives a great deal of media and public attention, civil society organizes, voters pressure their elected representatives to address the issue, and eventually elected officials and policy makers act. New laws or policies are created to address the issue. But soon disillusionment sets in as voters become aware of the costs of action and how long it will take to achieve results. Then as voters and officials become bored or disillusioned, attention wanes to the environmental issue and fewer resources are devoted to implementing the new policy. While democracy allows the potential for environmental action, it does not guarantee environmental protection in practice.

OPEN TECHNOLOGIES: CLEAN ENERGY

A third approach to environmental protection lies in inventing and applying greener and cleaner technologies. By this view, we can invent ourselves out of our environmental destruction, and technology will save us.

There are many promising new green technologies. Cell phones allow greater opportunities for environmental monitoring and transparency, as citizens can take pictures of environmental hazards, post and distribute them widely, and thus organize pressure on government or companies to improve environmental protection.

New technologies can directly improve environmental outcomes. For example, electric cars reduce carbon emissions as compared to fossil fuel burning cars.

As renewable energies become more available and more affordable, new technologies such as a "green grid" are needed to deliver clean energy. Researchers at Stanford University have devised a plan for each of the fifty US states to convert to a green power grid, based on the renewables already available in each state. From solar panels at homes, offices, schools and parking lots, to solar roads with embedded sensors that recharge electric vehicles as they drive on the roads, China is investing heavily in solar and renewable technologies.

Bill Gates, one of the world's richest men, is investing heavily in the next generation of nuclear energy. He envisions totally redesigned nuclear power plants that would not create nuclear waste but rather would use the nuclear waste created by old nuclear power plants as fuel, thus removing an environmental hazard rather than creating one. He calls for other inventors and investors to join him in creating an energy revolution, where zero carbon energy is readily and cheaply available at mass scale. His project is controversial because of the poor environmental history of nuclear power, and because some doubt the viability of the technological break-throughs which Bill Gates is advancing. Others, like Pope Francis, believe technology alone cannot save us from environmental problems. Instead he calls for a deeper change of heart and spirit. We must improve our relationships with nature and each other to be able to protect our common home, and improved relationships take real-world contact. Pope Francis calls us to stronger relationships with each other and with nature than we currently enjoy with our technologies.

Regardless of whether safe, zero carbon nuclear power is possible or advisable, it represents trying to solve environmental problems through new technologies and private sector solutions.

GOOD NEWS: COOPERATIVE ACTION WORKS

Throughout this chapter we have seen many examples of cooperative actions on environmental problems. They fall in three main categories.

Enhanced State Capacity

States can increase their capacity to address environmental problems. Individually, states can create new laws, policies, and enforcement, as when European countries banned motor vehicles from downtown city streets, or imposed carbon taxes or gas taxes. The United States, Canada, Europe, Japan, and other developed countries created environmental protection agencies in the 1970s, to enforce clean air and clean water laws that countries created. These enhanced state capacities helped clean up many toxic sites, such as the Cuyahoga River in Ohio, and the polluted sites in Eastern Europe as these countries democratized and cleaned up their toxic legacies. Democracy in action to improve state capacity and response are examples of a ballet of cooperation.

In many areas of the world greater sovereign state capacity is needed to protect the environment. For example, in the Amazon, Central Africa, and South Asia where illegal logging operations despoil the environment and rob people of their resources, stronger state capacities are needed to help protect indigenous peoples and their forests.

International Agreements are Just the Start

Many of the examples in this chapter have been of multilateral state action, or states creating new frameworks to cooperate on environmental action, such as the Montreal Protocol which helped to heal the "hole" in the ozone layer. The Biodiversity Convention, the United Nations Framework Convention on Climate Change, The Paris Agreement, the

Stockholm Convention, the Basel Convention, the Rotterdam Convention, the Geneva Convention on Long-range Transboundary Air Pollution, and the Minamata Convention are all examples of multilateral environmental agreements. The Sustainable Development Goals are an example of an international agreement that includes environmental commitments.

International environmental protection agreements can take many forms—conventions (which usually have many state parties) or treaties (which may have two or a number of state parties) or multilateral or bilateral agreements. Whatever the name, whether they are called Protocols or Conventions or Agreements, they share common characteristics. In international environmental agreements countries agree to take measures to protect some aspect of the environment and prevent some specified environmental harm or damage. These are important commitments, rightly heralded as progress in international cooperation. International conventions and treaties are law. But like any law, getting the law passed is only the first step toward addressing the problem. What follows the fanfare of international agreement signing ceremonies is the hard work of implementation and enforcement.

First, after the heads of state sign agreements, the convention or treaty has to be ratified by the governing authorities in each country.[25] Each country has its own ratification process, but for democracies, it generally means that the Parliament or Congress has some role in voting to approve ratifying the convention or treaty. This domestic ratification process can take some time. Some conventions or treaties, signed by presidents and heads of state, are never subsequently ratified by that state signatory. All laws have "born on" dates, when they enter into force, meaning when they take effect. The convention or treaty enters into force when it reaches some specified number of ratifications (as listed in the treaty, for example, when fifty states ratify). Upon entry into force the convention or treaty is officially binding on the signatories.

Second, after ratification, then the provisions of the convention or treaty have to be integrated into domestic law and policy regulations. Treaty commitments and language are often broad, general statements, and generally need to be made specific, into something that can be monitored and enforced at the national and local levels of government, and those specifics are left to each country to decide their own best approaches. Sometimes this means new laws or regulations are needed that cover the particular provisions of the treaty. Other times existing laws and policies can be updated to harmonize domestic law with international law. Sometimes the domestic law of a country already exceeds the international standards set in the treaty.

Third, after the translation and integration of the international treaty into the domestic context, (laws, regulations, and policies), then they become "part and parcel" of the local and national government's standard implementation procedures. Whether it is the local environmental protection agency, coast guard, fisheries agent, food inspector, or police, the law is implemented at the national and local level. Implementation of international law is therefore only as strong as the local government's capacity. States with more government capacity and with more professional and better-resourced law enforcement actors will have stronger enforcement than weak states with few resources and fewer, poorly trained or corrupt government agents.

This is too often where the gains made in negotiating international agreements can be lost in poor implementation. The 193 sovereign states (or however many have signed the particular treaty) have to be able and willing to implement and enforce their laws, including their domestic and international commitments to environmental protection. Some have strong capacity, some states have strong interest and political will, and will be the treaty's lead implementers. Other states have weak capacity or weak interest or political will, and will lag or neglect treaty implementation.

But international agreements do have means to help the laggers advance. Treaties often require signatories to monitor and report on their implementation and compliance, and this information is shared with all signatories, often through a Secretariat or designated agency. International environmental agreements usually include regular meetings of the state parties to the treaties; working groups of states with particular interest or capacity in specific subsets of issues; joint research activities, or coordination and information sharing of domestic research of issues pertaining to the treaty; capacity building measures and sharing of lessons learned and best practices; and conferences or other forums for joint deliberation and follow-up. Negotiations and interactions among states don't end once an international environmental agreement is signed. These features of international agreements provide channels for interaction and cooperation, that can be used to help laggers advance toward better implementation.

It is not a straight line from norm setting to rule implementation. Rather, there are a series of channels and interactions between a variety of domestic and international actors over time. But countries are creating more international agreements, building more channels of communication and cooperation than ever before. And for all the challenges of implementing these agreements, they provide leverage and a variety of avenues for cooperative action.

Private Sector Environmental Action

As the private sector increases in size and power, we are witnessing a huge increase in activities of private sector actors toward environmental protection, from both the nonprofit, legal side of the private sector, and the for-profit part of the private sector.

From the nonprofit side, from Pope Francis' environmental encyclical Laudato Si, to the activities of the Interfaith Center on Corporate Responsibility, NGOs and prestate actors are highly engaged on environmental issues. Behind changes in laws and international agreements are usually coalitions of NGOs known as transnational advocacy networks mobilized and pressuring states to change. For example, the Environmental Defense Fund has been very active in advocating that states create carbon cap and trade systems, coaching and advising countries such as Mexico on how to proceed. Children's campaigns such as Youth for Climate Change are becoming increasingly active. In Belgium, tens of thousands of school children have skipped school every Friday for weeks to protest climate change and demand that leaders implement the Paris Climate agreement. Led by Swedish high school student Greta Thunberg, who addressed the World Economic Forum and Davos in Switzerland demanding action, the children have formed networks around the world, with protests, marches, and school strikes in Sweden, Belgium, Ireland, Australia, Germany, etc. In the United States and separately in Canada, children are suing the government for failure to protect their rights to life, liberty, property, and a clean environment. These are examples of private sector nonprofit actions.

The for-profit side of the private sector is also working on environmental issues, as companies and investors invent and advance green technologies. TerraPower is the new company Bill Gates is hoping will develop a new and clean way to produce nuclear energy. Old companies can also develop new products and services, such as General Electric which built the world's largest wind turbine.

Illegal nonstate actors are also engaged on environmental issues, as criminal actors illegally fish, mine, log, dump toxic wastes, and trade in endangered species around the world.

Public–Private Partnerships

Another type of international environmental cooperation are the increasing numbers, scale, complexity, variety and reach of public–private partnerships. The United States. Canada Cap and Trade system for acid rain is an example of public–private-sector cooperation, including among academics, think tanks, and environmental NGOs such as the Environmental Defense Fund who provided advise and technical expertise to help establish the regime. The opening discussion of Dr. George Awuni and the sub-Saharan Agriculture Research Institute's efforts to help Ghana devise more climate change resilient crops and farming techniques are an example of an international public–private partnership. The Institute's work is supported by the US and Ghanain government, the SARI institute, Catholic Relief Services and Montsanto.

We have many models of cooperation. We have invented many new and creative modes and avenues for cooperation. But we need to speed up and scale up cooperation as quickly as environmental problems are speeding up and scaling-up. When the problems are this urgent, we need "all hands on deck," all approaches from all sectors, to protect our common home.

KEY TERMS

biopiracy, 217
black carbon, 227
cap and trade, 234
carbon sinks, 225
chlorofluorocarbons (CFCs), 224
communal land rights, 211
Convention on Biodiversity, 217
e-waste, 221
Elinor Ostrom, 235
environmental crimes, 213
environmental Kuznet's
    curve, 231
formal land title, 211
green revolution, 218
Intergovernmental Panel on
    Climate Change, 227
issue attention cycle, 236
Laudato Si, 210

Minamata convention, 223
Minamata disease, 223
Montreal Protocol, 225
particulate matter, 224
seed banks and gene banks, 218
Paris Climate Agreement, 227
Rotterdam Convention, 222
Stockholm Convention on
    Persistent Organic Pollutants
    (2001), 223
tragedy of the commons, 235
toxic trade, 222
United Nations Framework
    Convention on Climate
    Change, 227
Vienna Convention for the
    Protection of the Ozone
    Layer, 225

DISCUSSION QUESTIONS

1. How does climate change undermine food security, access to education and water?
2. For farmers in developed countries, climate change is a nuisance. For subsistence farmers in poor countries, climate change is a death

sentence. Why do poor farmers have fewer means to adapt to the changing climate affecting farming?

3. Describe cost shifting in environmental problems. Give examples. Have you experienced such cost shifting?
4. If the world's population were all able to live at US consumption levels, how many planet earths would we need?
5. What threatens biodiversity?
6. Environmental crimes are some of the largest international criminal activities in the world. Describe the types of activities undertaken. How have you experienced illegal dumping or other environmental crimes?
7. How much e-waste does the average American produce in a year? How much e-waste do you produce?
8. Why do seemingly small temperature changes, such as a 1.6 degree change in temperature, produce big results?
9. How has global health improved in recent decades? How is climate change undermining those hard-won gains in global health?
10. Why is the environmental Kuznet's curve theory attractive? What are some of the problems in applying this concept today?
11. When have cap and trade systems worked well? What are the challenges of applying them to global carbon emissions?
12. Why is Bill Gates in favor of new nuclear power designs?
13. Why are children around the world campaigning for environmental protection? What are they doing? Do their campaigns resonate with you? Why or why not?

Iraqi children learning to avoid IEDs and mines.

8

Terror in War and Peace

Weaponizing Fear

■ ■ ■

Terrorism almost always fails.

—Dr. Audrey Cronin[1]

Saudi Arabia is the world's biggest funder of terrorism. Saudi Arabia funnels our petro dollars, our very own money, to fund the terrorists that seek to destroy our people while the Saudis rely on us to protect them.

—President Donald Trump[2]

ISIS's use of unmanned aerial systems (drones) for surveillance and delivery of explosives has increased, posing a new threat to civilian infrastructure and military installations.

—U.S. Marine Corps Lt. Gen. Vincent R. Stewart, director of the Defense Intelligence Agency[3]

France is going to have to learn to live with terrorism.

—Manuel Valls, French Prime Minister[4]

ISLAMIC STATE TERRORISTS SET OFF a roadside bomb near a marketplace in western Anbar province in Iraq, using an IED (improvised explosive device). IEDs are the weapon of choice of terrorists in Iraq, Afghanistan, and Syria. Globalization inadvertently facilitates IED bomb making. The ready availability of cheap consumer electronics, from hobby drones to cellphones, and easily available Internet instructions on bomb making, means that inexpensive and easily

245

acquired circuits can be weaponized faster than governments can stop the bombmakers. No one was killed in this roadside attack, but two Iraqi civilians were severely injured by the blast. Security forces seek to apprehend members of the Islamic State, a terrorist group active in the ongoing civil wars in Iraq and Syria. The Iraqi media covered the story. Outside of Iraq, media and public attention was nearly nonexistent, as the attack seemed a routine part of the ongoing conflict in Iraq. The incident illustrates many of the common traits of terrorism. Most terrorism occurs in warzones. Most terrorist attacks fail, killing no one. Most terrorists are "homegrown," from the country in which they conduct attacks. Terrorists' ability to generate fear depends on their ability to command media and public attention for their misdeeds. Terrorism is an old problem, but globalization facilitates terrorism in unintended ways.[5]

Terrorism is not new. What is new is the way terrorists today can take advantage of globalization, broadcasting their message, organizing, and attacking beyond borders. Terrorists use drones for spying and to bomb with **IEDs**. Terrorists use cell phones to detonate bombs. Terrorists use cheap and instant social media and global infrastructure to video their violence and spread their messages; recruit members; radicalize people to commit violence; raise money; train individuals and cells; gather intelligence; move people, money and material; and conduct operations.

Most terror attacks kill no one, particularly in countries at peace. The vast majority of terror attacks globally are directed at property, not people. Most fatal terror attacks occur in warzones. Over 75 percent of deaths from terrorism occur in Iraq, Afghanistan, Syria, Somalia, and Nigeria.[6] Casualties outside of warzones are few, totaling only a few hundred people in the rest of the world combined. High casualty terror attacks, in which more than fifty people die, are increasing but are still very rare, accounting for less than one-half of 1 percent of all terrorist attacks. Most high casualty terrorism occurs in warzones. To end the world's worst terrorism, we must end the world's worst wars.

The good news is, terrorism ends. No terrorist group has ever felled a democratic state. While a few terrorist groups meet their short-term goal of survival for a few years, most do not, and nearly all terrorist groups fail to reach their long-term political objectives. More than 75 percent of terrorist groups dissolve within their first year. Terrorist groups have a poorer record than most new business startups. Terrorist groups are by definition minority groups that lack wide-scale popular support. War is defined as major armed conflict causing more than 1,000 battle-related deaths in a calendar year. Empirically, most terrorism is not war, as terrorist attacks are not usually very lethal. Terrorism is also rare in countries at peace. US citizens are more likely to die by being struck by lightning than they are likely to die in a terrorist attack.

Most terrorism and most high casualty terrorism occur in warzones. When wars end, the associated terrorism declines as well. When there were civil wars in Sri Lanka, Northern Ireland, and Colombia, terrorism was very high in those countries. Now that these countries have reached peace agreements and are building peace, terrorism has greatly declined there.

The bad news is that high casualty terrorist attacks are increasing, even though these primarily occur in warzones. Globalization allows terrorists to outsource casualties. Prior generations of terrorists limited the casualties they caused. For example, the Irish Republican Army in Northern Ireland and the Basque separatists in Spain, fought for autonomy, for control over territory and self- governance. They had self-imposed limits on killing, because their audience was local. The more Spaniards ETA killed, or the more Irish the **IRA** killed, the less local public support in Spain or Ireland the groups would be able to command. Mass casualty attacks did not serve their political objectives. This is not true of terror groups like Al Qaeda and Al Qaeda's splinter group, ISIS. These groups are globally networked, with political aims that go beyond borders, such as establishing a caliphate that would extend over many countries, from North Africa to Asia. Killing civilians in a foreign country may not undermine their local support in another country.

Consider these examples. ISIS and Al Qaeda use drones and cell phones to conduct terrorist attacks. Training is available cheaply and globally on the Internet 24/7. Terror recruits do not have to travel to Syria or Afghanistan or other locations for training at terror camps, risking detection by law enforcement. For example, Emanuel Lutchman was arrested in Rochester, NY, for conspiring with ISIS.[7] He had watched online radical videos, and communicated online with people who identified themselves as ISIS, but who were actually FBI undercover agents. Such "virtual" terrorism has been key to terror groups' survival. When United States and coalition forces destroyed terror-training camps in Afghanistan, according to Osama bin Laden biographer Hamid Mir, Al Qaeda scattered into exile with "every second al Qaeda member carrying a laptop computer along with a Kalashnikov." Online training videos and manuals include "how tos" for building and wearing a suicide bomber belt; creating biological weapons and spreading the plague; poisoning techniques; extracting and recycling explosives from missiles and land mines; bomb recipes, instructions, and country-by-country explosives shopping lists and availability information; hostage taking; assassination; shooting a rocket-propelled grenade; firing an SA-7 surface-to-air missile; blowing up cars; and using social media to organize a cell and plan an operation. In 1998 there were 12 terrorist-related Web sites; today there are over 7,000. At its height, ISIS had between 50,000 and 90,000 Twitter accounts alone. As government authorities or service providers shut down a terrorist Web site or twitter account, hundreds of successors crop up with mirror postings, in a digital game of "whack-a-mole." Violent extremists also use the dark web.[8]

In a historic demonstration of global terror networks, consider the case of the **millennium bomber**. The terror attacks of September 11, 2001, are well known. Less appreciated are the facts that numerous, terror plots were stopped by police in more than eight countries, including plans to hijack airplanes and fly them into landmarks. The millennium bomber was one of these attacks foiled by law enforcement.

On the evening of December 14, 1999, US Customs agent Deana Dean decided to search the last rental car leaving the ferry from Vancouver, British Columbia, into Washington state. The driver had a Canadian driver's license that identified him as Benni Antoine Noris of Montreal, but his answers to her routine questions seemed hesitant and nervous. Customs agents removed the cover over the spare tire in his trunk and found garbage bags of white powder, as well as aspirin containers and olive jars filled with liquid resembling honey. The suspect bolted, ran across lanes of traffic, bounced off a moving vehicle, and tried to commandeer a car. Customs agents apprehended and handcuffed him and continued to search his vehicle. Thinking the white powder they found was drugs, the border guards lifted, examined, and shook the containers, while the suspect ducked behind a car. Later, they learned they had by chance apprehended a 32-year-old Algerian man named Ahmed Ressam, who was wanted in France and Canada for suspected terrorist activities. Rather than narcotics, Ressam was carrying 100 pounds of volatile, high-powered explosives that could have detonated if accidentally dropped by the customs agents. His intended target had been the Los Angeles International airport. The press quickly dubbed him the "millennium bomber."[9]

Ressam worked with his father in a coffee shop in Algeria until civil war intensified in Algeria in 1992. An Islamic fundamentalist party was on the verge of winning national elections, but the government prevented it from taking power and a civil war broke out. Ressam became associated with Islamic extremists and then moved to France for the next two years. During that time, Algerian terrorists calling themselves the Group Islamique Armé (GIA), or Armed Islamic Group, conducted a series of bombings of the Paris Metro subway system, killing 22 people and injuring more than 200 others. In an eerie preview of the September 11 attacks, in 1994 they hijacked an Air France plane, which they intended to crash, fully loaded with fuel and passengers, into a Paris landmark, preferably the Eiffel Tower. French commandos successfully stormed the plane, freed the passengers, and shot the hijackers, thus spoiling the plan.[10]

Ressam left France, using a fake French passport, and applied for political asylum in Canada, which was denied. He moved in with a group of Islamic extremists in Quebec, where he supported himself on Canadian welfare assistance and petty theft and fraud, usually by robbing tourists and using or selling their traveler's checks, cash and credit cards, passports, driver's licenses, and other identification papers. When French police upset a GIA plot to bomb a G-7 economic meeting in France, they seized an electronic organizer filled with phone numbers and addresses of others in the terrorist network. Ahmed Ressam in Montreal was included in the electronic records. Bureaucratic obstacles and delays between the French and Canadian governments and within the Canadian government kept law enforcement from apprehending Ressam. In the meantime, he forged a false Canadian birth record and obtained a Canadian driver's license and passport as Beni Noris. Posing as Noris, he traveled to Pakistan, where he met with Al Qaeda members and was taken to Osama bin Laden's terrorist training camps in Afghanistan. He received training in explosives manufacturing, destruction of a country's infrastructure, use of chemical weapons, and other terrorist activities. He left with new skills, $12,000 in "seed money" from the Al Qaeda network to pursue terrorist activities, and a request from one of bin Laden's chief lieutenants to steal and send them original Canadian passports so they could help establish operatives in the United States. As investigating French Judge Jean-Louis Brugiere noted, "You can't move around if you don't have false papers and passports. For these groups, passports are as important as weapons."[11] Ressam returned to Canada via South Korea, with a layover in Los Angeles International Airport. While there, he surveyed the site, calculating how long he could leave explosives-laden luggage before it would be discovered and moved, and the length of time he would have to escape the premises (apparently, he did not plan a suicide bombing).

Ressam was arrested days before the millennium, and his cooperation with law enforcement helped secure the arrests of some of his associates in Canada and Brooklyn, New York. International law enforcement efforts foiled other millennium plots in Jordan, Yemen, the Philippines and elsewhere. After the September 11 attacks, Ressam was again interrogated in a high-security prison in Seattle. He said he did not know any of the September 11 hijackers, but he gave authorities additional information about terrorist sleeper cells and about Al Qaeda's interest in chemical and biological weapons. He was interviewed by terrorism investigators from seven countries more than seventy times. He provided the names of 150 terror suspects, and his testimony helped win several arrests and convictions, including the capture of Abu Zubaydah, Osama bin Laden's suspected lieutenant. Ressam was sentenced to thirty-seven years in prison; he will be sixty-five years old when he is scheduled to be released, if he lives that long.[12]

These examples illustrate many trends in modern terrorism: global operations, use of cheap and easily available modern technologies, networked organizational structures, and a desire to increase casualties. These same characteristics make it harder for states to stop terror attacks. States must share information, integrate action, and cooperate with a wider number of actors, including states, companies, and civil society groups, often in a short time frame.[13]

DEFINING TERRORISM

Terrorism has been around for centuries. The word terrorism was first used in describing the Reign of Terror phase of the French Revolution in 1793–1794 as a newly installed regime systematically attempted to consolidate power. In nineteenth-century Russia, the People's Will proudly admitted using terrorism in its fight against the autocracy, seeing its members as "noble, terrible . . . the martyr and the hero." A successor group later proclaimed, "The terrorists are the incarnation of the honor and the conscience of the Russian revolution."[14] Those first generation of terrorist groups were generally using violence to discredit monarchies.

Using the term "terrorism" has always been controversial. The British Army in Palestine in 1947 banned use of the word "terrorist" to describe members of Menachem Begin's Irgun group, the principal Jewish rebel force, because it implied that British forces had reason to be terrified by the resistance fighters.[15]

The twentieth century witnessed many terrorist groups of this type, using the tactic of terrorism in anti-colonialism, ethnic and nationalist violence. Other types of terrorism are ideological groups, whether they are right wing, such as the Ku Klux Klan and other white supremacist and antigovernment groups, or left wing, such as the Peruvian group, the Shining Path, and other communist groups. Left-wing terrorism has precipitously declined since the end of the Cold War, with many groups disbanding since the demise of the Soviet Union. Right-wing terrorism is on the rise. The final type of terrorist group is religious or spiritual, such as Al Qaeda and Aum Shinrikyo.

Besides the objectives they pursue, terrorist groups also vary by their organizational type. Today, many groups favor decentralized networks; others are organized in cells, or in traditional hierarchies. They also vary in their geographic reach, from domestic to international, and in the sources of their support, from states to individuals. State-sponsored terrorism has declined greatly since the end of the Cold War, although some state-sponsored terrorism remains, primarily in the Middle East. Saudi Arabia sponsors Al Qaeda–affiliated groups such as the al Nusra Front; Iran sponsors Hezbollah. Agreeing upon one common definition to cover so many different types of groups is difficult.

Defining terrorism today is no less controversial, in part because the concept is entwined with questions of justice, legitimacy, and values. Terrorists call into question the basic social contract of the state, the ability of the state to protect its citizens and the state's possession of a monopoly on the legitimate use of force. Because of the word's pejorative connotation, many people seek to label any use of violence they perceive as illegitimate or with which they disagree as terrorism. Israel tends to refer to any Palestinian violence as terrorism, whereas Palestinians call Israel a terrorist state. Pakistan regards Muslims fighting for the autonomy of Kashmir as freedom fighters, yet India regards them as terrorists. **Al Qaeda**, a Saudi Arabia–based terrorist organization, began to support Muslim fighters against the Soviet Union's invasion of Afghanistan; it contends that the United States engaged in terrorism because of civilians killed in Iraq, and because the United States used weapons of mass destruction against civilian populations—as when it dropped atomic bombs on Hiroshima and Nagasaki in 1945. Many commentators in the United States refuse to refer to violence by white supremacist groups as terrorism.[16]

Distinct from the word's use as an insult, however, is some core of agreement about the definition of terrorism. Why is terrorism considered to be an illegitimate use of force? One reason is that **terrorism** typically refers to force directed against noncombatants, which violates centuries of natural law and international law regarding the rules of war. Terrorists intentionally target noncombatants because it is a violation of deeply held moral and legal convictions. Killing noncombatants generates a greater response than killing soldiers, who expect personal risk in their line of work. Terrorists are minority groups without the conventional means to attack their enemies. They deliberately break conventions against killing noncombatants as a "force multiplier," in order to cause a psychological reaction (fear, shock, panic) out of proportion to the magnitude of the attack in order to perpetuate political goals, and to call into question the legitimacy of the state, whose job it is to protect civilians.[17] For example, more people die in the United States in their bathtubs than die by acts of terrorism.[18] Yet bathtub deaths do not command public outcry, media attention, and creation of special "Bathtub Death" government response units.

Unlike other "isms"—communism, fascism, and socialism—terrorism is a strategy or tactic, not an ideology. It is used by widely divergent groups, from Maoists in the mountains of Peru to white supremacists in the United States to conservative Wahhabi Salafi Islamic extremists in the Arabian desert. Combating terrorism is similar to other efforts to delegitimize particular tactics internationally, such as the bans on antipersonnel landmines, cluster munitions, chemical, biological, and nuclear weapons. Similar to these campaigns to ban landmines and cluster munitions as illegitimate tools of force against noncombatants, international coalitions, treaties, and conventions against terrorism also seek to globally undermine the use of terrorist violence against noncombatants. Combating terrorism is not a fight against a particular state, territory, group, person, or ideology. It is an effort to protect noncombatants, to curtail the use of a specific method of violence.[19]

Terrorism depends on surprise to gain attention and generate fear, so terrorists must constantly be innovative in their means of attack or they lose the power to shock. If terrorist violence becomes routine, then their actions will not pressure change and their goals will no longer receive attention. Surprise is one way of compensating for what they lack in numbers. "Terrorists rarely attack well defended targets. The two factors of weakness and the desire to excite passions encourage terrorists to attack ordinary civilians."[20]

Terrorism is an inherently political act designed to achieve particular goals, generally to bring public pressure to bear on government decisions. For example, Al Qaeda's terrorist campaign against the United States began as an attempt to pressure the United States to withdraw its support from the Saudi and Egyptian regimes, which Al Qaeda regards as illegitimate. The calculus assumes that raising the costs to the United States will undermine support and encourage change of US policies in the Middle East. Thus, even though some people regard such terrorists as "mad" due to their morally reprehensible means, terrorist groups are engaged in conscious, goal-directed, and premeditated rather than random behavior.

As opposed to mass insurgencies, mass uprisings or spontaneous violence, "Terrorism is clandestine violence organized by small groups. . . . [T]errorism is highly intentional or purposeful violence. It is not spontaneous or unplanned."[21] For example, the Paris attacks on Friday, November 13, 2015, revealed a highly organized conspiracy that spread across France, Belgium, Austria, and Syria. Learning from the Paris attacks, a British counterterrorism official noted, "We used to plan for three simultaneous attacks but Paris has shown that you need to be ready for more than that. We are ready if someone tries with seven, eight, nine, ten."[22]

Because terrorism aims to arouse or intimidate civilian audiences more than reduce an opponent's military effectiveness, "Victims are representative and symbolic. Their usefulness to the terrorist lies in the regard society has for them." In the past, terrorists often assassinated government leaders, until they realized they often did not get the response they wanted from these attacks. Terrorists changed targets to focus on "the common man or woman" as evidenced by attacks on people engaged in "everyday" activities in Germany, Belgium, and France.[23]

There are other official definitions of terrorism. The **International Convention for the Suppression of the Financing of Terrorism** sponsored by the United Nations defines terrorism as "an act intended to cause death or serious bodily injury to any person not actively involved in armed conflict in order to intimidate a population, or to compel a government or an international organization to do or abstain from doing any act."[24] Other UN documents stress that terrorists are nonstate actors motivated by political goals.[25]

The US Department of State defines terrorism as premeditated, politically motivated violence perpetrated against noncombatant targets by subnational groups or clandestine agents, usually intended to influence an audience. The term "international terrorism" means terrorism involving citizens or the territory of more than one country. The term "terrorist group" means any group practicing, or that has significant subgroups that practice, international terrorism.[26]

The definitions share the idea that terrorism is the use of violence against noncombatants, generally by nonstate actors to generate fear in furtherance of other political goals. The "nonstate" component of the definition is important, though controversial. If terrorism is conducted only by nonstate actors, then by definition US and Israeli actions against noncombatants are not terrorism, whereas similar actions by Palestinians may be so termed. If states like Syria and Sudan deliberately and intentionally target and terrorize noncombatants, it is a violation of the laws of armed conflict, not terrorism. State violence against civilians is also illegal, but it may be classified as war crimes, crimes against humanity, or genocide. International conventions, because they are signed by states, are likely to support definitions of terrorism that are more favorable to states.

All uses of violence by groups labeled as terrorist may not be terrorism, and not all violence by nonstate actors is terrorism. Terrorism is distinct from other forms of political violence by nonstate actors such as insurgency and guerrilla warfare, among others. **Insurgency** is a movement to overthrow a government, take over control of some or all of the territory of a country, or force a government into sharing power over the disputed territory. Insurgencies require the support of the population, either actively or indirectly. Insurgent violence targets government and military targets, whereas terrorists deliberately target civilians. Insurgencies are mass movements and aim to grab and hold territory and set up their own governing institutions. Terrorists are smaller, minority, clandestine groups, which do not enjoy much popular support. Insurgencies last long, while most terrorist groups do not last very long. The average length of an insurgency is ten years, while many last much longer (insurgencies in Colombia lasted over forty years). Insurgencies with more than two insurgent groups last longer, as is the case in Syria. Insurgencies are more likely to succeed in rural, less-developed countries, like Afghanistan. Government forces are more likely to win eventually against insurgencies in middle-income, urbanized countries, like Syria. Governments that are in transition from autocracy to democracy, an **anocracy**, like Iraq after the fall of Saddam Hussein, have the most difficulty in combatting insurgents. Nonstate groups may use a medley of tactics that includes both terrorism and other forms of political violence. For example, when ISIS broke away from Al Qaeda in Iraq they began as a terrorist group, but increasingly conducted mass insurgent warfare aimed at military targets, seizing and holding land and setting up governance. ISIS also engaged in terror attacks against civilians, to delegitimize the Iraqi state and expose it as being unable or unwilling to protect Iraqi citizens. Terrorism means not only conducting illegal actions (such as killing noncombatants) but also having certain intentions behind those actions (causing fear and psychological reactions to achieve political or other goals rather than destroy something of material value). Some terrorist groups aspire to winning more popular support to become a more widespread insurgency.[27] Traditional guerrilla or insurgent actions to diminish a government's abilities to project power into a disputed region may not be terrorism, but insurgent groups may also use terrorism.

These distinctions between terrorism and other forms of low-level violence can confuse policy makers and the public, because generally once a group is labeled as terrorist, all its actions are labeled as terrorism, even though groups may employ a variety of tactics, only some of which are terrorism. If Hamza bin Laden, an Al Qaeda leader, orders a cup of coffee, is it an act of terrorism? If a vendor was forced to give bin Laden a cup of coffee at gunpoint, is the vendor illegally giving material support to terrorism? These are not trivial questions—the **USA PATRIOT Act** is a hastily constructed law intended to help US law enforcement to deter and detect terrorist attacks. As currently and overbroadly interpreted, it categorizes a person as a criminal who gives material support to terrorists, even if the "support" was coerced at gunpoint. For example, people kidnapped by terrorists and forced to pay ransom for their lives to be spared are deemed by the Patriot Act as having provided support to terrorists; the law does not distinguish between victims and sponsors of terrorism.[28] Developing common definitions of terrorism is important as antiterrorism laws are increasingly enacted domestically and internationally. In the case of the millennium bomber, what difference does it make whether we call his actions terrorism? He committed fraud, theft, illegal immigration, and perjury, and he created and carried illegal explosives across state lines in a conspiracy to commit multiple homicides. Unlike many acts of cybercrime, which are not illegal in some states, terrorism is not primarily a problem of a lack of law. Most everything terrorist organizations do is already illegal: fraud, theft, murder, hijackings, bombings, and conspiracy. What value is added by enacting additional domestic and international legislation that labels these activities as terrorism? The purpose of additional antiterrorism legislation is primarily political: to help free additional resources to combat terrorism, to build international political consensus and harmonize international law regarding these acts, and to further undermine the tactic's legitimacy.

GOING GLOBAL

Additional international legal conventions are also sought against terrorism because, although terrorist networks are increasingly global, intelligence, military, and law enforcement efforts are still stymied by state borders and jurisdictions. For example, the US government complains that European governments are more lax in prosecution of suspected terrorists. Many of those apprehended in Germany in connection with the September 11 plot were either released or served minimal jail sentences. In contrast, the Saudi government beheaded suspects apprehended in connection with the USS Cole bombing. This was also a blow to officials in the US government, who were not afforded an opportunity to question the suspects. Because the suspects were Saudi citizens in Saudi territory, the Saudi government was well within its sovereign rights. Terrorists may go global, but state actions to pursue terrorists are constrained by sovereignty.

Although terrorism has existed for centuries, the modern period of globalization changes it. If terrorism is a form of "advertising discontent,"[29] then globalization offers terrorists the opportunity to easily and cheaply take their complaints to a global stage.[30] For example, in its heyday, ISIS had media units which took pains to film their violence in brutal detail, often doing several "takes" of beheadings and atrocities in order to get the best camera angles.

Globalization takes local fault lines farther afield. Terrorists can go global by using global media as shrewdly as other political actors. Journalist Peter Bergen recalls being contacted by Osama bin Laden's media advisors, who were considering appropriate venues for bin Laden's first television interview. The advisors had a large stack of media requests, but they had narrowed it down to the BBC, CBS News's 60 Minutes program, or CNN. Bergen, employed by CNN, recalled, "I pointed out that CNN's programs were shown in over a hundred countries, while CBS was broadcast only in the United States."[31] A month later, CNN was called on to do the interview. Bergen and his crew were blindfolded and escorted to an undisclosed location in Afghanistan and allowed to use only Al Qaeda's video equipment in case their cameras were bugged or rigged with explosives.[32] After the interview, the media advisor reviewed the tape and cut out any unflattering footage of bin Laden.[33]

Besides global media, terrorists use other cheap and easily available off-the-shelf technologies. Al Qaeda and ISIS use off-the-shelf drones, both for surveillance and to deliver bombs and IEDs. Cellphones are used to create improvised explosive devices. Terrorists use social media tracking technologies to customize messages to and recruit particular individuals. From cell phones to social media and the Internet, terrorist networks use the same technologies that global business networks use.

Globalization increases terrorists' casualties, due to greater access to lethal technologies and reduced taboos on killing. Experts have noted rising casualties and increased lethality in terrorist violence in recent years. Although the Japanese group Aum Shinrikyo's release of poisonous sarin gas into the crowded Tokyo subway system in 1995 "only" killed 12 people, more than 5,500 were injured. Many more would have died if the group had been more expert in its use of chemical agents. Local terrorist groups in the past faced diminishing returns on increased bloodshed. If their activities caused too many casualties, it could decrease critical social support, recruitments, financial support, and legitimacy. The **IRA** often faced this dilemma. But today, terrorism experts fear greater casualties in coming years as terrorist groups train in and explore the use of chemical, biological, and nuclear devices. Because terrorist groups are increasingly networked globally, with training, recruitment, financing, and operations carried out in several countries, increased deaths of one country's citizens may not reduce sympathy, support, and recruitment for the group in other countries. Increased casualties may actually build support as the group gains media exposure and international recognition that it is a force to be reckoned with. Terrorists may also capitalize politically on governments' increased use of violence to combat terrorism. For example, increased violence by British troops and Protestant paramilitary units in Northern Ireland—including the British Army's firing into a crowd of unarmed Irish Catholic civil rights protestors, killing thirteen civilians in Londonderry on "**Bloody Sunday**" (January 30, 1972)[34]—led to the establishment of the Provisional Irish Republican Army and increased sympathy for the IRA's cause for a time, as many people asked, "Who are the real terrorists here?"[35] No British soldiers were held accountable for the attacks until 2019, when only one soldier now faces charges for two of the murders.[36] Similarly the Iraq War proved to be a huge rallying point and recruitment tool for jihadist terrorists.

Globalization also facilitates the financing of terrorist groups, because dirty money moves in the same cross-border financial flows as clean money. Terrorists can finance their operations through private charitable foundations. These NGOs may conduct social service works (such as education, health care, and care of widows, orphans, war victims, and refugees), but some of the funds raised may be diverted to illicit activities. Terrorists also engage in strategic cooperative ventures with transnational criminal groups. Terrorist groups in Latin America, for example, often derive significant financial benefit from the drug trade, just as Al Qaeda profited from the Afghan heroin trade. Kidnappings for ransom are a common source of funding for terrorist groups in the Philippines and Colombia.

Terrorist organizations may also conduct legal businesses. The **Aum Shinrikyo** Japanese sect used its software development companies as a major source of revenue. The Japanese defense ministry even used Aum-developed communications programs at twenty ground bases across Japan. Aum programs were also used for airline-route management and mainframe computer operations. The software companies earned the business through indirect subcontracting relationships and by underbidding competitors by 30–40 percent because their employees, all Aum members, worked for virtually no pay. In an incredible irony, the Japanese government purchased software from the very group that perpetrated the sarin gas attacks in the hope of causing chaos that would lead to the overthrow of the Japanese government.[37]

Terrorist organizations may also network with other terrorist organizations. For example, the head of the US military's Africa Command, David M. Rodriguez, warned in congressional testimony of an "increasingly cohesive *network* of *Al Qaeda* affiliates and adherents" that "continues to exploit Africa's undergoverned regions and porous borders to train and conduct attacks."[38] While ISIS has been pushed from territory in Iraq and Syria, many are concerned that departing terrorist fighters will start new cells in other countries. Such terrorist networking is not new. The Provisional IRA historically prized "its links with foreign terrorist movements such as the Popular Front for the Liberation of Palestine, the Red Brigades, the Red Army Faction, and the ETA [Euskadi Ta Askatasuna, a Basque separatist group that inhabits the Spanish–French border region]. . . . Italian terrorists shared a huge consignment of Palestinian weapons between the ETA and the IRA."[39] IRA members were arrested in Colombia, helping to train the Revolutionary Armed Forces of Colombia (Fuerzas Armadas Revolucionarias de Colombia, or **FARC**).

THE MISSING LINK: THE PRIVATE SECTOR AND CURTAILING TERRORISM[40]

Global infrastructures were built for speed and profit, not security. People and packages now move faster, farther, more easily, and for a lower price than ever before—but at the cost of preventive, multilateral security measures. Although attention has been placed on increasing government activities against terrorism after the September 11 attacks, the private sector remains key in safeguarding infrastructure from terrorist attack. Eighty-five percent of US critical infrastructure are privately owned and operated—everything from roads and bridges to power plants, nuclear facilities, chemical and pharmaceutical manufacturers. Much of US critical infrastructure is old and was not built with security concerns in mind. Investments in critical infrastructure yield dividends every day whether or not a terrorist attack ever occurs, from better roads and bridges to better responses in hurricane or flu season.

While greater cooperation with the private sector is necessary, it is difficult. Businesses say they have few incentives to change the system and engage in greater public–private cooperation with government on security issues. They are rarely required to do so by law. Their clients, customers, and shareholders are concerned more with the bottom line than with security measures. They do not trust government competence or motives. Would information volunteered to government land in the hands of their competitors or result in higher tax bills? Without action by businesses, however, terrorists can easily exploit the vulnerabilities of the global trade and transportation infrastructure, as they did on September 11.

Because terrorists seek easy targets, private-sector responses are crucial. The private sector is increasingly partnering with states. For example, the financial sector works to curtail money laundering, and airlines share information with governments to screen passengers. Yet more private-sector cooperation is needed.

Border control has improved in the last decade, but greater real-time transparency within transportation and shipping infrastructure systems are still needed. Border walls, increasing the number of border control agents and the amount of equipment and increasing searches and seizures at borders are efforts that are still bound to fail, because even the most up-to-date and efficient government agents cannot keep up with the volume of global trade flows. Speed and volume are crucial to maintaining the economic health of global trade and transportation systems. Just-in-time shipping and narrow profit margins that are dependent on speed and volume mean that closing down borders for old-fashioned search and seizures is an unsustainable approach and equivalent to imposing an economic embargo on ourselves.[41] Luckily we have other choices.

Rather than focusing efforts on border control, security checks should be done at the point of origin in trade and transportation flows. As Stephen Flynn, a scholar on resilience and a retired Coast Guard Commander, notes trying to manage security at borders is like "trying to catch minnows at the base of Niagara Falls."[42] Border checks should be the last defense, not the first or main check for security. Thorough security background checks should be required of all private-sector employees in the shipping and transportation sectors. Governments and private-sector actors need to keep up with smart technologies, allowing more accurate real-time transparency and accountability about the contents of the shipping or transportation stream at any given time. This is how United Parcel Service and FedEx track packages in transit to customers. Businesses that comply with standards and do thorough and strict self-policing can be accorded fast-track processing at borders that would be the equivalent of an "EZ pass" lane. Border checks continue but are based on intelligence and risk management baselines rather than on hunches or profiling.

Ending Terrorism

All terrorism ends. Nearly all terrorist groups fail to achieve their objectives. Most fail quickly. But even those that are failing to meet their objectives may hang on and do damage even while they are ending. Terrorism does not end automatically. Policy makers must adopt skilled policies that exploit fissures and weaknesses within terrorist groups, without overreacting and playing into narratives that may help terrorists gain popular sympathy, resources, and recruits. If terrorist groups get larger, gain mass support and are able to transition to become an insurgent or guerilla group, as ISIS did, they become much harder to root out and will last longer.

Most terrorism ends through a combination of careful police and intelligence work to "roll up" the group (40 percent), with political work (43 percent) to address the group's grievances and/or to integrate group members who have eschewed violence into normal political processes; a combined 83 percent of terrorist groups end through intelligence, police, and political work. Thus, the Good Friday Peace agreement allowed the Irish Republican Army affiliated political party **Sinn Fein** to compete in elections and send representatives to Parliament. The Colombian peace accord likewise allows members of the FARC to enter politics. In the terrorism that occurs in warzones, ending the wars ends the terrorism.

Strengthening counterterrorism police and intelligence work requires building better networks, both horizontally and vertically. Horizontally, governments need to better share information and work together across sovereign borders. The private sector and government also need to work more closely together to disrupt and deter terrorist attacks, and to safeguard critical infrastructure. Vertically, local and national forces need to cooperate in real time. In theory, all agree on these points. In practice, it can be hard to share information and coordinate action among such a large number of different actors, among local law enforcement and national law enforcement, intelligence, and counterterrorism units

The most common state response to terrorism is to apply overwhelming military force to try to wipe out terrorist groups. This rarely

Figure 8.1 How Terrorism Ends

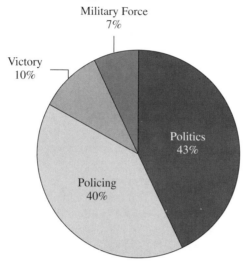

Source: RAND, "How 266 Terrorist Groups Worldwide Ended, 1968–2006"

works. Given the emotions of outrage that terrorist attacks on civilians incite, it is understandable how states are tempted to respond with "an eye for an eye" military attacks. Leaders also feel political pressure to "do something!," whether or not these actions are likely to be successful. The use of military force fails for a number of reasons. Terrorist groups do not provide a target-rich environment because they are not military organizations. They generally do not have land, armies, navies, air forces, bases, or much physical footprint. Thus there are few sites for military forces to strike. Because terrorists take refuge among civilians, the use of force by governments will create unintended civilian casualties, which terrorist groups will leverage to delegitimize the state and create a "moral equivalency" between their group and the state's use of violence. Endless war doesn't work because it plays into the narratives of terrorist groups. States have to carefully moderate their response, so as not to alienate citizens and create further recruits for terror group.

Terrorist groups seek to incite self-defeating over-reactions from states. The IRA was a weak and marginal group before the British and paramilitary attacks on peaceful protestors, shooting retreating civilians in their backs on "Bloody Sunday" breathed new life and new recruits into a faltering IRA. As Osama bin Laden recounted his strategy, "It has been easy for us to provoke and bait the Bush administration. All that we have to do is to send two mujahedeen to the furthest point east to raise a piece of cloth on which is written al Qaeda, in order to make generals race there to cause America to suffer human, economic and political losses without their achieving anything of note other than some benefits for their private corporations."

Most terrorism experts conclude that the US invasion into Iraq was a huge strategic error. Former secretary of defense Donald Rumsfeld noted this when he asked, "Are we capturing, killing, or deterring and dissuading more terrorists every day than the madrassas and the radical clerics are recruiting, training, and deploying against us? The cost-benefit ratio is against us! Our cost is billions against the terrorists costs of millions."[43]

Paul Wilkins concurs, noting that "It is a serious mistake to believe that the use of military force is sufficient to eliminate a terrorist threat. . . . When President George W. Bush stated, in the aftermath of 9/11, that the United States was declaring 'war on terrorism,' he misled many into assuming that the US military would be able to 'solve' the terrorism problem by defeating al-Qaida on the battlefields in the Middle East, and that with its superior military force the United States would rapidly defeat terrorists who hide among the civilian population."[44]

The use of military force may backfire, as when the 2003 US invasion of Iraq created Al Qaeda in Iraq, and the subsequent US de-Baathification policy created the Iraqi insurgency and unintentionally created ISIS. According to the CIA, there was no Al Qaeda presence in Iraq prior to the US invasion in 2003. Saddam Hussein's dictatorship repressed opposition groups, and Iraq is a predominantly Shia country, not disposed to a foreign Sunni/Saudi/salafi jihadist group like Al Qaeda. Opposition to the invading American forces, however, created an opportune recruiting ground for the newly created Al Qaeda in Iraq. Not only did the United States invade, but as part of the US occupation, it kicked out all Baathist party members from any government or security sector job. Unlike US military occupations in World War II, which made distinctions between Nazi ring leaders and rank and file conscripts, this de-Baathification policy made no distinctions between water sanitation engineers or government bureaucrats who were Baath party members simply to access a government job, and those who had committed war crimes or represented a threat of violence. In one stroke of the pen, the US government policy both crippled the Iraqi government by firing all competent government workers, and created enemies with guns who had nothing to lose by opposing the United States and the new Iraqi government. The Iraqi insurgency began with these disgruntled and armed former Baathists. After Iraq descended into violence and insurgency, the United States later worked to reverse the de-Baathification policy. As part of the "surge" attempt to counter the insurgency, the US government offered money to these Iraqi fighters, paying them not to fight. Through the "Sons of Iraq" and "Sunni Awakenings" movements, the US government paid former Baath fighters not to fight, and promised that the new Iraqi government would reverse the de-Baathification policy, hire back the soldiers, police, and security forces and integrate them into the new Iraqi security forces. The Iraqi government did not do this. When US payments to these fighters ended, and US forces left Iraq, the Sunni fighters again took up arms against the Iraqi Shia government. Former Iraqi military leaders who had served Saddam Hussein's government became the leaders of ISIS. US forces gave arms and money to the new Iraqi government. When Iraqi government forces retreated in the face of ISIS forces in 2014, ISIS seized arms and money provided by the United States. ISIS swept across Iraq and Syria, seizing large swaths of territory, oil fields, committing genocide against Christians and other minority communities, and destabilizing the region. The US invasion of Iraq, unintentionally, facilitated the creation, arming, and funding of ISIS. The US military invasion of Iraq to topple the regime of Saddam Hussein had the unintended consequence of increasing terrorism in Iraq, helping create new violent extremist groups, and destabilizing the larger region. Military counter terrorism strategies often backfire, because terrorism is not primarily a military threat, terrorists do not present good military targets, and decentralized terrorist networks are not easily targeted by centralized military force.

What works in preventing and managing terrorism? Terrorism is worst in war zones, so ending wars decreases terrorism, particularly high casualty terrorist attacks. More international cooperation, greater information sharing and cooperation across and within government bureaucracies, and more sustained and systematic cooperation between government and the private sector have worked to protect against terrorism.

Terrorism is an international problem and therefore requires policies that go beyond unilateral state actions. Money and weapons flow across borders, and supporters of terrorism (if not the terrorists themselves) often have established bases in other countries. Increasingly, law enforcement efforts aimed at stemming terrorism have an international component, and such a strategy will only require more international cooperation in the future. The nature of the terrorists' grievances matters. Although political violence by itself can rarely achieve its aims, it can sometimes do so in conjunction with less violent political action.

By the same token, deterring terrorism and prosecuting terrorists may be insufficient to end terrorism, especially when a large population supports the terrorists' cause. In this regard, the war on terrorism may be as unsuccessful as the war on drugs if efforts to curtail terrorism focus exclusively on military, defensive, and law enforcement approaches. Without addressing underlying factors of what terrorists are fighting for, where they draw their strength from, and how to address their grievances or separate organizations from their base, it will be difficult to manage or end terrorism. The means and targets of terrorism may be global, but grievances are often still local, ensuring that governments will need to use a range of responses to manage networked terror.

Which measures are chosen will depend on the nature of the terrorist threat as well as the domestic political context. The diffusion of power in democratic governments poses a challenge for formulating and coordinating policy.[45] In addition, democracies generally promote the idea of protection of the rights of the individual, bringing pressure on governments to respond to terrorist attacks on innocent civilians. "Democracies can survive the assassinations of leaders . . . but they cannot tolerate public insecurity."[46] However, choosing a response must be tempered by the fact that no democratic regime has ever been conquered by terrorism. Terrorists often miscalculate. Their attacks may rally support for their opponent and strengthen rather than undermine the power of the state. The magnitude of terrorist destruction must also be considered in context.

Terrorist destruction "is small compared not only to other forms of political violence such as civil wars or communal rioting but also to other sources of casualties in modern societies."[47] This is particularly true after September 11. The public perception of risk from terrorism generally far exceeds the reality. Citizens in developed countries are more likely to die from firearms or car accidents than from terrorism. In 2017, 40,100 Americans died in motor vehicle accidents.[48] Citizens in developing countries are more likely to die from tuberculosis, malaria, or AIDS than from terrorism. The spread of democracy and global media make open societies more vulnerable to terrorist attacks and place great pressure on governments to respond. Yet in choosing a response, democracies must be careful not to overreact. In fighting the war on terrorism, we must not become more like our opponents than we would like and less able to address the underlying vulnerabilities and grievances of globalization that can fuel terrorism.[49]

KEY TERMS

Al Qaeda, 247
anocracy, 254
Aum Shinrikyo, 256
Bloody Sunday, 257
de-Baathification policy, 262
FARC, 258
IED, 245
insurgency, 254

International Convention for the
    Suppression of the Financing
    of Terrorism, 253
IRA, 247
millennium bomber, 248
Sinn Fein, 260
terrorism, 250
USA PATRIOT Act, 255

DISCUSSION QUESTIONS

1. How does the explosion of a roadside IED in Iraq illustrate many of the characteristics of terrorism?
2. What is old about terrorism?
3. What is new?
4. What's the story of the millennium bomber? How was he apprehended? How does he illustrate trends in modern terrorism?
5. What is the definition of terrorism?
6. How do terrorists exploit new technologies?
7. How is terrorism different from insurgent movements?
8. How long do insurgencies tend to last? What types of government are least able to effectively combat insurgency?
9. What types of government attempts to counterterrorism are more successful? Which types of responses are more likely to backfire? Offer examples.
10. How can the private sector help to curtail terrorism?
11. "Terrorism almost always fails." Explain and offer examples.

Cyberattacks are increasing.

9

Cyber Attacks beyond Borders

■ ■ ■

Today an enemy doesn't need to travel thousands of miles to attack us. An enemy doesn't need to carry tons of iron bombs . . . . Today, because of the networked nature of our critical infrastructures, our enemies needn't risk attacking our strong military if they can much more easily attack our soft digital underbelly.

—Senator John Kyl, R-Arizona[1]

The moon shot for cyber security, in my view, is to find techniques that scale faster than the explosion in information.

—DARPA Director Arati Prabhakar[2]

The drone that landed today at the White House you can buy in a Radio Shack. You know that there are companies like Amazon that want to use small drones to deliver packages. . . There are incredibly useful functions that these drones can play in terms of farmers who are managing crops and conservationists who want to take stock of wildlife. But we don't really have any kind of regulatory structure at all for it.

—President Barack Obama[3]

Putin & I discussed forming an impenetrable Cyber Security unit so that election hacking, & many other negative things, will be guarded and safe.

—President Donald Trump

Russia leads the world in cybercrime. There is a close relationship between the Russian state and Russian organized

267

crime. . . . Russia provides sanctuary for the most advanced cybercriminals, who hack at the behest of the Russian state.

—McAfee[4]

WE ARE BEING ATTACKED BY ROBOTS all day, every day. Botnets are groups of computers or other smart devices which are compromised by malware and used as zombie robot IT armies to carry out and spread cyberattacks. Every 40 seconds a cyberattack is launched. Open technologies bring greater connectivity and productivity around the world. But they also bring new vulnerabilities, unintended consequences not imagined by the creators and propagators of the Information Age. Computers and information technologies are integrated into all aspects of life, including banks, stores, credit card machines, ATMs, hospitals, electric grids, gas stations, cars, ports, water systems, and militaries. The "internet of things" means that smart technologies are embedded in everything from our keys to cars to surveillance cameras to homes to nuclear power plants. These technologies were meant to make life easier and more efficient and prosperous, but they also make us vulnerable to attack by anonymous attackers exploiting the very IT we rely on daily. The "attack surface" of potential targets is huge.

The growing internet of things provides a large and vulnerable target set, from institutions such as banks, to personal devices. These devices were created to get products to market quickly, not to with security in mind. Through cyberattacks these devices can be turned into weapons. Or they can be used to provide precise information that can be used to conduct a traditional attack against a target. For example, through a hacked cell phone the Saudi government gained information they used to kill US-based journalist Jamal Khashoggi.

Ironically, the most powerful and technologically advanced countries are the most vulnerable, more at risk than less technologically integrated countries. From the internet to the dark web to drones, countries created many new technologies to make states stronger, but these had unintended consequences and users. The private sector rapidly adopted and adapted technologies built for speed and commerce, not security. Errors and vulnerabilities accidentally are written into computer code at the rate of approximately one vulnerability for every 2,500 lines of code. A smart phone or an Operating System, with millions of lines of code, contains thousands of vulnerabilities, generally unknown to its creators and users, leaving everyone using that product at risk. Every day adversaries test our systems, using armies of computers and malware code, searching for vulnerabilities to exploit. All day, every day, we are engaged in a global and dangerous game of "whack-a-mole." "**White hat**" hackers, the corporate and government cybersecurity experts who test IT system security, engage in "**patch and pray**" all day, every day, reactively working to patch the vulnerabilities in our IT structures faster than adversaries can find and exploit these vulnerabilities.

There are not warning signs, like troops massed at a border, before a cyberattack. Digital attacks can strike so quickly and quietly that victims may not initially know they have been hit. Malware may steal, spy, and compromise systems quietly for months or years before it is detected. For example, the Pentagon was infected with the Agent.btz malware for 14 months before it was detected. This is typically how Chinese government attacks work, trying not to draw attention. Even when victims are aware they have been attacked, victims may not want to admit they have been compromised or the full extent of the damage, not wanting to undermine confidence in their IT systems or to advertise their vulnerabilities and thus attract more attacks.

"**Watering hole**" attacks, in which attackers place malware in sites and code that users regularly use for automatic updates, turn cybersecurity upside down. The updates users expect to deliver greater security may unexpectedly harm them instead.

Cyberthreats instantly cross borders, blurring lines between government and non-state actors, crime, and warfare. Cyberattacks have costly and sometimes deadly real-world consequences. For example, on one warm summer day, trucks and ships backed up for miles in a massive traffic jam outside of the Maersk shipping center outside of New York City. The gates and cranes of the massive shipping terminal were frozen, stranding billions of dollars of freight that could not be loaded or unloaded for shipment. Nearly a quarter of Maersk terminals were simultaneously disabled around the world, from New York to Los Angeles to Mumbai, India, grinding a sizeable portion of global trade to a halt. Refrigerated, just-in-time shipping containers filled with food and medicine were in danger of spoiling. Tens of thousands-of-trucks were turned away from the disabled terminals. Factories waiting on just-in-time shipped parts went idle, costing millions. Trying to figure out what hit them, and with their computers, websites, email, and phones compromised, Maersk went silent. As one customer described it, "Maersk was like a black hole. It was just a clusterf***."[5]

Initially, the company thought it had suffered a **ransomware** attack, as many hospitals, governments, and companies in 150 countries had experienced the month before. Just as criminals kidnap people for ransom money, cyber attackers kidnap computers and data. Ransomware locks computers and encrypts data until victims pay the attackers a ransom in bitcoin or some other anonymous crypto currency. Victims then receive a key to unlock the encryption and release their data and computer systems.

Some cyberattackers are criminal groups or individual hackers, and some are states. North Korea was behind the Petna ransomware attack the month before Maersk was struck. North Korea uses cyberattacks to politically and militarily strike at its adversaries. North Korean attacks have targeted South Korea, the United States, and even actors and film companies, such as Sony, which it blames for negative portrayals of North Korea. But North Korea also conducts cyberattacks for money. The country needs the cash. It is a poor country which often suffers famine, and struggles under international economic sanctions designed to constrain the regime and punish its bad behavior.

But Maersk and the other victims of this attack soon learned that paying a ransom was useless in this case; the malware destroyed data and systems, and there was no key to undo the damage. Maersk hired the international consulting firm Deloitte to run an emergency response center in London to rebuild the company's electronic brain that ran the shipping system. Employees ran to electronics stores and bought as many laptops and Wifi hot spots as they could, not trusting any Maersk IT for fear it was compromised. Safe, back-up copies of destroyed shipping data and servers were found and retrieved in the company's global systems. But one key piece of the network could not be resuscitated, the Domain Controller which controls and sets the rules for how the units interact. While the company maintained multiple back-ups, all 150 Maersk Domain Servers had been simultaneously destroyed. As one CISCO cybersecurity expert tasked with fixing the problem explained, "To date, it was simply the fastest-propagating piece of malware we've ever seen. By the second you saw it, your data center was already gone."[6] Eventually the company located an intact Domain Server in a remote location in Ghana, West Africa, that had been spared from the attack by a local power outage. They had to physically shuttle the hard drive from Ghana to Nigeria to London, in order to restore the missing piece of the puzzle and get Maersk back up and running.

As devastating as the attack was to Maersk, the Danish headquartered shipping company was neither the target nor the most badly hurt victim. Simultaneously the same process unfolded at hundreds of other companies and countries, including Fed Ex shipping in Europe, the French construction giant St. Gabant, and the food company Mondelez (parent company of Nestle and Cadbury). While Maersk and Fed Ex suffered losses in the 300–400 million dollar range, Merck pharmaceutical suffered nearly a billion dollars in damage. Although these victims sustained losses, none of these customers and companies were the target of the attack.

The target was Ukraine. Russia has been at war with Ukraine since 2014, including cyberwar. Russia is still smarting at the demise of the Soviet Union in 1991. Russian president Putin describes the fall of the Soviet Union as "the greatest geopolitical catastrophe of the 20th century."[7] Ukraine disagrees. Ukraine is Russia's neighbor and a former Eastern European satellite state that suffered genocide and repression at the hands of the Soviets. While Putin does not seek a return of communism or a communist economy, Russia seeks to retain political power and influence in its neighbors, especially Ukraine, home of Russia's only warm water port for the Russian Navy, in **Crimea,** the area of Ukraine currently occupied by Russia. Ukraine was divided by the USSR. Ukrainian speakers in the west do not like Russia and desire stronger ties with the United States and the EU. But many former Soviet naval officers and their families retired in Crimea in the East, speak Russian, and desire close ties with Russia, not the EU. Russia seized Crimea, a strategic peninsula in eastern Ukraine, in 2014. Ten thousand Ukrainians were killed by Russians in the war, notably by Russian military who removed their Russian uniforms and spread out from the Russian naval base in Crimea. Russia denies this, saying the attacks were spontaneously undertaken by Russian-loving separatists in eastern Ukraine, with no support or orchestration from Russia. With the seizure of Crimea, Ukraine lost most of its navy that had been based in Crimea, and Russia now controls and impedes Ukraine's access to the sea. The conflict has split the Orthodox Church.

Russia conducts cyberwar against Ukraine constantly, simultaneously with Russia's military grab of Crimea. Russia undertook cyberwar against former satellite states in Estonia and Georgia in 2007. Russia follows the same playbook as it attacks Ukrainian government, military, and commercial targets. Russia unleashed the **NotPetya** attack on Ukrainian Constitution Day, to punish Ukraine on its independence day. By making the attack initially appear similar to the Petya ransomware attack conducted by North Korean agents the month before, Russia sought to confuse and misdirect, to cause greater damage and to cover their tracks and avoid culpability for the attacks. This is Russia's

M.O. in cyberwar, combining and weaponizing the talents and ingenuity of Russian organized crime in service of the Russian government with the support and resources of the Russian state, and mimicking criminal behavior in order to avoid military, political, legal, and economic consequences and punishments for their actions.

Russia targeted Ukraine in the NotPetya attacks, and took down the Ukrainian government, airports, hospitals, banks, energy companies, ATMs, credit card machines, and businesses.[8] Foreign companies that had business with Ukrainian companies, like Maersk, Merck, and Fed Ex, were also damaged in the attack. There is no downside to this "collateral damage" from Russia's point of view. Creating costs to businesses that work in Ukraine fosters Russia's foreign policy of trying to undermine and isolate Ukraine from Europe and the West.

THE ENEMY GETS A VOTE: CYBER OPERATIONS TO UNDERMINE DEMOCRACY

Russia interfered in elections in former Soviet satellite states from 2007 to the present using cyberattacks and information warfare. Russia interfered in Western European elections in Germany, the Netherlands, Finland, and the UK. Not surprisingly, Russia then interfered in the US Presidential elections in 2016, as they have done elsewhere. Internationally, the Russian interference in the US election case *is important because it reveals troubling structural vulnerabilities of democracies to cyberattacks and information warfare.* Greater and new forms of cooperation are needed to secure future elections against such interference, and in order to stop the undermining of democracy. Particularly challenging are the hijacking of social media by foreign information operations disguised as domestic free speech.

According to the Director of National Intelligence, the National Security Agency, CIA, and FBI, Russian interference in the US election, with the aim of electing Donald Trump and undermining US democracy, was ordered by Russian president Vladimir Putin.[9] They assess "with high confidence" that "Putin Ordered Campaign To Influence US Election; The Russian Campaign Was Multifaceted; The Influence Effort Was Boldest Yet in the US; and the Election Operation Signals 'New Normal' in Russian Influence Efforts."[10] Russian military units 26165 and 74455 engaged in criminal cyberoperations to help the Republican candidate and defeat the Democratic candidate. Russia wanted Trump to become president because Trump policies were more favorable to Russia. Trump favors removing economic sanctions against Russia that were placed to punish Russia for its invasion of Ukraine. Russia worked to defeat the candidate who favored continuing sanctions against Russia.[11]

Over a dozen Russian military and intelligence officials, private individuals and three Russian businesses have been indicted of a criminal conspiracy to defraud the United States, as well as other criminal charges of wire fraud, bank fraud, and aggravated identity theft, but these suspects currently remain at large; they live in Russia so the US government has not been able to bring them to trial. Because this illegal effort was so successful for Russia, the US intelligence agencies assess they will likely continue cyberattacks combined with other means to interfere in elections in the United States and elsewhere.

According to the US government indictment of Russian government operatives, "Russia engaged in large scale cyberoperations involving the staged release of documents stolen through computer intrusions. To hide their connections to Russia and the Russian government, the Conspirators used false identities and made false statements about their identities. To further avoid detection, the Conspirators used a network of computers located across the world, including in the United States, and paid for this infrastructure using cryptocurrency."[12] The stolen information was distributed by Wikileaks. Julian Assange, founder of Wikileaks, says the stolen emails were released at strategic points during the campaign, to draw attention away from bad news stories for Trump and to undermine good news stories for Democrats. For example, minutes after the release of the "Access Hollywood" tape in which Donald Trump was recorded saying that he enjoyed molesting women and "grabbing their pussies," the Russians released stolen emails from the opposing campaign. President Trump praised Wikileaks for their release of the stolen information, saying repeatedly "I love Wikileaks."[13]

Donald Trump's appointee to the Director of National Intelligence, former Republican Congressman Dan Coates, notes that Russian election hacking is an ongoing problem, not a one-time attack. Russia is still interfering with elections in the United States and other countries. This is not surprising, as Russia has conducted similar cyberoperations for over a decade. Russia has a well-developed play book and tools they have used in Estonia, Georgia, Ukraine, and other countries, to support pro-Russian candidates and undermine candidates critical of Russia, and to disrupt, create confusion and division, undermine elections, the media, and democracy. In 2016 they took their show on the road to the United States and Western Europe, beyond their own neighborhood of former Soviet satellite Eastern European states. They created fraudulent accounts with false identities to hide the Russian sources behind the propaganda messages favoring pro-Russian candidates and messages, and undermining democracy and candidates critical of Russia. They used social media such as Facebook and Twitter to spread lies about US Presidential candidates, to help Trump. Their tools included targeted electronic disinformation campaigns to suppress voter turnout of women and minorities in key swing districts. For example, they sent false messages to Clinton supporters that Clinton had already won so they did not need to vote. They also sent lies telling voters they could vote online and need not stand in long lines, sending voters to fraudulent "online voting sites," made to look like official government websites. These criminal attacks were targeted at specific districts in key swing states which the Trump campaign needed to win enough electoral college votes to win, despite losing the popular vote by over 3 million votes. Trump campaign director Paul Manafort delivered private Trump campaign information to Russia, allowing the Russians to carefully target their cyberattacks.

Congress has introduced new cybersecurity bills, but these have not passed, and the president has done away with the chief cybersecurity officer, at a time when independent assessments find government cybersecurity lagging behind all other industries.[14] Thus there has been little US federal government response to prevent such cyberattacks in the future. As the CIA concludes, because these cyber operations were so successful for Russia, they will continue to interfere in elections in the United States and elsewhere.[15]

Some aspects of this case are different from Russian cyberattacks in other countries' elections. What is unusual about the US case versus the many previous cases of Russian election interference was that President Donald Trump and members of his administration and campaign publicly encouraged this interference. Donald Trump publicly asked Russia, on national television and in public campaign appearances, multiple times, to help his campaign by hacking and releasing stolen electronic information from his opponent. On July 27, 2016, (at 5:30 pm Russian time) Donald Trump asked Russia in a public, televised news conference "Russia, if you're listening, I hope you're able to find the 30,000 [Clinton Democratic party] emails that are missing. I think you will probably be rewarded mightily by our press. Let's see if that happens. That'll be next." Russia immediately responded on the evening of July 27, 2016, and for the first time started trying to hack 76 email accounts of the Clinton campaign, and more email accounts used by Clinton's personal office.[16] Trump and members of his campaign publicly cheered on Russian interference, and many members of the Trump campaign and Trump administration were also criminally involved with Russia. Five members of the Trump administration and Trump campaign have pleaded guilty, and many more face criminal charges.[17] Russia has interfered in many other countries' elections before interfering in the United States. But in the other countries, the leaders fought the Russian election interference. Never before in history has any US president publicly criticized US law enforcement and intelligence agencies for their work to protect cybersecurity, while instead cheering on and defending the hackers. Partisanship is at an all-time high in the United States, in part facilitated by Russian cyberoperations sowing partisanship and discord. Attention to the US domestic political implications of the case has distracted from the larger international cybersecurity concerns that the case exposes.

STATES STRUGGLE TO KEEP UP WITH CYBERSECURITY

The exponential growth and dizzying speed of new information, communication, and transportation technologies present special challenges for states, which struggle to keep up with the technology changes and uses of private actors. Asymmetries in speed, information, and technological adaptation change not only the threats states must address, but also the tools actors have, and the way they do their jobs. The new technologies change the power and social dynamics under which governments operate. For example, the US government created the internet, drones, cyberweapons, and the dark net, for military and foreign policy purposes. But these technologies also are adopted by nonstate actors and adversaries, for legal as well as illicit and violent purposes. State cooperation in improving and harmonizing laws, enforcement, and international state-to-state cooperation on these issues are necessary, but not enough. The private sector is larger than the government, and develops and uses more new technology than the government. Private sector self-policing is necessary, but not sufficient. It is imperative that private companies police themselves, but private actors need governments and IGOs to help coordinate actions. Increasingly, states contract out their technology needs to the private sector, creating new vulnerabilities and challenges, as illustrated when contractor Edward Snowden captured and publicly released thousands of classified documents. States are expected to protect their citizens, yet 85 percent of critical infrastructure are privately owned and operated. Sovereign states have the authority and legitimacy to act, but the private sector often has more capacity and agility. States and IGOs urge public–private networks in technology areas. In practice, this is hard to do. Three examples of these themes will now be explored: drones, cyberweapons, and cybersecurity.

Cyberattacks and War

Similarly, the US government (particularly **DARPA,** the Defense Advanced Research Projects Agency) created both the internet and the dark net for use by the US military and defense organizations. The internet was created to facilitate information exchange among government military scientists. The **Dark Net** was "initially developed by the US military as a way of traversing the internet secretly, but since then had become an open source project."[18] DARPA helped develop the dark web, a place beneath the surface web for people who want to remain anonymous on the Internet. Military and intelligence units want to be able to use the internet without having their online activity detected. Military investments funded the research, as well as smaller seed money from human rights organizations, who want to help dissidents and whistle blowers be able to speak and associate online freely, without worrying about government detection, censorship, and reprisals, particularly in authoritarian countries. While the intention of creating the anonymous Dark Web may have been good, it also has had unintended consequences. The US government is now challenged in tracking down and stopping criminals and terrorists who use the Dark Web to sell drugs, recruit terrorists, launder money, etc., as discussed in the chapter on Global Crime.

A similar story is behind the creation of the internet. DARPA initiated and funded research during the Cold War in order to make a system of computer communication for the old war machine. They were worried that if a Soviet attack occurred (particularly a nuclear attack), it could sever US military communications. Seeking to create a means of computer communication that could survive a Soviet attack on the phone system, DARPAnet was created, which would later become the internet. The government created the Internet for military purposes. It did not envision how the technology might be used by the private sector, or how it could be used in warfare, by state and nonstate actors, against the United States.

In these cases, the US government imagined a monopoly on the use of these new technologies. It did not imagine how these technologies would be used against the US government, or others.

History of Cyberattacks

The new technologies change the nature of the threats countries face, create new or heighten existing international problems, and change the very jobs state organizations have to do. For example, in January of 1989 there were 80,000 Internet hosts. By January of 2000, there were 73,398,092, a 917-fold increase in 11 years.[19] In these years, cybersecurity threats were born, as well as initial government experimentation in how to respond.

The first information attacks occurred before there was an internet. "Spoofing" to steal free long-distance phone service (called "phreaking") was done in the 1970s and 1980s. The first computer worm was created in 1971; the first computer virus was developed in 1983. These means of attack just acquired more room to roam, and more ability to do greater damage, as billions of users and countless data all migrated to one system, the internet. While information technology has bolstered business productivity, reliance on IT has also made both the US government and private industry more vulnerable. The US military has always prided itself on being a very high-tech military, with information dominance. The much greater value of high-tech weapons are often automatically presumed, not tested. The US military is very high-tech dependent. Forces are completely computer equipped, from headcams and GPS trackers on troops to help avoid friendly fire, to computer-operated missiles and drones. This leads to unintended vulnerabilities.

For example, former secretary of defense Donald Rumsfeld argued when the United States invaded Afghanistan and Iraq, that technology was leading to a transformation in military affairs, where high-tech dominance would allow for lighter, faster forces. It did not exactly turn out that way. When the United States invaded two countries, Iraq and Afghanistan, soldiers faced low-tech opponents who quickly figured out ways to exploit the military's technology dependence. Hackers hijacked US drones, broadcasting the video feeds from drones for all to see, thus giving US opponents the same "eye in the sky" advantage that US forces have. Insurgents wired improvised explosive devises, using cell phones to detonate bombs. "Lighter" US troops were vulnerable to attacks. It took Secretary of Defense Robert Gates over a year to re-route money from high-tech old-war programs to low-tech body armor and armored tanks, to save lives and protect soldiers from tools of asymmetric warfare, such as IEDs (improvised explosive devices), used by their "low-tech" foes in Iraq and Afghanistan. The military was surprised to find itself vulnerable from the very information technology that was supposed to aid it. Instead, cyberattacks on military systems have increased exponentially. The military is under cyberattack every day. The political system is also under cyberattack.[20] Militaries in particular are geographically based. They are not well positioned to combat anonymous attacks that are not tied to geography.

When the enemy is an advancing army, the government can determine whom it is facing and calculate how to mobilize resources to respond. It also knows when it has been attacked. But when government organizations face cyber attackers, they may not know who is assailing them since the new technologies provide anonymity. They also may not know they have been hit until much later. Denial of service attacks or website take-downs are "noisy" attacks where the victims are aware that they have been hit. But most cyberattacks are not noisy. Attackers go to great lengths to prevent discovery of their sabotage. Data is copied or accessed, but the original data is often left in place, so it is not immediately apparent that security is compromised or that there has been a data theft. When the security breach is eventually discovered, the attackers may have had access for months or even years. It can be much more difficult to track the perpetrator after so much time has passed from the initial security breach. Even when the breach is recent, tracking is very difficult. Perpetrators operate anonymously at a distance and "cover their tracks" by routing activities through many servers and machines, so as to disguise their geographic position and identities. The inability to identify the perpetrator makes determining the appropriate response quite difficult.

For example, hackers penetrated a number of sensitive but unclassified Pentagon networks at precisely the time when US troops were deploying in the Persian Gulf against Iraq in February of 1998. In the Solar Sunrise case, the perpetrators later turned out to be two California teenagers and a hacker in Israel, but the intrusion alerted the Pentagon to vulnerabilities in its information systems,[21] calling "attention to how some of the department's open sites could provide entry to military files containing sensitive personnel and administrative data."[22]

The cyberthreat was taken more seriously after the Pentagon conducted what was at the time a top-secret, joint-staff-run exercise, code-named operation **"Eligible Receiver,"** to test the security of US critical infrastructure (such as phone lines, power grids, the Internet, financial networks) in 1997. A team of twenty National Security Agency agents, working for only three months and using software which was readily available on the Internet, showed how vulnerable US infrastructures were to cyberattacks. They accessed unclassified computer systems, demonstrating that (if they had wanted to) they could have shut down command and control functions for the military's Pacific Command as well as the entire US power grid merely by disrupting computer control networks.[23] The exercise "scared the hell out of a lot of people."[24] US technology superiority, long touted as only an advantage, now was revealed to bring real weaknesses as well. Senior US officials were stunned at how Eligible Receiver revealed the exposure of US "wireless and wireline networks, power grids, banking and financial operations and other vital support systems to sabotage."[25] Many were concerned that adversaries could launch an "**electronic Pearl Harbor**," a surprise and strategically devastating cyberattack. President Clinton noted in a commencement address at the US Naval Academy on May 22, 1998, "our foes have extended the fields of battle–from physical space to cyberspace."[26]

Ellie Padget, the Pentagon official heading the "Eligible Receiver" information war game, reported the ease of cyberattacks. "The bottom line is it doesn't take a lot of people to do this."[27]

Greater reliance on information systems provides a target-rich environment, with both many more potential points of attack and an unknown connectivity between them. Interconnected systems provide an unknown, unintended, and unpredictable domino effect: if one system is penetrated, it may have unanticipated adverse effects on other systems, even ones that are not clearly related to the point of entry. The then deputy secretary of defense John Hamre noted when the US government first began to consider cybersecurity,

Over the last ten years, most of America's infrastructure—and by this I mean everything from power utilities to water systems to natural gas pipelines to telephone networks—has been converted so that control is largely run through distributed processors. . . . America's infrastructure is largely controlled through remote computer-based technologies. Increasingly, these technologies are being linked up and actually operated over this very porous and inherently vulnerable technology of the Internet. Even in the Defense Department, 95 percent of our communications systems now ride over commercial lines.[28]

In wartime, information vulnerability grows, as spider webs of technology string our forward deployed forces together in the midst of combat. For example, the 1991 Persian Gulf War "required 7,000 radio frequencies, 1,000 miles of land links, 12 combat communications squadrons, and 29 million calls."[29] Unprecedented reliance on integrated information technologies helped win the Gulf War and maintain undisputed military superiority since, but it also makes the United States more vulnerable to attacks or disruptions on these systems.

In an embarrassing turn of events, the FBI and its **NIPC** cybersecurity unit (National Infrastructure Protection Center), charged with preventing and prosecuting cyberattacks, were forced to take down their own Internet websites due to cyberattacks against them. The attacks were launched by a Portuguese hacker identifying himself as M1crochip and his group FOrpaxe, in retaliation for the FBI and NIPC's investigations into computer crimes. They warned that "now it's our turn to hit them where it hurts by going after every computer on the Net with a .gov [suffix] . . . . We'll keep hitting them until they get down on their knees and beg. . . . We could have done worse, like destroying completely all servers. We can do it if we want. . . . "[30]

Years later, the same problems persisted. ISIS took over the Facebook and Twitter pages of US Central Command, the part of the military fighting ISIS in Iraq and Syria. The government maintained ISIS did not gain access to any sensitive information or systems, that this was merely a nuisance attack. But the US military is subject to a constant barrage of attacks, probing the US military's less secure systems such as human resources, academic, and others, looking for any way in to more important military systems. Due to the constant digital attacks, no one, not even employees, may use a thumb drive in a DoD or military computer.

Governments have tried to increase governmental capacity to fight cyberattacks. In response to the high tempo of digital attacks on DoD, the US military first created a Joint Task Force for Computer Network Defense, then the US Air Force created a Cybercommand unit in 2007, and finally a joint **US Cyber Command** was created in 2010 to integrate and strengthen the Department of Defense's expertise in cybersecurity. US military commands are usually organized geographically around territory, for example, Pacific Command. But cyberattacks are neither restricted nor attached to geography. The US military recognized it could not turn to its regional, geographic command centers to address a nongeographic threat.

PATCH AND PRAY DEFENSE

The lines between cyber defense and cyberattack are blurring. Cyber Command has both defensive and offensive responsibilities for the US military's cyber systems. Defensively, it is responsible for protecting DoD assets from cyberattacks. The US military is the largest employer in the world, and is completely dependent on networked technologies, so protecting these is a huge task. As retired Lt. General John Campbell describes it, "Defense is by far the most important of the cyber disciplines, because the consequences of mission failure are so enormous. On the battlefield, almost everything we do to plan, execute, and support military operations depends on networks of networks."[31]

Many states, like the response of the US military, have a reactive response to cyberthreats. After they have been probed or breached, they attempt to fix the newly revealed vulnerability. DoD owns over 7 million information devices, contractors use many more, and all these are vulnerable. 15,000 DoD organizational units are responsible for securing these devises, keeping their software patches and firewall protections up to date against the latest threats. *This defensive "patch and pray" approach is difficult, because security is only as good as the weakest link.*

States have been slow in creating new capacities to protect their cyber critical infrastructure. For example, the Pentagon established a Chief Information Officer late, only *in 2012*, because of the vast size and vulnerabilities of Pentagon military technologies. According to the Chief Information Officer (CIO),

> The DoD CIO supports an IT user base of 1.4 million active duty, 783,000 civilian, 1.2 million National Guard and Reserve personnel and over 5.5 million family members and military retirees. The DoD CIO provides this support in over 146 countries in over 5,000 locations and 600,000 buildings and structures. The DoD CIO also supports more than 10,000 operational systems (20% are mission critical). 1700 data centers, 65,000 servers, over 7 million computers and IT devices and thousands of networks/enclaves, email servers, firewalls and proxy servers. The DoD CIO supports the use of over 600,000 military and commercial mobile devices which includes 473,000 Blackberries, 41,000 iOS Systems and 8,700 Android Systems. The DoD CIO IT support budget is greater than $39.6 billion (6.6% of overall DoD Budget) of which $17.4 billion (2.8% of DoD) is allocated for IT Infrastructure and $5.4 billion (1.0 % of DoD) is allocated for Cybersecurity for Fiscal Year 2014.[32]

This defensive, "patch and pray" approach to cybersecurity is not limited to the US government or military. Other countries and civilian government agencies also take a reactive approach to cybersecurity, with fewer resources than those available to the military. Cybersecurity functions also are increasingly contracted out to private companies.

PLAYING OFFENSE: CYBERWEAPONS DEMOCRATIZE AND PRIVATIZE WAR

While still playing defense, government agencies also explore and sometimes use offensive cyberattacks, using the weapons and tactics of hackers against them and against other states. This is problematic, as some states such as the US government work at cross-purposes in cyber-security. *Cyber offense does not complement cyberdefense; it explodes it.* Government cyber offense activities may unintentionally undermine cybersecurity.

Offensive cyber operations at first were closely tied to traditional war efforts. For example, Israel is widely believed to have used cyber-weapons against Syria's radar system, to allow Israeli planes to proceed undetected into Syrian airspace in 2007. Israel took control over the Syrian Air Defense system, feeding it false information of no-intruder, while Israeli planes destroyed the Al Kibar site, where Israel contends Syria was secretly building a nuclear reactor. This example illustrates the use of cyber means to do traditional signals jamming and military disruption of air defense systems, using a cyberattack in place of kinetic bombing.

China's cyberattacks are primarily for espionage purposes. China seeks economic espionage, patent and source code information, as well as general information on other governments and entities.

Russia's cyberattacks originated as primarily **information warfare**, using cyber methods to implement traditional Soviet misinformation and propaganda campaigns. In attacking former Soviet satellite states, however, Russia has broadened its cyberattacks to include attacks on physical infrastructure such as banking systems, electric grids, government websites, and democratic elections from Brexit to the US 2016 Presidential election.

North Korea uses cyberattacks to generate revenue, to help it survive Western economic sanctions. Iran has also used cyberweapons for espionage, as well as to attack diplomats from countries that did not sign or those that broke their agreement on the Iran nuclear deal.

Similar to Israel, the first cyberattacks by the US military were traditional attacks on the military command, control, and communications systems of Saddam Hussein in Iraq in 2003, including disruptions of satellite and telephone networks. These targets were traditionally attacked and jammed prior to a conventional war; the innovation here was the ability to "turn off," deny service, or disrupt and jam command, control, and communication networks rather than bomb and destroy them, so they could more quickly be restored after Saddam

Hussein's government was defeated. Cyberattacks were used as part of the US "surge" in Iraq in 2007 against insurgents, to target and destroy cell phones used in IED (improvised explosive devices) attacks against Iraqi and coalition forces, to track insurgents, and to cripple command, control, and communications among insurgents. Cyberattacks were similarly used at the tactical level, in pursuing insurgents in Afghanistan.[33]

The bigger innovation has been the use of cyberweapons against the internet of things, exploiting the embedded electronics, software, sensors, and connectivity of physical objects in order to destroy them. The Bush administration was interested in pursuing greater unilateral, offensive capabilities. The United States proved this was possible in March 2007 at Idaho National Laboratory. The **Aurora Project** was a research effort to determine the vulnerability of critical infrastructure to cyberattacks which sought to destroy critical infrastructure, not just to shut it off or disrupt or deny service. In the exercise, an electric power generator was blown up by cyberattacks on the electronic controls. The US military are widely believed to have unleashed (with the Israelis) the very complex **Stuxnet** worm, which was a cyberweapon aimed at destroying the controversial nuclear centrifuges at Iran's Natanz nuclear plant. Iran has nuclear energy plants, and is suspected of enriching nuclear material from civilian use to make it bomb-grade fissile material, that would be able to be used in a nuclear weapon. Centrifuges are the machines that enrich uranium. Iran denies it is seeking nuclear weapons, while the United State and Israel fear Iran is trying to develop nuclear weapons, or is trying to develop bomb-grade fissile material as a sort of "insurance policy," that could be used in the future to create nuclear bombs quickly if dire circumstances ever required nuclear weapons. Because of the complexity of the computer code, the purpose of the worm to destroy the controversial Iranian centrifuges, and other evidence, most experts believe Stuxnet was a cyberattack made by the United States and Israel against Iranian nuclear centrifuges. For example, the worm contained no fewer than four **"zero day" vulnerabilities**. These are previously unknown vulnerabilities in computer software or operating systems, unknown even to the creators and vendors of the product, so they have "zero days" to prevent or patch the exposed vulnerabilities. Hackers and IT security firms work to find such vulnerabilities and sell them, either to the makers of the software or systems so they can repair them, or to the highest bidder on the black market. CyberComm has been buying "zero day" vulnerabilities for use as cyberweapons. It is estimated that the cost of producing the Stuxnet worm was approximately half a million dollars, as "zero day" vulnerabilities alone can cost about $100,000 each. The creator of Stuxnet was either extraordinarily lucky to find four "zero day" vulnerabilities of exactly the software used in the Natanz plant, or extremely well-funded to buy them, as the US government military agencies have been well-funded since 9/11. US Cyber Command has no comment on Stuxnet, but most experts attribute the attack to a joint effort between the US and Israeli governments to attack the Iranian government.[34]

Other offensive attacks of cyberwar have been broader and noisier. Russia took down Estonia's internet and Georgia's internet when the countries were involved in conflicts. Sony Entertainment company was attacked when Sony made a film which depicted the assassination of North Korean Supreme leader, Kim Jong Un. Experts widely believe the attacks against Sony were carried out by North Korea. North Korea is also credited with using cyberattacks such as ransomware to raise money for the poor country whose economy is further constrained by economic sanctions against North Korea.

In contrast, Stuxnet was a quiet intrusion. Different versions were unleashed over many months. And Stuxnet had a very specific target— the specific industrial controls that operated these particular Iranian nuclear centrifuges. There were several layers of constraint built into Stuxnet, to turn the worm off if it entered a system it was not targeting. These suggest it was not an indiscriminant hacker or a thief (who would not have cared what else they broke as long as they got what they came for), but a government with lawyers trained in the laws of war about limiting collateral damage.[35]

The results of the Stuxnet attack were mixed. On the one hand, the centrifuges may not have been destroyed; the damage to the centrifuges seemed not to have stopped activities at Natanz, but merely to have slowed the Iranians down. But these attacks may have convinced the Iranians to negotiate rather than face potentially worse cyberattacks in the future.

Cyberattacks "can cause real devices—real hardware in the world, in real space, not cyberspace—to blow up," noted Richard Clarke, former Cybersecurity Czar for the Bush White House (and the official who tried to warn the Bush administration of the impending 9/11 attacks).[36] All modern critical infrastructures use the types of industrial controllers that Stuxnet broke. Despite the specific damage done by Stuxnet, the ramifications of the attack are huge. In the past, an adversary would need an invading military force to enter another's territory and destroy a power plant or damage other physical targets within a country's borders. Stuxnet shows proof-of-concept to all of *the democratization and privatization of war*. Ubiquitous industrial controls that power and control all our critical infrastructure—power grids, dams, water systems, nuclear power plants, etc.—can be attacked remotely and electronically. The attack proved that cyberattacks can cause real destruction in the real world, not only thefts of data and disruptions of digital services. Few sectors have many security controls on these parts of these private systems.

Cyberweapons democratize and privatize war. Anonymous individuals and groups can physically destroy important international targets without wielding bombs and guns, without armies and militaries, and without setting foot on another country's soil. Stuxnet "leaked" to other computers around the world, beyond the Iranian computers at the Natanz nuclear fuel enrichment facility, so hackers around the world now have the Stuxnet worm, and are working to adapt this very dangerous cyberweapon. As Richard Clarke put it,

> You now have it, and if you're a computer whiz you can take it apart and you can say, "Oh, let's change this over here, let's change that over there." Now I've got a really sophisticated weapon. So you have it and are playing with it. And if I'm right, *the best cyberweapon the United States has ever developed, it then gave the world for free.*[37]

The blowback potential to the United States is huge for Stuxnet-type attacks. Who has the most of these types of targets? The United States does. The United States uses information technology pervasively across our industries and society. This creates economic efficiencies, while simultaneously making us a target-rich environment. The Stuxnet worm drew a huge red target logo on US infrastructure and wrote a "Kick Me" sign across them all. Previously, people who warned of the vulnerabilities of these systems were often dismissed as alarmist. Stuxnet proved them accurate. Stuxnet has dramatically demonstrated to the world exactly how to defeat the United States. Not surprisingly, attacks on the industrial controls of US critical infrastructure have mushroomed since the Stuxnet attack. A similar cyberattack to industrial control systems created catastrophic destruction of a German iron blast furnace. Industries do not have to (and do not like to) publicly report such incidents, but one cybersecurity expert for SANS Institute, a cybersecurity research and education organization, says he personally knows of seven such incidents.[38]

These threats go beyond sovereignty. Even when states create or adopt new technologies to increase sovereign capacity, these technologies may be used against them in unpredictable ways by adversaries and nonstate actors. Governments repeatedly seem to open Pandora's box, consistently overestimating short-term military utility of new technologies, from cyberweapons to drones, in state-to-state conflict, while underestimating the capacity of private and state actors to quickly exploit the new technologies for their own purposes, and to impose blowback costs to the private sector as well as to governments, over the long term.

Many states are adapting their institutions to address cyberthreats, but these governmental adaptations to increase sovereign capacity are not keeping pace with the speed of technological change. Most governmental actors look at cyberthreats in a siloed way, asking, for example, how their militaries can protect themselves from new sorts of attacks, and also use the new technologies of attack against state military adversaries.

Government intelligence agencies race to integrate new technologies to increase their capacities to gather information about the world. But public sector cyber capacity is not growing as fast as private sector cyber skills. This leads governments to increasingly contract out cybersecurity functions to private businesses, which can open new vulnerabilities.

For example, the US government spends more on its military than nearly the rest of the world combined. Congress allocated huge military and intelligence agency budget increases after the September 11 attacks. But most of that money was funneled to private contractors, personnel and technologies to do these large tasks. These private companies are contracted to governments. The NSA's (National Security Agency, intelligence organization) headquarters in Fort Mead, MD, is larger than the office space at the Pentagon. The NSA had long collected phone conversations and communications of foreign governments and terrorists, to integrate into the intelligence analysis provided to the president. Today, personal cell phone and digital devices mean that the NSA has much more importance in providing actionable intelligence. In fighting the wars in Afghanistan and Iraq, the military and CIA track communications devices not to listen in on the conversations, but to use the tracking data from the cell phones to kill those terrorists or insurgents who own the devices. Contractors increasingly provide the intelligence, even for military operations, adopting the slogan, "We Track 'Em, You Whack 'Em."[39]

The NSA has huge cyber intelligence operations; the exact size and parameters are classified. However, a large and growing percentage of NSA's budget goes to private companies, spies for hire, who do cyber intelligence work for NSA, and other government spy agencies.

In the past, it was easier for the government spy agencies such as the NSA to distinguish "foreign" targets to listen in on. Today, global companies and carriers provide the servers and infrastructure for global users, so the foreign and domestic lines of information gathering are blurring. The demand for real-time information to prevent terrorist attacks, and the computer processing ability to collect and mine patterns in "big data" have increased government's collection and analysis in controversial ways. Within weeks after the 9/11 attacks, the CEOs of private telecommunications companies were asked to provide data for the NSA to analyze. Most of the CEOs agreed, from companies such as AT&T, Verizon, MCI, and Sprint. A few did not, citing legal and liability concerns that cyber collection of information would violate constitutional protections of privacy and against unwarranted government search and seizure. Older laws created for telephones, not computers, barred the US government from spying on its own citizens without a court-approved warrant.[40] Government laws prohibiting domestic spying had not kept pace with the new methods of information collection by private sector actors.[41] Congress eventually updated and amended the **Foreign Intelligence Surveillance Act (FISA)** law which details the oversight procedures for government surveillance activities. FISA was amended to legalize NSA activities after-the-fact, and provided legal immunity for telecomm companies that gave data to the NSA. But the cyber skills of private companies now give private contractors unprecedented powers over states, even over governments. In 2012 a private contractor to the NSA, **Edward Snowden**, from the company Booz-Hamilton, identified himself as a "whistle blower," and released thousands of documents showing the extent of government surveillance, and unleashing a storm of international criticism of government abuse of cybersecurity.

In response to the public and international criticism raised by the Snowden documents, in 2014 the US administration began a review of the programs with an eye to the government providing better protection of privacy and civil liberties. President Obama noted that with the government continually on an open-ended war footing, "the danger of government overreach becomes more acute. And this is particularly true when surveillance technology and our reliance on digital information is evolving much faster than our laws . . . in this era of diffuse threats and

technological revolution." President Obama issued a presidential directive making changes to foreign surveillance programs, offering greater
transparency, greater Congressional, FISA, and executive branch oversight, greater accountability to the public and to allies abroad. "Just as
we balance security and privacy at home, our global leadership demands
that we balance our security requirements against our need to maintain
the trust and cooperation among people and leaders around the world."[42]
Regardless of whether one judges the NSA surveillance programs, and
the actions of private companies and contractors, effective and necessary
in combating terror and cyber threats, or unnecessary intrusions on civil
liberties, they demonstrate several themes of this book.

Sovereign states struggle to address the challenges of globalization
and nonstate actors, which move faster than government responses.
Policy makers respond to try to increase governmental capacity in
cybersecurity. But governments need expertise and technology from
the private sector to address cybersecurity issues. Governments' use
of cyber tactics to advance short-term military purposes may have the
long-term, unintended, negative effects, undermining efforts to protect
cybersecurity. While the private sector and some arms of the US government try to protect against and prevent cyberattacks, the NSA and
intelligence agencies want to keep back doors and holes in information infrastructure open, so that they can exploit them for intelligence
gathering purposes and offensive cyber operations. Citizens and private
companies, for example, would like to eliminate information vulnerabilities, such as "zero day" vulnerabilities, in order to protect personal
and corporate data. But the NSA and the US military's Cybercomm
would like to buy them, to stockpile as cyberweapons. Flush with huge
budget increases since 9/11, the US Department of Defense spends large
sums on buying "zero day" and other IT vulnerabilities, creating a
market in IT vulnerabilities that impede companies' abilities to fix these
vulnerabilities.[43] Offensive cyberattacks undermine the US government's
defensive cybersecurity.

Stuxnet is not an isolated example. The US government unit
involved in the creation of Stuxnet (experts cite the NSA and Cyber-
Comm) is said to be behind cyberattacks around the world that rewrite
the firmware that launches every time a computer is turned on, hiding
spyware that can effectively capture a computer's data and encryption
passwords. It is impossible to remove the malware which is "close to
the metal of the machines," and nearly impossible to detect it in the
computer's hardware. Infected computers cannot be "wiped clean,"
repaired and re-used, turning "even the most sophisticated computer

into a useless piece of metal. . . . You have to replace the computer to recover from that attack."[44] Iran, Russia, Pakistan, Afghanistan, China, Mali, Syria, Yemen, and Algeria have the highest rates of infection, with targets focused on government and military installations, nuclear research facilities, and Islamic groups. Attacks occurred even on computers that were not connected to the internet. Experts note that access to proprietary hard drive source codes was required to create these attacks, from leading computer-tech companies such as IBM, Micron, Seagate, and Toshiba. How could the US government get the source code for almost every hard drive on the computer market?

"According to former intelligence operatives, the NSA has multiple ways of obtaining source code from tech companies, including asking directly and posing as a software developer. If a company wants to sell products to the Pentagon or another sensitive US agency, the government can request a security audit to make sure the source code is safe. 'They don't admit it, but they do say, "We're going to do an evaluation, we need the source code,"'" said Vincent Liu, a partner at security consulting firm Bishop Fox and former NSA analyst. "It's usually the NSA doing the evaluation, and it's a pretty small leap to say they're going to keep that source code."[45]

While states are not publicly revealing their cyberactivities, it appears the US government created and has been using these cyberweapons since 2001, while blaming the Chinese government for similar behavior, hacking and planting malware and spyware on US computers. These cyberweapons are on the hard drives of adversaries, available to adversaries to reverse engineer these cyberweapons and use them against US systems. As Richard Clarke said of Stuxnet, *"the best cyberweapon the United States has ever developed, it then gave the world for free."*[46] The example and proof of concept have been set by the United States. The Chinese government has not surprisingly announced a policy, demanding any company selling technology in China to give the Chinese government their source codes.

US government officials have not denied these reports. If true, these activities follow a pattern similar to drones: new technologies are exploited for state military functions of spying on and destroying enemy government targets. Governments advance new military technologies assuming their state will have a monopoly on their use, and assuming they will be useful in state-to-state military confrontations. The technology moves faster than government responses, spreading to adversaries and nonstate actors in unintended ways. The US monopolies on new technologies does not last. The new technologies democratize and privatize war, in ways unanticipated by their creators.

DRONES AND CYBERWAR

Governments first developed drones, but governments no longer control drone technology. Drones are cheap and readily available for commercial purchase. Use by nonstate as well as state actors is increasing faster than governments' abilities to regulate their use. Every type of nonstate actor—nongovernmental organizations, multinational corporations, terrorist groups, and criminal cartels—all use drones for their activities. NGOs use drones to better direct humanitarian aid, to monitor refugee flows, to track global warming, to deliver medical supplies to remote areas. Companies like Amazon use drones to deliver their products, while other companies use drones to create their products, from photography to farm irrigation. Drug cartels use drones to make deliveries. And terrorist organizations use drones for surveillance and to drop bombs. None of these activities were expected or intended when governments developed drones for state military purposes.

The US government first started experimenting with **unmanned aerial systems,** vehicles without a human operator on board, in World War II. It did not go well. The US military continued research and development experiments with unmanned systems. The Defense Advanced Research Projects Agency (DARPA) developed two prototypes in 1973 which ran on lawn mower engines and could carry 28 pounds, but competitions among military organizations over who would control the new technology, and budget overruns, kept unmanned technologies from being part of US military forces or plans.

Israel developed and used drones, primarily for Intelligence, Surveillance, and Reconnaissance (ISR) purposes, in the 1973 Yom Kippur war. Israel showed the unmanned systems could be effective in war. Impressed with Israel's success with drones in their 1982 Lebanon war, the United States developed and deployed drones during the 1991 Iraq War. In one well-publicized case, some Iraqi Republican Guard troops surrendered to a drone. Afterward, the United States developed the Predator and other unmanned systems in air, land, and sea, and used them particularly in surveillance of terrorist camps. When nineteen hijackers attacked the United States on September 11, 2001, the United States had no war plan for fighting a nonstate actor, and no war plan for an invasion of Afghanistan. Afghanistan's mountainous terrain and poor infrastructure were a challenge. Plans underway to arm the Predator drone were quickly accelerated. Policy makers, facing changes in external circumstances, improvised and experimented. Existing military assets, 100 pound Hellfire missiles, were added to Predator drones. The first killer drones were used in combat in Afghanistan. The CIA began using drones to hunt down and kill terrorists "and associated forces" outside of the war zone, in Yemen and Pakistan in 2002. As the intelligence community hired more contractors, private companies also operated drones. Most drones are used for ISR, but the United States has expanded killer drone strikes to Somalia, Libya, Yemen, Pakistan, and Syria. The UK has used killer drone strikes against ISIL forces in Iraq, and Israel has used killer drone strikes in Gaza.

Unmanned systems are not actually unmanned. They require human operators to control them from a distance, using satellite and wireless links and computer technologies. Unmanned systems run the gamut. Microscopic robot nanotechnology can invade a human body. Insect-sized robots can swarm and inflict lethal injections. Bird-sized drones are well used for ISR and delivering small payloads—such as the 4 pound Ravens used by the US military for tactical surveillance. Quadricopters and larger helicopters (octocopters, etc.) are the most used and most available drones. Used by commercial and nonstate actors as well as states, they sell for as little as $250 or can be built yourself, and carry cameras and payloads of a few pounds to about 45 pounds, but the price and size of the drone increases with the size of the payload. Predator and Reaper drones carry cameras and multiple 100 pound Hellfire missiles, and have been the go-to combat drones of the US military. The 32,000 pound Global Hawk costs between $173 million and $222 million each, seven to ten times more than the price it was supposed to cost (and far more than the manned U-2 spy planes it was supposed to replace). Global Hawks and the Naval Triton variant have a 130 foot wing span, and are larger than most commercial airplanes.[47]

The United States imagined drone technologies would be an effective way to increase the capacity of the military, as can be seen by the role of DARPA (Defense Advanced Research Projects Agency) in drone development. The United States has often used new drone technologies in a very old-war way, building large, expensive, unmanned systems that look like the manned military planes they were replacing. The Global Hawk and the Triton are larger than a 757 Airplane. They are prone to accidents; a Global Hawk from Patuxent Air Base crashed near my home, and I watched it burn. They are so expensive that the US military has tried to cancel the contracts, as the old U-2 spy planes they were to replace are more reliable and cheaper to operate. The larger, more expensive drones fly higher and longer (when they are not grounded by bad weather that U-2s can fly through), able to spy for long periods of time without needing to return or refuel. By using expensive unmanned systems which look like planes, the US military has tended to insert the new technologies in ways consistent with its standard operating procedures and organizational culture. Military defense contractors and their Congressional defenders are also interested in selling more expensive, not less expensive technologies.[48] The US government allows sales of commercial, military, and killer combat drones to US allies.[49] Other militaries and nonstate organizations have gone in the other direction, acquiring smaller drones that more easily evade detection, are more reliable and less expensive if they crash or malfunction.

The United States developed and used drones as a high-tech tool for state-to-state conflict in Iraq. But drones soon proved less useful in fighting adversaries with modern defenses. When the United States invaded Iraq in 2003, few combat drones were used because the Iraqi Army had air defenses and an air force and were easily able to shoot down the drones. Drones have only been effective against militarily weak foes who do not have the ability to shoot them down.

It is not necessary to shoot down drones to defeat them. Because drones rely on computers and on the link to the drone base or handler, drones are easily hacked and spoofed. Drones are run by computers which use commercial computer code, built for speed and commerce not security, so drones are vulnerable to the same types of malware and other hacks that all computers are vulnerable to. The drone systems at Creech Air Force base in Nevada, which control drones used in the war in Afghanistan, were infected by malware in 2012 when a drone operator played a computer game at work and inadvertently allowed the military system to become infected. Drones use both encrypted and commercially available global positioning signals (GPS) to operate, which can be easily jammed (a GPS jammer can cost as little as $50). Hacked or spoofed drones no longer obey their controllers' commands, and may be "taken over" to instead obey the hackers' commands. US drones have been captured by Iran and ISIL. Iran claims they captured the US drone by "spoofing" it, fooling the drone's computer into following their false GPS signal, and getting it to land. The photos and video released by the Iranians show a perfectly intact drone, without any signs of being shot down. It is also possible the drone failed due to its own "bugs" or error. Publicly, the US military contests the Iranian claim, but government and private researchers have demonstrated this drone vulnerability as early as 2005.[50]

Drones are vulnerable to computer and technical errors. US drones often are grounded and cannot fly, due to computer, weather, and other technical problems. The high cost and high vulnerabilities of drones have led the military to try to cancel contracts for low-performing drones, such as the Global Hawk. Iran and ISIS are trying to reverse engineer the captured drones for their own use. The task is difficult, but not impossible. Al Qaeda and ISIS have drone units, creating killer drones from small drones and surveillance drones to attack Iraqi and coalition forces.[51]

The United States imagined they would be able to maintain a monopoly on drone technology and use. But all countries are expected to have drones by 2025, and all types of nonstate actors currently have and use drones. There are four types of nonstate actors—legal, illegal, for-profit, and nonprofit. All four types of nonstate actors currently use drones. Drug cartels use drones for surveillance and drug deliveries. Terrorists use drones for intelligence gathering, to direct ground forces and suicide bombers, and to kill, delivering bombs and improvised explosives. ISIS uses both killer drones and surveillance drones. ISIS acquired 88 pounds of uranium from Mosul University in July 2014. This uranium is not bomb-grade so could not be used to build a nuclear weapon. But such radioactive material could be used in an RDD, a radiological dispersal device that spreads radioactive material like a crop duster, to cause death, illness, and mayhem, or a dirty bomb, in which a conventional explosive spreads radiological material. Drones are commercially available and frequently used in farming for crop dusting and fertilizing. ISIS and other terrorist groups have plenty of bomb makers, and plenty of people with extensive experience in creating improvised explosive devices (IEDs) detonated by cell phones. ISIS and terrorist groups have the capacity to create and use *weapons of mass disruption* that would kill and sicken some people and destroy economies.

For example, in the 1994 Aum Shinryko terrorist attack on the Japanese metro, more people were killed from fear and panic (from strokes and heart attacks) than from the release of the sarin gas. Expensive commercial real estate in key locations could be rendered worthless by radiation, triggering economic recession or depression. If the radioactive levels were high, the land might have to be abandoned for generations, as happened to the 30 kilometer Chernobyl Exclusion Zone, after the Soviet Chernobyl nuclear power plant melt down in 1986. The Ukrainian government estimates the land will remain unfit for human habitation for 20,000 years. Even if the land and environment had low levels of radiation and thus were deemed safe for human health, it is likely that buyers and the market for those lands and properties would plummet, with severe economic impact. After the 9/11 attacks, the New York economy lost $178 billion, in the physical costs of rebuilding, lost travel and tourism, etc.[52]

Drones democratize and privatize war. Terrorists and other illegal, violent nonstate actors have drones, and are using them to project force abroad. In the past, actors had to build expensive, professional modern armies, navies, or air forces to be able to project force abroad. Drones allow a wider variety of nonstate actors to spy, bomb, and cause disruption and destruction across borders for a low cost.

In the past, the high cost of building and maintaining delivery vehicles for nuclear weapons has prevented and slowed nuclear proliferation. Intercontinental ballistic missiles, air forces and navies are costly and hard to build, acquire, and maintain. The information of how to build nuclear bombs is now easily available on the internet. Acquiring bomb-grade fissile material is harder, although not impossible given global smuggling markets. But after building or buying a nuclear bomb, actors still must have a way to deliver a nuclear weapon, and this barrier to entry has been a thorn-in-the-side of many would-be proliferators. North Korea, with the help of the A.Q. Khan smuggling network, has several nuclear bombs. North Korea has been trying to miniaturize its nuclear weapons to make them easier to deliver, but it has always struggled with delivery vehicles. The problems and misfires of its missile program are well known. Drone technologies allow would-be proliferators a way around this obstacle. Early in the Cold War, the United States experimented with small nuclear weapons, and with nuclear armed unmanned vehicles, but instead moved toward large weapons delivered by conventional means. Today, off-the-shelf, readily available, smaller, and less expensive drones can deliver payloads of small bombs, IEDs, nuclear or otherwise.

As commercial and civilian drones proliferate, small drones operated by illegal actors are difficult to detect and prevent among the increasing flow of legal drones. The US Federal Aviation Administration forecasts 30,000 drones in domestic airspace by 2020.[53] Drug delivery drones have only been detected by law enforcement when the drones crashed due to over-loading, when greedy drug smugglers exceeded the carrying capacity of the drones.

Dozens of drones flew over French nuclear power plants in 2014 and 2015. Some drones have also been detected over other countries' nuclear power plants. French authorities are alarmed. These drone flights occurred prior to the Charlie Hebdo terrorist attacks which put

France on high terror alert. The plans, design, and layout of French nuclear power plants were posted on the internet. States have no idea who flew these drones, or for what purpose. Were these spying missions by terrorists planning a future attack?[54]

Government officials around the world, not just in France, are concerned about these drone overflights of nuclear plants. Terrorists and other violent nonstate actors would not need to drop RDDs or dirty bombs to create a nuclear catastrophe. They could use drones to "do a Fukushima." On March 11, 2011, an earthquake and tsunami hit Japan, killing over 20,000 people. The Daiichi nuclear power plant survived the initial earthquake and tsunami tidal wave, more than the plant had been engineered to survive. But the power outage and damage to back-up generators disrupted the cooling system at the plant. Three core reactors melted down and three reactor building explosions caused radioactive releases, contaminated ground water and land in an agricultural area, and caused the evacuation of 300,000 people and a 20 kilometer mandatory exclusion zone area near the plant. There are thirty-two nuclear power plants around the world of the same GE Mark I design as Daiichi; many more have similar designs, such as twenty-three within the United States. Since 2001, many nuclear power plants around the world hardened the protections of their nuclear reactor cores against a 9/11-type attack from a large, commercial aircraft flying into the reactor from the sky. But drones allow violent actors other means to fly beneath the radar and undertake more targeted, but potentially devastating attacks. Drones could damage the non-hardened electricity, back-up generators and cooling systems of nuclear plants. Terrorists or other violent actors need not have a nuclear weapon to create a nuclear catastrophe. Fukushima provides a demonstration of the costly results that can come from disruption of a nuclear power plant's cooling system, particularly via its power system.

Drones are also used in cyberattacks. Drones can gather information on secured computers and locations, even off-line computers, that can be used to compromise these computers and locations. Drones can also be used to attack military systems, such as drones designed to electronically disrupt surface to air missile systems.

Currently, we have an explosion of drones and drone uses without common rules. Small, low-flying drones are not detected by radar. Within the United States, the FAA has issued initial rules on commercial drone use, requiring some certification (but not licenses) for operators, and exclusion zones around airports and above 400 feet.[55] The White House has issued some rules for government drones,[56] used in agriculture, law enforcement, border control, etc., to try to protect privacy rights. But these rules are not shared internationally, and noncommercial drone use under 400 feet high is little regulated. The FAA has asked a private body to self-regulate civilian hobbyists, and the government and private sectors have started a public–private partnership to increase safe use of noncommercial UAS flying under 400 feet high.[57]

Drones are anonymous; it can be difficult for states to trace the operators. When a small drone crashed on the White House grounds, the US government had no idea who the operator was, until a hobbyist turned himself in the next day, apologizing that he had lost control of his drone.[58] The private sector is full of drone operators. NGOs use drones for environmental monitoring, for land mine removal, for search and rescue operations, for exposing wild life poachers illegally hunting endangered species, for provision of humanitarian assistance in warzones, and for monitoring ceasefires and human rights abuses. The for-profit private sector uses drones for agriculture, photography, journalism, tourism, surveillance, and maintenance of power lines and other infrastructure, logging, fishing, medicine, pizza delivery, and delivery companies such as Amazon and Fed Ex are beginning to use drones for same-day delivery. Terrorists and violent nonstate actors such as Hamas and Hezbollah have and use drones. Governments also use drones, for environmental and wildlife monitoring, weather monitoring, border control, and law enforcement.

Cybersecurity becomes even more critical as companies and countries develop autonomous drones, without a human in the loop. Autonomous lethal drones make kill decisions without needing a human to sign off on the target or release the bomb. Artificial intelligence advocates argue that autonomous drones will make better decisions about whom to kill than humans, by removing human error from the decision chain. But killer robot advocates do not address how computer error, and also cyberattacks, could mistakenly kill people by machine error. Hacked drones would allow adversaries to take control of killer drones. Transnational Advocacy Networks have formed to combat autonomous drones, led by Jodi Williams, who led the successful transnational advocacy campaign to ban anti-personnel landmines.

States developed drones for military use, but states have lost any monopoly on the technologies created. Lacking enough military pilots to operate drones, the US military and intelligence agencies increasingly contract out drone operations to private companies. Sovereign states cannot control the use of drones, or the cyberattacks on drones, by nonstate actors. Drones democratize war, allowing a wider number of actors to project violence across borders, without armies, navies, and air forces, and in ways that may evade detection and identification.

CYBERSECURITY: DECENTRALIZED
PUBLIC–PRIVATE NETWORKS

When the first internet worm struck over thirty years ago, the first cybersecurity response was a decentralized network, a public–private partnership created between a US government agency (DARPA) and Carnegie Mellon University to combat it. Cooperation among academics, private sector and government IT experts created the first **Computer Emergency Response Team (CERT)**, to help detect and respond to information intrusion problems. Today that original CERT model has been advanced by CERTS founded in over ninety countries, which come together in an international federation, called FIRST.[59] Automated security measurement systems monitor network use. Systems administrators review audit trails on the information systems, and call in the CERTs when anomalies or attacks are detected. This system has been so successful that it is recommended as the preferred model for private sector–critical infrastructure protection. In most countries around the world, critical infrastructure (banks, electric grids, dams, nuclear power plants, health systems, media, etc.) are privately owned and operated. Computer networks are critical to the operation of all these critical infrastructures. Today, some call for strengthening the coordination and common guidelines of the private sector, voluntary CERTS, along the lines of a Red Cross for cybersecurity.[60]

That decentralized, network response continues. No single sovereign state government agency is responsible for cybersecurity due to the distributed and decentralized nature of the threat. All government agencies are IT users, all are subject to cyberattacks, therefore all agencies have cybersecurity responsibilities. The distributed nature of the threat led to distributed, decentralized responses, as each government agency built cybersecurity into their operating procedures.[61] All agencies must play defense, to protect and secure their IT infrastructure and data from attack and penetration. The lead agencies for different sectors in critical infrastructure protection also have responsibilities to help the private sector respond to cyberthreats impacting their sector (finance, etc.). Agencies are trying to move beyond a reactive approach to a proactive approach, "to predict and prevent attacks, rather than simply react after the fact," as described by the head of the FBI Cyber Branch, Robert Anderson, Jr.[62] This is easier said than done.

Some have greater responsibilities than others. As the only agency authorized with both an intelligence and law enforcement function, with both domestic and international operations, the FBI developed greater cyber capacity earlier. In the last chapter we discussed the FBI's development of a Cyber Division, as well as the creation (under the Clinton administration) of the interagency coordinating group. The FBI has "threat focus cells," interagency collaboration groups which integrate the subject-matter experts across government on various cyber threats. The FBI created cyber task forces across the country in all fifty-six field offices, which work with local and state governments. The FBI also established the Infragard program, geographically based (rather than industry sector based), regional, cybersecurity public–private partnerships, which build relationships and exchange information with the private sector. The FBI maintains a 24-hour Cy Watch cyber command center for cyberintrusion response and prevention. The FBI is the lead in the National Cyber Investigative Joint Task Force (**NCIJTF**), the interagency unit which includes twenty law enforcement and intelligence community agencies, tasked with coordinating, integrating, and sharing information on cyber threat investigations with domestic impact.

The FBI also works with and supports newly established cyber divisions internationally in Europol and Interpol, and bilaterally, for example, with Britain's MI5 intelligence agency. Liaison officers from the UK, Canada, and Australia serve in the National Cyber Investigative Joint Task Force (NCIJTF), the US government interagency integration group. But the mismatch in international jurisdictions complicates efforts to track and prosecute cybercrime. As former attorney general Janet Reno put it when the US government first began to respond to cybersecurity issues in the 1990s,

> Because of the technological advancements, today's international criminals can be more nimble and more elusive than ever before. If you can sit in a kitchen in St. Petersburg, Russia, and steal from a bank in New York, you understand the dimensions of the problem. Cyber attacks create a special problem, because the evidence is fleeting. You may have gone through this computer 1,500 miles away to break through another computer 5,000 miles away. Simply put, cyber criminals can cross borders faster than law enforcement agents can, as hackers need not respect national sovereignty, nor rely upon judicial process to get information from another country.[63]

This assessment remains accurate. Beyond the CERTs, other public–private partnerships were established as the government encouraged the formation of private sector ISACs (Information Sharing Analysis Centers) within each critical infrastructure sector, to coordinate and share information and action plans to improve cyber security. The FBI and Department of Homeland Security maintain public–private partnerships for sharing information about cybersecurity threats, investigations, and best practices. As discussed previously, simultaneously the NSA has relied on the private sector to provide communications metadata so that the NSA can analyze the "big data" to discern patterns that can help in counterterrorism operations. Since cooperating with the NSA, private companies have been sued for providing this data, and have been subject to Freedom of Information (FOIA) requests since they provided their information to the government. The private sector wants protection from legal liability and FOIA requests which could compromise their private business information (and aid business competitors), but Congress has failed to enact such legislation. The fallout from NSA surveillance has damaged trust and cooperation between the public and private sectors in cybersecurity. The private sector worries the government is simply trying to use them for spying, surveillance, and data collection, and that firms expose themselves to legal risk and risk of exposing key information by cooperating with the government. NSA spying has undermined public–private partnerships which are essential for cybersecurity. A persistent focus of National Cybersecurity plans has been coordination among the many government and private sector entities active in cybersecurity.[64]

Sovereign states are hesitant to regulate cybersecurity. States often lack the technological knowledge to create good rules. The mismatch between the slowness of government institutions and the speed of technological change presents challenges. Technology changes so quickly, that regulations would be obsolete by the time they emerged. For these reasons, public–private partnerships have become a means to develop rules, creating "fast soft law" to promulgate best practices in cybersecurity. In the United States, the National Institute of Standards and Technology (NIST) developed a **"Cybersecurity Framework,"** of voluntary standards and practices "to guide industry in reducing cyber risks to the networks and computers that are vital to the nation's economy, security and daily life." The Cybersecurity Framework was created with input from both the public and private sectors, and responding to a second set of feedback, adaptations were made in the second Cybersecurity Framework.[65] By using private sector technology standards, governments were able to jumpstart the creation of fast, soft law in the Cybersecurity Framework. These soft law, voluntary frameworks are quickly being adopted by private sector actors, who are eager to show they are using industry-best practices, in order to limit their legal liabilities in cases of security breaches. They also appreciate the Framework as a move toward harmonization of best practices and processes. Without such harmonization, firms can be torn in different directions, trying to meet a variety of compliance metrics, which is costly and inefficient. The Cybersecurity Framework focuses on cybersecurity *processes* applicable across many different types of IT environments and industries. The private sector welcomes NIST's voluntary framework instead of legislative mandates, as cyberthreats evolve faster than governmental ability to legislate. Public–private sector cooperation can update the Cybersecurity Framework faster than government is able to act. The private sector argues that hard law mandates would be the lowest common denominator in cybersecurity, whereas the flexible framework allows actors to reach for more proactive, higher performance processes in cybersecurity.

Although voluntary, industry understands that the soft law framework is laying the track for what may become mandatory, and what may become the baseline for legal liability. As one industry group notes,

> The Framework may become the de facto standard for cybersecurity and privacy regulation and may impact legal definitions and enforcement guidelines for cybersecurity moving forward. The Framework may also set cybersecurity standards for future legal rulings. If, for instance, the security practices of a critical infrastructure company are questioned in a legal proceeding, the courts could identify the Framework as a baseline for "reasonable" cybersecurity standards. Organizations that have not adopted the Framework to a sufficient degree—Tier 3 or Tier 4, for instance—may be considered negligent and may be held liable for fines and other damages. Using history as a guide, the Framework may become a business requirement for companies that provide services to critical infrastructure owners, operators, and providers. For example, an organization deemed to be a critical infrastructure provider that adopts the Framework may require that its vendors and suppliers achieve the same Implementation Tier ranking. Doing so will help the organization protect itself from a potential weak link in its supply chain . . . future requests for proposals (RFPs) and partnerships may require some level of implementation with the Framework.[66]

In other words, "fast soft law" works. **Soft law**[67] is not so soft. Voluntary frameworks that are quickly and widely adopted, tend to become industry standards and legal liability standards, achieving wide levels of compliance similar to hard law. Changing the law is only one way to change norms; changing norms may eventually change law.

The Cyber Framework is evolving as the threats evolve. It is an attempt to harmonize standards across private sector actors.

The EU is also working to improve and harmonize cybersecurity. The **General Data Protection Regulation** (GDPR) requires all organizations which collect data from EU citizens (whether or not the entity is located in the EU) to have standard data security and privacy protections in place, including strict rules on controlling and processing personally identifiable information (PII). The regulation notes that "personal data is any information relating to an individual, whether it relates to his or her private, professional or public life. It can be anything from a name, a home address, a photo, an email address, bank details, posts on social networking websites, medical information, or a computer's IP address."[68] Organizations must obtain prior consent of citizens for collection and use of their data, must notify people of why it is collecting their data, how long it is retaining their data, how it is safeguarding it, and must notify people of data breaches. People have the right to not have their data collected and used, and the right to have their data erased at any time. The law permits large fines for organizations that do not comply. The GDPR went into effect in 2018, and applies to any organization that does business with Europeans (the law excludes government law enforcement and national security agencies).

The European Union also created a **Directive on Security of Network and Information Systems (NIS)** that began to be implemented in 2018. The Directive requires all EU member states to create "Computer Security Incident Response Teams (the CSIRT s Network), dedicated to sharing information about risks and ongoing threats and cooperating on specific cybersecurity incidents . . . Businesses in these sectors that are identified by the Member States as operators of essential services will have to take appropriate security measures and to notify serious incidents to the relevant national authority. Also key digital service providers (search engines, cloud computing services and online marketplaces) will have to comply with the security and notification requirements under the new Directive." The EU Directive works to raise and harmonize cybersecurity among EU member states. It also helps states to implement the EU standards into national policies and legislation by providing an implementation toolkit. "The 'NIS toolkit' provides practical information to Member States, e.g. by presenting best practices from the Member States and by providing explanation and interpretation of specific provisions of the Directive to clarify how it should work in practice."[69] These norms are binding on EU members, although states that do business with the EU (such as the United Kingdom) are also complying with the measures.

The United Nations has also made several attempts to develop consensus norms for cybersecurity. For example,

> The UN Group of Government Experts on Developments in the Field of Information and Telecommunications in the Context of International Security (UN GGE) was established to develop a common approach to how governments should behave in cyberspace. Its 2015 report provided the foundation for an internationally recognized governmental cyber code of conduct. The 2015 report recommended eleven basic but important norms, including determinations that states should not knowingly allow their territory to be used for internationally wrongful cyber acts; should not conduct or knowingly support ICT activities that intentionally damage critical infrastructure; and should seek to prevent the proliferation of malicious technologies and the use of harmful hidden functions. In this consensus document, existing and emerging threats in cyberspace were spelled out; basic norms, rules, and principles for responsible behavior were proposed; and confidence-building measures, international cooperation, and capacity-building were given the attention they deserve.[70]

These UN norms are a start, but the members have not yet endorsed the **Cyber Code of Conduct** by a nonbinding United Nations General Assembly Resolution, or by a binding international convention.

Long-standing obstacles remain to public–private cooperation. There are conflicts of interest which can prevent closer partnerships. For example, the concerns of the FBI (gathering evidence for legal prosecution), NSA (leaving holes open for government surveillance), and of DHS (preventing terror attacks) may be at odds with the concerns of private actors, who first want to protect themselves and their IT infrastructure and data. Sharing company information vulnerabilities with others and the government may hurt them, particularly if the government cannot keep such information secure. Companies hit with cyberattacks may not want to advertise their vulnerabilities or liabilities to customers, investors, competitors, or hackers.

Intelligence and law enforcement agencies have long had such disagreements. The FBI wants to arrest criminals and terrorists, whereas intelligence organizations may want to observe them, in order to protect information about their intelligence collection methods, and in order to develop a larger understanding of threats. Law enforcement agencies might observe actors for a time in order to roll up the entire network in their arrests. In contrast to both these approaches, private sector actors want to stop attackers and close infrastructure vulnerabilities immediately in order to limit their companies' losses and liabilities, even if this means lost opportunities for understanding the larger picture. It is never in a company's interest to delay action and incur liabilities, losses, potential losses, and risks, in order that others might benefit. Companies have fiduciary responsibilities to turn a profit for their shareholders; helping others, including the government, is not part of the business plan.

Challenges of Public-Private Networks

Private sector concerns are warranted, regarding whether government partners can be trusted with their secrets about their most sensitive information vulnerabilities. Government IT systems are constantly attacked and hacked, and exposures of classified information are well known, from WikiLeaks to breaches of top-secret DoD systems.

All government agencies are not equal in their cyber capacities. Some, such as the US Department of Defense, have large budgets from which to buy the best IT and train and hire more personnel with cyber expertise. They have expertise and equipment, but also have such huge systems, often run by private contractors, that they also have huge risk exposure. Other government agencies are slower to get and master the new technologies than their cyber adversaries.

Cybersecurity is only as good as the weakest link. Countries with very different IT infrastructure, which lack resources and suffer from power outages, may lack resources to protect against cyberattacks. Poorly protected systems can spread attacks to others they are connected to, as exemplified in the Not Petya attack.

Most governments (the United States included) pay considerably less than the private sector for IT workers, and take a very long time to hire and process them through security clearance procedures. This inability to hire leads to a great dependence on IT contractors, which can impede institutional learning and change. If government's cybersecurity of its own IT systems is not good, why would the private sector want to share its most sensitive cyber vulnerabilities with an insecure and perhaps untrustworthy partner? The digital divide is not only an obstacle to effective information sharing within government; it also impedes the receptivity of the private sector to partnering with government.

As Janet Reno recognized in the early days of the information age,

> Infrastructure protection requires that we work together as never before. It demands a partnership among all federal agencies with responsibilities for different sectors of the economy or for certain special functions, like law enforcement, intelligence, and defense. It also requires a partnership with private industry which owns and operates most of the infrastructures. It calls for a partnership with academia . . . . It also requires a partnership with state and local law enforcement . . . . [And] if we are to protect our infrastructure we must reach beyond our borders. Cyber threats ignore the borders. The attack can come from anywhere in the world. We must work with our allies around the world to build the same partnerships that we talk about here at home.[71]

Why should private sector entities volunteer information about their most sensitive company vulnerabilities and losses with governments? In theory,

> The government, with unique access to foreign intelligence and law enforcement information, can develop a threat picture that no entity in the private sector could develop on its own. We need to share this with the industry. . . . At the same time, we need to learn from industry about the intrusion attempts and exploited vulnerabilities that it is experiencing. This will help us paint the vulnerability and threat picture more completely and will give us a head start on preventing or containing threats and incidents . . . this two-way dialogue is the only way to deal with our common concern about protecting our infrastructures.[72]

In practice, industry often already knows of the threats before government alerts arrive. Information may be dated or stale by the time they hear about it from government. In order to better work with the private sector on information and technology issues relating to foreign affairs, the foreign policy bureaucracies have to substantially improve their own technologies to be able to interact with the private sector. Only when private firms feel the information is secure at the other end, will they share it with the government. For US foreign policy organizations, technology upgrades, thinking about international affairs through technological lenses, and embracing the private sector to solve emerging global issues are not separate agendas. The success of any one of them requires the others. Insufficient government IT capacity creates large opportunities for contracting out foreign policy functions to private sector contractors. While this buys capacity, it also leads to risk, abuse, and liability, as illustrated in the Snowden leaks.

Sovereignty and Cybersecurity

New technologies change not only the way sovereign states do their jobs, but also the jobs they have to do. More fundamentally, new technologies change the way organizations think about themselves, whether government or private companies do the government's spying, intelligence, defense, and foreign policy functions, as well as internal and external power dynamics.

New technologies are never neutral. "Every technology is both a burden and a blessing; not either-or, but this-and-that . . . . The benefits of a new technology are not distributed equally. There are, as it were, winners and losers . . . to whom will the technology give greater power and freedom? And whose power and freedom will be reduced by it?"[73]

Often the power repercussions of technological developments are unanticipated. The US military, when developing drones and the internet, never intended to aid terrorists, pirates, or the Russians. New technologies can undermine the beneficiaries of old technologies in unanticipated and nonlinear ways, as we have seen with drones, cyberweapons, and cybersecurity.

Technology changes not only provide opportunities for efficiency gains: they also change the very social and power relationships that undergird states. The new technologies create and empower new actors, private sector actors and companies, while changing or undermining the power base of old actors. Governments too often adopt new technologies with a narrow focus on competing with other sovereign states, such as conducting drone attacks against Afghanistan and a cyberattack against Iran, without fully appreciating that nonstate actors and adversaries will use these same technologies in unanticipated ways against the state.

CONCLUSIONS: CREATE NEW WAYS TO COOPERATE

Globalization's open technologies present global issues that state and other actors are not well prepared to meet. We face today's global issues with institutions built for a different world. Foreign policy is wired for relations with other sovereign states, for government-to-government relations, while the number, resources, power, and expertise of nonstate actors are multiplying, bolstered by new technologies. Foreign policy struggles to keep up with the challenges of globalization's fast, interdependent open economy, open technology, and open society processes, driven by diffuse, decentralized, private sector actors. Globalization moves fast, while government foreign policy actors move slowly. Foreign policy is conducted in a closed system of states, but globalization is open to a variety of state and nonstate actors. States today struggle to change focus and to face emerging security challenges quite different than those of the mid-twentieth century. We have a mismatch between foreign policy and globalization that is particularly visible in the technology arena. The ability of states to cooperate in cybersecurity will be undercut by the cyberwarfare, cyber offense activities of states, which works at cross purposes with US government actors such as the FBI, working to stop and prevent cyber intrusions and close "zero day" exploits. Lacking technological capacity, government foreign policy organizations increasingly contract out spying and intelligence functions to private companies. This generates problems of transparency, accountability, and democracy. Whether cyber offense or cyber defense will predominate remains to be seen. Institutions must evolve or become extinct; innovation is mandatory, because the new technologies and their consequences are not going away.

Public–private partnerships in cybersecurity are creating global models for deeply integrated cooperation between states and the private sector. The EU General Regulation on the Protection of Data, and the EU Directive on Security of Network and Information Systems are models for creating common standards and practices among states. Because it is the first binding multinational effort to bring states to common cybersecurity standards, it may have spillover effects beyond EU member states and the organizations that do business in the EU. Because it is easier for companies to comply to a common standard than to meet several different standards, or to leave themselves legally liable for noncompliance by a unit not thought to be connected to the EU market, many companies and organizations may gravitate to the EU standard for ease, cost savings, efficiency, and to reduce legal liabilities. UN efforts to create an international Code of Conduct for Cybersecurity have the potential to reach all countries, but currently these measures are not binding.

All efforts are needed, quickly, as the cyberthreat risk environment is moving faster than sovereign states' efforts to respond and to cooperate. "Greater and new forms of cooperation are needed. There is an urgent need for cooperation among states to mitigate threats such as cybercrime, cyberattacks on critical infrastructure, electronic espionage, bulk data interception, and offensive operations intended to project power by the application of force in and through cyberspace. Emerging cyber threats could precipitate massive economic and societal damage, and international efforts need to be recalibrated to account for this new reality."[74]

Cybersecurity threats go beyond sovereignty; so must our cooperative responses.

KEY TERMS

Aurora Project, 283
botnets, 268
CERT, 297
Crimea, 271
Cyber Code of Conduct, 302
Cybersecurity Framework, 299
DARPA, 276
Dark Net, 276
Directive on Security of Network and Information Systems (NIS), 301
Edward Snowden, 287
electronic Pearl Harbor, 279
Eligible Receiver, 278
FISA, 287

General Data Protection Regulation, 301
IEDs, 277
information warfare, 282
internet of things, 283
NCIJTF, 298
NotPetya, 271
patch and pray, 269
ransomware, 270
soft law, 299
Stuxnet, 283
unmanned aerial systems, 290
US Cyber Command, 280
watering hole, 269
white hat hackers, 269
"zero day" vulnerabilities, 283

DISCUSSION QUESTIONS

1. We are being attacked by robots all day, every day. Explain this statement. What evidence of this trend have you experienced? Have you been a victim of a cyberattack?
2. What are the challenges with a "patch and pray" approach to cybersecurity?
3. Nearly a quarter of Maersk shipping terminals were simultaneously disabled around the world, from New York to Los Angeles to

Mumbai, India, grinding a sizeable portion of global trade to a halt. What caused this? How did Maersk figure out what had hit them? How did they get their systems back up and running? Who was the actual target of the attack?

4. How are democracies vulnerable to information warfare and cyberattacks?
5. Cyber offense does not complement cyberdefense; it explodes it. Discuss what is meant by this. How can offensive and defensive cyber policies sometimes work at cross purposes?
6. Give examples of offensive cyberoperations by various countries. How do countries differ in their cyberoperations?
7. What was the Stuxnet attack on Iran? Why do most experts attribute the attacks to the United States and Israel?
8. How can cyberweapons democratize and privatize war? Which kinds of countries and militaries are most vulnerable to cyberattacks?
9. What are "zero day" vulnerabilities? Who finds them? Who uses them?
10. How can adversaries undertake cyberattacks on drones?
11. Why are new forms of cooperation needed in cybersecurity?

Nobel Peace Prize winner Nadia Murad Basee Taha, who survived trafficking at the hands of ISIS, was appointed as UNODC (UN Office on Drugs and Crime) Goodwill Ambassador for the Dignity of Survivors of Human Trafficking.

10

Global Criminal Networks
Old Challenges, New Means

■ ■ ■

Human trafficking is a crime against humanity.

—Pope Francis

Illicit trade is developing rapidly in all sectors. . . . New technology, communications, and globalization fuel the exponential growth of many of the most dangerous forms of illicit trade.

—Louise Shelley[1]

Transnational crime is a business, and business is very good. Money is the primary motivation for these illegal activities. The revenues generated . . . not only line the pockets of the perpetrators but also finance violence, corruption, and other abuses. These crimes undermine local and national economies, destroy the environment, and jeopardize the health and wellbeing of the public.

—Channing May[2]

Today's crime wars hark back to a pre-Westphalian era of perpetual conflict involving feudal kingdoms and marauding bandits. . . . Today's crime cartels and gangs may not necessarily aim to displace governments, but the net result of their activities is that they do.

—John Sullivan and Robert Muggah[3]

Thank you very much for this honour [the Nobel Peace Prize], but the fact remains that the only prize in the world that can restore our dignity is justice and the prosecution of criminals.

—Nadia Murad[4]

NADIA MURAD WAS A TEENAGE student in a small town in Northern Iraq when ISIS killed her family, captured her and thousands of other minority Yazidi girls, and sold them as sex slaves, to make money for the terrorist group and to reward ISIS fighters and sympathizers. Human trafficking exists the world over, but women and girls in warzones are particularly vulnerable to the systematic business of slavery. Nadia describes her experience in the slave market.

> The buyers gravitated toward the most beautiful girls first, asking, "How old are you?" and examining their hair and mouths. "They are virgins, right?" they asked a guard, who nodded and said, "Of course!" like a shopkeeper taking pride in his product. Now the militants touched us anywhere they wanted, running their hands over our breasts and legs, as if we were animals.[5]

Nadia was beaten and gang-raped repeatedly. She eventually was able to make a heroic and lucky escape, with the help of a brave Iraqi family who risked their lives to help rescue a stranger.[6] Unlike most victims of human trafficking, Nadia was granted asylum in Germany, where she became the UN Goodwill Ambassador for human trafficking victims. Nadia started a foundation to help Yazidis and other victims of sex slavery. Nadia Murad won the Nobel Peace Prize for her work. Nadia uses the media spotlight, and her book *The Last Girl*, to draw attention to what she describes as an ancient crime facilitated by impunity, by the disinterest of the international community in helping victims and prosecuting criminals, and by modern technology.

> I was an ISIS sex slave. Taking girls to use as sex slaves wasn't a spontaneous decision made on the battlefield by a greedy soldier. Islamic State planned it all: how they would come into our homes, what made a girl more or less valuable, which militants deserved a sabaya [sex slave] as incentive and which should pay. They even discussed sabaya in their glossy propaganda magazine, Dabiq, in an attempt to draw new recruits. . . . I want to be the last girl in the world with a story like mine.[7]

Global criminal networks are not new. Ancient texts are filled with references to slavery, piracy, and smuggling networks. Biblical accounts tell of people like Joseph, seized into slavery from his homeland into forced labor in another country. The ancient Silk Road trade route was known for attracting international thieves. The Canterbury tales discusses the perils of bandits who plagued the international tourism

Figure 10.1 Global Criminal Activity Flows

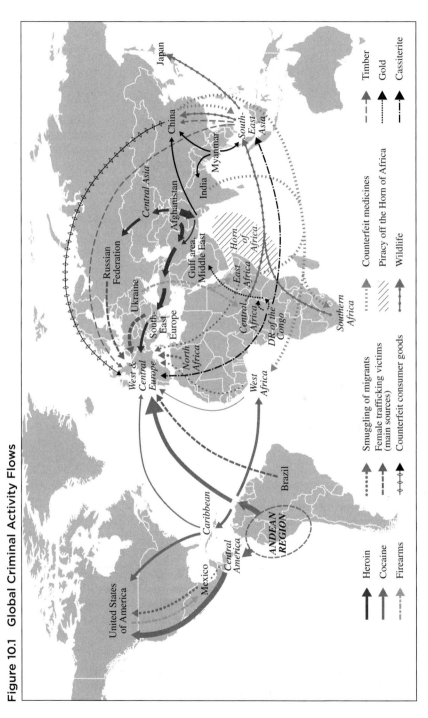

Source: UNODC

routes of medieval religious pilgrims. And in more recent centuries, two wars were fought over smuggling opium into China.

But these ancient global criminal practices are now enabled by modern technologies, open markets, and open societies with expanded private sector capacity and limited state control. Criminal networks parallel the growth, business models, anonymity, payment and distribution networks of legal global businesses. Global criminals have never had it so good.

Open economies, open societies, and open technologies mean that the private sector is everywhere growing, including the illicit private sector. How big is globalized crime? The criminals aren't telling, making estimates of the size of the problem difficult. Experts estimate that global crime is a 1.6 to 2.2 trillion dollars a year industry, but also admit that this is a conservative estimate, and the real size of the international black market is larger.

The largest global criminal enterprises are drug trafficking, human trafficking, smuggling counterfeit products (including medicines), and environmental crimes. Other major international criminal activities include arms smuggling, cybercrime, and piracy, as depicted in this map produced by the United Nations Office on Drugs and Crime (UNODC). Money laundering is necessary to and present alongside all of these criminal activities. Cyber methods increasingly accompany and facilitate criminal activities. For example, online illegal drug markets are increasing market share, just as online legal business (Amazon, etc.) are increasing market share against traditional, local retailers.

DECLINING VIOLENT CRIME AND WAR

The good news is that violent crimes of all types—murder, rape, assault, etc.—have been dramatically declining around the world and in the United States over the past three decades, in parallel with the global decline in war. Globally, intentional homicides account for more than two-thirds of the 560,000 violent deaths annually. Only 18 percent of violent deaths occur in war and conflict.[8] Contrary to popular perceptions (and to the self-serving rhetoric of many politicians), violent crime (and war) have dramatically declined across the globe and across the United States, in cities, suburbs, and rural areas, at the same time as global population has increased. While crime rates tick up and down from year to year, the overall trends have shown "the **Great Crime Decline**," dramatic decreases in the murder rate and other indicators of violent crime, from the high levels of the 1970s to the early 1990s.

While population levels have increased, the crime rate has decreased to historic lows. Immigrants are much more law-abiding, and much less violent, than native-born citizens, so immigrants have helped to decrease the rates of violence and crime. The year "2014 was not only the safest year of the past five decades, it was one of the safest years in U.S. history."[9] The "Great Crime Decline" is documented not just in official records collected by the FBI and other law enforcement databases, but also in household surveys of victims and families.[10] Declining crime has led to huge increases in public health, education, rejuvenation of cities, and prosperity.

The bad news is that for countries that remain in wars, particularly for those caught in "the **conflict trap**" of recurring cycles of violence and poverty, violent crime persists as well. Violent crime happens more frequently in warzones and postconflict societies. After peace treaties are signed to end wars, if disarmament, demobilization, and reintegration are not successful, violent crime can increase. If former combatants are not able to be retrained and reintegrated with jobs in the legal economy, they will apply their experience and skills in violence to make a living in crime. This has been the pattern in Central America and the Philippines, where countries like Honduras, Guatemala, and El Salvador, ended their civil wars, but then experienced an increase in violent criminal activity.

As Nadia's testimony illustrates, human trafficking is worst in war zones. Most human trafficking is for sexual exploitation; 72 percent of human trafficking victims are women and girls.[11]

Human trafficking is present in every war zone, for several reasons. All major armed conflicts in the world today are civil wars in which groups are fighting the national government. Many of these wars have been ongoing for extended periods of time, degrading government capacity and resources to address other issues. According to the UN report on human trafficking, "Areas with weak rule of law and lack of resources to respond to crime provide traffickers with a fertile terrain to carry out their operations. This is exacerbated by more people in a desperate situation, lacking access to basic needs. Some armed groups involved in conflict may exploit civilians. Armed groups and other criminals may take the opportunity to traffic victims—including children—for sexual exploitation, sexual slavery, forced marriage, armed combat and various forms of forced labour."[12]

Criminal groups operate in warzones or postconflict societies to take advantage of weakened institutions of law and order. And combatant groups also engage in criminal activities in warzones in order to finance their war and/or terrorism activities. For example, terrorist groups frequently kidnap people for ransom. If the ransom is paid, the terrorist group makes money to fund their terrorist activities. If the ransom is not paid, the kidnapping victim may be sold into slavery, to make money for the organization. Or the victim may be killed in order to further terrorize the population. Whether or not the ransom is paid, the group's terrorism objectives are furthered.

Increasing Types of Crime

There are over fifty-two types of transnational criminal activities, all growing with the growing global population, and the growing opportunities provided by new technologies and open markets. Some of the largest categories of transnational organized crime, by volume and profit, are drug trafficking, counterfeit medicines and goods, human trafficking, environmental crimes, and money laundering, which accompanies all types of crime.

HUMAN TRAFFICKING

Perhaps the most horrific transnational crime is human trafficking. Slavery is everywhere illegal, but modern-day slavery persists. There are over 40.3 million modern-day slaves, 25 million who live in conditions of slave and forced labor and sex trafficking, and another 15 million in forced marriages.[13] Human trafficking, or **trafficking in persons (TIP)**, is banned in International Law. All countries are supposed to ban and prosecute TIP in domestic law and law enforcement, to assist victims, and work to prevent TIP. But countries vary in their capacity and willingness to crack down on TIP.

> Article 3, paragraph (a) of the Protocol to Prevent, Suppress and Punish Trafficking in Persons defines Trafficking in Persons as the act of recruitment, transportation, transfer, harbouring or receipt of persons, by means of the threat or use of force or other forms of coercion, of abduction, of fraud, of deception, of the abuse of power or of a position of vulnerability or of the giving or receiving of payments or benefits to achieve the consent of a person having control over another person, for the purpose of exploitation. Exploitation shall include, at a minimum, the exploitation of the prostitution of others or other forms of sexual exploitation, forced labour or services, slavery or practices similar to slavery, servitude or the removal of organs.[14]

In addition to **TIP's three components (the Act, Means, and Purpose)** detailed in law, it is also illegal to attempt to commit trafficking, to serve as an accomplice to TIP, or to direct others to commit TIP.

There are many forms of human trafficking. The old system of **descent-based slavery** continues today in some areas of the world, including in countries in the Sahel region of Africa, such as Sudan, Chad, Niger, and Mauritania. Descent-based slavery is when slavery is continued across generations of a family and/or class. People are "born into slavery" and the status of slave passes from mother to child when a family or class is considered by a society to have "slave" status. Born without birth certificates and documentation, it can be difficult for descent-based slaves to procure identification documents needed to escape their conditions or attend school, open a bank account or obtain a driver's license. Without the ability to go to school, travel or work elsewhere, descent-based slaves lack basic opportunities for human development, and are unable to break away from their slave "masters."

According to an NGO who works to liberate and assist descent-based slaves in the Sahel region,

> People born into descent-based slavery face a lifetime of exploitation and are treated as property by their so-called "masters." They work without pay, herding animals, working in the fields or in their masters' homes. They can be inherited, sold or given away as gifts or wedding presents. Women and girls typically face sexual abuse and rape, and often have to bear their masters' children. In turn, their children will also be owned by their masters. Children can also be taken away from their mothers at an early age. They start work at an early age and never attend school. Escaping slavery is enormously challenging. It is hard for people to adapt to independent life and find decent work. Many thousands of people who have long left their masters (even generations before) still bear the social status of "slave" and as such face ongoing discrimination.[15]

Another form of modern slavery is **debt bonded labor**, which occurs when people are forced to work without pay to pay off a debt or supposed debt. Such "debt" can be passed on to the children and future generations. In South Asia it is estimated that over a million people are working to pay off the "debts" of their ancestors. Often people are tricked into debt-bonded labor, and their captors continually "move the goalposts." The forced laborers can never pay off the alleged debt, as their captors will continue to add fees to the "debt"—for job recruitment and employment processing, interest, food, room and board, etc.

Labor trafficking or forced labor occurs when deception, force, or threat of force are used in order to compel people to work for no or little payment. People may answer job advertisements or respond to job recruiters, only to later learn they have been trapped into forced labor, without payment. Forced laborers are often compelled to turn over their identity papers or travel documents to their employers, supposedly for the employer to "process" their job application. The employer then refuses to return their identity or travel papers. Forced laborers are isolated, without tools to escape or reach out to others for help. Particularly forced laborers working in foreign countries or far from their homes may find themselves unable to escape their captors. Migrant farm workers are particularly vulnerable to forced labor, as are migrant domestic workers.

Signs of forced labor and human trafficking include many exploitative practices: coercive recruitment; confiscation of identity papers or travel documents; physical or sexual violence; deception about the nature of work; forced overtime; limited freedom of movement or communication; withholding or delay of wages; denunciation to authorities; and a lack of freedom to resign in accordance with legal requirements.[16]

Foreign guest workers and workers in temporary worker programs are particularly vulnerable to forced labor or debt bondage. Their legal status in the country they have entered to work is entirely dependent on their employer, thus they are not able or willing to report or seek redress from their employer. For example, in the United Arab Emirates and many other Gulf states, 88.5 percent of the population, and 90 percent of the workers, are foreign guest workers who have almost no legal rights. To work in the UAE you must be "sponsored" by an employer, to whom you sign a contract to work for at least two years, under whatever terms the employer sets. The employer can change the terms at any time, and workers have no recourse. Workers are promised by recruiters that travel costs to the UAE will be reimbursed by the employer, and workers sign a contract for a wage. When they arrive in UAE, they are forced to sign a different contract for a lower wage, working every day without time off, they are made to pay the cost of the travel to the UAE, and their travel documents are seized and held by their employer. The law was changed in 2017 to supposedly outlaw this practice of seizing travel documents, but the law is generally violated, even by the government. Some international chains, like Hilton Hotels, make workers sign a document saying they have "voluntarily" given up their passports to their employers "for safe keeping." The practice is not voluntary, and it is not done for "safekeeping" to benefit the worker, but to be able to control the worker. Workers cannot leave, they cannot change jobs, they cannot take time off or return home, even for medical treatment or a death in the family. Employers can refuse to pay workers, garnish their wages, charge them with "crimes" such as "failing to adequately protect their employers' secrets (which carries a $27,000 fine), charge them "fines," or "processing fees" at any time. These fines then become debts, trapping workers in debt bondage. Workers cannot complain, protest, or strike; they have no free speech rights, unionization and strikes are illegal, and beatings, arbitrary arrest and torture are common.

As miserable as these forced labor conditions are, domestic workers in the UAE have even fewer rights. The "paper laws" which are supposed to protect guest workers (such as the law against holding passports, that is generally violated) do not apply to domestic workers, whose fate is controlled entirely by the family they work for. Working in private homes shut off from the world, with all conditions controlled by the employer, workers are vulnerable to exploitation and abuse. Their passports are seized, they have no days off, and no independent means to break free. Even outside of the UAE, private homes are often not subject to labor, safety, and inspection standards that apply to businesses. The risk of involuntary domestic service increases when the employer has diplomatic status, which offers diplomatic immunity to civil and criminal prosecution.

While the UAE exploits foreign workers, primarily from South Asia and Africa, North Korea exploits its own workers. North Koreans are made to serve in forced labor as foreign workers, remitting their "salaries" to the government. According to the US Department of Labor's report on forced labor and child labor, "The North Korean government reportedly earns hundreds of millions of dollars each year from its citizens working overseas. Foreign employers pay salaries directly to the North Korean government, or workers are forced to relinquish 70–90% of their earnings to the authorities. These revenues are used to support the regime."[17]

US employers also exploit foreign migrant workers, particularly in the agricultural and landscaping sectors. Migrant farm workers, working in remote agricultural areas, are frequently at the mercy of employers, who may be unscrupulous, withholding pay and forcing them to work in unsafe conditions.

Child laborers are particularly vulnerable to all forms of modern-day slavery. There are 152 million child laborers around the world; half work in dangerous, unhealthy conditions, at risk of death and injury, for example, working in mining, brick kilns, and making fireworks. Child labor harms children's health, keeps them out of school, and thus traps them in cycles of poverty and exploitation for their lifetimes. Children cost less than adult laborers, can be confined against their will, forced to work long hours, and may be more compliant. Thus exploited child laborers are in high demand in industries around the world, from the hand-made carpet industries in India, Pakistan, and Afghanistan, to coffee and cocoa farming in Africa. Children are in slavery as domestic labor, are trafficked for labor in criminal enterprises such as counterfeit goods and sexual exploitation, and are forced to serve as child soldiers. Seventy percent of the child laborers who work in hazardous conditions are working in the agricultural sector, often as migrant or temporary farm workers with little to no protections against exploitative, slave labor conditions. The poorest and youngest region of our planet, sub-Saharan Africa, has the world's largest concentration of child laborers, including child soldiers.[18]

The passage of the international law against the **Worst Forms of Child Labor Convention** twenty years ago has helped reduce the number of exploited children, even while the global population has grown dramatically. The Convention commits countries to stop child slavery and slave-like conditions, including buying and selling children, trafficking children, debt bondage, serfdom, children in the sex industry including child prostitutes and child pornography, and child soldiers. The convention has helped focus attention on recognizing and eliminating child slavery. Combined with the global efforts to implement the millennium development goals and sustainable development goals, which increase child education and reduce poverty, the number of child laborers has been reduced from over 250 million in 1999 to 152 million today.

Progress has been uneven, however. **UNICEF** reports that "in the least developed countries, around one in four children (ages 5 to 17) are engaged in labour that is considered detrimental to their health and development." In Africa the percentage is higher; about 30 percent of children in Africa are engaged in child labor.[19]

Orphans are also vulnerable to human trafficking and child labor. There are 140 million orphans around the world who have lost one or both parents. Lacking the economic and social support of two parents, orphans are vulnerable to exploitation. They may be left in the care of extended family or state institutions who lack resources for the children's care. They may be manipulated into turning these children over to traffickers in the hope of finding jobs and economic support. There are more orphans in war zones and natural disaster areas, vulnerable to trafficking.

People in war zones and natural disaster areas are displaced, struggling for resources, and without their normal social support structures, making them vulnerable to human trafficking. The decline in major armed conflicts helps reduce the conflict areas vulnerable to traffickers. But these gains are offset by the rise in global climate change and extreme weather events, which displace poor people in particular, thus increasing the populations vulnerable to trafficking.

Child soldiers are another form of modern slavery. Tens of thousands of children around the world, as young as 8, are forced to serve in government or paramilitary forces. Africa has the largest number of child soldiers in the world. The violent group Al-Shabab in Somalia kidnapped over 1,600 children in 2017, further harming many of them with sexual violence. Fifty-six nonstate actors (including ISIS, Al Shabaab, and Boko Haram) use child soldiers, along with the governments of seven countries—Afghanistan, Myanmar, Somalia, South Sudan, Sudan, Syria, and Yemen. Children are used in combat operations, including as suicide bombers, in fourteen countries: Afghanistan, Central African Republic, Colombia, Democratic Republic of Congo, Iraq, Mali, Myanmar, Nigeria, Philippines, Somalia, South Sudan, Sudan, Syria, and Yemen.[20]

Children are often forced to commit heinous war crimes, to sever their ties with their home communities. This helps ensure that they will not be accepted back into their home communities, therefore must stay and serve the armed group. Child soldiers can serve in various roles, as combatants, cooks, spies, or sexual slaves.

The creation of the **UN Special Representative for Children and Conflicts** brought greater transparency and urgency to child soldier and child protection issues. The office produces an annual report providing greater transparency and accountability on the issue, pressuring governments and nonstate actors to create action plans to improve their records, and publishing a blacklist shaming and naming the world's worst violators. Yet too often child soldiers are still put into jail, rather than recognized as victims needing assistance. Children suffer long-lasting damage from their time as child soldiers, particularly children who are raped and suffer sexual violence, such as girls forced to be "wives" and sex slaves of the armed fighters.

Early and forced "marriage" is another form of human trafficking. A total of 15 million girls and women are forced into "marriage," without their consent, often in order to earn money for their families or to relieve their families of responsibility for the costs of raising the child, or as a result of rape. Girls in refugee camps are particularly vulnerable. For example, in camps of families who have fled the wars in Syria and Iraq, girls aged between 11 and 13, but sometimes as young as 9, are "married" to older men who pay the families a "dowry." When forced into "marriage," the girls are raped and forced into sexual and domestic servitude. In warzones some families feel that "early marriage" is a way to protect girls from gang rape and human trafficking by armed groups. In many parts of the world, when a girl or woman is raped, they are forced into "marriage" with their rapist, as a way to restore the "honor" of their family, and to prevent the societal shame of a child being born out of wedlock.

Sex trafficking occurs everywhere, but it is particularly prominent in urban areas, at popular tourist destinations, and at large sporting events like the World Cup and the Olympics. At the 2019 Superbowl, 169 people were arrested for human trafficking.

Sex trafficking is the most profitable component of human trafficking, generating two-thirds of human trafficking revenue. According to the International Labor Organization, over 1 million children each year are forced into sex trafficking.

COOPERATION TO COMBAT HUMAN TRAFFICKING

Religious actors and NGOs are very active in anti-trafficking efforts. Religious sisters work together in an international network, **Talitha Kum**, named after Bible quote in which Jesus raises a little girl from the dead with the words "Rise up, little girl (talitha kum)." The sisters mobilize before every superbowl and major sporting event, calling hotels near the events, sending anti-trafficking materials, pressing hotel managers to train employees in how to recognize suspected trafficking and report it to law enforcement.

The good news is slavery is outlawed around the world, and governments have increased their commitments to ending modern-day slavery. Sustainable development goal 8.7 specifically calls for ending modern-day slavery. All countries committed to "Take immediate and effective measures to eradicate forced labour, end modern slavery and human trafficking and secure the prohibition and elimination of the worst forms of child labour, including recruitment and use of child soldiers, and by 2025 end child labour in all its forms."

Modern international laws against human trafficking and slavery stem from the United Nations Convention against Transnational Organized Crime and its two related protocols, the United Nations Protocol to Prevent, Suppress, and Punish Trafficking in Persons, Especially Women and Children, and the United Nations Protocol against the Smuggling of

Migrants by Land, Sea, and Air. These entered into force in 2003–2004. To support these laws, the UN created the Special Rapporteur on trafficking in persons, to focus attention on human trafficking and the rights of victims, especially of women and children. The United Nations Office on Drugs and Crime (UNODC) created the United Nations Global Initiative to Fight Human Trafficking (UN.GIFT) in 2007, which aims to help states build their capacity to fight trafficking. Other instruments include the **Convention on the Rights of the Child** on the Sale of Children, Child Prostitution and Child Pornography, and the Protocol to the Convention on the Rights of the Child in Armed Conflict (both entered into force in 2002, and almost all states have ratified).

The century-old International Labor Organization (ILO) also works to prevent and end human trafficking. Founded in 1919, the ILO is the only intergovernmental organization with a unique three-part structure, bringing together workers, employers, as well as governments to improve just labor conditions. Nearly all countries are members of the ILO.[21] Modern ILO conventions against human trafficking include Protocol of 2014 to the Forced Labour Convention (entered into force in 2016; the United States has not ratified); Convention 182, Elimination of Worst Forms of Child Labor (entered into force in 2000; almost all countries have ratified, except Eritrea); Convention 189, Domestic Workers (entered into force in 2013). These modern laws update the older laws ratified by almost all countries, Convention 29 Forced Labour (1930), and Convention 105, Abolition of Forced Labour (1957). As traffickers adapt, creating new forms of trafficking, the law adapts to shine a light on and stop these practices. Some of the updates in the new laws include commitments by employers to undertake "due diligence" actions to prevent human trafficking in their businesses and supply chains, and assistance for victims, including protection from being jailed for offenses related to trafficking, such as their being in another country without legal papers, or prostitution.

These modern laws are supported by older international laws that date back to the abolition of slavery, such as the Slavery Convention (1926) and the Supplementary Convention on the Abolition of Slavery, the Slave Trade, and Institutions and Practices Similar to Slavery (1956). Whether or not states are parties to all these modern anti trafficking laws (most are), they are still bound to protect against human trafficking by both customary international law and older instruments such as the Universal Declaration of Human Rights (1948), the International Covenants on Civil and Political Rights (1966), The United Nations

Convention for the Suppression of the Traffic in Persons and of the Exploitation of the Prostitution of Others (1949), and the Convention on the Elimination of all Forms of Discrimination Against Women (1979).

Improved national laws support these international commitments, such as the US Trafficking in Persons Act (2000), committing governments to track and report on progress in combatting human trafficking, and assist trafficking victims rather than jail them. Many countries have their own such laws, but the US annual report documents what each country around the world is doing (or not doing) to prevent trafficking and assist victims, and gives each country a "grade," of either best (Tier 1), worst (Tier 3), or making progress against TIP (Tier Two). Regions are increasing measures to strengthen antihuman-trafficking capacities and efforts of states, such as the Council of Europe Convention on Action against Trafficking in Human Beings (2008), the European Convention for the Protection of Human Right and Fundamental Freedoms (1950). Subregions are also making efforts, such as the Coordinated Mekong Ministerial Initiative against Trafficking (COMMIT), founded in 2005 by China, Laos, Thailand, Cambodia, Myanmar, and Vietnam.

The Walk Free Foundation, Project Polaris, and End Slavery are some of the many anti trafficking NGOs who lobby governments, corporations, and citizens to end modern-day slavery and protect victims. For example, the Rights Lab at the University of Nottingham partners with the Walk Free Foundation to track whether governments and corporations are upholding their commitments to end modern-day slavery. They release the annual Global Slavery Index and other independent assessments, separate from the government annual reports on government action, such as the US State Department and Justice Department's annual Trafficking in Persons reports. They track "approximately 104 indicators, covering criminal justice responses, victim assistance programming, coordination and accountability mechanisms, addressing risk factors, and actions governments are taking to engage with business."[22] They hope to identify and encourage best practices, and show where gaps exist and improvements are needed, by providing an independent, external assessment.

There is a great deal of overlap between human trafficking and human smuggling. Both are illegal and involve movement of people, but in human smuggling the person being transported has generally tried to leave his or her home country and consented to the transport, at least initially. However, people who begin a journey in a consensual transport-for-hire contract, may end up trafficked or captured into forced labor. For example, Sr. Aziza was awarded the Trafficking in Persons Hero award for her work with African victims of human trafficking and smuggling in the Sinai. Thousands had fled their homes as refugees, migrants, or been trafficked, and were kidnapped by gangs in the Sinai who held them for ransom. They were held as sex slaves, raped and tortured, often with their loved ones listening on the phone as a way to encourage their families to pay the ransom. Families did not have the monies asked for, so victims would be killed or held while families tried to beg or borrow the money. Sr. Aziza provides human rights reporting and medical, psychological and social services to victims who made it out into Israel. The government of Eritrea is corrupt and officials are complicit with the trafficking, according to the State Department annual report on human trafficking. Sr. Aziza has received many death threats for her work. She is undeterred.

According to the White House,

> Human smuggling is the facilitation, transportation, attempted transportation, or illegal entry of a person or persons across an international border, in violation of one or more countries' laws, either clandestinely or through deception, whether with the use of fraudulent documents or through the evasion of legitimate border controls. It is a criminal commercial transaction between willing parties who go their separate ways once they have procured illegal entry into a country. The vast majority of people who are assisted in illegally entering the United States and other countries are smuggled, rather than trafficked. International human smuggling networks are linked to other transnational crimes including drug trafficking and the corruption of government officials. They can move criminals, fugitives, terrorists, and trafficking victims, as well as economic migrants. They undermine the sovereignty of nations and often endanger the lives of those being smuggled.[23]

People who are trafficked often find themselves engaged as forced laborers in criminal enterprises, from prostitution to farm work to manufacturing. For example, to make counterfeit goods profitable, criminal organizations need to keep production costs low. One means to keep production costs low for labor-intensive goods is to use forced labor or trafficked labor.

MONEY LAUNDERING: FOLLOW THE MONEY

Money laundering is the father of all transnational crimes. Whenever you have crime, you also have the crime of money laundering, as the channel to use the profits from the original criminal activity (be it human trafficking, drug trafficking, counterfeit goods, environmental crimes, or arms trafficking). Money laundering is the ultimate make-over for criminals and their cash, taking criminals and their illegal money and dressing them up with new layers to make them appear to be legal businessmen with legal profits. Money laundering takes criminal income, moves it through a series of shell companies and opaque organizations designed to break the laws against money laundering, in order to hide the illicit origins of the cash, and make it appear as if the income were generated through a legal channel. Casinos and luxury real estate in New York, Florida, and London are some of the favorite ways criminals launder money. Here's how it works.

Money laundering takes place in three steps: placement, layering, and integration. These three steps can involve a variety of different businesses and techniques, and these may vary around the world, but the goals are the same, to hide the illegal origins of the money (**placement**), to deceive people into thinking that illegal cash came from a legitimate source (**layering**), and to be able to use the cash openly (**integration**).

The first step is to place the illegal criminal profits into some sort of business or financial institution in order to hide the illegal origins of the cash. This may be done in many different ways. Anti money laundering laws require banks and businesses to report **suspicious financial activities** including cash transactions of 10,000, or that add up to 10,000 in a day. Some banks and businesses look the other way, take the money, and do not report the suspicious transaction. Casinos are a favorite money laundering stop for criminals, because these are cash-heavy businesses. Criminals offer "loans" from loan sharks (of the illegal cash) to players, or may send in criminal employees to play with some of the illegal cash, but at the end the criminals will turn their chips in for a receipt or get a receipt for wins. With the casino receipt they have placed the cash, showing a legal source for it. This receipt then allows them to take their check to the bank or other financial institution, as they can now "show"

Table 10.1 Common Money Laundering Schemes

Region	Common Money Laundering Schemes
Africa	Informal banking, cash couriers, real estate
Americas	Casinos, wire transfers, trade-based money laundering
Asia	Informal value transfer systems
Europe	Cash-intensive businesses, real estate, high-value goods

Source: Organization for Security and Co-operation in Europe.

a seemingly legal source for the cash. Some criminals place the money into cash-heavy businesses that are friendly to criminals and don't ask too many questions, for example, casinos and hotels. The illegal cash is mixed with the legal cash; the friendly business breaks the law and does not file suspicious financial activity reports, and may even inflate its books to make it appear as if the illegal cash came from the legal cash-heavy business. For example, in a high-profile case, Donald Trump's Taj Majal Casino was repeatedly fined for breaking laws against money laundering and not reporting suspicious financial activities of large cash transactions, from as soon as the Taj Majal opened its doors through today.[24] Also, Canada has been working to crack down on money laundering at casinos.

Other methods of placing the cash are to send criminal employees called human cash "**mules**" who carry bags of currency to make smaller deposits in different banks and businesses. This is called **structuring** or **smurfing**, and the purpose of making several deposits is to avoid the $10,000 mandatory reporting threshold. Cash "mules" can also travel internationally over borders to deposit the money into lax banks or businesses that do not comply with anti money laundering laws.

Layering is deception. In this stage criminals move the money around through complex, opaque financial transactions, **shell companies** that do not disclose the owner's name, or using book keeping tricks in order to deceive people about the criminal source of the money. Think of the "slight of hand" magic trick in which a ball is placed under a cup or shell, next to three similar shells, and the three are then quickly mixed and moved, so that you will not be able to tell under which shell the item is. Criminals use a similar process to move and confuse people about where the illegal money is and its illegal origins. Off shore tax havens which hide wealthy people's money so they can avoid taxes, are often used to hide criminal profits as well.

Because the cash is huge, and the chance of detection low, even legitimate banks are often caught money laundering. Barclays, Deutsche Bank, ING, Lloyds Banking Group and the Royal Bank of Scotland are among top banks that have been fined for money laundering assets from Libya, Sudan, and Russia. HSBC paid $1.92 billion in fines in 2012 to the US government for failure to comply with anti money laundering laws, including failure to file suspicious activity reports for transactions involving Mexican drug cartels.

Most notably, HSBC admitted to violating the Bank Secrecy Act by failing to monitor over $200 trillion in wire transactions between its Mexico and US subsidiaries, among other crimes. $881 million in drug money from the Sinaloa and Norte de Valle drug cartels were found to have been moved through HSBC-Mexico's accounts to HSBC-USA via the unmonitored wire transactions.

After the money has been placed and layered, it can then be integrated or used. In this stage criminals buy things with the money, often high-priced real estate in places like New York, Miami, and London, where half of the real estate transactions are made in cash. Real estate transactions are costly, which is good for criminals looking to park large amounts of cash. And real estate is less regulated than other financial transactions, so it is less likely to draw the attention of law enforcement. Real estate may also increase in value over time, so it is a good investment that does not require many subsequent transactions after purchase, which could draw attention to the criminal customer. **Know Your Customer laws** and policies apply to banking, and require banks to authenticate who their customers are and where their money comes from. Know Your Customer laws are not generally applied in real estate.

According to international standards, for example, real estate agents should be required to refuse to do business with an intermediary or a shell company unless they disclose the identity of the customer they are representing first. A recent report, however, found that in three major markets—Australia, Canada and the US—this seemingly simple requirement is not yet in place in national law.

The United Kingdom is changing its laws to close this "loophole" for money laundering through high-end real estate. It has passed new transparency laws which require the true beneficiary of shell companies buying real estate to be disclosed and published in a public listing. The **Unexplained Wealth Order** gives real estate agents tools to ask buyers where their money comes from. It is these types of multi million, all cash transactions, made by shell companies, some of which are tied to organized crime, which has drawn investigations by law enforcement into Trump properties.[25]

There are many other ways in which criminals launder money, as criminals get creative and use new technologies to keep a step ahead of law enforcement. Online banking and various online currency transfer methods are easy ways for criminals to move money around. Bitcoin and similar **crypto currencies** are a haven for criminals, as these currencies are not issued by governments or regulated by governments, and are not transparent. Europol notes that bitcoin was used in 40 percent of illicit transactions in the European Union, including in payments between criminals in many high-profile investigations.[26]

Criminals also use online sites in the gig economy, such as Uber and Airbnb, for **ghost laundering**. By setting up a ghost account as a fake property or service provider, then paying money even without receiving the service, cash is effectively transferred. Since the gig economy is largely unregulated, this can be an effective means of avoiding anti money laundering laws and reporting requirements.

Some of the largest and most complex money laundering schemes involve **transfer pricing, trade misinvoicing, and trade-based money laundering.** In these schemes a fraudulent "bill of sale" is created for goods or trade that lists a false price, quantity, and/ or a false description of the goods, different than the goods are worth. A legitimate business would fail if it paid inflated prices for shoddy goods. But if the purpose of this exchange is to move large amounts of criminal money into the legal economy, not to make a profit from the sale of the goods, then the actual quality and price of the goods doesn't matter. What matters is the bill of sale showing a legitimate business transaction. This type of money laundering is very difficult to detect and prevent, as it is easy to hide illicit "sales" among the torrent of legal trade. This is becoming the preferred method of money laundering. It also facilitates the sale of counterfeit goods, as a "front business" to mask the transfers of illegal cash.

The world cooperates to stop money laundering through a variety of means. Although fraud and tax evasion are crimes, originally money laundering was not designated as a crime until the 1988 United Nations Convention Against Illicit Traffic in Narcotic Drugs and Psychotropic Substances first criminalized money laundering the profits of drug trafficking. In 1989 the Organization for Economic Cooperation and Development (OECD) created the Financial Action Task Force (FATF), and published forty recommended anti money laundering (AML) measures in 1990, as well as nine measures to counter terrorist financing. The now thirty-seven members conduct self-assessments of how well they are implementing the AML recommendations. To enhance transparency and accountability, AML experts and financial investigators from other countries also conduct external peer reviews, and this information is shared with all members. To encourage others to follow the best practices in AML, FATF engages in "name and shame" practices, periodically publishing blacklists of **noncooperative countries and territories (NCCT)** that have lax laws and practices that attract money laundering. These noncooperative countries and territories fear losing investors and international reputation, so they changed their AML laws to be compliant with FATF recommendations, even though these states are not parties to FATF. Through this type of leverage, FATF was able to pressure between one-fourth and one-third of all sovereign states to adopt FATF standards by 2006. Today eight regional FATF associate organizations have been founded, to bring the FATF principles to specific geographic regions, including the Caribbean, Africa, the Middle East/North Africa, and Asia/Pacific.

Interpol supports AML efforts by helping with investigations between countries. But implementation is left to countries themselves. Experts estimate that less than 1 percent of criminal money flows are stopped and seized around the world. Generally, when casinos, banks, or other organizations are caught money laundering they are fined, but the fines are generally less than the profits they received from money laundering, and bankers are not sent to jail.

Money laundering is not a "victimless, white collar" crime. Money laundering allows those who have committed heinous crimes, from drug trafficking to slavery, to get away with murder and to enjoy their stolen funds. Money laundering harms the legal economy. It puts legal businesses, goods and services at a disadvantage when they have to compete with the fraudulent prices of illegal front companies, counterfeit merchandise, and trade-based money laundering schemes. It encourages corruption, avoids taxes, and undermines government capacity, creating a negative feedback loop which facilitates more crime and undermines the state's ability to fight crime.

Raymond Baker and his NGO, Global Financial Integrity, notes that money laundering robs the poor, by siphoning more than $1 trillion a year out of developing countries. This stolen money flowing out of developing countries is larger than all foreign aid and direct investment going in to developing economies. This stolen money is not available for hospitals, schools, power, roads, and development. By undermining government, stealing money, resources, and tax dollars, money laundering hampers development and kills poor people. Global Financial Integrity urges stronger action against money laundering. "Bankers who knowingly commit crimes and allow bank accounts to be used to shelter criminal money should be held personally accountable. To date, enforcement has generally focused on moderate-sized fines and promises by banks to improve compliance. No bank should be "**too big to jail.**"[27]

ENVIRONMENTAL CRIMES

Taken together, environmental crimes are the second biggest category of international crime, costing the world over $276.3 billion a year in stolen timber, fish, minerals, species, and oil. The environmental and human damage from this illegal destruction of the ecosystems like the Amazon is priceless.

About one-third of the trees cut around the world are illegally logged, but in some regions such as the Amazon region of South

America, Central Africa, and Southeast Asia, between 50 and 90 percent of logging is illegal. Trees are often stolen and cut from public lands like national parks and endangered, protected ecosystems like the Amazon. Illegally clear-cutting trees decimates the habitat of the animals, birds, plants and life forms that live in there. Species become extinct and endangered, and biodiversity lost, as forests are cut down for illegal profits. Most of the world's illegal timber are imported by China.[28]

Most of the illegal fishing enterprises in the world steal fish from poor countries, who need the fish to feed their own people. Much of this illegal fishing relies on government subsidies to keep the fleets operating. Ships may be registered with **"flags of convenience"** by countries such as Panama, that exercise little oversight over vessels, and do not require transparency or accountability over who owns or operates the ship. Or they may be conducted by the huge Chinese fishing fleet. The Chinese government subsidizes fishing, which keeps the price of fish low and encourages Chinese fishing fleets to overfish. Illegal fishing operations set up off the coasts of developing countries, such as along the coast of the countries of West Africa, knowing that these governments have little capacity to prevent or catch the criminals stealing fish, or to seize their illegal catches. Equipped with the same technologies as legal fishing boats, such as fish finding GPS and commercial freezers, criminal fishing fleets are destroying and overfishing the world's fisheries. The UN estimates that 90 percent of the world's fisheries are fully or overfished. China is a big driver of illegal fishing, both in stealing fish and consuming the fish. China subsidizes a huge distant overseas fleet of 3,000 vessels, far more vessels than could fish sustainably or legally. Over 500 Chinese fishing fleets steal over $2 billion in fish from West African countries alone each year. Catches are supposed to be reported to the UN Food and Agriculture Organization, "but the statistics are very unreliable as a result of under-reporting, indifference to treaty quotas, illegal species catch, and stocks caught outside national jurisdictions. The European Union estimates that the actual Chinese catches may be over twelve times what is reported through official channels and is dominating and decimating supply particularly in developing nations in West Africa where there is no domestic fleet to compete."[29]

Illegal mining also takes place primarily in developing countries that cannot prevent criminal actors from stealing their precious resources such as gold, tin, tantalum, and tungsten, minerals used in cellphone and electronic circuits. This illegal practice often fuels conflict, such as in the Democratic Republic of Congo (DRC) where millions have died. Girls as young as 8 years and grandmothers as old as 80 are raped as a tool of war by the armed groups, to terrorize populations away from the lucrative mine sites. Peace accords have been signed in the DRC civil war, but splinter groups continue to fight in order to have access to the lucrative stolen resources. Illegal mining spurs and finances the violence. These groups kill, rape, and terrorize communities, kidnap women and girls into sexual slavery and kidnap children to serve as child soldiers or forced laborers in the illegal mines. This creates a negative feedback loop. Deprived of the legal income tax revenue, and legal development that such resources could provide, governments of developing countries lack the revenue and capacity to effectively prevent or catch the criminals, which encourages more illegal activities. Illegal mining operations dump toxic mining chemicals into the ground water and rivers, poisoning the environment near their illegal sites. Transparency measures have helped to reduce these practices. A US law (section 1502 of the Dodd Frank Wall Street Reform and Consumer Protection Act) required transparency of supply chains. Companies that listed on the Securities and Exchange Commission had to publicly disclose whether their products had conflict minerals in their supply chains. There were no fines or sanctions for companies that used minerals from conflict areas; it simply requires transparency so consumers can make informed choices. Although the Trump Administration has stopped enforcing the **Conflict Minerals Transparency law**, most companies continue to follow it. They believe it is a good business practice to reduce their risk of having their products linked to war, slavery, and environmental destruction. The law has worked to reduce the control of mines by armed groups. And despite the Trump administration's failure to enforce the law, the EU has enacted a similar measure. Companies that do business in the European market will have to comply with transparency reporting anyway. Many companies, including Apple and Intel, do not want the transparency rule scrapped.

Other environmental crimes include the illegal wildlife trade, which targets endangered species. Elephants are poached for their ivory. The government of Kenya seized and burned a record 105 tons of ivory in 2016, but that has not curbed the demand, particularly in Asia. Thirty percent of elephants were killed between 2007 and 2014.[30] Rhinoceros are killed for their horns. In Vietnam it is considered a male status symbol to ground rhino horn into one's drink, or to give it to one's boss to advance a career. Tigers are killed for their skins, bones, and body parts which are used in traditional medicine.

Criminals who commit environmental crimes are rarely caught, and rarely prosecuted. With rising consumption patterns and a growing global population, environmental crimes are not going away. "One reason is that China is the factory for the world. There is a large, rising middle class who want standards of living they haven't known before. It's an enormous pressure on the resources of the planet, on the fish, on the timber, and it leads to a massive illicit trade in these natural resources.[31]

THE UNITED STATES OF DRUGS

The United States leads the world in drug addiction. Russia leads the world in alcohol addiction. Over 72,000 Americans alone died from drug overdoses last year. A total of 100,000 died from alcohol consumption. Nearly 70 percent of those with substance abuse problems (alcohol or drugs) are men, and most drug addicts are young men in their twenties.

The world is experiencing an epidemic of drug addiction, fueled by the production of more opium and cocaine than ever recorded in history. Opioid addiction is up around the world. In the United States, opioid overdose is the single largest cause of death for people under the age of 50. Opioids are drugs created from the opium poppy plant, either as legal medicines or illicit narcotics. The current crisis in the United States began with overprescription of legal pain killers for medicinal use or surgery. As patients became addicted, they continued illicit use of prescription drugs, and also shifted to consuming other opioids, such as heroin and fentanyl, a powerful and deadly synthetic opioid that China exports to the United States. It is 80–100 times stronger than morphine.

Illegal drug trafficking is one of the most deadly, and most profitable, transnational crimes. Drugs are a half trillion dollar industry annually, and it is constantly growing. Financially drugs account for about one-third of all transnational crime profits.

Traffickers use the gamut of modern technologies to move their products from farm or pharma lab to consumers. Drones are the newest tool in the drug traffickers tool kit. Mexican drug cartels are expanding their use of drones to deliver drugs across the border. Drones are small and can travel low and undetected. They are not stopped by border walls. Drones are anonymous, don't steal profits, and don't testify against the drug organizations if they get caught by law enforcement. Mexican cartels are rapidly expanding their use of drones. Officials estimate there are hundreds of drug drone flights annually, transmitting many tons of contraband drugs. Drones are a perfect delivery vehicle as they are cheap, versatile, and can be used for both surveillance and delivery. The drones do not land in the United States, but merely drop their shipments and return to base. Drones are readily available and easily replaced, and don't require licenses to operate that would link the drone to people in the drug cartel.

While some of the drugs for the US market are domestically produced, such as cannabis (marijuana), others are imported: fentanyl
from China, cocaine from Colombia and Mexico, heroin from Afghan
opium. Traffickers use a variety of transport methods, from small boats
and planes, to shipping containers, to UPS and global mail delivery services, to submarines. Drugs enter through legal ports, airports, rails and
roads, thus border walls do not stop the flow of illegal drugs.

Cannabis is the most widely produced, used and distributed drug.
It is produced domestically, as well as imported. Cannabis is the largest component of the drug market, comprising about 44 percent of the
global drug trade. It is estimated that 2.5 percent of the world's population use cannabis.

That's different from **fentanyl**, which comes from China. As Louise
Shelley notes,

> Many of these drugs were purchased on Chinese web sites. The Chi-
> nese government doesn't bother with the sites, because it's meant
> for an external market. They are not being taken down by Chinese
> authorities, because they are not charging Chinese citizens. In the
> middle 1800s, China was brought down by England in the first opium
> war, France and the U.S. joined England in the second opium war, in
> the mid-1850s. They defeated China and this has been an enormous
> embarrassment, and it's something the Chinese haven't forgotten, and
> they still teach their children about it in school. I wonder if in some
> ways, this trade in fentanyl is revenge for the opium wars. In so much
> of illicit trade, the past shapes the present.[32]

New technologies give old criminal enterprises, like drug trafficking, new ways to reach customers and move product to market.
Drug traffickers and customers increasingly go online, using encrypted
DarkNet sites and online payment systems to traffic drugs, which are
then shipped using the post office or commercial shippers. When government finds and shuts down one of these illegal websites, they quickly
reopen with a slightly altered name.

Terrorist groups and insurgent groups use drug trafficking to raise
funds for war and violence. The Taliban are key to the opium trade in
Afghanistan. Guerrilla groups in Colombia used cocaine sales to finance
their insurgency. Drug profits undermine the government, deprive the
state of tax dollars, and overshadow the legal economy, making it difficult for government to gain capacity to shut down criminal networks.

Countries have been cooperating and creating international laws
to stop illicit drug trafficking for over a century, since the International
Opium Commission of 1909. Almost all countries, including the United

Figure 10.2   Share of Population with Drug Use Disorders, 2017

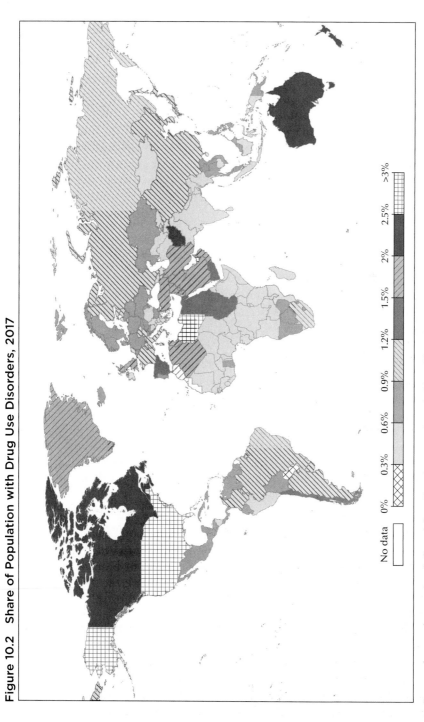

Drug dependence is defined by the international Classification of Diseases as the presence of three or more indicators of dependence for at least a month within the previous year. Drug dependency includes all illicit drugs.

Source: Our World in Data; IHME, Global Burden of Disease

States, are parties to the three main international agreements that form the backbone of international cooperation to stop illicit drugs: the 1961 Single Convention on Narcotic Drugs; the 1971 Convention on Psychotropic Substances; and the 1988 Convention Against Illicit Traffic in Narcotic Drugs and Psychotropic Substances. Countries have also created the UN Office on Drugs and Organized Crime, to research and disseminate reports tracking global trends, and the International Narcotics Control Board, to monitor treaty compliance. Most countries experience much lower drug usage, lower drug addiction, and lower drug overdose deaths than the United States. Most developed states focus government responses on health care, substance abuse treatment, and recovery from addiction, rather than jailing drug users.

COUNTERFEIT MEDICINES AND PRODUCTS

The sale of counterfeit goods is the largest segment of the contraband economy, totaling about $1.13 trillion annually. All major international crime groups are involved, from the Chinese triads, to the Japanese Yakuza, to the Italian Camorra and the Italian-American mafia. The production of counterfeit goods follows market demand for the legitimate good. Between two-thirds and three-quarters of all counterfeit goods are made in China.[33]

Counterfeiting may seem like a benign enterprise. Who is hurt by the sale of fake Gucci sunglasses? But the rising trade in counterfeit goods makes us all sicker and poorer. The Chinese government does not regulate its pharmaceutical companies that produce medicines for export. About one-third of the medicines in developing countries are counterfeit, but the number can be much higher in some places. In Nigeria, it is estimated that 70 percent of anti-malaria medications imported from China are counterfeit. When people use counterfeit medicines, lives are on the line. The medicines may contain no active ingredients, as when a shipment of cancer drugs was found to have no active ingredients. Or the fake medicines may have harmful ingredients, as when eleven people in the Boston area were killed by fake steroid medication, and people in Singapore died and others suffered brain damage when counterfeit erectile dysfunction drugs were laced with toxic levels of anti-diabetes medication.[34]

When farmers use counterfeit fertilizers that do not work as well as real fertilizers, less food is produced and people go hungry. Counterfeit fertilizers or other agricultural products that contain toxins leech into the food supply, and make people sick.

According to the UNODC, international cooperation in the fight against trafficking in counterfeit medicines is growing and needed.

As with other forms of crime, criminal groups use, to their advantage, gaps in legal and regulatory frameworks, weaknesses in capacity and the lack of resources of regulatory, enforcement and criminal justice officials, as well as difficulties in international cooperation. At the same time, the prospect of the comparatively low risk of detection and prosecution in relation to the potential income make the production and trafficking in falsified medical products an attractive commodity to criminal groups, who conduct their activities with little regard to the physical and financial detriment, and exploitation, of others.[35]

OPEN MARKETS, LEGAL AND ILLEGAL

The spread of open, legal markets around the world has facilitated the rise of illegal markets, often piggy backing on legal trade. The larger volume of legal trade makes it easy to hide illegal trade, and the vast size of the market challenges law enforcement to see and separate the legal from the illegal activities.

With the growing availability of online market places such as Amazon and eBay, and the illegal versions of these sites, criminals can easily sell their wares online. In the case of online pharmaceutical sites, people unknowingly purchase fake medicine. In the case of illegal drugs, people turn to online drug purchases to avoid detection.

The increase in legal trade makes the sale of illegal counterfeit goods difficult to detect. More traded hides more money laundering through trade-based money laundering methods such as misinvoicing and transfer pricing. Large global integrated markets have lots of good hiding places for illegal money and illegal trade.

OPEN SOCIETIES: DEMOCRACY ON DRUGS

The world's biggest and oldest democracy is also the world's biggest drug addict.

Voters have voted to legalize many drugs in many democracies, from the Netherlands to California. In the United States, nine states and the District of Colombia have voted to legalize cannabis, putting state laws at odds with federal regulations which still list it as an illegal substance. Those who favor drug legalization argue that decriminalizing the sale of drugs will remove money from the hands of criminal organizations, and will put resources back in the hands of police. Instead of tying up government law enforcement, courts, judges, and prison resources jailing drug users (particularly of high volume, lower-risk drugs like cannabis), governments could instead channel money to help provide medical and social help for drug addicts. Whether governments provide health support for people suffering from addictions varies widely among democracies, with Western European governments providing greater health support to help cure addictions, and the United States providing little to no assistance to addicts. This is one of the reasons why the US death rate from addiction is the highest in the world. Advocates for decriminalization of drugs argue that legalization will reduce violence and crime. Arguing from a comparison with alcohol, they say that just as alcohol prohibition helped the mafia, and legalization of alcohol removed a lucrative market from the hands of criminal actors, so they argue that decriminalization will take the drugs out of the hands of violent actors, and into the hands of corporate producers who they presume will behave more responsibly. Alcohol companies such as Corona, Coors, Molsen, and Budweiser are pursuing partnerships with cannabis producers, and tobacco companies such as Philip Morris (Marlboro) have long wanted to sell cannabis for many decades.

Opponents to decriminalization of drugs note that drugs are harmful, present a public health crisis, and are particularly harmful to children and youth. The human brain is not fully developed until the age of 25. Children and youth exposed to alcohol and/or drugs prior to age 21 (and by some experts, age 25) substantially increase their lifelong chances of addiction, reducing their life expectancy and increasing their risks of poverty and a host of other social and economic problems. Addictions undermine health and well-being in many ways. Drug use kills people and lowers life expectancy. Drug use makes it harder for people to hold onto their jobs or finish/do well in school, undermining their earning potential and making them poorer, breaking up relationships, families, and marriages, and harming health from a host of diseases. Opponents note that drug use reduces the capacity of the frontal cortex, the part of the brain responsible for executive function, for impulse control, decision-making, assessing consequences, thinking, planning, solving problems, and behaving appropriately. By impairing the part of the brain responsible for making good decisions, drug usage increases crime and other risky behaviors. Thus decriminalization of drug use will not reduce crime, but will increase crimes committed by people using drugs because their prefrontal cortex is impaired, so they cannot make appropriate decisions to control behavior and impulses. Opponents also argue that the use of seemingly less harmful drugs, such as cannabis, may lead to the use of more harmful and addictive drugs, such as opiates, via this pathway of the brain's decreased ability to make sound choices.

There's a libertarian sentiment among many drug users, and those who commit other crimes from hunting endangered animals to cybercrime, that "the government" should not tell people what to do. For example, **Dread Pirate Roberts**, also known as Ross Ulbricht, was the University of Texas alumni and Eagle Scout who founded Silk Road, one of the first and most successful black market sites on the darknet, where drugs and other illegal products were sold. Using bitcoin and Tor encryption, Ulbright believed the site would be anonymous to government authorities. He claimed he ran the site not for the money but because of his libertarian ideals. "Silk Road was supposed to be about giving people the freedom to make their own choices." When he was caught and imprisoned, he paid assassins to murder six people who might testify against him. He was convicted for drug trafficking, money laundering, and cybercrime, and is now serving two concurrent life sentences without possibility of parole. The Libertarian Party and some groups like the Gun Owners of America have petitioned President Trump to pardon Ulbricht.

OPEN TECHNOLOGIES AND CRIME

Drones on Drugs

Transnational Criminal Organizations are fast to adopt new technologies to crime. As we've seen, from cryptocurrencies like bitcoin, to ghost laundering using online sites, to using drones for drug deliveries, criminals use the same technologies as legal businesses use, in service of crime. The UN Office on Drugs and Crime notes that as criminals exploit new technologies, such as the darknet, it is changing the organizational structure and nature of the illicit drug trade, with more loose, horizontal networks, as well as changing the types of players involved. Old criminal networks relied on relationships, often family ties. New criminal networks are more anonymous and less based on personal relationships. While old transnational criminal cartels are still operative, new and smaller groups are becoming more important.[36] Just as new technologies and platforms are disrupting the legal business landscape, the same is true in the illegal criminal context.

According to Louise Shelley, the new technologies allow criminal activities to metastasize in scale, reach, and speed. But the speed and skills of technologically enhanced crime outpaces law enforcement's capabilities to respond. For example, Silk Road 2.0 was opened just four months after the original "illegal eBay," Silk Road was shut down.

> Illicit trade has been growing exponentially in the last 30 years in part because of the rise of new technology. The fact that most of the world's population is now connected to cell phones, and to the internet, has fueled illicit trade in rural areas that used to be inaccessible. For example, a third of rural India is now using illegal pesticides, purchasing the

goods through the Internet and cell phones, and directly affecting the health and food supply of the people. These counterfeit harmful products have shown up in the most remote areas of the world. If you look at the history of illicit trade, it was in ports and big cities; it was along rivers. Now, with transport links and communications, it's everywhere. The Silk Road site, which started out selling drugs, was the first large marketplace on the Dark Web. Within two years it had done $1.8 billion dollars' worth of corrupt business in the cyberworld. When things go into the cyber-world, they don't change fundamentally, but the scale and the speed becomes just enormous. Silk Road Two was over double the size of Silk Road One. Every new level of involvement in this gets larger, with more volume and greater profits. Part of what cyberspace does is help us understand the magnitude of illicit trade, and law enforcement can get some awareness of its dimensions. Law enforcement needs to be much more computer savvy. But the problem is that most of the tech world and the technology and information that goes alongside it is housed in the records of computers and software companies. So they have the data, they control access to data, and unless there is cooperation with the technology community, it is not really possible to combat illicit trade at any meaningful level.[37]

CONCLUSIONS: CRIMINALS GO BEYOND SOVEREIGNTY, SO MUST OUR COOPERATION AGAINST CRIME

Open markets, open societies, and open technologies create new opportunities for transnational criminal enterprises. Big government, and authoritarian government has declined since the mid-twentieth century, creating new opportunities for criminals. Open markets have spread, creating new opportunities for criminals. Open technologies built for speed and commerce, not security, create new opportunities for criminals. Some of the oldest criminal activities—human trafficking and drug trafficking—now are supported by global technologies, easier transportation and communication to facilitate global criminal distribution networks.

Sovereign states have come together to create modern laws against transnational organized crime, such as the UN Convention Against Transnational Organized Crime (UNTOC or **Palermo Convention**) and the UN Convention Against Corruption (UNCAC). The Palermo Convention entered into force in 2003, and almost all countries are parties to the treaty (except Somalia, South Sudan, and a few island states). The Convention Against Corruption entered into force in 2005, and almost all countries are parties to it (except Eritrea, North Korea, Somalia, and a few island states).

States have created new international organizations to fight crime, such as UNODC, the UN Special Rapporteur on trafficking in persons, especially women and children, the United Nations Office of the Special Representative of the Secretary-General for Children and Armed Conflict, and the UN Global Initiative to Fight Human Trafficking. These are intended to build cooperative capacity and shine a light on pressing problems of international crime.

States have also worked to increase state capacity to enforce these laws, offering greater training, education, sharing best practices and lessons learned, data bases and technologies. For example, the US and European anti trafficking laws work to build capacity of state actors to enforce laws against trafficking and to assist victims. Drones and big data programs are used to detect and disrupt criminal activity. Creating new laws against transnational organized crime and corruption are important first steps. But implementation and enforcement of the laws are key, and that is up to individual sovereign states, as well as regional shared sovereignty bodies such as the EU.

NGOs work to keep countries transparent and accountable, to keep their commitments, through monitoring, information sharing, dissemination of best practices and lessons learned, training and capacity building, and public naming and shaming. For example, the religious sisters of the Talitha Kum Network minister to trafficking victims, and pressure businesses and governments to better enforce anti trafficking measures. Through conflict minerals reporting and transparency, corporations are helping to take the profit out of illegal conflict minerals that fuel war.

Because governments who are engaged in criminal activities themselves will not help in the fight against crime, the NGO Transparency International monitors and creates a list every year, ranking countries from the most to the least corrupt. The most corrupt counties in the world are Somalia, South Sudan, Syria, North Korea, Yemen, and Afghanistan.[38] Five of six of these most corrupt countries are experiencing civil war, further eroding the sovereign state's ability to function. When countries like Afghanistan are caught in long-term cycles of conflict and corruption for decades, it perpetuates a negative feedback cycle. The state is unable to prevent crime, catch criminals, and support legal economic development, so youth are tempted to enter into crime and corruption, lacking other alternatives. When legal jobs and money are low, crime and corruption are high. In situations of economic scarcity, corruption can be perceived as necessary, as families and clans "take care of" their own.

The world has made progress. Child labor has decreased, and violent crime of all types has decreased in most places, even while global population levels are increasing. But drug use, environmental crimes, money laundering, and illegal counterfeit sales are also increasing, making people poorer and sicker.

Big data technology may be helpful to trace and stop criminal activities. Drones have been used to detect and stop illegal logging. Satellite information can track illegal fishing and direct law enforcement to intercept. And greater financial intelligence is needed to separate illegal money laundering from legal trade transactions. Transparency is increasing in many ways which can assist the fight against transnational crime.

International crime is done for money. The NGO Global Financial Integrity advocates for greater effort to stop the flow of dirty money, which would help in combatting all types of transnational crime. They advocate for "several steps governments and other regulatory bodies can take to increase the levels of detection and interdiction of the proceeds of transnational crime:

- Require that corporations registering and doing business within a country declare the name(s) of the entity's true, ultimate beneficial owner(s)
- Flag financial and trade transactions involving individuals and corporations in 'secrecy jurisdictions' as high-risk and require extra documentation
- Scrutinize import and export invoices for signs of misinvoicing, which may indicate technical and/or physical smuggling
- Use world market price databases to estimate the risk of misinvoicing for the declared values and investigate suspicious transactions
- Share more information between agencies and departments on the illicit markets and actors that exist within a country's borders."[39]

There are many sensible suggestions for better cooperation in combatting transnational crime. The challenge is whether states and the private sector can scale-up cooperation faster than criminal networks are scaling-up illegal activities.

KEY TERMS

DISCUSSION QUESTIONS

1. Who is Nadia Murad? Why did she win the Nobel Prize? Why did she title her book *The Last Girl?*
2. Why have global criminals never had it so good? What is new about global criminal activities?
3. What is "the Great Crime Decline?"
4. How does transnational organized crime thrive in war zones and former war zones? Why does this happen?
5. What are the types of human trafficking? Which forms are worst?
6. Imagine you are a young girl in a warzone. How are you vulnerable to criminal groups?
7. What do organizations such as Talitha Kum hope to achieve and how?
8. Describe the arguments for and against drug decriminalization. Which arguments and evidence are most persuasive to you, and why?
9. How do criminals launder money?
10. What measures do governments and businesses use to try to stop money laundering?
11. How do criminals work around anti money laundering laws and policies?
12. How are global actors trying to cooperate across borders to curtail money laundering? What are the pros and cons of these efforts?

Nuclear weapons survivors support a nuclear weapons ban.

11

Weapons of Mass Destruction

Challenges of Control and Elimination

■ ■ ■

No nation today boasts of being a chemical weapon state. No nation argues that it is acceptable, in extreme circumstances, to use sarin nerve agent. No nation proclaims the right to unleash on its enemy the plague or polio. That is because international norms have been set, perceptions have been changed. And now, at last, we have an unequivocal norm against nuclear weapons . . . . Nuclear weapons, like chemical weapons, biological weapons, cluster munitions and land mines before them, are now illegal. Their existence is immoral. Their abolishment is in our hands. The end is inevitable. But will that end be the end of nuclear weapons or the end of us? We must choose.

—Beatrice Finn, Nobel Peace Prize Winner[1]

As a country that voluntarily dismantled its nuclear weapons programme, South Africa is of the firm view that there are no safe hands for weapons of mass destruction. . . . We are making a clarion call to all member states of the UN to sign and ratify the ban treaty in order to rid the world and humanity of these lethal weapons of mass destruction.

—South African President Jacob Zuma[2]

Nuclear weapons are a threat to the world. Any large-scale nuclear exchange would have globally catastrophic consequences. . . . Now is not the time to build larger arsenals of nuclear weapons. Now is the time to rid the world of this threat.

—George P. Shultz, Secretary of State
to President Ronald Reagan[3]

We can expect more of these nuclear smuggling cases. As long as the smugglers think they can make big money without getting caught, they will keep doing it.

—Constantin Malic,[4] Moldovan official

Challenges to the disarmament and non-proliferation architecture are growing. The global strategic context is more fluid and dangerous than ever. Technological advances have made means of production and methods of delivery for chemical, biological, radiological and nuclear materials cheaper, easier and more accessible. Vicious non-State actors that target civilians for carnage are actively seeking chemical, biological and nuclear weapons... We see the reappearance of some of the discredited arguments that were used to justify nuclear weapons during the cold war. Those arguments were morally, politically and practically wrong 30 years ago, and they are wrong now.

—Ban Ki-moon, UN Secretary General[5]

Nuclear war cannot be won and must never be fought.

—President Ronald Reagan

Somebody hits us within ISIS; you wouldn't strike back with a nuke? Nothing is off the table.

—President Donald J. Trump[6]

WEAPONS OF MASS DESTRUCTION (WMD) are now banned. But they still exist, posing a danger to people and the planet. Open societies, open technologies, and open markets create more avenues for the proliferation of WMDs to terrorist groups as well as states, but these channels of globalization also create new opportunities for countering these weapons. WMD do not discriminate between civilians and soldiers. They violate the Geneva Conventions and the International Laws of War, laws which are also institutionalized in the US (and other countries') Military Codes of Justice. Chemical weapons were used in World War I. Most died from chlorine, phosgene, and mustard gas attacks. The use of chemical and biological weapons was banned in 1925 in the Geneva Protocol. Horrific experiments and stockpiles of new types of biological and chemical weapons were created during the Cold War. The ban on biological weapons was expanded in the **Biological Weapons Convention** in 1972 (which entered into force in 1975), banning development, possession, production, stockpiling, and transfer of biological weapons. Likewise, the ban on chemical weapons was expanded in the **Chemical Weapons Convention** of 1993 (which entered into force in 1997), which bans possession, development, production, stockpiling, and transfer of chemical weapons.

The bans on other WMD did not include a specific ban on nuclear weapons, although the very first UN Resolution, passed by the General Assembly January 24, 1946, called for the complete elimination of atomic weapons and the creation of an international body to ensure that atomic science only be used for peaceful purposes.[7] A majority of countries banned nuclear weapons through a series of **Nuclear Weapons Free Zone (NWFZ)** treaties, which prohibited the manufacture, use, testing, and possession of nuclear weapons. In 2017, 122 countries signed an international nuclear weapons ban, extending the previous NWFZ treaties globally. The Nuclear Ban is currently in the ratification period, so has not yet entered into force.

Nuclear weapons were exploded over 2,045 times over the years. The United States exploded over 1,100 nuclear weapons. The United States and other countries bombed using nuclear weapons on their own countries and indigenous territories in order to study the impact of the weapons and to understand whether the weapons would work. The nuclear detonations were entirely real, not limited in duration or impact as the term "test" implies. The Nevada Test Site is the "most bombed place on earth." Nearby Las Vegas turned these frequent nuclear explosions into a tourist attraction. The Atomic Bar, and other hotels and bars along the Vegas strip, hosted atomic bomb viewing parties, specialty drinks, and atomic beauty pageants. Families brought picnics to the desert to watch the explosions, which were advertised by the Chamber of Commerce, like fireworks displays. In addition to bombing the cities of Hiroshima and Nagasaki, Japan, the United States bombed in New Mexico, Nevada, Navajo Nation, Colorado, Mississippi, Alaska, Hawaii, the Marshall Islands, and the Bikini islands. Other countries bombed Australia, Algeria, Ukraine, Kazakhstan, Russia, China, India, Pakistan, French Polynesia, Kiribati, South Africa, and North Korea. The US military considered exploding nuclear weapons on the moon, in order to have a massive demonstration effect of the power of nuclear weapons.

During the Cold War, the United States and Soviet Union built and deployed over 66,000 nuclear weapons in the air, land, and sea (the **triad**). China, Britain, France, India, Pakistan, Israel, and North Korea later developed nuclear weapons in small numbers, from 20 to 290 weapons each (North Korea's arsenal may be lower), for a total of nine countries with nuclear weapons (out of 193 countries). More countries have given up nuclear weapons and programs than have them, concluding they were more of a liability than an asset. South Africa, Kazakhstan, Belarus, Ukraine, Argentina, Brazil, South Korea, Taiwan, Sweden, Japan, Libya, and many others voluntarily gave up their nuclear arsenals or programs.[8]

How did the United States, and later the Russians, go from a handful of nuclear bombs to enough to destroy the earth many times over? In the beginning, the United States was the only country with nuclear weapons. Some US policymakers believed this atomic monopoly would translate into a power advantage. Having "the bomb in our back pocket" would cause potential adversaries to accede to United States demands. It didn't work that way. Countries continued to press for their interests and concerns. And the Soviets soon stole the bomb design and detonated their own atomic bomb in 1949.[9] Most of the world argued that nuclear weapons were too dangerous and ought to be put under international control or banned. They expressed this position in the **first resolution** of the newly formed United Nations. Some scientists who helped build the weapons agreed.

Others argued that nuclear weapons ought to be used. US policies of "Massive retaliation," and "flexible response" were based on threatening to use nuclear weapons. Some US military and civilian leaders considered using nuclear weapons in Korea, Vietnam, and Europe. This **"Nuclear Utility Theory,"** or NUTs group, long a minority position, is reviving today. President Trump's **Nuclear Posture Review** orders the creation of new nuclear weapons, and threatens to use nuclear weapons in response to conventional attacks, including attacks against infrastructure of the United States and allies, which may include cyberattacks.

The predominant nuclear policy has been the theory of **nuclear deterrence**. According to this theory, a country maintains nuclear weapons, with all their costs and risks, in order to persuade other countries not to use their weapons against us. Deterrence seeks to persuade adversaries that they have nothing to gain from using nuclear weapons, because their nuclear attack will trigger a devastating response ensuring their own demise, in **Mutually Assured Destruction (MAD)**. Deterrence purports to prevent genocide by threatening genocide. In order to make MAD threats credible, policymakers increased the size of United States and Soviet nuclear arsenals, in order to have **"second strike survivability,"** to ensure that nuclear weapons would survive a nuclear first strike in order to deliver a crushing nuclear retaliation against the initiating party. In order to make MAD threats credible, policy makers increased the size of United States and Soviet nuclear arsenals, increased their geographic spread by dispersing weapons across land, air, and sea (the triad), diversified delivery vehicles, made smaller and easily movable battlefield **tactical nuclear weapons** (even suitcase nuclear bombs), hardened nuclear weapons sites in mountains and underground silos, and hid nuclear weapons, to ensure the arsenals would survive, even if the people did not.

Besides increasing the numbers of nuclear bombs, the superpowers also increased their delivery systems to get the bombs to their targets, such as long-range airplanes, ships, aircraft carriers, silos, and military bases around the world. They developed ever more sophisticated **ballistic missiles**, rocket-propelled, guided weapons that can carry either conventional or nuclear warheads (bombs) and follow a high arc trajectory toward a predetermined target. These include **intercontinental ballistic missiles (ICBMs),** and submarines armed with **Sub Launched Ballistic Missiles (SLBMs),** as well as computer systems, transportation, personnel, and security systems to keep track of and secure the arsenals. This is very costly, so weapons scientists created a way to put more nuclear bombs on a missile with **Multiple Independently targetable Re-entry Vehicles (MIRV)** on the missiles so that separate warheads could each reach different targets. Imagine the intercontinental missile as a bus bound from the United States to Russia, and each MIRVed nuclear warhead as a passenger departing at separate stops along the way (e.g., Moscow, Leningrad, Vladivlostok).

The nuclear weapons complexes also needed fissile material to use in the nuclear bomb cores. Uranium mines from the Congo, Canada, and Navajo nation fueled the first US nuclear bombs. Other US states also mined uranium (later used in nuclear energy plants): Arizona, Colorado, Idaho, Oregon, South Dakota, North Dakota, Texas, Utah, Washington, and Wyoming. Kazakhstan and Ukraine mined uranium for Soviet bombs.

Creating bombs required centrifuges, machines, and processes to transform the minerals taken out of the ground into highly enriched, bomb-grade fissile material, and factories to build the bombs in Oak Ridge, Tennessee, and Amarillo, Texas. These mining and production facilities were built for speed, to quickly deliver bombs for the Cold War arms race. The sites were not built for safety or security or environmental and public health even though some were located near big population centers. Controversies continue today over the polluted ecosystems and harmed health of workers and neighbors and "downwinders" to these nuclear sites.

Tens of thousands of scientists and technicians are needed to sustain these arsenals, at dozens of national laboratories, factories, and facilities. The more nuclear weapons there are, and the more sites in the nuclear complex there are, the more targets there are in the superpowers' war plans. The US nuclear war plan was called the **Single Integrated Operational Plan, or SIOP** (now called the O plan or operational plan). The nuclear arms race created a terrible feedback cycle of **vertical proliferation,** increasing the size and sophistication of nuclear arsenals among the existing nuclear powers, primarily the United States and Russia. More facilities and more arms created more targets, which in turn required more arms aimed at the targets. Thus, the United States and Russia drove the world from a handful of atomic weapons in 1945 to nearly 70,000 nuclear weapons, with much higher levels of destructiveness, at the height of the Cold War in the mid-1980s.

Concerned with the spread of nuclear weapons, the United States attempted to stop **horizontal proliferation,** the spread of nuclear weapons to more countries. President Eisenhower created the "**Atoms for Peace" program** in the 1950s, in which research and material for the "peaceful uses" of the atom for nuclear energy, medicine, and research were shared with other countries, in return for their pledge never to develop nuclear weapons. This "grand bargain" became the basis of the **Non Proliferation Treaty (NPT)** of 1968. Nonnuclear states agreed not to develop nuclear weapons (stopping horizontal proliferation of nuclear weapons among more countries), and committed to using nuclear material and research for peaceful purposes, not military arsenals. In return, nuclear armed states agreed not to share nuclear weapons with other countries and to decrease the size of their arsenals (to stop vertical proliferation of nuclear weapons), to move toward disarmament.

As the supreme commanding general in World War II, Dwight Eisenhower was against the nuclear bombings in World War II, which he and many other US generals argued at the time were unnecessary and immoral, as the Japanese were already in the process of surrendering.[10] Afterward, as a Republican president, Eisenhower proposed a ban on nuclear testing. A limited or partial ban on above ground nuclear tests was reached in 1963. The United States was the first country to sign the Comprehensive Test Ban Treaty in 1996, but the Senate has not ratified the CTBT, and the treaty has not yet entered into force.

Maintaining so many weapons, spread across so much territory, has led to nuclear weapons accidents. There have been dozens of nuclear weapons near-misses and accidents over the years. The US government admits losing eleven nuclear weapons, but experts believe the actual number is much higher, around fifty. The Cold War arms race was created to maximize fear and threat to the other side, not to maximize safety of the weapons and arsenals. The triad's widespread deployment and constant movement of nuclear weapons creates safety hazards, as nuclear weapons are transferred on aircrafts continually flying, on ships and submarines, and in silos. US nuclear bombs fell out of US airplanes in Spain, Canada, Greenland, and in North Carolina, Georgia, Maryland, and California. US nuclear bombs fell off US ships near Japan, and sunk with submarines near the Azores.

Other countries were horrified at the growth of the United States and Soviet nuclear arsenals, and did not appreciate having their countries and lives endangered by the nuclear arms race, and by nuclear weapons accidents. Beginning in the 1960s, countries around the world banned nuclear weapons from their territories, air space, and territorial waters. Mexico and Brazil led the charge, leading the creation of the world's first nuclear weapons free zone in Latin America in 1967. These **nuclear weapons free zones (NWFZs)** cover the entire Southern Hemisphere: Latin America and the Caribbean (thirty-three countries); the South Pacific (thirteen countries); Southeast Asia (ten countries); Africa (fifty-two countries); Central Asia (five countries), and Antarctica. Nearly 60 percent of countries have banned nuclear weapons through NWFZs. The nuclear armed states agreed to respect these nuclear weapons free zones.

Arms control and disarmament agreements between the United States and Russia from the 1970s until 2011 greatly reduced the size of the nuclear arsenals to a total of over 13,300 weapons today, still on "hair trigger" alert, and still spread around the world in the air, land and sea. Republican president Ronald Reagan first eliminated a whole category of battlefield nuclear weapons, in the **Intermediate Nuclear Forces (INF) treaty** with Russia, at the beginning of the end of the Cold War. Smaller, tactical nuclear weapons are the most destabilizing, the most vulnerable to theft and accident, so Reagan and Russian president Gorbachev began with eliminating these weapons, but Reagan saw the INF as just the start of creating a world free of nuclear weapons. Reagan wanted the elimination of nuclear weapons, noting "nuclear war can never be won and must never be fought." President Trump has reversed Reagan's policy, and announced he is withdrawing the United States from the INF treaty. The **Strategic Arms Reduction Treaties (START)** followed under Presidents Bush, Clinton, and Obama, greatly reducing the US and Russian nuclear arsenals. Today, no new arms control agreements are under negotiation, and the current US administration is withdrawing from existing arms control agreements. For example, the New START treaty is set to expire in 2021 unless the United States and

Russia take action to continue the Treaty, but US-Russian relations are currently at a low point.

CTR, the Cooperative Threat Reduction program, was a bipartisan program created by Senators Sam Nunn and Richard Lugar in late 1991, as the Soviet Union was collapsing. The program helped Kazakhstan, Ukraine, and Belarus safely dispose of over 7,000 nuclear weapons left behind by the Soviet Union, along with the weapons infrastructure. CTR also helped Russia to safely reduce its nuclear weapons and implement its arms control commitments under START, and to safely secure and protect its remaining weapons from theft or accident.

US nuclear arsenals, units, and officers have also been involved in accidents and dereliction of duty. After the Cold War, the decreasing prominence and prestige of nuclear weapons has led to increasing incompetence in the management of these systems. For example, US air force crews and pilots mistakenly loaded and flew a plane full of nuclear armed cruise missiles cross country, from North Dakota to Louisiana. Multiple air force crews made multiple mistakes, not noticing the dummy training warheads they were supposed to be transporting were actually nuclear warheads. No one reported the nuclear warheads missing from North Dakota, and no one noticed the nuclear warheads sitting unsecured in Louisiana for nearly two days. In another accident, nuclear bomb parts were mistakenly sent to Taiwan. No one reported them missing, and they remained unsecured in a foreign country for over a year. Twenty percent of Air Force officers responsible for nuclear weapons were involved in a cheating scandal, texting answers to pass the nuclear weapons safety and certification tests. The generals in charge of these nuclear weapons units have been fired for, in addition to the other scandals, drunkenness, gambling, and inappropriate behavior. Illegal drug use has also been found among military responsible for nuclear weapons. The units involved in these scandals are in several states, including North Dakota, Montana, New Mexico, Wyoming, and South Dakota. There are many reasons for the safety violations, accidents, and problems in US nuclear forces, documented since 2006 to the present. Warfighters get promoted in the armed services, and the wars in Iraq and Afghanistan provided paths for officers to advance. Nuclear weapons units are not seen as central or an avenue to promotion and do not attract the military's best talent. Concerns for nuclear safety, the increasing number of nuclear accidents, and threats of nuclear weapons ending up in the wrong hands have led senior military and defense officials in the United States and around the world to urge deeper and quicker nuclear disarmament. The larger the arsenals, the larger the risks.

In the past, key arms control and disarmament treaties were negotiated by government elites, usually shaped by those countries who possessed or used the weapons, without input from the people hurt by the weapons. Today, this is changing. The nuclear ban treaty (the Treaty on the Prohibition of Nuclear Weapons of 2017) was unlike previous WMD arms control treaties. Globalization's tools of open societies, open economies, and open technologies present new WMD challenges. Terrorists seek to acquire WMD technologies and capabilities, whether to kill a lot of people with WMD, or to scare a lot of people with RDD (radiological dispersal devices). For-profit smuggling rings offer WMD and their "dual-use" components for sale on the global market. Yet open societies, open technologies, and open markets also provide new tools for countering and eliminating WMD, as illustrated in the nuclear weapons ban.

Counterproliferation is the full range of operational, primarily military preparations and activities to reduce and protect against the threat posed by WMD weapons and delivery means. Counterproliferation is a blend of vertical and horizontal prevention efforts focused on preventing the use of WMD weapons. The concept of counterproliferation grew from a recognition in the early 1990s that nonproliferation geared to Cold War objectives ignored the growing concern over nonstate actors, and the concern that nonproliferation could fail (as states might not live up to their treaty commitments). Counterproliferation was envisioned as a tool to be used when diplomacy fails—when there is a threat of use or illicit trafficking in WMD weapons, components or technology.

OPEN ECONOMIES AND WMD

Open markets create new avenues for proliferation of WMD and WMD information, components, and materials. Past arms control and disarmament agreements were based on states, and stopping states from acquiring WMD and from passing WMD on to other states. Today, private sector actors sell WMD and WMD plans and component materials for a profit. Private sector actors which have nuclear materials, such as hospitals, universities, nuclear power plants, and research labs, are often unwitting sources of materials stolen by thieves and nuclear smugglers. In recent years, fifty-three countries and four international organizations gathered in a series of four Nuclear Security Summits to increase security of such sites and to reduce the risks of nuclear proliferation. Yet despite this progress on securing nuclear materials and private sector facilities, nearly 1,000 nuclear smuggling incidents or risks have been reported in the past five years alone.[11]

Sometimes private proliferation actors sell their WMD wares to states. The scientist and businessman, **A.Q. Khan**, is hailed in Pakistan as the father of the Pakistani nuclear weapons program. Outside of Pakistan, A.Q. Khan is known as a notorious nuclear smuggler, who sold nuclear secrets and centrifuge technologies (for refining uranium to make bomb-grade nuclear explosives) to North Korea, Libya, Iran, and other buyers. While working for the European Uranium Centrifuge Enrichment Corporation (EURENCO), Khan stole all the centrifuge plans and lists of suppliers for the parts. He gave this information to his homeland, Pakistan, and helped Pakistan develop nuclear weapons and he also sold this information to buyers shopping for nuclear bombs and know how. Nobel Prize winner and former head of the International Atomic Energy Agency, Mohamed El Baradei, described Khan's network as the "Walmart of private sector proliferation." Khan put out glossy sales brochures showing a mushroom cloud, and openly marketed nuclear technologies at arms sales trade shows. The Khan black market network had companies and associates in twenty countries, including Malaysia, Dubai, the Netherlands, Germany, and Sri Lanka. A.Q. Khan's companies provided "one stop shopping," selling "turnkey" nuclear programs, everything from plans to components to technical advisors. The network was uncovered by United States and British intelligence services. Initially, Khan was placed under "house arrest" by the Pakistani government when the illegal operation was first discovered, but he is since free and has returned to the import-export arms sales business.

The highest risk of the sale of WMD came after the fall of the Soviet Union in 1991. Concern over the sale and safety of WMD arsenals, materials, and research labs in the successor states to the FSU, presented a dangerous prospect, from the transfer of actual nuclear weapons out of weapons possessing states, the "loose nuke" problem in black market sales, to the stealing and selling of radiological material from nuclear power plants and nuclear medicine, such as Cobalt 60 or Cesium 137.

Open markets can also help prevent WMD proliferation. **DDR,** Disarmament, Demobilization, and Reintegration, is a standard tool of de-escalating conflict and restoring relations after a conflict. DDR often includes compensation to war victims and economic development opportunities to spur defense conversion to civilian economic activities.

DDR was quite effective in rebuilding Europe after World War II. As discussed in the chapter on IGOs, through the European Coal and Steel Community and Marshall Plan assistance, former adversaries converted their defense industries to civilian economic purposes and had economic incentives to work together. After the Cold War, some US and Russian programs helped create economic incentives for defense conversion and disarmament. The Megatons to MegaWatts program was an example of defense conversion; the fissile material from decommissioned nuclear bombs was turned into electricity. At the height of the program, 10 percent of electricity in the United States came from decommissioned nuclear bombs.

CTR aided in some disarmament and demobilization of the WMD in FSU states. But without wider demobilization thousands of US and Russian nuclear weapons remain on hair trigger alert, with a widely spread risk over air, land, and sea due to the triad force structure.

CTR provided some economic restoration and reintegration; former Soviet nuclear weapons scientists were offered other scientific jobs and relocation in order to prevent nuclear proliferation. By offering them other employment opportunities, CTR prevented a "brain drain" of Soviet scientists being hired by actors trying to acquire nuclear weapons.

Restoration did not move beyond FSU scientists, however. Restoration has not been offered to most victims of nuclear weapons. The Radiation Exposure Compensation Act of 1990 and the Nuclear Claims Tribunal were slow and inadequate in compensating those harmed by the nuclear weapons complex and the compensation fund ran out for Pacific island victims of nuclear testing. While some uranium miners and veterans received some compensation, many more died or were denied restoration, including native Americans, Pacific Islanders, women, children, and members of the wider community exposed to nuclear testing and the hazardous waste of nuclear weapons production. Children born in Navajo Nation today still exhibit high uranium levels, at a rate more than five times higher than the rest of the population.[12]

DDR processes, which have worked so well in other postconflict arenas, need to be used between the United States and Russia. Restoration of the safety of people and the planet requires not only decreased arms but also removing them from hair trigger status, reintegrating workers from the nuclear complex into new jobs and industries, reducing the spread and increasing safety of the weapons during drawdown, and clean-up of the nuclear weapons sacrifice zones. Other tools of postconflict peacebuilding, such as disarmament of the mind and heart, have also not occurred. The radiological contamination and environmental damage of the nuclear age have been long lasting, as has the cultural damage to impacted communities, particularly indigenous peoples forced from their homes. Restoration can use many practices, including economic development, environmental remediation, trauma healing, healing of memories, soul repair, medical interventions, as well as the rebuilding of the physical infrastructure of water supply, etc.

Open economies can also create opportunities for nuclear proliferation, as WMD materials can have legal use in economic pursuits and are sold for profit by smugglers or seized by terrorists. As discussed in the cybersecurity chapter, dual-use nuclear materials and centrifuges are used in nuclear power plants. Nuclear medicine hospitals and research labs also contain dual-use materials. The vulnerability of these open economy dual-use materials was highlighted when ISIS seized nuclear materials when it captured the University of Mosul in Iraq in August 2014. The materials seized were cobalt-60, a metallic substance with lethally high levels of radiation. The materials were low grade, not highly enriched, bomb-grade fissile material. The risk of the materials being used to make nuclear weapons was low. Yet while used to kill cancer cells in nuclear medicine, it can also be used to create a "dirty bomb," a conventional bomb used to disperse radiological materials in order to spread radiation, fear and panic.[13] Today, the Iraqi government has retaken Mosul, but similar unsecure nuclear medicine machines exist around the world, many in war zones. Four global Nuclear Security Summits convened government leaders, as well as businesses, and NGOs, to address the security of nuclear materials, particularly in scientific, medical, and research facilities outside of nuclear weapons facilities. The Summits made progress in improving the security of nuclear materials and sharing best practices, but the process has been discontinued due to deteriorating relations with Russia and the changed policies of the Trump administration.

Nuclear smugglers are active in Moldova, a poor, former Soviet country. The nuclear smugglers work with Russian criminal gangs to peddle radiological materials to ISIS and other violent groups in the Middle East. The US FBI (Federal Bureau of Investigation), working with Moldovan government officials, have stopped several sales of smuggled nuclear materials. But the nuclear black market remains, connecting criminal groups with terrorists and other violent nonstate actors.[14]

These black market concerns arose with Pakistan in late 2001, when there were serious concerns over the stability of the government and the security of Pakistan's nuclear stockpile,[15] particularly following

Figure 11.1 2018 Estimated Global Nuclear Warhead Inventories

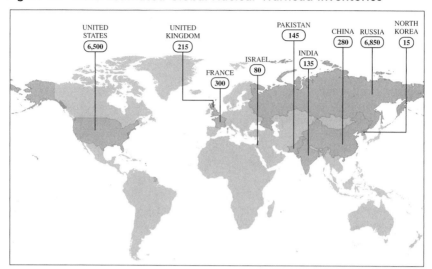

The world's nuclear armed states possess a combined total of roughly 15,000 nuclear warheads; more than 90 percent belong to Russia and the United States. Approximately 9,600 warheads are in military service, with the rest awaiting dismantlement.

Sources: Hans M. Kristensen, Robert S. Norris, U.S. Department of State, and Stockholm International Peace Research Institute. Updated: June 20, 2018. Courtesy of the Arms Control Association.

two attempts to assassinate the former Pakistan president, Pervez Musharraf, in December 2003. Pakistan's stability and the prospect of nuclear material leakage or direct acquisition of Pakistan's state program again arose, as the Taliban competed for control over much of the Northwest Territory and Swat River Valley. In the words of the Commission on the Prevention of WMD Proliferation and Terrorism, "Were one to map terrorism and weapons of mass destruction today, all roads would intersect in Pakistan. It has nuclear weapons and a history of unstable governments, and parts of its territory are currently a safe haven for al Qaeda and other terrorists."[16]

Open economies and new technologies can also help to prevent proliferation risks. For example, a coalition of small European countries are collaborating to create a WMD network of sensors to detect any nuclear, biological, chemical, or radiological "dirty bomb" threat.[17] Rather than create military equipment customized for any one country's military, their approach mounts sensors on "off the shelf" commercially available drones and other robots. The remotely piloted autonomous ground and air vehicles would enter a contaminated area, and communicate the sensor information back in real time via the software network. When complete, Austria, Croatia, Hungary, Slovenia, Slovakia, and the Czek Republic may lease access to the network to other countries, using a "Zipcar" type open economic model for WMD detection equipment. DTRA, the US Department of Defense unit responsible for implementing CTR, also works with the National Labs (that once helped invent nuclear weapons) to develop new technologies to detect WMD and counter proliferation. The four international Nuclear Security Summits focused on best practices to reduce proliferation threats from nonmilitary sources of radiological materials. New technologies can replace many old technologies that use radiological materials. For example, cesium-137 blood irradiators can be replaced by nonradioactive X-ray devices. Cancer treatment machines that use radioactive cobalt-60 can be replaced by linear accelerators (LINACs).

OPEN ECONOMIES AND NEW FORMS OF COOPERATION: THE PROLIFERATION SECURITY INITIATIVE (PSI)

Private sector involvement can help disrupt proliferation. An example of a new type of international cooperation on global issues is the growing coalition of like-minded countries plans, exercises, and executes interdiction operations aimed at disrupting the traffic in WMD- and missile-related materials and technologies. **The Proliferation Security Initiative (PSI) is a coalition of 106 participating and supporting states who cooperate to stem proliferation.**[18] The initiative was announced by US president Bush on May 31, 2003, in Krakow, Poland. The concept was largely developed as a result of a failure, the So San interdiction incident in 2002. In December 2002, US intelligence tracked the So San ship as it departed from North Korea, bound for Yemen. Acting on a request from the United States, Spanish special operations forces, staged from the Spanish frigate Navarro, intercepted and boarded the ship. While searchers found a great deal of cement, the declared cargo, they also discovered smuggled Scud-B missiles, warheads, and fuel oxidizer hidden in the cargo. But without agreements in place for interdiction, ultimately the cargo was released to Yemen.[19] Shortly afterward, eleven countries initially came together and pledged cooperation in countering WMD and interdiction activities. PSI was created to fill the gaps in existing counterproliferation policies and implementation. PSI are ongoing activities to create a community committed to addressing these problems, without a specific blueprint for action or organizational structure in mind. Rather than creating a new IGO (as happened frequently after World War II), or waiting for existing IGOs to take slow action, these states wanted to better cooperate quickly in interdicting questionable shipments of dual use technology that could be used to create WMD.

Applying lessons learned from the embarrassing So San incident, countries developed and implemented a general statement of PSI principles to work together to stop suspicious shipments and proliferation. Unlike other formal IGOs, the PSI is a group of like-minded countries that have agreed to harmonize practices and work together to combat counterprofileration. These principles are embedded in existing international and state-based agreements and laws, enabling partner states to disrupt and interdict the illegal proliferation of WMD. PSI requires both internal efforts to strengthen counterproliferation laws and policies, and external efforts to train and work effectively with other countries and companies, sharing intelligence, timely communication, and multilateral action.

The interdiction of the BBC China ship showed the effectiveness of PSI. The United States shared intelligence found in the investigations of the A.Q. Khan economic network with Germany and Italy. A Malaysian company was suspected of shipping nuclear technology to Libya via Dubai, using a German-registered vessel. Acting on that intelligence, and with operational assistance from the US Navy, German and Italian officials diverted the ship to Italy. After this interception, Libya's leader agreed to give up its WMD program.

PSI countries increased from 11 to 106, increasing the pressure against would-be proliferators, and strengthening nonproliferation norms. PSI is a concrete set of security cooperation activities with allies and friends, and demonstrating that coordinated actions among like-minded states can be achieved without having to create new organizations or more formalized bureaucracies. First, countries commit to a statement of common interdiction principles. Guidelines and processes are in place for the collection, analysis, and sharing of intelligence. Ship-boarding agreements extend available legal authorities. Operational experts from participating states meet regularly to develop improved intelligence, military, and law enforcement capabilities to support interdiction activities. These capabilities are practiced and refined through a robust exercise program.

The Trump administration has declared that it will continue the PSI framework and strengthen PSI activity.[20] Going forward, the

PSI model presents an interesting way to cooperate quickly, concretely, and adaptively, even among states that do not otherwise have a formal alliance. The drawbacks of this model are that without a formal IGO as the home or champion of the program, institutional memory and momentum can be lost. PSI participating countries seek to extend the functions and the geographic reach of the PSI framework, adding new participants.

OPEN TECHNOLOGIES, WMD, AND TERRORISM

ISIS created chemical weapons and used them in Iraq and Syria. Using information and plans for how to build WMD that are readily available online, they created mustard gas, chlorine, and other chemical weapons and used them over seventy-six times, before Iraqi and US forces destroyed ISIS production facilities.[21] While some of the terrorists engaged with the IS chemical weapons program were killed or captured, others remain at large.

Other terrorists can follow their example. The Dark Net can bring buyers and sellers of WMD materials together. Terrorists seek WMD and are unlikely to be deterred from using them to meet their political objectives. If used, these weapons can create catastrophic damage, particularly if used on a wide scale or in a multiple event campaign style, as terrorists have done with conventional attacks. WMD in the hands of terrorists is a nightmare scenario that pushed policy makers to make deeper cuts in WMD arsenals after the September 11, 2001 attacks. Policy makers today are faced with a difficult risk calculation regarding this low-risk, high-consequence threat. WMD in the hands of terrorists is a low-risk probability. It is unlikely that terrorists can easily acquire, weaponized and use WMD. But the magnitude of the consequences of use are high so that significant resources are allocated to prevent WMD acquisition by terrorists. The challenge is in striking the proper balance.

Preventing WMD acquisition by terrorists or other extremist organizations presents many dilemmas. Do policy makers and planners assume that "possession = use," meaning if terrorist groups develop or acquire WMD, they will use them and not merely retain WMD for deterrence purposes? Or is this a costly planning assumption that skews the real threat posed by WMD compared to other more likely threats, posed by conventional adversaries, terrorist activities or even criminals such as drug cartels? Planning for the worst-case scenario, not the most likely scenarios, is driven by the high consequences of WMD use, even if the risk of use is low. If possession equals use, then planning must include how to respond to WMD attacks, not only interdicting and stopping acquisition. Worst-case planning is a costly, although prudent assumption.

Historically, terrorist organizations and nonstate groups have obtained and used WMD. The Japanese violent extremist group Aum Shinrikyo conducted chemical and biological weapons attacks and attempted to acquire nuclear weapons. On March 20, 1995, Aum attacked the Tokyo subway, using the chemical agent Sarin. They killed thirteen commuters, injured fifty-four, and perhaps as significantly, sent almost 1,000 casualties to hospitals, effectively crashing the health-care system of metropolitan Tokyo. This was only one of many attempts by Aum Shinrikyo to acquire and use WMD. Aum conducted other attacks, such as an attack in Motsomoto which killed eight in June 1994 in the Nagano Prefecture in Japan. The cult also attempted to purchase a nuclear weapon on the black market. When this proved too difficult, they turned to seeking ways to acquire strains to anthrax with the ultimate goal of spreading anthrax over Tokyo. Aum Shinrikyo was successful in acquiring strains of anthrax, but the type acquired was a harmless veterinary strain that did not affect humans.[22]

The Aum Shinrikyo program illustrates several important lessons. First, a WMD attack can occur without notice and first responders may not understand the nature and consequences of the threat. Second, those same first responders and key medical personnel may be among the first casualties and subsequently will be unavailable for responding to the crisis, but instead may themselves be victims themselves in need of care. Third, attribution of the attacker may not be immediate or their motivations clear. Fourth, cell phones and other easily available information technologies make a campaign of coordinated attacks easier, as we see with terrorist use of IEDs. The Aum Shinrikyo attacks took place on five different subway trains on different lines. The attack was a campaign and not a single attack. Most response planning is based on single point attacks and not the more complex scenario with follow-on attacks that can occur either near simultaneously, as with the Aum case, and also over a prolonged period of time. For example, in October 2001, just after the attacks of September 11, deadly anthrax attacks took place in the United States. These attacks resulted in five deaths and seventeen other casualties and occurred over a matter of months, not days, and resulted in many falsely reported suspected anthrax attack cases by a justifiably concerned population. This and the Aum Shinrikyo case highlight the consequences where terrorist intent—the intent to cause mass causalities and terror-intersects with possibilities brought about by open societies, open technologies, and open borders. Globalization presents a difficult security environment to control the spread of WMD technologies.

The Aum case is not unique. Al Qaeda also sought WMD. Prior to the attacks of September 11, 2001, Osama bin Laden declared that the acquisition of WMD was a religious duty and its use justified. Intelligence collected in Afghanistan revealed that Al Qaeda was working to acquire nuclear, biological, and chemical weapons as well as a radiological dispersal device. Two Pakistani scientists allegedly shared WMD information with Al Qaeda sometime in or prior to 2001 and commented on the viability of a radiological bomb.[23] While these examples point to the more traditional concern over the nexus between WMD and terrorist aspirations, today's environment is more complex and harder to predict. WMD may be used to poison political rivals. A dangerous class of chemical agents developed by the former Soviet Union, known as Novichoks, poisoned several people in Salisbury, England, one of whom died. The targets were a former KGB agent and his daughter, but the policeman who answered the call and a couple who stumbled upon what they thought was a perfume bottle, but was actually the deadly military-grade nerve agent, were also poisoned.[24] These Novichock agents are reportedly six to eight times more lethal than VX and were designed by Cold War-Russian scientists to avoid chemical warfare treaty restrictions. VX remains highly lethal and was used to assassinate the North Korean dictator Kim Jong Un's half-brother in Malaysia.

Why are terrorist (and other nonstate groups) interested in WMD today? These organizations may be facing a shift in their motives and goals. As discussed in the chapter on terrorism, mass-casualty events are becoming more common, particularly in war zones. Globalization broadcasts the psychological shock value of large numbers of fatalities to a wider audience and allows mass casualties to be inflicted abroad, not undermining local audiences' sympathies for terrorist causes. However, there is debate over the extent to which terrorist organizations may possess the necessary technical and financial resources to acquire effective WMD capabilities.[25] In practice, it is not as easy to do as it sounds. Skeptics frequently note that even Aum Shinrikyo, with almost a billion dollars in assets and highly trained and educated scientists in the developed country of Japan, was unable to effectively develop biological weapons or a truly massive chemical weapons dissemination capability. At the same time, that group's partial success and their ability to conduct an attack in roughly three days, coupled with known interest in acquisition and continuing advances in technology, suggests that nonstate actors may become increasingly WMD capable.

Other terrorist organizations will likely also acquire WMD, either on their own, or with the help of another, whether a country or a smuggling entrepreneur. The intent to acquire these capabilities is clear, the requisite materials and information are readily available, advances in technology will make this job easier over time, and use is likely if these weapons are acquired. Many proliferators, such as North Korea, are willing to sell dual-use technologies for money, particularly as North Korea's economy is stressed and further impacted by international sanctions. This raises the possibility that such states could provide weapons or material/technical assistance to terrorist groups. However, the specific form of WMD-related assistance a state-sponsor would provide to a terrorist organization, and the circumstances under which that assistance would be provided, remain unclear.

Fragile states present another potential avenue for proliferation. When a government has limited capacity, a terrorist or subnational group may seize control over a portion of that state's WMD arsenal. This is the ongoing concern with the security of Pakistan's nuclear arsenal, and with black market nuclear smuggling from former Soviet states.

There are two to three dozen terrorist organizations believed to be interested in acquiring WMD. It is easier to acquire chemical weapons, given the relative ease in acquiring precursor materials. The use of chemical weapons by states such as Syria, North Korea, and arguably Russia may lower the barrier for use in the future. According to press accounts, Dr. Ayman al-Zawahri noted that Al Qaeda's decision to acquire chemical weapons and pursue biological weapons was due to their ability to cause mass panic and fear and their relative ease of acquisition.[26]

As states move to improve their ability to defend against the classical forms of WMD attack, terrorists increasingly are looking for novel and unconventional ways to use WMD to achieve strategic effects. The use of Novochocks and other unused and little-known-about agents will be highly attractive to terror networks. Those charged with defending their borders can expect more numerous—and more sophisticated—threats and hoaxes that will command ever-greater response resources.

NEW TECHNOLOGIES AND WMD

New technologies create new WMD challenges. Cybersecurity threats, drones, and hypersonic weapons present new challenges to nuclear arsenals and delivery systems.

The nuclear weapons complex is susceptible to cyberthreats in a number of ways. Command and control systems may be vulnerable. Nuclear arsenals are supposed to be "firewalled" from contact with Internet-generated threats. But cyberthreats are constantly evolving, as the discussion of Watering Hole attacks and the Internet of Things attacks illustrates in Chapter Nine. Human error also routinely compromises security protocols, even in nuclear arsenals, as evidenced by the decertification of multiple US military units and the firing of many military officers responsible for nuclear weapons. Human error or lapses in following security protocols can have extreme consequences with WMD. The Stuxnet attack on Iran's nuclear centrifuges may have been unleashed on an infected thumbdrive. As shown by the NotPetya attack that took down Maersk and others, new cyberattacks are fast and extremely destructive, with greater abilities to permeate supposedly "firewalled" systems. The larger the nuclear complex, the larger the risks of cyberattacks.

Information warfare can also degrade a country's ability to discern fact from fiction and "fake news" propaganda. In a nuclear crisis such a degraded information environment may make it difficult, if not impossible, for decision-makers to determine whether nuclear weapons systems had been activated. Spoofing, false warning, and overwhelming systems have been common lines of cyberattack. Applied to the nuclear weapons complex these could seriously degrade decision-making, and lead to nuclear escalation based on bad data.

The US nuclear arsenal employs tens of thousands of people at diverse and geographically dispersed sites, from the arsenals and deployed weapons sites on submarines, air force bases, and missile silos, to the large nuclear complex of nuclear research laboratories, nuclear weapons factories, nuclear fuel sites, and nuclear storage sites. All these sites use IT; therefore, all these sites are vulnerable to cyberattacks that may have strategic impact. For example, the Japanese Fukushima nuclear power plant meltdown demonstrated the damage that could be done by disabling a nuclear facility's power supply. Cyberattacks on power grids are common and could disable the security systems in place at nuclear complexes. The series of four Nuclear Security Summits from 2010 to 2016 made advances in securing nuclear materials and facilities, whether military, commercial, or academic. But the Nuclear Security Summits have been discontinued under the Trump administration.

Drones present another emerging technology challenge to the WMD landscape. Delivery vehicles have always been the difficult part of any actor's nuclear weapons aspirations. But drones provide cheap

and commercially available delivery vehicles for terrorists or other proliferators. Smaller drones cannot carry large payloads, but they could
easily carry radiological dispersal devices.

Drones are increasingly becoming more autonomous, equipped
with artificial intelligence, in an attempt to make them more efficient
and to remove the "fog of war." "Killer robots," automated systems
where the humans are not in the decision loop making the kill decision,
are increasingly being developed and deployed. Arms salesmen and
proponents argue that reducing human error means taking the humans
out of the decision loop. Skeptics point out that computers also often
make errors and misfire. Should machines be allowed literally to make
life-and-death decisions? Drones are being deployed in all aspects of the
military. Drones are increasingly used to do boring, dirty, or dangerous
jobs in the nuclear and energy fields, such as surveillance and upkeep of
systems. The prospect that drones, and particularly autonomous drones,
could be deployed in various capacities in the nuclear weapons complex
presents moral, legal, as well as practical and technological problems.
Drones rely on communications systems between the robot and the base
commander. This leads drones to be extremely vulnerable to hacking.
Drones can be hijacked by hackers. Drones in the nuclear weapons
complex could be hijacked by adversaries intent on gaining nuclear
information or materials. Drones can also be deployed to conduct cyberoperations, stealing data, jamming signals, and distributing malware.

Hypersonic weapons increase the speed of delivery systems faster
than the human decision-making processes. Combined with these other
technological developments, they can further degrade the command and
control, security, and decision-making systems.

Advances in science and technology, for example, in medicine and
health, have the potential to transform major aspects of how people
live—extending human life, reshaping the global economy—and also
changing how the world wages war. Yet devastating new weapons are
also possible through the application of these scientific and technological advances to weapons of mass destruction. Two technology areas
have the greatest potential to yield new kinds of WMD: biotechnology
and nanotechnology.

Gene research and "personalized medicine" can be weaponized.
A new generation of biological weapons based on genomic research has
the potential to create new capabilities not envisioned or restricted by
existing arms control treaties based on bipolar Cold War realities of the
time. Examples include genetic weapons, Aptamers, molecular poisons,
and nanotechnology.

As medical research works to customize medicines based on DNA and genetic attributes, those same technologies can be used to kill. Genetic weapons that target specific groups based on their genetic characteristics may be an unintended consequence of research into assessing human health by reading metabolic signatures in human respiration. As more people use DNA testing for ancestry and medical purposes, more genetic information is more publicly available than ever before.

Bioweapons could use aptamers, which are strands of nucleic acid that act in a manner similar to antibodies. They bind and block cell receptors responsible for a variety of life-sustaining biological functions, but could also be applied to cause harm.

New bioweapons could include molecular poisons. These are nano-sized, microscopic particles. They are capable of working at the subcellular level and could be engineered to create specialized effects that cross the blood-brain barrier, disrupt genetic material, or trigger counterproductive immune system responses.

Tiny nanotechnology can be used in health care, or for harm, bringing highly lethal effects (e.g., molecular poisons) as well as other forms of mass destruction/mass disruption warfare. The development of explosive microdust, an ultra-high-explosive/ultra-incendiary material several times more potent than an equivalent mass of TNT, is one area of research. Swarming micro drones, or "slaughterbots" are another area of research. Carrying chemical, biological, or radiological materials such as tiny devices could elude existing detection systems and defenses.

New technologies challenge traditional concepts of the WMD threat environment. They also are not included in traditional arms control and disarmament treaties.

WMD: DIFFERENT AVAILABILITIES AND IMPACTS

Countering WMD will vary by weapon type and context. The tendency is to lump nuclear, radiological, chemical, and biological weapons together under the term "weapons of mass destruction." While convenient, it is misleading since each weapon represents vastly different underlying technologies for development, weaponization, and delivery. Different concepts of operation apply to each, and countermeasures and response and consequence management procedures are implemented differently depending on the weapon used.

NUCLEAR WEAPONS

Nuclear weapons are, in a sense, the only "true" mass-destructive weapons with the power to destroy cities and injure and kill hundreds of thousands or even millions. Motivations for developing nuclear weapons are varied, but their unmatched destructive power make them a sought-after commodity by states and terrorist actors. Some seek nuclear weapons for their sheer destructive power and perceived deterrence value to their utility as instruments of coercion or blackmail. Others see them as a means to advance or achieve regional or geopolitical objectives while still others may see nuclear weapons as a way to bolster international prestige, or perhaps for enhancing domestic political credibility or cohesion.

Those seeking to acquire nuclear capabilities or those wanting to increase the effectiveness or destructive power of their own nuclear stockpiles benefit from the fact that most of the basic research, as well as the basics of weapons design, are understood and widely disseminated via the Internet and other readily available sources. This does not mean that the process of acquiring the skill, expertise, or components required to make a nuclear weapon is readily available or easy to acquire on the black market. The ability to garner all aspects of a nuclear program is daunting; just consider the cost involved in developing the state-based nuclear programs in North Korea, Pakistan, India, or Iran. Would-be nuclear powers remain constrained by financial considerations or the time-consuming, labor-intensive nature of the development process. The key hurdle in developing nuclear weapons remains acquiring the needed fissile material of plutonium or highly enriched uranium (HEU) to make a nuclear weapon.

The spread of nuclear technology may come from nuclear weapons states, those declared nuclear states under the NPT—Russia, the United States, China, France, and the United Kingdom, or those who are outside the NPT. India and Pakistan are not declared states under the NPT, and both countries—India in 1974 and 1998 and Pakistan in 1998—have tested nuclear weapons. Israel officially avoids the question as to whether or not it has nuclear weapons but is presumed to have between 98 and 172[27] nuclear weapons.[28] North Korea announced that it had successfully conducted the first of six underground nuclear tests in October 9, 2006, with most recent being in September 2017.[29]

Iran does not have a nuclear weapons arsenal. Iran has a legal nuclear energy program. But Iran was widely suspected of having clandestine programs to produce more highly enriched fissile material than needed for research, energy, and medicine, which could be diverted to military application in the future. At a minimum, Iran is interested in developing nuclear technology. Under the JCPOA Joint Comprehensive Plan of Action agreement with the UK, France, Germany, Russia, China and the EU (the United States signed then later withdrew from the agreement), Iran has abolished much of this controversial capacity, and has passed numerous international inspections by the IAEA.

While serious concerns remain over the potential for rapid production of nuclear weapons in North Korea and to a much lesser extent, with China, India, and Pakistan, today, the concern is less over the number of total nuclear weapons, but what countries such as Russia and China are doing to modernize their arsenals. This concern applies also to US plans to modernize its nuclear arsenal under the Trump administration. Modernization would make the nuclear weapons themselves more devastating, more usable, and would also make the delivery systems, especially the missile technology, less vulnerable to missile defense and other countermeasures.

In 2001, Al Qaeda leader Osama bin Laden stated that his terrorist network had acquired nuclear weapons, although he declined to indicate where they came from and failed to provide any proof that Al Qaeda did possess the weapons.[30] States such as North Korea have learned to mask their intentions, hide their programs and literally, bury the evidence that would indicate a nuclear weapons program, building underground storage, testing, and research facilities out of view of overhead intelligence and surveillance capabilities. As denial and deception capabilities become more sophisticated, the potential exists for a new or different model of nuclear proliferation: one in which the amount of fissile material required for entry-level weapon designs is significantly reduced, and the facilities and activities required to produce such material are correspondingly smaller and less observable. Such "latent proliferation" may fit many states' need to have access to strategic capabilities without the burdens associated with maintaining large industrial infrastructures or deploying large operational stockpiles. For example, Japan has a robust nuclear energy infrastructure and a world-class technology sector and though a global leader in disarmament, is widely recognized as having a latent nuclear weapons capability. Known as "the bomb in the basement," should Japan or other advanced countries perceive a threat to survival, the country could build a nuclear weapon in short order.

This mixed environment of nonstate and state actors with fast technologies is hard to predict and even harder to plan for. This environment also presents difficulties for countering proliferation. Intelligence and state-based approaches to nonproliferation focus on limiting and controlling fissile material and its production. If the amount of fissile material required to create a credible nuclear device is reduced, a strategy based on controlling fissile material becomes less effective.

RADIOLOGICAL DISPERSAL DEVICES

While nuclear weapons harness the power of chain reaction, the mere fuel for these weapons alone present a dangerous threat. A device that has the ability to spread nuclear fuel or any radiation can present a serious health hazard and create "no-go" areas due to the contamination threat. Any device that can spread radiation is referred to as a radiological dispersal device (RDD). RDDs are "designed to disperse radioactive material to cause destruction, contamination, and injury from the radiation produced by the material."[31] An RDD is not a nuclear weapon, and it does not have the destructive potential of such weapons. For this reason, some refer to RDDs as "weapons of mass disruption" rather than as weapons of mass destruction. Others refer to them as mass contamination devices since an RDD is designed to spread a radioactive contaminant over a large area. There are several types of RDDs, each using a different means of dispersing radioactive elements.[32] Explosive RDDs, popularly known as "dirty bombs," use conventional explosives to scatter radioactive material over a wide area, spreading contamination and causing sickness through radiation poisoning. However, weaponization of radiological material is not even needed. Passive RDDs involve simply placing an unshielded radiation source in a location where unsuspecting people may be exposed, as Chechen rebels placed radiological material in Russia's Ismailovsky Park. Essentially, any method that can effectively spread radiation may be all that is needed to cause panic and fear.

Since RDDs cause few actual casualties and rely instead on radiation sickness and fear, they are not considered militarily effective battlefield weapons. However, using RDDs may make certain areas of a battlefield, especially those in an urban environments, dangerous for military personnel to operate in effectively and for some, radiation contamination may make certain areas "no-go areas" of operation for a period of time.

Radiation sources are more readily available to terrorists. The fear of ISIS fashioning an RDD was a real concern when they overran Mosul, Iraq. The Chechen rebels used RDD contained cesium-137 and dynamite in 1995; the cesium was likely removed from cancer treatment equipment. Fortunately, after reporters were notified about its location, the RDD was defused and did not detonate. These materials are widely used in hospitals, educational and research facilities, industrial and construction sites, and laboratories. These facilities have fewer controls and security, have more individuals with access, and lack the robust screening measures for access than military or nuclear weapons–related research facilities,[33] which is why the Nuclear Security Summits focused on better securing these sites and materials.

RDDs may contaminate targeted sites for a long time. Depending on the type and amount of radioactive material used in the device and its half-life, the cost and time associated with decontamination may be prohibitive, and it is possible that some sites may be abandoned altogether until such time as the contamination remediates. Indeed, several towns around the Chernobyl nuclear power plant in Ukraine, such as the ghost town Pripyat, remain closed due to contamination more than three decades after the Chernobyl nuclear disaster.[34] As the Three-Mile-Island and the Chernobyl cases demonstrate, the release of radioactive materials will cause panic and if delivered by a terrorist organization when the next attack may be unknown, could present serious societal challenges. The prospect of RDDs being used by terrorists received considerable media attention when a suspected Al Qaeda operative was charged with plotting an RDD attack.[35] These materials are located in every major community.

BIOLOGICAL WEAPONS

Biological weapons (BW) use microorganisms or toxins derived from organisms to cause disease in humans, plants, or animals. They come in many different forms, ranging from viruses to bacteria to rickettsiae to toxin.

In many ways, the least-understood and most fearful weapon in the WMD arsenal remains the biological weapons threat. Even for older, better-understood traditional agents such as anthrax, there remain important gaps in knowledge such as the ability to accurately model a release within an acceptable margin of error. What these weapons can do, how the agents spread, how long they linger in the environment and how fragile they are—they are, after all, living biological organisms— remain difficult to predict, especially as they can adapt and change. As genetic engineering techniques become more widely available, will this translate to medically resistant biological weapons? Will biological weapons, previously reserved for the most technologically advanced states, be produced by small groups or individuals with the help of commercial off-the-shelf components and technology? The risks widen with the growing diffusion of advanced biological techniques pursued in a wide variety of settings from pharmaceutical labs to universities to corporate development labs. The "biotechnology industrial complex" becomes more global daily, and can be used for wellness or for harm. There is now more global access to biotechnology by terrorists and others who would exploit the expertise and materials needed to execute biological attacks.[36]

Sixteen countries, Canada, China, Cuba, France, Germany, Iran, Iraq, Israel, Japan, Libya, North Korea, Russia, South Africa, Syria, the United Kingdom, and the United States plus Taiwan are currently suspected of having or pursuing BW programs.[37] Although the Russian offensive BW program Biopreparat was ended by presidential decree in 1992, the restrictive nature of the Russian scientific culture and community raises lingering concerns that prohibited activities may continue. Many Russian civilian facilities possess pathogen and toxin collections that lack adequate security or accounting measures. As with nuclear and chemical weapons, there is also the possibility that Russian scientists and technicians with biological agent knowledge could seek to improve their personal economic status by accepting employment in countries of proliferation concern.

Several other countries are suspected of pursuing offensive biological weapons research, development, and possibly weaponization. These countries include North Korea, China, and Iran. Countries that have the potential to develop offensive biological weapons and that may possibly be conducting limited efforts include Pakistan, Cuba, Israel, India, and Syria.[38] Still other states retain a latent capacity to rapidly mobilize resources in support of biological weapons programs. Most of these countries are parties to or signatories of the Biological Weapons Convention,[39] which provides that "Each State Party to this Convention undertakes never in any circumstances to develop, produce, stockpile or otherwise acquire or retain: (1) Microbial or other biological agents, or toxins whatever their origin or method of production, of types and in quantities that have no justification for prophylactic, protective or other peaceful purposes; (2) Weapons, equipment or means of delivery designed to use such agents or toxins for hostile purposes or in armed conflict."[40] Therefore, any offensive programs undertaken would violate their obligations under that treaty.

Biological threats from plague to flu are not new. In the Middle Ages, corpses with plague were catapulted over walls to break sieges, and in the Second World War, the notorious Japanese Unit 731 dropped bombs filled with plague-infected fleas over cities in Manchuria to cause sickness and paralyze both military and relief efforts. With effects ranging from lower to higher lethality, biological agents risk contaminating the attackers as well as the attacked targets. Biological agents can be genetically modified to make effects more severe and more difficult to diagnose and treat, as genetically modified pathogens are not found in nature and hence would not have a medical track record or treatment protocol to follow. Biological agents are a weapon of terror. Infections may take hours, days, or even weeks to present themselves making attribution of an attack nearly impossible. Enforced quarantine and other efforts to stem contagion run counter to Western notions of freedom of movement and association. But biological threats need not even target humans. Biological agents may target plants, animals, food supplies or even types of materials, oil-based rubbers or polymers for example, with potentially devastating economic effect. In their unpredictable and psychological impact, biological attacks could rival nuclear weapons in their ability to terrorize and to present an existential threat to societies.

As living organisms, many biological agents are affected by variances in environmental conditions, including the temperature and UV radiation. Thus, the performance of a potential dissemination mechanism must be within certain tolerance levels in order to be effective. For an attacker using biological weapons, the challenge lies in finding a means of dispersal that does not kill the organism while spreading it in a form and in sufficient quantity that will increase the likelihood of infection.

Biological weapons tend to favor attackers over defensive response. Attackers have the benefit of choosing the time, place, and manner of the attack. Defenders may only become aware they have been attacked well after the sick present themselves to health-care providers and either symptoms suggest or tests confirm that an attack is suspected. Adversaries may find biological weapons attractive for several reasons. First, they may allow an attack with a low likelihood of discovery, since attribution is difficult. For example, the anthrax attacks that occurred in the United States in the fall of 2001 were not attributed to an attacker by the FBI until 2008. In that case, a series of anthrax-tainted letters were mailed to several media and government targets.[41] At least four anthrax-filled envelopes were sent, and twenty-two people were infected with pulmonary or cutaneous anthrax. Five died of pulmonary anthrax. Hundreds were exposed and tens of thousands were put on the preventative antibiotics ciprofloxacin (Cipro) and doxycycline (Doxy) in

Washington, DC, New York, Florida, and Connecticut. Contamination control efforts cost millions, not including the loss in productivity. Microbiologist Bruce Edwards Ivins was eventually identified by the FBI as the lone anthrax attacker, but the investigation alone took more than seven years and due to Ivins's suicide, the motivation for the attack may never be clear. Even today, there are some who believe that Ivins was not the "lone attacker" demonstrating just how difficult attribution can be.[42] If the agent used is one that is endemic to an area, an attack may be mistaken for a natural outbreak and it may take outbreaks in other locations or scientific evaluation to point to an attack. And in the case of a targeted killing, the symptoms leading to death may be confused for other naturally occurring maladies if tests are not conducted to rule out a deliberate biological attack.

The second reason biological weapons are useful to adversaries is that the equipment, technology, and materials needed to produce biological weapons are often quite similar to those used in the legal production of pharmaceuticals and other commercial products. Thus, they are widely available through global commerce and relatively easy to obtain, and may represent a relatively low-cost option (compared, for example, to nuclear weapons) for states or nonstate groups. Given the dual use nature of much of the equipment and the precursor agents used in the production of biological weapons, concealment of a clandestine development program is possible. As the Soviet Union's Biopreparat organization demonstrated, it is even possible to hide such a program in "plain sight," collocating BW development facilities with legitimate sites such as pharmaceutical plants.[43]

Third, the expertise needed to produce biological weapons is widespread, and the knowledge base is growing due to scientific advances in biotechnology and genetic engineering, leading to a risk of "designer" pathogens. Many advanced biotechnologies and techniques are beyond the current capabilities of terrorist groups, and in some cases would provide few advantages over existing "traditional" techniques. The literature on biological warfare and the growth of "communities of interest" focused on sharing BW information suggest that opportunities for weaponizing new biotechnologies are growing.[44]

Finally, biological weapons have a wide range of effects and can be used against a wide range of targets. This versatility can make it difficult for states to craft an appropriate response. For example, an anti-crop weapon, while potentially causing a great deal of economic damage, may not necessarily result in the loss of any human life. Thoughtful adversaries seeking to inflict maximum terror and confusion may also employ multiple agents simultaneously to cause a range of effects, hampering identification and treatment efforts.

As biotechnology creates more opportunities and a greater array of options for proliferators, this creates a difficult intelligence target. Thus, any future use of biological weapons will likely come as a surprise. Developing countermeasures under these conditions is a major challenge.

CHEMICAL WEAPONS

The use of chemical weapons is prohibited by treaty and managed by the Organisation for the Prohibition of Chemical Weapons. Classes of chemicals used in the development of weapons are controlled and the stockpiles of the largest chemical weapons possessors, the United States and Russia, have been destroyed, leading many to believe that chemical weapons were relegated to atrocities of the past. Yet, chemical weapons atrocities are again front-page news as the Assad regime in Syria uses them to attack its own people.[45]

Chemical weapons (CW) use the toxic properties of various chemical compounds to kill, injure, or incapacitate. These weapons, used by both the Allied and Central powers during World War I, were reportedly responsible for more than 1 million casualties with more than 50,000 tons of chemical weapons used in combat.[46] Chemical weapons were used in the 1980s-era Iran-Iraq war, by the Iraqi government against its Kurdish citizens, and in a 1995 terrorist attack by Aum Shinrikyo on Tokyo subway commuters. State actors have traditionally favored chemical weapons for a number of reasons. First, they have been viewed as force multipliers on the battlefield as a way to dislodge enemy forces or as ways to deny territory to the enemy contaminated by chemical agents. Second, the wide range of dispersal methods available, from very crude methods (such as that employed by Aum Shinrikyo in Japan) to crop dusters and other aerosol sprayers to sophisticated military munitions, leads to a range of different attack options. Third, some chemical weapons, especially "first-generation" weapons such as chlorine or phosgene used by Syria and IS, are relatively inexpensive and available compared to other WMD.

The production, stockpiling, and use of chemical weapons are outlawed by the signatory states of the Chemical Weapons Convention (CWC) and prohibited under customary international law by those states not signatories. The CWC builds on and expands the Geneva Protocol of 1925 for chemical weapons and includes verification measures such as onsite inspections.[47] The convention is administered by the Organisation for the Prohibition of Chemical Weapons (OPCW) and is charged with conducting inspections of suspect facilities of the member states. According to Article 1 of the Convention, States Parties are obligated never under any circumstances:

(a) To develop, produce, otherwise acquire, stockpile or retain chemical weapons, or transfer, directly or indirectly, chemical weapons to anyone;
(b) To use chemical weapons;
(c) To engage in any military preparations to use chemical weapons;
(d) To assist, encourage or induce, in any way, anyone to engage in any activity prohibited to a State Party under this Convention.

Syria presents a troubling problem for the CWC and OPCW. Syria did not join the CWC until 2013 when, with the urging of their Russian allies, they agreed to join or face the prospect of coalition military action based on a United Nations Security Council resolution. Syria had long claimed the right to chemical weapons as an asymmetric balance to Israel's nuclear weapons program and refused to join the CWC. But with evidence of chemical attacks mounting and a UN investigation pointing to the Assad regime as the chemical attackers, the Syrian regime acceded to the Chemical Weapons Convention (CWC) in the fall of 2013. As a member of the CWC, Syria was required to declare all of its chemical weapons stockpiles to the Organization for the Prohibition of Chemical Weapons (OPCW). According to media reports, the confidential declaration showed that Syria possessed large stockpiles of sulfur mustard, sarin, and VX nerve gas. Syria's declared chemical weapons stockpile was removed from the country by June 2014 and destroyed by January 2016. By joining the CWC, Syria removed the political cause for potential military action against the regime. But concern remained, especially by the United States, that Syria had failed to declare all of the chemical warfare stocks and that the Assad regime retained operational control of covert stockpiles. Chemical attacks continue to be reported in Syria, particularly using chlorine.

OPEN SOCIETIES AND CONTROLLING WMD

The growth of civil society and NGOs creates new models for arms control and disarmament. Countries and people impacted by nuclear weapons have used transnational advocacy networks to help establish

Nuclear Weapons Free Zones in Latin America and the Caribbean, in Africa, in Australia and New Zealand, in the Arctic and Antarctic. The Nuclear Ban Treaty expands the regional nuclear weapons free zones to the whole globe. Following the humanitarian arms control model of the Landmines treaty, the Nuclear Weapons Ban Treaty invited victims of nuclear weapons use and testing to participate in the treaty negotiations. They had been excluded from the previous decades of nuclear disarmament discussions. Widening participation beyond government officials and scientists to include civil society, helped to build a wider constituency in favor of deeper disarmament.

The nuclear ban is an example of the effectiveness of transnational advocacy networks (TANs), and resurrection politics, discussed in the chapter on NGOs. Scientists, indigenous people, human rights advocates, and religious actors have been advocating to ban the bomb since nuclear weapons were created. Resurrection politics takes issues thought previously "Dead on arrival" and raises them up, bring them to life on the international agenda, using the tools of transnational advocacy networks, such as information politics, transparency politics, accountability politics, leverage politics, Dracula politics, and shame and name politics. When countries such as Ireland, Mexico, South Africa, and New Zealand, working with NGO networks such as ICAN (the International Campaign to Abolish Nuclear Weapons), began holding meetings on the humanitarian impact of nuclear weapons, many dismissed their efforts. But successful mobilization of wider networks raised the issue onto the UN agenda, moving the issue outside of the fora blocked by the nuclear powers.

The nuclear ban followed the humanitarian arms control model created by the International Campaign to Ban Landmines (ICBL) and the International Campaign to Ban Cluster Munitions. At first glance, bans from antipersonnel landmines to nukes may seem to have little in common. Landmines are cheap, readily available, and were a weapon in wide use at the time they were banned. In contrast, only nine countries have expensive nuclear weapons. Yet in both cases, decades of advocacy on the issue in traditional fora had stalled, and advocates grew impatient with the stonewalling of states. Progress on the issue was blocked, often by a handful of powerful countries (including the United States) who were part of the problem and did not want to address it. The arms control issues were framed in narrow, technical terms, and complexities among policy experts, without much wider public engagement or understanding of the human costs of the issues. Advocacy on the issues was deemed a hopeless cause, a dead end.

Resurrection politics, moving a dead issue to life, follows a deliberate pattern, made possible by expansion of civil society actors, in numbers, reach, expertise, and networking capacity. A diverse coalition of civil society actors and like-minded countries comes together. The coalition includes doctors, scientists, scholars, and health-care providers, universities, religious actors, nongovernmental organizations concerned with victims, and often retired military and government officials. The coalition shines a light on the human face of the issue, particularly the humanitarian impact on society's most vulnerable women and children. The groups reframe the issue, using powerful pictures and stories of victims, shaming and naming perpetrators. As the victims tell their stories of the human impact, "the professionals"—the doctors, scientists, scholars, health-care providers, retired military and government officials—validate the narrative with facts, figures, scholarly, and academic analysis which parallels and bolsters the victims' perspectives. Religious actors practice solidarity with the poor and vulnerable, raising moral concerns. Like-minded states pursue fast-track multilateral negotiations that do not allow powerful states to veto or block the process. Nonstate actors are invited to speak and participate in the negotiations of states. Together these efforts delegitimize the status quo, and make it more difficult for opposing states to justify their activities.

The nuclear ban closely followed the playbook of the ICBL. Advocates adopted a wide strategy to reach consensus with the "most first," rather than a strategy of reaching agreement with the most powerful (and most opposed) states first. The ICBL differed from other disarmament treaty negotiations in a number of ways: in the actors present, in its focus on the humanitarian impact of the weapons, in its methods, in its contents, and in its strategy. The nuclear ban, like the landmine ban, kept a clear focus on a simple message—ban the use, production, spread, stockpiling, and possession of the weapons, assist victims and survivors, and restore the impacted environment. The process in both cases kept the focus on the humanitarian impact of the weapons, engaged victims and mobilized a growing network of NGOs, who helped bolster the leadership of countries and key government officials willing to "break" with powerful states anchored to the status quo. In both cases, the coalition removed the issue from the existing, moribund international forums blocked by powerful states, and pursued instead a fast-track process committed to negotiating a comprehensive ban regardless of whether the United States or other powerful states might initially join. In both cases advocates avoided expanding the parameters of the ban, arguing that other issues could be addressed after the ban was born. By stigmatizing and delegitimizing the weapons, the processes unleash a pincer movement of pressure on opposing states both from external actors and also from inside their own societies.

The nuclear ban aims to create a norm against nuclear weapons that will increase the pressure nationally and internationally on the nuclear weapons states to reduce their arsenals, even if they remain outside the Convention. This is what occurred in the landmines and cluster munitions conventions. Even the countries that did not sign the bans stopped using and producing the weapons. Most of the nine nuclear states and allies opposed to the nuclear weapons ban are democracies. As citizens rally in favor of the nuclear ban, more governments may engage the process. The ban is popular with citizens in US allies such as Germany, Japan, and Italy. Private sector banks are beginning to divest from companies that make nuclear weapons. Opponents say the nuclear weapons ban is dead on arrival. Resurrection politics supports Mark Twain; reports of its death have been greatly exaggerated.

Another example of how the advancement of open societies has advanced WMD agreements is the Nunn-Lugar, Cooperative Threat Reduction (CTR) program. CTR expanded participation in disarmament beyond political elites in Moscow and Washington, to people harmed by the Cold War nuclear weapons complexes in Kazakstan, Belarus, and Ukraine. Support for CTR expanded to European countries through the G-8 Global Partnership Against the Spread of Weapons and Materials of Mass Destruction, and included scientists and researchers, not only political and military leaders. Senators Nunn and Lugar wanted to further expand CTR to include the participation of other countries, especially India and Pakistan, but there wasn't political will in Congress for expanded participation.

Open societies created new channels for participation in counterproliferation. Scientists and researchers worked together to stop proliferation threats, even when government leaders were not engaged. The activism and engagement of nuclear scientists worried about FSU materials being stolen by scavengers and sold on the black market eventually secured FSU sites in Kazakhstan.[48]

Boomerang politics and forum shopping are important avenues when politics is blocked, as is currently the case regarding United States-Russian relations. When politics is blocked in one venue, you pursue alternate forums. Expanding participation *beyond bilateral approaches* is necessary for principled as well as practical reasons, particularly at a time when bilateral relations are strained. Nonstate venues can be pursued, as well as multilateral cooperation and multilateral processes. The Nuclear Security Summits, the Proliferation Security Initiative/Partnerships to Prevent Proliferation, the Global Threat Reduction Initiative that removed HEU and plutonium from eighteen countries, more than enough for 100 bombs—these are important models that can be revived and continued. Multilateral and NGO cooperation in all-hazard foreign consequence management agreements and exercises also deepen relationships among a wider variety of stakeholders. Foreign consequence management, capacity sharing, and joint training and exercises helpful in disaster relief, would also help if RDDs (radiological dispersal devices or dirty bombs) or nuclear weapons were detonated, whether by accident or by terrorists. Unfortunately, this is a real concern. Widening the net of participation and relationship building, and the issues that we use to encourage cooperation, can keep momentum moving while bilateral disarmament talks are stalled.

PROLIFERATION PREVENTION: STRENGTHENING THE NPT REGIME

Proliferation prevention seeks to constrain the spread of weapons of mass destruction, reduce the numbers and destructiveness of those weapons and limit the means of their means of delivery. Traditionally, prevention mechanisms were seen in terms of horizontal and vertical proliferation. Nonproliferation focuses more on horizontal proliferation, using the full range of political, economic, and diplomatic tools to prevent, constrain, or reverse the proliferation of NBC weapons and their associated delivery means, to prevent acquisition. Nonproliferation has a long history and is the traditional focal point for the US government's efforts. Such efforts include the Nuclear Suppliers Group, the NPT regime, export controls, and the Comprehensive Test Ban Treaty, among others. Nonproliferation controls, such as the NPT, rely on state parties to control weapons and technology from spreading outside their borders. For example, the NPT requires the five declared nuclear weapons states to seek disarmament and to share peaceful nuclear technology with nonnuclear declared states. The nonnuclear weapons states in return promise not to seek nuclear technology for military or strategic application. Both parties commit to disarmament principles. Therefore, nonproliferation relies primarily on diplomacy and is based on the concept that sovereign states will adhere to their treaty commitments, prevent the spread of WMD weapons, components and technology and ultimately, move toward disarmament.

The challenge posed by North Korea to the NPT regime, the preeminent global nonproliferation treaty, is a great concern to global peace. The NPT obligates the five acknowledged nuclear weapon states (the United States, Russian Federation, United Kingdom, France, and China) not to transfer nuclear weapons, other nuclear explosive devices, or their technology to any nonnuclear weapon state. Nonnuclear weapon states agree in return not to undertake acquisition or production of nuclear weapons or nuclear explosive devices. Nonnuclear weapon states are also required to accept safeguards that detect diversions from peaceful activities, such as power generation, to the production of nuclear weapons or other nuclear explosive devices and is done in accordance with an individual safeguards agreement. This agreement is negotiated and concluded between each nonnuclear weapon State Party and the **International Atomic Energy Agency (IAEA),** the UN's nuclear watchdog agency. These agreements require that all nuclear materials be declared to the IAEA, whose inspectors have routine access to the facilities for periodic monitoring and inspections. If information from routine inspections is not sufficient to fulfill its responsibilities, the IAEA may consult with the state regarding special inspections within or outside declared facilities.

The actions of North Korea and the new nuclear weapons and modernization programs of the nuclear states have created a crisis in the treaty regime. Some commentators have suggested that the NPT is now at a critical juncture.[49] Without substantial progress as well as some understanding of how to deal with the other three states outside the NPT, India, Pakistan, and Israel, states that have placed their faith in nonproliferation treaties may reconsider their nuclear weapons posture. This may include new considerations of how to balance other nonconventional weapons such as chemical and biological weapons as they reformulate security policy. There could be a cascade of WMD acquisition decisions resulting from further erosion of the NPT regime. Better verification mechanisms and assurance procedures must be put in place to signal to the international community that a state party is in compliance and not seeking nuclear weapons covertly and under the cover of compliance.

Other challenges face the NPT regime.[50] Many nonnuclear states are concerned that the nuclear powers have shown no movement toward or interest in actually disarming nuclear stockpiles, a condition embedded in the NPT agreement, but instead are moving in the wrong direction. They use the nuclear weapons ban treaty to pressure nuclear states to move toward deeper disarmament.[51]

WMD AND TERROR CAMPAIGNS

Terrorists think and act in terms of campaigns—an orchestrated series of violent acts intended to advance a strategic objective. It is hard to identify acts of terror that are not somehow part of a campaign, whether the time-span of that campaign is short or long. By contrast, crisis and consequence managers tend to think in terms of single events. Responding effectively to single events is daunting enough; responders have barely begun to think concretely about the challenges posed by multiple events. Yet this challenge must be faced in light of the risks and opportunities it presents.

The risks seem clear enough—a greater chance that policymakers and the responder community will make mistakes that exacerbate rather than ease fear and panic, impair response capability, or undermine the legitimacy of government at all levels. The opportunities presented by terror campaigns are principally to learn and adapt, gain the initiative, and exploit mistakes the terrorists might make. How these possibilities play out will be shaped by a number of factors, such as the speed and degree of simultaneity of attacks and the degree of clarity about the "who, what, when, where, and why" of the attacks. At early points when uncertainty on these questions is greatest, risks are likely to dominate. As terrorist capabilities and intentions become clearer, the prospects for an adaptive response should increase. And it is important they do so, because life under a prolonged state of emergency will undoubtedly create profound stresses to any society so affected.

If decision-makers assume, prudently, that after an initial biological or chemical attack terrorists are "re-loading" for follow-on attacks, then it is equally prudent to expect the demands of dealing with the aftermath of an event to grow commensurately—perhaps "only" cumulatively at the local level, but probably exponentially at the country and international level as state leaders confront an overwhelming volume of "day after" demands. At any level, the response to a biological terror campaign in particular will be resource-intensive in ways not fully understood today. Assistance from outside one's own borders almost certainly will be critical. How well a state can respond to an event and how well it can effectively communicate with its people in the face of a terror campaign will be far more challenging, and may lead to a lack of public confidence if not handled professionally and in a timely, accurate manner. All the keys to public information success will be more difficult to achieve when the threat is characterized by multiple events, perhaps with a variety of agents, and perhaps geographically dispersed.

What are the possible elements of a strategy directed at countering and preparing for a biological terror campaign? In the context of an extended terror campaign, states need to demonstrate their ability to adapt and steadily improve their response to multiple attacks, particularly with respect to public health, risk, and strategic communication, and the maintenance of social order, including governance issues such as continuity of operations. Strengthening resilience is also an important, if less tangible, imperative here, to include the psychosocial factors relevant to coping with prolonged stress and the ability to respond to incidents both efficiently and compassionately. Just as important is to attack the adversary's ability to adapt—for instance, by denying him information, funding, training capacity, and strategic partners. This may be a more effective strategy against a terrorist organization than a true terrorist network, which is likely to command greater resources and exhibit greater resilience. Additionally, certain topics that generally have been taboo need to be discussed seriously. Confronting issues such as quarantine, triage, and martial law may not be avoidable, however uncomfortable these discussions may be.

CONCLUSIONS: GOING BEYOND SOVEREIGNTY TO COUNTER WMD

The threat from the proliferation of weapons of mass destruction is global, networked, adaptable, and facilitated by private actors seeking to benefit financially by exporting the world's most dangerous technology. Individual states cannot solve the WMD problem single-handedly, let alone hope to safeguard their own borders isolated from important global actors, be they public or private. Because of this, proliferation control regimes premised on state-to-state agreement are likely to fail since they ignore the growing threat posed by nonstate actors and the role the private sector plays in proliferation. It is not enough to wish the NPT were "more verifiable" or to hope difficult states will cooperate more fully with the IAEA in the future. Nonproliferation agreements assume that states are capable and willing to fulfill their international commitments, with the ability to control what goes on within their borders. But is this a viable reality? There are many failing or failed states, and many opportunities for global networks, designed for speed, efficiency, and security in ways governments are not, to act globally.

An "all hands on deck" approach is needed, combining the traditional nonproliferation activities of states with greater engagement of the private sector, both the nonprofit and for-profit sectors. It is on private sector networks—their ships, planes, and trucks—and through their financial institutions—investment banks, insurance, transshipping concerns—that illegal weapons and components are moved and paid for, and it is here that the process of proliferation, may also be most vulnerable. Civil society networks have also shown great creativity in advancing arms control, on issues such as landmines, cluster munitions, and blinding radars, that had previously eluded states. Will nuclear weapons and killer drones be the next successful bans in the humanitarian arms control movement?

Intergovernmental efforts work to reduce the risks of WMD use and acquisition through UN Security Council resolutions. The Organization for the Prohibition of Chemical Weapons (OPCW) and state-based, self-adaptive models such as the Proliferation Security Initiative (PSI) and the Global Initiative to Combat Nuclear Terrorism (GICNT) have made contributions to reducing the risk of nuclear war and increasing nuclear safety. Yet such efforts, primarily based on state activity, cannot stand alone in the future proliferation landscape that is increasingly networked, private and global.

States, civil society, and corporations have different interests, motivations, and capabilities. But without engaging the private sector and finding mutual areas of interest to contain the spread of WMD, state-based initiatives alone are likely to be late and less likely to succeed given today's global threat environment.

KEY TERMS

"Atoms for Peace" program, 350
A.Q. Khan, 354
ballistic missiles, 349
Biological Weapons
    Convention, 346
Chemical Weapons
    Convention, 347
counterproliferation, 353
CTR, the Cooperative Threat
    Reduction program, 352
DDR, 354
horizontal proliferation, 350
ICBMs, 349
Intermediate Nuclear Forces
    (INF) treaty, 351

International Atomic Energy
    Agency (IAEA), 348
MIRV, 349
Mutually Assured Destruction
    (MAD), 348
Non Proliferation Treaty
    (NPT), 348
nuclear deterrence, 348
Nuclear Posture Review,
    348
"Nuclear Utility Theory," or
    NUTs, 348
Nuclear Weapons Free Zones
    (NWFZ), 351

DISCUSSION QUESTIONS

1. Why do weapons of mass destruction violate the laws of war? Why do militaries need law, especially during wartime? Can you think of any examples of soldiers tried for crimes, even during wars?
2. Where have nuclear bombs been dropped?
3. How did Las Vegas respond to nuclear weapons? What is the most bombed place on earth?
4. Did you know that 10 percent of your electricity was provided by decommissioned nuclear bombs? Describe other examples of defense conversion.
5. Who is A.Q. Khan? Why was he important? How does he illustrate new challenges in WMD proliferation?
6. What was CTR? What did it accomplish?
7. What is DDR? How does it apply to nuclear weapons?
8. Describe different terrorist organizations who have used WMD. Is this trend likely to go away?
9. What is the "Grand Bargain" of the NPT? What have been the NPT's contributions? How is the agreement challenged today?
10. How can private sector actors engage to prevent WMD proliferation?

The zero emissions global race of electric vehicles, co-sponsored by the
UN Environment Programme (UNEP).

12

The Future

Networked Sovereignty, Global Issues, and the Race between Cooperation and Catastrophe

■ ■ ■

We are in a race between cooperation and catastrophe, and the global threat is outpacing our response. We must act now.

—Senator Sam Nunn[1]

Economic systems around the world are failing their citizens, who are not able to fully participate and benefit from the growth process. Globalization merely accentuates this fact.

—Jennifer Blanke[2]

In today's interconnected and globalized world, it's now commonplace for people of different world views, faiths and races to live side by side. It's a matter of great urgency, therefore, that we find ways to cooperate with one another in a spirit of mutual acceptance and respect.

—Dali Lama[3]

In a world that tends toward economic and cultural globalization, every effort must be made to ensure that growth and development are put at the service of all and not just limited parts of the population. Furthermore, such development will only be authentic if it is sustainable and just, that is, if it has the rights of the poor and respect for the environment close to heart. Alongside the globalization of the markets there must also be a corresponding globalization of solidarity.

—Pope Francis[4]

A world connected by trade and technology must be bound by common values.

—Mary Robinson, Former President of Ireland[5]

The human family is a dysfunctional family. What is needed is a network of structures, institutions, principles and elements of law to help manage in the best possible way the world's common good, which cannot be protected only by individual governments.

—Archbishop Diarmuid Martin, Archbishop of Dublin[6]

The major threats we face in the 21st century _ whether it's global recession or violent extremism; the spread of nuclear weapons or pandemic disease _ these things do not discriminate. They do not recognize borders. . . . Moreover, no one person, or religion, or nation can meet these challenges alone. Our very survival has never required greater cooperation and greater understanding among all people from all places than at this moment in history. Unfortunately, finding that common ground—recognizing that our fates are tied up, as Dr. King said, in a "single garment of destiny"—is not easy.

—President Barack Obama[7]

GLOBAL PROBLEMS MOVE AT INTERNET speed; the governments of sovereign states do not move so quickly. This creates gaps in what citizens expect the state to do, and what countries have the capacities to do. This book investigates global issues that move beyond sovereignty in both the nature of problems and solutions. *How can we bridge the gaps between the sovereign states we have, and the coordinating capacities we need, to address the global issues we face?* Global challenges are fast, fungible, fluid, and decentralized, and borders are more permeable. This chapter will explain the capacity gaps, jurisdiction gaps, participation gaps, legitimacy gaps, and ethical gaps in addressing global issues. Most effort has been placed on addressing capacity gaps and jurisdiction gaps, with some smaller effort at addressing participation gaps, leaving legitimacy and ethical gaps to fester. Neglecting the legitimacy and ethics gaps undermines some of the institutions (the EU, NATO, and the UN) available to manage global issues. How can global issues be tackled in a system that is based on sovereignty? There are three main avenues of addressing global issues: state-centric responses (including both unilateral and multilateral approaches); private sector responses (including both the for-profit and nonprofit sides of the private sector); and partnerships between public and private actors. Global issues are the unintended consequences of globalization. These practical responses to address global issues also create some unintended effects on sovereignty. Greater innovation in devising methods of cooperation are needed to address global issues that move beyond sovereignty.

GLOBAL GAPS

Global issues move faster and farther than the responses of sovereign states, across a host of issue areas. The cyberthreats chapter clearly illustrated the gaps in speed and span, but all of the global issues discussed in this book share the same challenge. Economic and technological change is fast, while government, legal, and intergovernmental responses are slow. This creates institutional[8] gaps between the problems of globalization and attempts to manage them. Existing states and international regimes are having difficulties coping with global issues because globalization creates and exacerbates institutional gaps. These institutional gaps fall into several categories: capacity gaps, jurisdiction gaps, participation gaps, legitimacy gaps, and ethical gaps.

Capacity gaps are shortfalls in organizations or organizational strength, competence, resources, personnel, or standard operating procedures that hinder an actor's ability, particularly a state's ability, to effectively respond to problems of globalization. Strong states may lack capacity because the global issue is relatively new, such as cyberthreats or money laundering using crypto currency such as Bitcoin. Weak states may lack capacity because their sovereign states are relatively new and lack resources and competence. For example, when Ebola virus spreads in the Democratic Republic of Congo, the response of religious actors, NGOs, and IGOs are crucial, because the state does not have adequate governmental public health capacity to stop the outbreak. The disease outpaces the state's ability to effectively respond.

Jurisdiction gaps are found when the problem extends farther than the authority of the institutions charged with responding to the problem. Sovereign states are geographically based; their jurisdiction and authority stops at their territorial borders. But global issues easily transcend borders, creating difficulties in crafting responses among a host of sovereign states. Transnational crimes such as drug trafficking exploits jurisdiction gaps, since bringing international criminals to justice requires cooperation, information sharing, and evidence sharing of police and law enforcement agencies in different countries. The crimes of the nefarious drug kingpin "El Chapo" took place in several countries. Prosecuting him for his crimes required the cooperation of law enforcement agencies in the United States, Mexico, and Colombia, illustrating the practical challenges of jurisdiction gaps.

Participation gaps exist when people affected by globalization are excluded from partaking in the decision processes of managing or guiding globalization, earlier described as "democracy deficits." Indigenous peoples around the world are most likely to be excluded, marginalized both from their state's policy processes, and historically also from IGO and corporate policies. For example, MNCs decide economic and environmental policies that can impact much of the world, but citizens lack a participatory framework in which to impact or even make their voices heard to corporations. On issues from the extraction of minerals in war-torn areas, to logging and air pollution, people and the environment are often harmed by corporate policies that they have limited ability to participate in or impact. On the other hand, public sector IGOs, such as the UN, have worked to expand participation of civil society NGOs in their fora and practices. For example, the Treaty on the Prohibition of Nuclear Weapons (the Nuclear Ban treaty signed by 122 countries in 2017) was created with expanded participation by civil society. A coalition of NGOs won the Nobel Peace prize for their work bringing together civil society, including indigenous peoples, to help craft the treaty, working with like-minded states such as the Ireland, Mexico, Brazil, and South Africa. While states sign treaties, NGOs increasingly provide information and advocacy to create treaties, and work to monitor treaty compliance. For example, the International Campaign to Ban Landmines civil society coalition worked to bring about an international ban on landmines, and they continue to work to monitor countries' treaty compliance through the Landmine Monitor, which issues a report card on progress in implementing the treaty. These are examples of expanding participation.

Legitimacy gaps are found when the institutions that manage or regulate globalization are not perceived by society as rightfully representing them. The Brexit vote for the UK to exit the EU was driven in part by the slogan "take back control," venting a sense that the EU did not rightfully represent the interests and views of the British public. Political scientists too often assume that accepted authority is associated with the state, but the state does not have a monopoly on legitimate authority, which can derive from many sources. Trust may be one pathway to social acceptance as a legitimate authority.[9]

Scholars Deborah Avant, Martha Finnemore, and Susan Sell concur that there are "a range of different sources of authority. Expertise propels professional associations to the fore, while advocacy organizations appeal to principles for their authority, and corporations sometimes gain authority because others perceive them as capable of achieving results. . . . Broadly, we see five bases of authority: institutional, delegated, expert, moral, and efficacious."[10]

The legitimacy gap looms large, as seen in the Brexit vote and Trump's withdrawal from many IGOs and international conventions. Many, such as Lola Sánchez, Spanish member of the European Parliament, criticize the unelected institutions of the EU as illegitimate.

The European Commission is the most obscure power of all, nobody was elected there, nobody has voted for them, and they act in a completely obscure way around this issue, and all issues. It is the true heart of the EU, and it is completely coopted, full of revolving doors, wills bought, and with so much lobbying. There is a struggle between the real democratic powers, such as the European Parliament, where we are directly elected by European citizens, and a series of obscure powers that move within the European Commission, which is completely coopted by corporate power. . . . So in the end, there is a struggle between democracy and corporate power within the European Union.[11]

A lack of transparency, and/or a lack of accountability,[12] undermines legitimacy. Using modern information technologies creates more opportunities for transparency.[13] Transparency is necessary to be able to judge effectiveness. But many actors use transparency as a stand—in or substitute for participation and accountability, hoping greater transparency will bring greater legitimacy. Transparency may undermine legitimacy, if the transparency exposes a poor performance record, for example. While transparency is necessary in order to hold an actor responsible for behavior, transparency may exist without mechanisms of accountability or participation. For example, years ago I questioned the head of the World Bank about poor countries' concerns over the lack of transparency and accountability for World Bank policies, and how this undermined support and legitimacy for the World Bank. He replied that the World Bank has complete transparency because it now *posts* its decisions and actions on its website *after* they have been taken. His response is a bit tone deaf to the issue.

Ethical or values gaps arise when globalization is perceived either to have no ethical base or to promulgate values that are at odds with societal values or the common good. Pope Francis criticizes globalization's values gaps when he decries a "globalization of indifference" to the poor, and urges instead for "a globalization for all," "a globalization of solidarity," that protects the poor, the environment, and the common good, instead of a globalization that puts corporate profits before people and the planet.

Of all these gaps, most effort has been made to bridge the capacity gaps. All of the preceding chapters discussed efforts to address capacity gaps, from responding to transnational crime or containing terrorism. Capacity gaps vex state, IGO, multilateral, and private sector institutions. Besides the problem of speed (institutions moving slower than global problems), there are other reasons why governments alone cannot effectively respond to globalization's problems. Many regimes have only shaky control over their respective territories. Failed and fragile states are a persistent feature of global politics. Lack of institutional capacity and resources undermines many governments' abilities to respond to global problems.

Comparatively speaking, developed democracies are better equipped to meet the challenges of globalization because they have adaptive and generally better-resourced political and economic institutions that are capable of responding to the dislocations, disruptions, and unintended consequences that globalization brings. States with adequate educational and public health systems and access to technology, coupled with stable governance, allow people access, an on-ramp to the globalization highway. But for many developing and newly democratizing states, rule of law and political and economic institutions are weak; they lack the capacity and resources to respond to globalization's challenges. Even strong states may lack capacity, as growth in the private sector (legal and illegal) has outpaced growth in the public sector by design. Weak and strong states both have capacity gaps, as evidenced by cyberattacks. They are more severe for developing states, fragile states, collapsing states, and states undergoing transitions.

Jurisdiction gaps have also been a focus of intense international activity described throughout this book, arising when problems cross borders but governments are still constrained by borders in their abilities to respond. Even strong states cannot manage global problems alone because the issues cross jurisdictional and territorial boundaries. Cybercriminals and international terrorists attack from a distance. Bringing them to justice is complicated by these jurisdictional gaps. In addition, the private sector often has better information and technology for containing global problems, while public sector capabilities lag behind. For example, the transportation and information infrastructures exploited by the ransomware hackers were primarily privately owned and operated, further complicating government's jurisdictional reach. Terrorism crosses international and public–private jurisdictions, making governmental responses necessary but insufficient to successfully manage these problems. As democratization and capitalism have spread liberal political and economic systems globally, more states find themselves constitutionally limited in what interventions they may undertake in the private sphere. Even when states may wish to intervene, such as in the face of the global economic recession or grave public health threats, they may not have effective tools to do so. IGOs have increased in number, resources, functions, and power particularly to address jurisdiction gaps. But IGOs and states alone cannot solve globalization problems because many of the factors that constrain individual states also constrain collections of states. This again creates gaps between what institutions can do and what they are needed to do.

The legitimacy gap, participation gap, and values gap all have received less attention to resolve. They are also made worse by capacity gaps and jurisdiction gaps; when institutions don't work well (due to capacity and jurisdiction gaps), this undermines their legitimacy. Legitimacy, participation, and ethics gaps are exacerbated by institutional gaps that exist between rich and poor. Generally, the wealthy have institutions with more capabilities to act on their behalf; the poor often do not. The rural poor have less opportunity to access globalization's benefits. Poor countries and peoples face institutional gaps that fuel the increasing backlash against globalization. Lacking resources, the institutions of poor countries are disadvantaged when bargaining with more powerful countries' institutions over the rules and regimes that govern globalization. For example, in the "biopiracy" cases discussed in the chapter on environmental issues, a common bean plant in Mexico was patented by a Colorado company, and Mexican farmers charged a bill to grow a plant they had grown for generations. Biopiracy reveals biases in global institutions that allow rich countries and companies to claim genetic materials and indigenous knowledge as their intellectual property. Cases like this illustrate that the poor do not have much participation in the institutions such as the WTO, and the World Intellectual Property Organization, which manage the "rules of the road" for intellectual property rights. To many, the WTO and WIPO appear illegitimate, that these institutions do not rightfully represent poor people. To critics, their behavior reveals a bias to protect the profits of the rich at the expense of the poor, and thus exposes ethical gaps. Participation gaps, legitimacy gaps, and ethical gaps often occur together, and reinforce each other in a negative feedback loop.

Poor peoples and countries do not have adequate participation in the decision-making processes that channel globalization, from corporate boardrooms to annual World Economic Forum summits to the Group of Seven meetings. This is why the annual G7 meetings of the leaders of the world's richest countries draw protestors in the streets. Because they lack a seat at the table inside the conferences, the only way for the critics of globalization to express their concerns is in the streets outside the meetings of elites. To avoid and diminish the space and opportunities for protestors, G7 meetings have moved to more remote meeting sites, undercutting the limited "participation" the poor have in these conferences which set the agenda for global economic decision-making. For example, the remote Charlevoix region of Quebec was chosen to host the 2018 G7 meeting because it was so difficult for protestors to reach. A "free speech" area for protestors was set up, over 2 km away from where the world leaders were actually meeting.

The thirty poorest member states of the WTO cannot afford to send delegations to represent and negotiate on their own behalf in Geneva. The participation gaps, capacity gaps, and asymmetric distribution of costs and benefits intensify dissatisfaction and backlash against globalization. Institutions that do not adequately protect developing countries and those that exclude them from decision-making processes are increasingly seen as illegitimate by those who are excluded.

These various institutional gaps are self-reinforcing in a negative feedback loop. Institutions must be perceived as legitimate to be effective, and participation gaps exacerbate legitimacy gaps, which in turn intensify capacity gaps.

The participation and legitimacy gaps also fuel the ethical and values gap. Many observers believe that corporations rule the world[14] and that globalization puts profits ahead of people. Growing income inequality, both across states and within states, undermines political support for globalization.[15] Sixty one men own as much wealth as half of humanity. Income for the top 1 percent has grown rapidly since 1980 when globalization advanced, while median incomes have flatlined and declined, particularly since the 2007 recession. In 1950, the income of a CEO was twenty times higher than the income of the average worker in his business, a rate that had been the same for 200 years prior. Today, average CEO income is more than 200 times that of the average worker in their firms and can be much higher. These income inequalities are a moral scandal when basic human needs for the bottom earners are not met. The growing inequality is an economic problem, because wealth concentration in the highest earners can lead to financial instability, risky investments, and "Casino Capitalism,"[16] as investments seek short-term profits in the financial sector. This exacerbates boom and bust patterns and does not spur wider and more long-term economic growth. Middle-class and poor people spend their incomes on basic needs, spurring more stable economic growth and "spillover effect" to the wider economy, not just the financial sector. Economies with high levels of inequality are inefficient. High levels of inequality are a political problem when it leads to political instability due to dissatisfaction with political leaders and the political system. Rising food prices and inequality in the Middle East caused protests and the "Arab Spring" revolutions. Rising dissatisfaction with economic stagnation of the middle and lower classes led to the "Occupy" protests around the world, and to the rise of increasing political polarization.

To the extent that globalization favors the few at the expense of the rest, many people suggest that the violence and backlash against globalization will increase. When the benefits of globalization are not shared widely, but reach too few people and countries, the public support for sustaining globalization become politically unsustainable.[17]

Today's growth of nationalist, nativist, isolationist, and fascist policies and leaders are evidence of people who feel that globalization has left them behind. In the United Kingdom, the areas with declining industries, stagnant or declining economies, and aging populations, were much more likely to vote to leave the EU than the cities and tech economy areas, where people derive benefits from economic integration. The same pattern appears in the United States. Rural areas and "rustbelt" areas with declining economies and aging populations, and areas with the highest levels of drug addiction and opioid deaths, were much more likely to vote for Trump's anti-globalization policies, while younger, tech economy areas did not vote for Trump.

Globalization's ethical gaps are large and growing. Today, about half of the world's citizens are not receiving the benefits of globalization, either because they are not plugged into the global economy or because they do not have institutions that can advance or protect their interests as participants in the global economy. Human life is lost, human development unfulfilled, and creation destroyed. This disparity between those who benefit from globalization and those who are left behind or vulnerable to its challenges is increasing. The world's youngest populations are growing and are the world's poorest people, while the populations of developed countries, who control most of the world's wealth, are aging and declining with the graying of the baby boomers. For example, world population is expected to grow from its current 7.6 billion to 9–11 billion by 2050. Ninety-five percent of that population growth will occur in developing countries and in already stressed urban areas—megacities such as Lagos and Mexico City. How will enough jobs and economic opportunities be created for the young in

Africa and the Middle East? Without jobs, young men are vulnerable to recruitment for crime and violence. If globalization does not create enough economic opportunities and jobs for the young of Africa, Asia, and the Middle East, the recent decades' gains in peace may be lost, and violence may come roaring back. There is some evidence for this; while major armed conflicts are still much lower today than in the twentieth century, minor armed conflicts are on the rise. Globalization's moral and ethical problems will intensify as the youth bulge in poor countries struggles to live and advance.

The values gap is exacerbated by the legitimacy, participation, jurisdictional, and capacity gaps. When governments fail in capacity and jurisdiction, failing to provide basic services, when governments exclude participation, governments lose legitimacy, and support. As Benjamin Barber notes, we must combat a malevolent interdependence (of criminals and human smugglers, etc.) with a benevolent "democratic architecture of interdependence."[18] In practice, this is hard to do. Efforts to expand capacity and jurisdiction may make the participation, legitimacy, and ethics gaps worse.

GLOBALIZATION'S UNINTENDED CONSEQUENCES

Much of this book has been about globalization's unintended consequences. States, IGOs, and MNCs worked to build international markets and to create the political, economic, and technological infrastructure that made the global marketplace possible. States courted foreign direct investment and technological advancement. Through a variety of economic and political liberalization policies, states deliberately worked to increase the size of the private sector while curtailing public sector expenditures so the private sector would not be "crowded out." They pursued these policies to increase economic development and prosperity, believing that wealthy states are strong states.

Western states sought to promote open societies, believing that democratic states are less likely to go to war with one another, are more likely to protect basic human rights, and are more stable trade partners. States did not intend, however, to create the infrastructure for global problems to thrive. State governments did not realize that the new actors and dynamics created by globalization would also drain some autonomy, choice, and freedom of action away from states. Sovereignty is based on territory (and generally taxes are based on territory), yet the information economy is less dependent on territory, making the new economic elites less beholden to states. How can these new dynamics and actors be managed within a system of sovereign states? How can states maintain law and order, justice and peace in a system of licit and illicit private sector actors who are increasingly powerful?

POLICY PRESCRIPTIONS

Policy prescriptions for managing globalization and the global issues facilitated by open societies, economies, and technologies, fall into three main categories: state-centric (public sector) approaches, nonstate-centric (private sector) responses, and mixed (public–private) responses.

The State-Centric Approach

The **state-centric approach** to global problems aims at strengthening state capacity to fight global problems, both individually and together, enhancing law and order institutions, control over borders, markets, multilateral cooperation among states, and interagency cooperation within states to increase states' efficacy of response.[19] Most attention and effort to address global issues has been focused on state-centric approaches, increasing capacity within states, and increasing coordination among states. The pendulum swings back and forth. Some leaders, countries, and time periods focus on improving internal state capacity. Examples include the decolonization period of the emergence of new states, the post-Soviet period of newly independent states, and the post-9/11 period of greater attention to preventing terrorist attacks via enhanced state structures. The emergence of new issue areas also creates political support for expanding state capacity to address an emerging issue area. For example, the creation of state cybersecurity units discussed in the cyberthreats chapter, and the creation of Cyber Command, is an example of state-centric responses.

Simultaneously, many focused on creating better means for states to collaborate together to manage global issues: examples include creating and enhancing regional and international regimes such as the EU, the WTO, enhanced UN PKOs, NAFTA, WIPO, and many others. The internal and external, unilateral and multilateral state-centric approaches are not necessarily opposed, but often work together. For example, the Proliferation Security Initiative collaborative network of 101 states shares lessons learned and best practices to stop the proliferation of weapons of mass destruction, and encourages states internally to create and strengthen their capacities to address the issue.

The state-centric approach argues that the same forces that facilitate global problems and undermine sovereignty (open technologies, economies, and societies) can be harnessed or managed to fight global problems. In essence, the answer to global issues which go beyond sovereignty is more sovereignty, either individual autonomous sovereignty or pooled sovereignty. The assumption is that we must make states (or groups of states) better, stronger, and especially faster, in order to catch global problems which move quickly across state borders. States need to better use the same new technologies and market forces that are being used against them in global problems. If we could just make states more capable and smarter and get them to work together better, then states would be able to meet these challenges more effectively. If states were equipped with better technologies, with a stronger tax base (without companies and individuals hiding income from taxes through elaborate off shore schemes), with enhanced state capacity, then cooperating and sharing information and implementation would be possible and would bring more effective action across and within governments. After all, terrorists and drug traffickers are using the most advanced emerging technologies and are developing strategic relations with other criminal cartels. Why can't states do the same in their efforts to stop these illicit activities? State-centric responses can be unilateral, focusing on building the capacity of states internally. They can also be multilateral, focusing either on increasing IGO capacity or on federal, functional cooperation among government agencies (as when police or judges network to share information and cooperate across borders).

Anne-Marie Slaughter argues that government agencies and officials at all levels are working together across borders in unprecedented government networks to manage global problems. These networking, harmonization, enforcement, and information networks help address capacity and jurisdiction gaps. And to the degree that government actors are democratically elected, these government-to-government networks are more legitimate, democratic, and accountable than partnerships with unelected actors such as MNCs, and NGOs. Horizontal networks coordinate action and information across governments, while vertical networks allow international coercion through state-to-IGO delegation. The result is "disaggregated sovereignty." Sovereign units respond to global problems, but they do so through government networks. These can be task networks, resilience networks, or scale networks.[20]

State-centric responses are seen most often in the efforts to fight the global problems of terrorism, drug smuggling, cyberthreats, transnational crime, and WMD proliferation. This is not surprising: These issues touch most closely to the security sectors where state identity and activities are strongest and where states have always been active. Interdiction, improved intelligence and law enforcement capabilities, interagency and IGO efforts to improve information sharing, cooperation, and enforcement are all examples of state-centric responses to global problems. The Proliferation Security Initiative is an example of a state-centric approach to improve countries' abilities to interdict WMD weapons and materials. Even progressive and creative programs that are fully in the cooperative security rubric—such as the Nuclear Security Summits and the Cooperative Threat Reduction programs to stem proliferation from the former Soviet Union (FSU)—fit into this category. Efforts to increase nuclear material protection, control, and accountability (MPC&A) by increasing security at nuclear labs and facilities by installing security cameras, detection devices, modern accounting and storage procedures, etc., were oriented at strengthening the capacity of states to control nuclear and dual use materials.

The Nonstate-Centric Approach

The **nonstate-centric policy approach** emphasizes the importance of the private sector in responding to global problems. It also emphasizes the limitations of trying to work through the state for help in curtailing activities that largely fall in the social and economic sectors where the reach of capitalist, liberal states is the shortest. If state capacity is (or should be) weakening, then why ask the state to solve global problems? Why not go directly to the private sector, where the resources exist to address the problem?

Examples include ICANN, the private organization that assigns domain names on the Internet. Corporate social responsibility programs, and corporations' efforts to clean up their supply chains from conflict minerals are examples of private sector responses to global issues, without government orders to do so. Religious actors work to persuade the hospitality and transportation industries to stop human trafficking. Religious actors and NGOs use their own institutions to directly serve human trafficking victims, refugees, and IDPs, and protect the environment, whether or not sovereign states act.

This approach emphasizes developing new responses and infrastructure that utilize nonstate actors such as NGOs and MNCs. Examples include corporate codes of conduct, which aim to improve international environmental and labor standards. Shareholder and consumer activism works to change MNC policies. Religious actors and NGOs advocate for pharmaceutical companies to voluntarily reduce prices and increase access to essential medicines for poor countries and people. Market-based approaches to reducing poverty through microcredit, FDI, increased trade, and microbusiness (e.g., Grameen Bank) are nonstate-centric policy prescriptions.

The private sector has primary responsibility for critical infrastructure protection and cybersecurity efforts, because 85 percent of critical infrastructure and information infrastructure is privately owned and operated.

Direct action campaigns by NGOs to change corporate or consumer behavior effect change regardless of governmental participation. For example, convincing the tuna industry to adopt dolphin-safe fishing techniques was a nonstate-centric approach. Efforts to fight global problems of refugee flows, disease, and environmental degradation tend to focus more readily on nonstate-centric approaches, particularly when state action is not engaged. NGOs, religious actors, and MNCs are focused on direct private sector reductions of carbon emissions, particularly since the United States has withdrawn from its Paris Climate Accords commitments to reduce emissions. Nonstate actors have traditionally been strongest in social and economic issue areas. Ancient, prestate religious actors have been healing, educating, fighting poverty and slavery, and welcoming strangers for millennia, but they now partner with NGOs and sometimes businesses to work in common cause.

Mixed or Public–Private Approaches: Networked Sovereignty

Finally, there is a third way. If public- and private sector responses alone cannot effectively manage global issues, then why not combine the two? **Public–private partnerships** have the potential to reap the benefits of each separate approach while minimizing some of the problems of one approach alone. In theory, by combining the benefits of state legitimacy and enforceability with the flexibility and resources of the private sector, more traction can be brought to bear on difficult global issues. Public–private partnerships have succeeded in global health efforts to reduce HIV/AIDS infection rates, and to help HIV/AIDs infected patients to manage their disease with anti-retroviral medicines. The Gates Foundation often partners with religious actors and pharmaceutical companies and the governments of countries in common efforts to immunize children and fight HIV/AIDs in Africa.

Cybersecurity efforts and critical infrastructure protection efforts include a heavy reliance on public–private partnerships. Examples include the Computer Emergency Response Teams (CERTS).

Cooperation among academics, private sector, and government IT experts in CERT teams to respond to cyberattacks has been such a successful model of public–private partnerships that it has been replicated around the world. The model is now being adopted to other areas of critical infrastructure protection.

The state still has important levers that can be used to fight global problems. A state can serve as negotiator or facilitator of private sector interactions, can backstop private sector initiatives with a safety net baseline of law that provides more universally implementable and enforceable norms, and can sometimes provide threats or force. States provide not only the sticks but also the carrots of incentives, and they can focus direction. The state has the added advantage of being familiar and available. States can facilitate discussion and action through their convening functions, and through collecting and releasing reports and information that can help spur and inform action.

I contend that we are in an era of networked sovereignty. Neither the state nor the private sector can manage global issues alone. The choices are not either/or, between multilateralism and unilateralism, integration and fragmentation, federal government and local government, and public sector and private sector. To manage global problems, we must use "both/and" approaches, using all of the networks at our disposal, while inventing some new ones. Choice of the institutional network and instrument will be based on who has the established network assets in a sector. She who has the network becomes the partner.

Networked sovereignty differs from old time, autonomous sovereignty. Historically, sovereignty is associated with law and order, autonomy, and independence. Today, other actors increasingly provide laws and order, and globalization curtails autonomy and independence. Sovereignty is increasingly networked—sideways to other states and nonstate actors, upwards to pooled sovereignty organizations, and downward to local actors. There is no "one size fits all" network model. Choice of the linked networks varies by issue area and political forces.

"Governance has gone global—and so have questions of legitimacy and accountability. The old 'club model' of international politics as a closed shop involving just governments is defunct. International organisations, nongovernmental organisations (NGOs), transnational companies—all play vital roles alongside national officials in global policymaking. Why bother with partnerships? A more appropriate question should be: What other useful mechanisms are available?"[21]

Problems of transparency, accountability, and legitimacy can be addressed by building checks and balances into the networks, not with a single mechanism but through what Benner and Witte term "pluralistic systems of accountability." These can include leveraging reputational accountability, peer accountability, financial accountability, process accountability, transparency about sources and uses of funding, and performance accountability.[22]

If states alone cannot adequately respond to global problems, then why is it important that they be part of the pluralistic approach? The most important advantage states have is that they exist. They do not have to be built from scratch. They are familiar, with addresses and known processes that are understood and available for interaction, allowing the opportunity for transparency and accountability. States may not have the ability to command or compel resolution of a global problem, but they are uniquely positioned to coordinate, communicate, facilitate, and cajole action from a variety of other actors who look to the state to fill that conduit function. States are a focal point for citizen imagination and demands. Whether or not states can solve global problems alone, the question is still raised by the public and the media, "What is the state doing about it?"

In addition, governments are often perceived to have the political legitimacy to act on behalf of the populace in foreign affairs. Although foreign policy bureaucracies in democracies are generally not staffed by elected officials, they are created and funded by elected officials, and they can be held responsible to elected officials. Thus, state institutions must have some degree of political support to exist at all. On the other hand, it is not clear whom MNCs and NGOs represent, to whom they are accountable or how they can be held accountable, or how much political legitimacy and support they command. Why not use the institutional advantages states have of being available as a forum, to convene nonstate actors through a public forum?

Underlying these different policy debates over how to best respond to global problems are different assumptions about the future of the

Table 12.1 Different Approaches to Global Issues and the Future of Sovereignty

Mixed Approaches Networked Sovereignty (Love)	
State-Centric Approaches	**Nonstate-Centric Approaches**
Autonomous Sovereignty (Krasner)	Private Authority (Haufler)
Pooled Sovereignty (EU)	Retreating Sovereignty (Strange)
Disaggregated Sovereignty (Slaughter)	

sovereign state. Is the sovereign state retreating, its power becoming more diffuse in a globalized economy? Susan Strange argues that power is moving from states to markets as states either abdicate more functions to nonstate actors or vacate certain functions altogether.[23] There is some evidence throughout this book of **retreating sovereignty**. Nonstate actors are increasingly taking on functions that were traditionally performed by states, even in the security sector. The chapter on cybersecurity supports Rosecrance's idea of the declining importance of territory relative to the rising importance of market forces.[24] If states are losing power to nonstate actors and market dynamics, then responses to global problems should be aimed at nonstate actors and market forces.

Others argue that the sovereign state is still the fundamental unit in the international system. Sovereignty took centuries to develop and will not disappear in a few decades, and there are no well-developed alternative organizing units ready to replace autonomous sovereign states.[25] The preceding chapters offer some evidence to support this view. Terrorism highlights that the state is still important enough to be worth fighting for. If this is the case and state actors still reign supreme, then efforts to fight global problems should still be aimed at states and strengthening state institutions or perhaps at developing more cooperative mechanisms among states.

There is a third way. If sovereignty is changing but not dead, then fighting global problems may require a combined approach in which a wide spectrum of policy responses are undertaken and coordinated, aimed at both state and nonstate sectors. If we are in a period of transition or turbulence[26]—in which a changed economic system has created new actors and dissipated the power of states in crucial economic, public health, and social sectors, but in which state actors are still important, particularly in the law enforcement and security sectors—then a combined approach is necessary. Just as new interstate highways are often built alongside existing two-lane highways, new networks using new actors must be built while the old state actors are still functioning.

For all of the advantages of pursuing public–private partnerships, there are also obstacles. They suffer from democracy deficits, participation gaps, legitimacy gaps, and ethical gaps, as discussed in previous sections. There are also complexity problems; working with many different actors and integrating a wide variety of responses is challenging, and there are no clear rule books for how to do this. More actors require greater coordination, communication, cooperation, prioritization, transparency, and accountability, which increases the level of difficulty. Pursuing a combined approach also necessitates vigilance for threshold effects and unintended consequences. For example, policy responses may need a certain level of funding for a protracted period of time before a program may yield results. But if policy responses are split over a variety of state and nonstate venues, then resources may be diluted or a plan of attack may be pursued for too short a period, never reaching the threshold necessary for effective action. Unintended consequences apply to every approach. Because action must be coordinated among a wider variety of players, it may be more difficult to anticipate the full ramifications of a wider array of actions in public–private partnerships. For example, funneling attention and funding to nonstate actors and sectors could further undermine state sectors and actors. As new highways are built, sometimes the old roadways fall into disuse.

Continued monitoring and attention to coordination, prioritization, and accountability are necessary. Yet none of these critiques is unique to public–private approaches, though they may be more intense with them. State-centric and nonstate-centric prescriptions also share these obstacles. For example, government bureaucrats are not elected, and government bureaucracies are not necessarily transparent, accountable, democratic, or legitimate. Combating terrorism, organized crime, or drug trafficking in one sector or region may merely drive it into another area. All approaches require building political support, coordination, communication, prioritization, transparency, and accountability—and all may encounter resistance to change by existing organizations, threshold effects, and unintended consequences.

DOES SOVEREIGNTY STILL MATTER?

Sovereignty—who cares? Why write a book about it, much less five books on the topic? For the world's youngest and fastest growing countries, for those living in fragile, failed, or failing states, sovereignty matters.[27] They would like to see more sovereignty, in the form of a state's ability to provide basic capacity to the people living within its borders, such as law and order, good governance, education and health services, a generally effective and fair public sector—what academics call internal sovereignty, **positive sovereignty**, or domestic sovereignty. Nigerians traveling to the West are awed by the simple things: the fact that people obey traffic rules, that cars move in predictable patterns, that there are regular, routine, and transparent procedures for obtaining a driver's license in the Department of Motor Vehicles, and that money or connections will not excuse you from these procedures. They know a world in which blind men can obtain driver's licenses for the right fee, in which cars and trucks jump median strips and head the wrong way down highways in a high stakes game of "chicken" if it will get drivers around traffic tie-ups.

For the families of the millions killed in civil wars in Syria, Iraq, Afghanistan, the Democratic Republic of Congo, and South Sudan, sovereignty matters. Many are fighting for control over the sovereign state; others are fighting for self-rule, to break away and form their own sovereign state. Some are fighting for democratic sovereignty, to have the institutions of the state accountable to the people. For people of Syria, of the Democratic Republic of Congo, of South Sudan, and Palestine, democratic sovereignty matters.

For the 37 percent of the world's population living in repressive states, and the 24 percent of the world's population living in only partly free countries, sovereignty matters. It matters when the police throw your loved one in prison for criticizing the government, or for some unnamed or fabricated offense.[28] When the sovereign state kills its own people instead of protecting and serving them, sovereignty matters. The 170 million killed at the hands of their own government leaders over the past century[29] knew the evils of sovereignty intimately. All these people daily experience **predatory sovereignty** (when the state preys on its own people), **personal sovereignty** (law is whatever the leader says it is, without democratic process or constraints), and **criminal sovereignty** (the co-optation of the state by criminal elements). What academics call **negative sovereignty** or the right of noninterference in states' internal affairs is what former UN secretary-general Kofi Annan decried when he noted that "The sovereignty of States must no longer be used as a shield for gross violations of human rights."[30]

For the millions of immigrants out of 192 million migrants killed, imprisoned, or deported due to failure to obtain proper entry permission, and for the 25.4 million refugees in the world today,[31] and 27 million victims of human trafficking, pushed out of one country's borders but unable to begin life anew in another country, sovereignty matters, as the sovereign state effectively denies access to jobs, food, shelter, health care, education, travel—opportunities that glimmer out of reach across the border.

Yet for those of us lucky enough to live in functioning, developed, democratic states, with positive sovereignty and democratic sovereignty, sovereignty is not enough. It is better than living in failed states, predatory states, and nondemocratic states, to be sure, but sovereignty isn't all it is cracked up to be. For the families of the 72,000 US citizens who died from illicit drugs last year, the unquestioned sovereignty of the United

States could not protect or save them from the international drug trade. For the 33 million people around the world infected with HIV or AIDS, sovereignty cannot save them from traveling, devastating pathogens.

As people everywhere move beyond sovereignty, they do so for different reasons. For people in fragile, failed, and failing states, and for people in predatory and criminal states, they look beyond sovereignty to networks of IGOs, NGOs, and even MNCs to help save them from their crumbling or abusive sovereign structures. For people in developed, democratic states, we look beyond sovereignty because even generally fair and functioning states cannot save us from pressing global problems that go beyond borders.

Sovereignty is not extinct; it persists, but in new forms and functions. We reinvent it in practice each day in our struggles to manage global issues.

NETWORKED SOVEREIGNTY

If state-centric responses are still necessary, along with other approaches in dealing with global problems, then does this mean that sovereignty hasn't changed much? Is there no competitor to the sovereign state out there right now, so sovereignty still reigns by default?

Not exactly, because sovereignty is changing in significant ways. We are in an era of **networked sovereignty**. Vertical and horizontal linkages may still tie sovereignty in place, but the links are changing. States are increasingly connecting to nonstate actors, while also deepening their links and connections with other states and IGOs/clubs of states.

It is instructive to remember Hendrik Spruyt's story of how fundamental change came about the last time and ushered in the sovereign state: the economy changed. New elites were created who benefited from the new economic system and needed a new form of political organization to better accommodate them and their economic practices. Ideas changed, new organizational forms emerged and competed, and, after centuries of flux, the sovereign state eventually won out.[32]

There are many parallels today. The economy has changed. The new economic system is increasingly based on information, technology, and services, which are less dependent on the control of territory. The means of production, capital, and labor are mobile, not fixed. Players who make use of modern information, communication, transportation, and financial technologies reap the benefits of increasingly open borders and economies.

Political systems that make room for the new economic system reap profits in foreign direct investment, and so regime types as distinct as the Chinese communist system, the Mexican emerging democracy, and the Iranian theocracy are all simultaneously undertaking reforms to make themselves more attractive to investors' capital and technology flows.

New elites are emerging who profit from the new economic system. Typified by Bill Gates, Carlos Slim, Warren Buffet, Mark Zuckerberg, Jeff Bezos, George Soros and Sergey Brin, these "new imperialists"[33] increasingly follow no flag. They are passionate about expanding technologies and markets, and they are frustrated by what they see as anachronistic state barriers to information, investment and trade flows, and to addressing global issues. The international business classes attend the same schools, fly the same airlines, vacation at the same resorts, eat at the same restaurants, and watch the same movies and television shows. Independent of national identities, these elites mobilize to try to make states facilitate technological and market dynamics. Some call it the "Davos culture" after the Swiss luxury resort where the annual World Economic Summit met. Sociologist Peter Berger believes these cultural ties made peace talks in South Africa and Northern Ireland go more smoothly: "It may be that commonalities in taste make it easier to find common ground politically."[34] Can it be that leaders who share cultural connections find political antagonisms unhelpful and unnecessary? In what he dubs the "Golden Arches Theory of Conflict Prevention," and the "**Dell Theory**," Thomas Friedman argues that economic interdependence brings peace, as "no two countries that are both part of a major global supply chain, like Dell's [computers], will ever fight a war against each other as long as they are both part of the same global supply chain," and no two countries with McDonald's restaurants have ever gone to war with one another.[35] Even though clearly there are many economically underprivileged people around the world who do not partake in this lifestyle, the values of this new elite percolate into the rest of society as people mimic the behavior of the elites and strive to better their economic situations to one day rise into the wealthier classes.

Ideas are changing (including ideas of authority, identity, and organization), facilitated by the new information technologies and changes in the economy. Never before in human history have we been able to spread ideas so quickly and widely. Modern communication technologies allow an ever-wider swath of the planet to be tuned in to the same advertisements, the same websites and social networking sites, the same entertainment shows, and, thereby, to some of the same ideas about consumerism and personal freedoms. Identity is becoming less tied to territory. If identity and authority do not stem from geography, then what is our identity tied to? In the European Middle Ages, identity came from Christendom, the Church, while authority stemmed from spiritual connections. In the modern era, identity was tied up with the sovereign state; authority corresponded with geography. Now authority and identity are increasingly contested. Strange believes we now have Pinocchio's problem: The strings of state control, authority, and identity have been cut, but no new strings have been fastened.[36] States no longer are the supreme recipient of individual loyalties, especially because they no longer fulfill basic services and functions and other actors have stepped into the gap. Firms, professions, families, religions, and social movements have all significantly challenged the state's territorial and security-based claim to individual loyalty. We are left to choose among competing sources of allegiance, authority, and identity, with no strings to bind us like puppets to one source of authority, and with more freedom to let our conscience be our guide.

Certainly, the integrated economy would like identity to be formed around consumer products—you are what you wear, what you consume. Advertisers spend billions to imprint brand loyalty at an early age, and all the advertising of Apple/iPod, Nike's swoosh, and I'd-like-to-buy-the-world-a-Coke, share a common theme: that identity stems not from national borders but from consumer products. Identity is therefore just as mobile as the economy. You are not born with it. You can buy it. Alternatively, some see identity as increasingly flowing from professions and firms: You are what you do, and your commitment is to your profession rather than to a specific state. As Rosecrance describes it, "Today and for the foreseeable future, the only international civilization worthy of the name is the governing economic culture of the world market."[37] Benjamin Barber refers to this popular, consumer market culture as "McWorld."[38] As market values permeate various cultures, certain ideas emerge as prized: the value of change, mobility, flexibility, adaptability, speed, and information. As capitalism becomes our creed, with technology as our guide, distinct national and religious cultures are becoming permeated with common market values.

There are alternatives to market values, however. Religious organizations and NGOs promulgate alternative ethics to materialism, a globalization in which we are not merely consumers or a governance problem but human beings, each with irreducible sacred dignity. This vision of globalization prescribes putting people before profits, ethical values before market values. These organizations use the tools of globalization to promote their views of humanizing globalization. For example, social media and the Internet are popular tools for organizing and proselytizing by many ancient faith groups, including traditional Islam. Pope Francis uses Twitter, Facebook, YouTube, websites, and instant technologies to communicate regarding ancient principles and texts.[39]

Ideas of organization are also changing and are based on models from the marketplace and technology. Cell and computer networks, the Internet, and the market are diffuse, decentralized, loosely connected networks with a few central organizing parameters but strong ties to the activities of individual entrepreneurs. Foreign policy organizations are, in some instances, going beyond hierarchical state bureaucracies, creating flexible, innovative, coordinating networks. Network theory provides models for new ways of organizing. But the private sector is more comfortable with flexible networks than the state. Sovereign foreign policy organizations are created by law, and so may have less flexibility in their organizational structures, which can create friction in working with private sector actors.

Creating public–private partnerships are another means of addressing global problems. Rather than trying to become draconian, big brother states (which would conflict with the goals of open societies, open economies, and open technologies), it makes sense for governments to look toward the private sector for help in managing global problems. But the greater complexity of these arrangements creates challenges.

How can the "public" be kept primary in public–private partnerships? The public and states must be aware of the costs of contracting out. Public–private partnerships without transparency and accountability create ripe opportunities for corruption. In privatizing, not only do governments lose some control over policy but also private entities may present obstacles to the public good or the government's agenda, as profit or other motives conflict with important public policy goals.[40] When governments pay private sector actors to address global issues, profit motives may distort policy. Although privatization and "moving beyond bureaucracy" are popular buzzwords in today's political climate, changes in state architecture have consequences for how we think about political authority, identity, and organization.

Ideas and networks drawn from experience of global information and economic systems shape new ideas of political organization. A resurgence of IGOs simultaneous with increased attention to local governance may not seem at all strange to a civilization used to surfing the Internet and using a system that is simultaneously globally connected and only as good as the local link.

Rosenau believes that as individuals become more analytically skillful, the nature of authority shifts. People no longer uncritically accept traditional criteria of state authority based on historical, legal, or customary claims of legitimacy. Instead, authority and legitimacy are increasingly based on how well government authorities perform.[41] The high numbers of refugees and migrants voting with their feet seems to support this claim. Thus, while scholars disagree about the sources of identity and authority in the emerging era, they agree that these ideas are changing.

Finally, new forms of political organization have emerged, as evidenced by the European Union and the increasing roles and profile of IGOs. Thus, even if, as Spruyt maintains, the sovereign state is still supreme, three out of four of his indicators of fundamental change are already here: Changes in economy, elites, and ideas are in evidence, and even though no new form of political organization has dethroned the sovereign state, new forms have emerged around the sovereign state that are chipping away at functions previously performed by it and changing its role.

GOING GLOBAL VERSUS GOING LOCAL: LOCAL NETWORKS

New forms of political organization are emerging to accompany these changes. Many cities are prestate actors, many of which existed millennia before the sovereign state. Urbanization accompanies globalization. Urbanization is rapidly increasing; by 2050, two-thirds of the world's populations will live in cities. The mayors of cities are actively creating cooperative networks to address global issues, from climate change and environmental problems to nuclear disarmament to human trafficking. Networks include the Global Covenant of Mayors and the C40 Public–private network, linking city governments with philanthropic foundations, to address climate change and environmental issues. The Mayors for Peace network works to deepen nuclear disarmament.

A Vatican official explained why the Pope has repeatedly convened conferences of mayors to discuss global issues from migration to pollution. "Mayors are the fundamental structures directly elected by the people, and they are the first to feel the real problems and give responses. . . . If mayors commit seriously, people follow them."

Ivo Daalder also lauds **City Diplomacy**, noting that

> the real action is not in nations; it is in their urban centers. It is in cities that the real power beyond sovereign states lies . . . today's

international politics is beginning to resemble the Hanseatic League of medieval cities, with global centres trading and working together to address common problems in ways that large nations do not . . . driving policies that stimulate wider change.[42]

Cities are closer to the issues and more focused on practical solutions, so can provide helpful capacity in addressing global issues. Barber builds a case for a global parliament of mayors to tackle problems. Cities, he argues, are less hamstrung by global tensions as well as by national-level partisan politics. City governments are more closely tied to their citizens and are practical, problem-solvers. They must produce concrete, more immediate results than national-level officials.[43]

Many commentators have noted the irony that globalizing forces are spreading and deepening at the same time that local networks are strengthening, sometimes destructively, as virulent forms of nationalism or tribalism are evident in internal wars.[44] There are several reasons why this is not surprising. First of all, scholars on nationalism note that ties to ethnic or national groups increase under threat.[45] Therefore, it makes sense that at precisely the time when globalizing forces threaten local identities, there is resurgent attention to local ways of life.

Threat is only one piece of the puzzle, however. Transitions to liberal economic and political forms are destabilizing. Virulent nationalisms can be resuscitated as a means of finding a scapegoat for tough times. The fact that there once was a violent form of nationalism does not mean, however, that future conflicts will break out along national or ethnic lines. Many of the most highly developed states today once endured bloody civil wars—the United Kingdom, the United States, and France.

Previous conflict by itself is neither an indicator nor an explanation for later conflict. For example, most journalists and pundits described the cause of conflict in the Balkans as "ancient ethnic hatreds."[46] But this no more explains the conflict than does noting that the sun rose before the fighting took place, and because A came before B, A therefore caused B. Poland and Czechoslovakia also experienced "ancient ethnic hostilities," yet violent nationalism did not plunge these societies into internal war as occurred in the former Yugoslavia. Economic decline was a pivotal trigger in bringing violent nationalism to Yugoslavia, while Poland and Czechoslovakia had gentler transitions from communism. As the economic situation deteriorated in Yugoslavia, politicians sought to protect their own national groups. Leaders exploited nationalist tensions to explain away economic woes and distance themselves from their communist pasts, often using the media as their megaphones of hate.[47] Michael Brown notes that bad leaders, bad neighbors, bad internal problems, and bad neighborhoods can also fire nationalism into internal conflict.[48] Paul Collier notes that countries dependent on natural resource economies, with a youth bulge, a history of conflict in the past five years, and flat or declining economies are particularly vulnerable to "the conflict trap." Conflicts over natural resources fuel and fund continued conflict, and youth are available for recruitment to violence as there are not enough other jobs and economic opportunities. Without other attractive, diversified economic engines there are high incentives to control the public purse by controlling the resources. There is no straight causal line between violent nationalism in the past and violent nationalism in the future. However, states undergoing difficult transitions are more vulnerable to such violent forms.

Going global and going local are connected in another way as well. Many studies over the past twenty years show a correlation between indicators of open societies, open economies, and open technologies and government decentralization. States that increased in globalization (and market, technological, and societal openness) over the time period also increased in government decentralization (the amount of money and decision-making power that went to the local government level as opposed to the central government). States that stayed closed in the same time period did not experience government decentralization. This correlation between globalization and decentralization occurred around the world, in countries as diverse as the United States, India, China, Latin America, Italy, the United Kingdom, and Western Europe. Correlation is not causation, and so the forces of open economy, open technology, and open society and government decentralization might be caused by some third factor (the IMF, for example, as international investors pressure states both to decentralize governments and to privatize markets). But evidence does show that there are "simultaneous trends in globalization and decentralization."[49] Decentralization and open society, open market, and open technology forces go together.

By this view it is not an accident that the highly centralized states of the communist Soviet Union and Eastern Europe, the apartheid state of South Africa, the military regimes in Argentina, and the social welfare states of the United Kingdom and the United States all underwent decentralization simultaneously. Big government has been downsized all over the planet. Even when leaders and populations have wanted to increase government activity in response to the economic recession, it has been difficult to do;[50] power increasingly moves to local governments in federated systems, and to nonstate actors. Sometimes the central state government retains authority over certain functions but no longer performs the functions itself, as when Australia contracts refugee camps out to private companies or the United States hires private military companies to serve as soldiers, and hires private companies to spy.

Global changes occurring today are creating new, complex, and decentralized systems of networks that are radically different from the old centralized systems of governance which controlled the process of international activities and decision-making.[51]

How can it be that local government is making a comeback all over the globe at the same time that IGOs are becoming more important? The state is networking with several actors simultaneously: IGOs, NGOs, MNCs, and local governments. Horizontal networking now matches vertical hierarchy as an organizing principle. The strong, hierarchical central governments of the twentieth century—the fascist states, the communist states, even the Roosevelt social security state—are receding. In the twenty-first century, the sovereign state remains. But it increasingly must network with a wide variety of actors in order to address global issues. The sovereign state is changing and new forms of political organization are emerging, will change take centuries this time around? When sovereignty emerged, competing political forms coexisted for centuries before feudalism receded and the sovereign state emerged as the standard. Skeptics believe that it will take a similarly long time before current changes in economic or social structures mount a fundamental challenge to the sovereign state system, in part because those who benefit from the existing state system will fight to keep it. But the end of feudalism and the rise of sovereignty took place in an era when the modes of transportation and communication were horseback and slow-moving ships. Might change occur more quickly now in an era of cell phones, jet planes, e currency, and the Internet?

The rate of change is different from what it used to be. As Susan Strange notes,

> What is new and unusual is that all (or nearly all) states should undergo substantial change of roughly the same kind within the same short period of twenty or thirty years. The last time that anything like this happened was in Europe when states based on a feudal system of agricultural production geared to local subsistence gave way to states based on a capitalist system of industrial production for the market. The process of change was spread over two or three centuries at the very least and in parts of eastern and southern Europe is only now taking shape. In the latter part of the twentieth century, the shift has

not been confined to Europe and has taken place with bewildering rapidity.[52]

Ideas spread instantaneously in an era of wireless, mobile satellite networks, as fast as a cellular network connection. The "one world" advertising themes of Nike, Microsoft, and Coca Cola are reality, not aspirational, for many parts of the planet, particularly for urban areas. Technological and economic change has been rapid, while democracy moves slowly. But people make politics. Experiences of networked connectivity bring political changes, particularly as democracy spreads across the globe, bringing more people into participatory self-governance.

The idea of punctuated equilibrium draws the analogy that institutional change may occur rapidly over a limited period of time in unexpected ways. Rather than the Darwinian idea of change as slow, steady, continuous, and gradual, punctuated equilibrium stresses that change is "usually accomplished rapidly when a stable structure is stressed beyond its buffering capacity to resist and absorb. . . . These evolutionary shifts can be quirky and unpredictable as the potentials for complexity are vast."[53]

The fast rate of change that open economy, society, and technology forces have unleashed has outpaced the rate of change of sovereign states to keep up with new environmental circumstances. This is particularly important as more states become democratic, because democratic state institutions are often slow to act, with opportunities for gridlock and delay built into the state structure. Democracy was never organized to be effective or efficient. Shared powers and separate institutions with checks and balances among them is a hedge against tyranny, not a recipe for efficiency. By putting different parts of government at each other's throats, it was hoped that government might stay off the people's backs and that deliberation and perspective might result from democratic procedures. Tyranny has many faults, but it can act quickly. The government does what the ruler says, whether it is right, just, legal, or in the public interest. The Nazi government, for example, was chillingly systematic and efficient in its use of industrial technology to conduct the Holocaust. The Syrian government was efficient in attacking its own citizens with chlorine barrel bombs. Government becomes much more slow and bothersome when those in charge have to consult others about what to do, and when they have to factor in civil rights, civil liberties, and accountability to the law. In an era of cell phones, high-speed Internet, and laptop computers, where the economy and technology place great value on speed and efficiency, we forget that democratic institutions were not built for speed. As Alexis de Toqueville noted, the miracle of the system is that it works at all.

If the rate of external change vastly exceeds the institution's ability to respond, then will sovereign institutions be stressed beyond their ability to evolve and adapt? Buffeted by external blows, sovereignty continues to limp along, pocked by capacity, jurisdiction, and other institutional gaps. But as the speed of technological change outpaces the sovereign state's ability to hobble and hotwire responses, the limp may become more pronounced and perhaps (though no time soon) eventually alter or overtake the sovereign state.

SOVEREIGNTY AND THE CHANGING SHIP OF STATE

At what point do we have a new ship of state? Scholars agree that change is occurring. The sovereign state is not obsolete and will continue to play a role along with other actors on the international scene. But there is disagreement over sovereignty's future. We are in a period of transition. We do not know yet whether the state can be retrofitted to weather the storms of changes in technology, economy, elites, and ideas, or whether these changes will someday bring about new forms of political organization.

The situation is analogous to a famous puzzle in the study of philosophy: the ship of Theseus. There are three different ways the ship of Theseus problem is discussed. The first stems from its origins in Greek mythology. Theseus was the son of Aegeus, the king of Athens. Theseus sailed away to fight a heroic battle, but after slaying the Minotaur, he forgot to change the sails to indicate the victory to his father. Sailing in the same old sails unwittingly brought about tragedy, as his father did not realize the battle had been won because the changed situation was not immediately apparent by viewing his son's ship. In a fit of despair, Theseus's father committed suicide, throwing himself from a cliff into the sea.[54] The analogy here is to the adaptability of our state institutions. Many of our foreign policy institutions were built to fight strong states, not weak states and global problems. We have not changed our institutional sails consistent with the new situation, and we flirt with disaster and unintended consequences by traveling with our old sails.

The more pressing analogy, however, concerns the other two ways in which the problem of the ship of Theseus is discussed, questioning the nature of change and identity. If the planks of a ship are removed one by one over intervals of time, and each time an old plank is removed it is replaced by a new plank, then is it a new vessel? At what point did it reach critical mass to call it something new?[55]

This is the question we now face in considering the sovereign state. In chapter 1, we considered ten functions of states that Susan Strange believed are either no longer being performed or are at least being shared with other, nonstate actors. William Zartman posts his own list. In discussing failed or weak states that are collapsing, he lists five basic roles states perform: as the decision-making center of government; as a symbol of identity; as controller of territory and guarantor of security; as an authoritative and legitimate political institution; and as a system of socioeconomic organization, the target of citizen demands for providing supplies or services.[56] Although Zartman offers this list as a litmus test for when weak states are failing because basic state functions are no longer being performed, many of these functions correspond with Strange's and other authors' observations of roles that all states (weak and strong) formerly undertook but no longer fulfill.

The chapters of this book show that states are no longer the sole decision-making centers. MNCs, IGOs, and NGOs increasingly make decisions about matters that were traditionally handled by states. Economic decisions increasingly take place in corporate boardrooms, on the floors of international stock exchanges, and in the conference rooms of the IMF, and states increasingly react to, rather than generate, these key decisions. States are being challenged as symbols of identity and as authoritative, legitimate political institutions. Even strong states no longer can unilaterally control territory or borders or secure territory from external threats.

Alternative institutions—from MNCs to NGOs and IGOs—are increasingly the targets of citizen demands for services that citizens do not believe the state can supply. If the sovereign state is no longer performing the basic functions associated with sovereign states, then at what point does sovereignty cease? If the primary innovation of the sovereign state was its connection of exclusive authority to territory, then what does it mean for sovereignty if the state's connection to territory is being changed, and states derive less authority or power from territory, and if authority is becoming disaggregated and overlapping, particularly as the state contracts out functions to the private sector? Rosenau argues that authority is no longer automatically conferred to the traditional sources on the basis of customary legitimacy claims, be they legal or geographic, but that people are instead judging legitimacy and authority on the basis of performance. If sovereignty is no longer about territory, then what is it about? If territory is at the heart of sovereignty and territory is removed, then is what's left still sovereignty?

War and violence are declining. If sovereignty was about protecting people from the security threats of war, and war and violence of all forms are declining, and states increasingly pay private companies to provide security, is sovereignty less relevant as its main function becomes less threatened? How many planks must be pulled for us to recognize sovereignty today as something different than sovereignty in the past?

There are differences in the analogy between sovereignty and the changes that occurred to the ship of Theseus. The ship's planks were replaced exactly in the same manner and to fulfill the same functions. The planks were not altered to turn the ship into a rocket. In the case of sovereignty, however, both the structures and the functions of sovereignty are changing. The changes this volume discusses are not just changes in sovereignty's face or outward appearance; they are changes in its nature. Unlike the ship of Theseus, the ship of state is changing the very functions it performs and how it performs them. If sovereignty is as sovereignty does, and what sovereignty does is changing, is sovereignty itself changing?

The final analogy with the ship concerns the nature of change. Some philosophers argue for foundationalism—that sound principles need to be laid out first before new concepts can be built on them. But Otto Neurath argues that we seldom have the luxury of changing our ideas in a pristine vacuum and starting from scratch. Instead he argues that "we are like sailors who must rebuild their ship on the open sea, never able to dismantle it in dry dock and to reconstruct it there out of the best materials."[57]

Certainly this is analogous to the descriptions of change offered by political psychologists, as forged in experience. Humans learn by doing. As we experiment with states contracting out, networking with various organizations including public–private partnerships, we learn new ways of thinking about human organizations. These experiences are changing how we exercise and think about sovereignty. The ship's wheel is being replaced while the ship is still in operation. New planks are added and old functions are jettisoned while we are under way. Private sector actors are arising and assuming functions that states used to perform. New policies toward global problems are evolving, utilizing nonstate sectors at the same time that state responses are being fine-tuned. We are not dry-docked and awaiting the emergence of a new ship of political organization, but we must go forward while we are in the midst of major construction.

The problem with our ability to track changes in the sovereign state is that we are used to the system. We are not good even at contemplating what the alternatives to sovereignty might look like. We are truly conceptual prisoners. Cognitive psychology tells us that we are often not able to see or register change, even when it is right in front of our eyes. We see the world and process information through the prism of our past expectations, and so are often unable to even process new information that does not conform to our preconceptions. Ideas matter, and outdated ideas can kill. Changes can occur in unintended ways, and they can occur rapidly when threshold effects are reached. Even though Krasner concludes that the sovereign state "will not be dislodged easily, regardless of changed circumstances in the material environment" and that sovereignty is so entrenched that "[i]t is now difficult to even conceive of alternatives," he acknowledges that surprises are possible.[58]

The *Titanic* was a supposedly unsinkable ship that hit an iceberg in the dark and sank within hours, killing more than 1,500 passengers and crew members. Similarly, the sovereign state is hitting many unforeseen obstacles in the dark side of globalization. Gaps in our institutions are already painfully apparent. Because the seas of change are turbulent, we have a moral obligation to think about the unthinkable, build better institutions, and consider alternatives if the impossible were to occur and the ship of sovereignty turned out not to be unsinkable after all.

CONCLUSIONS: COOPERATE OR DIE

We have more people and more countries, in more close connection, than ever before in human history. Remarkably, so far we have been able to reduce war and extreme poverty, even while population is rising into unprecedented high numbers. Global problems are increasing in speed; some are also increasing in number, such as environmental degradation and transnational crime. To coordinate among more people and more countries in more contact than ever before, we must build better means of coordinating and cooperating than ever before. We need to scale up and speed up, our cooperative processes, to keep pace with the scale and speed of the global problems we face, from climate change to nuclear weapons to cyber security. We urgently need to create new models, plural, of how to better organize humans. **Networked sovereignty** is a practical way to leverage existing networks to address global issues. This organizational pluralism does not portend creation of a singular replacement for sovereignty. Networked sovereignty develops out of our experiences of technological, economic, and social change as our ideas about organization are informed by the new organizational networks we use in everyday life, in the marketplace, cellular networks, social media, and the Internet.

Sovereignty is not going away, but it is networking, evolving, decentralizing, and contracting out. States increasingly coordinate policy among a wider variety of networks of public and private actors. Richard Neustadt describes a US political system in which the president is more powerful than other political actors but rarely has the ability to command or compel. Instead, the president must persuade others to pursue his preferred outcomes.[59]

The sovereign state is in a similar position. It rarely has the power to command or compel outcomes on global problems. Instead, states have to serve roles as coordinators, facilitators, initiators, and salesmen in order to persuade action on global problems among groups of networks. This places burdens on state institutions, requiring organizational changes and adding more functions for states to undertake though not necessarily control. Neustadt notes that an increase in duties does not equate to an increase in power or in the capacity to fulfill new duties, and that adding more duties without means is equivalent to being a glorified clerk, not a powerful entity. Sovereignty remains important in the mix of organizational pluralism, but networked sovereignty is messy. We are experiencing competing and collaborating mixes of cross-cutting, nonhierarchical, ad hoc, and relative forms of order and organization.

Yet integrating action among a wider variety of networks and players also opens new opportunities for policy and offers greater possibilities for effectively managing global issues than old-style, unilateral state responses. NGOs and MNCs frequently "forum shop"—that is, move an issue across borders to a more hospitable institutional venue for a chance at better resolution. We are no longer stuck with autonomous sovereignty only. We can often choose from and move among a variety of networks and institutions. We are engaged in an exciting period of organizational pluralism and experimentation. Global issues have gone beyond sovereignty. We must also go beyond sovereignty in theory and in practice, changing our ideas and our institutions to better respond to the life-and-death challenges of globalization's gaps.

We are cooperating in a variety of networks. States have created many formal regional organizations, IGOs, conventions and treaties, to better cooperate and coordinate action on a host of global issues, from human trafficking to healing the hole in the ozone layer. Private sector MNCs coordinate action informally to manage cybersecurity threats and threats to their global supply chains. NGOs have effectively worked together in transnational advocacy networks, advancing issues from the anti-poverty millennium development goals to bans on landmines, cluster munitions, and nuclear weapons. Public–private partnerships are effectively fighting diseases from HIV/AIDS to ebola. Local and regional governments are building effective networks to combat climate change and environmental problems, such as the Global Covenant of Mayors, and C40 network. State and nonstate networks must develop better ways to work together and leverage networks on global issues, for example, on environmental issues, particularly climate change.

We have creatively constructed new channels of cooperative action on many global issues. But we face a time constraint. We have more people and more countries on the planet than ever before. We are continuing to expand the size of our human family, from 7.6 billion today to upward of 9 to 11 billion people living on planet earth. Can we scale up and speed up our cooperative networks, before more people die from the fast and massive scale global issues we face? People die every day from pollution. People are dying every day from climate change, of malnutrition as climate change kills traditional farming's ability to bring food to the table. Record numbers of refugees die every day while running for their lives, trying to hike or swim or boat to safety, away from violent actors, and from the storms and floods and droughts of climate change that have taken their homes. Fish die every day from pollution and overfishing. Animals, birds, etc., are dying every day from loss of habitat. Entire species are dying every day from loss of habitat, pollutants, and other killers of biodiversity. We must create better ways to cooperate, before we kill our planet and ourselves.

We have created better cooperation before. At the end of World War II, we created the United Nations, the IMF, the World Bank, the EU, NATO, and many other channels of cooperation and coordination, in order to stave off World War III. These creative methods worked, and we were able to effectively lessen the problem of war. Wars are now much less prevalent, and much less deadly, despite the increase in countries and population.

After the bloodiest century in human history, we created better means of advancing peace and prosperity. Democratization and economic development averted wars saved lives and averted wars. But democratization has now stalled. And economic development has yet to unlock the education and employment potential of the world's youngest countries. Any solutions must scale up to handle much larger populations than in any previous period of human history.

Globalization's open societies, open economies, and open technology infrastructure are not random or automatic creations. These were each the work of human hands, labors of cooperation. Cell phones, social media, computers, the Internet—all these technologies that have transformed our lives, and the connections among them, were not created by a single individual. All these technologies connect us, and are themselves evidence of our cooperative abilities to invent new forms of cooperation. The same is true of the spread of democratization globally. Nonviolence resistance movements have succeeded in ending authoritarian regimes and moving countries on the path to greater citizen participation and cooperation in self-government. Stephan and Chenoweth show that expanded participation and mobilization is key to the success of nonviolent movements. Ironically, participation is key in order to create new democratic, participatory political systems. Likewise, while we often envision economics as a zero-sum game of competition, in reality markets are cooperative. No business, no marketplace, especially a global marketplace, is possible without building extensive cooperative and coordinating networks. These inventions were created by groups working together, globally. The global market allows us to cooperate in commerce, and is itself built by networks that allow and facilitate cooperation.

Humanity has survived these 200,000 years due to our prosocial capacities that created ever more complex cooperation. Now we must deepen and expand our circle, to include living in more healthy relationships with the environment and with each other. We live in an era of greater connectedness. We are learning how to create networks of networks, to leverage our relationships and connections in order to address global challenges whose scope and speed exceed the reach of autonomous sovereignty. Networked sovereignty is practical and resilient, a needed way to try to increase our connections and address the capacity and jurisdiction gaps exacerbated by globalization. But networked sovereignty is also messy, shifting, and complex, and needs methods of transparency and accountability, in order to address globalization's participation, legitimacy, and ethics gaps. We need to scale up our cooperation, and speed up the pace of our cooperative inventions. Through networked sovereignty, we are working to better connect diverse networks, to coordinate and cooperate in addressing global issues that move beyond sovereignty. We've done it before; we can do it again.

KEY TERMS

DISCUSSION QUESTIONS

1. How can we bridge the gaps between the sovereign states we have, and the coordinating capacities we need, to address the global issues we face?
2. Give examples of the five different types of institutional gaps (capacity gaps, jurisdiction gaps, participation gaps, legitimacy gaps, and ethical gaps). What experiences have you had with these types of gaps?
3. Most attempts to address global issues have used state-centric approaches, of internal state capacity building and building capacity for cooperation among states. What are the pros and cons of this approach? Offer some examples.
4. What examples have you experienced of private sector approaches to address global issues?
5. What are the pros and cons of public–private partnerships?
6. How do globalization and decentralization go together?
7. What is City Diplomacy?
8. What is the Ship of Theseus puzzle in philosophy? How does it apply to changes in sovereignty?
9. What is networked sovereignty?
10. Cooperate or die. What is the reasoning behind this statement? What evidence supports this statement? Describe why, or why not, you find this conclusion persuasive?

Glossary

■ ■ ■

3 "I's" Religious actors bring 3 "I's" to global issues institutions, ideas, and imagination. Institutions provide the "goody bag" of health, food, education, development, and emergency services, provided by networks of religious institutions, hospitals, schools, charities, etc. Ideas are the religious norms and reasons for actions on global issues. Imagination is the ability to reframe or think about current issues through the lens of religious symbols, stories, metaphors, or ideas.

1948 Convention on the Prevention and Punishment of the Crime of Genocide International law which outlawed genocide, defined as acts committed to "destroy, in whole or in part, a national, ethnical, racial or religious group." This includes killing, causing serious bodily or mental harm to members of the group, and it applies whether the offenses took place in war or peacetime, and applies not only to individuals but also to communities.

1948 Universal Declaration of Human Rights The international agreement that forms the foundation of international human rights law

1951 UN Convention on Refugees The cornerstone of national and international laws on treatment of refugee. 145 countries are party to the refugee convention.

accountability politics Is holding governments, corporations and organizations responsible to comply with their previously stated commitments. NGOs contrast an organization's words with their deeds, and challenge them to live up to their legal and moral obligations, and to their mission statements, corporate advertising image, and values.

African Union (AU) The regional organization of fifty-five African countries, created in 2002 as the successor organization to the previous Organization of African Unity (or OAU, which was active from 1963 to 1999).

agricultural subsidies Payments to local farmers and agricultural producers, to prevent goods from developing countries from reaching their markets.

Al Qaeda A Saudi Arabia–based terrorist organization, which began to support Muslim fighters against the Soviet Union's invasion of Afghanistan, and went on to conduct the September 11, 2001, attacks against the United States.

anocracy Governments which are in transition from autocracy to democracy. This form of government is not very effective in combating insurgency.

"Atoms for Peace" program President Eisenhower created this program in the 1950s, in which research and material for the "peaceful uses" of the atom for nuclear energy, medicine, and research were shared with other countries, in return for their pledge never to develop nuclear weapons. This "grand bargain" became the basis of the NPT.

Anti-Apartheid movement The nonviolent social movement in South Africa that led to the peaceful transition of power away from a regime based on racial segregation.

arbitration clauses Determine who has the authority to decide controversies and usually include a reference to the specific rules that will guide arbitration. Arbitration courts have established procedures and remedies that can be adopted or amended by the terms of a contract, and the arbiters have powers similar to those of sovereign courts.

ASEAN The Association of Southeast Asian Nations, a regional human rights body, a regional human rights charter this body can only reference general international rights

Asian Infrastructure Investment Bank (AIIB) Belt and Road Initiative China's effort to boost trade by building a global network of ports, highways, railways, and pipelines to enhance China's dominance of regional trade routes.

asylum An ancient legal principle, codified in the Refugee Convention and in Article 14 of the Universal Declaration of Human Rights, which states that "Everyone has the right to seek and to enjoy in other countries asylum from persecution."

Aum Shinrikyo Japanese terrorist group.

Aurora Project A research effort to determine the vulnerability of critical infrastructure to cyberattacks which sought to destroy critical infrastructure, not just to shut it off or disrupt or deny service. In the exercise, an electric power generator was blown up by cyberattacks on the electronic controls.

ballistic missiles Rocket-propelled, guided weapons which carry either conventional or nuclear warheads (bombs) and follow a high arc trajectory toward a predetermined target

Biological Weapons Convention International law banning the use, development, possession, production, stockpiling and transfer of biological weapons, signed in 1972, which entered into force in 1975.

biopiracy In which seeds and plants and indigenous knowledge from poor countries are patented by individuals and companies in rich countries.

black carbon Sooty, particulate matter from burning fossil fuels in gas or diesel engines, coal-fired power plants, and also from burning wood and other biomass. The particulate matter from black carbon inserts itself into the tissue of the lungs.

Bloody Sunday The British Army's firing into a crowd of unarmed Irish Catholic civil rights protestors, killing thirteen civilians in Londonderry on January 30, 1972, which led to the establishment of the Provisional Irish Republican Army and increased sympathy for the IRA's cause for a time.

boomerang politics A type of forum shopping that moves an issue to a different arena in order to escape blocked local politics.

botnets Groups of computers or other smart devices which are compromised by malware and used as zombie robot IT armies to carry out and spread cyberattacks. Every 40 seconds a cyberattack is launched

cannabis Another name for the drug marijuana

cap and trade A system that creates incentives for companies to engage in deeper environmental protection by putting a price on pollution and allowing companies to profit from environmental protection.

capacity gaps Shortfalls in organizations or organizational strength, competence, resources, personnel, or standard operating procedures that hinder an actor's ability, particularly a state's ability, to effectively respond to problems of globalization.

carbon sinks Trees capturing carbon so it is harmless. With fewer trees, more carbon is released into the atmosphere, exacerbating global climate change. Carbon levels are at their highest levels ever, and so are global temperatures, and extreme weather events.

Casino Capitalism The economic system's drive for short-term, quick profits over slower, lower risk growth. This pressure for fast, risky, high returns, creates banks and financial companies who gamble with investor's money, creating and spreading high risk over the larger financial system.

Computer Emergency Response Team (CERT)   Public–private partnerships to help detect and respond to information intrusion problems

Chemical Weapons Convention   International law signed in 1993 (which entered into force in 1997), which bans the use, possession, development, production, stockpiling, and transfer of chemical weapons.

child laborers   Workers who are children, who often work in hazardous working conditions, rather than attending school.

child soldiers   Soldiers who are sent to battle as children. Children are often forced to commit heinous war crimes, to sever their ties with their home communities. This helps ensure that they will not be accepted back into their home communities, therefore must stay and serve the armed group. Child soldiers suffer long-lasting damage from their time as child soldiers, particularly children who are raped and suffer sexual violence, such as girls forced to be "wives" and sex slaves of the armed fighters.

Chinese triads, Japanese Yakuza, Italian Camorra and Italian-American mafia   International criminal cartels from China, Japan, Italy, and the United States, respectively.

chlorofluorocarbons (CFCs)   A chemical widely used in refrigerators and air conditioners, had created a "hole" in the atmosphere's protective layer of ozone, which shields humans from the most harmful UVB rays of the sun.

choice of law   An agreement which allows a party to avoid local law and remove issues from local courts by predetermining where controversies will be resolved and under whose law the controversy will proceed.

City Diplomacy   A policy approach which focuses on cooperation among cities in addressing global issues. Cities are closer to the issues and more focused on practical solutions, so can provide helpful capacity in addressing global issues.

Cluster Munitions Coalition   A global civil society network active in over 100 countries, working to eradicate cluster munitions, prevent further casualties, and end the suffering caused by these weapons.

communal land rights   Property held by a community or group. Most indigenous societies have communal land rights.

Conflict Minerals Transparency law   A US law (section 1502 of the Dodd Frank Wall Street Reform and Consumer Protection Act) which required transparency of company supply chains and reporting of the use of conflict minerals. Companies that listed on the Securities and Exchange Commission had to publicly disclose whether their products had conflict minerals in their supply chains. There were no fines or sanctions for companies that used minerals from conflict areas; it simply requires transparency so consumers can make informed choices.

conflict trap   A pattern of recurring violence that occurs in countries with a youth bulge, flat or declining economy, a natural resource-dependent economy, and a history of previous violence.

Convention on Cluster Munitions   An international law that bans the use, production, transfer, and stockpiling of cluster munitions, and requires removal of the weapons and assistance to victims of cluster munitions. A majority of countries, including a majority of NATO countries, are parties to the treaty. The United States is not, but has not used cluster munitions since 2003 and had a policy from 2008 to 2018 of removing cluster munitions from US arsenals and war plans. The Trump administration has reversed course.

Convention on the Rights of the Child   International treaty to ban the Sale of Children, Child Prostitution and Child Pornography

Convention on Biodiversity   It commits countries to consider biodiversity protection a common concern of humankind, and to take measures to conserve all levels of biodiversity—of genetic material, of species, and of entire ecosystems. The Convention entered into force on December. 29, 1993, and calls for conservation, sustainable use, and fair sharing of the benefits derived from the use of genetic materials.

corporate social responsibility (CSR)   Businesses self-regulate (or work together with other businesses and NGOs) to improve their environmental and human rights impacts.

counterproliferation   The full range of operational, primarily military preparations and activities to reduce and protect against the threat posed by WMD weapons and delivery means. Counterproliferation is a blend of vertical and horizontal prevention efforts focused on preventing the use of WMD weapons.

Crimea   The area of Ukraine currently occupied by Russia.

criminal sovereignty   The co-optation of the state by criminal elements.

crypto currencies   Currencies are not issued by governments or regulated by governments, and are not transparent. Europol notes that bitcoin was used in 40 percent of illicit transactions in the European Union, including in payments between criminals in many high-profile investigations.

Cooperative Threat Reduction program (CTR)   A bipartisan program created by Senators Sam Nunn and Richard Lugar in late 1991, as the Soviet Union was collapsing. The program helped Kazakhstan,

Ukraine, and Belarus safely dispose of over 7,000 nuclear weapons left behind by the Soviet Union, along with the weapons infrastructure. CTR also helped Russia to safely reduce its nuclear weapons and implement its arms control commitments under START, and to safely secure and protect its remaining weapons from theft or accident.

Cyber Code of Conduct A set of voluntary cybersecurity norms, proposed by UN members, which include eleven basic but important norms, such as that states should not knowingly allow their territory to be used for internationally wrongful cyber acts; should not conduct or knowingly support ICT activities that intentionally damage critical infrastructure; and should seek to prevent the proliferation of malicious technologies and the use of harmful hidden functions.

Cybersecurity Framework Voluntary standards and practices "to guide industry in reducing cyber risks to the networks and computers that are vital to the nation's economy, security and daily life." The Cybersecurity Framework was created with input from both the public and private sectors, in an attempt to harmonize best practices. The Cybersecurity Framework focuses on cybersecurity *processes* applicable across many different types of IT environments and industries.

DARPA The Defense Advanced Research Projects Agency, a US government agency which created both the internet and the dark net for use by the US military and defense researchers.

Dark Net A place beneath the surface web for people who want to remain anonymous on the Internet.

de-Baathification policy The US policy of firing all Iraqi government workers, making no distinction between those who were guilty of war crimes and those who were simply government workers, in an attempt to minimize the influence of former followers of deposed dictator Saddam Hussein. This policy backfired, undermining the Iraqi government's capacity, and creating animosity toward the United States which brought about the creation of Al Qaeda in Iraq, ISIS, and the insurgency in Iraq and Syria.

debt bonded labor When people are forced to work without pay to pay off a debt or supposed debt. Such "debt" can be passed on to the children and future generations.

Dell theory The idea that economic interdependence brings peace, as Thomas Friedman notes that "no two countries that are both part of a major global supply chain, like Dell's [computers], will ever fight a war against each other as long as they are both part of the same global supply chain."

democratic peace theory The idea and the empirical record showing that democratic states do not go to war with other democratic states.

descent-based slavery Slavery which is continued across generations of a family and/or class. People are "born into slavery" and the status of slave passes from mother to child when a family or class is considered by a society to have "slave" status.

differentiation of political and religious institutions Autonomy and separation between state and religious institutions and authorities.

digital divide The gap between those who have access to computers, the Internet, and modern information technology world

Directive on Security of Network and Information Systems (NIS) An EU regulation which requires all EU member states to create "Computer Security Incident Response Teams" (the CSIRT s Network), dedicated to sharing information about risks and ongoing threats and cooperating on specific cybersecurity incidents.

Disarmament, Demobilization, and Reintegration (DDR) A standard tool of de-escalating conflict and restoring relations after a conflict. DDR often includes compensation to war victims and economic development opportunities to spur defense conversion to civilian economic activities.

"Dracula" politics A type of transparency politics that works to expose particularly bad deeds to public light. The fictional character Dracula could not survive in the light of day. NGOs apply the same process to global issues. Will a particular policy or practice be able to survive in the daylight?

early and forced "marriage" A form of human trafficking in which over 15 million girls and women are forced into "marriage," without their consent, often in order to earn money for their families or to relieve their families of responsibility for the costs of raising the child, or as a result of rape. Girls in refugee camps are particularly vulnerable.

Economic and Social Council (ECOSOC) The UN's main forum for addressing economic and social issues, and is tasked with coordinating the activities of the many specialized agencies, some of which existed before the UN, such as the International Labor Organization and the World Meteorological Organization.

electronic Pearl Harbor The threat of a surprise and strategically devastating cyberattack

Eligible Receiver The Pentagon conducted this early top-secret, joint-staff-run exercise, to test the security of US critical infrastructure (such as power grids, the Internet, financial networks) in 1997. A team of twenty National Security Agency agents, working for only three months and using software which was readily available on the Internet, showed how vulnerable US infrastructures were to cyberattacks. They accessed unclassified computer systems, demonstrating that (if they had wanted to) they could have shut down command and control functions for the military's Pacific Command as well as the entire US power grid merely by disrupting computer control networks. The exercise scared many people.

environmental crimes The third largest category of global illegal activities, behind drug trafficking and counterfeit goods and medicines. Environmental crimes include illegal logging, fishing, mining, oil extractions, hazardous waste dumping, etc.

environmental Kuznet's curve Based off the inverted (upside-down) U-shaped graph economists call a Kuznet's curve, this theory maintains that economies go through a "dirty development" phase of economic development, so initially as countries develop their economy, the levels of pollution increase. But that reaches a limit (at the top of the inverted U curve), after which increased economic prosperity tends to correlate with increased environmental protection. The idea draws from an implied "levels of need" whereby only after basic economic needs are met do people worry about environmental protection.

environmental refugees The increasing number of people fleeing increased high-intensity storms, "natural disasters," and other environmental problems.

ethical or values gaps Arise when globalization is perceived either to have no ethical base or to promulgate values that are at odds with societal values or the common good.

European Union (EU) A supranational IGO which binds its twenty-eight members into a common market, money, and laws.

e-waste Electronic waste such as phones and computers. The United States leads the world in e-waste. Each American throws away an average 176 pounds of e-waste per year. The global average is far less waste, about 13 pounds per person per year.

FARC The Fuerzas Armadas Revolucionarias de Colombia, or Revolutionary Armed Forces of Colombia, the largest guerrilla group in Colombia's long civil war. The Colombian peace accord disarmed FARC and allows members of the FARC to peacefully enter politics.

fentanyl A powerful and deadly synthetic opioid that is 80–100 times stronger than morphine, which China exports

Finn, Beatrice Awarded the Nobel Peace Prize in 2017 for her work as a leader of ICAN.

First Amendment of the US Constitution A key foundation of international religious freedom of belief and conscience, which states that the US "Congress shall make no law respecting an establishment of religion, or prohibiting the free exercise thereof; or abridging the freedom of speech, or of the press; or the right of the people peaceably to assemble, and to petition the Government for a redress of grievances." While binding only to the United States, this has inspired many other countries to include similar language in their laws and constitutions.

Foreign Intelligence Surveillance Act (FISA) A US law which details the oversight procedures for government surveillance activities

foreign direct investment (FDI) When an individual or company in one country buys control or a significant degree of influence on the management of a business in another country. FDI may take many forms: buyouts of a foreign subsidiary, joint ventures, licensing agreements, or strategic alliances.

foreign guest workers Non-citizen workers in temporary worker programs. These workers are particularly vulnerable to forced labor or debt bondage. Their legal status in the country they have entered to work is dependent on their employer.

formal IGOs Intergovernmental organizations established by treaties, charters, or conventions. These generally have permanent headquarters, secretariats, have member states, and a structure.

formal land title Written property rights for land.

Food and Agriculture Organization's (FAO) An IGO which issues nonbinding recommendations concerning food and agriculture, such as the early warning recommendations for famine assistance to countries experiencing food shortages.

forum shopping Moving and pressing an issue of concern in a more favorable arena.

four types of nonstate actors There are four categories of nonstate actors, for profit, nonprofit, legal, and illegal nonstate actors. For example, nonprofit legal nonstate actors are NGOs. For-profit legal nonstate actors are MNCs. Nonprofit, illegal nonstate actors are terrorist organizations. For-profit illegal nonstate actors are criminal cartels. IGOs are groups of state actors, so are more accurately classified as associations of states, but are not properly classified as "nonstate."

"fourth wave" of democratization The spread of participatory, electoral forms of government, which included the dramatic fall of authoritarian dictatorships in the former Soviet states in the 1990s. This fourth wave was "more global in its reach . . . affecting far more countries and more thorough than its predecessors." Democracy is not new and has been around in one form or another since the ancient Greeks. What is new, however, is the number of states from a variety of regions that are turning to representative government forms with free multiparty elections and the protection of individual and minority rights including free speech and free press, freedom of association, freedom of movement, and freedom of religion. For the first time in history, about half of the world's governments are either democracies or in transition to democracy.

General Data Protection Regulation An EU information security regulation, which requires all organizations which collect data from EU citizens (whether or not the entity is located in the EU) to have standard data security and privacy protections in place, including strict rules on controlling and processing personally identifiable information (PII). The regulation notes that "personal data is any information relating to an individual, whether it relates to his or her private, professional or public life. It can be anything from a name, a home address, a photo, an email address, bank details, posts on social networking websites, medical information, or a computer's IP address." Organizations must obtain prior consent of citizens for collection and use of their data, must notify people of why it is collecting their data, how long it is retaining their data, how it is safeguarding it, and must notify people of data breaches. People have the right to not have their data collected and used, and the right to have their data erased at any time. The law permits large fines for organizations that do not comply.

ghost laundering A type of money laundering in which criminals use online sites in the gig economy, such as Uber and Airbnb, set up a fake or ghost account (such as a fake rental property or service provider). Money is paid without receiving the service, in order to transfer cash and create a legal "receipt" for the profit. Since the gig economy is largely unregulated, this can be an effective means of avoiding anti money laundering laws and reporting requirements.

globalization Is the fast, interdependent spread of open economy, open technology, and open society infrastructures.

globalization of solidarity Pope Francis' call for an international, systematic concern for the poor and marginalized, for a global economy that serves people, rather than the globalization of indifference to the poor and vulnerable that too often is promoted.

Great Crime Decline Dramatic decreases in the murder rate and other indicators of violent crime, from the high levels of the 1970s to the early 1990s

green revolution   The effort in agriculture in the 1960s to create more productive and resilient crops which fed millions of people and saved the growing people from starvation. The downside of the green revolution is the overreliance on a few strains of crops and seeds, and the loss of the biodiversity of the food supply.

Hajj   The fifth principle of Islam, which requires that Muslims make a Pilgrimage to Mecca in Saudi Arabia once in their lifetimes, if the individual has the means to do so.

hard law   Legal obligations

honor killings   The practice of murdering a woman in order to reclaim the family's reputation or "honor." A woman who is accused of socially unacceptable behaviors may be killed or brutally mutilated in order to wipe out the "blemish" on a family's good name. Offenses include if the woman is a victim of rape, women who walk without a male relative escort, kissing or engaging in sexual behavior out of wedlock, flirting, failing to serve a meal on time, seeking divorce, or seeking to choose one's own marriage partner rather than accede to an arranged marriage.

horizontal proliferation   The spread of nuclear weapons to more countries that do not currently have nuclear weapons.

house churches   Groups who meet to worship in people's homes to avoid the persecution that might ensue from meeting publicly in official churches.

hyperglobalization   The rapid changes in the scope, speed, and spread of globalization in the information age

International Atomic Energy Organization (IAEA)   Which works to advance safe, secure and peaceful nuclear technologies,

ICBMs   Intercontinental ballistic missiles, long-range missiles capable of carrying nuclear warheads.

International Criminal Court (ICC)   The court only hears cases of genocide, war crimes, and crimes against humanity, and then only as a "court of last resort," when countries ask the ICC to hear a case, either because they are unable or it would be difficult for them to address it, or when the UN Security Council refers a case to the court.

IDP   Internally Displaced Persons

IED   Improvised explosive device, or bomb.

International Monetary Fund (IMF)   Created during World War II at the Bretton Woods conference in order to rebuild and stabilize the global economy after the shocks of the global economic depression and wars. The IMF focuses on stabilizing exchange rates, monetary and fiscal policy. As a nearly universal IGO, with 189 member states (only North Korea, Cuba, Andorra, Lichtenstein, and Monaco are not IMF members), the IMF works to prevent financial crises and contagion, to stop financial problems in one country from spilling over and dragging down the wider international financial, currency and economic system.

informal IGOs   Groups of countries which meet regularly to address common issues, but do not have permanent headquarters, staff, or membership dues. Examples include the G-7 and G-20 meetings of countries with the world's largest economies.

information politics   Credibly gathering information and moving it to where it may have the most impact

information warfare   Using cybermethods to implement traditional misinformation and propaganda campaigns.

insurgency   Is a movement to overthrow a government, take over control of some or all of the territory of a country, or force a government into sharing power over the disputed territory. Insurgencies require the support of the population, either actively or indirectly. Insurgent violence targets government and military targets, whereas terrorists deliberately target civilians. Insurgencies are mass movements and aim to grab and hold territory and set up their own governing institutions. Terrorists are smaller, minority, clandestine groups, which do not enjoy much popular support. Insurgencies last long, while most terrorist groups do not last very long. The average length of an insurgency is ten years

integration   To be able to use illegally obtained cash openly because it appears to be legally derived, the final stage of money laundering

Inter-American Human Rights Commission   Based in Washington, DC, an international human rights body for countries in the Americas.

Intergovernmental Panel on Climate Change   A process by which thousands of preeminent scientists around the world provide the best and cutting-edge research on the state of climate change, in order that the countries of the world share information, and base policy on high-quality scientific consensus.

Intermediate Nuclear Forces (INF) treaty   An arms control agreement made by Republican president Ronald Reagan, which first eliminated a whole category of battlefield nuclear weapons. Smaller, tactical nuclear weapons are the most destabilizing, the most vulnerable to theft and accident, so Reagan and Russian president Gorbachev began with eliminating these weapons, but Reagan saw the INF as just the start of creating a world free of nuclear weapons. Reagan wanted the elimination of nuclear weapons, noting "nuclear war can never be won and must never be fought." President Trump has reversed Reagan's policy, and announced he is withdrawing the United States from the INF treaty.

internal codes of conduct   A company's voluntary, internal standards. They vary from broad, general statements of company core values, to specific guidelines for concrete and specific practices.

International Atomic Energy Agency (IAEA)   The UN's nuclear watchdog agency

International Campaign Against Nuclear Weapons (ICAN)   A global civil society network modeled after the ICBL, which successfully advocated for the international ban on nuclear weapons. ICAN was awarded the Nobel Peace Prize in 2017.

International Campaign to Ban Landmines (ICBL)   A global network of actors in over 100 countries working to ban landmines and help landmine survivors.

International Convention for the Suppression of the Financing of Terrorism   Sponsored by the United Nations defines terrorism as "an act intended to cause death or serious bodily injury to any person not actively involved in armed conflict in order to intimidate a population, or to compel a government or an international organization to do or abstain from doing any act."

International Court of Justice (ICJ)   Based in the Hague, the Netherlands, the ICJ is available to hear international law disputes of UN member states if states ask the ICJ for its interpretation. The ICJ is not an international supreme court. It has no jurisdiction over individuals, is not a criminal court, cannot pursue cases or investigations independently, and serves only when member states ask it to hear a specific case between countries and both disputants agree to abide by ICJ findings. The court can hear two types of cases: contentious cases of international legal disputes between UN member states who submit the case to the ICJ, and requests for advisory opinions on legal issues submitted by UN specialized agencies and organs. Fifteen judges are elected by the UN General Assembly and UNSC to serve on the ICJ for nine-year terms. By tradition, these judge positions are distributed geographically, with three judges from Africa (one from Francophone Africa, one from Anglophone Africa, one from Arab Africa), three from Asia, two from Latin America and the Caribbean, two from Eastern Europe, and five from Western states. These totals include one judge from each permanent member of the UNSC. By law, no country can send more than one judge concurrently. The ICJ meets at the Peace Palace, facilities owned and operated by an NGO, the Carnegie Foundation.

Internet Corporation for Assigned Names and Numbers (iCANN) An NGO, not an IGO, that manages the internet address book. Quite deliberately iCANN is not an IGO, as the United States and Internet users fear an IGO would allow repressive governments to try to censor and distort the Internet. But iCANN has some IGO-like characteristics, including a Governmental Advisory Committee with representatives from 170 sovereign states to provide input on Internet governance.

internet of things Computers and information technologies are integrated into things we use in all aspects of life, including banks, stores, credit card machines, ATMs, hospitals, electric grids, gas stations, cars, ports, water systems, and militaries. Theses smart technologies embedded in everything from our keys to cars to surveillance cameras to homes to nuclear power plants were meant to make life easier and more efficient and prosperous, but they also make us vulnerable to attack by anonymous attackers exploiting the very IT we rely on daily.

Irish Republican Army (IRA) A terrorist group in Northern Ireland

issue attention cycle A theory created by Anthony Downes, which shows that when an environmental issue reaches an "alarm" stage and receives a great deal of media and public attention, civil society organizes, voters pressure their elected representatives to address the issue, and eventually elected officials and policy makers act. New laws or policies are created to address the issue. But soon disillusionment sets in as voters become aware of the costs of action and how long it will take to achieve results. Then as voters and officials become bored or disillusioned, attention wanes to the environmental issue and fewer resources are devoted to implementing the new policy. While democracy allows the potential for environmental action, it does not guarantee environmental protection in practice.

Jubilee A transnational advocacy network promoting debt relief for poor countries, based on religious invectives to forgive debt for the poor.

jurisdiction gaps Found when the problem extends farther than the authority of the institutions charged with responding to the problem. Sovereign states are geographically based; their jurisdiction and authority stops at their territorial borders. But global issues easily transcend borders, creating difficulties in crafting responses among a host of sovereign states.

Khan, A.Q. Hailed in Pakistan as the father of the Pakistani nuclear weapons program. Outside of Pakistan, A.Q. Khan is known as a notorious nuclear smuggler, who sold nuclear secrets and centrifuge technologies (for refining uranium to make bomb-grade nuclear explosives) to North Korea, Libya, Iran, and other buyers.

Know Your Customer laws Anti money laundering legislation and policies which apply to banking, and require banks to authenticate who their customers are and where their money comes from. Know Your Customer laws are not generally applied in real estate.

Laudato Si Care for Our Common Home, a Catholic encyclical concerning religious responsibilities to care for the environment, God's creation. This high level of religious teaching, an official letter from Pope Francis, includes the common ground of many religious traditions regarding care for creation. It decries that environmental problems disproportionately kill and harm the world's poorest people.

laws of war The national and international military rules that govern behavior of combatants during conflict (such as the Geneva Conventions and the US military code of justice).

layering Moving illicit profits around through complex, opaque financial transactions to deceive people into thinking that illegal cash came from a legitimate source, the second step of money laundering

legitimacy gaps Found when the institutions that manage or regulate globalization are not perceived by society as rightfully representing them.

leverage politics Using the power, platform, or resources of stronger network members, such as celebrities, on behalf of weaker network members to move a global issue forward.

Lumbini A world heritage site and pilgrimage site in Nepal, by tradition the birthplace of Buddha.

major armed conflicts Wars in which more than 1000 people die in battle-related deaths in a year

megachurches The more than one thousand churches that exist internationally, each drawing congregations of over two thousand worshipers per week, using organizational methods that consciously mimic corporate culture.

migrants Foreign workers who move primarily from middle-income countries to developed countries who lack younger workers willing to do manual labor.

millennium bomber   Benni Antoine Noris, or Ahmed Ressam, who was apprehended by law enforcement before he could conduct an attack in December 1999.

Millennium Development Goals (MDGs)   An agreement of aims by the UN member countries to cut extreme poverty by half by 2015. The MDGs created specific goals and benchmarks for reducing poverty, from increasing girls' education to decreasing maternal mortality rates. NGOs worked with governments to implement the goals, and kept the pressure on to reach these commitments. The MDGs were largely successful, and were replaced with more specific SDGs in 2015.

Mine Ban Treaty   Another name for the quickly formed and highly effective Ottawa Convention, a historic treaty banning the use, stockpiling, production and transfer of a weapon in widespread use, antipersonnel Mines. The Mine Ban treaty also mandates their destruction, and assistance to landmine victims. In each year since the Mine Ban Treaty entered into force, landmine use, production, and stockpiling has decreased while landmine decommissioning, education, and services to landmine victims has increased.

Minamata convention   International environmental agreement limiting and safeguarding mercury use, a highly toxic chemical used extensively in industrial processes and products, from thermometers to lights.

Minamata disease   Health damage caused by mercury poisoning, which harms the brain and sensory system, causing loss of sight, hearing, touch, tremors, brain damage, and birth defects.

Multiple Independently targetable Re-entry Vehicles (MIRV)   A way to put more nuclear bombs on a missile so that separate nuclear warheads could each reach different targets. Imagine the intercontinental missile as a bus bound from the United States to Russia, and each MIRVed nuclear warhead as a passenger departing at separate stops along the way (e.g., Leningrad, Vladivlostok).

Montreal Protocol   International agreement which banned the production of CFCs. Through these actions, ozone coverage is increasing and is expected to heal by 2070, if present trajectories continue.

moral entrepreneurs   Agents who act as reformers or crusaders to change rules out of an ethical concern to curtail a great evil.

mules   Criminal employees who carry bags of currency to make smaller deposits in different banks and businesses, or who travel internationally over borders to deposit the money into lax banks or businesses that do not comply with anti money laundering laws.

multinational corporations (MNCs) Enterprises that control and manage commercial ventures and operations outside their countries of origin. Fueled by open economies and distributed technology, enhanced financial mechanisms and the ease of transborder trade, their power and influence is growing dramatically.

Mutually Assured Destruction (MAD) The key threat in nuclear deterrence theory. Deterrence purports to prevent genocide by threatening genocide.

"name and shame" A type of transparency politics in which bad behavior or policies are exposed, and the specific bad actors and actions are exposed, specifically identified by name, and held up for public scrutiny. Entities with brands, reputations, or images to protect may be particularly vulnerable to name and shame politics.

nation A group with a common cultural, linguistic, ethnic, racial, or religious identity—such as the Navajo nation of the US west or the Kurds in Iraq, Turkey, and Syria. There are 8,000 nations. National boundaries—where various ethnic or linguistic groups are located—are elastic and often do not coincide with sovereign state boundaries. For example, the Basques live on either side of the border between Spain and France, and the Kurds live in Iraq, Turkey, Iran, Armenia, and Syria.

nation-state There is no such thing as a nation-state. All sovereign states are multinational, and have people of more than one national group living within the state's borders. The closest thing to a nation-state, with a one-to-one correspondence between the people of one nation living in the state's borders, is the hermit kingdom of North Korea, but Chinese nationals live in North Korea, and also in most other countries around the world.

North Atlantic Treaty Organization (NATO) A military defensive alliance among 29 countries.

National Cyber Investigative Joint Task Force (NCIJTF) The US government interagency integration unit which includes twenty law enforcement and intelligence community agencies, tasked with coordinating, integrating, and sharing information on cyber threat investigations with domestic impact. Liaison officers from other countries, such as the UK, Canada, and Australia, may also be included.

negative sovereignty A sovereign state's legal right to nonintervention from other states, even in cases when a state abuses its own citizens.

This is sometimes called external sovereignty, Westphalian sovereignty, or nonintervention sovereignty.

network power The benefits in increased speed and adaptability provided by a weblike organizational mode. NGOs are typically organized as flatter, more flexible organizations than governments, IGOs, or MNCs. This may give NGOs greater speed and adaptability to respond to pressing global issues or to get their views to the media faster than some government bureaucracies.

networked sovereignty States increasingly connect in networks, rather than guarding their autonomy from external actors. States link—sideways to other states and nonstate actors, upwards to pooled sovereignty organizations, and downward to local actors. There is no "one size fits all" network model. Choice of the linked networks varies by issue area and political forces. This messy mix is not fixed and hierarchical, but relational and changing. Which actors or network will prevail on any global issue area are context and network dependent.

new security dilemma Actors' efforts to protect against global issues, leveraging networks of state and nonstate actors, without taking actions that make these issues more severe.

National Infrastructure Protection Center (NIPC) A cybersecurity unit of the FBI, later blended into the Department of Homeland Security

noncooperative countries and territories (NCCT) Countries that do not use best practices to curtail money laundering, but instead have lax laws and practices that attract money laundering. Naming noncooperative countries and territories is a way to try to shame them into taking AML action.

Non Proliferation Treaty (NPT) of 1968 An international law in which Nonnuclear states agreed not to develop nuclear weapons (stopping horizontal proliferation of nuclear weapons among more countries) and committed to using nuclear material and research for peaceful purposes, not military arsenals. In return, nuclear armed states agreed not to share nuclear weapons with other countries and to decrease the size of their arsenals (to stop vertical proliferation of nuclear weapons), to move toward disarmament.

nonrefoulement A key principle of refugee law, stating that a refugee must not be returned to a country where they face serious threats to their life or freedom.

nonstate-centric policy approach A policy perspective that emphasizes the importance of the private sector in responding to global problems. It also emphasizes the limitations of trying to work through the state for help in curtailing activities that largely fall in the social and economic sectors where the reach of capitalist, liberal states is the shortest. If state capacity is (or should be) weakening, then why ask the state to solve global problems? Why not go directly to the private sector, where the resources exist to address the problem?

nontariff barriers Measures other than taxes that restrict imports or exports, such as quotas, "buy local"/rule of origin mandates, arcane licensing procedures, or domestic subsidies of local companies to protect them from foreign competition.

NotPetya A cyberattack that mimicked the Petya ransomware, but which destroyed data rather than encrypting it and releasing it for money. Russia targeted Ukraine with the NotPetya attack, and took down the Ukrainian government, airports, hospitals, banks, energy companies, ATMs, credit card machines, and businesses. Foreign companies that had business with Ukrainian companies, like Maersk, Merck, and Fed Ex, were also damaged in the attack.

nuclear deterrence The predominant policy approach to nuclear weapons in countries that have nuclear weapons. According to this theory, a country maintains nuclear weapons, with all their costs and risks in order to persuade nuclear armed adversaries not to use their weapons against us. Deterrence seeks to persuade adversaries that they have nothing to gain from using nuclear weapons because their nuclear attack will trigger a devastating response ensuring their own demise.

Nuclear Posture Review A US overview of nuclear weapons policy. The current NPR orders the creation of new nuclear weapons, and threatens to use nuclear weapons in response to conventional attacks, including attacks against infrastructure of the United States and allies, which may include cyberattacks.

Nuclear Utility Theory (NUT) The policy approach that contends that nuclear weapons ought to be used. US policies of "Massive retaliation," and "flexible response" were based on threatening to use nuclear weapons. Some US military and civilian leaders considered using nuclear weapons in Korea, Vietnam, and Europe. This group, long a minority position, is reviving today.

Nuclear Weapons Free Zones (NWFZ) A majority of countries banned nuclear weapons in their regions through a series of multinational treaties.

Organization for Security and Cooperation in Europe (OSCE) The world's largest regional IGO devoted to security issues, in which fifty-seven European countries share information and coordinate on issues from arms control to counter terrorism.

Organization of American States (OAS) The world's oldest regional organization, consisting of all 35 independent countries in the Americas.

Ostrom, Elinor Nobel Prize winner who studied communities which successfully cooperated to manage environmental common resources. She showed that eight principles work to avoid the destruction of a common resource. Democracies are more likely to have conditions which allow groups to develop these institutions for commons management than nondemocracies.

Ottawa Convention An international treaty banning antipersonnel landmines, a historic treaty due to the speed with which it was reached, its widespread acceptance and implementation against a cheap weapon that had previously been in widespread use. In one of the world's most widely accepted treaties, one hundred sixty-four states are parties to the Ottawa Convention officially titled the Convention on the Prohibition of the Use, Stockpiling, Production and Transfer of Anti-Personnel Mines and on Their Destruction, despite opposition from the United States.

Palermo Convention Another name for the UN Convention Against Transnational Organized Crime (UNTOC or Palermo Convention) which entered into force in 2003. Almost all countries are parties to the treaty (except Somalia, South Sudan, and a few island states).

Panama Papers An investigative journalism project that exposed corporations and individuals who avoided taxes through off shore tax havens, loopholes, and clever, complex processes that manipulate accounting to show "losses," and which move profits to shell company "affiliates" and locales such as Panama.

Paris Climate Agreement A multilateral commitment reached at the COP 2015 meeting, which committed countries to developing their own national plans to reduce emissions, in order to limit the global temperature rise to under 1.5 degrees C.

participation A principal of Just Peace that expands the peace process to include women, youth, and victims of the conflict.

participation gaps Exist when people affected by globalization are excluded from partaking in the decision processes of managing or guiding globalization, earlier described as "democracy deficits."

particulate matter A mixture of solid particles and liquid droplets that can include smoke, soot, dirt, and dust, is dangerous for our lungs, whether the particles are coarse (larger) or fine (smaller). Deforestation adds to the release of particulates, as soils no longer contained by tree roots dry out and blow away as dust. Construction, industrial-scale farming, clear-cutting, mining, especially mountain top removal coal mining, and fracking all release particulates.

pastorpreneurs Religious leaders who use the same niche marketing and economies of scale principles as other successful businesses. They integrate the language and methods of business entrepreneurship with religious organizations, believing their religion to be an "excellent product" deserving of the best sales pitch.

patch and pray A reactive approach to cybersecurity, whereby experts fix known vulnerabilities, hoping they can repair the vulnerabilities in our IT structures faster than adversaries can find and exploit these vulnerabilities.

People's Power The nonviolent social movement that removed the Marcos dictatorship in the Philippines.

perestroika Reform efforts made by the last Soviet leader, Mikhail Gorbachev, to improve the productivity and efficiency of the USSR's state-controlled economy and polity.

personal sovereignty Law is whatever the leader says it is, without democratic process or constraints.

placement To hide the illegal origins of criminally obtained profits, the first step in money laundering.

pooled sovereignty The sharing of decision-making power among states in a cooperative system.

positive sovereignty A state's ability to provide basic capacity to people within its borders, such as law and order, good governance, a generally effective and fair public sector, services to citizens such as education and health services—what academics call internal sovereignty.

positive sovereignty The actual, empirical ability of a state to control its political and economic space, to provide public safety and public services for the people living within a country's territory.

predatory sovereignty When the state preys on its own people.

prestate actors Organizations that existed before the advent of modern sovereign states in 1648, such as religious actors and tribes. Thousands of years before the concept of sovereign countries was ever invented, religious organizations created institutions and performed (and still perform) functions that are today associated with sovereign states. Religious organizations had laws, courts, schools, universities, hospitals, media, humanitarian aid departments, diplomatic emissaries, etc., and registered births, marriages, and deaths, millennia before sovereign states ever created such institutions or engaged in these activities.

Proliferation Security Initiative (PSI) A coalition of 105 participating and supporting states who cooperate to stem proliferation.

protectionist measures Policies which shield local companies from competition from foreign companies through a variety of means including tariffs, subsidies, and quotas. Protectionist obstacles are high in agriculture, the products in which developing countries enjoy comparative advantage.

public–private partnerships A policy perspective to address global issues by combining the benefits of state legitimacy and enforceability with the flexibility and resources of the private sector. In theory this can bring more traction to bear on difficult global issues. In practice, there is a high level of complexity in coordinating such different actors.

Responsibility to Protect (R2P) An international norm established in 2006 which recognizes that states have "the responsibility to protect populations from genocide, war crimes, ethnic cleansing, and crimes against humanity." Primary responsibility lies with the state itself for protection of its own citizens and people living within a state's borders. But in cases where states are unable or unwilling to protect their own people, others also have responsibilities to act to protect civilians from violent mass atrocities.

ransomware Just as criminals kidnap people for ransom money, cyberattackers kidnap computers and data. Ransomware locks computers and encrypts data until victims pay the attackers a ransom in bitcoin or some other anonymous crypto currency. Victims then receive a key to unlock the encryption and release their data and computer systems.

reconciliation Healing the wounds of war, using truth telling, acknowledgment, and other means of restorative justice; it is one of the principals of Just Peace.

refugee Any person who "owing to well-founded fear of being persecuted for reasons of race, religion, nationality, membership of a particular social group, or political opinion, is outside the country of his nationality, and is unable to return to it."

remittances Funds migrant workers send back to their families and communities in their countries of origin. Remittances are a significant source of external capital.

remittance management Systems developed to decrease the cost and increase the benefits of financial transfers from migrant workers to their home economies.

REPAM A transnational advocacy network formed by indigenous religious leaders and Catholic leaders from the Amazon region, in order to protect the indigenous peoples of the Amazon from personal, community, and environmental destruction.

restoration A principal of Just Peace that focuses on people building, rebuilding the whole human person and communities, economically, psychologically, and socially, not simply rebuilding roads and bridges destroyed by war, but rebuilding the human infrastructure.

resurgent religion Rising religiousity around the world at precisely the time when states are challenged. During the mid-twentieth century, states were strong and religion was repressed by a variety of regime types. Religious beliefs and actors went underground during periods of repression, but were not "wiped out." Religious actors helped to end repressive regimes, and rebounded at the end of the twentieth century.

resurrection politics Taking an issue previously deemed "dead on arrival" and raising it up onto the political agenda.

retreating sovereignty Nonstate actors increasingly taking on functions that were traditionally performed by states, even in the security sector.

right relationship Building respectful social connections among groups polarized and harmed by conflict, one of the principals of Just Peace.

Rotterdam Convention International law which requires accurate labeling, prior informed consent, and sharing information about bans of certain toxic chemicals and pesticides such as asbestos and DDT. Information sharing and informed consent are the goals of this treaty, so that companies from countries which banned certain chemicals from domestic use and production, could not sell those products abroad without notification. Nearly all countries, including Canada and the European Union, are parties to the Convention, which took effect in 1998. The United States is not a party to the convention.

Schengen Zone A freedom of movement "neighbor admission" policy of coordinated, preclearance screening activities. Nearly one-third of countries have agreements with their neighbors to enforce common external border policing and customs policies, in return for open movement among citizens of these neighboring countries. The largest region allowing open movement for citizens of member states is the Schengen Zone in Europe among twenty-six countries and over 400 million people. Other similar zones are the CARICOM zone of twelve Caribbean countries with good neighbor, preclearance admissions policies.

"second strike survivability" The policy of ensuring that nuclear weapons would withstand a nuclear first strike in order to deliver a crushing retaliation (or second strike) against the initiating party. In order to make MAD threats credible, policy makers increased the size of United States and Soviet nuclear arsenals, increased their geographic spread by dispersing weapons across land, air, and sea (the triad), diversified delivery vehicles, hardened nuclear weapons sites in mountains and underground silos, and also hid nuclear weapons, to ensure the arsenals would survive, even if the people did not.

Second Vatican Council A historic ecumenical gathering, also called Vatican II, which created religious laws more clearly supportive of institutional separation with state structures, and unambiguously supportive of human rights, religious freedom, democracy, and development. After Vatican II, the Catholic Church became a powerful aid to democratization in many places around the world. Seventy-five percent of the thirty countries that democratized after the Second Vatican Council were predominantly Catholic countries.

sector-wide agreements Pacts among companies within an industry to adopt certain standards or shared best practices. Sector-wide agreements can vary from narrow technical codes on specific industrial processes to broader statements of larger CSR commitments such as the Apparel Industry Partnership to improve working conditions in the garment industry.

seed banks and gene banks Efforts to preserve biodiversity by creating collections of preserved seeds and genetic materials to serve as "back up" systems for our food supply, to help reconstitute a crop or area devastated by drought or disaster. But these conservation and research centers are often threatened by poor support from governments and sponsors.

shareholder activism The practice of stockholders pressuring companies to improve their practices on social or environmental issues, or threatening to withdraw investments from companies with poor practices or ratings.

shell companies Businesses or corporations that do not disclose the owner's name, and use complex, opaque financial transactions to disguise or hide the source of the cash or true nature of the business.

Sinn Fein The Irish Republican Army affiliated political party, legalized to peacefully compete in elections and send representatives to Parliament in the Good Friday Peace agreement.

Single Integrated Operational Plan (SIOP) The US nuclear war plan, later called the Operational Plan or O Plan.

Sub Launched Ballistic Missiles (SLBMS) Rocket-propelled, guided missiles that follow.

Snowden, Edward US defense contractor to the National Security Agency, from the contractor Booz-Hamilton, who released thousands of classified government documents to the WikiLeaks organization.

soft law Voluntary frameworks that can be quickly and widely adopted, and may become industry standards and legal liability standards, achieving wide levels of compliance similar to hard law. Changing norms may eventually change law.

sovereign state A sovereign state or country is an internationally recognized unit of political authority over a given territory, such as the United States of America or Iraq. There are 193 sovereign states. Sovereign states have four characteristics: land, population, a government in control of the land and population, and international recognition. In practice, international recognition is key and nonnegotiable; the borders, population, and government of sovereign states may all be contested, but only the other sovereign states determine who is "in the club" of sovereign states.

sovereignty The theory, in international relations, that each geographic territory has one autonomous, recognized governing authority.

S.S. *St. Louis* Deemed the "voyage of the damned," a ship of German Jews fled the Holocaust in Hitler's Nazi Germany. The ship was refused entry in the United States and other countries, and most were returned to Europe and killed in the Holocaust.

stabilization clause An agreement to freeze the law at the time the contract is entered into, which prevents law made after a contract enters into force from having any effect on a controversy's ultimate disposition.

state-centric approach A policy prescription toward addressing global problems that aims at strengthening state capacity to fight global problems, both individually and together, enhancing law and order institutions, control over borders, markets, multilateral cooperation among states, and interagency cooperation within states to increase states' efficacy of response. Most attention and effort to address global issues have been focused on state-centric approaches, both increasing internal capacity within states, and increasing coordination among states.

Stockholm Convention on Persistent Organic Pollutants (2001) Bans the most toxic chemicals, which do not break down but last a long time, persist in the environment and bio-accumulate through the food web, and pose a risk of causing adverse effects to human health and the environment. The law is nearly universal. The United States and Israel are not party to the ban.

Strategic Arms Reduction Treaties (START) Followed under Presidents Bush, Clinton, and Obama, greatly reducing the US and Russian nuclear arsenals.

structuring or smurfing Making several smaller cash deposits in different banks and businesses in order to avoid the $10,000 mandatory reporting threshold of suspicious financial activities. Cash "mules" can also

Stuxnet A complex worm, which was aimed at destroying the controversial nuclear centrifuges at Iran's Natanz nuclear energy plant. Centrifuges are the machines that enrich uranium. Because of the complexity of the computer code, the purpose of the worm to destroy the controversial Iranian centrifuges, and other evidence, most experts believe Stuxnet was a cyberattack made by the United States and Israel against Iranian nuclear centrifuges.

suspicious financial activities Cash financial transactions of over $10,000 per transaction or that add up to $10,000 in a day. Banks and businesses must report these transactions in countries with anti money laundering laws (most countries).

Sustainable Development Goals (SDGs) The successor agreement to the MDGs, member states of the UN agreed to this set of 17 aims with associated benchmarks, to decrease poverty, and increase prosperity, environmental quality, peace, and justice by the year 2030.

sustainability Putting in place just social structures so that peace will last; it is one of the principals of Just Peace.

symbolic politics Using potent symbols, pictures, colors, flags, or religious images, to connect or make sense of an issue far away with something closer to heart or more understandable. Symbols can work on a more intuitive or emotional level than facts and figures, and can cut through the noise or the apathy regarding an issue.

tactical nuclear weapons Battlefield nuclear weapons that were smaller and more easily movable and thus more usable in a military campaign.

Talitha Kum A global network of religious women committed to stopping human trafficking, protecting victims, and advocating for better anti-human trafficking laws and policies.

terrorism Force directed against noncombatants, which violates centuries of natural law and international law regarding the rules of war. Terrorists intentionally target noncombatants because it is a violation of deeply held moral and legal convictions. Killing noncombatants generates a greater response than killing soldiers, who expect personal risk in their line of work. Terrorists are minority groups without the conventional means to attack their enemies. They deliberately break conventions against killing noncombatants as a "force multiplier," in order to cause a psychological reaction (fear, shock, panic) out of proportion to the magnitude of the attack in order to perpetuate political goals, and to call into question the legitimacy of the state, whose job it is to protect civilians.

third sector The growing societal groups of nonprofit and nongovernmental organizations, distinct from the public sector of governmental actors and distinct from for-profit businesses.

TIP Trafficking in persons

TIP's three components The legal definition of trafficking in persons includes Act, Means, and Purpose

toxic trade Hazardous waste from rich countries is shipped to poor countries for disposal, to avoid "cradle to grave" accounting and safe disposal costs in developed countries.

Trafficking in Persons Victims Protection Act A law that seeks to prevent human trafficking, protect victims, and prosecute traffickers.

tragedy of the commons A dilemma in which a common resource is destroyed.

transfer pricing, trade misinvoicing, and trade-based money laundering A large, complex, difficult to stop, detect, and prevent type of money laundering, in which a fraudulent "bill of sale" is created for goods or trade that lists a false price, quantity, and/ or a false description of the goods, different than the goods are actually worth. The purpose of this exchange is to move large amounts of criminal money into the legal economy, not to make a profit from buying or selling goods. It is easy to hide illicit "sales" among the torrent of legal trade that have lax laws and practices that attract money laundering. This is becoming the preferred method of money laundering. It also facilitates the sale of counterfeit goods, as a "front business" to mask the transfers of illegal cash.

transnational advocacy networks (TANs) Organizations of NGOs across international borders who work together to raise common issues and values.

Transparency International An NGO that rates countries according to how corrupt they are, and publishes an annual, public report about global corruption. No country wants to be on Transparency International's annual list of most corrupt places.

transparency politics Efforts to create greater openness and public access, in order to allow greater scrutiny, honesty, and detection of corruption and poor practices.

Treaty on the Prohibition of Nuclear Weapons Like the landmine and cluster munitions ban, the treaty bans using, developing, testing, producing, manufacturing, acquiring, possessing, transferring, basing, stockpiling, using, or threatening to use nuclear weapons or other nuclear explosive devices, and calls for assistance to victims. A majority of countries had already banned nuclear weapons; the Nuclear Ban Treaty unites and extends the separate nuclear weapons free zone treaties into one international treaty.

triad The practice of placing nuclear weapons in the air, land, and sea, in order to increase second strike survivability, and mutually assured destruction.

twin tolerations Mutually agreed-upon boundaries that respect the institutions of both state and religious organizations.

UN The United Nations, a universal membership organization consisting of 193 countries. This IGO is an umbrella organization, which includes many IGOs within the UN system. The United Nations organizations are open forums which can be used to address multiple issue areas.

unbranded products Generic products that companies do not advertise or invest in to develop a particular name, image, or following.

Unexplained Wealth Order A transparency law which requires real estate businesses to authenticate who their customers are and where their money comes from.

UN Global Compact A voluntary UN initiative in which businesses promise to adopt sustainable and socially responsible practices in their businesses, and to report on how well they are keeping their promises.

UNICEF United Nations Children's Fund

United Nations Framework Convention on Climate Change An international agreement created to marshal the countries of the world to tackle the problems of climate change. It entered into force in 1994. The Convention committed states to reduce greenhouse gas emissions in order to prevent the worst impacts of climate change. The convention did not create binding emissions limits, but created means by which states could negotiate such limits.

United Nations High Commissioner for Refugees The Office of the UNHCR is traditionally the lead agency for refugee relief, helping to gather information and statistics to help coordinate action among states and private sector actors.

United Students against Sweatshops (USAS) A student-created and student-led NGO, which advocates that the businesses that produce college sportswear uphold good human rights, labor, and environmental practices and allow independent verification of factory conditions. If companies do not abide by corporate social responsibility standards, USAS urges colleges to cut ties with those companies for lucrative college contracts.

unmanned aerial systems Commonly called drones, or vehicles without a human operator on board

UNPKOs United Nations peacekeeping operations

UN Security Council (UNSC) The UN body responsible for addressing issues of international peace and security, including voting to send in UN peacekeeping forces to a conflict. The UNSC has fifteen countries as members: five countries are permanent members with a veto—the United States, Russia, China, the UK, and France. The remaining ten member countries serve two-year terms and are elected by the General Assembly to serve on the UNSC.

UN Special Representative for Children and Conflicts A United Nations office created to bring greater transparency and urgency to child soldier and child protection issues. The office produces an annual report providing greater transparency and accountability on the issue, pressuring governments and nonstate actors to create action plans to improve their records, and publishing a blacklist shaming and naming the world's worst violators.

USA PATRIOT Act A US law passed quickly after the September 11, 2001, attacks, intended to help US law enforcement to deter and detect terrorist attacks.

US civil rights movement The nonviolent social movement that used peaceful protest to end Jim Crow laws of racial segregation and exclusion.

US Cyber Command A joint military command, created in 2010 to integrate and strengthen the Department of Defense's expertise in cybersecurity.

Vienna Convention for the Protection of the Ozone Layer An agreement over how to work together to protect the ozone layer.

Velvet Revolutions The nonviolent social movements in the former Soviet—allied republics, such as Poland and East Germany, which peacefully removed communist regimes from power.

vertical proliferation Increasing size and/or advancing the sophistication of nuclear arsenals among the existing nuclear powers, primarily the United States and Russia.

Washington Consensus The belief that free markets and sound monetary policy are the key factors to economic development. The consensus included policies of liberalizing trade, privatizing state enterprises, balancing the budget, and pegging the exchange rate, to lay stable foundations for an economic takeoff.

watering hole Attacks, in which attackers place malware in sites and code that users regularly use for automatic updates (the "watering hole"). These attacks turn cybersecurity upside down. The updates users expect to deliver greater security may unexpectedly harm them instead.

Weapons of Mass Destruction (WMD) Armaments capable of widespread, indiscriminant death and destruction.

white hat hackers Corporate and government cybersecurity experts who work to find vulnerabilities in IT structures so that they can fix them, not exploit them.

WHO The World Health Organization

Williams, Jody Leader of the ICBL who won the Nobel Peace prize for her work banning landmines.

World Bank The international lending group created in 1944 to help European countries rebuild after World War II. The World Bank originally focused on providing loans to governments for large infrastructure projects—dams, road, bridges, electrical grids and irrigation systems. Today, the World Bank's mission has shifted to eradicating extreme poverty and increasing prosperity for the world's poorest by helping both government and the private sector have access to finance.

Worst Forms of Child Labor Convention An international convention in which countries commit to stop child slavery and slave-like conditions, including buying and selling children, trafficking children, debt bondage, serfdom, children in the sex industry including child prostitutes and child pornography, and child soldiers. The convention has helped focus attention on recognizing and eliminating child slavery.

WTO World Trade Organization, which works to coordinate common trade rules for its 160 members.

Yunus, Muhammed   Nobel Peace Prize winner, who pioneered micro-credit lending to poor people.

"zero day" vulnerabilities   Previously unknown flaws in computer software or operating systems, unknown even to the creators and vendors of the product, so they have "zero days" to prevent or patch the exposed weaknesses. Hackers and IT security firms work to find such vulnerabilities and sell them, either to the makers of the software or systems so they can repair them, or to the highest bidder on the black market.

Notes

■ ■ ■

1: GLOBAL PROBLEMS, COORDINATED SOLUTIONS, NETWORKED SOVEREIGNTY

1. Wisława Szymborska, Nobel Laureate, "Psalm," in *Map: Collected and Last Poems* (New York: Houghton Mifflin Harcourt, 2016).

2. Musra Mardini, *Butterfly: From Refugee to Olympian, My Story of Rescue, Hope, and Triumph* (New York: St. Martin's Press, 2018).

3. President Donald Trump, "Remarks to the 73 Session of the General Assembly of the United Nations," September 25, 2018, https://www.whitehouse.gov/briefings-statements/remarks-president-trump-73rd-session-united-nations-general-assembly-new-york-ny/.

4. North Korea is the closest thing to a nation-state, but even North Korea has Chinese people who live and work there. North Korea's poor economy and poor human rights record are hardly good advertisements for the attempt to create a nation-state.

5. For example, the state of Alabama waited until the year 2000 to overturn its ban on interracial marriage in its state constitution, while 40 percent of Alabamans voted to continue outlawing interracial marriage. Also, Fund for Peace, *Fragile State Index*, http://fundforpeace.org/fsi/2018/04/19/fragile-states-index-2018-issues-of-fragility-touch-the-worlds-richest-and-most-developed-countries-in-2018/.

6. Thomas Friedman, *Thank You for Being Late: An Optimists Guide to Thriving in an Era of Accelerated Change* (New York: Farrar, Straus and Giraux, 2016); Nicholas Kristoff, *Half the Sky: Turning Oppression into Opportunity for Women* (New York, 2010); Jagdish N. Bhagwati, *In Defense of Globalization* (New York: Oxford University Press, 2012); Martin Wolf, *Why Globalization Works* (New Haven, CT: Yale University Press, 2004); John Micklethwait and Adrian Wooldridge, *A Future Perfect: The Challenge and Hidden Promise of Globalization* (New York: Random House, 2000); Thomas Friedman, *The Lexus and the Olive Tree* (New York: Farrar, Straus, & Giroux, 1999).

7. Patrick Stewart, *The Sovereignty Wars: Reconciling America With the World* (New York: Council on Foreign Relations, 2018).

8. Josh Dawsey, "Trump Derides 'Shithole' African Countries, Applauds Immigrants from Norway," *The Washington Post,* Januray 12, 2018; Thomas Colson, "Brexit Campaign Chief Praises Very Clever Nazi Propaganda," *Business Insider*, April 17, 2018.

9. Dani Rodrik, *The Global Paradox: Democracy and the Future of the World Economy* (New York: Norton, 2011); Richard Baldwin, *The Great Convergence: Information Technology and the New Globalization* (Cambridge: Harvard University Press, 2016); Joseph E. Stiglitz, *Globalization and Its Discontents* (New York: Norton, 2003); Amy Chua, *World On Fire: How Exporting Free Market Democracy Breeds Ethnic Hatred and Global Instability* (New York: Anchor, 2004); Robin Broad (Ed.), *Global Backlash* (Lanham, MD: Rowman & Littlefield, 2002); Lester R. Brown, *Outgrowing the Earth: The Food Security Challenge in an Age of Falling Water Tables and Rising Temperatures* (New York: Norton, 2005); William Easterly, *The Elusive Quest for Growth: Economists' Adventures and Misadventures in the Tropics* (Cambridge, MA: MIT Press, 2002); John Cavanagh, *Alternatives to Economic Globalization: A Better World Is Possible*, 2nd ed. (San Francisco: Berrett-Koehler Publishers, 2004); Noreena Hertz, *The Silent Takeover: Global Capitalism and the Death of Democracy* (New York: Simon & Schuster, 2002); James H. Mittelman, *The Globalization Syndrome: Transformation and Resistance* (Princeton, NJ: Princeton University Press, 2000); Dani Rodrik, *Has Globalization Gone Too Far?* (Washington, DC: Institute for International Economics, 1997); Benjamin R. Barber, *Jihad vs. McWorld: How Globalism and Tribalism Are Reshaping the World* (New York: Ballantine Books, 1995); Hans-Henrik Holm and Georg Sorensen, *Whose World Order?* (Boulder, CO: Westview Press, 1995).

10. Thomas Piketty, *World Inequality Report*, 2018, https://wir2018.wid.world/; Thomas Piketty, *Capital in the 21st Century* (Cambridge: Harvard University Press, 2014); International Labor Organization, "The World of Work: Income Inequality Is Growing," Geneva, October 16, 2008, http://www.ilo.org/public/engl ish/region/ampro/cinterfor/news/world_r.htm; "In the United States in 2007, the chief executive officers (CEOs) of the 15 largest companies earned 520 times more than the average worker. This is up from 360 times more in 2003. Similar patterns, though from lower levels of executive pay, have been registered" in 70 percent of other countries. According to the World Bank, "Global inequities are massive!" World Bank, World Development Report 2006, http://siteresources.worldbank.org/ INTWDR2006/Resources/477383-1127230817535/WDR2006overview.pdf, 6.

11. Piketty, *Capital in the 21st Century*; Piketty, *World Inequality Report*.

12. World Health Organization, "Global Hunger Continues to Rise," September 11, 2018, http://www.who.int/news-room/detail/11-09-2018-global-hunger -continues-to-rise—new-un-report-says; World Food Program, World Health Organization, UN Children's Fund, *State of Food Security and Nutrition in the World*, September 2018, http://www.who.int/nutrition/publications/foodsecurity/state-food -security-nutrition-2018/en/.

13. World Bank, *Poverty in a Rising Africa* (Washington: International Reconstruction and Development Bank, 2016).

14. Ibid., and The Borgen Project, "How Many Africans Live in Poverty," July 2017, https://borgenproject.org/how-many-africans-live-in-poverty/.

15. Michael Meacher (UK minister for the environment), Speech to the Royal Society of Arts, April 1998.

16. L. Craig Johnstone, *Strategic Planning and International Affairs in the 21st Century* (Washington, DC: U.S. Department of State, November 18, 1997).

17. F. H. Hinsley, *Sovereignty* (London: C. A. Watts, 1966); The Treaty of Westphalia is a commonly used if somewhat controversial marker for a historical process that took centuries. Scholars such as Bruce Bueno de Mesquita claim that the move toward sovereignty actually came much earlier, whereas others such as Stephen Krasner note that even after Westphalia there were struggles between religious and secular leaders and contested and overlapping authority claims, for example, Stephen Krasner, "Sovereignty: Think Again," *Foreign Policy*, November 20, 2009.

18. Hendrik Spruyt, *The Sovereign State and Its Competitors* (Princeton, NJ: Princeton University Press, 1996), 40.

19. Ibid., 47.

20. Friedrich Kratochwil, "Sovereignty as Dominium: Is There a Right of Humanitarian Intervention?" in Gene M. Lyons and Michael Mastanduno (Eds.), *Beyond Westphalia: State Sovereignty and International Intervention* (Baltimore: Johns Hopkins University Press, 1995), 21–42.

21. Ibid., 62, 75.

22. Nicholas Onuf, "Intervention for the Common Good," in *Beyond Westphalia*, (Baltimore, MD: The Johns Hopkins University Press, 1995), 43–58.

23. Daniel Philpott, *Revolutions in Sovereignty: How Ideas Shaped Modern International Relations* (Princeton, 2001).

24. Ibid.; Nicholas Onuf, "Sovereignty: Outline of a Conceptual History," *Alternatives* 16 (1991): 425–446.

25. Charles Tilly, *The Formation of National States in Western Europe* (Princeton, NJ: Princeton University Press, 1975).

26. Spruyt, *The Sovereign State and Its Competitors*.

27. Michael Ross Fowler and Julie Marie Bunck, *Law, Power, and the Sovereign State: The Evolution and Application of the Concept of Sovereignty* (University Park: Pennsylvania State University Press, 1995), 5–6.

28. UN secretary general Kofi Annan, Nobel Prize for Peace acceptance speech, December 10, 2001; International Commission on Intervention and State Sovereignty, *The Responsibility to Protect* (Ottawa, Canada: International Development Research Centre, 2001), http://www.iciss-ciise.gc.ca/pdfs/Commission-Report.pdf.

29. Patrick Stewart, "Trump's Sovereignty Doctrine," *U.S. News and World Report*, September 17, 2017; Steward, *The Sovereignty Wars*.

30. Fund for Peace, "The Fragile State Index 2018."

31. Stockholm International Peace Research Institute (SIPRI), "Major Armed Conflict," *SIPRI Yearbook 2018*, http://yearbook2018.sipri.org/; and *SIPRI Yearbook 2017*, https://www.sipri.org/yearbook/2017/02. See also, Project Ploughshares, "Armed Conflict Report," http://www.ploughshares.ca/libraries/monitor/monj09h.pdf.

32. I. William Zartman, *Collapsed States* (Boulder, CO: Lynne Rienner, 1995), 1–11. State collapse is more than a succession struggle over which group will control the levers of state—it is the failure of function of those very state institutions.

Although groups may be involved in leadership contests, state collapse continues no matter who wins the helm, because state authority, legitimacy, and competence have badly disintegrated. States that have protracted or persistent leadership battles are vulnerable to collapse as state institutions atrophy during continued warfare and as the legitimacy and authority enjoyed by these institutions are undermined by the conflict. *Civil war* and *state collapse* are not synonymous terms. Internal war can occur in states that are not in the process or in danger of collapse—as in Britain and Israel. More rarely, states can collapse without violence—as in the breakup of Czechoslovakia. Not surprisingly, however, state collapse is highly correlated with internal violence, which can weaken state institutions and precede and contribute to state collapse. Alternatively, state collapse can provide the opportunity for groups to use violence as they try to assert authority in the power vacuum left by state failure. See also the Fund for Peace, "Fragile State Index"; Gurr, "The State Failure Project"; and Jackson, *Quasi-States*.

33. Jackson, *Quasi-States*, 29.

34. Morton Halperin, *Self-Determination in the New World Order* (Washington, DC: Carnegie Endowment for International Peace, 1992).

35. Jackson, *Quasi-States*, 27.

36. SIPRI, *SIPRI Yearbook 1995* (New York: Oxford University Press, 1995), 23–24.

37. Zartman, *Collapsed States*, 7–10.

38. Terry Lynn Karl and Philippe C. Schmitter, "Democratization around the Globe: Opportunities and Risks," in Michael Klare (Ed.), *World Security: Challenges for a New Century* (New York: Palgrave McMillan, 1998).

39. Edward D. Mansfield and Jack Snyder, "Democratization and War," *Foreign Affairs* (May–June 1995): 79–97.

40. Max Singer and Aaron Wildavsky, *The Real World Order: Zones of Peace and Zones of Turmoil* (Chatham, NJ: Chatham House, 1993).

41. Jeffrey Garten, "Business and Foreign Policy," *Foreign Affairs* (May/June 1997): 68.

42. George Kennan, "Moscow Embassy Telegram #511: 'The Long Telegram,' February 22, 1946," in *Foreign Relations of the United States: 1946*, vol. I, 696–709.

43. Paul Krugman, "Dutch Tulips and Emerging Markets," *Foreign Affairs* (July–August 1995): 28–43.

44. Susan Strange, *Casino Capitalism* (New York: Blackwell, 1986).

45. Establishing and protecting formal property rights for the world's poor, and transparent and accountable record keeping, would lift millions out of poverty, and help them move from the shadow, unofficial economy to the formal economy, thus paying taxes and helping the state. De Soto's critique is that open market property right principles have not been respected for the world's poor. Hernando de Soto, *The Mystery of Capital: Why Capitalism Triumphs in the West and Fails Everywhere Else* (New York: Basic Books, 2000).

46. Friedman revised his "Golden Arches Theory of Conflict Prevention" to the "Dell Theory of Conflict Prevention" in light of conflicts between countries with McDonald's franchises (e.g., Russia and Georgia in 2008), however these conflicts

never rose to the level of a war or major armed conflict with 1000 dead. Thomas Friedman, *The World Is Flat: A Brief History of the Twenty-First Century* (New York: Farrar, Straus and Giroux, 2005), 421; Thomas Friedman, *The Lexus and the Olive Tree* (New York: Anchor, 2000).

47. WTO, "WTO IP Rules Amended to Ease Access to Essential Medicines for Poor Countries," January 23, 2017, https://www.wto.org/english/news_e/news1 7_e/trip_23jan17_e.htm.

48. Many more costs have been attributed to global economies than those discussed here. These include exploitation of labor; the exploitation (even the apartheid) of the developing South by the developed North (Richard Falk, "Democratizing, Internationalizing, and Globalizing," in Yoshikazu Sakamoto [Ed.], *Global Transformation: Challenges to the State System* [Tokyo: United Nations University Press, 1994], 475–502); and environmental degradation and endangerment of indigenous peoples and their civilizations (Falk, "Democratizing, Internationalizing, and Globalizing," 475–502).

49. Chua, *World On Fire*.

50. As quoted in Tim Shorrock, *Spies for Hire: The Secret World of Intelligence Outsourcing* (New York: Simon and Schuster, 2008), 9.

51. Sean McFate, "America's Addiction to Mercenaries," *The Atlantic*, August 12, 2016.

52. The founder of the Blackwater company, an early Trump supporter and brother to Trump's Secretary of Education Betsy DeVos, is the chief enthusiast for the plan to privatize the war in Afghanistan; he would also like to be awarded the contract to do the operation.

53. The Special Inspector General for Afghanistan, and Special Inspector General for Iraq, Senate hearings on oversight of contractors, and the Wartime Contracting Commission, all brought attention to the need for greater governmental oversight. The Obama administration Office of Management and Budget did a review, and produced guidance of what constitutes an "Inherently governmental" function. The guidance produced was better than no guidance, but agencies can still contract out functions listed on the "inherently governmental" list, based on need, context, and the decisions of agency personnel.

54. Lawrence Katz and Alan Krueger, "The Rise and Nature of Alternative Work Agreements in the U.S., 2005–2015," *Princeton University*, March 29, 2016, https://krueger.princeton.edu/sites/default/files/akrueger/files/katz_krueger_cws_-_march_29_20165.pdf.

55. Michael Weber, *Congressional Research Report R45344, Global Trends in Democracy* (Washington, DC: Congressional Research Service, October 17, 2018), https://fas.org/sgp/crs/row/R45344.pdf.

56. Francis Fukuyama, *The End of History and the Last Man* (New York: Free Press, 1992), xi.

57. Ibid., 337; see also Michael Mandelbaum, *The Ideas That Conquered the World: Peace, Democracy, and Free Markets in the Twenty-First Century* (New York: Public Affairs, 2003).

58. Weber, *Congressional Research Report R45344, Global Trends in Democracy*; Karl and Schmitter, "Democratization around the Globe," 43–44. This

description of the four waves of democratization is based on Karl and Schmitter's work. Other theorists, such as Samuel Huntington, merge waves one and two into an overly long and undifferentiated category and thus count only three waves of democratization.

59. Ibid., 60.

60. Thomas Carothers, "Democracy Aid at 25: Time to Choose," *Journal of Democracy* 26, no. 1 (January 2015): 59–73; Thomas Carothers, "Is the United States Giving Up on Supporting Democracy Abroad?" *Foreign Policy*, September 8, 2016.

61. Michael Doyle, "Liberalism and World Politics," in *Conflict after the Cold War* (Longman, 2007), 263–279.

62. Mansfield and Snyder, "Democratization and War," 88.

63. Fareed Zakaria, *The Future of Freedom: Illiberal Democracy at Home and Abroad* (New York: Norton, 2004), www.freedomhouse.org.

64. Internet World Usage Stats, June 2018, http://www.internetworldstats.com/stats.

65. Burton, "The Brave New Wired World," 26.

66. Nick Routley, "How Computing Power Has Changed Over Time," *Business Insider*, November 6, 2017, https://www.businessinsider.com/infographic-h ow-computing-power-has-changed-over-time-2017-11.

67. Kenichi Ohmae, *The End of the Nation State: The Rise of Regional Economies* (New York: Free Press, 1995).

68. Ohmae, *The End of the Nation State*.

69. Stephen D. Krasner, *Sovereignty: Organized Hypocrisy* (Princeton, NJ: Princeton University Press, 1999).

70. Robert Jackson, *Sovereignty* (Cambridge: Polity Press, 2007); Stephen D. Krasner, *Problematic Sovereignty: Contested Rules and Political Possibilities* (New York: Columbia University Press, 2001); K. J. Holsti, *Taming the Sovereigns* (Cambridge: Cambridge University Press, 2004); Samy Cohen, *The Resilience of the State* (Boulder, CO: Lynne-Reinner, 2006); Beatrice Hibou (Ed.), *Privatizing the State* (New York: Colombia University Press, 2004).

71. Stephen D. Krasner, "Sovereignty: An Institutional Perspective," *Comparative Political Studies* 21 (April 1988): 74.

72. Kenneth Waltz, "Globalization and Governance," *PS: Political Science & Politics* (December 1999): 693–700.

73. William H. McNeill, "Territorial States Buried Too Soon," *Mershon International Studies Review* 41 (1997): 269.

74. PRIO, Uppsala University.

75. Maria Stephan and Erica Chenoweth, *Why Civil Resistance Works: The Strategic Logic of Nonviolent Conflict,* Columbia Studies in Terrorism and Irregular Warfare (New York: Columbia University Press, 2013).

76. Paul Collier et al., *Breaking the Conflict Trap* (World Bank Policy Research Report, 2003).

77. Martha Finnemore, Deborah Avant, and Susan K. Sell, *Who Governs the Globe?*

78. Anne-Marie Slaughter, *The Chessboard and the Web* (Yale University Press, 2017).

79. Susan Strange, *The Retreat of the State: The Diffusion of Power in the World Economy* (Cambridge, UK: Cambridge University Press, 1996), 189.

80. Ibid., 78.

81. Ibid., 79.

82. Ibid., 81.

83. Ibid., 77, 199.

84. James N. Rosenau, "Sovereignty in a Turbulent World," in Gene M. Lyons and Michael Mastanduno (Eds.), *Beyond Westphalia? State Sovereignty and International Intervention* (Baltimore: Johns Hopkins University Press, 1995), 193; James N. Rosenau, *Turbulence in World Politics* (Princeton, NJ: Princeton University Press, 1990).

85. James N. Rosenau and W. Michael Fagen, "A New Dynamism in World Politics: Increasingly Skillful Individuals?" *International Studies Quarterly* 41 (December 1997): 660.

86. Rosenau, "Sovereignty in a Turbulent World," 204.

87. Ibid., 206–207; Rosenau, *Turbulence in World Politics*, 90–113.

88. Rosenau, "Sovereignty in a Turbulent World," 206–207; Rosenau, *Turbulence in World Politics*.

89. Edgar Grande and Louis W. Pauly, *Complex Sovereignty: Reconstituting Political Authority in the 21st Century* (University of Toronto Press, 2007).

90. Richard Rosecrance, *The Rise of the Virtual State: Wealth and Power in the Coming Century* (New York: Basic Books, 2000); and Richard Rosecrance, "The Rise of the Virtual State," *Foreign Affairs* (July–August 1996): 59–60.

91. Ibid., 59–61.

2: NONGOVERNMENTAL ORGANIZATIONS: POLITICS IN TRANSNATIONAL NETWORKS

1. Bono, "Poverty Is Sexist," *ONE Campaign*, January 4, 2018.

2. John McArthur and Krista Rasmussen, "How Successful Were the Millennium Development Goals," *Brookings Institution*, January 11, 2017, https://www.brookings.edu/blog/future-development/2017/01/11/how-successful-were-the-millennium-development-goals/.

3. International Campaign to Ban Landmines, http://www.icbl.org/.

4. Jody Williams, Speech at Vatican Conference on Integral Disarmament, Rome, November 2017; International Campaign to Ban Landmines, www.icbl.org; Richard Price, "Reversing the Gun Sights: Transnational Civil Society Targets Land Mines," *International Organization* 52, no. 3: 613–644; Anne Peters, "The International Campaign to Ban Landmines," case study for the Global Public Policy Network, www.f2.efresh.de/public/peters%20gpp%202000.pdf.

5. The Trump administration's new policy will keep the remaining, unreliable cluster munitions "in active U.S. stocks until the "capabilities they provide are replaced with enhanced and more reliable munitions." How that might occur remains unclear. The last US manufacturer who produced cluster munitions that Washington claims meet the safe 1 percent threshold stopped making them in 2016 and does not intend to renew production, according to The New York Times. The United States stopped buying new cluster munitions for its military in 2007." "U.S.

Undoes Cluster Munitions Ban," *Arms Control Today*, The Arms Control and Disarmament Association, https://www.armscontrol.org/act/2018-01/news-briefs/us-undoes-cluster-munitions-ban.

6. Maryann Cusimano Love, "Resurrection Politics and Banning the Bomb," Peace Policy, Notre Dame University, November 2017, https://peacepolicy.nd.edu/2017/11/06/resurrection-politics-and-banning-the-bomb/.

7. Maryann Cusimano Love, "Just Peace and Nuclear Disarmament," Stanford University, Hoover Institute, September 24, 2018.

8. Setsuko Thurlow, Nobel Prize Acceptance Speech, December 10, 2017, https://www.wagingpeace.org/setsuko-thurlow-nobel-peace-prize-acceptance-speech/.

9. Margaret E. Keck and Kathryn Sikkink, *Activists Beyond Borders* (Ithaca, NY: Cornell University Press, 1998), 1.

10. Lester Salamon, *Explaining Civil Society Development* (Baltimore: Johns Hopkins University Press, 2017). Lester M. Salamon, "Interview on Global Civil Society," *Johns Hopkins Gazette*, January 3, 2000, www.jhu.edu/~gazette/2000/jan0300/03lestxt.html; Lester M. Salamon, *Global Civil Society: Dimensions of the Nonprofit Sector* (Baltimore: Johns Hopkins University, Institute for Policy Studies, Center for Civil Society Studies, 1999).

11. Union of International Associations (Ed.), *Yearbook of International Organizations 2017* (Brussels: K.G. Saur Verlag, 2017).

12. Howard S. Becker, *Outsiders: Studies in the Sociology of Deviance* (New York: Free Press, 1963), 148; Ethan A. Nadelmann, "Global Prohibition Regimes: The Evolution of Norms in International Society," *International Organization* 44, no. 4: 482.

13. Maryann Cusimano Love, "Catholic Women Peacebuilders," in Katherine Marshall and Susan Hayward (Eds.), *Women, Religion, and Peacebuilding: Illuminating the Unseen* (Washington, DC: U.S. Institute of Peace Press, 2015); Maryann Cusimano Love, "Religious Transnational Networks," in Dan Philpott (Ed.), *Under Caesar's Sword* (New York: Oxford University Press, 2018).

14. Love, "Resurrection Politics and Banning the Bomb."

15. "The Murder Case of Oscar Romero Has Been Re-opened," *Catholic News Agency*, May 19, 2017, https://www.catholicnewsagency.com/news/the-murder-case-of-blessed-oscar-romero-has-been-reopened-42609; The Center for Justice and Accountability, "What is Hoped to be Achieved with these Cases?" http://www.cja.org/cases/Romagoza_News/RomagozaFAQs.htm#eight.

16. Keck and Sikkink, *Activists Beyond Borders*, 12.

17. Martha Finnemore notes that actors and interests are constituted in interaction. Martha Finnemore, *National Interests in International Society* (Ithaca, NY: Cornell University Press, 1996).

18. Keck and Sikkink, *Activists Beyond Borders*.

19. Lester M. Salamon, "The Rise of the Nonprofit Sector," *Foreign Affairs* (July–August 1994): 113.

20. Felice D. Gaer, "Human Rights, Nongovernmental Organizations, and the UN," in Weiss et al., (Eds.), *NGOS, the UN and Global Governance*, 52–53.

21. Jack Donnelly, *International Human Rights*, 2nd ed. (Boulder, CO: Westview Press, 1998), 43; John Simpson and Jana Bennett, *The Disappeared: Voices from a Secret War* (London: Robson Books, 1985), 110.

22. Donnelly, *International Human Rights*, 39; Simpson and Bennett, *The Disappeared*, 225.

23. Donnelly, *International Human Rights*, 44–45.

24. Gaer, "Human Rights," 52–53.

25. "Nailing Jello in China," *Washington Post*, August 26, 2000: A16.

26. Steven Livingston, "Satellite Imagery Augments Power and Responsibility of Human Rights Groups," Brookings Institution, June 23, 2016, https://www.brookings.edu/blog/techtank/2016/06/23/satellite-imagery-augments-power-and-responsibility-of-human-rights-groups/; Relief Web, "Drones and Satellites for Good Report," July 2015, https://reliefweb.int/report/world/drones-and-satellites-good-how-drones-and-satellites-are-helping-world; Tech for Good, "2018 Global NGO Technology Report," http://techreport.ngo/.

27. Salamon, "Interview on Global Civil Society."

28. Charles Downs, "Negotiating Development Assistance: USAID and the Choice between Public and Private Implementation in Haiti," in *Pew Case Studies in International Affairs* (Washington, DC: Georgetown University, Institute for the Study of Diplomacy, 1994), 7.

29. Downs, "Negotiating Development Assistance," 7.

30. Ibid.

31. Peter Sollis, "The State, Nongovernmental Organizations, and the UN," in Willetts (Ed.), *The Conscience of the World*, 194–195.

32. Peter Willetts (Ed.), *The Conscience of the World: The Influence of Nongovernmental Organisations in the UN System* (Washington, DC: Brookings Institution, 1996), 6.

33. Kal Raustiala, "States, NGOs, and International Environmental Institutions," *International Studies Quarterly* 41 (December 1997): 719–724.

34. Jessica Tuchman Mathews, "Power Shift: The Age of Nonstate Actors," *Foreign Affairs* 76 (January–February 1997): 55.

35. Paul Wapner, "Politics Beyond the State," in John S. Dryzek (Ed.), *Debating the Earth* (New York: Oxford University Press, 1999), 518–519.

36. Barber, *Jihad vs. McWorld*; Samuel Huntington, *The Clash of Civilizations* (New York: Simon & Schuster, 2011).

37. Love, "Religious Transnational Networks."

38. Keck and Sikkink, *Activists Beyond Borders*, 37.

3: MULTINATIONAL CORPORATIONS: POWER AND RESPONSIBILITY IN GLOBAL BUSINESS NETWORKS

1. Daniel Zager, Angeles Solis, and Sonia Adjroud, "These Georgetown Students Fought Nike, and Won," *The Nation*, September 15, 2017, https://www.thenation.com/article/these-georgetown-students-fought-nike-and-won/.

2. James Keady, Interview in Corporate Crimes Reporter, November 23, 2015, https://www.corporatecrimereporter.com/news/200/james-keady-and-the-coming-boycott-of-nike/.

3. Jason Lemon, "Nike Factory Workers Still Work Long Hours for Low Pay," *Newsweek*, September 6, 2018, https://www.newsweek.com/nike-factory-workers-still-work-long-days-low-wages-asia-1110129.

4. Miguel Korzeniewicz, "Commodity Chains and Marketing Strategies: Nike and the Global Athletic Footwear Industry," in Frank J. Lechner and John Boli (Eds.), *The Globalization Reader* (Malden, MA: Blackwell, 2000), 158–159.

5. Ibid., 157.

6. Nike, Inc. Annual Report, http://invest.nike.com/phoenix.zhtml?c=100529 &p=irol-finReporting.

7. United Nations, United Nations Statistics Division National Accounts, December 2017 www.unstats.un.org.

8. Chris Isadore, "How Nike Became King of Endorsements," *CNN Money*, June 5, 2015, https://money.cnn.com/2015/06/05/news/companies/nike-endorse ment-dollars/index.html; Emmett Knowlton, "Lebron James Nike Deal Exceeds $1 Billion," *Business Insider*, May 17, 2016, https://www.businessinsider.com/lebron-j ames-nike-deal-exceeds-1-billion-maverick-carter-says-2016-5.

9. Peter Schwartz and Blair Gibb, *When Good Companies Do Bad Things: Responsibility and Risk in an Age oef Globalization* (New York: Wiley & Sons, 1999), 51, 53.

10. Michael Clancy, "Sweating the Swoosh: Nike, the Globalization of Sneakers, and the Question of Sweatshop Labor," in *Pew Case Studies in International Affairs* (Washington, DC: Georgetown University, Institute for the Study of Diplomacy, 2000), 5.

11. Ibid.

12. Schwartz and Gibb, *When Good Companies Do Bad Things*, 51, 53.

13. Clancy, "Sweating the Swoosh," 9.

14. Nike Web site, corporate responsibility page, www.nikebiz.com/labor/index. shtml.

15. Clancy, "Sweati"Nikng the Swoosh," 13.

16. "Firms are considered to be more multinational if (1) they have foreign affili-ates or subsidiaries in foreign countries; (2) they operate in a wide variety of coun-tries around the globe; (3) the proportion of assets, revenues, or profits accounted for by overseas operations relative to total assets, revenues, or profits is high; (4) their employees, stockholders, owners, and managers are from many different coun-tries; (5) their overseas operations are much more ambitious than just sales offices, including a full range of manufacturing and research and development activities. . . . MNCs are firms that have sent abroad a package of capital, technology, managerial talent, and marketing skills to carry out production in foreign countries." Joan E. Spiro and Jeffrey A. Hart, *The Politics of International Economic Relations* (New York: St. Martin's Press, 1997), 96, 98.

17. "Study: Big Corporations Dominate List of World's Top Economies," *The Guardian*, September 12, 2016, https://www.theguardian.com/business/2016/sep /12/global-justice-now-study-multinational-businesses-walmart-apple-shell.

18. *Economist* (July 30, 1994): 57, reprinted in James Lee Ray, *Global Problems* (New York: Houghton Mifflin, 1998), 465.

19. United Nations Conference on Trade and Development (UNCTAD), *World Investment Report 2008*, 10, http://www.unctad.org/en/docs/wir2008overview_en.pdf.

20. "Fortune Global 500," *Fortune magazine*, 2017, http://fortune.com/ global500/.

21. United Nations Conference on Trade and Development, *World Investment Report 2018*, overview, https://unctad.org/en.

22. Schwartz and Gibb, *When Good Companies Do Bad Things*, 85.

23. United Nations International Labor Organization, "Modern Slavery and Child Labor," September 19, 2017, https://www.ilo.org/global/about-the-ilo/news room/news/WCMS_574717/lang--en/index.htm; Megha Bahree, "Child Labor," *Forbes*, March 10, 2008, http://www.forbes.com/global/2008/0310/062.html. Sixty-one percent of these are in Asia, 32 percent in Africa, and 7 percent in Latin America. Human Rights Watch, *Child Labor*, http://www.hrw.org/children/labor.htm.

24. Layna Mosley, "Does Globalization Hurt Poor Workers? It's Complicated," *The Washington Post*, September 15, 2016, https://www.washingtonpost.com/news /in-theory/wp/2016/09/15/does-globalization-hurt-poor-workers-its-complicated/?u tm_term=.54e3cda95001.

25. A. Claire Cutler, Virginia Haufler, and Tony Porter, *Private Authority and International Affairs* (Albany: SUNY Press, 1999), 16.

26. Chris Arsenault, "Study: Rich Nations Spend 250 Billion in Subsidies, Hurting Poor Growers," *Reuters*, October 16, 2015, https://uk.reuters.com/article/uk-f arming-subsidies/rich-nations-spend-250-billion-on-farm-subsidies-hurting-poor-g rowers-study-idUKKCN0SA2BF20151016; World Bank, *World Development Report 2008*, 97, http://siteresources.worldbank.org/INTWDR2008/Resources /2795087-1192112387976/WDR08_08_ch04.pdf.

27. Alan Taylor, "Bhopal The World's Worst Industrial Disaster 30 Years Later," *The Atlantic*, December 2 2014, https://www.theatlantic.com/photo/2014/12/bho pal-the-worlds-worst-industrial-disaster-30-years-later/100864/; Ward Morehouse and M. Arun Subramaniam, *The Bhopal Tragedy: A Report for the Citizens Commission on Bhopal* (New York: Council on International and Public Affairs, 1986); William Board, *The Bhopal Tragedy: Language, Logic, and Politics in the Production of a Hazard* (Boulder, CO: Westview, 1989); Paul Shrivastava, *Bhopal: Anatomy of a Crisis* (Cambridge, MA: Ballinger, 1987); Rama Lakshmi, "India Seeks to Reduce Charge Facing Ex-Union Carbide Boss," *Washington Post*, July 8, 2002: A12.

28. Suketu Mehta, "Bhopal Lives," *Village Voice*, December 3, 1996: 51.

29. Ibid., 55; Lakshmi, "India Seeks to Reduce Charge Facing Ex-Union Carbide Boss." Warren Anderson, CEO of Union Carbide at the time of the accident, was charged with culpable homicide in India and faced a civil suit in the United States over the accident. In June 2003, the Indian government requested Anderson's extradition to stand trial. A year later, on July 13, 2004, the US government rejected Anderson's suit and the extradition request on technical grounds.

30. Amnesty International, "Injustice Incorporated," March 7, 2014, https://ww w.amnesty.org/en/documents/POL30/001/2014/en/.

31. Mr. Austin Onuoha, "African Oil an"d Poverty," speech at Catholic University of America, Washington, DC, October 17, 2005.

32. The Global Corruption Report 2018, Transparency International, https:// www.transparency.org/country.

33. Fr. Antoine Berilengar, SJ, "African Oil and Poverty," speech at Catholic University of America, Washington, DC, October 17, 2005.

34. Bret L. Billet, "Safeguarding or International Morality? The Behavior of Multinational Corporations in Less Developed Countries, 1975–86," *International Interactions* 17 (1991): 171, 184; quoted in Ray, *Global Problems*, 476.

35. Deborah L. Spar, "The Spotlight and the Bottom Line: How Multinationals Export Human Rights," *Foreign Affairs* 77 (March–April 1998): 7–12.

36. Cutler, Haufler, and Porter, *Private Authority and International Affairs*.

37. David C. Korten, *When Corporations Rule the World* (West Hartford, CT: Kumarian Press, 1995).

38. Will Fitzgibbon, "Second Panama Papers," *International Consortium of Investigative Journalism*, August 16, 2018, https://www.icij.org/investigations/panama-papers/.

39. These include the power to compel discovery, dispose of property and property rights, order monetary damages, and, depending on the nature of the contract and the rules of arbitration chosen, even order specific performance.

40. United Nations Office on Drugs and Crime, "Money Laundering and Globalization," https://www.unodc.org/unodc/en/money-laundering/globalization.html. Other such as Australian scholar John Walker, make a higher estimate of 2.8 trillion dollars annually, https://www.businessinsider.com/the-economics-of-money-laundering-2011-6; Raymond W. Baker, *Capitalism's Achilles Heel* (Hoboken, NJ: Wiley & Sons, 2005), 163.

41. Jan Martin Witte and Wolfgang Reinicke, UN Global Compact Office, "Business UN Usual," 2005, http://globalpublicpolicy.net/businessUNusual/; Witte and Reinicke, "Partnerships: Opportunities and Challenges of Partnering with the UN," *Global Compact*, July 10, 2005, www.globalpublicpolicy.net.

42. Keck and Sikkink, *Activists Beyond Borders*.

43. Virginia Haufler, *A Public Role for the Private Sector: Industry Self-Regulation in a Global Economy* (Washington, DC: Carnegie Endowment for International Peace, 2001), 106.

44. Karen DeYoung and Shane Harris, "Erik Prince, in Kabul, Pushes Privatization of the Afghan War," *The Washington Post*, October 4, 2018, https://www.washingtonpost.com/world/national-security/erik-prince-in-kabul-pushes-privatization-of-the-afghan-war/2018/10/04/72a76d36-c7e5-11e8-b1ed-1d2d65b86d0c_story.html?utm_term=.94a32347b50e.

4: INTERGOVERNMENTAL ORGANIZATIONS: COALITIONS OF COUNTRIES

1. Eleanor Roosevelt, "My Day," October 30, 1950, https://www2.gwu.edu/~erpapers/myday/displaydoc.cfm?_y=1950&_f=md001739.

2. Dwight Eisenhower, "Address Before the General Assembly of the United Nations," December 8, 1953, http://www.presidency.ucsb.edu/ws/?pid=9774.

3. Helmut Schmidt, "Miles to Go: From American Plan to European Union," *Foreign Affairs*, May/June, 1997, https://www.foreignaffairs.com/articles/europe/1997-05-01/miles-go.

4. John Bolton as quoted in Mathew Haag, "Examples of John Bolton's Long Time Hardline Views," *The New York Times*, March 22, 2018, https://

www.nytimes.com/2018/03/22/us/politics/john-bolton-national-security-adv.html?mtrref=www.google.com&gwh=0C73EAFF414C367974818D1EF63C5D85&gwt=pay.

5. Madeline Herren, "International Organizations 1865–1945," in *The Oxford Handbook of International Organizations* (Oxford University Press, 2016), 96–97.

6. United Nations, "Charter of the United Nations."

7. Joshua Goldstein, *Winning the War on War: The Decline of Armed Conflict Worldwide* (New York: Penguin Publishing, 2012).

8. Håvard Hegre, Lisa Hultman, and Håvard Mokleiv Nygård, "Peacekeeping Works: Evaluating the Effectiveness of UN Peacekeeping Operations." *PRIO*, June 2017, https://www.prio.org/utility/DownloadFile.ashx?id=1526&type=publicationfile.

9. International Monetary Fund, "About the IMF," http://www.imf.org/en/About.

10. International Monetary Fund, "About the IMF," http://www.imf.org/en/About.

11. International Monetary Fund, "About the IMF," http://www.imf.org/en/About.

12. John Williamson, "Did the Washington Consensus Fail?" speech at the Peterson Institute of International Economics, Washington, DC, November 6, 2002, https://piie.com/commentary/speeches-papers/did-washington-consensus-fail.

13. Pascual Fontaine, *The European Union*, EU Directorate General for Education, April 4, 2018, https://publications.europa.eu/en/publication-detail/-/publication/2d85274b-0093-4e38-896a-12518d629057.

14. International Telecommunications Union, https://www.itu.int/en/about/Pages/default.aspx.

15. International Civil Aviation Organization, "ICAO: Making a Standard," https://www.icao.int/safety/airnavigation/Pages/standard.aspx.

16. President Dwight Eisenhower, "Atoms for Peace Speech," December 8, 1953, https://www.iaea.org/about/history/atoms-for-peace-speech; International Atomic Energy Agency; "60 Years of Atoms for Peace," December 6, 2013, https://www.iaea.org/newscenter/news/60-years-atoms-peace.

17. Gar Alperovitz, "The War Was Won Before Hiroshima, and the Generals Knew It," *The Nation*, August 6, 2015, https://www.thenation.com/article/why-the-us-really-bombed-hiroshima/; Mark Weber, *Was Hiroshima Necessary?* Institute for Historical Review.

18. President Dwight Eisenhower, *Mandate for Change* (New York: Doubleday, 1963).

19. Article 2, "Universal Declaration of Human Rights," http://www.un.org/en/universal-declaration-human-rights/.

20. Many countries also have border preclearance agreements. For example, US government border agents work in foreign countries, at most Canadian ports of entry, as well as in Bermuda, the Bahamas, Aruba, Ireland, and the United Arab Emirates. These US government agents apply US law and border clearance rules and procedures in these foreign points of departure, before passengers board planes for the United States.

21. European Commission, "Accession Criteria," https://ec.europa.eu/neighbour hood-enlargement/policy/glossary/terms/accession-criteria_en.

22. Amy J. Sennett, "Lenahan vs. United States: Defining Due Diligence," *Harvard International Law Journal* 53, no. 2 (Summer 2012): 537–547, http://www .harvardilj.org/wp-content/uploads/2012/10/HLI208.pdf.

23. Convention on the Prevention and Punishment of the Crime of Genocide, http://www.un.org/en/genocideprevention/genocide.html.

5: RELIGIOUS ACTORS AND GLOBAL ISSUES: GOD AND GLOBAL GOVERNANCE

1. John Micklethwait and Adrian Wooldridge, *God is Back: How the Global Revival of Faith Is Changing the World* (New York: The Penguin Press, 2009), and book excerpt, "God is Back," *The Fox News Forum*, April 9, 2009, http://foxforum. blogs.foxnews.com/2009/04/06/god_faith_religion/.

2. Polio Global Eradication Initiative, October 29, 2018, http://polioeradicat ion.org/news-post/religious-leaders-fuelling-demand-for-polio-vaccines-and-healt h-services-in-nigeria/.

3. David Agren, "Mexican Bishops Announce Security Protocols for Priests, Religious," *Crux*, June 21, 2018, https://cruxnow.com/global-church/2018/06/21/ mexican-bishops-announce-security-protocols-for-priests-religious/.

4. Second Vatican Council Promulgated by His Holiness Pope Paul VI, Gaudium et Spes, Pastoral Constitution on the Church in the Modern World, December 7, 1965, 26, http://www.newadvent.org/library/docs_ec21gs.htm.

5. Pope Benedict XVI argued that globalization limits the power of sovereign states, thus there is a need to create new political authorities and to strengthen the principle to protect in "Caritas in Veritate," Vatican City, June 29, 2009. As the US Catholic Bishops put it, "The church is not bound to any particular economic, political, or social system; it has lived with many forms of economic and social organization and will continue to do so, evaluating each according to moral and ethical principles: What is the impact of the system on people? Does it support or threaten human dignity?" US Bishops, "Economic Justice for All," 1986, 130, http: //www.osjspm.org/economic_justice_for_all.aspx. This is not an exclusionary or triumphalist position. Other nonstate actors, both religious and secular institutions, privilege attention to human persons and communities over the interests of sovereign states, in both principles and practices. Because the Catholic Church is so large and has UN observer status and diplomatic missions, the higher levels of the Church (The Vatican and the various Bishops' Conferences) have sustained relations with states. But the dominant focus of the church's work is not at the state, but at the community level.

6. Although recognizing the importance of human rights, the US government and the United Nations begin from the default position of recognizing sovereign states regardless of the government's treatment of its own citizens. While a "responsibility to protect" norm is emerging at the United Nations and within the United States to justify humanitarian response in cases of genocide, war crimes, ethnic cleansing, and crimes against humanity, in practice this is controversial, partial, and

difficult to implement, as the anemic responses to the ongoing genocide in Darfur indicate. The International Commission on Intervention and State Sovereignty in 2001 recommended to the UN secretary-general "'The Responsibility to Protect," the idea that sovereign states have a responsibility to protect their own citizens from avoidable catastrophe, but that when they are unwilling or unable to do so, that responsibility must be borne by the broader community of *states*." http://www. iciss.ca/report-en.asp. This principle was established in U.N. Security Council 1674, adopted April 28, 2006, accepting "the responsibility to protect populations from genocide, war crimes, ethnic cleansing, and crimes against humanity." http://dac cessdds.un.org/doc/UNDOC/GEN/N06/331/99/PDF/N0633199.pdf This moves the UN and US a step closer to the position of the church and other non-state actors. But the fact that such a principle is only recently emerging and was needed shows the established default position is a deference to state sovereignty over protection of human persons.

7. Holy See, Catholic Church Statistics 2018, http://www.fides.org/en/news/64944-VATICAN_CATHOLIC_CHURCH_STATISTICS_2018.

8. Barber, *Jihad vs. McWorld*; Friedman, *The Lexus and the Olive Tree*; Huntington, *The Clash of Civilizations*.

9. Previous versions of the arguments in this article appeared in Maryann Cusimano Love, *Beyond Sovereignty: Issues for a Global Agenda* (New York: Thomson/Wadsworth, 2006); address to Georgetown University, The International Conference Prayer for Peace, "Religion and Terrorism: Resurrection Politics," Washington, DC, April 27, 2006; keynote address to the International Conference of the World Union of Catholic Women's Organizations, "Women Peacemakers," Arlington, VA, June 1, 2006; address at the Chicago Theological Union, to the Catholic Peacebuilding Network Conference, "Emerging Peacebuilding Institutions and Norms," Chicago, IL, April 19, 2006; address to the Executive Leadership of the Roundtable, Georgetown June 16, 2006; and address to Catholic University Conference on Globalization, "Globalization and Faith-Based NGOs: Opportunities for Political Action," Washington, DC, April 15, 2005.

10. Keck and Sikkink, *Activists Beyond Borders*.

11. Rick Noack, "Megachurches Outside the U.S.," *The Washington Post*, July 24, 2015, https://www.washingtonpost.com/news/worldviews/wp/2015/07/24/how-u-s-style-megachurches-are-taking-over-the-world-in-5-maps-and-charts/?utm_term=.bd63d4b2614c; John Jackson, *Pastorpreneur* (Vision Quest Ministries, 2004).

12. Tyler Mathisen, "Do God and Money Mix?" *CNBC*, April 1, 2005, http://www.msnbc.msn.com/id/7346446/.

13. Micklethwait and Wooldridge, *God is Back*, 189.

14. Eleanor Albert, *Christianity in China*, The Council on Foreign Relations, May 2018, https://www.cfr.org/backgrounder/christianity-china; Emily Rauhala, "Christians in China Feel Full Force of Repression," *The Washington Post*, December 23, 2015, https://www.washingtonpost.com/world/asia_pacific/christians-in-china-feel-full-force-of-authorities-repression/2015/12/23/7dd0ec5a-a736-11e5-b596-113f59ee069a_story.html?utm_term=.62bea4ca7183; Micklethwait and Wooldridge, *God is Back*, 19.

15. Eleanor Albert, *Christianity in China*, The Council on Foreign Relations, May 2018, https://www.cfr.org/backgrounder/christianity-china; John Micklethwait and Adrian Wooldridge, "God Still Isn't Dead," *The Wall Street Journal*, New York, April 7, 2009, A15.

16. Pope Francis, "Globalization of Solidarity," Rome, March 13, 2018.

17. Micklethwait and Wooldridge, *God is Back*, 9.

18. Pippa Norris and Ronald Inglehart, *Sacred and Secular: Religion and Politics Worldwide* (London: Cambridge University Press, 2004).

19. Grace Davie notes that Americans and Europeans "are differently religious." A similar point may hold for developed and developing countries. Grace Davie, "Pew Forum On Religion and Public Life: Believing without Belonging—Just How Secular Is Europe?" FL: Key West, December 5, 2005, http://pewforum.org/events/?EventID=97.

20. Grace Davie, *Religion in Britain since 1945: Believing without Belonging* (New York: Blackwell, 1994).

21. USCCB, "Catholics Confront Global Poverty," http://www.usccb.org/sdwp/globalpoverty/ccgp_index.shtml; "A Place at the Table," http://www.usccb.org/bishops/table.shtml.

22. Fr. Ferdinand Muhigirwe, S.J., Centre d'Etudes Pour l'Action Sociale (CEPAS), Democratic Republic of Congo, "Natural Resource Extraction and Conflict in the Democratic Republic of Congo," Conference on The Future of Catholic Peacebuilding, Washington, DC, The Catholic University of America, August, 2016.

23. Catholic Relief Services, "Catholics Confront Global Poverty: Natural Resources and Our Catholic Response," http://www.usccb.org/sdwp/globalpoverty/pdfs/Natural_Resources.pdf.

24. Mike Sweitzer-Beckman, "Shareholder Activism Really Does Work," *National Catholic Reporter,* April 30, 2009; Interfaith Center on Corporate Activism, "ICCR Marks 40th Anniversary Chronicling the History of Faith-Based Shareholder Activism," June 18, 2009.

25. United Nations World Tourism Organization, "World Tourism Barometer," http://www.unwto.org/facts/eng/barometer.htm.

26. Coalition on the Environment and Jewish Life, "What's Jewish About Protecting the Environment? Ten Year Report," http://www.coejl.org/~coejlor/about/TenYearReport.pdf.

27. Timothy Shah and Robert Woodberry, "The Pioneering Protestants," *The Journal of Democracy* 15, no. 2 (April 2004): 47.

28. Daniel Philpott, "Explaining the Political Ambivalence of Religion," *The American Political Science Review* 101, no. 3 (August 2007): 515.

29. Alfred Stepan, "Religion, Democracy, and the 'Twin Tolerations,'" in Larry Diamond (Ed.), *World Religions and Democracy* (Baltimore: The Johns Hopkins University Press, 2005), 5.

30. Alfred Stepan, "The Multiple Secularisms of Modern Democracies," September 2006 SSRC Working Group paper for a volume *Rethinking Secularism*, edited by Mark Juergensmeyer, October, 2007, 1.

31. Archbishop John Onaihekan, Interview with the Author, Rome, December 2015; also "The Future of Catholic Peacebuilding Conference," April 13–15,

2008, The University of Notre Dame, South Bend, Indiana, http://cpn.nd.edu/pa pers_2008CPN/Role%20of%20Bishops%20in%20Peacebuilding%20_%20Onaiy ekan.pdf.

32. Elliot Abrams, "Religious Freedom: An American Perspective," International Coalition for Religious Freedom Conference on "Religious Freedom and the New Millenium," Tokyo, Japan, May 23–25, 1998.

33. Philpott, *Revolutions in Sovereignty*, 5.

34. Sociologist Peter Berger's 1999 book, *The Desecularization of the World*, turned away from his previous decades of work promoting secularization theory.

35. Micklethwait and Wooldridge, *God is Back*, and book excerpt, "God is Back," *The Fox News Forum*, April 9, 2009, http://foxforum.blogs.foxnews.com/2 009/04/06/god_faith_religion/.

36. Philpott, *Revolutions in Sovereignty*, 9.

37. Quoted in Winston Churchill, "The Gathering Storm," in *The Second World War*, vol. 1, ch. 8 (1948).

38. Anna Machowska, "Soviets Sent Bulgarian Assassin to Kill Pope John Paul II during Cold War," *The Daily Mail UK*, February 16, 2009, online http://www.dail ymail.co.uk/news/worldnews/article_1146559/Soviet_spies_sent_Bulgarian_assa ssin_kill_Pope_John_Paul_II_Cold_War_claims_priest.html#.

39. Scott Appleby, *The Ambivalence of the Sacred* (Lanham, MD: Rowman and Littlefield, 1999); Thomas Farr, *World of Faith and Freedom: Why International Religious Liberty Is Vital to American National Security* (New York: Oxford University Press, 2008); Philpott, "Explaining the Political Ambivalence of Religion," 505–525; Daniel Philpott, "The Challenge of September 11th to Secularism in International Relations," *World Politics 55* (Baltimore, MD: Johns Hopkins University Press, October 2002): 66–95; Scott M. Thomas, "Taking Religious and Cultural Pluralism Seriously: The Global Resurgence of Religion and the Transformation of International Society," *Millennium Journal of International Studies* 29, no. 3 (Sage 2000): 815–841; Thomas Farr, "Diplomacy in an Age of Faith: Religious Freedom and National Security," *Foreign Affairs* (New York: Council on Foreign Relations, April/May 2008); Max L. Stackhouse, *God and Globalization*, Vols. 1–4 (Princeton: Center of Theological Inquiry, 2000–2009); Karen Armstrong, *The Battle for God* (Toronto: Ballantine Books, 2001); Gabriel Almond, Scott Appleby, and Emmanuel Silvan, *Strong Religion: The Rise of Fundamentalisms around the World* (The Fundamentalism Project) (Chicago: University of Chicago Press, 2003); Scott Thomas, *The Global Resurgence of Religion and the Transformation of International Relations* (Palgrave Macmillan, 2007); Robert Seiple and Dennis Hoover, *Religion and Security: The New Nexus in International Relations* (Lanham, MD: Rowman and Littlefield, 2004); Jonathan Fox and Schmuel Sandler, *Bringing Religion into International Relations* (Palgrave Macmillan, 2006); Eric O. Hansen, *Religion and Politics in the International System Today* (London: Cambridge University Press, 2006); Jeff Haynes, *An Introduction to International Relations and Religion* (Boston: Longman, 2007); Micklethwait and Wooldridge, *God is Back*, and similar works.

40. Barber, *Jihad vs. McWorld*; Friedman, *The Lexus and the Olive Tree*; Huntington, *The Clash of Civilizations*.

41. Liora Danon and the Center for Strategic and International Studies, "Mixed Blessings," August 2007, 2–3.

42. Appleby, *The Ambivalence of the Sacred*.

43. David Singer and David Small, *The Correlates of War*; The Stockholm International Peace Research Institute (SIPRI), *Annual Yearbook of Major Armed Conflicts* (Stockholm: SIPRI, 2009); Monty Marshall and Ted Robert Gurr, *Peace and Conflict: A Global Survey of Armed Conflicts, Self-Determination Movements, and Democracy* (College Park, MD: Center for International Development and Conflict Management University of Maryland, 2007).

44. Milton Leitenberg, *Deaths in Wars and Conflicts Between 1945 and 2000*, Cornell University Peace Studies Program (Occasional paper # 29, June 2006), http://www.cissm.umd.edu/papers/files/deathswarsconflictsjune52006.pdf; Walter Wink, *The Powers that Be* (New York, 1998).

45. Vesselin Popovski, Gregory M. Reichbert, and Nicholas Turner (Eds.), *World Religions and Norms of War* (New York: United Nations University Press, 2009).

46. Robert D. Kaplan, *The Coming Anarchy: Shattering the Dreams of the Post–Cold War World* (New York: Vintage Books, 2001); Robert D. Kaplan, *Balkan Ghosts: A Journey through History* (New York: Vintage Books, 1994).

47. Susan Woodward, *Balkan Tragedy* (Washington, DC: Brookings Institution, 1995).

48. Appleby, *The Ambivalence of the Sacred*, 70–71.

49. Maryann Cusimano Love, *Morality Matters: Ethics and Combating Terror* (Ithaca, NY: Cornell University Press, forthcoming).

50. Love, *Morality Matters*.

51. Associated Press, "A Rabbi, A Priest, and an Imam Discuss their Painful Verses," May 6, 2008.

52. Armstrong, *The Battle for God*.

53. Michael Gerson, "The Sultan and the Archbishop," *The Washington Post*, May 22, 2009; John L. Allen Jr., "Tough Love With Islam: Church in Nigeria may be a Model of Dialogue," *National Catholic Reporter*, March 30, 2007.

54. Philpott, "Explaining the Political Ambivalence of Religion," 505–525; Philip Jenkins, "The Politics of Persecuted Religious Minorities," in *Religion and Security: The New Nexus in International Relations* (Lanham, MD: Rowman and Littlefield, 2004); Seiple and Hoover (Eds.), *Religion and Security*; Alfred Stepan, "The World's Religious Systems and Democracy: Crafting the 'Twin Tolerations,'" in *Arguing Comparative Politics* (Oxford: Oxford University Press, 2001), 213–254; Farr, *World of Faith and Freedom*.

55. Appleby, *The Ambivalence of the Sacred*.

56. Ibid., 86.

57. Ibid., 88.

58. "(1) multigenerational Protestant fundamentalism in North America; (2) Comunione e Liberazione, the Roman Catholic movement active in Italy and other parts of Europe; (3) international branches or offshoots of the original Egyptian Muslim Brotherhood, including Hamas and Hassan Turabi's National Islamic Front of Sudan; (4) the Sunni jama'at extremist cells influenced by the ideology of

Maududi and Qutb and led by charismatic figures such as Omar Abdel Rahman of Egypt and Marwan Hadid of Syria (Algeria's Islamist movement, as it developed in the 1970s and 1980s, was also influenced by this ideological strain, as are the aforementioned global terrorist networks of bin Laden); (5) Shi'ite movements in Iran (led by the Ayatollah Khomeini and his successors) and Lebanon (Hizbullah): 9^) Maududi's Jamaat-i-Islami organization in southern Asia, which remains strongest in Pakistan; (7) the haredi, or ultra-Orthodox, Jewish enclaves in Israel and North America; (8) Habad, the movement of Lubavitcher Hasidim, another Jewish messianist enclave but with missionary outreach toward the larger jewish community; (9) Gush Emunim, the extremist backbone of the Israeli settler movement; and (10) the Sikh extremists agitating for a separate state (Khalistan) in the Punjab." Appleby, *The Ambivalence of the Sacred*, 103.

59. Adapted from Love, *Morality Matters*, chapter two.

60. Michael Walzer, *Just and Unjust Wars: A Moral Argument with Historical Illustrations*, Third ed. (New York: Basic Books, 1977), 21.

61. Clement and Augustine (whom many consider the "father" of JWT), were Africans whose thought inspired later generations of European just war thinkers.

62. John Kelsay and James Turner Johnson (Eds.), *Just War and Jihad: Historical and Theoretical Perspectives on War and Peace in Western and Islamic Traditions* (New York: Greenwood Press, 1991); Karen Armstrong, *The Battle for God* (New York: Random House, 2000); George W. Gawrych, *Jihad, War, and Terrorism* (Fort Leavenworth, KS: U.S. Army Command and General Staff College). Combat Studies Institute, 29 October 2002. http://www_cgsc.army.mil/csi/research/writing/JihadGawrych.asp.

63. The greater jihad (to which all Muslims are called) is personal conversion and continued spiritual transformation. The lesser jihad (which is only necessitated under limited circumstances) is the defensive resort to arms to protect the Islamic community from attack. "The defensive jihad (*jihad al-dafaa*)... is a widely accepted concept that is analogous to international norms of self-defense and Judeo-Christian just-war theory. According to most Islamic scholars, when an outside force invades Muslim territory, it is incumbent upon all Muslims to wage jihad to protect the faith and the faithful. Mutual protection is seen as a religious obligation intended to ensure the survival of the global Muslim community. At the root of defensive jihad is a theological emphasis on justness, , as embodied in chapter 6, verse 151 of the Quran: "Do not slay the soul sanctified by God except for just cause." Defending the faith-based community against external aggression is considered a just cause *par excellence*." (Quintan Wiktorowicz and John Kaltner, "Killing in the Name of Islam: Al-Qaeda's Justification for September 11," *Middle East Policy Council Journal* X, no. 2 [Summer 2003]). Defensive jihad not only parallels the *jus ad bellum* condition of just cause, but "the jihad tradition also requires right authority. Historically, the leader of the community—the caliph for the Sunnis and the imam for the Shiites—had to authorize the use of force... to defend against an attack on Islamic society. But there were very stringent restrictions placed on this... Furthermore, the jihad tradition includes very explicit limits on whom you may fight. There are a number of traditions associated with the prophet Mohammed which include the language 'you shall not kill the women and children.' Some of the traditions

also include other groups of people: the aged, the infirm, the mentally incompetent. These are exactly the same kinds of lists we find in the just war tradition and in the contemporary international law of armed conflict."(James Turner Johnson, "Just War Tradition and the New War on Terrorism," Pew Forum on Religion and Public Life Panel Discussion, New York, October 2001, 8. http://pewforum.org/publicatio ns/reports/PFJustWar.pdf).

63. Citing Islamic tradition concerning limitations on war, many prominent Islamic scholars and clerics condemned the September 11th terrorist attacks as inconsistent with Islam.

64. Shannon E. French, *The Code of the Warrior: The Values and Ideals of Warrior Cultures Throughout History* (Lanham, MD: Rowman & Littlefield, 2003).

65. Love, *Morality Matters*, chapter two. Currently there are approximately 12 major armed conflicts going on around the world, most taking place in Africa and Asia. That number is down from the high of 33 major armed conflicts immediately after the Cold War ended, but the number has been rather stable over the past ten years. Most of these conflicts are civil or internal wars fought between government and rebel groups over who will control the country. In most of these wars serious *jus in bello* violations are routinely committed by both government and rebel groups (and are well-documented by many NGOs and IGOs, such as the International Committee of the Red Cross and Red Crescent societies, Amnesty International, Human Rights Watch, Doctors Without Borders, and the UN High Commission for Human Rights and the UN High Commission for Refugees). Wars in which non-combatant immunity and discrimination are routinely and deliberately violated are not just wars (*jus in bello* criteria are not met), regardless of the rationales behind these conflicts. Further, we know that many wars are conducted for personal power or aggrandizement, by brutal, corrupt, self-interested dictators, governments, and rebel groups, at times supported by private mercenary groups; these wars do not meet *jus ad bellum* conditions (just cause, right intention, legitimate authority). Yet we also know that sometimes innocents are slaughtered and in need of protection (September 11th; Rwanda). So the empirical record of recent decades has been that while most wars are unjust, under rare conditions war may be just. This rough, rule of thumb generalization can serve as a baseline to evaluate whether commentators (or we ourselves) are applying JWT responsibly. If all wars are deemed just or all wars are deemed unjust, we should be suspicious. Similarly, since no country or decision maker has a lock on virtue or vice, we should be similarly skeptical should all wars by one country or leader be judged just or unjust (e.g., the United States only fights just wars, or all US military interventions are unjust). While the evaluation in any particular case may prove true upon further inspection, it also may be a red flag that jingoist, nationalist, ideological or political biases are distorting judgment.

66. Erica Chenoweth and Maria Stephen, *Why Civil Resistance Works* (New York: Columbia University Press, 2011).

67. Maryann Cusimano Love, "What Kind of Peace Do We Seek? Emerging Peacebuilding Norms and Institutions," chapter in Scott Appleby (Ed.), *The Ethics and Theology of Peacebuilding* (New York and London: Oxford University Press, forthcoming).

6: REFUGEES, IDPs, AND MIGRANTS: PEOPLE BEYOND BORDERS

1. Bill O Keefe, quoted in Madd Hadro, "Latest Migrant Crisis Prompts Call to Address Root Problem," *Crux*, May 15, https://cruxnow.com/global-church/2017/0 5/15/latest-migrant-tragedy-prompts-call-address-root-problem/.

2. Yusra Mardini, quoted in "Yusra Mardini Appointed UNHCR Goodwill Ambassador," *UNHCR*, April 27, 2017, https://www.unhcr.org/ph/11691-yusr a-mardini-appointed-unhcr-goodwill-ambassador.html.

3. Knaan, *When I Get Older* (Toronto, ON: Tundra Books, 2012).

4. Madeleine Albright, quoted in "Five Refugees Who Changed the World," November 5, 2017, https://www.weforum.org/agenda/2015/11/5-refugees-who-changed-the-world/.

5. Henry Kissinger, "Remarks to the International Rescue Committee," March 2012, https://www.rescue.org/video/six-former-secretaries-state-speak-out-refugees.

6. Interview with author, Iraq, March 2016.

7. Ibid.; "Becoming Self Reliant," *JRS*, April 1, 2017, https://en.jrs.net/campai gn_detail?TN=PROJECT-20170327092155.

8. Interview with author, Iraq, March 2016.

9. Cindy Wooden, "Pulled from the Sea, Rescue Puts Spotlight on Italian Policies," *Catholic News Service*, July 18, 2018, https://cnstopstories.com/2018/07/18/pulled-from-the-sea-migrants-rescue-puts-spotlight-on-italian-policy/.

10. US Agency for International Development, "Cameroon Food Assistance Fact Sheet," October 13, 2017, https://reliefweb.int/report/cameroon/cameroon-food-ass istance-fact-sheet-october-13-2017.

11. Sarah Mardini was imprisoned without bail for 6 months during pre-trial detention. She has now been released, but despite no factual evidence of the charges against her, the charges have not been dropped. Piper French, "Rescue a Refugee: Get Charged with Trafficking?" *The New Republic*, March 5, 2019.

12. UNHCR, "Global Trends," June 2019, https://www.unhcr.org/5b27be547. pdf; International Organization for Migration, Migration Report, January 5, 2018, https://www.iom.int/news/mediterranean-migrant-arrivals-reached-171635--dea ths-reach-3116.

13. United Nations Conference of Plenipotentiaries on the Status of Refugees, 04/22/1954, Preamble, available at http://www.refugee.net/legal/un.html.

14. UNESCO (United States Educational, Scientific, and Cultural Organization) 2004, [Convention of 1951, Article 1A (2)] The United Nations High Commissioner for Refugees (UNHCR) and the Executive Committee of the High Commissioners Programme, http://portal.unesco.org/shs/en/ev.php-URL_ID=3138&URL_DO=DO _TOPIC&URL_SECTION=201.html.

15. Karen Musalo, Director, "Gender Asylum Facts: Background on Gender and Asylum," *Center for Gender & Refugee Studies (CGRS)*, http://cgrs.uchastings.edu/about/facts.php.

16. Maryann Cusimano Love, "Against All Odds," America, May 5, 2008.

17. Human Rights Watch, "World Report 2018: DRC," https://www.hrw.org/world-report/2018/country-chapters/democratic-republic-congo.

18. Robin M. Maher, "Female Genital Mutilation: The Modern Day Struggle to Eradicate a Torturous Rite of Passage," *Human Rights* 23, no. 4 (Fall 1996). Maher suggests that the term "female genital mutilation" generally describes three different forms of genital mutilation. The most common form is female circumcision, in which the clitoris is partially or completely cut away, often with razor blades or broken glass, and rarely with anesthesia. The most extreme form of FGM is infibulation, in which the entire genital area and outer tissues are cut away. The external sides of the vagina are then sewn together using catgut or thorns, leaving only a tiny opening for the passage of urine and for menstruation. The procedure, often performed by female family members, is carried out in nonsterile conditions and frequently results in serious and sometimes fatal infections. In some areas in West Africa, dirt, ashes, or pulverized animal feces are thrown into the wound to stop the bleeding, which contributes to the opportunity for infection, shock, and uncontrolled hemorrhaging. Following the procedure, the girl's legs are bound together for as long as forty days, during which time (if she survives) her wound heals and scars. The long-term effects of this procedure include complications and pain with menstruation, urination, intercourse, and childbirth. The association suggests that it is no coincidence that the highest maternal and infant mortality rates in the world are recorded in regions where FGM is practiced. The scarring and complications associated with FGM frequently result in delayed and obstructed labor, tearing, and hemorrhaging. Unassisted childbirth is impossible following infibulation; many women and infants die during childbirth as a consequence of the procedure.

19. Musalo, "Gender Asylum Facts"; and "Update on Rodi Alverado's Case," September 2008, http://cgrs.uchastings.edu/campaigns/alvarado.php.

20. Hillary Mayell, "Thousands of Women Killed for Family 'Honor,'" *National Geographic*, February 12, 2002, http://news.nationalgeographic.com/news/2002/02/0212_020212_honorkilling.html.

21. Mirren Gidda, "Women Are Dying in Honor Killings, and No One Knows How Many," *Newsweek*, May 12, 2017, https://www.newsweek.com/2017/05/12/honor-killings-violence-against-women-seeta-kaur-india-pakistan-593691.html.

22. International Labor Organization, "2017 Global Estimates of Modern Slavery," September 19, 2017, http://www.ilo.org/global/publications/books/WCMS_575479/lang--en/index.htm.

23. UNODC, "Global Report on Trafficking in Persons," February 12, 2009, http://www.unodc.org/unodc/en/frontpage/unodc-report-on-human-trafficking-exposes-modern-form-of-slavery-.html; Anderson Cooper, "Modern Day Slavery on the Rise," February 19, 2009, http://ac360.blogs.cnn.com/2009/02/19/modern-day-slavery-on-the-rise/; UNODC, Kevin Bales, "Modern-Day Slavery," *Testimony Before the Congressional Human Rights Caucus*, June 17, 2003, www.house.gov/lantos/caucus/TestimonyBales061703.htm; Kevin Bales, "How We Can End Slavery," *National Geographic*, September 2003, http://magma.nationalgeographic.com/ngm/0309/feature1/online_extra.html; Andrew Cockburn, "Twenty-First Century Slaves," *National Geographic*, September 2003, http://magma.nationalgeographic.com/ngm/0309/feature1/index.html.

24. US State Department, "2017 Trafficking in Persons Report," June 27, 2017, https://www.state.gov/j/tip/rls/tiprpt/2017/.

25. Musalo, "Gender Asylum Facts."

26. UN High Commission on Refugees, "Figures At a Glance," http://www.unhc r.org/en-us/figures-at-a-glance.html.

27. UN High Commission on Refugees, "Global Trends 2017," http://www. unhcr.org/globaltrends2017/.

28. United Nations Department of Economic and Social Affairs, "International Migration Report 2017," https://www.unhcr.org/5b27be547.pdf.

29. Philip Connor, "International Migration: Key Findings," *Pew Research Center*, December 15, 2016, http://www.pewresearch.org/fact-tank/2016/12/15/interna tional-migration-key-findings-from-the-u-s-europe-and-the-world/.

30. Charles M. Sennott, "An Immigrant Rush Stirs British-French Friction Eurotunnel Lure Draws Foreigners," *The Boston Globe*, June 9, 2002, A6.

31. UN News, "Mediterranean Crossing World's Deadliest for Migrants," November 24, 2017, https://news.un.org/en/story/2017/11/637162-mediterrane an-crossing-still-worlds-deadliest-migrants-un-report.

32. Old endnote 24.

33. Crisp, "Politics of Asylum," 83.

34. Louise Hunt, "The Mental Distress of Detained Asylum Seekers," *Community Care*, April 9, 2009. "Home at Last," *Economist*, June 25, 2005, 42.

35. UNHCR, *2008 Global Refugee Trends*, 5

36. The United Nations Economic Commission for Latin America and the Caribbean (ECLAC), Productive Development in Open Economies (June 18, 2004): 53.

37. World Bank, Migration and Remittances Team, "Migration and Development Brief: Remittances Trends," May 21, 2018.

38. Amy Budiman and Phillip Connor, "Migrants From Latin America Sent a Record Amount of Remittances," *Pew Research*, January 23, 2018, http://www .pewresearch.org/fact-tank/2018/01/23/migrants-from-latin-america-and-the-caribb ean-sent-a-record-amount-of-money-to-their-home-countries-in-2016/.

39. UN, *World Economic Survey 2004*, 105, 111; "Dollars Without Borders," *The New York Times*, May 13, 2004, 26; Peter Wise, "A Mainstay of the Economy: Portugal's Banks Have Been Singled Out as Model for How Remittances Can Be Used to Build National Wealth," *Financial Times*, October 20, 2004, 3.

40. World Bank, "Digital Remittances," March 3, 2017, http://blogs.worldba nk.org/peoplemove/digital-remittances-and-global-financial-health; "World Bank to Support Remittance Transfer Via Mobile Phones," *The Financial Express*, May 5, 2009.

41. José A. Muñoz and José L. Collazo, "Looking Out for Paisanos: Latino Hometown Associations as Transnational Advocacy Networks," *Migration and Development* 3, no. 1 (2014): 130–141.

42. UN, *World Economic Survey*, 105.

43. Jonathon Blitzer, "Inside the Campaign to Register Mexicans in the U.S. to Vote—in Mexican Elections," *The New Yorker*, April 12, 2018, https://www.new yorker.com/news/news-desk/inside-the-campaign-to-register-mexicans-in-the-us-to-votein-mexico; Benedict Mander, "Mexicans Abroad Win the Right to Vote by Post," *Financial Times*, June 30, 2005, 6.

44. BUA, "Ex-Patriot Voters Acknowledged," *South Africa Information*, April 24, 2009, http://www.southafrica.info/abroad/voters.htm; Roel Landingin and Justine Lau, "Philippine Presidential Race Moves Overseas," *Financial Times*, February 16, 2004, 2; Simon Montlake, "Filipinos Abroad Get Vote," *Christian Science Monitor*, March 17, 2004, 7.

45. Mark Raper, "Changing Role of NGOs in Refugee Assistance," in Leonore Loeb Adler and Uwe P. Gielen (Eds.), *Migration: Immigration and Emigration in International Perspective* (Westport, CT: Greenwood Publishing Group, 2003), 355; Stephen C. Lubkemann, "Refugees," in World at Risk: A Global Issues Source Book (Washington, DC: CQ Press, 2002), 531.

46. Raper, "Changing Role," 359.

47. Ibid., 356–357.

48. Quoted in Chen, "Confinement and Dependency," 10.

49. Benjamin Gidron, Phillip Quarles van Ufford, and Abdulhamid Bedri Kello, *NGOs Dealing with Refugee Resettlement in Ethiopia*, NIRP Research for Policy Series 12 (Amsterdam, NE: Royal Tropical Institute, 2002), 40.

50. Interviews with the author, 2016.

51. Maryann Cusimano Love, "Christian Transnational Networks," in *Under Caesar's Sword* (Oxford University Press, 2017).

52. Fr. William Headley, "Catholic Relief Services, Caritas Internationalis and Catholic Peacebuilding Network as 'Practical Peacebuilders," San Diego, CA, June 9, 2005, available at http://cpn.nd.edu/beyond_merton.htm.

53. US Holocaust Memorial Exhibit and Frank Davies, "Ill-Fated WWII Voyage Created a Mini Holocaust," *The Miami Herald*, June 1, 1999.

54. In 2003, more than fifty years after the UNHCR was founded, the UN General Assembly decided to change it into a permanent mandate until the resolution of all refugee problems was achieved. UNHCR, *Basic Facts: Helping Refugees*, www. unhcr.ch/cgibin/texis/vtx/basics/opendoc.htm?tbl=BASICS&id=420cc0432.

55. Lubkemann, "Refugees," 530.

56. United Nations, "Milosevic Case Information Sheet," April 5, 2005, www. un.org/icty/glance/milosevic.htm.

57. Jolene Kay Jesse, "Humanitarian Relief in the Midst of Conflict: The UN High Commissioner for Refugees in the Former Yugoslavia," Institute for the Study of Diplomacy, Case 471 (Georgetown University, 1996), 1–7.

58. Ibid., 8.

59. US Department of State, Bureau of Population, Refugees, and Migration, "Refugee Admissions and Resettlement."

60. The USA PATRIOT antiterrorism law itself is also an obstacle to legitimate refugees. A provision of the Patriot Act excludes from refugee admission anyone who has provided "material support" to any organization involved in terrorist activities. Unfortunately this clause has been broadly interpreted without exceptions for "support" forced at gunpoint or under duress, or for minimal or unknowing support. This means that Colombian families forced to pay ransom for the return of kidnapped loved ones are deemed to be terrorist supporters rather than being recognized as victims of terrorism. Most Colombians identified by the UNHCR as in need of resettlement are thus excluded, as extortion by paramilitary forces is

routine. Even Iraqis who worked with US forces to overthrow the government of Saddam Hussein were excluded by this law that was intended to catch terrorists.

61. The Economist, "Why Climate Migrants Do Not Have Refugee Status," March 6, 2018, https://www.economist.com/the-economist-explains/2018/03/06/why-climate-migrants-do-not-have-refugee-status.

62. US Department of State, "Global Report on Trafficking in Persons," Washington, DC, June 2018, https://www.state.gov/documents/organization/282798.pdf.

63. Maryann Cusimano, "Operation Restore Hope: The Bush Administration's Decision to Intervene in Somalia," Pew case study published by the Institute for the Study of Diplomacy, Georgetown University, 1995, www.guisd.org.

7: ENVIRONMENT AND HEALTH: CARING FOR OUR COMMON HOME

1. Philip J. Landrigan, Richard Fuller, Nereus J. R. Acosta, Olusoji Adeyi, Robert Arnold, Niladri (Nil) Basu, Abdoulaye Bibi Baldé, Roberto Bertollini, Stephan Bose-O'Reilly, Jo Ivey Boufford, Patrick N. Breysse, Thomas Chiles, Chulabhorn Mahidol, Awa M. Coll-Seck, Maureen L. Cropper, Julius Fobil, Valentin Fuster, Michael Greenstone, Andy Haines, David Hanrahan, David Hunter, Mukesh Khare, Alan Krupnick, Bruce Lanphear, Bindu Lohani, Keith Martin, Karen V. Mathiasen, Maureen A. McTeer, Christopher J. L. Murray, Johanita D. Ndahimananjara, Frederica Perera, Janez Potočnik, Alexander S. Preker, Jairam Ramesh, Johan Rockström, Carlos Salinas, Leona D. Samson, Karti Sandilya, Peter D. Sly, Kirk R. Smith, Achim Steiner, Richard B. Stewart, William A. Suk, Onno C. P. van Schayck, Gautam N. Yadama, Kandeh Yumkella, Ma Zhong. "The Lancet Commission on Pollution and Health," *The Lancet*, 2017, 1.

2. Stacy VanDeever, "Still Digging: Extractive Industries, Resource Curses, and Transnational Governance in the Anthropocene," TransAtlantic Academy Paper Series, Washington, DC, 2013, file:///C:/Users/CUAUser/Downloads/1358285161VanDeveer_StillDigging_Jan13_web.pdf.

3. Christian Nellemann et al. (Eds.), *The Environmental Crime Crisis*, A Rapid Response Assessment (Oslo: United Nations Environment Programme, 2014), 8, http://www.unep.org/unea/docs/RRAcrimecrisis.pdf.

4. Pope Francis, *Laudato Si: Care for Our Common Home.* 2015, No. 146.

5. Mike Barrett, as quoted in "Humanity Has Wiped Out 60% of Animal Populations Since 1970, Major Report Finds," *The Guardian*, October 30, 2018, https://www.theguardian.com/environment/2018/oct/30/humanity-wiped-out-animals-since-1970-major-report-finds.

6. Damian Carrington, "Why Does Biodiversity Matter to Us?" *The Guardian*, March 12, 2018, https://www.theguardian.com/news/2018/mar/12/what-is-biodiversity-and-why-does-it-matter-to-us.

7. "The U.S. Patent Office Rejects Claim for Bean Plant Commonly Grown in Mexico," April 2008, https://www.eurekalert.org/pub_releases/2008-04/bc-upo043008.php.

8. Cristiana Palma, as quoted in, "Stop Biodiversity Loss or We Could Face Our Own Extinction," *The Guardian*, November 6, 2018, https://www.theguardian.

com/environment/2018/nov/03/stop-biodiversity-loss-or-we-could-face-our-own-extinction-warns-un.

9. United Nations Environment Program, "Tackling Global Water Pollution," https://www.unenvironment.org/explore-topics/water/what-we-do/tackling-global-water-pollution.

10. World Health Organization, "Press Release for Report: 2.1 Billion People Lack Safe Drinking Water at Home," July 12, 2017, https://www.unicef.org/press-releases/21-billion-people-lack-safe-drinking-water-home-more-twice-many-lack-safe-sanitation.

11. Nicholas Mallos, "The Problem With Plastics," *Ocean Conservancy*, https://oceanconservancy.org/trash-free-seas/plastics-in-the-ocean/.

12. Food and Agriculture Organization of the United Nation, *The State of World Fisheries and Aquaculture 2016: Contributing to Food Security and Nutrition for All* (Rome: Food and Agriculture Organization of the United Nations, 2016), 38, http://www.fao.org/3/a-i5555e.pdf;London Zoological Society, "Living Planet Index Report," London, http://assets.wwf.org.uk/custom/stories/living_blue_planet/?_ga=1.19969916.537450017.1442235973.

13. NOAA, "Understanding Ocean Acidification," https://www.fisheries.noaa.gov/insight/understanding-ocean-acidification.

14. USDA, "Food Waste Challenge," https://www.usda.gov/oce/foodwaste/faqs.htm.

15. University of Utah, "How Much Do Americans Throw Away," http://students.arch.utah.edu/courses/Arch4011/Recycling%20Facts1.pdf.

16. International Telecommunications Union and United Nations University, "The Global E-Waste Monitor 2017," https://www.itu.int/en/ITU-D/Climate-Change/Pages/Global-E-waste-Monitor-2017.aspx.

17. EPA, "The Minamata Convention," https://www.epa.gov/international-cooperation/minamata-convention-mercury.

18. Lisa Rapaport, "Air Pollution Linked to Asthma in Children, Teens," *Reuters*, November 20, 2015, https://www.reuters.com/article/us-health-airpollution-children-asthma-idUSKCN0T92DB20151120.

19. United Nations, *Millennium Development Goals Report 2015*, July 7, 2015, http://www.un.org/millenniumgoals/2015_MDG_Report/pdf/MDG%202015%20rev%20(July%201).pdf.

20. All the MDG data in these paragraphs comes from the United Nations, *Millennium Development Goals Report 2015*.

21. United Nations, "Sustainable Development Goal 3," https://sustainabledevelopment.un.org/sdg3.

22. The Lancet Commission on Public Health, "Key Findings," Lancet Report on Pollution and Public Health, http://gahp.net/the-lancet-report-2/.

23. Dan Soloman, "Is a Texas Town the Future of Renewable Energy?" *Smithsonian Magazine*, April 2018, https://www.smithsonianmag.com/innovation/texas-town-future-renewable-energy-180968410/.

24. Elinor Ostrom, *Governing the Commons* (Cambridge University Press, 1990).

25. A small number of treaties or conventions, such as in specific areas of arms control, are self-executing. These are for issues that are "terra nova' in law; there

are no local laws in the legislative record on the topic, so by function of how they were written, no change in domestic law has to be written in order for them to go into effect. There are no preexisting local laws in the legislative record that need to be changed to reconcile with the convention or treaty provisions. Most international agreements, as described in this section, are non-self-executing treaties or conventions, in which states have to go through additional steps to reconcile new obligations of the treaty, with existing obligations, especially if the agreement is criminalizing a new class of activity, which will require passage of new criminal codes in alignment with what the new treaty provisions are. States may also officially register reservations as to how the state interprets a treaty. The Vienna Treaty says that if a state signatory has reservations, the state must put the other parties on notice, and addend the reservations to the treaty. Reading the reservations a country has with a treaty is an important way to understand how that signatory "reads," interprets, and understands its treaty obligations.

8: TERROR IN WAR AND PEACE: WEAPONIZING FEAR

1. Audrey Cronin, remarks at, author of *How Terrorism Ends: Understanding the Decline and Demise of Terrorist Campaigns* (Princeton, NJ: Princeton University Press, 2009).

2. Donald Trump, "On Meet the Press," transcript reprinted in the *Washington Post*, August 17, 2015, https://www.washingtonpost.com/news/the-fix/wp/2015/08/17/donald-trump-on-meet-the-press-annotated/?utm_term=.0f22f17bdd98.

3. Testimony to the Senate Armed Services Committee, May 23, 2017.

4. Manuel Valls, quoted in *The New Republic*, July 15, 2016, https://newrepublic.com/minutes/135104/france-going-learn-live-terrorism.

5. Mohammed Ebraheem, "Roadside Bomb Explosion in Kirkuk Leaves Two Civilians Severely Injured," *Iraqi News*, January 5, 2019, https://www.iraqinews.com/iraq-war/roadside-bomb-explosion-in-kirkuk-leaves-two-civilians-severely-injured/.

6. Department of State, "Country Reports on Terrorism 2016: Annex of Statistical Information," July 2017, https://www.state.gov/j/ct/rls/crt/2016/272241.htm.

7. Department of Justice, "N.Y. Man Sentenced for Conspiring to Provide Material Support to ISIL," January 26, 2017, https://www.justice.gov/opa/pr/new-york-man-sentenced-20-years-conspiring-provide-material-support-isil-connection-planned.

8. Kaveh Waddell, "Shutting Down Jihadist Websites Won't Stop Terrorism," *The Atlantic*, November 24, 2015; Chen Hsinchun and Cathy Larson, "The Dark Web Terrorism Research Project," University of Arizona Artificial Intelligence Lab, http://ai.arizona.edu/research/terror/index.htm;Gabriel Weimann, "Using the Internet for Terrorist Recruitment and Mobilization," in Boaz Ganor, Katharina Von Knop, and Carlos Duarte (Eds.), *Hypermedia Seduction for Terrorist Recruiting*, NATO Science for Peace and Security Series, 47–58. Steve Coll and Susan B. Glasser, "Terrorists Turn to the Web as Base of Operations," *The Washington Post*, August 7, 2005, A01.

9. Andrew Duffy, "The Millennium Bomber: Terror Plot Foiled by Border Agent," *The Ottowa Star*, August 15, 2017; Terrence McKenna, "Trail of a

Terrorist" (transcript of Frontline documentary, *Public Broadcasting Service [PBS]*, October 25, 2001, www.pbs.org/wgbh/pages/frontline/shows/trail/etc/script.html); Ahmed Ressam, testimony in July 2001 as a witness for the prosecution at the New York trial of co-conspirator Mokhtar Haouari, federal district court of the Southern District of New York, www.pbs.org/wgbh/pages/frontline/shows/trail/inside/testimony.html.

10. McKenna, "Trail of a Terrorist"; Ahmed Ressam testimony, July 2001.

11. Ibid.

12. Ibid., and Vernon Loeb, "Terrorists Plotted Jan. 2000," *Washington Post*, December 24, 2000, A01; Frontline, "Other Millennium Plots," *PBS*, October 25, 2001, www.pbs.org/wgbh/pages/frontline/shows/trail/inside/attacks.html.

13. Maryann Cusimano Love, "Globalization, Ethics, and the War on Terrorism," *Notre Dame Journal of Law, Ethics, & Public Policy* (Violence in America issue, 2002): 65–80; Maryann Cusimano Love, "Morality Matters: Ethics, Power, Politics, and the War on Terrorism," *Georgetown Journal of International Affairs* (Summer–Fall 2002): 7–16.

14. Martha Crenshaw, "Organized Disorder: Terrorism, Politics, and Society," in Ray C. Rist (Ed.), *The Democratic Imagination* (New Brunswick, NJ: Transaction Publishers, 1994), 140.

15. Ibid.

16. Jesse J. Norris, "Why Dylann Roof is a Terrorist Under Federal Law, and Why It Matters," *Harvard Journal on Legislation*, March 30, 2017, http://harvardjol.com/wp-content/uploads/2017/03/54.1-HLL105.pdf. Because of the unwillingness to call white supremacist violence terrorism, many analysts instead refer to "violent extremism." Over the past decade in the United States, right-wing violent extremist groups were responsible for 71 percent of deaths by extremist groups, while Islamic groups caused 26 percent of US–extremistrelated violence. Anti Defamation League Report, "White Supremacist Murders More than Doubled in 2017," January 17, 2018, https://www.adl.org/news/press-releases/adl-report-white-supremacist-murders-more-than-doubled-in-2017.

17. Love, "Morality Matters"; Saint Augustine, *City of God*, trans. Thomas Merton (New York: Modern Library Paperback Classics, 2000).

18. John Mueller and Mark Stewart, "Terrorism and Bathtub Deaths: Comparing and Assessing the Risks," American Political Science Association Paper, Boston, MA, August 13, 2018, https://politicalscience.osu.edu/faculty/jmueller/bathtubs8APSA.pdf.

19. Love, "Globalization, Ethics, and the War on Terrorism," 65–80; Love, "Morality Matters."

20. Crenshaw, "Organized Disorder," 150.

21. Ibid., 143–144.

22. Danny Boyle, "London Braces for Ten Simultaneous Terror Attacks in the Wake of Paris Atrocities," *The Guardian*, March 21, 2016, https://www.telegraph.co.uk/news/uknews/terrorism-in-the-uk/12199959/London-braced-for-ten-simultaneous-terror-attacks-in-wake-of-Paris-atrocities.html.

23. RAND, "Mumbai Terror Attacks Show Rise of Strategic Terrorist Culture," January 16, 2009, http://www.rand.org/news/press/2009/01/16/; Crenshaw, "Organized Disorder," 143.

24. United Nations, "International Convention for the Suppression of the Financing of Terrorism," December 9, 1999, http://untreaty.un.org/English/ters umen.htm#4.

25. Jonathan R. White, *Terrorism and Homeland Security* (Belmont, CA: Wadsworth, 2005), 12.

26. US Department of State, *Country Reports on Terrorism 2008* (Washington, DC: U.S. Government Printing Office, April 27, 2009), http://www.state.gov/s/ct/rls/crt/2008/122450.

27. Ben Connable and Martin C. Libicki, *How Insurgencies End* (RAND, 2010), Summary Findings.

28. Maryann Cusimano Love, "Broken Promises," America, May 14, 2007; Senator Patrick Leahy, "The Material Support Bar: Denying Refuge to the Persecuted," Senate Judiciary Committee Subcommittee on Human Rights and the Law, September 19, 2007.

29. Irving Louis Horowitz, "Political Terrorism and State Power," *Journal of Political and Military Sociology* (Spring 1973): 145–157.

30. Love, "Globalization, Ethics, and the War on Terrorism," 65–80; Crenshaw, "Why America?" 425.

31. Peter L. Bergen, *Holy War, Inc.: Inside the Secret World of Bin Laden* (New York: Free Press, 2001), 6.

32. It is ironic that Afghan rebel leader Ahmad Shah Massoud, an ardent opponent of the Taliban government and the Al Qaeda camps in his country, was later assassinated by opponents disguised as a camera crew.

33. Bergen, *Holy War, Inc.*, 23.

34. Prime Minister Tony Blair, "Prime Minister's Statement, Bloody Sunday Inquiry," House of Commons Official Report, January 29, 1998, Parliamentary Debates (Hansard) (London), www.bloody-Sunday-inquiry.org.uk/index2.asp?p=7.

35. Paul Wilkinson, "The Orange and the Green," in Martha Crenshaw (Ed.), *Terrorism, Legitimacy and Power* (Middletown, CT: Wesleyan University Press, 1983), 117.

36. "Bloody Sunday: Soldier F Faces Murder Charges," *BBC*, March 14, 2019, https://www.bbc.com/news/uk-northern-ireland-47540271.

37. Maryann Cusimano Love, "Public Private Partnerships and Global Problems: Y2K and Cybercrime. Paper delivered at International Studies Association," Hong Kong meeting, July 2001; Calvin Sims, "Japan Software Suppliers Linked to Sect," *The New York Times*, March 2, 2000, A6.

38. Congressional testimony quoted in "Jihadists Deepen Collaboration in North Africa," *The New York Times*, January 1, 2016, https://www.nytimes.com/2016/.../jihadists-deepen-collaboration-in-north-africa.html.

39. Wilkinson, "The Orange and the Green," 120.

40. This section derived from Love, "Globalization, Ethics, and the War on Terrorism," 65–80.

41. Stephen Flynn, "Homeland Insecurity," *The American Interest*, May/June 2009; *The Edge of Disaster: Building a Resilient Nation* (New York: Random House, 2007); Stephen E. Flynn, *America the Vulnerable: How Our Government Is Failing to Protect Us from Terrorism* (New York: Harper Collins/Perennial, 2005); Stephen E. Flynn, *The Age of Disaster: Terror, Catastrophe, and the Unmaking of a Great Nation* (New York: Random House, 2006).

42. Ibid.

43. Donald Rumsfeld, Memo, October 16, 2003, *Fox News*, http://www.foxn ews.com/story/2003/10/22/raw-data-rumsfeld-memo-to-inner-circle.html.

44. Paul Wilkins, chapter on terrorism in Security Studies edited volume.

45. Martha Crenshaw, "Counterterrorism Policy and the Political Process," *Studies in Conflict & Terrorism* (October 2001): 329–337.

46. Crenshaw, "Organized Disorder," 149; Irving Louis Horowitz, "The Routinization of Terrorism and Its Unanticipated Consequences," in Martha Crenshaw (Ed.), *Terrorism, Legitimacy, and Power* (Middletown, CT: Wesleyan University Press, 1983).

47. Crenshaw, "Organized Disorder," 145.

48. US Department of Transportation, National Highway Traffic Safety Administration, "2017 Traffic Safety Annual Assessment."

49. Cusimano Love, "Globalization, Ethics, and the War on Terrorism," 65–80; Love, "Morality Matters," 7–16.

9: CYBER ATTACKS BEYOND BORDERS

1. Sen. John Kyle, quoted in "Feds, Firms Lack Information Protection Security, Experts Tell Congress," *National Security Institutte's Advisory*, July 1998, 2.

2. Jim Garamone, "DARPA Director Discusses Cybersecurity Challenges," U.S. Department of Defense, October 1, 2014, http://www.defense.gov/news/newsart icle.aspx?id=123307.

3. President Barack Obama, "Obama Responds to Drone Landing at the White House, Wants More Drone Regulation," Interview with *CNN* Fareed Zakaria, January 27, 2015, http://www.cnn.com/videos/us/2015/01/27/sot-obama-zakaria-dr ones-white-house.cnn.

4. McAfee, "A Map of the Most Dangerous Sources of Cybercrime," March 6, 2018, https://securingtomorrow.mcafee.com/business/map-dangerous-source s-cybercrime/ "the combination of massive budgets, access to talent and protection from law enforcement make nation-states the most dangerous source of cybercrime, which our report estimates takes about a $600 billion toll on the global economy."

5. Andy Greenberg, "The Untold Story of NotPetya, the Most Devastating CyberAttack in History," *Wired*, an excerpt from his book *Sandworm* (New York: Penguin, 2019), https://www.wired.com/story/notpetya-cyberattack-ukraine-rus sia-code-crashed-the-world/.

6. Greenberg, "The Untold Story of NotPetya, the Most Devastating CyberAttack in History."

7. Vladimir Putin, quoted in "Putin Says He Wishes He Could Change the Collapse of the Soviet Union; Many Russians Agree," *The Washington Post*, March 3, 2018, https://www.washingtonpost.com/news/worldviews/wp/2018/03/03/puti n-says-he-wishes-he-could-change-the-collapse-of-the-soviet-union-many-russians-agree/?utm_term=.08e22c22d1d3.

8. Ellen Nakashima, "Russian Military Was Behind NotPetya Attacks in Ukraine, CIA Concludes," *The Washington Post*, January 12, 2018, https:// www.washingtonpost.com/world/national-security/russian-military-was-behind-no

tpetya-cyberattack-in-ukraine-cia-concludes/2018/01/12/048d8506-f7ca-11e7-
b34a-b85626af34ef_story.html?utm_term=.57ab313a2df4.

9. Director of National Intelligence, https://www.dni.gov/files/documents/ICA_
2017_01.pdf.

10. Director of National Intelligence, https://www.dni.gov/files/documents/ICA_
2017_01.pdf.

11. The Mueller Report, released Apri18, 2019.

12. United States of America versus Victor Borisovich Netyksho et al., United
States District Court for the District of Columbia, "Indictment of Russians for Election Interference," July 13, 2018, http://cdn.cnn.com/cnn/2018/images/07/13/gru.
indictment.pdf; The Mueller Report.

13. Julian Assange faced rape charges in Sweden, but took refuge in the Ecuadorian Embassy in London to evade facing criminal charges in Sweden, the UK,
and elsewhere. The Ecuadorian Embassy turned Assange over to police in April
2019; the president of Ecuador denounced Assange as "a miserable hacker." PBS,
"Charges Against Assange," April 11, 2019, BBC, "Transcript of Donald Trump's
Obscene Videotape," October 9, 2016, https://www.bbc.com/news/election-us-201
6-37595321.

14. State of Software Security Report, "Trump Eliminates National Cybersecurity Position," NBC News, May 15, 2018, https://www.nbcnews.com/politics/wh
ite-house/trump-eliminates-job-national-cybersecurity-coordinator-n874511.

15. DNI, January 6, 2017, https://www.dni.gov/files/documents/ICA_2017_01.
pdf.

16. United States of America versus Victor Borisovich Netyksho et al., United
States District Court for the District of Columbia, "Indictment of Russians for
Election Interference," July 13, 2018, http://cdn.cnn.com/cnn/2018/images/07/13
/gru.indictment.pdf; Office of the Director of National Intelligence, Intelligence
Community Assessment, "Assessment of Russian Election Activities and Intentions
in Recent U.S. Elections," January 6, 2017, https://www.dni.gov/files/documents
/ICA_2017_01.pdf; as Secretary of State, his opponent Hilary Clinton had used
both government and personal email accounts to conduct government business, as
had every Republican and Democratic secretary of state before her, and as Trump
administration officials continue to do today. Mixing use of personal and professional email and twitter accounts is legal, although perhaps not wise.

17. National Security Advisor Michael Flynn admitted guilt to a felony, lying
to the F.B.I. about his interactions with the Russian government, and to violating
law about lobbying for foreign governments, failing to disclose money he received
to represent foreign governments while working for Trump. Paul Manafort, head
of Trump's presidential campaign, pleaded guilty to multiple felonies of conspiring
against the United States, conspiring to obstruct justice, tamper with witnesses,
and lying about his contacts with Russia. He gave detailed polling information
to Russia that they were able to use in targeting their information attacks. He
was also convicted of eight felonies involving tax evasion and fraud, and failure to disclose pro-Russian lobbying work he did for pro-Russian groups in
Ukraine. Trump's lawyer Michael Cohen pleaded guilty to multiple felony crimes.
These include lying about work to land a real estate deal in Moscow during the

campaign. Cohen violated campaign finance laws by making hush money payments to pornography stars and prostitutes who had sexual relations with Donald Trump, to help Trump win the election by preventing voters from having access to this information prior to the election. Campaign aides Rick Gates and George Papadapolous also pleaded guilty to crimes of financial fraud and perjury, lying about contacts with Russia during the campaign. Trump advisor Roger Stone also faces such charges.

18. Peter Shadbolt, "Is the Darknet a Glimpse of the Future?" *CNN*, December 8, 2014, http://www.cnn.com/2014/12/08/tech/web/tomorrow-transformed-darknet-bot/.

19. Internet Software Consortium, "Internet Domain Survey: Number of Internet Hosts, 1981–2000." http://www.isc.org/ds/host-count-history.html.

20. Reuters, "U.S. Spy Chief Resolute on Russian Cyberattacks of U.S. Election, Differs with Trump," January 6, 2017, http://www.reuters.com/article/us-usa-ru ssia-cyber-clapper-idUSKBN14P0G5.

21. Maryann Cusimano Love, *Beyond Sovereignty*, 4th ed. (New York: Cengage, 2011).

22. Bradley Graham, "Pentagon Orders Security Review of Its Web Sites," *The Washington Post*, September 26, 1998, A5.

23. Love, *Beyond Sovereignty*.

24. Lt. General John Campbell, "Cyberdefense: A Retrospective," *University of Maryland University College*, March 13, 2013, http://www.umuc.edu/cybersecur ity/news/upload/cyber-defense-retrospective.pdf.

25. Jeffrey Silva, "Pentagon May Want 3G Spectrum for Protection," *Crain Communications Report*, September 7, 1998, 8.

26. President Clinton quoted in article by Andrew Rathmell, "Information Warfare: USA Takles Cyber Threat," *Jane's Intelligence Review*, September 1, 1998, 14.

27. Ellie Padget, quoted in "Feds, Firms Lack Information Protection Security, Experts Tell Congress," *National Security Institute's Advisory*, July 1998, 2.

28. Dr. John J. Hamre, Deputy secretary of defense, "Remarks at the 2nd Annual Leaders Conference Microsoft Corporation," Seattle, Washington, April 15, 1999.

29. Rathmell, "Information Warfare: USA Takles Cyber Threat," *Jane's Intelligence Review*, September 1, 1998, 14.

30. Associated Press, "Hackers Hit More Federal Web Sites," *The Washington Post*, June 1, 1999, A5.

31. Lt. General John Campbell, "Cyberdefense: A Retrospective."

32. Department of Defense, "Office of the Chief Information Officer," http://dodcio.defense.gov/AboutCIO.aspx, accessed March 14, 2015.

33. Lt. Gen Richard P. Mills, Deputy Commandant for Combat Development and Integration, US Marine Corps Commanding General, US Marine Corps Forces Cyberspace Command, remarks atTechNet Land Forces Conference, Baltimore, MD, August 15, 2012, http://www.afcea.org/events/tnlf/east12/intro.asp "I can tell you that as a commander in Afghanistan in the year 2010, I was able to use my cyber operations against my adversary with great impact. I was able to get inside his nets, infect his command and control, and in fact defend myself against his almost constant incursions to get inside my wire, to affect my operations."

34. Kim Zetter, *Countdown to Zero Day: Stuxnet and the Launch of the World's First Digital Weapon* (New York: Crown/ Random House, 2014), also excerpted in *Wired*, November 3, 2014, http://www.wired.com/2014/11/countdown-to-zero-day-stuxnet/.

35. Richard Clarke, "Who Was Behind the Stuxnet Virus," *Smithsonian Magazine*, April 2012, http://www.smithsonianmag.com/history/richard-clarke-on-who-was-behind-the-stuxnet-attack-160630516/?no-ist.

36. Clarke, "Who Was Behind the Stuxnet Virus."

37. Ibid.

38. "BSI Admits Cyberattack Caused Physical Damage to Iron Plant," *Computer Business Review*, December 19, 2014, http://www.cbronline.com/news/cybersecurity/data/bsi-admits-cyber-attack-caused-physical-damage-to-iron-plant-4473814.

39. Dana Priest, "NSA Growth Fueled by the Need to Target Terrorists," *The Washington Post*, July 21, 2013, http://www.washingtonpost.com/world/national-security/nsa-growth-fueled-by-need-to-target-terrorists/2013/07/21/24c93cf4-f0b1-11e2-bed3-b9b6fe264871_story.html.

40. Kevin Bankston, "Court Rules Warrantless Wiretapping Illegal," March 31, 2010, https://www.eff.org/deeplinks/2010/03/court-rules-warrantless-wiretapping-illegal.

41. National Security Agency, Office of the Inspector General, History of NSA surveillance program, March 21, 2009, http://www.theguardian.com/world/interactive/2013/jun/27/nsa-inspector-general-report-document-data-collection; Electronic Frontier Foundation, timeline of NSA Domestic Spying, https://www.eff.org/nsa-spying/timeline.

42. President Obama, "Transcript of Speech on NSA Reforms," January 17, 2014, http://www.washingtonpost.com/politics/full-text-of-president-obamas-jan-17-speech-on-nsa-reforms/2014/01/17/fa33590a-7f8c-11e3-9556-4a4bf7bcbd84_story.html.

43. Joseph Menn, Reuters Special Report, "U.S. Cyberwar Strategies Stokes Fears of Blowback," May 10, 2013, http://in.reuters.com/article/2013/05/10/usa-cyberweapons-idINDEE9490AX20130510?type=economicNews.

44. Nicole Perlwath and David Sanger, "U.S. Embedded Spyware Overseas, Report Claims," *The New York Times*, February 16, 2015, http://www.nytimes.com/2015/02/17/technology/spyware-embedded-by-us-in-foreign-networks-security-firm-says.html?_r=0.

45. Joseph Menn, "Russian Researchers Expose Breakthrough U.S. Spying Program," *Reuters*, February 16, 2015, http://www.reuters.com/article/2015/02/16/us-usa-cyberspying-idUSKBN0LK1QV20150216.

46. Clarke, "Who Was Behind the Stuxnet Virus."

47. Christopher Harress, "The U2 and Global Hawk," *International Business Times*, August 14, 2014, http://www.ibtimes.com/u-2-global-hawk-us-spy-planes-will-help-hunt-isis-syria-1671272.

48. Aram Roston, "Will Congress Let the Air Force Abandon the Global Hawk?" *Defense News*, June 24, 2013, http://www.defensenews.com/article/20130624/C4ISR01/307010011.

49. Department of State, "U.S. Export Policy for Military Unmanned Aerial Systems," February 17, 2015, http://www.state.gov/r/pa/prs/ps/2015/02/237541.htm.

50. Katia Moskvitch, "Drones Can Be Hacked," *BBC*, February 6, 2014, http://www.bbc.com/future/story/20140206-can-drones-be-hacked.

51. Lori Hinnant and Susannah George, "ISIS Using Drones, Innovating Tactics, with Deadly Effects," *Associated Press*, February 1, 2017, http://www.military.com/daily-news/2017/02/01/isis-using-drones-other-innovating-tactics-deadly-effect.html.

52. Shan Carter and Amanda Fox, "9/11 Tally: 3 Trillion Dollars," *The New York Times*, September 8, 2011, http://www.nytimes.com/interactive/2011/09/08/us/sept-11-reckoning/cost-graphic.html.

53. "The FAA Modernization and Reform Act of 2012," February 1, 2012, http://www.gpo.gov/fdsys/pkg/CRPT-112hrpt381/pdf/CRPT-112hrpt381.pdf.

54. David Chazan, "Drones Spotted Over French Military Sites," *The Telegraph*, March 8, 2015, http://www.telegraph.co.uk/news/worldnews/europe/france/11458116/Drone-spotted-over-French-military-site.html.

55. FAA, "FAA Proposes New Rules for Small, Unmanned Aircraft Systems: Regulations Will Facilitate Integration of UAS Into U.S. Aviation System," February 15, 2015, http://www.faa.gov/news/press_releases/news_story.cfm?newsId=18295.

56. White House, "Fact Sheet on Presidential Memorandum: Promoting Economic Competitiveness While Safeguarding Privacy, Civil Rights, and Civil Liberties in Domestic Use of Unmanned Aircraft Systems," February 15, 2015, http://www.whitehouse.gov/the-press-office/2015/02/15/fact-sheet-promoting-economic-competitiveness-while-safeguarding-privacy.

57. FAA, "FAA and Academy of Model Aeronautics Work Together on UAS Safety," January 13, 2014, http://www.faa.gov/news/updates/?newsId=75599.

58. Joan Lowy, "Drone Crashes at White House; Hobbyist Says It's His," *Associated Press*, January 26, 2015, https://www.militarytimes.com/news/your-military/2015/01/26/drone-crashes-at-white-house-hobbyist-says-it-s-his/.

59. FIRST, https://www.first.org/about.

60. Duncan Hollis and Tim Maurer, "A Red Cross for Cyberspace," *Time Magazine*, February 18, 2015, http://time.com/3713226/red-cross-cyberspace/.

61. Most other countries follow this pattern. See, Neil Robinson, Luke Gribbon, Veronika Horvath, Kate Robertson, Rand Corporation Report 235, *Cyber Security Threat Characterization: A Comparative Analysis*, Prepared for the Center for Asymmetric Threat Studies (CATS) (Stockholm: Swedish National Defence College, 2013); OECD, 2012, "Cybersecurity Policy Making at a Turning Point: Analysing a New Generation of National Cybersecurity Strategies for the Internet Economy," *OECD Digital Economy Papers*, No. 211 (OECD Publishing). http://dx.doi.org/10.1787/5k8zq92vdgtl-en.

62. Robert Anderson, Jr., Executive Director Cyber Services Branch, FBI, "Testimony to the Senate Committee on Homeland Security and Governmental Affairs," Washington, DC, September 10, 2014, http://www.fbi.gov/news/testimony/cyber-security-terrorism-and-beyond-addressing-evolving-threats-to-the-homeland.

63. Attorney General Janet Reno, "Address to the Conference on Critical Infrastructure Protection," February 27, 1998, Lawrence Livermore Laboratory, California, 19.

64. Roy Mark, "Obama's Cybersecurity Plan: Deja Vu All Over Again," *E-Week*, May 29, 2009, http://www.eweek.com/c/a/Security/Obamas-Cyber-

Security-Plan-Deja-Vu-All-Over-Again-469231; Declan McCullough, "A Cybersecurity Quiz: Can You Tell Obama from Bush?" *CNet*, May 29, 2009, http://www.cnet.com/news/a-cybersecurity-quiz-can-you-tell-obama-from-bush/.

65. Congressional Research Service, "The 2013 Cyber security Executive Order," December 15, 2014, http://fas.org/sgp/crs/misc/R42984.pdf.

66. Price Waterhouse Cooper, "Why You Should Adopt the NIST Cybersecurity Framework," May 2014, http://www.pwc.com/en_US/us/increasing-it-effectiveness/publications/assets/adopt-the-nist.pdf.

67. Diane Shelton, *Commitment and Compliance: The Role of Non-binding Norms in the International Legal System* (Oxford, 2003), 6; Deborah Avant, Martha Finnemore, and Susan Sell, *Who Governs the Globe*; Eleanor Ostrom, *Governing the Commons: The Evolution of Institutions for Collective Action* (Cambridge: Cambridge University Press, 1990).

68. European Commission, "Press Release on Comprehensive Data Protection Reform," Brussels, Belgium, January 25, 2012, http://europa.eu/rapid/press-release_IP-12-46_en.htm?locale=en.

69. European Union, NIS Directive, https://ec.europa.eu/digital-single-market/en/network-and-information-security-nis-directive.

70. Global Governance Working Paper, "Increasing International Cooperation on Cybersecurity," The Council on Foreign Relations, February 23, 2018, https://www.cfr.org/report/increasing-international-cooperation-cybersecurity-and-adapting-cyber-norms.

71. Attorney General Janet Reno, "Address to the Conference on Critical Infrastructure Protection," February 27, 1998, Lawrence Livermore Laboratory, California, 4–5, 19.

72. National Infrastructure Protection Center, Federal Bureau of Investigations, "Frequently Asked Questions," Washington, DC.

73. Neil Postman, *Technopoly: The Surrender of Culture to Technology* (New York: Vintage Books, 1993), 4–5, 11.

74. "Increasing international Cooperation Needed in Cybersecurity," The Council on Foreign Relations, https://www.cfr.org/report/increasing-international-cooperation-cybersecurity-and-adapting-cyber-norms.

10: GLOBAL CRIMINAL NETWORKS: OLD CHALLENGES, NEW MEANS

1. Louise Shelley, *Dark Commerce: How A New Illicit Economy Is Threatening Our Future* (Princeton: Princeton University Press, 2018).

2. Channing May, *Transnational Organized Crime* (Washington, DC: Global Financial Integrity, 2017).

3. John Sullivan and Robert Muggah, "The Coming Crime Wars," *Foreign Policy*, September 21, 2018.

4. Nadia Murad, "Nobel Prize Acceptance Speech," December 10, 2018, https://www.nobelprize.org/prizes/peace/2018/murad/55705-nadia-murad-nobel-lecture-2/.

5. Nadia Murad, *Excerpt from her Autobiography the Last Girl* (New York: Random House, 2018), as excerpt appeared in *The Guardian*, October 6, 2018,

https://www.theguardian.com/commentisfree/2018/oct/06/nadia-murad-isis-sex-slave-nobel-peace-prize.

6. Nadia's captor, a judge in Mosul, left the house unlocked for a moment. She escaped unnoticed, but had nowhere to run to. The entire city of Mosul was occupied by ISIS; she had no way out. Her home village was many miles away and destroyed. Her family members were either killed or scattered in remote camps of refugees and internally displaced persons. Signs everywhere promised $5,000 rewards for returning escaped slaves, and penalties including death for helping slaves escape. If she spoke her accent would reveal her to be a hated Yazidi minority. If she asked for help she risked being returned to ISIS. In a city savaged by war, filled with people either afraid of ISIS or sympathetic to ISIS, and desperate for money and subsistence, her chances of escape were small. She eventually knocked on the right door, of a family who did not support ISIS, but like Nadia had nowhere else to go. A brave Iraqi family risked their own lives and took her in, hid her, created a fake ID, and dangerously smuggled her out of ISIS territory. The young Iraqi father left behind his pregnant wife and toddler son, created a "cover story" that she was the man's wife and they were traveling to visit family in the region outside of ISIS control. They faced close calls at the numerous ISIS checkpoints, where the car was searched and they were asked questions. Nadia's photo was posted at the checkpoints as a "wanted" runaway slave, but miraculously the ISIS soldiers did not force her to remove the niqab covering her face. Nadia was released into Kurdish territory, and made her way to a refugee camp. She told her story to journalists and eventually to a UN agency. A German province selected her and a small number of other escaped Yazidi survivors of genocide and sexual slavery for refugee resettlement in Germany. The Iraqi man and his family who rescued her have not been as fortunate. ISIS immediately came after them. The man jumped from the roof of his apartment and fled. His pregnant wife and son tried to join him and be smuggled out in a gas tanker, but the rough attempted escape was too hard on the pregnant wife and child, who had to turn back. The man was jailed in Bulgaria along with other asylum seekers as "undocumented migrants." Eventually Germany granted him temporary protection, but rising right-wing nationalism in Germany undermines his chances to stay. There are swastikas spray painted on the buildings near his room. Even though he still receives death threats from ISIS and ISIS sympathizers, the United States has declared ISIS "defeated," so Germany might not allow him to stay but force him to return to Iraq. Rebecca Collard, "He Helped Iraq's Most Famous Refugee Escape: Now He's the One Who Needs Help," *Time*, July 13, 2018, http://time.com/longform/nadia-murad-isis-refugee-omar-jabar/.

7. Murad, *Excerpt from her Autobiography the Last Girl.*

8. Claire McEvoy and Gergeley Hideg, "Global Violent Deaths 2017," Small Arms Survey, Graduate Institute of International and Development Studies, Geneva, December 2017, http://www.smallarmssurvey.org/fileadmin/docs/U-Reports/SAS-Report-GVD2017.pdf.

9. Patrick Sharkey, *Uneasy Peace: The Great Crime Decline* (New York: W.W. Norton, 2018). Justin Fox, "Crime Near an All Time Low; Why Do Americans Remain Unconvinced by the Data?" *Bloomberg News*, February 12, 2018, https://www.bloomberg.com/opinion/articles/2018-02-12/pssst-crime-may-be-near-an-all-time-low.

10. Gains are not uniform, however. Some cities, like New York City, have seen even greater declines in crime than the national averages, while other cities, like Baltimore and Cinncinati, continue to struggle with violent crime rates. Sharkey, *Uneasy Peace*. Fox, "Crime Near an All Time Low."

11. United Nations Office on Drugs and Crime, "UN Global Report on Human Trafficking," 2018, http://www.unodc.org/documents/data-and-analysis/glotip /2018/GLOTiP_2018_BOOK_web_small.pdf.

12. United Nations Office on Drugs and Crime, "Global Report on Trafficking in Persons 2018," New York, United Nations, 2018, 11, http://www.unodc.org/docu ments/data-and-analysis/glotip/2018/GLOTiP_2018_BOOK_web_small.pdf.

13. Walk Free Foundation, *Global Slavery Index*, https://www.walkfreefounda-tion.org/; The UN and other bodies often refer only to the 25 million in forced labor, omitting the women who live in slave labor conditions in forced "marriages."

14. United Nations Office on Drugs and Crime, "What Is Human Trafficking?" https://www.unodc.org/unodc/en/human-trafficking/what-is-human-traffic king.html.

15. Anti-Slavery International, "Descent Based Slavery," https://www.antislav ery.org/slavery-today/descent-based-slavery/.

16. ILO, *Hard to See, Harder to Count: Survey Guidelines to Estimate Forced Labour of Adults and Children*, 2012.

17. Department of Labor, "Report on Forced Labor and Child Labor," 2018, https://www.dol.gov/sites/default/files/documents/ilab/ListofGoods.pdf.

18. Statistics from the International Labor Organization of the UN, as quoted in "Half of World's 152 Million Child Laborers Do Hazardous Work," *Voice of America*, June 10, 2018, https://www.voanews.com/a/half-the-world-s-152-million-child-laborers-do-hazardous-work/4432362.html.

19. UNICEF, "Child Labor Data," https://data.unicef.org/topic/child-protection/ child-labour/.

20. United Nations, "Annual Report of the Secretary General on Children and Armed Conflict," 2018, https://childrenandarmedconflict.un.org/children-faced-with-unspeakable-violence-in-conflict-as-number-of-grave-violations-increased-in -2017/.

21. Andorra, Bhutan, Liechtenstein, Micronesia, Monaco, Nauru, and North Korea are not members of the ILO.

22. Walk Free Foundation, https://www.walkfreefoundation.org/.

23. White House, "Transnational Organized Crime: A Growing Threat," https:// obamawhitehouse.archives.gov/administration/eop/nsc/transnational-crime/threat.

24. The Trump Taj Mahal casino broke anti money laundering rules 106 times in its first year and a half of operation in the early 1990s, according to the IRS in a 1998 settlement agreement. US Treasury Department, "Financial Crimes Enforcement Network fines Trump Taj Mahal $10 Million for Significant and Long Standing Money Laundering Violations," March 6, 2015, https://www.fincen.gov/news/news-release s/fincen-fines-trump-taj-mahal-casino-resort-10-million-significant-and-long.

25. Anita Kuman, "Buyers Tied to Russia Paid $109 Cash for Trump Properties," *McClatchy News*, June 19, 2018, https://www.mcclatchydc.com/news/politics-government/white-house/article210477439.html; "Narco–a-Lago: Money Laundering at Trump Panama," Global Witness Report, https://www.globalwitness.org/

sv/campaigns/corruption-and-money-laundering/narco-a-lago-panama/?accessible= true.

26. Europol, "Internet Organized Crime Threat Assessment," 2015, https://www. europol.europa.eu/activities-services/main-reports/internet-organised-crime-threat-assessment-iocta-2015.

27. Global Financial Integrity, "Money Laundering," https://www.gfintegrity. org/issue/money-laundering/.

28. Channing May, *Transnational Crime and the Developing World Report* (Washington, DC: Global Financial Integrity, March 2017), 15, https://www.gfi ntegrity.org/report/transnational-crime-and-the-developing-world/.

29. Peter Neill, "China's Insatiable Appetite for Fish Is a Colossol Disaster in the Making," *The Huffington Post*, April 25, 2017, https://www.huffingtonpost.com /entry/chinas-insatiable-appetite-for-fish-a-colossal-disaster_us_58ffa0dce4b063 1b8fc9c531.

30. "The Great Elephant Census," August 2016, http://www.greatelephantcen-sus.com/.

31. Louise Shelley, "How Dark Commerce Is Making Us Poorer and Sicker," https://thecrimereport.org/2018/11/13/how-dark-commerce-is-making-us-poorer -and-sicker/.

32. Shelley, "How Dark Commerce Is Making Us Poorer and Sicker."

33. May, *Transnational Crime and the Developing World Report.*

34. WHO, "Growing Threat from Counterfeit Medicines," https://www.who. int/bulletin/volumes/88/4/10-020410/en/

35. UNODC, http://www.unodc.org/unodc/en/fraudulentmedicines/introducti on.html.

36. UNODC, *UN Drug Report Booklet 2017*, 4.

37. Shelley, "How Dark Commerce Is Making Us Poorer and Sicker."

38. Transparency International, Global Corruption Perceptions Index, https:// www.transparency.org/cpi2018?gclid=EAIaIQobChMIsOPlj-Os4AIVh56fCh0g -QjvEAAYASAAEgIdNPD_BwE

39. May, *Transnational Crime and the Developing World Report.*

11: WEAPONS OF MASS DESTRUCTION: CHALLENGES OF CONTROL AND ELIMINATION

1. Beatrice Finn, Nobel Prize Acceptance Speech, 2017.

2. Jacob Zuma, September 2017, United Nations signing ceremony of the Treaty on the Prohibition of Nuclear Weapons.

3. George P. Shultz, interview with the author, September 25, 2018; "We Must Preserve This Nuclear Treaty: This is the Time to Expand, not Abandon, an Impor-tant Nuclear Weapons Agreement with Russia," *New York Times*, October 25, 2018, https://www.nytimes.com/2018/10/25/opinion/george-shultz-nuclear-treaty.html.

4. Quoted in Steve Anderson, "FBI Foils Smugglers' Plot to Sell Nuclear Mate-rials to ISIS," *The Independent*, October 7, 2015, https://www.independent.co.uk/ news/world/middle-east/smugglers-tried-to-sell-nuclear-material-to-isis-a6684051. html.

5. Ban Ki-moon, "Addressing Security Council, Secretary-General Calls for Recommitment to Eradicating Weapons of Mass Destruction 'Once and for All'," Secretary-General Statements and Messages, SG/SM/17996-SC/12486-DC/3647, August 23, 2016.

6. Interview with Donald J. Trump, MSNBC 2016.

7. United Nations Resolution 1, https://undocs.org/en/A/RES/1(I).

8. Only the weapons development programs in Iraq and Syria were stopped by foreign military attack.

9. The Soviets stole the US and British bomb design from the Manhattan Project, primarily through Klaus Fuchs, a German scientist who fled the Nazis, became a British citizen and key scientist in the project to develop nuclear weapons. He served 14 years in prison for spying for the Soviets, then was returned to East Germany, where he lived out the rest of his life working as a scientist.

10. Six out of seven five-star officers were against the use of the atomic bomb at the time, including Admiral Leahy, Admiral Nimitz, General Curtis LeMay, General Hap Arnold, and General Eisenhower. Eisenhower frequently recounted that during a July 1945 meeting with Secretary of War Henry Stimson he voiced his deep opposition: "I told him I was against it on two counts. First, the Japanese were ready to surrender and it wasn't necessary to hit them with that awful thing. Second, I hated to see our country be the first to use such a weapon."

11. Center for Non Proliferation Studies, 2018 Global Incidents and Trafficking Database and Annual Report, https://www.nti.org/analysis/articles/cns-global-i ncidents-and-trafficking-database/.

12. Laurel Morales, NPR, "For Navajo Nation, Uranium Mining's Lingering Deadly Legacy Continues," April 10, 2016, https://www.npr.org/sections/health -shots/2016/04/10/473547227/for-the-navajo-nation-uranium-minings-deadly-le gacy-lingers.

13. Joby Warrick and Loveday Morris, "How ISIS Nearly Stumbled on the Ingredients for a 'Dirty Bomb'," *The Washington Post*, July 22, 2017, https://www.was hingtonpost.com/world/national-security/how-isis-nearly-stumbled-on-the-ingredie nts-for-a-dirty-bomb/2017/07/22/6a966746-6e31-11e7-b9e2-2056e768a7e5_story. html?utm_term=.c6d2e1af49e2.

14. Matthew Bunn, Martin Malin, William Potter, and Leonard Spector (Eds.), *Preventing Black Market Trades in Nuclear Technology* (Cambridge University Press, 2018).

15. Douglas Frantz, "U.S. and Pakistan Discuss Nuclear Security," *The New York Times*, October 1, 2001, A3; John J. Fialka and Scott Neuman, "Will Pakistan's Warheads Stay Secure? If a War Topples Leader, Control Is Uncertain; Some Call Threat Slim," *Wall Street Journal*, October 4, 2001, A17; Paul Richter, "Pakistan's Nuclear Wild Card," *Los Angeles Times,* September 18, 2001, A2; Nigel Hawkes, "Pakistan Could Lose Control of its Arsenal," *Times*, London, September 20, 2001, n.p.

16. See, Graham Allison, "Nuclear Disorder: Surveying Atomic Threats," *Foreign Affairs*, January/February 2010.

17. Elisabeth Braw, "Here's a 6 Country Effort that Might Work," *Defense One*, October 15, 2018, https://www.defenseone.com/ideas/2018/10/heres-6-country-def ense-cooperation-effort-just-might-work/152016/?oref=d-river.

18. "PSI endorsing states," Proliferation Security Initiative Info Website, undated, http://www.psi-online.info/Vertretung/psi/en/Startseite.html.

19. Bush, Statement, December 11, 2002, www.whitehouse.gov/news/releases/20 02/12/20021211-8.html.

20. "Joint Statement From Proliferation Security Initiative (PSI) Partners in Support of United Nations Security Council Resolutions 2375 and 2397 Enforcement," Media Note, U.S. Department of State, January 12, 2018.

21. Joby Warrick, "Iraqi Scientist Helped ISIS Make Chemical Weapons," *The Washington Post*, January 21, 2019, https://www.washingtonpost.com/worl d/national-security/exclusive-iraqi-scientist-says-he-helped-isis-make-chemical-weapo ns/2019/01/21/617cb8f0-0d35-11e9-831f-3aa2c2be4cbd_story.html?utm_term=.bad d2111334f; Columb Strack, "The Evolution of Islamic State's Chemical Weapons Efforts," *West Point Counter Terrorism Center Sentinel*, October 2017, 10, no. 9, https://ctc.usma.edu/the-evolution-of-the-islamic-states-chemical-weapons-efforts/.

22. In 1993, the Aum Shinrikyo cult aerosolized Bacillus anthracis spores over Kameido, Japan. The isolates were consistent with strain Sterne 34F2, which is used in Japan for animal prophylaxis against anthrax. Paul Keim, Kimothy L. Smith, Christine Keys, Hiroshi Takahashi, Takeshi Kurata, and Arnold Kaufmann, "Molecular Investigation of the Aum Shinrikyo Anthrax Release in Kameido, Japan," *Journal of Clinical Microbilology, American Society of Microbiology*, 2001, http://jcm.asm.org/content/39/12/4566.full.

23. Peter Baker, "Pakistani Scientist Who Met Bin Laden Failed Polygraphs, Renewing Suspicions," *Washington Post*, March 3, 2002.

24. "Unusual Activity at Russian Embassy Before Novichok Attack," *The Guardian*, March 4, 2019, https://www.theguardian.com/uk-news/2019/mar/04/un usual-activity-russian-embassy-novichok-attack-skripal-poisonings; Steve George, "Russian Spy Attack Nerve Agent was Rare, Dangerous and Sophisticated," *CNN*, March 13, 2017, https://www.cnn.com/2018/03/13/europe/what-is-novichok-nerve -agent-intl/index.html.

25. See, Stephen Hummel, "The Islamic State and WMD: Assessing the Future Threat," *CTC Sentinel, Combating Counterterrorism Center, West Point*, 9, no. 1, January 2016, https://ctc.usma.edu/the-islamic-state-and-wmd-assessing-the-futu re-threat/.

26. This memo was discovered in 2001 on a computer acquired by the Wall Street Journal that had been used by Al Qaeda members in Afghanistan. Government officials are reported to have confirmed the authenticity of the files found on the computer's hard drive, which also contained a table of lethal doses for poisons according to body weight and a list of disease agents, including anthrax. See "Al-Qaeda: New Evidence of Chemical and Biological Weapons Pursuit," *Global Security Newswire*, January 2, 2002.

27. Joseph Cirincione, Jon B. Wolfsthal, and Miriam Rajkumar, *Deadly Arsenals, Carnegie Endowment for International Peace* (Washington, DC: The Brookings Institution Press, 2005), 55.

28. William Greider, "It's Official: The Pentagon Finally Admitted That Israel Has Nuclear Weapons, Too," *The Nation*, March 20, 2015.

29. Lily Hay Newman, "North Korea''s Nuke Test Reveals Terrifying Capabilities," *Wired*, September 3, 2017.

30. "Bin Laden 'has Nuclear Weapons,'" *BBC*, November 10, 2001, http://new s.bbc.co.uk/1/hi/world/south_asia/1648572.stm.

31. Central Intelligence Agency, "Terrorist CBRN: Materials and Effects" June 2003, 4.

32. Ibid.; US Nuclear Regulatory Commission, "Fact Sheet on Dirty Bombs," March 2003.

33. Central Intelligence Agency, "Terrorist CBRN: Materials and Effects," June 2003, 4; U.S. Nuclear Regulatory Commission, "Fact Sheet on Dirty Bombs," March 2003.

34. See, "Inside the Abandoned City of Pripyat, 30 Years after Chernobyl – in Pictures," *The Guardian*, April 5, 2016, https://www.theguardian.com/cities/galle ry/2016/apr/05/inside-abandoned-city-pripyat-30-years-chernobyl-in-pictures.

35. Michael Eisenstadt and Omar Mukhlis, "The Potential for Radiological Ter- rorism by al-Qaeda and the Islamic State," PolicyWatch 2671, *The Washington Institute*, August 10, 2016, http://www.washingtoninstitute.org/policy-analysis/ view/the-potential-for-radiological-terrorism-by-al-qaeda-and-the-islamic-state.

36. Aimee Amiga and Ruth Schuster, "EU Report: ISIS Could Commit Chemi- cal or Biological Terror Attack in West," *Haaretz*, December 13, 2015, https://ww w.haaretz.com/middle-east-news/isis/eu-isis-could-commit-chemical-biological-att ack-in-west-1.5436111.

37. "The Biological Threat," *Nuclear Threat Initiative (NTI)*, December 30, 2015, http://www.nti.org/learn/biological/.

38. See, variously, Central Intelligence Agency, Unclassified Report to Congress on the Acquisition of Technology Related to Weapons of Mass Destruction and Advanced Chemical Munitions, 1 January through 30 June, 2001 (January 30, 2002); *Proliferation: Threat and Response*; John R. Bolton, "Beyond the Axis of Evil," Remarks Made at the Heritage Foundation, May 6, 2002.

39. The official title of the Biological Weapons Convention is "The Convention on the Prohibition of the Development, Production, and Stockpiling of Bacteriologi- cal (Biological) and Toxin Weapons and on Their Destruction." It entered into force on March 26, 1975.

40. Article I, Biological Weapons Convention, is the Convention on the Prohibi- tion of the Development, Production and Stockpiling of Bacteriological (Biological) and Toxin Weapons and on their Destruction, 1975.

41. Saskia V. Popescu, "New Biosecurity Threats Appear in Less Familiar Forms," *Contagion: Infectious Disease Today*, November 1, 2017.

42. Scott Shane, "Panel on Anthrax Inquiry Finds Case Against Ivins Persua- sive," *The New York Times*, March 23, 2011.

43. Jens H. Kuhn and Milton Leitenburg, "The Soviet Biological Warfare Pro- gram," in Lentzos Filippa (Ed.), *Biological Threats In The 21st Century: The Poli- tics, People, Science and Historical Roots* (Imperial College Press, 2016), 87.

44. The Increasing Threat of Biological Weapons: Handle with Sufficient and Proportionate Care, The Hague Centre for Strategic Studies (HCSS), 2016.

45. Ben Hubbard, "Dozens Suffocate in Syria as Government is Accused of Chemical Attack," *The New York Times*, April 8, 2018.

46. D. Hank Ellison, *Handbook of Chemical and Biological Warfare Agents*, Second ed. (CRC Press, August 24, 2007), 567–570.

47. The official title of the Chemical Weapons Convention is "The Convention on the Prohibition of the Development, Production, Stockpiling and Use of Chemical Weapons and on Their Destruction." It entered into force on April 29, 1997.

48. David Hoffman and Eben Harrell, "Saving the World at Plutonium Mountain," *The Washington Post*, August 16, 2013, https://www.washingtonpost.com/opinions/saving-the-world-at-plutonium-mountain/2013/08/16/1d43dd3a-0381-11e3-88d6-d5795fab4637_story.html?utm_term=.b93e0883c86f.

49. Tom Sauer, "Crossroads: Why the Nuclear Nonproliferation Treaty Could Become Obsolete," *The National Interest*, December 8, 2017.

50. Paul Meyer, "The Nuclear Nonproliferation Treaty: Fin de Regime?" *Arms Control Today*, Arms Control Association, April 2017.

51. For a great resource on the Non-Aligned Movement and disarmament, see, "Non-Aligned Movement (NAM)," *Nuclear Threat Initiative*, April 14, 2017, http://www.nti.org/learn/treaties-and-regimes/non-aligned-movement-nam/.

12: THE FUTURE: NETWORKED SOVEREIGNTY, GLOBAL ISSUES, AND THE RACE BETWEEN COOPERATION AND CATASTROPHE

1. Senator Sam Nunn, Interview with Author, Washington, DC, 2018.

2. Jennifer Blanke, "World Economic Forum: More Inclusive Growth Is Needed to Reap the Benefits of Globalization," July 18, 2016, https://www.weforum.org/agenda/2016/07/more-inclusive-growth-is-needed-to-reap-the-benefits-of-globalization/.

3. Dali Lama, Twitter post, June 8, 2018, https://twitter.com/dalailama/status/1005019375957471232?lang=en.

4. Pope Francis, "Address in Apostolic visit to Albania," September 21, 2014.

5. Mary Robinson, "The Ethical Globalization Initiative: Realizing Rights."

6. Archbishop Diarmuid Martin, Speech to the Humanizing the Global Economy Conference, Catholic University, Washington, DC, January 28, 2002.

7. President Barack Obama, May 17, 2009.

8. Institutions range from "formal organizations, which have explicit rules and forms of administration and enforcement, to any stabilized pattern of human relationships and actions." Jack Knight, *Institutions and Social Conflict* (Cambridge, UK: Cambridge University Press, 1996), 2.

9. Maryann Cusimano Love, "Trust in Ghana," in *Living in an Age of Mistrust* (Routledge, 2017).

10. Deborah Avant, Martha Finnemore, and Susan Sell, *Who Governs the Globe?* 2010, 1.

11. "The European Commission is the Most Obscure Power of All," *Real World Radio*, October 19, 2018, http://www.cadtm.org/The-European-Commission-is-the-most-obscure-power-of-all.

12. Grant and Keohane describe seven different accountability mechanisms. Ruth Grant and Robert O. Keohane, "Accountability and Abuses of Power in World Politics," *American Political Science Review* 99 (2005): 29–43.

13. Ann Florini (Ed.), *The Right to Know: Transparency for an Open World* (New York: Columbia University Press, 2007).

14. David C. Korten, *When Corporations Rule the World* (West Hartford, CT: Kumarian Press, 1995); Richard Falk, *Predatory Globalization: A Critique* (Malden, MA: Blackwell, 1999); John Gray, *False Dawn: The Delusions of Global Capitalism* (New York: New Press, 1998).

15. Branco Milanovic, *Income Inequality*, 2016; Thomas Piketty, *Capital in the 21st Century* (Harvard University Press, 2014); Joseph E. Stiglitz, *Globalization and Its Discontents* (New York: W. W. Norton, 2003); Ignacio Ramonet, "Dueling Globalizations: Let Them Eat Big Macs," *Foreign Policy* (Fall 1999): 116–121, 125–127; S. J. Thierry Linard de Gueterchin, "A Christmas Present for the Ford Workers in the ABC of Sao Paulo," Centro Cultural de Brasilia: Global Economies and Culture Project, in conjunction with the Woodstock Theological Center, Georgetown University, Washington, DC, April 6, 1999; Dani Rodrik, *Has Globalization Gone Too Far?* (Washington, DC: Institute for International Economics, 1997).

16. Susan Strange, *Casino Capitalism* (Oxford University Press, 1986).

17. Chua, *World on Fire*; Mittelman, *The Globalization Syndrome*; Mark Juergensmeyer, "The Worldwide Rise of Religious Nationalism," *Journal of International Affairs* 50, no. 1; Barber, *Jihad vs. McWorld*; Huntington, "Clash of Civilizations," 22–28.

18. Benjamin Barber, "Mutual Aid Society on a Grand Scale," *Los Angeles Times*, November 17, 2002, www.democracycollaborative.org/publications/books/barber_111702.html.

19. Francis Fukuyama, *State-Building: Governance and World Order in the 21st Century* (Ithaca, NY: Cornell University Press, 2004).

20. Anne-Marie Slaughter, *The Chessboard and the Web: Strategies of Connection in a Networked World* (Yale University Press, 2018); "America's Edge: Power in the Networked Century," *Foreign Affairs*, January/February 2009; *A New World Order* (Princeton, NJ: Princeton University Press, 2004).

21. Thorsten Benner and Jan Martin Witte, "Everybody's Business: Accountability, Partnerships, and the Future of Global Governance," in Susan Stern and Elisabeth Seligmann (Eds.), *The Partnership Principle: New Forms of Governance in the 21st Century* (London, Archetype Publishers, 2004); Mirjam Bult-Spiering and Geert Dewulf, *Strategic Issues in Public Private Partnerships*, Blackwell 2007.

22. Ibid.

23. Strange, *The Retreat of the State*, 189.

24. Rosecrance, "The Rise of the Virtual State," 59–60.

25. Krasner, *Problematic Sovereignty*; Krasner, *Sovereignty: Organized Hypocrisy*; Krasner, "Sovereignty: An Institutional Perspective," 74; Waltz, "Globalization and Governance," 693–700; McNeill, "Territorial States Buried Too Soon," 269.

26. Rosenau, *Turbulence in World Politics*.

27. Foreign Policy and the Fund for Peace, "Fragile State Index 2018," http://fundforpeace.org/fsi/2018/04/24/fragile-states-index-2018-annual-report/; "The Failed State Index," *Foreign Policy* (July/ August 2005), www.foreignpolicy.com/story/cms.php?story_id=3098.

28. Freedom House, Freedom in the World 2018, https://freedomhouse.org/repor t/freedom-world/freedom-world-2018.

29. Greg Noone, "Genocide and Crimes Against Humanity," presentation 2004.

30. Kofi Annan, Nobel Prize Acceptance Speech, December 10, 2001.

31. UNHCR, https://www.unhcr.org/figures-at-a-glance.html.

32. Hendrik Spruyt, *The Sovereign State and Its Competitors* (Princeton, NJ: Princeton University Press, 1994), 62, 75.

33. Mark Leibovich, *The New Imperialists* (New York: Prentice Hall, 2002).

34. Peter L. Berger, "Four Faces of Global Culture," *The National Interest* (Fall 1997): 24.

35. Friedman, *The World Is Flat*, 421; Friedman, *The Lexus and the Olive Tree*, 195–196. Some question the "Golden Arches theory" after conflict between Russia and Georgia in August 2008, but the conflict never reached the level of a war or major armed conflict with over 1000 deaths in battle, as 365 deaths were estimated by Human Rights Watch and government officials. Thomas Friedman, *Hot Flat and Crowded* (New York: Farrar, Straus & Giroux, 2008).

36. Strange, *The Retreat of the State*, 199.

37. Rosecrance, *The Rise of the Virtual State*, 59–60.

38. Benjamin R. Barber, *Jihad vs. McWorld* (New York: Ballantine Books, 1996).

39. Reuters, "Pope Benedict Wants to Meet You on Facebook," May 22, 2009; Jon W. Anderson and Dale F. Eickelman (Eds.), *New Media in the Muslim World: The Emerging Public Sphere* (Bloomington: Indiana University Press, 1999).

40. McFate, "America's Addiction to Mercenaries"; Shorrock, *Spies for Hire*; Paul Verkuil, *Outsourcing Sovereignty* (Cambridge, 2007); Peter Passell, "U.S. Goals at Odds in a Plan to Sell Off Nuclear Operation," *The New York Times,* July 25, 1995, A1.

41. Maryann Cusimano, "James Rosenau and Monica Lewinsky," *PS: Political Science and Politics,* December 1999. Interestingly, Rosenau's thesis explains why President Clinton's approval ratings did not diminish and even improved during his impeachment hearings. The media and conservative thinkers were at a loss to explain why the US public was not more exercised about President Clinton's extra-marital affair, its moral implications, and its effects on the dignity of the presidential office. But if the public judges legitimacy and authority by performance criteria, not by appeals to tradition or moral authority, then breaches of tradition and morality would not affect the public's perception of Clinton's legitimacy or authority. If performance criteria are all that matters, then Clinton's poll ratings made sense given the low unemployment rate and strong performance of the US economy during his administration, especially while European and Asian economic growth rates were simultaneously flat or declining. According to Rosenau, it would seem that political leaders can "get away with" quite a bit as long as it does not interfere with their record of concrete achievements.

42. Ivo Daalder, "Global Cities," *Financial Times*, May 26, 2015, https://ww w.ft.com/content/a5230756-0395-11e5-a70f-00144feabdc0#axzz3bKPqcdmE.

43. Benjamin Barber, *If Mayors Ruled the World: Dysfunctional Nations, Rising Cities* (New Haven, CT: Yale University Press, 2013).

44. Chua, *World On Fire.*

45. Ted Robert Gurr, "Minorities, Nationalists, and Ethnopolitical Conflict," in Chester Crocker, Fen Osler Hampson, and Pamela Aall (Eds.), *Managing Global Chaos* (Washington, DC: U.S. Institute of Peace, 1996), 53–78; David Little, "Religious Militancy," in Crocker et al., *Managing Global Chaos*, 79–92; Ernest Gellner, "Nations and Nationalism," in Richard Betts (Ed.), *Conflict after the Cold War: Arguments on the Causes of War and Peace* (New York: Macmillan, 1994), 280–292; Louis Kriesberg, "Regional Conflicts in the Post–Cold War Era: Causes, Dynamics, and Modes of Resolution," in Michael Klare and Daniel Thomas (Eds.), *World Security: Challenges for a New Century* (New York: St. Martin's Press, 1994), 155–174; Donald L. Horowitz, "Ethnic and Nationalist Conflict," in Klare and Thomas, *World Security*, 175–187.

46. Kaplan, *The Coming Anarchy*; Kaplan, *Balkan Ghosts.*

47. Woodward, *Balkan Tragedy.*

48. Michael Brown, *The International Dimensions of Internal Conflict* (Cambridge: MIT Press, 1996), 579.

49. Jong S. Jun and Deil S. Wright, *Globalization and Decentralization: Institutional Contexts, Policy Issues, and Intergovernmental Relations in Japan and the United States* (Washington, DC: Georgetown University Press, 1996), 1.

50. President Clinton declared the era of big government dead, referring to the end of welfare as we knew it and reforms that downsized the federal government to the smallest it had been since the Kennedy administration. Similar downsizing efforts have been underway internationally as privatization and "e-government" spread. Structural adjustment policies trim government spending in developing countries.

51. Jun and Wright, *Globalization and Decentralization*, 3–4.

52. Strange, *The Retreat of the State*, 87.

53. Krasner, "Sovereignty: An Institutional Perspective," 79.

54. Robert E. Bell, *Dictionary of Classical Mythology: Symbols, Attributes and Associations* (Santa Barbara, CA: ABC-Clio, 1982), 207.

55. Zartman, *Collapsed States*, 5.

56. Rosecrance, *The Rise of the Virtual State.*

57. Otto Neurath quoted in A. J. Ayer (Ed.), *Logical Positivism* (Glencoe, IL: The Free Press, 1959). This is sometimes referred to as "Neurath's ship."

58. Krasner, "Sovereignty: An Institutional Perspective," 80.

59. Richard E. Neustadt, *Presidential Power and the Modern Presidents: The Politics of Leadership from Roosevelt to Reagan* (New York: The Free Press, 1990).

Index

■ ■ ■

Page references for figures and tables are italicized.